Is There a Court for Gaza?

Chantal Meloni · Gianni Tognoni
Editors

Is There a Court for Gaza?

A Test Bench for International Justice

T·M·C·ASSER PRESS  Springer

Chantal Meloni
Criminal Law Department
Cesare Beccaria
Law Faculty
University of Milan
Via Festa del Perdono 7
20122 Milan
Italy

Gianni Tognoni
International Section
Lelio Basso Foundation
Via Della Dogana Vecchia 5
00186 Roma
Italy

ISBN 978-90-6704-819-4
DOI 10.1007/978-90-6704-820-0

e-ISBN 978-90-6704-820-0

Library of Congress Control Number: 2011943565

© T.M.C. ASSER PRESS, The Hague, The Netherlands, and the authors/editors 2012

Published by T.M.C. ASSER PRESS, The Hague, The Netherlands www.asserpress.nl
Produced and distributed for T.M.C. ASSER PRESS by Springer-Verlag Berlin Heidelberg

No part of this work may be reproduced, stored in a retrieval system, or transmitted in any form or by any means, electronic, mechanical, photocopying, microfilming, recording or otherwise, without written permission from the Publisher, with the exception of any material supplied specifically for the purpose of being entered and executed on a computer system, for exclusive use by the purchaser of the work. The use of general descriptive names, registered names, trademarks, etc. in this publication does not imply, even in the absence of a specific statement, that such names are exempt from the relevant protective laws and regulations and therefore free for general use.

Printed on acid-free paper

Springer is part of Springer Science+Business Media (www.springer.com)

Foreword

Palestine first surfaced as a subject of international litigation in the second contentious case before the Permanent Court of International Justice. The matter concerned certain legal consequences of the British mandate and was not unrelated to London's encouragement of the establishment of a Jewish state in Palestine, although the precise dispute is far from issues of contemporary concern.[1] Indeed, for about eighty years subsequent to the Permanent Court's decision, in 1924, the Palestine issue remained far from the docket of international courts and tribunals. Only very recently there has been any serious prospect of the Israeli occupation and its consequences being addressed through the mechanisms of international justice and international courts. To some extent this is because the institutions themselves did not previously exist or were not available. But it is also the result of an increasingly robust use of international law as a means to deal with international disputes.

Some have dismissed this as 'lawfare'. Recently, the term has been used to attack the Advisory Opinion of the International Court of Justice on the Wall and the Report of the Fact-Finding Mission presided over by Richard Goldstone. 'Lawfare' was apparently coined by General Charles Dunlap, an American military lawyer, in a lecture at Harvard University in November 2001. He said it was a practice whereby 'the rule of law is ... hijacked into just another way of fighting (lawfare), to the detriment of humanitarian values as well as the law itself'. Dunlap said 'the use of law as a weapon of war, is the newest feature of twentyfirst century combat'.[2]

Were not the British, French and Russians using 'lawfare' in 1915 when they said that Ottoman leaders would be prosecuted for 'new crimes of Turkey against humanity and civilization', what we call today the Armenian genocide? What of

---

[1] *Mavrommatis Palestine Concession* (*Greece v. United Kingdom*), P.C.I.J., Series A, No. 2, 30 August 1924.

[2] Charles J Dunlap, 'Law and Military Interventions: Preserving Humanitarian Values in 21st Conflicts', Humanitarian Challenges in Military Intervention Conference, Carr Center for Human Rights Policy, Harvard University, 29 November 2001.

the Americans, the British and the Soviets who, in October 1943, spoke of 'evidence of atrocities, massacres and cold-blooded mass executions which are being perpetrated by Hitlerite forces in many of the countries they have overrun and from which they are now being steadily expelled'? The Allies said they would 'pursue them to the uttermost ends of the earth and will deliver them to their accusers in order that justice may be done'. The Nazis were doing the same, accusing their adversaries of war crimes in the fire-bombing of cities, for example.

The 'lawfare' libel is nothing more than frustrated resistance to the availability of new mechanisms and institutions whereby international law can be applied to present conflicts, including those involving Israel and Palestine. For decades, international law was a largely theoretical proposition, something invoked by academics and activists, and in debates within political bodies of the United Nations. Now, there is a realistic prospect that the great conflicts of our time can actually be brought to court.

This volume asks: 'Is There a Court for Gaza?' The answer is a resounding yes. Indeed, there are at least two courts capable of addressing the armed conflict in Gaza that took place in December 2008 and January 2009: the International Court of Justice and the International Criminal Court. But neither of them has jurisdiction *prima facie*. The challenge, then, is to resolve the difficulties in establishing jurisdiction. Once this is done, the merits, which have only partially been addressed in the Goldstone report, can be litigated. Even then, there are limits to the subject-matter jurisdiction that are likely to confine the judicial debate.

The International Court of Justice is the more challenging of the two. Israel could consent to jurisdiction of the Court, in accordance with Article 36 of the Statute. But it is not likely to do so. Even if it did, it would be necessary to identify a dispute with another State, and one that was prepared to submit an application to the Court. The Advisory Opinion procedure is also available, as the 2004 ruling shows. But considerable creativity would be required to develop a question immune to the complaint that it amounts to blatant misuse and a disguised attempt to litigate a contentious matter. Although the Goldstone Commission Report cited the 2004 Advisory Opinion in several places, it did not even contemplate the possibility that the violations of international law it had identified be addressed in that forum.

A far more promising prospect is the International Criminal Court. It was the forum seriously considered by the Goldstone Report. As a general principle, the International Criminal Court may exercise jurisdiction over virtually any violation of its Statute committed anywhere in the world. This is a direct consequence of Article 12(3) of the Rome Statute by which any State may make a declaration accepting the exercise of jurisdiction by the Court, regardless of whether it has ratified or acceded to the Statute. The only significant restrictions on this result from other jurisdictional provisions: the alleged crime must fall within the subject-matter jurisdiction of the Court and the act must have been perpetrated subsequent to the entry into force of the Statute, on 1 July 2002. Neither of these criteria poses a problem with respect to the recent Gaza conflict.

Foreword

Several years ago, in *An Introduction to the International Criminal Court*, I suggested that the Palestinian Authority might make a declaration to the effect that when Palestine becomes a state, it pledged to give the Court jurisdiction over crimes committed on its territory in the past by means of a declaration in accordance with Article 12(3). I did not then think seriously about the argument that it is already a state for the purposes of Article 12(3), although I now acknowledge the strength of the arguments to that effect. At the time, there were already two cases in which the provision had been relied upon, but they concerned Member States of the United Nations, Côte d'Ivoire and Uganda, whose claim to be 'a State' within the meaning of Article 12(3) could not reasonably be in dispute. My thesis then was that such a measure by the Palestinian Authority would at the very least sound a warning, and that this might generate a deterrent effect. Perhaps the proposal was superfluous. International lawyers working for Israel have analyzed the details of the Rome Statute and already appreciated the possibility that everything carried out on Palestinian territory since 1 July 2002 is potentially subject to the Court's jurisdiction.

By the time this book is published, Palestine's existence as a State may be established beyond dispute. This important development may eliminate a significant portion of the debate with which the contributions in this volume are concerned. Then our attention will be focused principally on the substantive charges rather than on the jurisdictional issues. That a State may give jurisdiction retroactively pursuant to Article 12(3) is unquestionable, as the Côte d'Ivoire and Uganda declarations demonstrate. After all, retroactive application is precisely the purpose of the provision. Israel may nevertheless argue that a state of Palestine cannot employ Article 12(3) to give jurisdiction over its territory for a period in the past when it may not have been a state. There is no convenient precedent to provide an answer to this argument. However, the consequence of such a claim leads to an absurdity, or at least to a proposition that defies the object and purpose of the Rome Statute. It would mean that one portion of the globe, due to the fact that it was occupied illegally by a foreign power, would become more or less permanently insulated from the International Criminal Court. The judges of the Court are exceedingly unlikely to accept such an interpretation.

The Fact-Finding Mission chaired by Richard Goldstone documented a large number of violations of international humanitarian law and international human rights law. There has been much noise about a subsequent statement of Richard Goldstone expressing hesitation with respect to some of the conclusions. The extent of his remarks has often been exaggerated, as they only dealt with one set of the alleged violations concerning intentional targeting of civilians during combat operations. Judge Goldstone said that he doubted whether the evidence showed this had taken place as a matter of policy. Careful reading of the Report indicates that the Fact-Finding Mission never made such a claim in any case. That individual soldiers may have targeted civilians is a separate question from whether they did so as a matter of policy. It can only adequately be addressed with detailed analysis of specific incidents, and it is virtually impossible to reach an accurate conclusion on such matters without hearing both sides. In any case, the issue of intentional attacks on civilians does not get to the heart of the matter. The core of the Goldstone Report dealt with the planned destruction of the entire infrastructure of a community, aimed at punishing Palestinians in Gaza for their support of Hamas. That this was Israeli policy seems to have been admitted. It was a strategy that had already been used in Lebanon in 2006. No member of the Fact-Finding Mission has repudiated the conclusions on this important point.

The Fact-Finding Mission found that war crimes may have been perpetrated by both sides in the conflict. This is a source of satisfaction to many in the human rights movement, who cherish the neutrality of such a perspective. Others, including Richard Falk in this volume, contend that the critique of Hamas introduces a distortion into the analysis. And from the other side, supporters of Israel claim that essentially all of the acts perpetrated by the Israeli Defence Forces were a legitimate response to the Hamas rockets. These quarrels bring us to the heart of the real challenge in finding a court for Gaza. If the International Criminal Court were to proceed on the basis of the referral by the Palestinian Authority, whom would the Prosecutor target? What crimes would be addressed? Would he deal with Hamas and the Israeli Defence Forces equally, or with only one to the exclusion of the other? If he were to pursue both sides, what would be the proportions of such prosecutorial alchemy?

The question of even-handed prosecution has dogged international criminal justice since its beginnings, when the victors of the First World War included punishment provisions in the Treaty of Versailles. The great trials at Nuremberg and Tokyo have been constantly criticized because they only dealt with violations on one side of the conflict. The more recent *ad hoc* tribunals are purportedly more balanced in that they are established not by the victors but by the United Nations Security Council. The prosecutors of the *ad hoc* tribunals are not appointed by one side in the conflict, as was the case at Nuremberg and Tokyo, and the jurisdictional framework makes prosecution of all parties a possibility. However, the Yugoslavia, Rwanda and Sierra Leone tribunals have all required decisions to be made about the selection of defendants. In each, there has been controversy, demonstrating that the alleged shortcomings of Nuremberg and Tokyo have not been solved.

Nor has the International Criminal Court yet to provide the answer. To date, the Prosecutor has selected situations for prosecution that are confined to a group of contiguous states in Africa. He has achieved this by either exercising his *proprio motu* power to choose situations, pursuant to Article 15 of the Rome Statute, or by his concurrence with such decisions when they are initially made by either the Security Council or a State Party (in accordance with Articles 13(b) and 14, respectively). The Prosecutor has located the activity of the Court within the comfort zone of the United States and other prominent 'western' powers. This is not 'victors' justice' in the institutional sense, as was the case at Nuremberg and Tokyo, but the result is about the same.

Ultimately, if prosecutions concerning Gaza are to proceed, the Prosecutor will have to agree. A declaration under Article 12(3) does not trigger jurisdiction.

An additional step is required. This can come from the Security Council (improbable), a State Party or the Prosecutor himself. But in all cases, the Prosecutor must concur both with the decision to investigate and with the choice of the accused. To the extent that there is any anxiety about operating close to an exposed nerve of the United States, a positive decision by the Prosecutor would seem unlikely, no matter how solid the legal arguments for jurisdiction may be. The biggest hurdle is not convincing the Prosecutor that he may exercise jurisdiction but rather convincing him that he should. Moreover, even if he were to proceed, his choice of individual targets for prosecution may generate a narrative of the conflict with which many will disagree.

At present, the subject-matter jurisdiction of the International Criminal Court is confined to genocide, crimes against humanity and war crimes. The Fact-Finding Mission quite correctly ignored the occasional demagogic invocation of the 'g-word' and focused its attention on crimes against humanity and war crimes. In the context of international humanitarian law, these might be categorized as the *jus in bello*. They concern the conduct of hostilities rather than their legality. This is perhaps one of the great conundrums of bringing law to bear on the Gaza conflict. The general public does not properly understand the distinction between *jus in bello* and *jus ad bellum*. Many undoubtedly believe that there should be prosecutions with respect to the Gaza conflict because Israel is responsible for the occupation, for the blockade and for the initiation of the recent conflict. These are matters that cannot at present be addressed directly in proceedings before the International Criminal Court.

The famous statement signed by the late Ian Brownlie and several other prominent academics, including a member of the Fact-Finding Mission, published in *The Sunday Times* in January 2009, criticized Israel not only for the conduct of hostilities but also for waging the war in the first place. A focus solely on the battlefield as such leads us toward the more balanced position whereby both sides bear responsibility for violations. It implies that the root cause of the conflict as a secondary matter, and is premised on the apparent neutrality of the *jus in bello* perspective. We search for solutions that involve punishment of individual soldiers rather than turning to the only real answer, which is full affirmation of the right of the Palestinian people to self-determination.

Palestine's entitlement to a sovereign state within fair borders reflecting its historic territory is an agenda that international litigation may help to advance, but probably not one for which the International Criminal Court is particularly suited. In 2017, the Court may be able to exercise jurisdiction over the crime of aggression. But this will not be possible retroactively, even if the new provisions were to be applicable to an armed attack like the one made by Israel in 2008.

In the past, theorizing about using international law in order to resolve the conflict in the Middle East was an interesting exercise but one whose significance was essentially hortatory. There was no court capable of providing a forum for the debate. That no longer is the case. Over the past decade, both the International Court of Justice and the International Criminal Court have been confronted with aspects of the crisis. Neither institution provides an adequate remedy. But nor should the contributions that both can make to the debate be gainsaid. The legal arguments are inexorably intertwined with advocacy strategies, which they nourish, assist and orient.

William Schabas
Professor of International Law
Middlesex University
UK

Acknowledgments

This book would not have been possible without the help and support of the International Section of the Lelio Basso Foundation in Rome.

The editors wish to thank in particular the Collective of Women of the town of Lecco, Italy, who assured the financial support for the project, as expression of their long term commitment for the Permanent Peoples' Tribunal and more broadly for the peoples' right to self-determination.

August 2011
Chantal Meloni
Gianni Tognoni

Contents

1 Introduction 1
Chantal Meloni and Gianni Tognoni
1.1 Introduction 1
1.2 Chronology of Events Related to the UN Fact Finding Mission on the Gaza Conflict 5
1.3 Map of Gaza 9

Part I International Conference 'Is There a Court for Gaza?' 22 May 2009, Rome

2 Selected Materials from the International Conference 'Is There a Court for Gaza?' 22 May 2009, Lelio Basso International Foundation, Rome 13
Chantal Meloni and Gianni Tognoni
2.1 Introduction 14
2.2 Selected Conference's Papers 15
    2.2.1 Raji Sourani 16
    2.2.2 Eric David 24
    2.2.3 Giuseppe Palmisano 30
    2.2.4 Gabriele Della Morte 36
    2.2.5 Chantal Meloni 41
    2.2.6 Flavia Lattanzi 48
    2.2.7 François Rigaux 56
2.3 Presentation of the Complaint Filed Before the International Criminal Court by Gilles Devers and Mireille Fanon Mendes-France 61
    2.3.1 Introduction 61
    2.3.2 Violations of International Law 62

		2.3.3	Violations of International Humanitarian Law and Human Rights Law....................	66
		2.3.4	The Commission of War Crimes	69
		2.3.5	The Commission of Crimes Against Humanity......	70
		2.3.6	Consequences in Terms of the Individual Criminal Liability of Israeli Authorities	71
		2.3.7	The Consequences of the Violations of International Law by the State of Israel...................	72
		2.3.8	Conclusions..............................	74
	2.4	States that have Recognised Palestine as a State...........		76
	References			79

Part II The UN Fact Finding Mission on the Gaza Conflict and Follow-up at the International and Domestic Level

3 The Goldstone Report and the Goldstone Retreat: Truths Told by Law and Reviled by Geopolitics...................... 83
Richard Falk
	3.1	A Preliminary Observation on the Goldstone Retreat	83
	3.2	Assessing the Goldstone Report	87
	3.3	Why the Goldstone Report Broke the Sound Barrier........	88
	3.4	Conclusions and Recommendations of the Goldstone Report..	93
	3.5	A Polarized Debate: Liberal Legality and Geopolitical Reality	96
	3.6	International Law and the Peace Process.................	101
	3.7	Conclusion..	102
	References		103

4 The Follow up to the Goldstone Report and its Legal Impact in Israel and Beyond 105
Sharon Weill
	4.1	Introduction......................................		105
	4.2	The Recommendations of the FFM Report		107
	4.3	The Monitoring of Israeli Investigations		108
		4.3.1	United Nations Monitoring	108
		4.3.2	Israeli Monitoring: The Turkel Commission	110
	4.4	The Israeli System of Investigation.....................		111
		4.4.1	Structural Deficiencies	111
		4.4.2	Policy Deficiency...........................	114
	4.5	Domestic Investigations and Prosecutions Conducted in the Aftermath of Cast Lead		115
	4.6	Conclusion..		117

	4.7	Annex: Cases Prosecuted by Israel in the Aftermath of Cast Lead 118
	References	120

5 Initial Reactions to the Goldstone Report and Reflections on Israeli Accountability 123
Jennifer Barnette
- 5.1 Introduction 124
- 5.2 Initial Reactions to the Goldstone Report 127
  - Not So Easy to Sweep Under the Rug 130
- 5.3 The Legitimacy War 134
  - H.Res.867 135
  - Attacking Goldstone ... and his report 137
- 5.4 Conclusion 139
- References 141

6 Investigating the Investigations: A Comment on the UN Committee of Experts Monitoring of the 'Goldstone Process' 145
Daragh Murray
- 6.1 Introduction 145
- 6.2 Background: The Creation of the Committee 146
  - 6.2.1 Mandate and Methodology 147
  - 6.2.2 The Committee's Principal Findings 147
- 6.3 The International Regulation of Domestic War Crimes Investigations 148
- 6.4 The Committee's Findings 152
  - 6.4.1 Israel 152
  - 6.4.2 The Palestinian Side 158
- 6.5 Concluding Remarks 159
- References 160

7 The Importance of Fact-Finding Missions Under International Humanitarian Law 161
Liesbeth Zegveld
- 7.1 Inability of IHL to Protect Civilians 161
- 7.2 Importance of Facts 162
- 7.3 Goldstone Report and Fact Finding 163
- 7.4 Evidence Gathering in International Law 164
- 7.5 Conclusion 166
- References 167

Documents Attached to Part II 169
[1] UN Human Rights Council Resolution S-9/1 of 12 January 2009, establishing the Fact Finding Mission on the Gaza Conflict 169
[2] Report of the United Nations Fact Finding Mission on the Gaza Conflict (the 'Goldstone Report'): Executive Summary, 23 September 2009 173
[3] Report of the United Nations Fact Finding Mission on the Gaza Conflict: Conclusions and Recommendations, 24 September 2009 199
[4] UN Human Rights Council Resolution S-12/1 of 16 October 2009, endorsing the Goldstone Report 227
[5] UN General Assembly Resolution 64/10 of 5 November 2009 and Official Records with individual States' votes 233
[6] Follow-up to the Report of the United Nations Fact Finding Mission on the Gaza Conflict: Report of the UN Secretary General, Ban Ki Moon, of 4 February 2010, with annexed Israeli and Palestinian Reports on internal investigations 251
[7] UN General Assembly Resolution 64/254 of 26 February 2010 323
[8] UN Human Rights Council Resolution 13/9 of 25 March 2010, establishing a Committee of independent Experts 325
[9] First Report of the Committee of Experts, Pres. Tomuschat, of 23 September 2010. 329
[10] Second Report of the Committee of Experts, Pres. McGowan Davis, of 18 March 2011 357
[11] UN Human Rights Council Resolution 16/32 of 25 March 2011 385

Part III Gaza and the International Criminal Court: The Legal Debate on the Admissibility of the Palestinian Declaration Pursuant to Article 12(3) of the Rome Statute

8 Why Statehood Now: A Reflection on the ICC's Impact on Palestine's Engagement with International Law 391
Michael G. Kearney
8.1 Introduction 391
8.2 De-Politicisation and Human Rights Advocacy 393
8.3 From the Partition Resolution to the ICC 396
    8.3.1 The 1988 Declaration of Independence and Engagement with International Law 398
    8.3.2 The Palestinian Declaration to the ICC 401
8.4 The Fact-Finding Mission Report and the Pressures on the PA to Defer the Vote at the UN 403

	8.5 Summary	405
	References	407

9 The Effects of Palestine's Recognition of the International Criminal Court's Jurisdiction 409
Allain Pellet
9.1 Introduction 409
9.2 The Relevance of a Functional Approach 411
9.3 The Validity of the Palestinian Declaration of 21 January 2009 415
9.4 Postscript 425
References 428

10 The Palestine Declaration to the International Criminal Court: The Statehood Issue 429
John Quigley
10.1 Prior Episodes that Raised the Issue of Palestine Statehood ... 431
10.2 Palestine's Declaration of Statehood 432
10.3 Possible Claimants to Palestine Territory 434
10.4 Entitlement to Self-Determination 435
10.5 Reaction of States 435
10.6 A Continuing Statehood 436
10.7 Conclusion 439
References 439

11 Is Palestine a "State"? A Response to Professor John Quigley's Article, "The Palestine Declaration to the International Criminal Court: The Statehood Issue" 441
Robert Weston Ash
11.1 Introduction 441
11.2 That Palestinian Officials Repeatedly and Openly Admit that Palestine is not a "State" Conclusively Establishes that Palestine Does not Meet the Conditions Required to Accede to ICC Jurisdiction 443
11.3 That Palestine is not Recognized as a "State" by Key International Institutions is Additional Indication that the International Community Does not Recognize Palestine as a "State" 449
11.4 That no Arab Palestinian State Currently Exercises Sovereign Control Over Claimed Palestinian "Territory" Also Confirms that Palestine is not a "State" 455
11.5 Conclusion 458
References 459

12	Palestine Statehood: A Rejoinder to Professor Robert Weston Ash	461
	John Quigley	
	12.1 Professor Ash's Sect. 11.2: Statements by Palestinian Officials and Palestinian Participation in the Peace Process...	462
	12.2 Professor Ash's Sect. 11.3: The International Community....	463
	12.3 Professor Ash's Sect. 11.4: The Attributes of Statehood.....	466
	12.4 Conclusions.	467
	References	468
13	ICC Jurisdiction Over Acts Committed in the Gaza Strip: Article 12(3) of the ICC Statute and Non-State Entities	469
	Yaël Ronen	
	13.1 Introduction.	469
	13.2 Preconditions for ICC Jurisdiction	473
	13.3 Admission of the Palestinian Declaration as that of a Full-Fledged State	476
	13.4 Admission Under Article 12(3) of a Declaration by a Quasi-State	481
	13.5 Institutional Considerations	485
	13.6 Conclusion.	491
	References	492
14	In Defence of Functional Interpretation of Article 12(3): A Response to Yaël Ronen	497
	Yuval Shany	
	14.1 The Statute's Delegation-Based Jurisdiction.	498
	14.2 The Interpretative Question: Can a Non-State Entity be Regarded as a State?.	500
	14.3 The Rome Statute's Object and Purpose is Well-Served by a Functional Approach to Delegation	503
	14.4 The Plot Thickens: The Oslo Accords.	506
	14.5 Conclusions.	510
	References	511
15	Note on the Legal Effects of Palestine's Declaration Under Article 12(3) of the ICC Statute	513
	Vera Gowlland-Debbas	
	15.1 A Functional Approach to Statehood for Purposes of Article 12(3)	514
	15.2 Interpretative Approaches to Article 12(3) of the Statute.	515
	15.3 The International Status of Palestine Under the Relevant Rules of International Law	517
	15.3.1 Obligations Toward the United Nations.	517

		15.3.2	Palestine's International Status and the Legitimacy of Statehood	518
		15.3.3	Obligations Under International Law of the States Parties to the ICC Statute	523
	References			524

Part IV Non Judicial Responses: The Russell Tribunal on Palestine

16 The Russell Tribunal on Palestine 527
Frank Barat and Daniel Machover
    16.1   Introduction 527
    16.2   Background to the RToP 530
    16.3   The First International Session of the Russell Tribunal on Palestine 532
    16.4   The Call for the Suspension of the EU-Israel Association Agreement 535
    16.5   The Second International Session of the Russell Tribunal on Palestine 537
    16.6   Corporate Liability for Complicity in International Law Violations 538
    16.7   The Third International Session of the Russell Tribunal on Palestine 540
    16.8   Russell Tribunal on Palestine: An Enduring Legacy 541
    References 542
    Annex to Chapter 16: Executive Summaries of the Findings of the International Sessions of the Russell Tribunal on Palestine, Barcelona, March 2010, and London, November 2010 543

Part V Concluding Remarks

17 International (In)Justice and Palestine 581
John Dugard
    Annex to Chapter 17: Report of the Independent Fact Finding Committee on Gaza Presented to the League of Arab States, 30 April 2009—'No Safe Place', Executive Summary 586

Chapter 1
Introduction

Chantal Meloni and Gianni Tognoni

Contents

1.1 Introduction 1
1.2 Chronology of Events Related to the UN Fact Finding Mission
    on the Gaza Conflict 5
1.3 Map of Gaza 9

1.1 Introduction

'Is there a Court for Gaza?' was the straightforward question that emerged in the wake of the Israeli military operation in the Gaza Strip (the so-called 'Operation Cast Lead') of 27 December 2008–18 January 2009. Serious allegations of grave violations of international humanitarian law and of war crimes' commission were immediately raised by a number of sources with regard to this operation. International and local independent human rights organisations—as Amnesty International, Human Rights Watch, FIDH, B'Tselem, PCHR—all issued reports detailing the extent of the alleged violations, and the disregard for the basic principles of international law, in particular of the principles of necessity, proportionality and of distinction between civilian and military targets.

C. Meloni is Researcher in Criminal Law, University of Milan, and Alexander von Humboldt scholar, Humboldt University of Berlin. G. Tognoni, Medical Doctor, is Secretary General to the Permanent Peoples' Tribunal, residing in the Lelio Basso Foundation, Rome.

C. Meloni (✉)
University of Milan, Milan, Italy

G. Tognoni
Lelio Basso Foundation, Rome, Italy

C. Meloni and G. Tognoni (eds.), *Is There a Court for Gaza?*,
DOI: 10.1007/978-90-6704-820-0_1,
© T.M.C. ASSER PRESS, The Hague, The Netherlands, and the authors/editors 2012

An independent Fact Finding Committee, led by Professor John Dugard, managed to enter the Gaza Strip few weeks after the end of the offensive, and released a Report which was presented to the Arab League on 30 April 2009, assessing the responsibility of both Israel, for the commission of war crimes, crimes against humanity and other grave violations of international law, and of Hamas, for the indiscriminate rocket firing (see *infra* Chap. 17, Annex).

Moreover, in the aftermath of the operation a UN Fact Finding Mission was established, which was led by the South-African Judge Richard Goldstone and composed by well-respected and qualified independent experts. The Commission released a highly detailed report (the 'Goldstone Report') in September 2009, outlining the commission of war crimes and possible crimes against humanity by the Israeli and, on a different scale, by the Palestinian side. It called for urgent implementation of accountability mechanisms at the domestic level or—in case of failure by the national authorities to conduct prompt, independent, credible investigations, in line with international standards—at the international level.

The UN General Assembly, Human Rights Council and European Parliament amidst high political pressure and criticism endorsed the Report and its recommendations. Several resolutions followed, calling for proper investigations and accountability for the alleged violations of international law. An independent Committee of Experts was established by the Human Rights Council, tasked with the assessment of the investigations conducted at the domestic level. The Committee, which was led by German Professor Christian Tomuschat, released a first report in September 2010, which pointed out the flaws of the domestic system and the lack of proper criminal investigations at the national level.

A second report by a second Committee of Experts was released in March 2011 which, while giving account of some sets of military investigations carried out by Israel and of the findings of the commission of inquiry that was established by the Palestinian Authority in Ramallah, substantially confirmed the findings of the first Report. Indeed in March 2011 the UN Human Rights Council adopted a last Resolution recommending the General Assembly to reconsider the Report of the Fact Finding Mission at its 66th session (i.e. the September 2011 one) and urged the Assembly to submit that Report to the Security Council for its consideration and appropriate action, including considering a referral of the situation in the occupied Palestinian territory to the Prosecutor of the International Criminal Court (ICC).

What emerges clearly after more than two and a half years is that recourse to mechanisms of international justice is urgently needed. Victims are still in quest of justice: no proper criminal investigation was carried out, no reparation was granted so far. As Justice Goldstone affirmed when presenting the Report before the UN Human Rights Council:

> A culture of impunity in the region has existed for too long. The lack of accountability for war crimes and possible crimes against humanity has reached a crisis point; the ongoing lack of justice is undermining any hope for a successful peace process and reinforcing an environment that fosters violence. Time and again, experience has taught us that overlooking justice only leads to increased conflict and violence.

1 Introduction

Against this complex background, the idea came to us to put together a book that would serve to thoroughly document the actual situation from a legal perspective, and focus on the role of international bodies and institutions in the delicate blend of law and politics that connotes international justice in general, and specifically when it comes to the Israeli–Palestinian conflict.

This is particularly evident today, in a moment when—at the time of closing this book—the debate is burning about the 'September bid' (Palestinian President Abbas' request of September 2011 for UN membership and statehood recognition of Palestine), and the 'Goldstone Report' appears to have been intentionally forgotten, as if it were incompatible the contemporary pursue of justice for the victims and an advancement at the political stage. Surely such a UN vote will potentially have a big impact also on the legal mechanisms available to the Palestinians, in case Palestine were to be recognised as an independent State under international law and/or accepted as a UN member. However, it appears also clear that no real sovereignty will be achieved and no self-determination enjoyed by the Palestinians as far as the occupation of their territory will continue.

In any case the perspective that we decided to adopt, as editors of this book, is a strictly legal one, and is aimed at inquiring the judicial alternatives which are at hand for the victims of the alleged grave crimes committed in the occupied Palestinian territory, and in particular in Gaza.

The book collects important contributions by distinguished professors and scholars in the field of international law, and it puts together essential official documents that were produced at the international level before and as follow-up to the 'Goldstone Report'. The material is structured along five parts, each of them outlining different aspects of the same issue.

In particular, *Part I* collects a selection of papers from the International Conference that was organised by the Lelio Basso Foundation in Rome on 22 May 2009, and that actually inspired the present book. During that early conference (when the 'Goldstone Report' had yet to be released), eminent professors, lawyers and human rights experts discussed the possibility of an intervention of the International Criminal Court and its hurdles, and imagined possible alternatives to achieve justice for the victims, including the recourse to the principle of universal jurisdiction.

Part II is focusing on the UN Fact Finding Mission on the Gaza Conflict and its follow-up at the international level. Richard Falk, the UN Special Rapporteur on the Occupied Palestinian Territory, thoroughly analyses the issue in its whole complexity, also in the light of the recent 'retreat' by Judge Goldstone, which sparked so much criticism among the international jurists community. The papers of Jennifer Barnette, Sharon Weill, Daragh Murray and Liesbeth Zegveld further analyse the follow-up process to the UN Fact Finding Mission Report from an international law perspective, outlining both the importance of the process and the specific problems and obstacles encountered, including the adverse reactions to the Report in the USA and in Israel. The chapter is complemented by the essential UN documentation produced on the 'Goldstone process' up to date.

The possible intervention of the International Criminal Court is treated in *Part III*. A declaration under Article 12(3) of the ICC Statute was submitted by the

Palestinian Government back in January 2009, accepting the jurisdiction of the Court for the purpose of 'identifying, prosecuting and judging the authors and accomplices of acts committed on the territory of Palestine since 1 July 2002.' Indeed, the ICC Prosecutor opened a 'preliminary examination' of the situation in Palestine but the actual opening of an investigation is put on hold, allegedly due to the unclear jurisdiction of the Court on the facts at stake. In fact Israel is not a State Party of the Court and Palestine is currently not in a position to ratify the Statute either. Michael Kearney's paper, which opens the chapter, well outlines the effects of a possible ICC intervention on the Palestinian situation and of Palestine's engagement with international law. Whereas the existence or otherwise of a State of Palestine remains—at the time of writing—moot at best for the purpose of international law generally speaking, a convincing argument has been made by professor Alain Pellet that according to a functional interpretation of the concept of statehood, thus for the purposes of the ICC Statute only, a determination by the ICC that Palestine is a State that can be under the jurisdiction of the Court would be valid and in line with the Statute's requirements. Pellet's opinion—which was submitted to the ICC Prosecutor—has been shared by a vast number of International Law professors. Other important opinions, both in favour of the Palestine's declaration and against it, are also presented in the same Part.

In the face of all the difficulties which are so far impeding the pursuit for justice in the occupied Palestinian territory, the on-going experience of the Russell Tribunal on Palestine is presented as a particularly interesting non-judicial response, which can well complement, although not replace, proper judicial mechanisms (*Part IV*). This Tribunal is organised according to the long tradition of Peoples' Tribunals, starting from the Tribunal on Vietnam (1966–1967), which Bertrand Russell set up in the wake of the Vietnam war to document, denounce and judge the responsibilities of the United States. Few years later, Lelio Basso (who had been Rapporteur for the Sessions on Vietnam) launched the Russell Tribunal 2, on the dictatorships which were dominating Latin America with the substantial support of the international community (1974–1976), and inspired and founded the Permanent Peoples' Tribunal (1979) which has been since then active on more than 30 cases of violations of human and peoples rights not admitted to judicial international instruments.

The outspoken and lucid concluding remarks by Professor John Dugard (*Part V*) do not leave much space for optimisms or for easy answers: when it comes to the Palestinian situation, political interests have been hindering justice for so many decades that a dramatic change would be needed, at the international level, in order to overcome such an impunity crisis and restore the rule of law. Surely a strong call for the implementation of international justice mechanisms comes from the international community; therefore it is critical that the process which has been put in place following the Report of the UN Fact Finding Mission on the Gaza Conflict—which is now blocked for political reasons—is brought to its envisaged conclusion.

In the end, as the sub-title of this book suggests, Gaza can be seen as a test case for international justice, a still imperfect and developing discipline, which is looking for a realistic balance between political equilibrium and justice requirements. In order to reaffirm the rule of law and to avoid bringing the system to a shortcut, it is crucial to assure a minimum of credibility into an international order capable of being accountable first and above all for the human-individual and collective rights of the victims. While it is clear that international juridical institutions and instruments (such as the most recent of them, the ICC) are expressions of the broader international scenarios and actors, it is even clearer that the prolongation, and the worsening, of the dissociation between the principles and the formal declarations, and their real life implementation could represent a truly fatal threat for the whole international community.

1.2 Chronology of Events Related to the UN Fact Finding Mission on the Gaza Conflict

12 January 2009: UN Human Rights Council adopts Resolution S-9/1 calling for the appointment of a UN Fact Finding Mission on the Gaza Conflict (27 December 2008–18 January 2009).

3 April 2009: President of the Human Rights Council establishes an international independent Fact Finding Mission (FFM) with the mandate "to investigate all violations of international human rights law and international humanitarian law that might have been committed at any time in the context of the military operations that were conducted in Gaza during the period from 27 December 2008 and 18 January 2009, whether before, during or after."

4 May 2009: UN Fact Finding Mission on the Gaza Conflict convenes for first time in Geneva.

The United Nations Fact Finding Mission Members—The Mission was headed by **Justice Richard Goldstone**, former member of the South African Constitutional Court and former Chief Prosecutor of the International Criminal Tribunals for the former Yugoslavia and Rwanda, and composed by three other mission members: **Professor Christine Chinkin**, Professor of International Law at the London School of Economics and Political Science and member of the High Level Fact Finding Mission to Beit Hanoun (2008); **Ms. Hina Jilani**, Advocate of the Supreme Court of Pakistan and former Special Representative of the Secretary General on Human Rights Defenders and member of the International Commission of Inquiry on Darfur (2004); and **Colonel Desmond Travers**, former officer in the Irish Armed Forces and member of the Board of Directors of the Institute for International Criminal Investigations.

1–5 June and 19–26 June 2009: Mission members conduct two field visits to the Gaza Strip, during which they hold meetings, conduct interviews with victims and witnesses and visit the sites of incidents. On 28 and 29 June, the Mission holds public hearings in Gaza, including victims and experts from the Gaza Strip. On 6 and 7 July, the Mission holds public hearings in Geneva, consisting of victims and experts from Israel and the West Bank, as well as military and legal experts.

1–4 July 2009: The Mission is refused collaboration by Israel and thus cannot enter the West Bank. Members of the Mission travel to Amman, Jordan, to interview witnesses and meet with people and organizations from Israel and the West Bank.

15 September 2009: Report of the Fact Finding Mission on the Gaza Conflict (i.e. the 'FFM Report') is released, recommending that the sides to the conflict openly investigate their own conduct and, should they fail to do so, that the allegations to be brought to the International Criminal Court.

16 October 2009: UN Human Rights Council Special Session endorses the 'FFM Report' (Resolution S-12/1).

5 November 2009: UN General Assembly endorses the Goldstone Report by a vote of 114 in favour to 18 against, with 44 abstentions (Resolution 64/10). The Resolution calls upon the Government of Israel and the Palestinian side to conduct investigations "that are independent, credible and in conformity with international standards into the serious violations of international humanitarian and international human rights law reported by the (United Nations) Fact Finding Mission (on the Gaza Conflict), towards ensuring accountability and justice", within 3 months, and requests Secretary-General Ban Ki-Moon to send the 'FFM Report' to the Security Council.

3 December 2009: UN Secretary-General Ban Ki-Moon sends notes verbales to the Permanent Mission of Israel to the United Nations, the Permanent Observer Mission of Palestine to the United Nations and the Permanent Mission of Switzerland to the United Nations, drawing their attention to the relevant provisions of Resolution 64/10, and requesting written information by 29 January 2010 concerning any steps that may have been taken or were in the process of being taken in relation to their implementation.

29 January 2010: Permanent Observer Mission of Palestine to the United Nations conveys to UN Secretary-General Ban Ki-Moon a 27 January letter from Palestinian Prime Minister Salam Fayyad including a preliminary report on the internal investigations conducted by the Independent Investigative Committee established by the Palestinian Authority in follow-up to the recommendations of the 'FFM Report'.

29 January 2010: The State of Israel submits a report of its internal investigation into serious violations of international humanitarian and international human rights law committed by the Israeli side to the Gaza conflict to the Office of the High Commissioner of Human Rights, entitled "Gaza Operation Investigations: An Update."

2 February 2010: Hamas government communicates to the Office of High Commissioner of Human Rights the establishment of a commission of inquiry, with international members, into serious violations of international humanitarian and international human rights law committed by the Palestinian side during the Gaza Conflict.

4 February 2010: Report of UN Secretary-General Ban Ki-Moon is released, with annexed the responses and materials received by the State of Israel, the Palestinian Authority and Switzerland. The Secretary-General notes that "the processes initiated by the Government of Israel and the Government of Switzerland are ongoing, and that the Palestinian side initiated its process on 25 January 2010. As such, no determination can be made on the implementation of the resolution by the parties concerned."

4 March 2010: The European Parliament passes a resolution endorsing the 'FFM Report'. The Resolution calls on European Union member states to "publicly demand the implementation of [the Report's] recommendations and accountability for all violations of international law, including alleged war crimes."

25 March 2010: UN Human Rights Council endorses Resolution on Follow-up to the Report of the United Nations Fact Finding Mission on the Gaza Conflict, thereby establishing an independent Committee of Experts in international humanitarian and international human rights law to monitor and assess and domestic, legal or other proceedings undertaken by both the Government of Israel and the Palestinian side with regard to recommendations made by the 'FFM Report' (Resolution13/9 dated 14 April 2010).

14 June 2010: UN Human Rights Council appoints a Committee of Experts for Gaza investigation, as outlined in Resolution 13/9 of 25 March. The Committee is chaired by Prof. Christian Tomuschat, Professor Emeritus at Humboldt University of Berlin, former member of the United Nations Human Rights Committee and former president of the International Law Commission. The other two members are: Judge Mary McGowan Davis, former Justice of the Supreme Court of the State of New York and former federal prosecutor; and Mr. Param Cumaraswamy, jurist and former Special Rapporteur of the Commission on Human Rights on the independence of judges and lawyers.

19 July 2010: Israeli Defense Forces (IDF) submit to the Office of the UN High Commissioner of Human Rights a second report of the IDF's internal investigation on the Gaza conflict entitled "Gaza Operation Investigations: Second Update."

26–30 July 2010: The Committee of Experts, which has been refused collaboration by the Israeli government and thus cannot enter either Israel or the West Bank, convenes in Amman, Jordan.

28 July 2010: The Hamas government submits to the Office of the UN High Commissioner of Human Rights a second communication regarding its internal investigation on the Gaza Conflict.

15–16 August 2010: The Committee of Experts convenes in Gaza, where it meets with representatives from governments and NGOs as well as witnesses and victims of the incidents mentioned in the 'FFM Report'.

23 September 2010: The Report of the Committee of Experts is submitted to the UN Human Rights Council; it assesses the domestic, legal or other proceedings undertaken by both the government of Israel and the Palestinian side with regard to the recommendations made by the 'FFM Report'.

6 October 2010: UN Human Rights Council Resolution 15/6 renews and resumes the Committee of Expert's mandate.

18 March 2011: The second Report by the Committee of Experts is submitted to the UN Human Rights Council pursuant to its Resolution 15/6, which "renews and resumes" the mandate of the Committee established in Human Rights Council Resolution 13/9. The Committee is composed by Justice Mary McGowan Davis (chairing member, following to Professor Tomuschat's resignation) and Judge Lennart Aspegren, former Judge and Director-General for Legal and International Affairs at different Swedish Ministries, and Judge at the ICTR.

25 March 2011: UN Human Rights Council endorses the conclusions of the Committee of Experts and urges the General Assembly to submit the 'FFM Report' to the Security Council "for its consideration and appropriate action, including consideration of referral of the situation in the Occupied Palestinian Territory to the Prosecutor of the International Criminal Court, pursuant to Article 13(b) of the Rome Statute" (Resolution 16/32).

1 Introduction

1.3 Map of Gaza

Map created by the Office for the Coordination of Humanitarian Affairs (OCHA), occupied Palestinian territory.

Part I
International Conference
'Is There a Court for Gaza?'
22 May 2009, Rome

Part I
Information and Communication:
Is There a Future for eLearning?
An EDEN 2004 Research...

Chapter 2
Selected Materials from the International Conference 'Is There a Court for Gaza?' 22 May 2009, Lelio Basso International Foundation, Rome

Chantal Meloni and Gianni Tognoni

Contents

2.1	Introduction	14
2.2	Selected Conference's Papers	15
	2.2.1 Raji Sourani	16
	2.2.2 Eric David	24
	2.2.3 Giuseppe Palmisano	30
	2.2.4 Gabriele Della Morte	36
	2.2.5 Chantal Meloni	41
	2.2.6 Flavia Lattanzi	48
	2.2.7 François Rigaux	56
2.3	Presentation of the Complaint Filed Before the International Criminal Court by Gilles Devers and Mireille Fanon Mendes-France	61
	2.3.1 Introduction	61
	2.3.2 Violations of International Law	62
	2.3.3 Violations of International Humanitarian Law and Human Rights Law	66
	2.3.4 The Commission of War Crimes	69
	2.3.5 The Commission of Crimes Against Humanity	70
	2.3.6 Consequences in Terms of the Individual Criminal Liability of Israeli Authorities	71

C. Meloni is Researcher in Criminal Law, University of Milan, and Alexander von Humboldt scholar, Humboldt University of Berlin. G. Tognoni, Medical Doctor, is Secretary General to the Permanent Peoples' Tribunal, residing in the Lelio Basso Foundation, Rome.

C. Meloni (✉)
University of Milan, Milan, Italy

G. Tognoni
Lelio Basso Foundation, Rome, Italy

C. Meloni and G. Tognoni (eds.), *Is There a Court for Gaza?*,
DOI: 10.1007/978-90-6704-820-0_2,
© T.M.C. ASSER PRESS, The Hague, The Netherlands, and the authors/editors 2012

	2.3.7 The Consequences of the Violations of International Law by the State of Israel..	72
	2.3.8 Conclusions...	74
2.4	States That Have Recognised Palestine as a State..	76
References...		79

2.1 Introduction

On 22 May 2009, four months after the end of the devastating Israeli attack on Gaza (the so-called 'Operation Cast Lead') the International Section of the Lelio Basso Foundation organised an international conference in Roma (Italy), which eventually inspired the present book.

The conference brought together a number of eminent international law professors, lawyers and human rights experts, political figures and high profile personalities, who are variously involved in the struggle for justice of the Palestinian People. The invited speakers included Eric David, François Rigaux, Flavia Lattanzi Giuseppe Palmisano, Antoni Pigrau Solé, Gilles Devers, Franco Ippolito, Raji Sourani, Roland Kessous, Mario Lana, Luisa Morgantini, Leila Shahid, Moni Ovadia, Mireille Fanon Mendes-France and Gabriele Della Morte, besides the present editors and several other members of the Lelio Basso Foundation.

Notwithstanding the political implications of virtually *anything* that involves the Israeli–Palestinian context, the question at the heart of the conference, whether there is a Court for Gaza, was of course strictly juridical. Although the question remains still a current and unfortunately unsolved one, many interesting inputs and suggestions came from the speakers during that early conference, in a sort of anticipation of the issues which are developed more in depth in the following Parts of this book. Of course, back in May 2009 the UN Fact-Finding Mission's Report (the 'Goldstone Report') had not been published yet; still, allegations of commission of crimes during the 3-weeks military operation were consistent and coming from several independent sources.

Moreover, on 21 January 2009 the Government of Palestine, acting through its Minister of Justice, had lodged a declaration with the Registrar of the International Criminal Court (ICC) accepting the jurisdiction of the Court pursuant to Article 12(3) of the Statute.[1] The declaration did not refer to any specific crimes but accepted the jurisdiction of the Court on the crimes committed in the territory of Palestine after 1 July 2002 (the date of the entry into force of the ICC Statute). The Court Registrar, Silvana Arbia, accepted the declaration and notified the

---

[1] According to this article, "If the acceptance of a State which is not a party to this Statute is required under para 2 that State may, by declaration lodged with the Registrar, accept the exercise of jurisdiction by the Court with respect to the crime in question."

Palestinian authorities of the reception with the following *caveat*: "without prejudice to a judicial determination on the applicability of Article 12, para 3, to your correspondence."

As one of the first legal actions that were undertaken in the aftermath of Israeli 'Operation Cast Lead', the French lawyer Gilles Devers and Mireille Fanon Mendes-France, filed a complaint to the International Criminal Court on behalf of a number of associations representing the victims of the attacks (see *infra* 2.3). The debate around the possible intervention of the ICC was of course very intense and animated the discussion among the panellists of the conference for several hours.

In this part of the book we thus decided to give account of the discussion that took place during that early conference in Rome, focusing in particular on the legal issues that emerged in the different panels, namely the question of the Palestinian statehood; the possible jurisdiction of the ICC and the principle of complementarity; the crime of aggression; the recourse to the principle of universal jurisdiction and the flaws of the domestic systems.

The 'proceedings of the conference'[2] are opened by a paper of Raji Sourani, Director of the Palestinian Centre for Human Rights, introducing the factual, legal and political situation of Gaza and framing Israel's military 'Operation Cast Lead' and its consequences in the broader Palestinian context (2.2.1), include the legal analysis and interventions of scholars Eric David (2.2.2), Giuseppe Palmisano (2.2.3), Gabriele Della Morte (2.2.4), Chantal Meloni (2.2.5) and Flavia Lattanzi (2.2.6) and are concluded by the observations of François Rigaux, Professor emeritus of international law and member of the Permanent Peoples' Tribunal (2.2.7).

2.2 Selected Conference's Papers

The following contributions are based on the papers that the speakers have been invited to submit following to the conference, which have been partly re-elaborated by the editors and assembled as needed for the purposes of this publication.[3]

---

[2] *Infra*, Sect. 2.2.

[3] The editors wish to thank once again all the eminent speakers that found the time to put in writing their oral interventions, and in particular Professors Eric David, Flavia Lattanzi, Giuseppe Palmisano and François Rigaux, Dr. Gabriele Della Morte, Lawyers Raji Sourani and Gilles Devers and Ms Mireille Fanon Mendes-France.

2.2.1 Raji Sourani[4]

(1) Israel's recent 23 day **military offensive on the Gaza Strip** (codenamed operation 'Cast Lead' by the Israeli Army), claimed the lives of approximately 1,400 Palestinians and resulted in the decimation of the Gaza Strip. The overwhelming majority of the dead and wounded were non-combatants, including hundreds of women and children. The sheer scale of the destruction, and the consequent suffering and trauma is hard to imagine. Today, four months after Israel's declaration of a unilateral ceasefire, the Gaza Strip remains as it was on the 18 January 2009.[5] The siege of Gaza—a form of collective punishment, which has been tightened and consecutively imposed since June 2007—means that reconstruction, and thus recovery, is impossible. Rubble still litters the Gaza Strip, thousands of people remain homeless, and most importantly the 1.7 million population of Gaza are imprisoned in this little territory, unable to enjoy their most basic rights: most of the injured from the last offensive—over 5,300—not even have the chance to get a proper medical treatment. Every day the citizens of Gaza confront the reality of the offensive, and the reality of the occupation, as they struggle to reclaim some semblance of 'normality' amidst an escalating manufactured humanitarian crisis.

(2) A preliminary note on the Palestinian context. Operation 'Cast Lead' was only the latest horrific incident in 42 years of occupation. On 14 May 1999, the Oslo Peace-Process was to have resulted in a final political solution and an independent Palestinian State. Ten years have now passed since this date, and what have been the results? Today, we human rights Organisations are talking about cement, freedom of movement, and access to medicine. We are talking about basic survival. For Palestinian civilians, Oslo has not resulted in progress, but in regression. Life now is worse that it was before. There is a de facto apartheid system in place in the West Bank, economic and social suffocation in the Gaza Strip, and continuing violence, as dramatically illustrated by the recent Israeli offensive. The possibility of a real and lasting peace seems more elusive than ever before.

Following the death of President Arafat—a man once hailed as a 'partner for peace', but who, as the Oslo process crumbled, was transformed into a 'terrorist' and placed under siege—the Palestinians chose the rule of law. In democratic elections, internationally recognised as free and fair, Palestinians voted for a new

---

[4] Director of the Palestinian Centre for Human Rights (PCHR), http://www.pchrgaza.org. Executive member of the International Commission of Jurists (ICJ); Vice President of the International Federation of Human Rights (FIDH) and President of the Arab Organization for Human Rights.

[5] At the time of editing the present book (July 2011), the situation is unfortunately not substantially different than two years ago. The illegal closure of the Gaza Strip has prevented any real reconstruction, and has worsened the economic and social conditions of the civilian population, which continues to be cut off from the rest of the world, without access to the most basic needs, including a decent health care [ChM].

leadership. In a serious blow for democracy and self-determination, their decision was rejected by the international community. In rejecting the 2006 Legislative Council election results, and endorsing Israel's decision to isolate Hamas and collectively punish the Palestinian people, the international community apparently adhered to an antiquated Roman ideal of democracy: that democracy was for masters and not for slaves. These events generated a momentum that has resulted in the reality currently faced by Palestinians.

The complicity of the international community—evidenced, *inter alia*, by its endorsement of the decision to isolate Hamas and *de facto* support for the siege of the Gaza Strip—effectively granted Israel permission to escalate crimes perpetrated in the occupied Palestinian territory (oPt), and to reinforce the economic and cultural suffocation of the Palestinian people. In the absence of accountability, the rule of law has been disregarded.

In June 2007, in response to the Hamas takeover of the Gaza Strip, Israel closed Gaza's borders to the movement of both people and goods. In spite of the devastating consequences of both the offensive and the siege itself, Israel has maintained its closure policy to this day.

This illegal form of collective punishment has now been imposed on the population of the Gaza Strip for nearly two years, bringing Gaza to its knees. By December 2008, on the eve of Operation Cast Lead, the Gaza Strip was the scene of a humanitarian crisis. Unemployment was at 80 percent, poverty at 60 percent. There was no wheat for bread, bakeries either closed or were forced to resort to animal feed. There was not enough electricity to power hospitals and other essential services, such as the water and sanitation networks. Cooking gas, medicines and essential food stuff were scarce, or unavailable. In the aftermath of the offensive, the situation in the Gaza Strip is dire. An estimated 21,000 homes have been completely or partially destroyed, thousands of dunums of agricultural land have been razed, 1,500 factories, workshops and commercial establishments have been damaged or destroyed, and public infrastructure is in a state of near collapse.[6] Today, four months after Israel's declaration of a unilateral ceasefire, the Gaza Strip remains in a limbo; though the offensive has ended, the occupation continues. The Israeli imposed siege makes recovery impossible. Civilians cannot rebuild their homes. The 600,000 tonnes of rubble littering the Gaza Strip cannot be cleared. There is not even the concrete with which to construct a tombstone. Palestinians cannot enter or leave the Gaza Strip. Patients continue to die because they are denied access to medical treatment. Under the siege, the economy continues to contract. There are ever-increasing levels of unemployment, poverty, destitution, and despair.

At the 2 March 2009 conference in Sharm el-Sheikh, international donors pledged US$4.5 billion for the reconstruction of the Gaza Strip. Such funds are urgent and necessary given the extent of the unfolding humanitarian disaster. However, although international donors pledged a seemingly impressive sum of

---

[6] These figures are based on initial estimates.

money, what does this mean? Without the political pressure necessary to end the siege and make reconstruction possible, Sharm el-Sheikh is nothing but a show presented to the world's media.

It is claimed that what is happening in Gaza now is a result of Hamas' takeover of the Gaza Strip, a situation which the Palestinian Centre for Human Rights has documented and condemned in detail. But this is a disingenuous argument. One need only look at the situation in the West Bank for proof that events in the Gaza Strip merely form part of Israel's overall occupation policy. Despite the existence of a 'friendly' government in Ramallah, illegal settlement expansion continues. By-pass roads link settlements to major cities in Israel leading to the cantonization of the West Bank (a process of de facto Bantustanisation). Construction of the Annexation Wall continues. Nearly 680 checkpoints restrict freedom of movement and contribute to economic stagnation. Over 40 members of the Palestinian Legislative Council are currently imprisoned in Israeli jails. The annexation of East Jerusalem continues. Incursions, killings and house demolitions, all have become features of life in the West Bank.

This reality has been extensively documented. It has been the subject of an Advisory Opinion of the International Court of Justice; it has been addressed by the United Nations Security Council; it has been the subject of numerous reports by various UN agencies and bodies, including the Human Rights Council, and the reports of several Special Rapporteurs. The evidence is overwhelming.

We must ask ourselves why it happened? What has happened to the rule of law, was it replaced by the rule of the jungle?

(3) International Humanitarian Law (IHL) extends explicit protections to civilians in times of occupation and armed conflict. It is founded upon the concept of human dignity, and is intended to spare civilians—as far as possible—from the effects of hostilities. To this end, explicit laws regulate the conduct of hostilities. They detail who is a combatant and who is not, they establish measures that must be taken to ensure the protection and welfare of civilian populations, they expand upon the precautions necessary in attack, and limit the methods and means of warfare. These laws are not ambiguous, they detail explicit rights and obligations. The Geneva Conventions have been universally ratified, while customary IHL extends their principles to form a comprehensive body of international law.

Yet, over the course of the occupation, IHL and international human rights law, have been consistently violated and disregarded, often under the glare of the world's media. How, and why, has this happened? In light of the offensive this conference has asked "Is there a court able to shed a light on these tragic events, apportion liability, and tell the truth about what happened?"

Let me begin by stating the obvious. It is essential that these cases are heard before a competent court, and that those responsible are held to account. The simple truth is that violations of international legal obligations have been a consistent part of Israel's policy in occupied Palestinian territory. The reason for this is clear: Israel has been permitted to operate outside the law. It has been granted impunity. Not once has a competent court—acting in accordance with international legal standards relating to the effective administration of justice—sat in judgment of those accused of the numerous crimes of the occupation. These crimes have included torture, grave breaches of the Geneva Conventions, and crimes against humanity.

If the rule of law is to be upheld, if it is to be relevant and capable of protecting those it seeks to protect, then it must be enforced. There is no alternative: as long as a State is permitted to act with impunity, it will continue to violate the law. Enforcement and accountability are thus necessary mechanism to combat impunity and promote deterrence: to ensure that the rule of law remains relevant. However, we must not forget the victims. As recognised in Article 2 of the International Covenant on Civil and Political Rights (ICCPR), the victims are entitled to an effective judicial remedy. They are entitled to justice: to see those responsible tried and punished. It is these victims that we work for.

So, what court is capable of meeting their needs? I will address three potential avenues available to Palestinian victims of international crimes. Although countless other crimes, not amounting to international crimes were committed, in light of the relevance of this conference, I will deal only with those violations capable of giving rise to international jurisdiction.

But let me first turn to the Palestinian institutions and their possible jurisdiction over such crimes.

(4) The Palestinian Authority (PA) was established consequent to the 'Oslo Accords', an agreement reached between the Palestine Liberation Organisation (PLO)—as the recognised representative body of the Palestinian people—and the State of Israel. Though the PLO has been granted special observer status at the United Nations, the remit of the PA is expressly limited, both by the Oslo Accords and the resultant Israeli–Palestinian Interim Agreement. For example, although the PA has established a functioning judicial system capable of upholding the rule of law in the oPt, its jurisdiction is severely limited. Article XVII of the Israeli–Palestinian Interim Agreement stipulates that "the territorial and functional jurisdiction of the [Palestinian] Council will apply to all persons, *except for Israelis*."[7] This explicitly removes Israeli citizens, and members of its armed forces, from the jurisdiction of the PA; therefore, no Israeli may be brought before a Palestinian court. When dealing with the prosecution of alleged Israeli war criminals, this legally binding restriction effectively removes the Palestinian judicial system from the ambit of legal options available to victims.

Additionally, consequent to its legal status, the PA cannot ratify or accede to any of the major international criminal law treaties, such as the Statute of the International Criminal Court (ICC), or to other international human rights law or international humanitarian law treaties such as the Geneva Conventions, the International Covenant on Civil and Political Rights (ICCPR), or the United Nations Convention against Torture (UNCAT). Consequently, the jurisdiction of inter alia, the ICC, the Human Rights Committee, or the Committee against

---

[7] Interim Agreement on the West Bank and the Gaza Strip, Israel–Palestine, September 28, 1995 (emphasis added).

Torture, cannot currently extend to the oPt. However, it must be noted that, as the Occupying Power, Israel has extensive extraterritorial human rights obligations.[8] As such it is required to report to the abovementioned bodies regarding its activities in the oPt. However, no individual petitions on behalf of Palestinian victims can currently be brought before these bodies, and so they cannot offer effective judicial remedy.

The current lacuna in the international legal system, with respect to Palestinian victims of grave breaches of the Geneva Conventions and war crimes, results in a situation whereby there are no legal remedies available to Palestinian victims within the Palestinian system.

(5) **The State of Israel**, as the Occupying Power, is bound by a number of pressing legal obligations. The State of Israel has ratified several relevant international treaties, such as the Geneva Conventions, the ICCPR, and UNCAT, and is therefore bound by the provisions contained therein. For example, Article 146 of the Fourth Geneva Conventions requires that Israel enact "any legislation necessary to provide effective penal sanctions for person committing, or ordering to be committed" any grave breaches of the Geneva Conventions. Equally, the ICCPR obliges Israel to facilitate victims in their pursuit of an effective remedy, and to guarantee their protection before the law. Given the jurisdictional limitations of the PA, Israel has a primary responsibility with respect to Palestinian victims of Israeli violations of international law. In this regard, Israeli courts offer the only domestic mechanism wherein Palestinians can pursue justice.

To date, however, Israel's investigations have proved inadequate, while prosecutions—particularly at the command level—have not been forthcoming. It is presented that, in this respect, Israel must be regarded as shirking its legal obligations, and denying its victims effective legal remedy.

A number of cumulative factors have been identified which fundamentally frustrate Palestinian's pursuit of justice before the Israeli courts. These are: the perceived status of the Gaza Strip and the classification of its civilian population as 'enemy aliens', Israel's legal and judicial mechanisms, the mechanisms of investigation and the lack of a timely remedy. These issues will be explained briefly as they illustrate the bias and lack of independence inherent in the Israeli legal system, and Israel's unwillingness to genuinely investigate and prosecute those suspected of committing crimes against the Palestinian population.

(6) **As for the status of Gaza**, the Israeli authorities—including the Attorney General (AG), the Supreme Court and the legislative—have consistently advanced the position that the Gaza Strip is a 'hostile territory' and that its inhabitants are 'enemy aliens'.[9] In a statement issued on 19 September, 2007, the Israeli Ministry of Foreign Affairs stated that: "Hamas is a terrorist organisation that has taken

---

[8] *Legal Consequences of the Construction of a Wall in the Occupied Palestinian Territory*, Advisory Opinion, ICJ, July 9, 2004, paras 111, 112, 113.

[9] See, Israel Government Communiqué, Security Cabinet Declares Gaza Hostile Entity, September 19, 2007.

control of the Gaza Strip and turned it into hostile territory. This organisation engages in hostile activity against the State of Israel and its citizens and bears responsibility for this activity."[10] This statement followed former Prime Minister Ariel Sharon's claim—made before the General Assembly of the United Nations on 15 September, 2005—that disengagement represented "the end of Israeli control over and responsibility for the Gaza Strip."[11] Israel has used the allegedly modified status of the Gaza Strip to renounce its obligations as an Occupying Power,[12] and to justify the imposition of methods of collective punishment which fail to distinguish between the civilian population, and armed groups.

With respect to the effective administration of justice, it must be highlighted that the "enemy aliens" doctrine effectively treats all inhabitants of the Gaza Strip as enemies, and thus as potential 'terrorists'. In Adalah v. the Interior Minister,[13] the Israeli Supreme Court expanded upon this doctrine:

> The Palestinian public plays an active part in the armed conflict. Among the Palestinian public there is enmity to Israel and Israelis. Large parts of the Palestinian public—including also persons who are members of the organs of the Palestinian Authority—support the armed struggle against Israel and actively participate in it […] *It follows from this that the residents of the territories—Judaea, Samaria and the Gaza Strip—are enemy aliens.*[14]

The Court further noted that Palestinians: "are presumed to endanger national security and public security."[15]

The claim—presented and accepted at the highest levels of the Israeli political and legal system—that all residents of the Gaza Strip are presumed to endanger the State of Israel's national security and public security, has clear and evident repercussions with respect to the pursuit of justice. The straightforward presumption that all Palestinians pose a direct threat to Israel, comes into direct conflict with the presumption of innocence, a fundamental tenet of international law.[16] It is difficult to argue that, under such circumstances, Palestinian victims can expect to receive a fair trial, or an effective judicial remedy.

(7) The mechanisms of the **Israeli legal and judicial system** prevent the impartial pursuit of justice. There is no separation of powers between the military and the military legal system (preventing independent investigation), the hierarchical structure of the military has evident implication with respect to any claim of impartiality, while ineffective civilian oversight and significant—in some cases

---

[10] Ibid.

[11] Ariel Sharon, Prime Minister of the State of Israel, Speech before the General Assembly of the United Nations, September 15, 2005.

[12] Despite these assertions, Israel remains the Occupying Power in the Gaza Strip, based, *inter alia*, on the level of effective control—including control of all land, sea, and air borders—which it still exercises.

[13] The Citizenship and Entry into Israel Law (temporary provision) 5763—2003.

[14] HCJ 7052/03, *Adalah v. The Interior Minister* (decision delivered on 14 May 2006), para 12 (emphasis added).

[15] Ibid., para 78 (emphasis added).

[16] Article 14(2), ICCPR.

virtually indefinite—delays within the judicial system contribute to promote a climate of impunity.

Within the Israeli military system, the Military Attorney General (MAG) serves a twofold function: acting as legal advisor to the military authorities, and enforcing penal laws intended to represent the rule of law and the public interest. In this respect, the MAG performs a similar role to that of the AG in the civilian sphere. However, the MAG remains subordinate—in terms of command—to the Chief of Staff. While the Chief of Staff does not have the authority to instruct the MAG regarding arraignments, the military hierarchy within which the MAG operates cannot be ignored.[17]

This situation presents clear implications with respect to the impartiality of any investigation.[18] The extensive 'margin of appreciation' awarded to the AG and the MAG by the Israeli Supreme Court results in the lack of effective civilian judicial oversight, which fundamentally undermines the possibility of justice for Palestinian victims.[19] As noted by the High Court of Justice: the decision made by the prosecuting authorities to close an investigation file on the basis of a lack of sufficient evidence […] normally falls within the 'margin of appreciation' that is afforded to the authorities and curtails—almost to nil—the scope of judicial intervention.[20]

When combined with the Israeli military system's independence and impartiality deficit, the absence of effective civilian judicial oversight and review fundamentally violates Palestinian victims' right to an effective judicial remedy. Israeli Colonel Daniel Reisner, deputy Judge Advocate General, remarked: "Every commander determines whether he's reached the truth… There is no textbook on investigations … We see a great variety."[21] Further, the Military Justice Law and the General Security Services Law stipulate that all materials related to an operational probe, including what is said during the course of a probe, the protocols of its hearings, its findings, conclusions and recommendations, shall not be used as evidence in court, and are confidential.[22]

---

[17] HCJ 425/89, *Zofan v. the MAG*, 43(4) P.D. 718, 725.

[18] See, PCHR Report 2010a.

[19] See, *inter alia*, Israeli Supreme Court decisions: HCJ 5699/07, *Jane Doe (A) v. The Attorney General* (decision delivered on 26 February 2008); and HCJ 425/89, *Suffan v. The Military Advocate General*, PD 43(4) 718, 727 (1989).

[20] HCJ 5699/07, *Jane Doe (A) v. The Attorney General* (decision delivered on 26 February 2008), para 10 of Deputy Chief Justice Rivlin's ruling.

[21] Wilkinson 2002.

[22] Article 539A of the Military Justice Law—1955 states that, "Anything that is said during the course of a military probe, in a protocol of a probe, or any other materials prepared during a probe, as well as its summaries, findings and conclusions, shall not be accepted as evidence in court, except for in a trial for providing false information or concealing an important piece of information in a probe." Article 17(a) of the General Security Services Law—2002 states that, "Anything that is said during an internal probe or in a report prepared following an internal probe, including protocols, findings, conclusions or recommendations […] shall not be accepted as evidence in court, except for in a disciplinary procedure or a criminal trial for providing false information or knowingly concealing an important piece of information in a probe".

These probes, which constitute an integral component of the legal system, are patently ineffective, and cannot be considered either independent or impartial. They give rise to a clear conflict of interest, wherein the accused is intrinsically involved in the investigation.

(8) A note on **'Operation Cast Lead'** and the **conflict of interest of the Israeli Attorney General**. Both the MAG and the AG were heavily involved in the planning and execution of 'Operation Cast Lead'. As revealed in the Israeli media, the offices of the MAG and the AG provided the legal framework regulating the attacks on Gaza.[23] In light of this close relationship, it is unsurprising that the AG rejected Israeli human rights organisations' demands that an independent mechanism be established in order to investigate the killing and injuring of civilians during 'Operation Cast Lead'.

The Israeli authorities opened a number of internal investigations into events associated with 'Operation Cast Lead'. These investigations are inadequate and inappropriate, *inter alia*, on the basis of the fundamental flaws inherent in such investigations, as outlined above. The investigations so far concluded that Israeli forces acted in accordance with the law, closing most of the inquiries into Israeli soldiers accounts of alleged crimes committed in the Gaza Strip.[24]

As has been illustrated, the Israeli system—as it relates to Palestinian victims of Israeli violations—does not meet the necessary international standards with respect to the effective administration of justice. The presumption that all Palestinians are 'enemy aliens' or 'potential terrorists' has evident implications regarding the presumption of innocence, and the right to a fair trial. The hierarchical nature of the military, the ineffective manner in which investigations are conducted, and the lack of civilian oversight—as epitomised by the wide margin of discretion awarded by the Israeli Supreme Court—all combine to fundamentally frustrate the pursuit of justice.[25] Justice for Palestinians is not attainable within this system.

(9) When national legal systems are unable or unwilling to offer effective judicial remedy, the demands of justice require resort to **international legal mechanisms**. In light of the recent presentation to the ICC, and in the absence of a Security Council resolution, there are two potential options. First, the Prosecutor may decide that the ICC has jurisdiction, and second, the pursuit of universal jurisdiction before national courts.

It is hoped that the ICC will develop into the Court that it is intended to become, that it will be widely ratified and that it will prove capable of holding to

---

[23] Feldman and Blau 2009, available at http://www.haaretz.com/hasen/spages/1057648.html.

[24] See, PCHR Press Release 2009a and 2009b.

[25] Additionally, since the beginning of the second *intifada* the number of investigations into cases of death and injury of Palestinians has dramatically dropped, even when not involved in hostilities; B'Tselem reports that between 2000 and 2008 only 287 such exceptional investigations were opened; only 33 of these cases resulted in actual indictments. See http://www.btselem.org/English/Accountability/Investigatin_of_Complaints.asp.

account those accused of crimes falling within its jurisdiction. This is an essential step on the road to universal justice, and all efforts must be made in this regard. Unfortunately, however, that day is not yet with us. In the context of the recent offensive, Israel has not ratified the ICC, and the PA is unable to do so. So while it is essential to promote the work of the ICC, presently it is unable to meet the needs of Palestinian victims.

Under the current scenario, the pursuit of universal jurisdiction is the only legal mechanism currently capable of meeting victims demands for justice. With respect to grave breaches each and every State is under an obligation to enact national legislation—in accordance with Article 146 of the Fourth Geneva Convention—so that those accused of grave breaches may be tried in national courts.

The continued violations of international law and the continued suffering of civilians are the direct consequence of impunity. If the Oslo process has taught us anything it is the consequences—and costs—of deviating from the rule of law and allowing politics to take precedence over justice.

These examples illustrate the fundamental importance of accountability; in order to be relevant, the rule of law must be enforced. Impunity cannot be allowed to prevail. Those responsible for international crimes must be held to account. Such accountability ensures victims' rights to an effective judicial remedy; significantly, it also combats impunity and promotes deterrence, measures which are essential if the cycle of violence and suffering is to be broken. In light of the new government in Israel, it is of paramount importance that the protections of international human rights and humanitarian law are guaranteed.

We must now rely on European civil society, and those who fight for the rule of law to protect the independence of their judiciaries. Recent, politically motivated, measures intended to restrict universal jurisdiction must be opposed, and prevented. Politics must not be allowed to take precedence over justice. It is a testament to the will of the Gazan people that, three days after the end of the offensive, schools and businesses were reopened. This spirit, the power of individual civilians, is what we must seek to protect.

In conclusion, is there a court capable of meeting victims' demands? Yes, there are many, we must tirelessly pursue universal jurisdiction, using it as a stepping stone on the road towards universal justice.

2.2.2 Eric David[26]

(1) The declaration of acceptance by the Palestinian Authority of the jurisdiction of the International Criminal Court (ICC) on 21 January 2009, in the wake of the shelling of Gaza earlier that month, raises the issue of whether the Registrar of the

---

[26] Professor Emeritus, Law of Armed Conflicts, Université Libre de Bruxelles.

ICC can consider Palestine as a State pursuant to Article 12(3) of the Statute, which, in turn, poses the question: **what is a State**?

Curiously enough, even though the State is a central subject in international relations and in international law, it has never been given a universally accepted official definition. Just as the civil code does not define the parties—that is to say, the persons—to whom its rules apply, except to draw a distinction between different categories (natural persons and corporations, nationals and aliens, adults and children, etc.), conventional international law does not define the State, which is both its primary subject and its object.[27] The only official definition we have of a State is found in a regional instrument: the Convention on the Rights and Duties of States, adopted at Montevideo on 26 December 1933 by the 7th Panamerican Conference, in which Article 1 provides that:

> The State as a person of international law should possess the following qualifications:
>
> (a) a permanent population;
> (b) a defined territory;
> (c) government; and
> (d) capacity to enter into relations with the other States [...].

But this Convention has only been ratified so far by 16 States,[28] and its definition has not been globally confirmed. It is, however, significant that the International Law Commission ultimately refrained from defining the notion of State when it set about laying down the rights and duties of States in 1949, after extensive discussions on the subject.[29]

(2) Yet, the State exists (!), and we know that the **elements** the most commonly repeated to define it are: territory, population, government and sovereignty, or the independence of the community concerned. But these criteria are not sufficient to fully define a State. For it is the case that:

- Communities without real sovereignty have also been considered as if they were States: for example, Ukraine and Belarus were admitted as full members of the United Nations as early as 1945, even though these entities did not become fully independent until 1991, following the break-up of the Soviet Union;
- Communities without real control over their territory have nevertheless been considered States. For example: Palestine was admitted to take part in the work of the Council of the League of Arab States in 1945 (in the annex to the Arab League Pact of 22 March 1945),[30] before becoming a member in 1976,[31] and a full member of the United Nations Economic and Social Commission for Western Asia (ESCWA); the participation of the *Gouvernement provisoire* of

---

[27] Cf. Spiropoulos 1949, p. 35.
[28] http://www.oas.org/juridico/english/sigs/a-40.html.
[29] Spiropoulos 1949, pp. 61–81, 289.
[30] Comp. U.S. Court of App., 2nd Cir., 21 June 1991, *Klinghoffer*, paras 73–74.
[31] http://www.universalis.fr/encyclopedie/MAP0002/LIGUE_ARABE.htm and, http://www.arabsummit.tn/fr/ligue.htm.

the Algerian Republic as a full member of the Inter-African Conferences that preceded the Organisation of African Unit (OAU); Guinea-Bissau was admitted to membership of the OAU in 1973 when it was still under the control of the Portuguese forces, about one year before Portugal withdrew in 1974; the Sahrawi Arab Democratic Republic (Western Sahara) was admitted to the OAU in 1980 at a time when Morocco controlled three-quarters of the territory[32]; Namibia was admitted as a full member of the ITU, FAO, UNESCO, the AIEA, ILO and UNIDO[33] while still occupied by South Africa.
- Communities with a government, a population, a territory and claiming sovereignty have virtually never been recognised as States and have never been admitted as States to any international organisation: Mandchoukouo (1931–1945), Katanga (1960–1962), Biafra (1969–1970), Bantustans (1977–1994), The Turkish Republic of Northern Cyprus (1984–),[34] and Taiwan (1971–).[35]"

(3) There is a contrast between the reality and the legal implications: in some cases, there is a community with no territory and no real sovereignty but is considered to be a State, while in others there is a community which is *de facto* sovereign, and possesses a territory, but is not considered to be a State. Most importantly, this shows that, despite all the hesitations in the literature,[36] it is difficult to ignore the **role of recognition in terms of the legal effects of the existence of a State.** Like it or not, a State is an 'inter-subjective being'[37] which, **in legal terms,** only exists internationally as a State in relations with the States that recognise it as such.[38] Recognition therefore has an effect that is not declaratory alone.[39]

(4) Certainly, however, the cautious reaction of **Switzerland, as the depositary State of the Geneva Conventions** (GCs) of 1949 and their Additional Protocols (APs) of 1977, issued in 1989, reflects a certain amount of reticence:

> On 21 June 1989, the Swiss Federal Department of Foreign Affairs received a letter from the Permanent Observer of Palestine to the United Nations Office at Geneva informing the Swiss Federal Council 'that the Executive Committee of the Palestine Liberation Organisation, entrusted with the functions of the Government of the State of Palestine by

---

[32] Regarding these examples, Bennouna 1980, pp. 193–200; Bedjaoui 1984, pp. 35–58.
[33] Selected Legal Opinions, UN Juridical Ybk., 1989, 373.
[34] Cf. Salmon 1988, pp. 59–60.
[35] Cf. A/Res. 2758 (XXVI), 25 Oct. 1971; a number of small States supported Taiwan's candidature to the United Nations, see Doc. ONU A/55/227, 4 August 2000, add. 1 et 2.
[36] See Carpentier 1991, p. 650.
[37] Carpentier 1986, 98, cited by Ruiz Fabri 1992, p. 168.
[38] Cf. Lapidoth and Calvo-Goller 1992, pp. 802–803.
[39] For the Arbitration Commission of the Commission on Yugoslavia, "La reconnaissance par les autres Etats a des effets purement déclaratifs", opinion of 29 November 1991, para 1, a. We consider the reality to be rather more nuanced: see Ruiz Fabri 1992, pp. 153–154, 163.

decision of the Palestine National Council, decided, on 4 May 1989, to adhere to the Four Geneva Conventions of 12 August 1949 and the two Protocols additional thereto'.
On 13 September 1989, the Swiss Federal Council informed the States that it was not in a position to decide whether the letter constituted an instrument of accession, '**due to the uncertainty within the international community as to the existence or non-existence of a State of Palestine**'.[40]

In other words, as the depositary State of GCs, Switzerland refused to include Palestine on the list of States Parties to the GCs of 1949 and the APs of 1977.

(5) Nevertheless **the reluctance of Switzerland** to register Palestine as a State Party to these Treaties was, and remains, **highly controversial**, for various reasons:

(i) It was on 15 November 1988 that the Palestinian National Council proclaimed the independence of the State of Palestine. One month later, the United Nations General Assembly adopted a resolution confirming this proclamation; in the Preamble to the Resolution, the General Assembly recalled «its resolution 181 (II) of 29 November 1947, in which, *inter alia*, it called for the establishment of an Arab State and a Jewish State in Palestine»[41] and also declared itself «*Aware* of the proclamation of the State of Palestine by the Palestine National Council in line with General Assembly Resolution 181 (II) and in exercise of the inalienable rights of the Palestinian people.»[42] In the same Resolution the General Assembly further:

(a) *Acknowledges* the proclamation of the State of Palestine by the Palestine National Council on 15 November 1988;
(b) *Affirms* the need to enable the Palestinian people to exercise their sovereignty over their territory occupied since 1967;
(c) *Decides* that, effective as of 15 December 1988, the designation 'Palestine' should be used in place of the designation 'Palestine Liberation Organisation' in the United Nations system, without prejudice to the observer status and functions of the Palestine Liberation Organisation within the United Nations system, in conformity with relevant United Nations resolutions and practice.

This Resolution was adopted with 104 votes in favour and two against (Israel and the USA) with 36 abstentions, signifying that 104 States recognised Palestine as a State.

(ii) In addition to this resolution, which appears to be the expression of multilateral recognition by 104 States, Palestine has been recognised as a State, bilaterally, by 97 States (48 African States, four American States, 30 Asian States, 14 European States and one State in Oceania (see Section 2.4 *infra*); Palestine has also been a full member of the League of Arab States since 1976[43] and of ESCWA; it is therefore not some fictitious or imaginary State, because Palestine is recognised as a 'State' by 97 States [In the meanwhile the number of States that

---

[40] http://www.cicr.org/dih
[41] A/RES 43/177, 15 December. 1988, 2nd considering.
[42] Ibid., 4th considering.
[43] http://www.arableagueonline.org/wps/portal/las_en/home_page/

according to public available sources, as of December 2011, recognised Palestine has grown to 128, see *infra* Annex 2.4, ChM].

(iii) The Swiss attitude is open to criticism in particular in terms of the Vienna Convention on the Law of Treaties of 23 May 1969, which provides that « The functions of the depositary of a treaty are international in character and the depositary is under an obligation to act **impartially** in their performance » (Article 76(2), emphasis added); in its commentary of the draft Convention, the International Law Commission explained that while the depositary State was entitled to express its point of view, as a party to the Treaty, in its capacity as depositary it was nevertheless under an obligation to show objectivity and to perform its functions impartially. Switzerland manifestly failed to do so, because its refusal to include Palestine in the list of States parties to GCs and the APs was tantamount to espousing the position of the States which do not recognise Palestine; by so doing, the Swiss attitude was partisan and not impartial.

(iv) The practice followed by the United Nations Secretary General in the matter of registering and publishing treaties appears to be considerably more compliant with the requirements of Article 76 of the Vienna Convention on the Law of Treaties: in the note annexed to the regulations for implementing Article 102 of the United Nations Charter (the registration and publication of treaties), the United Nations Secretariat pointed out that:

> Registration of an instrument submitted by a Member State, therefore, **does not imply a judgement by the Secretariat** on the nature of the instrument, the **status of a party** or any similar question. It is the understanding of the Secretariat that its action **does not confer on the instrument the status of a treaty or an international agreement if it does not already have that status and does not confer on a party a status which it would not otherwise have** (emphasis added).

In the *Qatar/Bahrain* (1994) case, Bahrain objected to the registration of the '*Minutes*' of an agreement concluded with Qatar. The United Nations legal advisor pointed out that it was the practice of the General Secretariat to register all the texts submitted to it as treaties, without pronouncing on the legal nature of those texts.[44] The Secretary General was therefore ready to register Bahrain's objection as well as the text deposited by Qatar.[45]

This attitude is both honest and impartial. It is the attitude that every depositary of a treaty should adopt. As soon as a community demanding recognition of statehood declares its intention to become party to a treaty, and once this community is recognised as a State by other States, the depositary cannot challenge that status, because otherwise it would cease to be acting **impartially** in the performance of its functions required by Article 76(2) of the Vienna Convention on the Law of Treaties. Refusal to register this community as a State party to the Convention of which it was the depository constituted interference in the internal affairs of the recognised State and the States recognising it, because it was

---

[44] A/Res. 97 (I) of 14 December 1946.
[45] See *Bahrain's Counter-Memorial*, 11 June 1992, II, p. 135.

tantamount to criticising the political stance of the States that had proceeded to recognise it.

(6) Therefore, the Swiss Department made a mistake in 1989 when refused to register the PLO decision to adhere the Geneva Conventions. If Switzerland had included Palestine among the States parties to the GCs and their APs, it would have properly performed its role as the depositary and would have acted impartially without implying its recognition of the status of the State of Palestine. It was then up to the other States to object to the registration, if they evaluated this to be appropriate, and it was the responsibility of Switzerland to register and also publish the protests and the reactions of all the parties concerned, consistently with the neutral and impartial position that the depositary of a treaty is required to adopt.

(7) *Mutatis mutandis*, this is also the way that the Registrar of the ICC should act. Since the Statehood of Palestine has been recognised, first of all, by 104 member states of the United Nations General Assembly within the framework of Resolution 43/177,[46] and subsequently bilaterally by 97 States, of which 34 were parties to the ICC Statute, the Registrar had no option but to take account of this legal reality and take note of the fact that in the opinion of these States, Palestine is a full State. Consequently, the declaration of acceptance by the Palestinian Authority of the jurisdiction of the ICC met the conditions of Article 12(3) of the Statute and must be considered to have been issued by a State. The Registrar's failure to do so would be tantamount to a lack of objectivity, an implicit criticism of the recognition of Palestine as a State by 34 States parties to the Statute, and interference in the domestic policies of these States, which is manifestly not the Registrar's role.

(8) Although it is true that the United Nations did never say that Palestine was a State, when the Security Council has addressed one or other episode in the Israeli–Palestinian conflict, for instance calling '*upon* Israel scrupulously to observe the provisions of the Geneva Conventions and international law governing military occupation [...],'[47] it implicitly treated Palestine as a State, because, by definition, **occupation** is the outcome of conflict between States.

The Security Council has frequently reiterated the fact that Israel is under an obligation to apply the Fourth Geneva Convention[48] when this convention, taken as a whole, only applies to **international** armed conflicts. Likewise, on the subject of the *Wall*, the ICJ, without going so far as to call Palestine a State, nevertheless noted that: « Section III of those Regulations, which concerns 'Military authority over the territory of the hostile **State**' is particularly pertinent in the present case » [49]. The Court also « further reminded the Contracting Parties [of the fourth

---

[46] Detail of the vote on UN Resolution 43/177 at http://unbisnet.un.org: 104 in favour, 2 against, 36 abstentions, 17 did not vote.

[47] UNSC Resolution. 271, 15 September 1969, para 4.

[48] UNSC Resolution 446, 22 March 1979, para 3; Resolution 681, 20 December 1990, para 4; Resolution 726, 6 January 1992, para 2; Resolution 904, 18 March 1994, preamble, 6th recital.

[49] Legal Consequences of the Construction of a Wall in the Occupied Palestinian Territory, Advisory Opinion, ICJ, 9 July 2004, para 89 (emphasis added).

Geneva Convention], the parties to the conflict, and the State of Israel as occupying Power, of their respective obligations ».[50]

Recently, the Chamber of First Instance of the Special Tribunal for Sierra Leone confirmed this conclusion when it ruled that:

> The rights and duties of occupying powers, as codified in the 1907 Hague Convention and the Fourth Geneva Convention, apply only in international armed conflicts. This is also the case at Customary International Law, which defines an occupying power as a military force present **on the territory of another State** as a result of an intervention.[51]

(9) Thus, the express recognition of Palestine as a State by one-half of the international community, including the majority of the members of the United Nations General Assembly, and implicit recognition of its statehood by the United Nations Security Council and the ICJ, show that the condition required to qualify as a State for the purposes of enabling the ICC to exercise its jurisdiction as required by Article 12(3) of the ICC Statute, has been met *in casu*. The declaration deposited on 21 January 2009 by the Palestinian Authority, accepting the jurisdiction of the ICC, therefore meets the conditions of Article 12(3) of the ICC Statute.

2.2.3 Giuseppe Palmisano[52]

(1) The Palestinian ICC declaration raises the fairly urgent problem of its relevance for the purposes of enabling the Court to exercise its jurisdiction over the grave crimes alleged to have been committed by the Israeli military in the course of Operation Cast Lead which, according to reliable sources, claimed the lives of hundreds of civilians, including over 300 children and more than 100 women. It was specifically by reference to these events that, as to February 2009, the Court Registrar's office received as many as 326 complaints lodged by NGOs and private individuals.

The conditions required by the ICC Statute for the Court to open an investigation would appear, *prima facie*, to be fulfilled. The available information reveals a *fumus* of numerous violations falling within the jurisdiction of the court, *ratione materiae*, and in particular war crimes and crimes against humanity.[53] With

---

[50] Ibid., para 96.

[51] SCSL, Case SCSL-04-15-T, *Sesay* et al., 9 March 2009, para 982 (emphasis added), in http://www.sc-sl.org.

[52] Professor of International Law at the University of Camerino. This contribution is based on the author's article "La Corte penale internazionale di fronte all'operazione 'Piombo Fuso' e al problema della statualità della Palestina", which was published in *I diritti dell'uomo. Cronache e battaglie*, 3, 2009, 54–60, following the Conference in Rome of 22 May 2009.

[53] See the report *No Safe Place*, produced by an independent committee of experts chaired by Prof. John Dugard and presented on 30 April 2009 to the League of Arab States (see *infra* Chap. 17, Annex), and the Report prepared by the 'UN Headquarters Board of Inquiry' commissioned by the UN Secretary General and presented to the Security Council on 5 May 2009.

respect to the complementarity principle (regulating the relation between the Court and domestic jurisdictions), so far no indication has been received of criminal proceedings opened in Israel against any soldier or any other individual in connection with actions performed in the course of Operation Cast Lead, and it does not appear likely that any proceedings will follow. Neither does it appear likely that third countries will be conducting any criminal investigations on the basis of the dual nationality of some Israeli soldiers who took part in the operation, or of some of the Palestinian victims.

Prior acceptance of the Court's jurisdiction would not, however, be necessary if the UN Security Council were to decide to adopt a Resolution under Chapter VII of the UN Charter, and make a referral to the ICC pursuant to Article 13(b) of the Statute regarding the situation in the occupied Palestinian territories (and particularly in the Gaza Strip).[54] However, there are political reasons that make such an eventuality highly improbable and, for the moment, as unrealistic as the acceptance by Israel of the jurisdiction of the International Criminal Court.

Against this unfavourable background, the Palestinian declaration pursuant to Article 12(3) of the ICC Statute, would therefore appear to be the only possibility for the purposes of meeting the conditions required for the Court to exercise its jurisdiction in respect of the serious and tragic events in Gaza.

(2) However, the fact that the Palestinian declaration requires the ICC to appraise the 'statehood' status of Palestine gives rise to a number of procedural and substantial questions that require further discussion.

In terms of the **procedure** to be followed, under the system created by the ICC Statute and its Rules of Procedure, the organ charged with the task of pronouncing on the issue of the 'Palestinian statehood' appears to be in the first place the Prosecutor. The Prosecutor could in fact directly decide to reject the complaints received, arguing that one of the preliminary conditions for the exercise of the Court's jurisdiction would have not been met. Such a decision by the Prosecutor would be tantamount to deciding on the current international status of Palestine, and, in particular, it would imply taking the responsibility for denying Palestine the status of a State, which would be decisive for the purposes of invoking the jurisdiction of the ICC.

It is most unlikely that the Prosecutor would decide to act by his own on this issue and take the responsibility for such an extremely sensitive decision on the international political level. What is, conversely, more likely to happen is that the Prosecutor might refer the matter to the ICC Pre-Trial Chamber. In this case, the appraisal of the thorny point at issue—that is to say, the question of Palestinian statehood for the purpose of applying Article 12(3) of the Statute—would be placed in the hands of the ICC judges. Such a decision could eventually be challenged before the Appeals Chamber, pursuant to Article 19 of the

---

[54] A request to this effect has already been submitted to the Chairman of the Security Council by Amnesty International and by Bolivia, as a non-permanent member of the Security Council.

Statute.[55] That said, this would be an unusual and in some respects anomalous situation, in which a panel of international criminal law judges (whether the Pre-Trial Chamber or the Appeals Chamber) would have to take a legally binding decision, on a matter which is essentially political: whether the political entity of 'Palestine' has taken on a character defining it as an independent and sovereign State, in other words, as being in possession of the features of the members *par excellence* of the international community.

For these reasons, and because of the high political responsibility that any decision on Palestinian statehood entails, it is most unlikely that any of the Court organs will ever issue a determination on this point without a prior indication—which must be political—coming from the States Parties to the Statute.

(3) The opportunity for the **Assembly of the States Parties to the ICC** to pronounce itself on the Palestinian declaration under Article 12(3) could be fairly imminent—namely at the intergovernmental conference to revise the ICC Statute, convened in May 2010 in Kampala, Uganda. The question of Palestinian acceptance of the Court's jurisdiction could be considered there, in order to reach a sufficiently wide-ranging consensus specifically on the Palestinian move, without at the same time generically attributing the same status to every national liberation movements, or other entities claiming or aspiring to some form of statehood.

It is also unlikely that the Prosecutor or the Chambers would consider the Palestinian declaration under Article 12(3) as a sufficient basis for establishing the Court's jurisdiction over the events in Gaza, if the Assembly of States Parties were to prefer not to formally deal with this matter, thereby demonstrating an inadequate level of support, or some diffidence or concern, regarding the exercise of the Court's jurisdiction over criminal acts committed by reference to the Israeli–Palestinian conflict.

One not purely abstract possibility might be for the Assembly of the States Parties to issue a determination to refer the matter to the **International Court of Justice** (ICJ), requesting its advisory opinion. This could be done if the States Parties were to agree to submit a request to this effect at the UN General Assembly, which (by a simple majority vote) could resolve itself to request the ICJ to issue an advisory opinion pursuant to Article 96 of the UN Charter. This

---

[55] Such a procedure would also apply even should the Prosecutor not take the initiative to request authorisation to institute an investigation on the basis of complaints made by NGOs or individuals, and also in the event of a referral made to the Prosecutor by a State Party under Article 14 of the Statute. In that case, the Prosecutor would not have to request prior authorisation from the Pre-Trial Chamber to commence investigations, but there would be the possibility for the Prosecutor to refer any problems to the Pre-Trial Chamber until the moment the charges are formally confirmed. And even if no issue regarding jurisdiction in connection with the problem of Palestinian statehood had been raised before that moment, the Pre-Trial Chamber could at all events take the initiative to raise the issue when deciding on the confirmation of the charges. Lastly, even in this case, the Pre-Trial Chamber's decision for or against the jurisdiction of the Court could be appealed before the Appeals Chamber pursuant to Article 19 of the Statute.

procedure would considerably lengthen the process, but it would offer the advantage of providing the ICC with the support of the most competent Court (the ICJ) to address the issue of the Palestinian statehood from the international law perspective.[56]

However, the difficulties related to the opening of an investigation in the Palestinian situation would not end even if the ICC organs would eventually accept the effectiveness of the Palestinian declaration of acceptance on the basis of a favourable stance by the Assembly of States Parties. Apart from the countless obstacles that would certainly be raised by Israel's refusal to cooperate with the Court, the Security Council could still block the investigation pursuant to Article 16 of the Statute (in other words, the Security Council could consider that the suspension of the investigation was a necessary measure to maintain or restore international peace and security, as provided by Chapter VII of the UN Charter).

(4) Turning to the substance of the problem regarding the Palestinian declaration of acceptance of the ICC jurisdiction, the following question needs to be answered: is Palestine currently a State, and can it therefore, in that capacity, declare the *ad hoc* acceptance of the jurisdiction of the ICC? This question can be approached at least in two different ways. The first approach is more general and more theoretical, and that is to ask whether Palestine is, or is not a 'State under international law'. In order to try to answer this question we must necessarily begin by clarifying a fundamental issue, i.e. what a 'State under international law' actually means, if such a notion actually exists and has any *raison d'être* at all. Another, more minimalist and pragmatic, approach is to ask whether there are any convincing arguments to show that Palestine might be considered a State for the purposes of the jurisdiction of the ICC. It is precisely on this second aspect that we wish to offer some remarks.

First and foremost, it should be recalled that the question of Palestinian statehood was first raised twenty years ago following the *Declaration of Independence of the State of Palestine on our Palestinian Territory with its Capital Jerusalem* issued by the Palestine Liberation Organisation (PLO) on 15 November 1988.[57] Following that declaration, some 100 States recognised that political entity as an 'official' international interlocutor. Also in the wake of the declaration, the UN General Assembly, in Resolution 43/177 of 15 December 1988, vested 'Palestine' (rather than the previously indicated PLO) with observer status, thereby empowering it to participate (without the right to vote) in the deliberations of the General Assembly. Since then, the Security Council has always invited Palestine to take part to its sessions whenever debating Middle Eastern issues or other agenda items of direct interest. In 1989, the PLO tried twice to secure international recognition

---

[56] In this connection, the ICJ was recently asked by the UN General Assembly to issue an opinion on the international subjectivity and statehood of what we might call an 'untypical political entity'. We are referring to the 10 October 2008 request for an opinion on the "Accordance with International Law of the Unilateral Declaration of Independence by the Provisional Institutions of Self-Government of Kosovo."

[57] On this point see Quigley 2009, *infra* Chap. 10.

of the State of Palestine, but without success. In the one case it sought Palestine's admission to the World Health Organisation (WHO), and in the other, it deposited the instruments ratifying the four Geneva Conventions of 1949 and Additional Protocols with the Swiss government. In the first case, due to the fierce opposition of the USA, the WHO Assembly resolved to postpone *sine die* any decision on its admission. In the second case, the Swiss Government as the depositary of the Geneva conventions, replied that it was 'not in a position to decide whether this communication can be considered as an instrument of accession in the sense of the relevant provisions of the Conventions', because of 'uncertainty within the international community as to the existence or the non-existence of a State of Palestine and as long as the issue has not been settled in an appropriate framework'.[58]

(5) Certainly, the above mentioned situation dates back to a particular historical moment, that is before the 1993 Oslo Accords, when the 'PLO/Palestine' political entity was not able yet to exercise any effective, however limited, power of governance over the Palestinian community of the West Bank and Gaza Strip. However, the fact that, despite the exercise by the PNA of certain powers of governance over the Palestinian territorial community, Palestine is not yet a member of the United Nations, has not been granted membership in the WHO or any other UN agency and is not considered a Party to the 1949 Geneva Conventions, is a sign that these difficulties still persist up to this day.[59]

So that, at the present time, recognising Palestine as an independent and sovereign State would flatly contradict the opinions, plans and commitments regarding the Palestinian situation that have been agreed and endorsed not only by the majority of the States, which are members of the concerned international institutions, but also by the parties most directly involved, i.e. Israel and Palestine. In fact, since the Oslo Accords, every document adopted at the interstate level regarding the 'peace-process', refers to the political process and intermediate phases to be achieved according to the *Roadmap*, in order to reach *the hoped-for final outcome*, that is the *birth of an independent and sovereign Palestinian State*. These phases require Israel to withdraw from the occupied territories and the dismantling of the settlements, and investing the PNA with further powers of governance.

In this perspective, one also needs to take account of the legal assessment, which was made by the ICJ in its Advisory Opinion dated 9 July 2004 on 'Legal Consequences of the Construction of the Wall in the Occupied Palestinian Territory'. In this Opinion, the Court indicated a number of internationally illegal acts committed by Israel in relation to the construction of the Wall, pointing out that it

---

[58] Note from the Swiss Government of 13 September 1989, in respect of which see the critical comments by Eric David, *supra* in this Chapter.

[59] The situation is different in the case of the regional interstate lawmaking bodies which are geopolitically close to Palestine, and sensitive to Palestinian demands for statehood. One only has to think of the fact that *ever since 1976* Palestine has been considered a full member State of the League of Arab States.

constituted a violation of the right to self-determination of the Palestinian people, in the perspective of eventually arriving to the establishment of an independent and sovereign Palestinian State (para 162 of the Opinion). However, nothing in the Opinion suggests that the Court considered Palestine as enjoying, at the present, the status of an independent and sovereign State.[60]

The fact that both the ICJ, in its Opinion on the Wall, and the various international organisations with quasi-judicial powers, always refer to the 'Occupied Palestinian Territories' and to Israel as the 'Occupying power' is not in contradiction to the conclusion that Palestine is not a State yet. For these expressions just describe the reality of the Palestinian territories, and suggest Israel's obligation with regard to the Palestinian territories and the human community living there, until the time comes for the Palestinian people to exercise their right of self-determination, and finally succeed in establishing an independent and sovereign State.

These difficulties, related to seeking recognition for Palestinian statehood, could have been overcome if in the past few years an independent Palestinian Authority had succeeded in establishing itself over the West Bank and Gaza and was capable of exercising effectively the power of governance on this territory in a sustainable way. This would have made much easier for Palestine, as a political entity, to achieve recognition in the world interstate *fora*. However, such step in fact did not happen, due both to the repressive military grip that Israel imposed on the Palestinian people and territory, and also to the inadequacy of the support provided by the international community for the Palestinian cause, and lastly because of the inability of the Palestinian authorities (more evident today than ten years ago) to create a single power structure able to effectively, and independently, governing the territory and authentically represent the Palestinian community, presenting itself as a credible interlocutor in the relations with Israel and more generally at the international level. The failure of this political entity to establish itself as an effective authority is hampering the achievement of Palestine's statehood recognition, also *vis-à-vis* the possible intervention of international judicial bodies (such as the ICC or the ICJ).

(6) The problems related to achieving recognition of Palestinian statehood, could prove to be non-decisive for the purposes of establishing the jurisdiction of the ICC, and in the end might not prevent this recognition from being achieved. For, on more than one occasion, the rationales of the international balancing of powers, the pursuit of political goals supported by the majority of the States (such as the decolonisation process), or other contingent reasons, have previously led to the result that political entities have been accepted as States (and admitted as members of international organisations) despite the fact that their status as independent and sovereign States has been even less evident than today's Palestine.

---

[60] In this latter sense, one might consider the fact that the Court rejected Israel's claim of lawful self-defence to justify its conduct, because the terrorist attacks organised in, and launched from the Palestinian territories, would not qualify as an armed attack *launched by another State* (Opinion, para 139).

One only has to think of the admission of Ukraine and Belarus in October 1945 as members of the United Nations, or the admission of Guinea-Bissau in September 1974 (at a time when Portugal still exercised powers of governance over it); or the admission of Namibia to the FAO in 1977 (when South Africa still occupied Namibia and exercised full control and effective powers of governance over the country).

Therefore, and despite the difficulties, there is no reason to exclude a priori a change of climate and a new international political convergence in the near future, leading to a recognition of Palestine's acceptance of the ICC (pursuant to Article 12(3) of the Statute) and thus enabling the ICC to exercise jurisdiction over the events in Gaza. For what is worth it, personally I hope that this will come about. A result of this kind, regardless of the inevitable repercussions on the 'peace-process' (which will not necessarily be positive), would send out a signal of historic importance for the international criminal justice system, in the sense of combating impunity of perpetrators of international crimes. If the ICC were to succeed in putting an end to the impunity which Israeli military and political authorities have so far enjoyed in perpetrating grave crimes to the detriment of the Palestinian people over the past forty years, no criminals, whatever their rank and nationality (whether they are an African dictator, or an Israeli soldier, a Palestinian militant, a NATO officer or a Taliban leader) could feel completely safe and immune again.

2.2.4 Gabriele Della Morte[61]

(1) The Treaty establishing the International Criminal Court (ICC), which was 'in process' for over 50 years, was eventually adopted in Rome on 17 July 1998, with 120 votes in favour, 21 abstentions and 7 votes against (China, Libya, Iraq, Israel, the United States, Qatar and Yemen). On 1 July 2002, after the sixtieth ratification required, the Court entered into force for conducts qualifying as war crimes, crimes against humanity, and crimes of genocide (and eventually aggression).[62]

As for the Court's jurisdiction, there are four parameters, according to which it can be defined: the jurisdiction *ratione personae, temporis, loci* and *materiae* (the *who, when, where* and *what* of the criminal offences). Beginning with the **jurisdiction *ratione personae***, the conduct must be attributable to individuals aged over 18 years,[63] whether *intelligent bayonets* or *senior commanders/officials*. Looking at the list of the individuals indicted by the ICC Prosecutor so far, one finds both lower ranking suspects and heads of State. This *Big/Little Fish Dilemma* is an endemic problem for a system of justice which is '*toujours partielle (plus que*

---

[61] Lecturer in International Law, Università Cattolica del Sacro Cuore, Milan.
[62] See Rome Statute, Article 15 *bis* and Article 15 *ter*.
[63] See Rome Statute, Articles 25 and 26.

partiale).[64] Moreover, the Statute rules out the defence of 'superior orders'(which might be used only in mitigation of sentence)[65] and hierarchical superiors can be charged also of the crimes committed by their subordinates, in the event that they knew, or should have known, of the criminal conduct of their subordinates and have failed to take all necessary and reasonable measures to prevent their commission.[66] Lastly, the Statute provides the non-applicability of the statute of limitations,[67] and the irrelevance of official capacity.[68]

From the temporal point of view (**jurisdiction *ratione temporis***), the Court's jurisdiction is limited by the principle of non-retroactivity (*nullum crimen sine lege*): the Court has jurisdiction only with respect to crimes committed after the entry into force of the Statute (*dies a quo*: 1 July 2002). However, if a State becomes Party to the Statute after its entry into force, the Court may exercise its jurisdiction only with respect to crimes committed after the date of ratification by that State, unless that State has made a declaration under Article 12(3) of the Statute. The same provision is now used to attempt to establish the Court's jurisdiction over the events in Gaza.

The spatial scope of the Court's jurisdiction (**jurisdiction *ratione loci***) largely depends on the preconditions for the exercise of jurisdiction,[69] i.e. the Court's trigger mechanism. In general, apart from the case in which the Court is triggered by a Security Council's referral, it is necessary that the conduct occurred on the territory of a State Party. If the conduct did not occur in the territory of a State Party, the Court can also exercise its jurisdiction in the event that the conduct can be attributed to a citizen of the State Party.

The Court's **jurisdicion *ratione materiae*** covers the crime of genocide,[70] crimes against humanity,[71] war crimes[72] and (in the future) the crime of aggression. It is clear from the reports that the alleged criminal conducts committed during 'Operation Cast Lead' can be defined as war crimes and crimes against humanity.

---

[64] "Always partial (rather than partisan)", Garapon 2002, p. 84.

[65] See Rome Statute, Article 33. The second paragraph of this article adds that, "For the purposes of this article, orders to commit genocide or crimes against humanity are manifestly unlawful."

[66] See Rome Statute, Article 28 (Responsibility of commanders and other superiors). With the significant difference that whereas for military commanders it is necessary that they "either knew or, owing to the circumstances at the time, should have known" that the forces were committing such crimes, for other superiors is sufficient that they "either knew, or consciously disregarded information which clearly indicated", that the subordinates were committing such crimes.

[67] See Rome Statute, Article 29.

[68] See Rome Statute, Article 27.

[69] See Rome Statute, Article 12.

[70] See Rome Statute, Article 6.

[71] See Rome Statute, Article 7.

[72] See Rome Statute, Article 8.

(2) What has been said so far with regard to the crimes falling within the material scope of the Court's jurisdiction is more complicated in the case of **aggression**, because this crime, which stays in between the *ius in bello* and *ius ad bellum* regime, is partly different from and more complex than the others. The crime of aggression can only be committed by senior political and military leaders. Moreover an *act of aggression* gives the UN Security Council the power to declare the use of force in international relations lawful (one of its main purposes of the UN is indeed 'the suppression of acts of aggression').[73] For this reason, i.e. for its political implications, it is extremely difficult to define this crime. While the invasion of Kuwait by the Iraqi Army in 1990 was an undisputed case of aggression (even though it was not qualified as such by the Security Council), the shelling of Serbia by NATO in 1999, the terror attack on the Twin Towers on 11 September 2001, or the latest military operation led by the USA in Afghanistan and Iraq are still widely debated.

In 1998, at the end of the preliminary works of the ICC Statute, the compromise agreed-upon by the delegates was to establish a 'dormant jurisdiction over the crime of aggression',[74] meaning that aggression would fall within the ICC jurisdiction *ratione materiae*, but at the same time its definition was deferred to some future date, to be addressed within a Statute review conference.[75]

An 'act of aggression' means the use of armed force by a State against the sovereignty, territorial integrity or political independence of another State, or in any other manner inconsistent with the UN Charter. An example of aggression would be the 'bombardment by the armed forces of a State against the territory of another State or the use of any weapons by a State against the territory of another State'.[76] Clearly this could theoretically apply to what happened in Gaza during 'Operation Cast Lead'. However, it is imperative to specify **theoretically,** for the jurisdiction of the Court *ratione temporis* is limited to the future, and thus can not apply to any acts committed before the definition of aggression was adopted. Moreover, before the Court will actually be able to exercise its jurisdiction over the crime of aggression, a number of conditions must be met.[77] It can be noted that

---

[73] United Nations Charter, Preamble and Article 1.

[74] See, Kirsch and Robinson 2002, p. 78.

[75] That review was carried out in Kampala in June 2010, and produced a definition of the crime based on a non-binding resolution of UN General Assembly adopted in 1974, cf. Res. 3314 (XXIX) adopted by United Nations General Assembly on 14 December 1974. See Rome Statute, Article 8 *bis* [ChM].

[76] See Rome Statute, Article 8 *bis*(2)(b).

[77] The main conditions are that there must be a minimum of thirty ratifications by the Member States that have accepted the amendment to incorporate this crime, secondly that a further resolution must be adopted with at least a two-thirds majority of the States parties after 2017. Last, if the trigger mechanism is not activated by the Security Council consent is required from the aggressor state. A restriction of this kind is not provided for any other crimes: for example, in order for the prosecutor to investigate the crime of aggression acting on his or her own initiative after 2017, it will not be sufficient for the territorial State to have accepted the amendment, but it will *also* be necessary to secure the consent of the aggressor (and this is highly improbable).

serious restrictions have been adopted in this regard, for political reasons, but apparently *'La diplomatie l'emporte sur le droit. Seul le juriste s'étonne de cette contradiction'*.[78]

(3) As for the trigger mechanism of the ICC, as well known, the Court has complementary jurisdiction to the national courts: the international prosecutor may take action when the domestic courts are unable, or unwilling, to investigate and/or prosecute the alleged crimes. If the jurisdiction is triggered by a UN Security Council referral, acting under Chapter VII of the UN Charter, the Court's jurisdiction is potentially worldwide, even over countries which have not ratified the Rome Statue and therefore are not Parties to the ICC.[79] Otherwise, when the Prosecutor initiates an investigation on the basis of a State referral or *proprio motu*, the crime must have been committed in the territory of a State Party to the Treaty or by one of its citizens.

Furthermore, in addition to the right to trigger the jurisdiction of the Court, the Security Council also enjoys a specular/correspondent power, enabling it to suspend the investigations for a period of 12 months (renewable), if this is required in the 'interests of peace'.[80] Thus, the highest political organ of the international community is the sole custodian of a *dual key*, enabling it to activate or to stay the judicial action of the ICC. It follows that the permanent members of the Security Council vested with veto power, possess a copy of this key. So far, only two out of the five permanent members have ratified the Rome Statute (France and the UK).

(4) As for the jurisdiction of the ICC over acts committed during 'Operation Cast Lead', this appears to be a timely debate in light of the 'Declaration Recognising the Jurisdiction of the International Criminal Court', which was deposited by the Palestinian Authority with the ICC Registrar, pursuant to Article 12(3) of the ICC Statute.

The question that arises here is whether the Palestinian Authority has the status to be able to lodge such a declaration. Because of Article 12(3) of the ICC Statute uses the term 'State', one might infer that only States are authorised to deposit an *ad hoc* declaration accepting the Court's jurisdiction and even though the Palestinian declaration uses such expressions as 'Government of Palestine', recognition of this authority as a 'State' is a highly controversial matter both in political and legal debate. A further complication is the present internal division of the Palestinian Authority (the PA in Ramallah, which is recognised as the 'Government of Palestine' outside, is flanked by a *de facto* Hamas government in the Gaza Strip).

Interestingly, the ICC Registrar, in declaring its acceptance of the declaration submitted by Palestinians, specifically stated that notice of its reception would be 'without prejudice to a judicial determination on the applicability of Article 12,

---

[78] "Diplomacy prevails over law. Only jurists are surprised by this contradiction." Dupuy 1999, p. 293.

[79] Cf. Resolution 1593 adopted by the Security Council on 31 March 2005 (Darfur) and Resolution 1970 adopted by the Security Council on 26 February 2011 (Lybia).

[80] See Rome Statute, Article 16.

para 3 to your correspondence'. As has been rightly observed, '[t]his can be read as saying something like: we receive this as something that looks like a declaration, without determining whether you can actually make such a declaration'.[81] So, in the end the whole issue depends on whether it is possible to accept such a declaration from an entity which is not internationally recognised as a State.[82] **The functional approach** advanced by Professor Pellet, according to which the Court 'has to determine whether Palestine is a State *in the meaning of Article 12, para 3, of the Statute*', and not 'the issue of whether, *in absolute*, Palestine is or not a State' seems acceptable. It is no different from the question posed by the UN General Assembly to the International Court of Justice in Resolution A/RES/63/3 of 8 October 2008 in view of an Advisory Opinion on the Kosovo situation. In this latter case, the General Assembly was meticulous not to ask the ICJ about the status of Kosovo as a State 'in general'; rather it asked whether 'the unilateral declaration of independence by the Provisional Institutions of Self-Government of Kosovo [is] in accordance with international law'.[83]

(5) In short, in terms of triggering the ICC jurisdiction, there are essentially three mechanisms for opening an investigation: (*i*) via referral of a situation to the Prosecutor by the United Nations Security Council acting under Chapter VII of the United Nations Charter (consequently without compliance with the territorial and national preconditions); (*ii*) via referral of a situation to the Prosecutor by a State Party to the Rome Statute; or (*iii*) via the Prosecutor acting *proprio motu*.

Each of these three scenarios encounters objective practical difficulties: in the first case, it appears highly unlikely that the Security Council's permanent members with veto power (USA *in primis*) would endorse such a solution. In the second case, apart from the fact that it is quite rare for a third State to decide to denounce another State, the same problem as in the third case would arise: the crimes must fall in the jurisdiction *ratione loci* of the ICC (meaning that territorial State or the State of nationality of the alleged perpetrators must be Party to the Rome Statute).

Yet, in the third case, if the Prosecutor intends to open an investigation *proprio motu* (rather than on the basis of a *referral* from any State Party or from the Security Council), he needs to get an authorisation by the Pre-Trial Chamber. After examining the Prosecutor's request, the Pre-Trial Chamber may authorise the investigation to begin, 'without prejudice to subsequent determinations by the Court with regard to the jurisdiction and admissibility of a case'."[84] It would be in

---

[81] See Glasius 2009.

[82] One interpretation in support of the legitimacy of the Palestinian declaration has been advanced by Alain Pellet, and endorsed by a significant number of co-signatories, in an opinion entitled *The Effects of Palestine's Recognition of the ICC's Jurisdiction*, 2010, reprinted in Chap. 9 of this Volume.

[83] "Likewise in this instance, the ICC is not called to "recognise" the State of Palestine, but only to ensure that the conditions necessary for the exercise of its jurisdiction are fulfilled." Ibid., para 7. See also the contributions of Ronen and Shany, *infra* Chaps. 13 and 14 in this Volume.

[84] See Rome Statute, Article 15(4).

any case highly significant to reach a determination by the Pre-Trial Chamber—perhaps also using the dual nationality of the possible authors of the crimes as a jurisdictional basis.

Even though the exercise of judicial examination over Operation Cast Lead would probably attract critics of politicisation of the ICC, at the same time it would give a clear signal of the Prosecutor's independence, which the Court has yet to enjoy, and make the Court able to cover situations relating not only to Africa (the ICC is currently dealing with seven African situations, making it appear a sort of *African* International Criminal Court), but also to other countries as Afghanistan, Colombia and Guinea, beside of course Palestine, which are since long waiting to see the opening of the investigation.

Of course, since the Court does not allow for trials *in absentia,* and in order to arrest the suspects it relies on the cooperation of States (not having its own police forces), the outcome of these efforts might be practically unsatisfactory. *Vis-à-vis* the huge expectations that the Court raises among the victims, in fact there appear to be a very small number of proceedings. Should one therefore conclude that the Court is more a tribune than a tribunal? No, or at least not entirely so: for the international justice system requires a very long time to become effective, during which it nevertheless exerts considerable influence. The ICC is no longer an institution for the *victor's justice* (as it was the case regarding the tribunals after the Second World War)*:* on the contrary, the Rome Statute is an international treaty open to all States, and the Court is meant to be open and accessible worldwide, to all victims.

2.2.5 *Chantal Meloni*[85]

(1) We are focusing today, in particular, on the possible jurisdiction of the International Criminal Court following the Article 12(3) Declaration lodged by the 'Palestinian Government' on 21 January 2009. For sure this international *forum* would be, for many aspects, in the best position to adjudicate the responsibilities for the alleged war crimes and crimes against humanity committed in the Gaza Strip in the context of 'Operation Cast Lead', and in the occupied Palestinian territory in general. As an alternative to the ICC, one other tool needs to be addressed, as we shall see in a moment, i.e. the principle of **universal jurisdiction**.

I would also like to focus on another aspect, that trascends the Palestinian struggle for justice, and that pertains the *quality* of justice that we wish to achieve. In fact the call for justice and accountability presents in my opinion a twofold problem: not only it is critical to find a *forum*, a judge having jurisdiction on the

---

[85] Researcher in Criminal Law, Università degli Studi of Milan.

alleged crimes, but also that this judge be in a position to administer real justice and *not just an appearance* of it. It is thus necessary to avoid any kind of 'mock justice', which would be for instance the one targeting only low-level soldiers and covering up high level responsibilities. Indeed international justice in the last years is focusing more and more on those who are regarded as the 'most responsible ones', i.e. those who took the decisions at the highest political and military levels, those who unlawfully advised the military analysts, those who provided the soldiers with vague rules of engagement, let alone with unlawful ones. In this sense this justice that we are invoking today must be administered by a truly independent judge, empowered with the proper instruments to ascertain the responsibility of the higher—political and military—leaders. I will come back to this aspect in a moment, to delineate the so-called **command responsibility** principle, one of the most important international criminal law instruments to target the higher echelons implicated in the commission of serious crimes.

(2) With regard to the first aspect, **universal jurisdiction** is a legal principle which evolved in order to overcome jurisdictional and impunity gaps in the international legal order. It allows suspected perpetrators of international crimes to be prosecuted in the courts of third countries, regardless of the place where the crimes were committed or by whom. It is intended to ensure that those responsible for international crimes are brought to justice. It is the horrific nature of the crimes which establishes the basis of universal jurisdiction: War crimes, crimes against humanity, torture, genocide. These grave crimes 'threaten the peace, security and well being of the world' and therefore offend and are 'of concern to the international community as a whole'.[86]

Universal jurisdiction of course is not and shall not be regarded as something specific to the Israeli–Palestinian context. It is sufficient to have a look at the studies compiled, among others, by Human Rights Watch (HRW)[87] or Amnesty International (AI)[88] to realise how many countries have enacted this principle in their legislation and how many cases lawyers have brought all over the world, seeking the arrest of war criminals and their prosecution before foreign tribunals.

The fact that the principle is enacted in the domestic legislation of a large number of countries does not mean, however, that it also finds proper application worldwide: several practical obstacles are still there when prosecuting war criminals at the domestic level pursuant to the universal jurisdiction principle, especially due to political restraints and interference. Notwithstanding such obstacles it can be certainly affirmed that the trend is in the direction of a broader recognition of the principle of universal jurisdiction (at least in theory and regardless of the governments' efforts to limit it).

---

[86] See the Preamble of the Rome Statute of the International Criminal Court.
[87] See HRW Report 2006.
[88] See the various country reports by Amnesty International 2009.

This is due also to the on-going process of ratification of the Statute of the International Criminal Court, which is based on the premises that the duty to investigate and prosecute international crimes stays in the first place with the States' domestic courts.

Similarly to the principle of complementarity that regulates the relationship between the ICC and the States' domestic courts, universal jurisdiction shall come into play when States with a more traditional jurisdictional nexus to the crime (related to the place of commission, the perpetrators' or the victims' nationality) prove unable or unwilling to genuinely investigate and prosecute: when their legal system is inadequate, or when it is used to shield the accused from justice. As such universal jurisdiction does not represent an attempt to interfere with the legitimate affairs of the State. It can be rather seen as a sort of 'last resort' judicial mechanism to restore the value of the rule of law which has been violated in cases of particular relevance. It is in fact nowadays broadly recognised that the protection of fundamental human rights and the reaffirmation of the rule of law passes also through the ascertainment of individual responsibilities.[89]

Individual criminal responsibility is indeed one of the modern conquer of international justice system. Traditionally only States were held responsible at the international level. This has been overcome in Nuremberg, where the principle was affirmed that 'crimes against international law are committed by men, not by abstract entities, and only by punishing individuals who commit such crimes can the provision of international law be enforced'. The principle of individual criminal responsibility, which is now recognised as a well established element of international customary law, means that individual perpetrators of international crimes cannot longer shield themselves behind the doctrine of the act of State, where only the State bears responsibility for the conduct of its agents.

(3) For sure the lack of justice at the domestic level with regard to the alleged Israeli crimes in the occupied Palestinian territory is no surprise: war crimes, crimes against humanity and other international crimes typically occur in situations where it is unlikely that the concerned State will exercise its criminal jurisdiction because the very perpetrators are State authorities or agents of the State. Lacking proper criminal investigations at the domestic level, then recourse has to be done to international justice mechanisms.

Typically international justice—which is selective justice—is addressed to those who are said to be 'the most responsible ones'. If we have a look at the praxis of the International Tribunals we notice that both the *ad hoc* Tribunals (ICTY and ICTR) and the ICC started with cases involving 'small fishes' for practical reasons of opportunity, but aimed at targeting the responsibility of the top leaders: the Yugoslav Milosevic and Karadzic, the Rwandan Kambanda or the Sudanese Al Bashir, just to mention some names.[90]

---

[89] See Werle 1997, p. 822.
[90] See ICTY, *Prosecutor* v. *Karadzic* et al.(IT-95-5/18), Trial Chamber Decision, 16 May 1995, paras 25–26.

Significantly, under international law the responsibility of high level perpetrators originates not only from the actual perpetration or complicity in the commission of the crimes but also from acts of omission. Thus, when referring to the responsibility of the higher echelons, we mean not only the ones who gave the order, planned or organised the military operation, but also those who—having the power to do so—failed to prevent or punish the crimes by the subordinates.

This is the so-called principle of **command responsibility**,[91] which was expressly recognised in international criminal law (cf. Article 28 of the ICC Statute). It stipulates that military commanders and civilian leaders can be criminally responsible for their subordinates' crimes, under the following three conditions:

(a) that they were the superiors of those who committed the crimes;
(b) that they knew or should have known of the crimes;
(c) that they failed to take the necessary measures in order to prevent or punish the crimes.

Thus, not only commission of unlawful acts, but also culpable omissions—i.e. failure to act when under a duty to do so—can lead to the criminal responsibility of the individual in a position of command and control. The failure to take the proper measures to prevent or punish the crimes becomes as grave as having committed them under certain conditions.

Particular attention shall be paid, in my view, to the second requirement of command responsibility that we could refer as the 'knowledge element'. Pursuant to this element the superior is responsible if he knew or *should have known* of the subordinates' crimes, meaning that there is a duty which is placed on those individuals bearing a position of command and control, to keep themselves informed about the actual circumstances of their troops/subordinates' actions. In this regard, it is interesting to recall what was previously stated by Raji Sourani, that the work of documentation of the crimes committed in Gaza, which his Centre (the Palestinian Centre for Human Rights) is carrying on since many years, is aimed also at ensuring that no one in the future can say: 'I did not know it'. And Sourani added that, at least from a moral point of view, everyone (who knew of the crimes, and, having the possibility of, failed to act in order to stop and prevent them) becomes responsible. I would just like to add that not only we are dealing with a 'moral responsibility'; in the circumstances that we indicated above, we are actually dealing with a full criminal responsibility under international law, a criminal responsibility for failure to act.

It is interesting to note that the command responsibility principle was used by the Israeli '**Khan Commission**' that investigated the massacre, which took place

---

[91] For a comprehensive study on this form of liability, may I refer you to, Meloni 2010.

on the 16 September 1982 in the Palestinian refugee camps of Sabra and Shatilla, in Lebanon, two days after the assassination of the Lebanese Prime Minister, Bashir Jemayel, in Beirut.[92] The Commission was charged with investigating any Israeli responsibility in the massacre. Though the Israeli troops had not been directly involved in the crimes, the commission found that Israel had an 'indirect responsibility' for the massacre which was materially carried out by Lebanese Christian Phalangist militias. The responsibility of the IDF consisted in the fact that they allowed the Phalangist troops to enter the camps, disregarding the risks of a massacre, which should have been foreseen given the information at their disposal (in particular following the assassination of the Lebanese Prime Minister). The enquiry focused in particular on the responsibilities of the Israeli military commanders in charge of the operation, the top members of the Israeli secret services, several ministries and other political leaders, including Ariel Sharon, who was the Minister of Defence at that time. The Commission was particularly severe in assessing the responsibility of the latter one: the failure to evaluate the danger of bloodshed, when he authorised the Phalangists to enter the Palestinian refugee camps, was judged as unjustifiable. He was also held responsible for not having ordered the adoption of appropriate measures to prevent or reduce the risk before letting the Phalangists enter the camps.

Although the Commission did not have any sanctionary or judicial power, the Kahan Report of 1983 had a significant impact in the ascertainment of the facts and responsibilities related to the events. Also, it was one of the first examples of application of the principle of command responsibility to civilian superiors, a precedent which gained particular importance for the development of the notion of command responsibility under international law.

(4) Going back to the first point, the **principle of universal jurisdiction**, it can be noted that over the years a number of criminal complaints were brought against senior Israeli political and military figures, some of them in third countries under the principle of universal jurisdiction.[93] Among the Israeli high ranking individuals that were targeted by the emission of a warrant of arrest issued under the principle of universal jurisdiction there are Ehud Barak (Israel's defence minister), Tzipi Livni (former Foreign Minister), Benjamin Ben-Elizer (former Minister of Defence); Shaul Mofaz (former Minister of Defence and IDF Chief of Staff), Avi Dichter (former Director Israeli General Security Services) and Doron Almog (Major General, former Commander IDF Southern Command).

In 2005, Doron Almog returned to Israel without leaving his plane at Heathrow after a tip-off from the Israeli embassy in London that a warrant of arrest had been issued for him over allegations of war crimes in relation, among other things, to

---

[92] The commission, and relative report, was named after its President, Yizhak Kahan, former president of the Israeli Supreme Court. The other members were Aharon Barak, judge of the Supreme Court, and Yona Efrat, Major General.

[93] See PCHR Report 2010b.

the destruction of 59 houses in the Rafah refugee camp, in the Gaza Strip, in January 2002.

A serious attempt to open a case against former Prime Minister Ariel Sharon was done in Belgium, precisely for his responsibility for the Sabra and Shatilla massacre in Lebanon of 1982. This investigation—along other cases targeting high ranking officials of various foreign (and powerful) States—led to the amendment of the Belgian law on universal jurisdiction in 2003.[94] Also Spain, where a number of high profile universal jurisdiction cases were brought, is considering an the amendment of its legislation, which aims at restricting Spanish jurisdiction on violations of international law committed abroad.[95]

More attempts to investigate alleged crimes committed by the Israeli army on Palestinian territory have been made in recent years in other European countries, as in Norway, which is one of the few countries to dispose of a unit specialised in investigating international crimes: Norway's National Criminal Investigation Service (NCIS).[96]

(5) Finally, I would like to conclude with some personal critical remarks. In my view, the principle of universal jurisdiction cannot be regarded as the ultimate solution; Prosecuting international crimes in third countries is not, in my opinion, the *panacea* for every impunity gap around the world, mainly because of the significant hurdles that arise in implementing the principle in practice in front of third States' courts.

Problems arise at various levels, starting at the stage of the police investigations, arrest of the suspect, immunity issues, lack of resources and, most importantly, the already mentioned political pressures. Criminal matters are traditionally a domestic issue: as the old saying goes, 'You don't hang your dirty clothes outside'.

Some of the above mentioned problems could instead be resolved at the international level. For instance, the immunity issue appears to be an obstacle only at the domestic level: functional immunity maintains its validity with regard to national courts, but not before international ones (see Article 27 ICC Statute).

---

[94] See HRW Report 2006, p. 37.

[95] The new Bill was enacted in November 2009; the amendment limits Spanish jurisdition on international crimes to cases where (i) the alleged perpetrators are present in Spain, (ii) the victims are of Spanish nationality, or (iii) there is some relevant link to Spanish interests. Moreover Spain will not have jurisdiction if another 'competent court or international Tribunal has begun proceedings that constitute an effective investigation and prosecution of the punishable acts'.

[96] Evidence indicating the commission of war crimes during operation Cast Lead in Gaza were not wanting before the Norwegian prosecutor. However, the prosecutor, Siri Frigaard, eventually decided not to open the investigation, purportedly for administrative/practical considerations.

Moreover, international institutions have certainly more resources and better structure to investigate such complex crimes. International courts also have the advantage of being immune from political pressures, at least in principle.

Yet, even before international courts, it still remains to be solved the not irrelevant issue of the cooperation of State authorities, which is a necessary precondition for the effectiveness of the investigations and, of course, for the arrest of the suspect, a necessary condition for the celebration of the trial.

Recourse to universal jurisdiction can be regarded as an 'interim' phase, looking forward to achieving a truly universal International Criminal Court, through universal ratification of the Rome Statute, and through the creation of an integrated system of universal justice which is able to combine domestic and international judicial resources in a proper manner. For the time being, however, international justice still has to rely on the work, efforts and determination of some lawyers who bring cases before third states' courts relying on the principle of universal jurisdiction.

Though, if we wanted to analyse things from the perspective of costs/immediate benefits there is no doubt that the balance would be probably negative. A lot of work, costs and complications for the involved lawyers, high expectations for the victims, very little results. However, even what we could call 'lost cases' make the law advance. We shall not forget that international criminal law is a fairly new subject and is still developing. Moreover, as the Pinochet case has clearly shown, international law develops also through failures and attempts. The reality is that only 20 years ago it would have been unthinkable that a serving chief of State (as for instance the Sudanese President Al Bashir) could be charged with war crimes and genocide counts in front of an international court.

Moreover recourse to the universal jurisdiction principle has some practical, immediate effects, which—to some extent—can be regarded as a success: travelling to certain countries (especially in Europe) became more difficult for war criminals, as it is recently shown by the cases of several Israeli officials, who had to cancel their travels abroad for fear of being arrested.

The more countries will actually implement the principle of universal jurisdiction the more international criminal law will advance. It can be regarded as a 'domino effect': States do not want to become and be regarded as safe havens for war criminals. For instance, as mentioned above, a new police unit has been recently established within Norway for investigating international crimes. One of the reasons why the issue of prosecuting international crimes attracted attention in Norway is related to the creation of a similar war crimes unit in Denmark. Following the establishment of this unit, suspected perpetrators of international crimes left Denmark for Norway. Norwegian authorities soon realised the problems posed by this development and called for a study to determine the best arrangements for a new unit.

It is not much, especially in the perspective of the victims, just some first and small stepping-stones in the direction of a more just and global international justice.

2.2.6 Flavia Lattanzi[97]

(1) The more natural way to seek for accountability for the crimes allegedly committed by Israeli militaries in particular against the Gaza civilian population during the three weeks operation of 27 December 2008–18 January 2009—as well as for the crimes allegedly committed by the Hamas fighters against Israelis—would be before domestic courts. In this regard, the most convenient domestic *forum* would be the territorial one, i.e. the jurisdiction of the State exerting its sovereignty over the territory where the crimes occurred, regardless by whom committed. However, in the situation of Palestine, the **territorial judicial sovereignty is problematic**.

(a) With regard to the possible Palestinian territorial jurisdiction, it is not necessary to address first the issue of the international statehood of Palestine. In fact, the exercise of the judicial power by an entity endowed with some governmental functions is independent from the *status* it enjoys at the international level. Even an autonomous—not independent—state or other entity is able to exercise this kind of internal sovereignty.[98] According to the 'Oslo–Washington Agreements' the Palestinian territories acquired a limited self-government in different fields, including the judicial one. So that it could be argued that the territorial jurisdiction on the individuals responsible for the crimes committed during the so-called Operation Cast Lead might be exercised by the judicial organs organised on the Palestinian territories by the PNA.[99] On the basis of the unilateral Declaration to respect the Geneva Conventions lodged by PLO in 1982 with Switzerland as the State depositary, the PNA would even be obliged to investigate and prosecute war crimes, regardless by whom committed, to the extent that is able to do so through the—limited—functions received by the said Agreements. The Geneva Conventions establish, indeed, the obligation of all the States parties—and thus also of every non-State party to a conflict having declared its willingness to respect these Conventions—to repress the grave breaches pursuant to the universal jurisdiction principle (see for instance, Article 146 of the IV GC).

Two problems however arise with regard to the territorial jurisdiction of Palestine on the Israeli militaries: the first one is represented by the exclusion, in accordance with the Interim Agreement, of the Palestinian jurisdiction on Israelis (citizens, soldiers, settlers, corporations), in all Palestinian territories. Therefore, Israeli nationality holders are exempted from Palestinian jurisdiction. The second problem is represented by the fact that—after the political split of 2006/7—there

---

[97] Professor of International Law, Università Roma Tre.

[98] This is what the federate States of USA, as well as the Bosnian entities do, although not being independent at the international level.

[99] The PNA being precisely the entity endowed with self-government functions and working in coordination of PLO, the entity representing at the international level all the Palestinian, regardless of their residence on the territories (Israel also having recognised in 1993 its representing role) and still enjoying an observer *status* at UN and other international institutions.

are currently two self-governments on the Palestinian territories: 1) the Al Fatah self-government in the West Bank, exercising limited governing functions under the enduring military control by Israel (and the overall control by Israel on the security and order in the all area); and, 2) the Hamas government, exerting its internal powers on the Gaza Strip after the formal disengagement of Israel, which, nevertheless, is still controlling borders, see and air-space of the whole territory of Gaza.

Undoubtedly, the critical relations inside the Palestinian Authority render the situation extremely complex: even the validity of the Declaration lodged by Palestinian Authority, represented by the Al Fatah government in the West Bank, whereby it accepts the ICC jurisdiction, is put at risk by the internal political split, given that the authority which lodged this Declaration—self-qualifying as the 'Government of Palestine'—does not coincide with the authority governing Gaza. Reconciling the two Palestinian Authority sides is necessary in order to resuming the negotiations with Israel and taking steps towards the hoped-for final outcome of the Palestine independence.

Given such a complex internal situation of Palestine and the non recognition by Hamas of the Oslo Agreements, it can be imagined that the Israeli militaries could be subjected (if captured) to the territorial jurisdiction of the Hamas self-government in Gaza, in disregard of the Interim Agreement. But, apart from the dubious ability of the Hamas jurisdiction to prosecute Israeli militaries, such prosecutions would certainly be problematic also from the point of view of their impartiality and fairness according to international standards.

Could it be argued that the disruption of the 'peace-process' and the violation of the Oslo–Washington Agreements, in particular by the construction of the 'security Wall', which has been declared illegal by the ICJ in 2004, have nullified the provisions of these Agreements, including the obligation of the Palestinian authorities not to exercise their territorial jurisdiction on the Israelis? This consequence could be envisaged, but the PNA has never made this argument explicitly and it is not likely that the Al Fatah government will make it. In any case, even if the Hamas government were willing to exercise the territorial jurisdiction on the Israelis, in disregard of the commitment taken by the PLO during the Oslo process, it would not be able to start even the initial investigations. This would happen not only because of the lack of Israeli cooperation, but also because of the harsh limitations on Gaza sovereignty imposed by Israel, including the *embargo* along the entire Gaza coasts.

Instead the **alleged crimes committed by Palestinian groups from Gaza,** through the indiscriminate rocket attacks against Israel,[100] certainly fall under the Palestinian jurisdiction. The Hamas Gaza government would acquire some credibility among the international community if it were to decide to bring to justice the suspects of these crimes, thereby respecting the Geneva Conventions; but it seems unwilling to do so.

---

[100] Which have been qualified by the Fact-Finding Mission as 'blind attacks'.

(b) As for the **Israeli territorial jurisdiction**, this could be exercised **on the said indiscriminate rockets attacks** from the Gaza Strip into the Israeli territory, which threatened and injured civilians and civilian property. But from the point of view of the impartiality and fairness of the potential prosecutions of the Palestinians (and in particular of Hamas members), the Israeli jurisdiction would also pose some actual challenges with respect to international standards.

On the other hand, **Israel has certainly its full power to prosecute members of its armed forces** suspected of the crimes committed during the military operation in Gaza, on the basis of the national jurisdiction nexus. The State, as a Party to the Geneva Conventions, is directly under the obligation to proceed with criminal investigations. But, as it appears evident from the first investigations, until nowadays Israel is unwilling to carry out serious and genuine criminal investigations and prosecutions, as required by international standards.[101] The only investigations carried out so far have led to the incredible conclusion that all the Palestinian civilians killed (among whom hundreds of elderly, women and children)[102] and the thousands wounded were **not intentionally** targeted: thus, are all these victims the result of military errors? In my view, errors can certainly not be alleged when systematic, indiscriminate attacks are conducted. Such attacks prove a policy of targeting deliberately the civilian population, as the Israeli authorities consider the inhabitants of Gaza Strip as terrorists or collaborators with terrorists. Moreover, a military inquiry is not the best way for assessing potential responsibilities of the members of armed forces. Independent and impartial criminal investigations would need to be conducted by ordinary domestic jurisdictions. But it is very doubtful that independence and impartiality can be guaranteed by the Israeli ordinary jurisdiction, in the light of how the Israeli Supreme Court has qualified the territory of Gaza and its inhabitants: the first as a hostile territory, and the latter ones as enemy aliens.

With regard to the **possible jurisdiction of other States**, the recourse to the jurisdictional criterion of nationality to prosecute Israeli soldiers could be also used on the basis of the double nationality enjoyed by many of them and even, as it seems, by some military commanders who planned and executed Operation Cast Lead. Given that 194 States are parties to the Geneva Conventions, their obligation to investigate the grave breaches of the Conventions according to the universal jurisdiction implies that almost every State in the world has the duty to investigate such crimes, regardless of the presence of the suspect on its territory (which presence could instead be required to proceed with the actual prosecution if a trial *in absentia* is not allowed).

Extraterritorial investigations even if not arriving to actual prosecution, still have an impact in terms of limiting the freedom of movement of the suspects.[103]

---

[101] PCHR Press Release 2009a.

[102] See the paper by Raji Sourani, *supra* in this Chapter.

[103] See the paper by Chantal Meloni, *supra* in this Chapter.

The deterrent effect of such investigations could be reinforced if all States parties to Geneva Conventions would implement their obligation to bring to justice the perpetrators of the grave breaches independently of any link with the crimes or the authors (on the basis of the absolute universal jurisdiction). Unfortunately, the egoistic political interests of the single States prevail on the humanitarian values often only rhetorically re-affirmed. Indeed, very few States have implemented at the national level the universal jurisdiction principle; as specific implementing legislation is required, the problem is at the level of law-making rather than of law enforcement.

Moreover, leaving aside the question of the controversial assessment given by the ICJ on immunity, some more hurdles arise in applying the universal jurisdiction principle with specific regard to the issue of immunity[104] (although I would argue that the Geneva Conventions, by providing for the universal jurisdiction and the principle of command responsibility with no exception for any official qualification, represent precisely one of the conventional derogations to the customary—not peremptory—international rules on immunity, as was envisaged by the ICJ, although referring only to conventions creating international tribunals).

The lack of national legislations implementing the Geneva universal criterion of jurisdiction as well as the immunity rules as extensively applied by the ICJ show clearly that the optimistic attitude of some lawyers and NGOs (as Amnesty International and Human Rights Watch), affirming the existence of an international general principle on universal jurisdiction for crimes of international concern, is not founded. The principle still lacks States' *opinio iuris* and practice, and the territorial or the nationality nexus required for the ICC to exercise its jurisdiction are clear *indicia* of this. Thus, it can only be said that there *should* be in general international law a principle on universal jurisdiction, but unfortunately there is not.[105]

(2) The international community created international criminal tribunals precisely to fill this vacuum and put an end to impunity for the gravest crimes of international concern. But the jurisdiction of the ICC is subjected to many conditions, as it appears clearly by the contribution of Gabriele Della Morte.[106]

First, the ICC jurisdiction is complementary to the domestic jurisdiction of any State in the world, not only of the States parties.[107] This means that the Court cannot exercise its jurisdiction if any domestic jurisdiction is willing and able to investigate/prosecute it or has already fairly and genuinely prosecuted it. In any

---

[104] See ICJ, Arrest Warrant case, I.C.J. Reports 2002, at 3 ff. Particularly controversial is the question with respect to former high state officers suspected of criminal behaviours in execution of their official functions even where these criminal behaviours are to be qualified as crimes of international concern.

[105] See, more thoroughly, Lattanzi 2009, pp. 461 ff.

[106] See the paper of Gabriele Della Morte *supra* in this Chapter.

[107] See Lattanzi 2010, pp. 181 ff.

case, with regard to the alleged crimes committed during Operation Cast Lead, it appears that such a condition is satisfied in the current situation.

Second, the Court was not endowed with a universal jurisdiction: it can prosecute only the crimes committed on the territory of a State party to the Statute or by a national of a State party, except for the case of a Security Council referral. Had Israel ratified the ICC Statute then, according to the national link, every other State party could have referred the 'Gaza situation' to the Court and the Prosecutor could have started an investigation even *proprio motu*—after getting authorisation by the Pre-Trial Chamber—following the number of complaints and *notitiae criminis* he received. Furthermore, according to the territorial link, the same procedures could have been followed for the crimes allegedly committed by Hamas members against Israel, the 'blind attacks', which caused their criminal effects on the territory of Israel. However, Israel (like the USA, China, Russia, India and many other States) did not ratify yet the Rome Statute, precisely for protecting its nationals from the ICC jurisdiction, with the consequence that the ICC has no jurisdiction neither on Hamas rockets attacks against Israel.

There is still the possibility to open an investigation, pursuant to a State referral or a *proprio motu* action by the Prosecutor, on the basis of the national jurisdictional link, provided that some of the Israeli suspects possess double nationalities of a State party to the Statute, as it seems to be the case. I am surprised that the Prosecutor, having received some *notitiae* about a possible national link of some suspects with a State party to the Statute did not proceed yet with the investigation, requesting the authorisation of the Pre-Trial Chamber, the sole ICC body able to ascertain the effectiveness of the link.

In addition, as already noted, the UN Security Council could refer this situation to the Court, even in absence of any territorial or national link with a State Party to the ICC. Of course, the Security Council is always selective in its activity, and its decisions are submitted to the veto of the permanent members, which makes very unlikely a referral against Israel to the Court. Also the option, proposed by someone, of a possible referral by the UN General Assembly, pursuant to the *'Uniting for Peace'* Resolution, is not realistic in my view, because the Security Council is not inoperative in general, it is inoperative only with regard to certain situations, as for the violations committed on the Palestinian territories, where it limits its intervention to a general condemnation, without operative measures.

All these obstacles make it appear that the alleged crimes committed during the military operation against Gaza of 2008–2009, will go unpunished. This is certainly not the only case where grave crimes of international concern suffer a vacuum of justice, but there is not another situation in the world where the large-scale commission of war crimes and crimes against humanity lasted so long and remained completely unpunished.

(3) A last possibility to invest the ICC with the Israel/Palestine situation needs to be explored. And that is to analyse whether the Declaration lodged at the ICC by the Palestinian Authority, according to Article 12(3) of the Statute had the effect to

create the *ad hoc* jurisdiction of the Court on the crimes linked with 'Operation Cast Lead'.

Notwithstanding the numerous opinions expressed in favour of the existence of an international *status* of Palestinian statehood, only a minority of lawyers are claiming that 'Palestine', according to the term used in UN documents since 1988, may even ratify the Rome Statute. I will not address this issue since the power to ratify the ICC Statute is not claimed by the PNA or PLO, showing that even the PNA is aware of the fact that Palestine does not enjoy the same statehood as all other States parties to the Statute. But the question of Palestine's international statehood has to be addressed.

Most of the difficulties on this issue come from the failure to distinguish between internal and external **sovereignty**, the latter being more precisely also indicated as **independence**. These two notions are confused in all the analysis of the Palestinian situation, even if worldwide there are many instances of States enjoying internal sovereignty and lacking the external one.

The fact that Palestine is endowed with self-governmental functions in some fields, i.e. with an internal—even if limited—sovereignty, is difficult to deny. This internal sovereignty was even granted by some international agreements—the Oslo–Washington Agreements—concluded between Israel and PLO under the sponsorship of other countries (as the USA, Russia, Egypt, Jordan, Norway and the EU). These agreements recognised the legitimate aspiration of the Palestinian people to pursue the gradual realisation of their self-determination in the form of an independent State.

Denying to this status even the qualification of **internal statehood** because Palestine territories would lack precise borders is only a political move, contrary to UN Resolutions. These Resolutions always refer to the Green Line as the border and include East Jerusalem as part of the Palestinian territory.[108] After all, the UN adopted the term 'Palestine' for indicating these territories as a single political unity on their way to enjoy a full independent statehood. Considering the Palestinian territories as not defined in their borders not only is contrary to UN Resolutions, but indirectly implies that even the territory under the full sovereignty of Israel is indefinite. Would it mean that also the Israeli statehood is not clearly defined?

The internal statehood does not yet imply Palestine's international independence, which is still claimed by the Palestinian people and authorities, and supported by the international community. In sum, this State is not a State in the international law sense, for it is still on its way towards the construction of its independence. I do not exclude that the occupation regime, as some underline, entails the existence of two States—one being the occupying one and the other the occupied, but since Israel in 1967 has occupied the home of the Palestinians but

---

[108] The Green Line was fixed the 3rd April 1949 in the armistice between Israel and Jordan. The ICJ considers as territories occupied by Israel the territories between the Green Line and the former eastern boundary of Palestine under the mandate, occupied by Israel in 1967 (including East Jerusalem).

not a Palestinian independent State, I consider that the occupation regime of the Palestinian territories is *sui generis*, deriving from occupation of territories which were previously internationally administrated but not internationally independent.[109] And the enduring occupation by Israel impedes the independence of Palestine, but not its internal statehood.

Thus although this **occupation** is not exactly what was envisaged under the Fourth Geneva Convention, which assumes the existence of two States at the international level, yet, this regime of occupation is totally compatible with the obligations of the occupying State and the rights of the occupied one. Indeed the United Nations consider still in force the regime of military occupation of all the Palestinian territories and the consequent Israel's human rights obligations in respect to their residents, regardless of the formal disengagement of Israel from the Strip. So, it can be argued that Palestine—which has been recognised by almost 120 States and is handled by the UN as an entity occupied by a foreign State, with definite borders and even a definite (partial) capital—enjoys at the international level **a *sui generis* status**, which implies some positive features, but also many negative ones, included an apparent vacuum of justice for the crimes committed on its territory.

It is interesting, in this regard, the example of the Republika Srpska before the ICTY, in relation to which the Plenary Assembly of the Judges, decided to endorse, in the Rules of Procedure of the Tribunal, a broad definition of the term 'State' as used in the Statute. Pursuant to Rule 2A, is a State for the purpose of the ICTY Statute: (i) A State Member or non-Member of the United Nations; (ii) an entity recognised by the constitution of Bosnia and Herzegovina, namely, the Federation of Bosnia and Herzegovina and the Republic Srpska; or (iii) a self-proclaimed entity *de facto* exercising governmental functions, whether recognised as a State or not. This shows that also entities, not independent at the international level, but endowed with some self-governmental powers, are able to take measures functional to the repression of crimes, both at the internal and international level.

Also the limited internal statehood of Palestine, as a political entity represented by PNA and to certain extent governed by it, would allow it to cooperate with the ICC according to Chapter IX of the ICC Statute, which is applicable also in case of *ad hoc* jurisdiction. Therefore, from this limited viewpoint, it could be recognised to Palestine the power to lodge a declaration of acceptance of the ICC jurisdiction, and thus an international statehood in the limited sense of Article 12(3) of the Statute (as elaborated by Prof. Pellet in his opinion).[110]

In this regard it could assume some relevance also the fact that, since the approval of the Rome Statute in 1998, international law developed further towards humanitarian values, which imply that this justice vacuum has to be filled. It is worth noting **Article 10 of the ICC Statute**, stating: 'Nothing in this Part [of the Statute] shall be interpreted as limiting or prejudicing in any way existing or

---

[109] Egypt has never, and Jordan no longer is claiming sovereignty over the Palestinian territories.
[110] See *infra* in this Volume, Chap. 9.

developing rules of international law for purposes other than this Statute'. Among these developments, it could even be considered the broad notion of State given by the ICTY Plenary Assembly of Judges, as referred to above.

But it is also true that every rule has to be interpreted in the light of the legal context. In this regard, it cannot be denied that at the **Rome Conference** the concept of State was clearly that of an independent State at the international level, able to accept the jurisdiction of the Court by ratifying the Statute, or to lodge an *ad hoc* declaration. The Assembly did not envisage the possibility of a declaration by a State, or a different political entity, enjoying only 'autonomy'. This reading is also confirmed by the wording of Article 12, paras 2 and 3, of the Statute, which, dealing with the States' ratification and declarations, endorses the same concept of State.

In any event, I consider that such a controversial legal issue cannot be solved by the ICC Prosecutor. It cannot even be solved by the Assembly of the States parties, a political organ which would only go to assess the *status quo* of the uncertainty of the Palestine statehood in the international relations, similarly to what Switzerland, as the depositary of the Geneva Conventions, did. This issue needs to be solved by the **ICC Chambers**, the only organ that has the capacity and can interpret the Statute (including Article 10) in the light of all the applicable rules according to human rights law (pursuant to Article 21 of the ICC Statute), including the obligation to repress the crimes by all available means.

Why should the ICC Chambers not be able to assess the *status* of Palestine, whereas the ICJ judges, as some argued,[111] would be more able to do it? The ICC Chambers have the power to interpret all the provisions of the Statute, not only those having a criminal nature but also the provisions having a stricter international nature. Precisely for this reason, it was decided, at the Rome Conference, to have among the ICC judges also international law experts.

(4) Now, the question is: how can the Palestine situation arrive before an ICC Chamber, given that the procedure has been stopped—since the beginning of 2009—at the Prosecutor assessment stage? According to Article 15 of the ICC Statute, the Prosecutor has to evaluate the seriousness of the *notitiae criminis* that he received, seeking further information, and also receiving oral or written testimonies at the seat of the Court. This is to be done for determining whether there is a reasonable basis for requesting to the Pre-Trial Chamber an authorisation to open a formal investigation on the basis of any supporting material collected. Article 53 of the Statute stipulates that the Prosecutor shall consider whether 'the information available to the Prosecutor provides a reasonable basis to believe that a crime within the jurisdiction of the Court has been or is being committed'. Thus, according to this wording, the reasonable basis could include also the issue of the jurisdiction.

Yet, given that when requested to authorise the opening of a *proprio motu* investigation by the Prosecutor, the Pre-Trial Chamber evaluates again the

---

[111] See the paper of Giuseppe Palmisano, *supra* in this Chapter.

reasonable basis for such an investigation and, pursuant to Article 15, it has to assess the Court's jurisdiction, I consider that the Prosecutor, shall not focus on the jurisdiction issue when evaluating the existence of a 'reasonable basis' for the opening of the investigation according to the Statute. In any event, the Prosecutor shall limit its assessment only to a *prima facie* analysis.

According to this reading, in the current case the Prosecutor should not deal with the issue of the validity and legal effects of the Palestinian Declaration, but—if a reasonable basis exists—should request the Pre-Trial Chamber the authorisation and leave this delicate issue to the judicial assessment. In this regard, it is of great significance that, as provided by Article 15, the victims can make representations before the Chambers, both at the Pre-Trial and Appeals level, given that the hearings are public for security reasons. The impact of such a public procedure would be huge and could even push a third State to exercise its extraterritorial jurisdiction.

Unfortunately, there is a gap in these rules as they were included in the Rome Statute: in fact, if the Prosecutor is obliged to ask the authorisation of the Pre-Trial Chamber in order to open an investigation *proprio motu*, on the opposite he is not subjected to any judicial control when deciding *not* to open any investigation. In this case, the Prosecutor's discretionary power is absolute: he just has to inform those who provided the information 'that the information provided does not constitute a reasonable basis for an investigation'. Which means that if the Prosecutor simply decided not to follow up on the Palestine situation, this decision could not be judicially challenged. And nothing will remain—in the judicial documentation of the ICC—about the crimes committed during, as well before or after, Operation Cast Lead!

2.2.7 François Rigaux[112]

Concluding remarks: State Law, Peoples' Law and International Law

The legal problems raised by the situation of Palestine and the violations of the law of war perpetrated by Israel on the territory of Gaza bring into focus the difference between international law and peoples' law. The international legal order is made of States and rules on interstate relationships. Some (apparent) exceptions, not relevant in the present context, do not need to be dealt with for our purpose. The recognition of the Palestinian State as such entails many consequences in the field of international relationships. Should the governing authorities of that entity lodge a complaint before the International Court of Justice, the question of law would be adjudicated by the Court: only States (still neglecting non-relevant exceptions) can be parties before the Court and its decision would settle the controversy. The

---

[112] Professor Emeritus of International Law, Université Catholique de Louvain, and Member of the Permanent Peoples' Tribunal.

advisory opinion of the International Court of Justice, upon which Professor David's correctly relies, did not explicitly characterise Palestine as a State.

The bias through which eminent scholars are trying to bring Israel before another jurisdiction, the International Criminal Court, is very interesting but does not answer the question: were the Palestinian authorities entitled to make the declaration recognising the jurisdiction of that tribunal? This process must be pursued and the present writer cannot but sustain it. The circumstance that such legal difficulties need to be smoothened if one wants to remain within the bounds of international law highlights the difference between that branch of law and peoples' law.

The first and more striking difference lies in the separation between State and law and between State and people. It is not necessary to be a Kelsenian to adhere to the identification of law and State and of State and people. By laying down that double equation Hans Kelsen has given some scientific justification to the most commonly accepted philosophy of practicing lawyers. With due respect to Kelsen's genius, it is necessary to discard both affirmations.

First, let us get rid of the assimilation of law and State. States are only one—as well as the latest, in chronological order—of the 'entities' capable of being a source of law. Not only were legal systems in force long before the crystallisation of State power, but non-State law is still in effect and has been proliferating up to date. For instance, the legal system, which most disturbed Kelsen at his time, was religious law. Other more contemporary legal orders require the voluntary adhesion of their subjects. Such is the case with sport law. However, it entails compulsory elements: if someone wants to take part in a tennis or a football competition, he or she must be a member of an appropriate club or organisation. Just like a church, such organisations possess the power of a unique sanction, the exclusion of the member who does not carry out his or her duties. Such penalty is perhaps worse than excommunication: the sportsman who is barred from participating in a competition is deprived access to an activity which constitutes the main aim in his life.

One difference between State and non-State law remains: only the first one exerts a power of coercion on its territory. But that power can be evaded and the power of exclusion of non-State orders have an equal dissuasive force.

The second false assumption which needs to be clarified is the assimilation of State and people. The German legal theory uses the expression *Staatsvolk* (the people of the State) to indicate that State and people are one and the same. One State, one people. Such assimilation is in fact false and entails dangerous consequences. Every State is made of diverse peoples both since its origin (for instance through conquest) or later on, through immigration. The State rules on the attribution of nationality express, on an unequal mode, such plurality within the State. A political regime which tries to deny any difference between State and people incurs the risk of denying the fundamental rights of collective or individual differences within the national sovereignty.

Nazi Germany tried to lay down rules submitting all persons within State jurisdiction to its coercive power. However, the success of this attempt was short-lived. Even in the heyday of its regime it could not curb all churches and was forced to accept disrupting elements of liberal capitalism. Not only was Germany defeated by foreign powers, but as soon as the Nazi leadership was thwarted, the buds of liberal Germany and of clerical influence immediately covered every sector of the new German State. Even the system of regional autonomy, which was flourishing at the time of the German Empire, redefined itself under new denominations in the Federal Republic of Germany. The continuity of the German State was affirmed by the political establishment and by the highest judiciary authorities in contradiction with the position taken in the German Democratic Republic and with the Kelsenian dogma of the identity between State and law.

Religious controversies are offering a clear test of the problems raised by a plurality of religious affiliations within a State. Most of all, one can assume that the Jewish people was created through their exclusion from all political communities. But even Christianity could not bring together all denominations of disciples of Christ. From the time of the Lutheran Reform no European State would tolerate religious dissidents. A strong cohesive line was adopted: *cujus regio illius religio*. But even before that, the European history is rich in heresies, in popular superstitions which were often linked with the demand of a better life, which in turn encouraged a repression by the associated powers of State and dominant church. The advent of religious tolerance did necessarily coincide with the diminishing impact of religion as such. As long as religious faith represents a strong appeal to human beliefs, religious indifference entails a risk of subversion of the social fabric.

Not only the assimilation of State and law could be seen as a regrettable error generated by healthy juridical principles, but it entails a similar confusion between State and people. It has already been shown that peoples are endowed with legal institutions using a common language, that they are apt to produce a respectable civilisation, and that the State itself must relinquish the illusory conviction of its exclusive aptitude to be the unique source of legal institutions. What is called the people of the State (*Staatsvolk*) is an ideological contribution to the dogma of State supremacy. There is no embodying of a whole people within the State. Every society is made of a plurality of communities, of collective groups of diverse nature and origin. The *Staatsvolk* is a chimera invented in order to bestow on the political organisation called "State" the popular symbol it needs. No State presents such a harmonious combination of a community (*the* people) and a system of regular and authoritative institutions. Any individual is a member of heterogeneous collectivities or communities: a village, a province, a religious community, a movement of opinion, a trade or professional membership. Each individual belongs to different affiliations; hence, everyone is deprived of some peculiar character if he or she is condemned to surrender all of them except for the sole quality of subject of a State.

The emergence of Peoples' law has been made explicit under the visionary conceptions of Lelio Basso, and such legal order is embodied in the Universal Declaration of Peoples' Rights adopted on July 4, 1976 in Algiers. One of its institutions is the Permanent Peoples' Tribunal.[113] To be characterised as a people, a collectivity does not need a State's blessing. It exists through its own institutions, its myths poetising the most original aspects of its history. Indian population in America or aboriginals in Australia have been subjected by an alien State power for a long time. They are trying now to reaffirm their own institutions, their legal capacity to be recognised as a people. Had they not withstood without submitting to State power, they could not have resumed their right to be recognised as such.

Peoples' law cannot be properly understood unless it is compared with State law on the one hand and international law on the other. State law is constructed around a particular collective entity. Without adhering to the assimilation of State and people they have some common features. Both States and peoples could be identified as a particular collective entity. Peoples are just as different as States: they compete for the enjoyment of rare goods, most of all for the exclusive occupation of a territory. As soon as communities emerged from nomadism, they needed to exert some kind of appropriation of dwellings. The land appeared relatively empty, and could easily be shared by various city States, by different peoples. The dissemination of groups of peoples and, later on, colonisation, both offer vacant territories to the invaders. Such emptiness, however, is conspicuously illusory. Some fictions as old as Roman law, as the idea of vacant territory, of *terra nullius*, are useful means to deprive the local populations of their ancestral rights.

Under such approach, peoples are as competitive as States. From that perspective peoples' law does not deliver a peaceful image of the relationships between their subjects. As soon as collective entities—peoples or States—claim some exclusive right on a rare commodity—land or any other possession—such challenge entails a risk of war. When defending peoples' rights, one is exposed to a conflict between the concurrent claims of different peoples. At that level peoples are not different from States. Besides the fiction of *terra nullius*, it belongs to the victorious party to provide some legitimation for the subjugation of another people. It is well known that history is written by the victor.

How does international law deal with conflicting situations? Very badly for three main reasons: one is that this branch of law does not enjoy the same degree of enforceability as State law. The second reason is that the superior force of the victorious party rules the conflict. The success of war does not depend on the legitimacy of the victor's case but on pure force. This is also the main deficiency within the doctrine of just war. Once in possession of the war's booty, the victorious party can easily resist any claim from its victim. The third reason for the inadequacy of international law to rule 'fairly' on disputes between peoples or between States is that, as it has already been pointed out, history is written by the victor, and actual possession of the prize bestows a title upon the victor which will easily formulate some kind of justification.

---

[113] See, for further information on the Peoples' Tribunal, the website of the Lelio Basso Foundation, http://www.leliobasso.org, under the international section [ChM].

Like Janus, peoples' law presents two faces. It invests every people with fundamental rights. Such was the main purpose of the Algiers Declaration of 1976. Under that approach peoples' law is solidly grounded on the doctrine of human rights. But is goes a step further by affording people collective rights. The analogy with human rights is very profound: individual rights are denied if the community to which the individual belongs is itself deprived of its basic rights. For instance under a foreign domination, individual rights are also downtrodden.

The most difficult task for the law of peoples consists in performing the same kind of function which pertains to international law. The Algiers Declaration is rather evasive on the question. What kind of duties does people have towards all other people? Here we meet another analogy with human rights. It is easy to conceive negative fundamental rights (*Abwehrrechte*), of which liberty is the most typical instance. The individual has to be protected against any invasion of its fundamental rights: he has to be guaranteed against any encroachment on his or her life, corporal integrity and so on. It is more difficult to assess the nature and the extent of solidarity rights. Hunger and poverty are evils which should be improved by the action of other peoples, all the more so since economic exploitation can be the reason why such torments are inflicted on other peoples. The doctrine of human rights suffers the same dilemma. Some fundamental rights—to food, to health care, to a job—cannot be granted without some positive action of public authorities. At the level of peoples' law it seems much more difficult to State how far rich peoples are under a duty to help other peoples enjoy a minimum level of well being.

Under Peoples' law, the Palestinians are a people deserving consideration and recognition. Their case against Israel is valid under the same legal order. They shall not be denied their fundamental rights, which are embodied in the Universal Algerian Declaration of 1976.

The use which has been made of that instrument with some success and which is embodied in the numerous decisions delivered by the Permanent Peoples' Tribunal does not prevent us from submitting it to the same critique with respect to its position towards State law and the inadequacy of the international legal order as it stands.

Struggling for the rights of the Palestinian People, one has to be aware of the relativity of the very concept of people. Within the present international context, one has to assume that the independence of the Palestinian people whose success could lead to the institution of a Palestinian State does not allow to disregard the plurality of affiliations comprised under the denomination 'the Palestinian people'. The future State should take into account such plurality.

This leads to a semantic critique of the very terminology of the Universal Declaration. 'Peoples' are deemed enclosed entities, as an abstract concept which does not admit any kind of plurality within the group having been granted such characterisation. The struggle of a people tends basically to institute itself, following a pattern of *autopoiesis*. The task seems easier with respect to States: in the presence of a "great" leader (such as Louis XIV in France, Friedrich II in Prussia, Catherine the Great Empress of Russia and most of all, Napoleon) there was a recognition of State power, insofar as they were convincing albeit unsatisfactory impersonations of the State upon which they ruled. They transformed the aggregation of men and women into something that did not exist before them: a State.

The Universal Declaration of Peoples' Rights constitutes a framework to dismantle the traditional subservience to any form of State power, and to the illusory power of a so-called international legal order, with which the Declaration shares a prospective approach. The so-called norms of international law are not obeyed and they offer a scheme for future achievements. The decisions of the Permanent Peoples' Tribunal are not enforced either. Both international law and peoples' law are akin to religious faiths, promising rewards or threatening punishments to be delivered in an afterlife. In fact, what is done here and now is the *conditio sine qua non* to make the future something more than wishful thinking. The enforcement of international law and of peoples' law embodies a hope for the future, but inspire—and compel—immediate action.

2.3 Presentation of the Complaint Filed Before the International Criminal Court by Gilles Devers and Mireille Fanon Mendes-France[114]

2.3.1 Introduction

As the bombs were still lighting up the skies over the Gaza Strip, sowing death and destruction on the ground, national and international Palestinian solidarity organisations were doing everything possible to save the lives of the civilians of Gaza, calling for the end of this offensive, which was broadcast live by numerous television networks and that had been condemned by many sources, from the outset, as criminal. One of the prime demands regarded specifically international law, its enforcement and its effectiveness, to make sure that these crimes would not go unpunished, as they had in 2006, after the Israeli war against Lebanon.

We felt immediately that it was essential to remind the authorities of every State and government that they had committed themselves to comply with international law, at all times and under all circumstances, even in the course of an armed conflict. Their commitments entailed the international protection of human rights and the respect for international humanitarian law, placing them under an obligation to respect the right of peoples to self-determination, the sovereignty and territorial and political integrity of States, and to ban the use of armed force.

---

[114] Gilles Devers, Lawyer in Lyon, Doctor in Law; Mireille Fanon Mendes-France, Member of the International Association of Democratic Lawyers and President of Frantz Fanon Foundation, http://www.frantzfanonfoundation-fondationfrantzfanon.com

These same organisations,[115] while expressing their solidarity with the people of Gaza, also sought to remind the international community of the very purpose of its existence, that was to represent the People of Nations, the vast majority of whom were utterly convinced of the validity and relevance of international law and the need for all the rules and principles of international law to be enforced against all States and against all political, military and other leaders, without distinction and without discrimination.

Therefore, one of our first concerns was to contribute to prosecuting these crimes, to put an end to impunity, as advocated by the Preamble to the Statute of the International Criminal Court, which provides that *"the most serious crimes of concern to the international community as a whole must not go unpunished and that their effective prosecution must be ensured by taking measures at the national level and by enhancing international cooperation."*

The many organisations and associations, on which behalf we have filed a complaint before the International Criminal Court with regard to the Israeli attack on the Gaza Strip of December 2008–January 2009, have thereby reaffirmed their endorsement of the provisions of the United Nations Charter and their conviction of the soundness and topical relevance of the ban on the use of force (one of the greatest achievements after Second World War), even though this rule has now been radically eroded.

In the following pages we will briefly outline the main legal arguments on the basis of which, on 22 January 2009, we filed a first complaint to the Prosecutor of the International Criminal Court, seeking to trigger the jurisdiction of the Court pursuant to Article 15(1) of the Rome Statute.[116]

2.3.2 Violations of International Law

2.3.2.1 Violation of Article 2(4) of the UN Charter

The obligations imposed by the UN Charter and by international law include the prohibition on the State of Israel to use armed force against an illegally occupied people—one part of which was declared to be a 'hostile entity'[117] and was

---

[115] The complaint was signed by 350 NGOs, from Europe, the Middle East, Africa and South America. It was signed by a team of forty lawyers.

[116] The Declaration by the Minister of Justice of PA and the forum of discussion opened by the ICC Prosecutor.

[117] Israeli Security Cabinet, 19 September 2007: http://www.mfa.gov.il/MFA/Government/Communiques/2007/Security+Cabinet+declares+Gaza+hostile+territory+19-Sep-2007.htm.

subsequently placed under an illegal and illegitimate blockade by the Occupying Power.

Article 2(4) of the UN Charter absolutely prohibits the threat and actual use of armed force. This prohibition is a normative guarantee, designed to ensure peace and international security for all States and peoples. The ban on the use of force also includes the use of armed force in all its forms: war, reprisals, or all other kinds of use of arms, including—of course—acts of aggression.

To resort to the use of armed force is not prohibited in case of 'self-defence', as provided under Article 51 of the UN Charter. However, if the State of Israel was acting, as it claimed, in response to an act of aggression against it, it was under an obligation to inform the Security Council of this fact.[118] And it failed to properly do this.

Moreover, in the case of the offensive against the Gaza Strip launched by Israel, it is very debatable under international law that the notion of lawful self-defence can be invoked, in the light of the right of the Palestinians to resist the long-standing illegal Israeli occupation of their territory. The wording of Article 2(4) of the UN Charter is unambiguous regarding the substance and the scope of the ban on the threat and the use of armed force. It leaves no doubt that "All Members shall refrain in their international relations from the threat or use of force against the territorial integrity or political independence of any State, or in any other manner inconsistent with the purposes of the United Nations."

One of the most important international instruments for interpreting Article 2(4) is the UN General Assembly Resolution 2625 of 24 October 1970: Declaration on Principles of International Law Concerning Friendly Relations and Co-operation among States in accordance with the Charter of the United Nations.[119] Adopted by consensus, this Resolution develops the principles and the rules of the United Nations Charter, particularly with regard to the ban on using armed force. This resolution unambiguously states that every State is duty-bound to "refrain from the threat or use of force to violate the existing international boundaries of another State or as a means of solving international disputes." The prohibition on the use of force as expressed in Article 2(4) of the UN Charter is part of international

---

[118] According to Article 51 of the UN Charter: "Nothing in the present Charter shall impair the inherent right of individual or collective self-defence if an armed attack occurs against a Member of the United Nations, until the Security Council has taken measures necessary to maintain international peace and security. Measures taken by Members in the exercise of this right of self-defence shall be immediately reported to the Security Council and shall not in any way affect the authority and responsibility of the Security Council under the present Charter to take at any time such action as it deems necessary in order to maintain or restore international peace and security."

[119] UN General Assembly: http://daccess-dds-ny.un.org/doc/RESOLUTION/GEN/NR0/348/90/IMG/NR034890.pdf?OpenElement.

customary law principles, and has particular importance with regard to international peace and security.

By conducting the so-called 'Cast Lead' operation against the Gaza Strip, the Israeli authorities ordered the execution of wide-ranging military operations which, by all evidence, violated the UN Charter. They have therefore violated one of the most fundamental rules of international law, including the obligation to pursue every means of reaching a peaceful settlement of disputes, as required by Article 33 of the same Charter—thereby directly posing a threat to international peace and security.

2.3.2.2 The Prohibition on Armed Reprisals

Resolution 2625 broadened the scope of Article 2(4) of the UN Charter to include other cases such as reprisals, providing that "States have a duty to refrain from acts of reprisal involving the use of force." It clearly follows from this that all States are prohibited from using armed reprisals, whatever purposes they may be pursuing. The State of Israel, however, failed to take account of this commitment, as it did in 2006 during the war against Lebanon, which Israel also claimed to be justified as an act of reprisal.

The International Court of Justice has explicitly recognised that this Resolution is an authentic interpretation of the UN Charter, affirming that: "The effect of consent to the text of such resolutions…may be understood as an acceptance of the validity of the rule or set of rules declared by the resolution by themselves".[120] The International Law Commission also clearly expressed its view in favour of banning armed reprisals. Article 50(1) of the Draft Articles on Responsibility of States for Internationally Wrongful Acts stipulates that: "Countermeasures shall not affect: (a) The obligation to refrain from the threat or use of force as embodied in the Charter of the United Nations."[121] Therefore, it is apparent that contemporary—both treaty-based and customary—international law formally prohibits recourse to the use of force in the form of armed reprisals. The only exception would be for the purposes of lawful self-defence with the authorisation of the Security Council.

It is thus clear that Israel's offensive on the Gaza Strip was, legally speaking, an unlawful use of armed force which is a flagrant violation of Article 2(4) of the UN Charter, and as such constitutes a violation of the fundamental and basic rules governing international peace and security, for which the State of Israel—and in consequence its State authorities—must be held accountable.

---

[120] ICJ, *Case concerning military and paramilitary activities in and against Nicaragua*, 1986, para 188. See also: ICJ, *Namibia case*, Advisory Opinion, 21 June 1971, para 96; ICTY, *Kupreskic* case, Judgement, 14 January 2000, para 535; US, Military Tribunal at Nuremberg, *List (Hostages Trial)* case, 8 July 1947–19 February 1948.

[121] Article 50(1)(a) of the UN Draft Articles on Responsibility of States for Internationally Wrongful Acts. http://www.ilsa.org/jessup/jessup06/basicmats2/DASR.pdf.

As ruled by the International Court of Justice, in its advisory opinion on the threat or use of nuclear weapons, "many rules of humanitarian law applicable in armed conflict are so fundamental to the respect of the human person and elementary considerations of humanity [that] they constitute intransgressible principles of international customary law."[122]

2.3.2.3 The Act of Aggression: An International Crime

At 11.30 on the morning of 27 December 2008, as the children were leaving schools, and without any prior warning to the civilian population, Israel started a widespread military offensive on the Gaza Strip. The argument of the Israeli authorities was that they were merely exercising their right to self-defence, in response to rockets fired from Gaza against southern Israel.

The wide sweep and full scope of the Israeli armed action, however, fell outside the scope of the definition of an armed response in the category of 'proportionate' or 'disproportionate reprisals'; in fact, the Israeli attack could amount to an armed aggression as defined and prohibited by Resolution 3314 of 14 December, 1974, which defines aggression as "… the use of armed force by a State against the sovereignty, territorial integrity or political independence of another State, or in any other manner inconsistent with the Charter of the United Nations, as set out in this Definition."[123]

Article 6 of the Nuremberg Military Tribunal Statute already included aggression under the notion of "crime against peace." The United Nations International Law Commission has made it clear that the crime of aggression has consequences in terms of individual criminal liability, and in fact the Rome Statute of the International Criminal Court includes it among the crimes under its jurisdiction (although not yet prosecutable).[124]

---

[122] ICJ, *Legality of the Threat or Use of Nuclear Weapons*, Advisory Opinion, 8 July 1996, paras 37, 50 and 63; D'Amato 1971, p. 88; Tirlway 1972, p. 58.

[123] This provision was recognised as part of customary law, as the International Court of Justice remarked, cf. ICJ, *Case concerning military and paramilitary activities in and against Nicaragua* 1986, para 195.

[124] ICC Statute under Article 8 *bis* Article 8 *bis*, inserted by Resolution RC/Res.6 of 11 June 2010.

2.3.3 Violations of International Humanitarian Law and Human Rights Law

2.3.3.1 Relevant Legal Framework

The State of Israel is party to the four Geneva Conventions of 1949, but has never ratified the Additional Protocols I and II of 1977. Moreover, Israel is also party to a number of other international treaties, among which: the Hague Convention on the Protection of Cultural Property in the Event of Armed Conflict of 14 May 1954 and Protocol I of 1954; the Convention on Certain Conventional Weapons, the Protocol on Non-Detectable Fragments, and the Protocol on Prohibitions or Restrictions on the Use of Mines, Booby-Traps and Other Devices, adopted in Geneva and dated 10 October 1980.

Many other prohibitions and obligations, although not treaty-based, also arise from customary law. These two corpuses of law, conventional and customary, mutually strengthen and complete each other.[125]

2.3.3.2 The Geneva Conventions

Israel has violated a number of provisions of the Geneva Conventions relative to the Protection of Civilian Persons in Time of War. In particular we can mention the provisions protecting civilian hospitals from attacks and requiring respect for the wounded, sick, and infirm people, including the safeguard that transport of wounded and sick civilians be guaranteed, which are grave breaches and must be investigated or prosecuted before the courts of any State party.

---

[125] On the principle of distinction cf.: Hague Regulations, Article 3; Fourth Geneva Convention, Article 27 and 51; Additional Protocol I, Article 43(2), 50 and 51(3); ICC Statute, Article 8, 2, a, i. Jurisprudence: ICJ, *Nuclear Weapons* case, Advisory Opinion, 8 July 1996, paras 78–79; ICTY, *Tadic* case, Prosecutor's Pre-Trial Brief, 10 April 1996; ICC, Pre-Trial Chamber I, Decision on the confirmation of charges, *Katanga and Ngudjolo Chui*, 30 September 2008, No ICC-01/04-01/07. On the principle of proportionality: Article 51(5)(b) and 57(1) of Additional Protocol I; ICC Statute, Article 8(2)(b)(iv). Jurisprudence, ICJ, *Nuclear Weapons* case, Advisory Opinion, 8 July 1996, paras 30 and 41; ICTY, *Kupreskic*, Judgement, 14 January 2000, para 524. See also the Report "No Safe Place" http://www.arableagueonline.org/las/picture_gallery/reportfullFINAL.pdf [the Executive Summary of the Report is reprinted in this Volume as Annex to Chap. 17].

On the principle of precaution in attack cf.: Article 2(3) of the 1907 Hague Convention; Article 57(1) of Additional Protocol I; Second Protocol to the Hague Convention for the Protection of Cultural Property, Article 7. Jurisprudence: ICTY, *Kupreskic*, Judgement, 14 January 2000, paras 524 and 525. See also the 'Goldstone Report', A/HCR/12/48, Conclusions [the Executive Summary and the Conclusions of the Report are reprinted as Documents 2 and 3 in Part II of this Volume, ChM].

Moreover, Article 53 of the Fourth Geneva Convention (IV GC) provides that

> "Any destruction by the Occupying Power of real or personal property belonging individually or collectively to private persons, or to the State, or to other public authorities, or to social or cooperative organisations, is prohibited, except where such destruction is rendered absolutely necessary by military operations."

The mass destruction of civilian property by the Israeli forces cannot be considered to be "for the purpose of fighting." And under no circumstances can it be argued that the shelling and indiscriminate destruction of civilian movable and immovable property, and of villages, towns and civilian neighbourhoods, as it happened during operation Cast Lead, were "absolutely necessary". They were not part of a "lawful military operation" covered by the provision of Article 53 IV GC. The destruction of property by shelling civilian targets can amount to collective punishment under Article 33 IV GC, which is a grave breach of the Convention itself.

2.3.3.3 Violations of the First Additional Protocol of 1977

Israel has also violated the First Additional Protocol of 1977 (I AP) to the Geneva Convention on the Protection of Victims of International Armed Conflicts, and in particular Article 35—on the Methods and Means of Warfare; Article 48—on the need at all times to distinguish between the civilian population and combatants; Article 51—on the protection of the civilian population; Article 54—on the protection of objects indispensable to the survival of the civilian population; and Article 56—on the protection of works and installations containing dangerous forces.

Article 85 I AP describes a number of serious violations:

> "In addition to the grave breaches defined in Article 11, the following acts shall be regarded as grave breaches of this Protocol, when committed wilfully, in violation of the relevant provisions of this Protocol, and causing death or serious injury to body or health: (a) making the civilian population or individual civilians the object of attack; (b) launching an indiscriminate attack affecting the civilian population or civilian objects in the knowledge that such attack will cause excessive loss of life, injury to civilians or damage to civilian objects, as defined in Article 57, para 2 (a)(iii); (c) launching an attack against works or installations containing dangerous forces in the knowledge that such attack will cause excessive loss of life, injury to civilians or damage to civilian objects, as defined in Article 57, para 2(a)(iii); (d) making non-defended localities and demilitarised zones the object of attack...".

The ban on attacking the civilian population forms part of international customary law, and as such it applies also to the State of Israel regardless of the non-ratification of this Protocol by the State.

2.3.3.4 Violations of the Protection of Cultural Property

Israel is a party to the Hague Convention for the Protection of Cultural Property in the Event of Armed Conflict of 1954 and the relative Regulations. The State of

Israel is thus committed to protecting cultural property as such as part of the obligations it entered into under the terms of that Convention. Moreover, Article 27 of the Hague Convention of 1907—which acquired the character of customary law as recognised by the International Court of Justice,[126] and therefore is binding also on Israel—states that

> "all necessary steps must be taken to spare, as far as possible, buildings dedicated to religion, art, science, or charitable purposes, historic monuments, hospitals, and places where the sick and wounded are collected, provided they are not being used at the time for military purposes."[127]

By carpet-bombing villages and towns, the Israeli forces committed serious violations of the laws of war, which fall in the grave breaches category, thereby constituting war crimes.

Article 3 of the Hague Convention of 1907 provides that "A belligerent party which violates the provisions of the said Regulations shall, if the case demands, be liable to pay compensation. It shall be responsible for all acts committed by persons forming part of its armed forces." Therefore, the State of Israel is wholly liable for the violations of the laws and customs of war, and the violation of these provisions places it under an obligation to compensate the Palestinian victims and institutions. Ultimately, it is the Israeli State which is directly responsible for all the acts committed by its armed forces.

2.3.3.5 The Obligation to Respect Human Rights

Article 2 of the International Covenant on Civil and Political Rights (ICCPR) places an obligation on the States parties

> "to respect and to ensure to all individuals within its territory and subject to its jurisdiction the rights recognised in the present Covenant, without distinction of any kind, such as race, colour, sex, language, religion, political or other opinion, national or social origin, property, birth or other status."

Furthermore, the International Court of Justice has ruled that the Pact applies equally to any acts perpetrated outside the territory of the State.[128]

---

[126] ICJ, *Legality of the Threat or Use of Nuclear Weapons*, ICJ Reports, 1996, para 80.

[127] Hague Regulations, Article 56; ICC Statute, Article 8(2)(b)(ix) and 8(2)(b)(xiii); also: Article 8(2)(e)(iv) and 8(2)(e)(xii); Hague Convention for the Protection of Cultural Property, Article 4 and Article 19; ICC Statute Article 8(2)(b)(ix); ICTY, *Blaskic* case, Judgement, 3 March 2000, para 185.

[128] ICJ, *Legal Consequences of the Construction of a Wall in the Occupied Palestinian Territory*, Advisory Opinion, 2004, para 111; UN Human Rights Committee, General Comment No. 29 (Article 4 of the International Covenant on Civil and Political Rights), 24 July 2001, para 3.

By causing the destruction of business enterprises, civil infrastructures, hospitals, mosques and other healthcare and cultural infrastructures, Israel failed to honour its obligation to respect the right to life, the right to housing, the right to work, the right to education, the right to medical care and health, and other fundamental human rights, including the right to an adequate standard of living. The shelling and destruction of welfare and health care centres, farms and livestock ranges, the destruction of schools, and of water and electricity systems, all constitute grave breaches of human rights, violating various Human Rights instruments as the International Covenant on Economic, Social and Cultural Rights and Convention on the Rights of the Child.

As the UN High Commissioner for Human Rights, Navanethem Pillay, has made it clear

> "The indiscriminate rocket attacks against Israeli civilian targets are illegal [but that] Israel's responsibility to fulfill its international obligations is totally independent of compliance by Hamas of its own obligations. States' obligations in respect of civilians are not subject to the principle of reciprocity."[129]

She also described as *unacceptable* "Israeli strikes against facilities clearly marked with the initials of the UN, where civilians had sought refuge."[130]

2.3.4 The Commission of War Crimes

Under Article 147 IV GC,

> "Grave breaches ... shall be those involving any of the following acts, if committed against persons or property protected by the present Convention: wilful killing, torture or inhuman treatment, including biological experiments, wilfully causing great suffering or serious injury to body or health, unlawful deportation or transfer or unlawful confinement of a protected person, compelling a protected person to serve in the forces of a hostile Power, or wilfully depriving a protected person of the rights of fair and regular trial prescribed in the present Convention, taking of hostages and extensive destruction and appropriation of property, not justified by military necessity and carried out unlawfully and wantonly."[131]

---

[129] While indiscriminate rocket attacks against civilian targets in Israel are unlawful, Israel's responsibility to fulfill its international obligations is completely independent from the compliance of Hamas with its own obligations under international law. States' obligations, particularly those related to the protection of civilian life and civilian objects, are not subject to reciprocity.

[130] Special Session on "serious violations of human rights in the occupied Palestinian territory, including the recent aggression in the occupied Gaza Strip," Council of Human Rights of 9 January 2009, http://www2.ohchr.org/english/bodies/hrcouncil/specialsession/9/index.htm.

[131] Article 85(5) of Protocol I of 1977 also states that "[...] subject to the application of the Conventions and this Protocol, grave breaches of these instruments are considered war crimes."

Any systematic and large-scale violation of the conventional rules and customs governing conduct in time of war or armed conflict by the unlawful use of weapons, violations of obligations towards the civilian population and civilian property and violations of the obligation to protect the environment, among other things, constitutes war crimes. Article 8 of the ICC Statute details such acts in its definition of war crimes *"for the purpose of this Statute."* The notion of war crime is very broad and applies not only to grave violations provided by the Geneva Conventions and its Additional Protocols, but also other violations, particularly with regard to conduct of hostilities and the unlawful use of weapons.

By using white phosphorus and cluster bombs, Israeli officials violated their obligation not to use them unlawfully, least of all against the civilian population. This was a case of using weapons likely to cause superfluous harm to the civilian population, but the use of these bombs against civilians and children nevertheless constitutes a war crime. By scattering bombs on farms and croplands, Israeli officials deprived the population of their livelihoods and committed a crime of particularly heinous nature. Similarly, the deliberate shelling of villages and towns and refugee camps were all war crimes.

While directing indiscriminate attacks against the civilian population, and against civilian property is *per se* a violation of the rules governing the conduct of armed conflicts, the fact that it was done intentionally, or wilfully, or in full knowledge of what was being done, certainly also constitutes a war crime, and is punishable as such.

2.3.5 The Commission of Crimes Against Humanity

The notion of crimes against humanity has gradually acquired an autonomous character, and today it is distinct from the notion of war crimes. Accordingly, any act committed in wartime can, simultaneously, be both a war crime and a crime against humanity. As the International Law Commission has pointed out "… war crimes and crimes against humanity go hand in hand. As will be seen, most war crimes are also crimes against humanity."[132] Article 7 of the ICC Statute defines crimes against humanity as a list of criminal acts "when committed as part of a widespread or systematic attack directed against any civilian population."[133]

---

[132] Fourth Report on the Draft Code of Crimes against Peace and Security of Mankind, by Mr. Doudou Thiam, Special Rapporteur, Yearbook of the International Law Commission, A/CN.4/398 and Corr. 1-3, 1986, vol. II (1), para 6. The ICTR also considered that "That the crimes against humanity may indeed be committed either within or outside of an armed conflict…." *Prosecutor* v. *Kayishema and Ruzindana*, Trial Chamber, Judgement of May 21, 1999, para 127.

[133] ICJ, *Nuclear Weapons* case, Advisory Opinion, 8 July 1996, para 25; ICTY, *Delalic* case, Judgment, 16 November 1998, paras 422–423, 452 and 454 and Part IV.

The International Criminal Tribunal for Rwanda (ICTR) has interpreted the meaning of a widespread or systematic attack in the following terms: "A widespread attack is one that is directed against a multiplicity of victims. A systematic attack means an attack carried out pursuant to a preconceived policy or plan."[134] According to Article 7 of the ICC Statute, it is not necessary for an attack to be at the same time 'widespread' and 'systematic' to fall in the category of crimes against humanity. An attack may be either widespread or systematic, or both at the same time, and must be directed against a civilian population. For, as the ICTR ruled in the Akayesu case, the existence of an act constituting a crime against humanity presupposes that: "An act must be directed against the civilian population if it is to constitute a crime against humanity. Members of the civilian population are people who are not taking any active part in the hostilities ...."[135] The ICTR has construed the notion of *civilian population* in the broad sense of the term: the presence of certain non-civilians in no way affects the status of the civilians or the civilian population and therefore in no way entitles one of the warring parties to attack the civilian population. This interpretation is, furthermore, consistent with the provisions of Article 50 I AP, which emphasises that "The presence within the civilian population of individuals who do not come within the definition of civilians does not deprive the population of its civilian character."

Some of the Israeli actions, as committed during the military operation 'Cast Lead', can integrate, according to the case law of the International tribunals, both war crimes and crimes against humanity. In particular, crimes against humanity were committed in light of the fact that the operations conducted on the Palestinian territory and against the Palestinian people were actually targeting the civilian population on a *widespread* or *systematic* basis.

These crimes are deemed to be so heinous by the international community that they follow a special regime, which derogates to a certain extent to the ordinary criminal law principles. For instance, international crimes are not subjected to statute of limitations. The first article of the Convention on the Non-Applicability of Statutory Limitations to War Crimes and Crimes Against Humanity accordingly states that they can always be prosecuted, regardless of the time when they have been committed.

2.3.6 Consequences in Terms of the Individual Criminal Liability of Israeli Authorities

The UN General Assembly, in its Resolution 95 (I), confirmed the principles of international law recognised by the Nuremberg International Tribunal. In

---

[134] Ibid., para 123.
[135] ICTR, *The Prosecutor* v. *Jean Paul Akayesu*, Chamber I, Judgement of 2 September 1998, para 582.

Resolution 488 (V) of 12 December 1950, it enshrined the validity of the Nuremberg Tribunal's principles in international law by adopting the "Principles of international law recognised in the Charter of the Nuremberg Tribunal and in the judgment of the Tribunal." Principle I recognised that "Any person who commits an act which constitutes a crime under international law is responsible therefore and liable to punishment."[136] Principle 3, furthermore, provided that "The fact that a person who committed an act which constitutes a crime under international law acted as Head of State or responsible government official does not relieve him from responsibility under international law."

Individual criminal responsibility for international crimes is now explicitly recognised in Articles 25 and 27 of the ICC Statute, which unequivocally rule out the relevance of official capacity as a ground to excluding criminal responsibility. The Parties to the Four Geneva Conventions committed themselves to comply with their international obligations also in times of war, including bringing those individuals responsible for international crimes to justice, according—*inter alia*— to Articles 146 and 147 IV GC. One of the primary obligations on the State of Israel, and consequently of its tribunals, is to enforce the relevant legislation to bring Israeli nationals to trial and prosecute them for their alleged crimes. Thus, Israeli nationals (including political and military officials) suspected of infringing the provisions of the Geneva Conventions and customary international law in relation to the conduct of the military operation against Gaza, should be investigated and prosecuted in the first place by the Israeli courts, which have primary jurisdiction by virtue of the principle of territorial jurisdiction.

However, in the light of the fact that the competent Israeli authorities: failed to take action; clearly showed no intention of prosecuting anyone responsible for the alleged crimes; have not been able to demonstrate their independence; and have shown to be incapable of exercising their jurisdiction and disciplinary powers, it is therefore up to other parties and competent authorities to take action in order to put an end to the impunity that those responsible for international crimes are enjoying within Israel's territory.

2.3.7 The Consequences of the Violations of International Law by the State of Israel

2.3.7.1 The International Responsibility of the State of Israel for Grave Violations of International Law

The first Article of the Draft Principles on the International Responsibility of States elaborated by the International Law Commission, states that: "Every

---

[136] Report of the International Law Commission on its second session from June 5 to July 29, 1950, Official Records, Fifth Session, Supplement No. 12 (A/1316), United Nations, New York, 1950, pp.12–16.

internationally wrongful act of a State entails the international responsibility of that State." Article 2 then provides that: "There is an internationally wrongful act of a State when conduct consisting of an action or omission: (a) is attributable to the State under international law; and (b) constitutes a breach of an international obligation of the State."[137] In the case of the Israeli military attack against the Gaza Strip the regime of international responsibility applies in full. Furthermore, pursuant to Article 5 the Israeli authorities acted not only as organs of the State: the top of the hierarchical chain of command, i.e. the Prime Minister, the Defence Minister, the Foreign Affairs Minister and the General Chief of Staff (among others) are all individually responsible for the crimes committed in the course of the military operation. Those actions met all the conditions to be considered as internationally unlawful acts entailing the international responsibility of the State of Israel and triggering other obligations incumbent upon the State, in particular the obligation to pay reparations for the wrongful acts committed.[138]

2.3.7.2 The Obligation to Make Reparations

International law clearly establishes that where an internationally unlawful act has been committed that is attributable to a State, thereby affecting that State's international responsibility, the State is obliged to make reparation for the internationally unlawful act. The basic rule is quite clear: the responsible State is required to make full compensation for any loss and damage caused by its internationally unlawful act.

The International Law Commission's Draft Articles on State Responsibility addresses this issue under Article 37, as follows:

> "1. The State responsible for an internationally wrongful act is under an obligation to give satisfaction for the injury caused by that act insofar as it cannot be made good by restitution or compensation. 2. Satisfaction may consist in an acknowledgement of the breach, an expression of regret, a formal apology or another appropriate modality."

This requires the State to make reparation, in an appropriate manner, for the loss and damages caused to both the people and civilian infrastructure and properties, including reparation covering damage to hospitals, ambulances, places of worship and others. The I AP also considers the responsibility of the State which violates the provisions of international humanitarian law. Article 91 expressly

---

[137] United Nations ILC Draft Articles on Responsibility of States for Internationally Wrongful Acts, Article 2.

[138] First Geneva Convention, Article 51; Second Geneva Convention, Article 52; Third Geneva Convention, Article 131; Fourth Geneva Convention, Article 148; Germany, Federal Supreme Court, *Reparation Payments* case, Judgement, 26 February 1963; Israel, District Court of Jerusalem, *Eichmann* case, Judgement, 12 December 1961, para 28; Italy, Military Tribunal of Rome, *Priebke* case, Judgement in Trial of First Instance, 1 August 1996. ICTY, *Tadic case*, Judgement on Appeal, 15 July 1999, paras 137–145 and 147–157.

provides that a Party to the conflict which violates the provisions of the Conventions or of the Protocol shall, if the case demands, be liable to pay compensation and *"shall be responsible for all acts committed by persons forming part of its armed forces."*

The State of Israel is therefore under an obligation to make full compensation by way of reparation for all the material, human, environmental and other damage it caused to the Palestinian population. As already noted, this obligation to make reparation in no way prejudges the matter of the criminal liability of individuals. Yet the Israeli authorities are continuing to ignore and deny the validity of the resolutions, which were adopted both by the UN Security Council and the General Assembly, with regard to the occupied Palestinian territory, continuing to perpetrate internationally illegal acts, thereby further aggravating their international responsibility.

The civilian victims and their assigns, entitled to compensation for the damage and destruction caused by Israeli military actions, are certainly entitled to benefit from this obligation to make reparations. The victims therefore have the right to seek a remedy "for gross violations of international human rights law and serious violations of international humanitarian law" including "the victim's right to the following as provided for under international law: (a) Equal and effective access to justice; (b) Adequate, effective and prompt reparation for harm suffered."[139] This is further corroborated by Article 75 of the Rome Statute, which makes it clear that the International Criminal Court may establish principles relating to reparations, including restitution, compensation and rehabilitation. In 2007, a Trust Fund was established by the Assembly of the States parties, for victims of crimes falling within the jurisdiction of the ICC and for their families.

2.3.8 Conclusions

Throughout the whole period of the offensive, the conduct of the Israeli armed forces demonstrated their total defiance and repeated infringements of the most basic principles of general international law and the rules governing armed conflicts, in relation to the prohibition on attacking the civilian population, the prohibition on causing superfluous injury or unnecessary suffering, and the prohibition on attacking civilian targets. One of the most serious consequences of Israel's breaches of its international obligations was the death of many hundreds of innocent civilians as a result of indiscriminate shelling. Whatever the nature of the armed conflict started by Israel against Palestine and whatever the reasons for it, the Israeli political and military authorities were required, at the time of the events,

---

[139] Basic Principles and Guidelines on the Right to a Remedy and Reparation for Victims of Gross Violations of International Human Rights Law and Serious Violations of International Humanitarian Law, adopted Resolution 60/147 by the General Assembly, December 16, 2005.

to comply with the laws and customs of war, including the Geneva Conventions of 1949 and the binding rules of international law or *jus cogens*, customary law rules and those stemming from obligations *erga omnes*.

In the wake of the repeated violations and wilful acts perpetrated by the Israeli military authorities and political leaders, it is important to ensure that all those who have violated human rights, international humanitarian law and the basic rules of international criminal law are brought to justice. It is urgently necessary to take measures against those responsible because those violations cannot be left, once again, unpunished. For the surviving victims and the relatives of the civilians and children who were killed—and for the whole of humanity itself—it is crucial that the Israeli officials who are responsible of the violations are made accountable for their acts before a criminal court to ensure that this long-standing impunity comes finally to an end and that the responsibilities are ascertained. These prosecutions are important to restore credibility for the rule of law, as the means of protecting and safeguarding human rights and the individuals.

In sum we can say, in respect of the acts perpetrated by the Israeli authorities, that:

(1) The State of Israel seriously violated the prohibition on the use of force, under Article 2(4) of the UN Charter, by attacking the Gaza Strip;
(2) No military justification existed for the wilful and widespread attacks against the civilian population. No political or military justification is acceptable for the systematic killing of civilians, the attacks and the destruction of towns and villages, and of the environment;
(3) The Israeli authorities were responsible for large-scale violations of both the laws and customs of war and the conventional and customary rules governing conduct in armed conflicts;
(4) Through its authorities, the State of Israel committed international crimes, and in particular the crime of aggression;
(5) The State of Israel and its authorities are required, under international law, to make full reparations for all the damages caused to the civilian population, civilian property and the environment;
(6) The Israeli authorities that ordered, designed or planned the military operation against the Gaza Strip, knowing that this would have resulted in the commission of international crimes, are individually criminally responsible for these acts, in particular as war crimes and crimes against humanity;
(7) The crimes committed by Israeli officials fall within the jurisdiction of national and international courts. Israeli officials could therefore be investigated and prosecuted by the competent courts of any State, under the principle of universal jurisdiction, and can be tried before the International Criminal Court.

2.4 States that have Recognised Palestine as a State[140]

The list below is based on the list maintained by the Palestine Liberation Organization during the campaign for United Nations recognition in 2011. Of the 193 UN member States, 127 (65.8%) have recognised the State of Palestine as of September 2011 [1 more State, Island, recognised Palestine in November 2011]. 72 of the 128 States that have so far recognised the State of Palestine are also members of the International Criminal Court, representing the 60% of the ICC member States [120 as of December 2011].

Nr.	Name	Date of recognition	ICC member State
1	Afghanistan	November 16, 1988	yes
2	Albania	November 17, 1988	yes
3	Algeria	November 15, 1988	no
4	Angola	December 6, 1988	no
5	Antigua and Barbuda	September 22, 2011	yes
6	Argentina	December 6, 2010	yes
7	Azerbaijan	April 15, 1988	no
8	Bahrain	November 15, 1988	no
9	Bangladesh	November 16, 1988	yes
10	Belarus	November 19, 1988	no
11	Belize	September 9, 2011	yes
12	Benin	May 1989 or before	yes
13	Bhutan	December 25, 1988	no
14	Bolivia	December 22, 2010	yes
15	Bosnia and Herzegovina	May 27, 1992	yes
16	Botswana	December 19, 1988	yes
17	Brazil	December 1, 2010	yes
18	Brunei	November 17, 1988	no
19	Bulgaria	November 25, 1988	yes
20	Burkina Faso	November 21, 1988	yes
21	Burundi	December 22, 1988	yes
22	Cambodia	November 21, 1988	yes
23	Cape Verde	November 24, 1988	yes
24	Central African Republic	December 23, 1988	yes
25	Chad	December 1, 1988	yes
26	Chile	January 7, 2011	yes
27	China, People's Republic of	November 20, 1988	no
28	Comoros	November 21, 1988	yes
29	Congo, Democratic Republic of the	December 10, 1988	yes
30	Congo, Republic of the	December 5, 1988	yes

(continued)

---

[140] Public available sources, http://en.wikipedia.org/wiki/International_recognition_of_the_State_of_Palestine (last consulted December 2011)

2 Selected Materials from the International Conference   77

(continued)

Nr.	Name	Date of recognition	ICC member State
31	Costa Rica	February 5, 2008	yes
32	Côte d'Ivoire	2008 or before	no
33	Cuba	November 16, 1988	no
34	Cyprus	November 18, 1988	yes
35	Czech Republic	November 18, 1988	yes
36	Djibouti	November 17, 1988	yes
37	Dominican Republic	July 14, 2009	yes
38	East Timor	March 1, 2004	no
39	Ecuador	December 24, 2010	yes
40	Egypt	November 18, 1988	no
41	El Salvador	August 25, 2011	no
42	Equatorial Guinea	May 1989 or before	no
43	Ethiopia	February 4, 1989	no
44	Gabon	December 12, 1988	yes
45	Gambia	November 18, 1988	yes
46	Georgia	April 25, 1992	yes
47	Ghana	November 29, 1988	yes
48	Guinea	November 19, 1988	yes
49	Guinea-Bissau	November 21, 1988	no
50	Guyana	January 13, 2011	yes
51	Honduras	August 26, 2011	yes
52	Hungary	November 23, 1988	yes
53	Iceland	November 26, 2011	yes
54	India	November 18, 1988	no
55	Indonesia	November 16, 1988	no
56	Iran	February 4, 1989	no
57	Iraq	November 15, 1988	no
58	Jordan	November 16, 1988	yes
59	Kazakhstan	April 6, 1992	no
60	Kenya	May 1989 or before	yes
61	Korea, North	November 24, 1988	no
62	Kuwait	November 15, 1988	no
63	Kyrgyzstan	November 1, 1995	no
64	Laos	December 2, 1988	no
65	Lebanon	November 30, 1988	no
66	Lesotho	June 6, 2011	yes
67	Liberia	July 2011	yes
68	Libya	November 15, 1988	no
69	Madagascar	November 16, 1988	yes
70	Malawi	April 19, 2011	yes
71	Malaysia	November 15, 1988	no
72	Maldives	November 28, 1988	yes
73	Mali	November 21, 1988	yes
74	Malta	November 16, 1988	yes
75	Mauritania	November 15, 1988	no

(continued)

(continued)

Nr.	Name	Date of recognition	ICC member State
76	Mauritius	November 17, 1988	yes
77	Mongolia	November 22, 1988	yes
78	Montenegro	July 24, 2006	yes
79	Morocco	November 15, 1988	no
80	Mozambique	December 8, 1988	no
81	Namibia	November 19, 1988	yes
82	Nepal	December 19, 1988	no
83	Nicaragua	November 16, 1988	no
84	Niger	November 24, 1988	yes
85	Nigeria	November 18, 1988	yes
86	Oman	December 13, 1988	no
87	Pakistan	November 16, 1988	no
88	Papua New Guinea	October 4, 2004	no
89	Paraguay	March 25, 2005	yes
90	Peru	January 24, 2011	yes
91	Philippines	September 1, 1989	yes
92	Poland	December 14, 1988	yes
93	Qatar	November 16, 1988	no
94	Romania	November 24, 1988	yes
95	Russia	November 18, 1988	no
96	Rwanda	January 2, 1989	no
97	Saint Vincent and the Grenadines	August 30, 2011	yes
98	São Tomé and Príncipe	December 10, 1988	no
99	Saudi Arabia	November 16, 1988	no
100	Senegal	November 22, 1988	yes
101	Serbia	November 16, 1988	yes
102	Seychelles	November 18, 1988	yes
103	Sierra Leone	December 3, 1988	yes
104	Slovakia	November 18, 1988	yes
105	Somalia	November 15, 1988	no
106	South Africa	February 15, 1995	yes
107	Sri Lanka	November 18, 1988	no
108	Sudan	November 17, 1988	no
109	Suriname	February 1, 2011	yes
110	Swaziland	July 1991 or before	no
111	Syria	July 18, 2011	no
112	Tajikistan	April 2, 1994	yes
113	Tanzania	November 24, 1988	no
114	Togo	November 29, 1988	no
115	Tunisia	November 15, 1988	yes
116	Turkey	November 15, 1988	no
117	Turkmenistan	November 2004 or before	no
118	Uganda	December 3, 1988	yes
119	Ukraine	November 19, 1988	no
120	United Arab Emirates	November 16, 1988	no

(continued)

(continued)

Nr.	Name	Date of recognition	ICC member State
121	Uruguay	March 15, 2011	yes
122	Uzbekistan	September 25, 1994	no
123	Vanuatu	August 21, 1989	yes
124	Venezuela	April 27, 2009	yes
125	Vietnam	November 19, 1988	no
126	Yemen	November 15, 1988	no
127	Zambia	November 16, 1988	yes
128	Zimbabwe	November 29, 1988	no

References

Amnesty International (2009) No Safe Haven Series. End Impunity through Universal Jurisdiction. http://www.amnesty.org

Bedjaoui M (1984) L'Admission d'un Nouveau Membre à l'Organisation de l'Unité Africaine, in Mélanges Offerts en l'honneur de Charles Chaumont, Pedone, Paris, pp 35–58

Bennouna M (1980) L'Admission d'un Nouveau Membre à l'Organisation de l'Unité Africaine, in 26 Annuaire Français de Droit International, pp 193–198

Carpentier C (1991) L'Appréciation de la Qualité d'Etat Par Les Organisations Internationales. Paris I, Panthéon-Sorbonne

D'Amato A (1971) The Concept of Custom in International Law. Cornell University Press, Ithaca, New York

Dupuy R-J (1989/1999) L'Illusion Juridique—Réflexions Sur le Mythe de la Paix Par le Droit, Initially in Mélanges Offerts à Guy Ladreit de Lacharrière, Paris, and Later in Dialectiques du Droit International—Souveraineté des Etats, Communauté Internationale et Droits de l'Homme, Paris

Feldman Y, Blau U (2009) How IDF Legal Experts Legitimized Strikes Involving Gaza Civilians, Haaretz. http://www.haaretz.com/hasen/spages/1057648.html

Garapon A (2002) Des Crimes qu'on ne Peut ni Punir ni Pardonner. Odile Jacob, Paris

Glasius M (2009) The ICC and the Gaza War: Legal Limits, Symbolic Politics. http://www.opendemocracy.net

HRW (2006) Universal Jurisdiction in Europe. The State of Art. http://www.hrw.org

Kirsch P, Robinson D (2002) Reaching Agreement at the Rome Conference. In: Cassese A, Gaeta P, Jones J (eds) The Rome Statute of the International Criminal Court—A Commentary. Oxford University Press, Oxford, p 78

Lapidoth R, Calvo-Goller NK (1992) Les Elements Constitutifs de l'Etat et la Declaration du Conseil National Palestinien du 15 Novembre 1988, 96 Revue Generale de Droit International Public, p 777

Lattanzi F (2009) Quelques Réflexions sur le 'Principe de Jurisdiction Universelle'. In: Venturini G, Bariatti S (eds) Droits Individuels et Justice Internationale, Liber Fausto Pocar. Giuffré, Milano, p 461

Lattanzi F (2010) Concurrent Jurisdictions Between Primacy and Complementarity. In: Belelli R (ed) International Criminal Justice: Law and Practice from the Rome Statute to its Review. Ashgate, Farnham, p 181

Meloni C (2010) Command Responsibility in International Criminal Law. T.M.C. Asser Press, The Hague

PCHR Press Release (2009a) Israel Closes Investigation into Alleged War Crimes Committed in the Gaza Strip, 31 March 2009. http://www.pchrgaza.org
PCHR Press Release (2009b) PCHR Condemns Israeli Attempts to Legitimise Crimes in Gaza and Shield Perpetrators from Justice, 27 April 2009. http://www.pchrgaza.org
PCHR Report (2010a) Genuinely Unwilling. An Update. http://www.pchrgaza.org
PCHR Report (2010b) The Principle and Practice of Universal Jurisdiction: PCHR's Work in the Occupied Palestinian Territory. http://www.pchrgaza.org
Quigley J (2009) The Palestine Declaration to the International Criminal Court: The Statehood Issue, 35 Rutgers Law Record, pp 1–10 (and in this Volume, Chap. 10)
Ruiz Fabri H (1992) Genèse et Disparition de l'Etat à l'époque Contemporaine, Annuaire Français de Droit International, pp 153–178
Salmon J (1988) La Proclamation de l'Etat Palestinien, Annuaire Français de Droit International
Shaw Y (2010) In the Matter of the Jurisdiction of the International Criminal Court with Regard to the Declaration of the Palestinian Authority—Supplementary Opinion. http://www.icc-cpi.int (visited on 10 March 2011)
Spiropoulos J (1949) In: Yearbook of the International Law Commission, p 35. http://untreaty.un.org/ilc/publications/yearbooks/1949.html
Tirlway H (1972) International Customary Law and its Codification. A. W. Sijthoff, Leiden
Werle G (1997) Menschenrechtsschutz Durch Völkerstrafrecht, Zeitschrift für Die Gesamte Strafrechtswissenschaft, p 822
Wilkinson T (2002) Israeli Army Probes Slaying of Palestinian Grandmother. Los Angeles Times, Los Angeles

Part II
The UN Fact Finding Mission on the Gaza Conflict and Follow-up at the International and Domestic Level

Chapter 3
The Goldstone Report and the Goldstone Retreat: Truths Told by Law and Reviled by Geopolitics

Richard Falk

Contents

3.1 A Preliminary Observation on the Goldstone Retreat 83
3.2 Assessing the Goldstone Report 87
3.3 Why the Goldstone Report Broke the Sound Barrier 88
3.4 Conclusions and Recommendations of the Goldstone Report 93
3.5 A Polarized Debate: Liberal Legality and Geopolitical Reality 96
3.6 International Law and the Peace Process 101
3.7 Conclusion 102
References 103

3.1 A Preliminary Observation on the Goldstone Retreat

The Goldstone Report gained its prominence because of its UN auspices and the high credibility of Richard Goldstone as the Chair of the Fact Finding Mission appointed by the Human Rights Council.[1] Other reputable inquiries (John Dugard's parallel mission set up by the Arab League, Amnesty International,

---

Richard Falk is Albert G. Milbank Professor of International Law Emeritus, Princeton University, and currently research professor of global studies at the University of California, Santa Barbara. Since 2008, he has been the Special Rapporteur on the Occupied Palestinian Territories for the UN Human Rights Council.

[1] On the establishment of the Fact Finding Mission on the Gaza conflict, see J. Barnette, Chap. 5 *infra*.

R. Falk (✉)
University of California, Santa Barbara, CA, USA

Human Rights Watch), aside from a host of journalistic and credible eyewitness accounts, converged on the overall criminality under international law of Operation Cast Lead. The video reports, together with the 100:1 casualty ratio, reinforced this impression, which has since been further validated by the testimony of IDF soldiers, diaries of persons living in Gaza at the time, by the Norwegian film *Tears of Gaza*, as well as by informal reports by UN staff stationed at the time of the attacks in Gaza.[2] What the Goldstone Report did was to provide greater detail, especially in relation to several incidents, a set of recommendations for further action, and significantly, encouragement for accountability by way of the less conventional means of Universal Jurisdiction (application of norms of international criminal law by national courts against persons charged with violations regardless of where perpetrated) and civil society action.

The report of the commission, known as 'The Goldstone Report,' when released in September 2009, was greeted with savage hostility by the political leadership of Israel, repudiated by the United States Government, and endorsed in subsequent months by a vote of 25-6 (with 11 abstentions) in the UN Human Rights Council and by a vote of 114-8 (with 44 abstentions) in the General Assembly. The report was mainly critical of Israel, but also criticized the behavior of Hamas, and contained recommendations for implementation premised on giving the accused political actors considerable time to act on its own, calling for implementation of its call for accountability only in the event that Israel and Hamas failed to act on their own in a manner that corresponds to international standards.

As I have pointed out in the past, in many respects the Goldstone Report was unduly favorable to Israel in two major respects. First, it somewhat unfairly highlighted Hamas's wrongdoing by failing to take account of Israel's provocative attack on November 4, 2008 that broke the truce—a truce that had effectively reduced cross border violence for several months, and which Hamas proposed extending indefinitely, provided only that Israel end its unlawful blockade. Israel never even responded to such a proposal, seeming to be disinterested in restoring security on its southern border by normalizing its relationship with Gaza, or at least testing whether this would be possible.

More serious in some respects was the failure of the Goldstone Report to consider several key issues that might have led to even more damaging conclusions from Israel's perspective: whether, given the truce, it was permissible for an occupying power to launch such an attack in the first instance, and more fundamentally whether a military assault on a densely populated urban society can ever be reconciled with international humanitarian law; and, further, whether the Israeli denial to Gaza civilians of the opportunity to leave the war zone during the period of combat was not itself a distinct crime against humanity. There were other issues that were not sufficiently investigated, including whether the casualty total should

---

[2] This is substantiated by the casualty figures, which suggest somewhere between 1,387 and 1,444 Palestinians were killed, mainly civilians, and more than 300 children, while three Israeli civilians died as a result of rocket and mortar fire from Gaza, and this could not clearly be attributable to Hamas due to the role of independent militias not under its control.

include those suffering from a variety of forms of post-traumatic stress, which was reportedly widespread among Gaza civilians, especially children.

The high visibility of the Goldstone Report highlights both the strengths and weaknesses of international law and the UN. Its strengths are shown by the extent to which findings of unlawfulness and criminality are influential with respect to world public opinion, and help to mobilize solidarity initiatives in civil society. There is no doubt that the BDS Campaign and the Freedom Flotilla were strengthened in resolve and capabilities due to the Goldstone Report. In what I call the Legitimacy War being waged, "lawfare" is an important battleground, and the outcome of the Goldstone mission was a major victory for those supporting the Palestinian struggle for self-determination.

At the same time, the refusal of the United States to back the recommendations of the Goldstone Report—on the contrary to use its political muscle to block and minimize its institutional impact within the UN—meant that the recommendations would likely remain stillborn, as has turned out to be the case. The UN cannot challenge unlawful and criminal behavior unless a geopolitical consensus is present. For instance, the use of force in Libya was backed by a geopolitical consensus, although a weak one due to the abstention of five Security Council members, including China and Russia, with regard to the crucial Resolution 1973.

In effect, the UN is strategically important as a site of struggle in the Legitimacy War, but it has been unable to protect the Palestinian people or safeguard their rights under international law. In this respect, its relevance is *symbolic*, and its frustrations and impressions of futility are *behavioral*. For external behavioral support, the Palestinians must look mainly to civil society as well as to their own tactics of resistance, of which the soft power challenge mounted by the first intifada was the most notable, creative, and effective to date.

Meanwhile, as mentioned earlier, the issue of the lawfulness of Israel's recourse to an armed attack on this scale, given the situation that existed, seemed entirely unreasonable, and likely motivated by considerations other than providing security for southern Israel (i.e. influencing the outcome of imminent Israeli elections; striking at Hamas before Obama took office; sending a message to Iran; restoring the reputation of the IDF after its failures in the Lebanon War of 2006). It may be illuminating to analyze the issue both from the perspective of international law, which overwhelmingly regards Gaza as subject to the legal regime of "occupation" as set forth by the Fourth Geneva Convention, as supplemented by Protocol I agreed upon in 1977, and from the perspective of Israeli foreign policy, which views Gaza as a foreign entity due to the Israeli disengagement by way of the withdrawal of ground forces in 2005.

With regard to occupation, the basic character of the operation is manifestly incompatible legally with the fundamental obligation of the occupying power to rely on the minimum force with the least disruption of civilian life. The operation equally violates international law if the Israeli foreign policy view is adopted, as Israel's right to use force would then be subject to the Charter framework that limits a right of self-defense to a response against a prior border-crossing armed attack. There is no way in which rockets that rarely caused human or property damage can be viewed as an armed attack or as creating a security threat that could only be reasonably met by such a large-scale military operation. There is some flexibility that has grown up over the years with respect to interpreting the right of self-defense, but nothing in past practice or legal authority would provide support for the scope and intensity of the military operation carried out by Israel in 2008–2009.

As I have tried to explain, relying on UN inquiries to establish illegality and criminality is of great symbolic relevance in promoting Palestinian objectives by way of conducting a Legitimacy War. The limitations are due to the geopolitical unwillingness to regard such findings as entailing behavioral consequences, such as activating the accountability procedures available by way of the International Criminal Court. Even should the ICC get the opportunity to indict and prosecute, it would in all likelihood have no capacity to apprehend and punish. At the same time, such a conviction would be a further success from a legitimacy perspective. Also relevant is the heightened possibility that national courts would rely on Universal Jurisdiction to investigate allegations of criminality of Israeli political and military commanders associated with policies that were previously condemned by UN inquiries. In recent years, several European countries have been sufficiently threatening about the possibility of detaining and prosecuting Israeli officials before their national courts as to discourage their travel, which is itself a weak sanction.

What is evident, then, is the weakness of international law and the UN when it comes to the enforcement of international criminal law. Here, too, this weakness is selective. When the geopolitical will exists, as with Saddam Hussein or Slobodan Milosevic, the implementation of international legal standards will be self-righteously insisted upon. This reality of double standards is greatly discrediting to international law as a just and fair legal regime.

In terms of the recent editorial by Richard Goldstone [published by the Washington Post on 2 April 2011, and titled "Reconsidering the Goldstone Report on Israel and War Crimes"—ChM], it should be remembered that Goldstone, although the chair of the mission, is only one of its four members. More significantly, after the notorious Goldstone editorial was published, the other three members of the fact-finding mission in a published joint statement reaffirmed the report in its entirety, and although Goldstone's name was not mentioned, their intent was obvious. Without being invidious, it seems appropriate to note that Christine Chinkin, a distinguished professor of international law at the London School of Economics, was the most expert member of the group when it comes to international humanitarian law. So fairly considered, Goldstone's retreat should not count for much, but unfortunately the retreat is being spun by the U.S. Government as a retraction that justifies demanding that the Human Rights Council repudiate the report retroactively.

It is unfortunate and ironic that it should be Judge Goldstone who steps forward to undermine the Goldstone Report. Of course, if there was some new truth that genuinely undermines the original conclusions and recommendations, then we should have been ready to applaud Goldstone's courage and integrity to acknowledge a past mistake. But here, the grounds for reconsiderations are flimsy to the point of being non-existent, making the Goldstone position seem more like a belated plea for Zionist redemption. Sure enough, invitations to Israel have already been issued by Netanyahu cabinet ministers and praise bestowed by the right wing extremist Foreign Minister, Avigdor Lieberman.

Beyond this, Goldstone's reconsiderations touch on a review of facts relating to some of the incidents, and rely unconvincingly on Israel's self-investigations as providing a reliable basis for assessment. This flies in the face of almost all other accounts, which view these investigations as little more than self-serving public relations exercises. Goldstone wildly over-generalizes to conclude that he does not now ascribe intentionality to Israeli attacks on civilians and civilian targets in Gaza. Again, this seems completely untenable given the overall weight of testimony, including the damning confessional evidence of IDF soldiers contained in the publications of Breaking the Silence.

Of course, lawfare cuts both ways, and it is now Netanyahu who is calling upon the UN Human Rights Council to repudiate the Goldstone Report and indirectly lend support to the claim of the Israeli Minister of Defense, Ehud Barak, that the IDF is "the most moral army in the world." Let us hope that the UN holds its symbolic ground, and not only reaffirms confidence in the Goldstone Report, but feels a new stimulus to take seriously its recommendation for further action long overdue in the General Assembly and Security Council. And even if the UN fails to act responsibly, civil society has many options to show that even if governments and international institutions do not take issues of criminal accountability seriously, the peoples of the world do.

3.2 Assessing the Goldstone Report

I wish to draw a fundamental distinction between (1) the Goldstone Report as *a text* to be considered from the perspective of international law and world politics; and (2) the Goldstone Report as *an event* that has achieved remarkable salience given its nature as a rather tediously detailed account, covering 575 pages, of the investigation of the four-person fact-finding mission. This mission was established by the Human Rights Council of the United Nations on 12 January 2009.[3] On one side, the text of the report has the quality of ordinariness that makes it somewhat reminiscent of Hannah Arendt's famous characterization of Adolph Eichmann's criminality as "the banality of evil."[4] Such banality, if attributed to a UN report, usually means its total neglect, which makes it particularly intriguing that on this occasion the Goldstone Report attracted worldwide attention and scrutiny, generated controversy, and made the distinguished international jurist, Richard Goldstone, a lightning rod for praise and calumny. Despite this prominence, I suspect that there have been few close readers of the report, with most commentary deriving from casual perusals of the rather lengthy Executive Summary and Recommendations section of the report.

---

[3] UN Human Rights Council Resolution S-9/1 (12 January 2009).
[4] Arendt 1964.

A first challenge, then, for any interpretation of the Goldstone Report, is to make sense of why this particular report touched the raw nerve of global moral and political consciousness. On this basis, some attempt will be made to evaluate substantively the harshly critical responses of Israel and the United States, followed by a more detached assessment as to whether the recommendations of the Goldstone Report that seem entirely reasonable from *liberal legalist perspectives* are practical given the *geopolitical realities* of the situation. In light of this posited tension between the imperatives of international criminal law and the constraints of geopolitics, it seems unlikely that the sound and fury generated by the release of the Goldstone Report will lead to the implementation of its principal recommendations on an intergovernmental level or in the form of enforcement initiatives on the part of the United Nations, much less the International Criminal Court. Such an outcome does raise questions as to whether international law and the UN system are capable of upholding the rights of the weak under circumstances where an offending state enjoys the protection of the strong. In line with this view, the burden of implementation shifts our focus to the potentialities of global civil society as an arena of implementation for the Goldstone recommendations, and reminds us of the relevance of "legitimacy wars" of the sort waged by the anti-apartheid campaign during the 1980s that so significantly and, at the time unexpectedly, contributed to the transformation of the racist regime in South Africa.

3.3 Why the Goldstone Report Broke the Sound Barrier

Strong global expectations

The Goldstone Report was commissioned in the aftermath of the major attacks launched by Israel on December 27, 2008, and continued until January 18, 2009. These attacks by an advanced military power on an adversary with no relevant means of self-defense or meaningful retaliatory capability were a shocking instance of one-sided warfare. This impression was accentuated by widespread media coverage of the events, by eyewitness accounts of the deliberate targeting of civilians and the destruction of targets protected by international humanitarian law (including medical facilities, educational institutions, UN buildings, and civilian infrastructure) and, perhaps most of all, by the ratio of casualties (more than 1,400 Palestinians killed compared to thirteen Israelis of whom only three were civilians). This one-sidedness made most commentators reluctant to call the attacks an example of "war." Critics tended to call it a "massacre" while supporters relied on the anodyne language of "military operation," or avoided the problem of naming by using the Israeli official designation, Operation Cast Lead.

Indicative of this perception of the Gaza attacks were the urgent calls for some kind of response by the United Nations. High UN officials, including the Secretary-General and the High Commissioner for Human Rights, both expressed concern about the military action involving the commission of war crimes, and called for some kind of investigation. Such calls, although without much political prospect of implementation, did give rise to special sessions of both the General Assembly and the Human Rights Council, the latter producing the resolution establishing the Goldstone Commission. This kind of initiative, normally a low profile kind of initiative unnoticed by the media, here seemed responsive to the acute sense of frustration and outrage about the Israeli attacks that was prevalent around the world and at the United Nations, although much less so in the United States. Given this mood, there existed in the weeks following the attacks on Gaza a rather unrealistic expectation on the part of those who supported the Palestinian struggle that this effort would finally exert serious external pressure on Israel after years of frustration. At the very least, it was believed that the continuing daily ordeal of the Gazan population due to the blockade could be brought to an end. It was deeply troubling that Israel had not ended the blockade of Gaza at the same time as the January 18, 2009 cease-fire took effect. In fact, Israel has continued the blockade, with significant Egyptian cooperation, a policy in flagrant, ongoing, and massive violation of Article 33 of the Fourth Geneva Convention that prohibits collective punishment.[5] The cumulative impact of the blockade has been described as a form of "slow genocide," and would certainly seem to qualify as a crime against humanity.[6]

It was also believed that a report identified with such a distinguished and impeccably qualified chair of the mission would be both authoritative and difficult to discredit or ignore. After all, Richard Goldstone was not only widely-known and respected in international circles, but was also a prominent Zionist with continuing personal and professional ties to Israel. In this respect, those who were critical of Israel's occupation policies believed that it might be possible to bring meaningful international pressure to bear by way of the UN system, especially because Israel seemed intentionally to attack UN facilities during the Gaza attacks.[7] Due to Judge

---

[5] The motivations for this blockade have been variously described as: punishment of the Gazan population for its show of support for Hamas in the January 2006 elections; a response to the Hamas forcible takeover of Gazan governance in July 2007; a strategy of undermining Hamas by making the life of the civilian population both unbearable and highly unfavorable as compared to life in the West Bank under the Palestinian Authority; a bargaining tactic to secure the return of the single captured Israeli soldier, Gilad Shalit. Because nothing is acknowledged, such explanations are obviously speculative. What is not speculative, and yet significant, is that the blockade has little if anything to do with Israeli concerns about the Qassam rockets fired from Gaza in the direction of Israeli towns. The rocket fire virtually disappeared during a ceasefire, and Hamas frequently offered to extend the cease-fire even for a period of ten years, an offer ignored by Israel.

[6] See column by Hijab 2009.

[7] A summary of a comprehensive report prepared by UN Board of Inquiry details damage to UN facilities, and concludes that Israel deliberately targeted such facilities despite knowing their identity and that they were being used as a shelter for Gazan civilians. The full report has been treated as an internal document and never made public, although a rather extensive Executive Summary is available that includes a recommendation that compensation be sought from Israel for damage done. See "Transcript of Press Conference by Secretary-General Ban Ki-moon, UN Headquarters" (SG/SM/12224) (5 May 2009). For commentary emphasizing Israel's reaction, see Rabinovich 2009.

Goldstone's experience in relation to international criminal law and reputation for integrity as well as the prior consensus as to the criminality of the Israeli tactics in carrying out the attacks, it was generally assumed that the report would find Israel guilty of war crimes.[8]

In this sense, the findings of the Goldstone Report did live up to the strong expectations that it would confirm prior allegations of criminality, and it even went beyond these expectations by setting forth a series of recommendations that presupposed that the United Nations could and should implement the international rule of law even in the face of anticipated well-organized geopolitical opposition. The fact that Hamas was also found to have pursued tactics that violated international humanitarian law gave an appropriate balance to the report, but did not seem to avoid the assessment that the importance of the report resulted from its conclusions critical of Israel. An added weight of these conclusions arose from the seeming caution of the mission, expressed by its careful investigatory methodology, its reluctance to rely on speculation, and its insistence on providing detailed explanations for any allegation of criminality.

Touching an Israeli raw nerve

Interest in the Goldstone Report was undoubtedly enhanced by the high-profile angry responses by Israeli political leaders, and the outraged tone struck in the Israeli media. The supposedly more peace-minded Shimon Peres, President of Israel and Labor Party leader, called the report "a mockery of history" that somehow lent legitimacy to terrorism.[9] Prime Minister Benjamin Netanyahu devoted a portion of his 2009 speech in the General Assembly to a denunciation of the report that adopted the sort of inflammatory rhetoric that President George W. Bush deployed after the September 11 attacks. Netanyahu declared that "Israel justly defended itself against terror. This biased and unjust report is a clear-cut test for all governments. Will you stand with Israel or will you stand with the terrorists?" He went on, "We must know the answer to that question now. Now and not later. Because if Israel is again asked to take more risks for peace, we must know today that you will stand with us tomorrow."[10] The contrary logic of the Goldstone Report can also be formulated as a question to the United Nations: Will you confer impunity upon Israel and its leaders or will you stand behind this call

---

[8] It was at Justice Goldstone's insistence that the Human Rights Council's original mandate be expanded to include inquiry into the conduct of Hamas. For Goldstone's own reflections on his involvement in this inquiry, see Goldstone 2009; see also for his underlying orientation, Goldstone 2000.

[9] Shimon Peres even mounted an entirely inappropriate and ill-fitting personal attack on Goldstone calling him "a small man, devoid of any sense of justice, a technocrat with no real understanding of jurisprudence" who led "a one-sided mission to hurt Israel." As quoted in Sadeh 2009; see also Zarchin 2009.

[10] Netanyahu speech of 24 September 2009; compare President George W. Bush 2001.

for the implementation of international humanitarian and criminal law? The Israeli Defense Minister, Ehud Barak, echoed the sentiments of Netanyahu, saying the report was "false, distorted and promotes terror." He added that "adopting the report will cripple" the capacity of governments in democratic countries "to deal with terror organizations, and terror in general."[11] Even putting aside the rest of the problematic character of such statements, they seem to suggest that, if the adversary can be characterized as terrorist, then there should be no operative legal limitations on the use of force. Here, it also seems diversionary to attach the label of "terrorist" to a democratically elected political grouping that has repeatedly called for a long-term cease-fire and diplomatic solution to the underlying conflict, and was a de facto governmental actor representing the people of the Gaza Strip. In addition, Hamas had repeatedly proposed a cease-fire of long-term duration, provided that Israel lift the blockade and open the crossings, and peaceful coexistence up to 50 years if Israel were to implement Security Council Resolution 242 and withdraw to 1967 borders.

Note that the condition of the cease-fire was limited to the demand that Israel terminate its unlawful blockade, what was legally and morally required in any event. Of course, Hamas was in effect proposing to stop firing rockets into Israel, which was an unlawful form of resistance regardless of Israel's provocation. In effect, the cease-fire would have restored a semblance of legality to the regime of occupation. The main point here is not so much a substantive rebuttal of the Israeli response, but a need to interpret this unprecedented intensity of response at leadership levels in Tel Aviv. It is necessary to base our understanding on circumstantial considerations because the actual reasons for such a posture of defiance is unlikely to be ever honestly disclosed by any government. What, then, is the most plausible explanation of why Israel reacted with such hostile intensity to the Goldstone Report?

One plausible reason was to counteract the high expectations of those who had applauded the outcome of the Goldstone Mission, compounded by the difficulty of discrediting someone of Goldstone's stature and known Israeli sympathies. Furthermore, the implications of repudiating Israel's claim that its anti-terrorist Gaza operation was legitimate struck directly at the main rationale for the extent and severity of Israeli violence throughout the occupied Palestinian territories, and not just in the Gaza Strip. The Goldstone Report also directly rejected the Israeli claim that international humanitarian law must be adjusted to accommodate counter-terrorist tactics even if directed at targets with heavy civilian components and, as the reactions of Israeli leaders made clear, this obviously agitated Israeli sensitivities. Finally, the conclusion that Israeli leaders and military personnel were potentially guilty of war crimes, possibly even crimes against humanity, seemed to disturb the government in Tel Aviv for a combination of symbolic, substantive, and practical reasons. Symbolically, there was a subtle resonance with the Nazi

---

[11] Haaretz 2009.

past where Jews were massively victimized. Substantively, there was the sense that the failure of Israel to act in accordance with the Geneva Conventions was not just wrongful, but criminal. And practically, there was anxiety that Israeli political and military leaders could be detained and charged with international crimes either by recourse to some international mechanism or through a national procedure relying on the authority of "universal jurisdiction."[12] Undoubtedly, the great interest in the Goldstone Report was increased as a result of this furious response by the highest levels of Israeli officialdom. This response departed dramatically from the past Israeli treatment of external criticism, especially emanating from the United Nations, and particularly from the Human Rights Council, which had long been demonized by Israel and the United States as being obsessively anti-Israeli. Habitually, Israel would simply reject such criticism and adverse policy directives with a curt government statement of dismissal. It did this routinely and effortlessly, almost always with the backing of the United States. A clear instance of this pattern is illustrated by Israel's rejection without making any special effort to provide a legal rationale of the near unanimous conclusions of the International Court of Justice that the construction of a separation wall on occupied Palestinian territory was unlawful, that the wall should be dismantled, and Palestinians who had been harmed should be compensated.[13] What is surprising with respect to the Goldstone Report is that Israel greeted the release of the report as if shocked and taken by surprise, whereas the general contours of the outcome should have been anticipated, given the similarity of conclusions reached by other prior respected inquiries under liberal auspices and even by a group of testimonies of participating soldiers from the Israel Defense Forces (IDF).[14] In fact, Israel's refusal to cooperate with the Goldstone Mission, even to the extent of denying entry to Gaza by way of Israel, was widely interpreted as a kind of pre-emptive repudiation of the report, fully expecting that the allegations of war crimes would be confirmed.[15] That the Goldstone Report so ruffled Israeli feathers was itself a surprising public relations success for the UN initiative, although this publicity victory could easily

---

[12] For exploration of and support for universal jurisdiction, see various contributions to Macedo 2004.

[13] See *Legal Consequences of the Construction of a Wall on Occupied Palestinian Territory*, I.C.J. Advisory Opinion (9 July 2004); the fact that it was an advisory opinion should not make it less authoritative, especially given the acceptance of the conclusions by a formal resolution passed in the General Assembly.

[14] See reports of Amnesty International, Human Rights Watch, and Breaking the Silence, the latter collecting the testimony of thirty IDF soldiers.

[15] An internationally respected Israeli activist and former member of the Knesset, Uri Avnery, expresses this facet: "People around the world know that it is as honest a report as could be expected after our government's decision to boycott the investigation." Uri Avnery, 2009. Avnery earlier had written, "So why did the Israeli government boycott the commission? The real answer is quite simple: they knew full well that the commission, any commission, would have to reach the conclusions it did reach."

morph into disillusionment in the event that Israel succeeds in discouraging implementing moves at the UN.

3.4 Conclusions and Recommendations of the Goldstone Report

As indicated above, the conclusions of the Goldstone Report were mainly confirmatory of prior reports that were already sufficiently authoritative to convey an impression to worldwide public opinion that Israel's attacks at the end of 2008 on Gaza involved the widespread commission of war crimes, if not crimes against humanity. I consider only three aspects of the conclusions in the report to be of sufficient note to warrant mention. The first involves the degree to which the attacks were declared to be applications of the so-called Dahiya doctrine that had explicitly endorsed the use of "disproportionate force and the causing of great damage and destruction to civilian property and infrastructure, and suffering to the civilian population." In damning language, the Goldstone Report says that the Dahiya doctrine "appears to have been precisely what was put into practice" in Operation Cast Lead.[16] Such a conclusion comes close to raising the issue as to whether waging a one-sided war against an essentially defenseless civilian population can ever be reconciled with international humanitarian law or the customary international law of war.[17] I believe this issue needs to be addressed more comprehensively by the International Committee of the Red Cross in hosting an international negotiating conference tasked with the job of producing a protocol

---

[16] "Human Rights in Palestine and Other Occupied Arab Territories: Report of the United Nations Fact-finding Mission on the Gaza Conflict," (Goldstone Report), para 62, available at http://www2.ohchr.org/english/bodies/hrcouncil/specialsession/9/FactFindingMission.htm. The Goldstone Report also notes that these same elements were present in the Israeli tactics during the Lebanon war of 2006, almost equally a one-sided war in terms of damage and casualties. For a range of critical assessments, see Hovsepian 2008; on the Dahiya doctrine, see discussion in Barnette 2010, pp. 15–20. The essence of the Dahiya doctrine was expressed by Maj. Gen. Gadi Eisenkot, Israeli Northern Command chief, in October 2008: "What happened in the Dahiya quarter of Beirut in 2006 will happen in every village from which Israel is fired on …. We will apply disproportionate force on it and cause great damage and destruction there. From our standpoint, these are not civilian villages, they are military bases …. This is not a recommendation. This is a plan. And it has been approved." Ynet 2008, also see Siboni 2008.

[17] I have argued elsewhere, without a focus on the Gaza attacks, that such one sided war resembles "torture" more than "war," wondering why the former disturbs public sensibilities so much more than the human impacts of war. See Falk 2011, pp. 119–133.

criminalizing such one-sided warfare, the Dahiya doctrine, with possible allowance of limited force applied to strictly military targets. There admittedly are complexities because alleged adversary forces using violence could hide weapons and personnel in protected civilian structures. Again, allowances could be made, but what would be prohibited unconditionally are attacks that are deliberately disproportionate and designed to inflict punitive damage on the civilian infrastructure as an avowed objective.[18]

Second, "in the context of increasing unwillingness of Israel to open criminal investigations that comply with international standards," the report explicitly encourages reliance on universal jurisdiction "as an avenue for States to investigate violations of the provisions of the Geneva Conventions of 1949, prevent impunity and promote international accountability."[19] A recommendation at the end of the Goldstone Report is more directive as it recommends that States Parties to the Geneva Conventions of 1949 start criminal investigations in national courts, using universal jurisdiction, where there is sufficient evidence of the commission of grave breaches. Where so warranted, following investigation, alleged perpetrators should be arrested and prosecuted in accordance with internationally recognized standards of justice.[20]

This is an important reminder that states can use their national criminal law systems to reinforce claims of international criminal law in the event that the principal state fails to act responsibly in relation to its own accused nationals. At present, universal jurisdiction for serious crimes of states exists mainly in several Western European countries, and is under great pressure from Israel and the United States to renounce such legal authority. It was reported recently that Tzipi Livni, head of the Israeli opposition and foreign minister during the Gaza attacks, cancelled a speaking engagement in London after being informed that an arrest warrant had been issued by a British magistrate. The warrant was withdrawn after it was known that she had canceled her plans for the visit.[21]

What seems evident is that even the threat of detention on the basis of universal jurisdiction is likely to inhibit travel of high Israeli political and military officials prominently associated with Operation Cast Lead. It is also quite possible that legislation empowering national courts to exert universal jurisdiction may spread to other countries, especially if such a result becomes one tactic of the Palestinian solidarity movement.

And finally, the recommendations of the Goldstone Report break some new ground by suggesting that their findings as to war crimes allegations require the

---

[18] For insightful discussion of "disproportion" in the setting of air strikes by Israel, see Farer 2009.

[19] Goldstone Report, Executive Summary, para 127; reprinted in this Volume, *infra* Document 2 in Part II.

[20] Goldstone Report, para 1772, Recommendations section.

[21] See Black and Cobain 2009.

establishment of an accountability mechanism. Their principal call is for the UN Security Council to insist that Israel conduct its own investigation of allegations in a manner that is "independent and meets international standards," with the process to be completed within six months. The Executive Summary "concludes that there are serious doubts about the willingness of Israel to carry out genuine investigations … as required by international law."[22]

More significant than the call for investigation is the report's recommendation that, if such an investigation and implementation of accountability are not carried out in a satisfactory fashion after six months, the Security Council should "refer the situation in Gaza to the Prosecutor of the International Criminal Court pursuant to Article 13(b) of the Statute."[23] It seems unlikely that Israel will mount a sufficiently credible investigation to satisfy the United Nations because it seems so far to be relying on self-investigations by the IDF and has not made any moves to undertake a process of assessment independent of the government. The Secretary-General of the UN reported inconclusively to the General Assembly on February 5, 2010 about Israeli and Hamas developments in response to the recommended investigative procedures proposed by the Goldstone Report.[24] Nevertheless, the Israeli military advocate-general seems to believe that, as soon as the IDF published its findings showing nominal responsiveness to the call for an investigation, pressure from the UN would decline.[25] His assessment may have assumed quite realistically that an ebbing of international concern after some nominal Israeli effort at investigation, reinforced by the assured diplomatic support of the United States and some European governments, would effectively discourage any additional UN efforts to implement the accountability recommendations in the Goldstone Report.

There are a number of other recommendations, the acceptance of which would substantially close part of the gap between the legal obligations of Israel as the occupying power and the present occupation policies being pursued. Of particular importance is the recommendation that Israel review its rules of engagement and operating practices to ensure conformity in the future with "the principles of proportionality, distinction, precaution and non-discrimination" in a manner that protects Palestinian rights and avoids "affronts to human dignity."[26] There has been a rather elaborate debate about whether Israel is acting properly when it shifts

---

[22] Goldstone Report, para 122.

[23] Goldstone Report, paras 1766 and 1767.

[24] See BBC report of 11 Palestinian human rights organizations directing an identical letter to Palestinian Authority president Mahmoud Abbas and Hamas prime minister Ismail Haniya urging the initiation of investigations of allegations made against Hamas and Palestinian forces during the Israeli "military offensive" in Gaza that took place between 27 December 2008 and 18 January 2009. See "Palestinians Urged on Gaza Crimes", BBC 2010.

[25] See Izenberg 2009; in the same article, there was speculation as to whether the International Criminal Court might investigate a complaint filed by the Palestinian Authority.

[26] Goldstone Report, para 1769, point 4.

risks of harm to enemy civilians that might be normally unacceptable in order to uphold the security of its soldiers and its own citizenry. This debate is mainly conducted by supporters of Israel, and in terms of the ethics of violence in the context of Israeli security and combat engagement rather than adherence to the requirements of international humanitarian law.[27] There are a series of other important recommendations, including upholding "the inviolability of UN premises and personnel," release of Palestinians being held in detention by Israel, and establishment of freedom of movement for Palestinians throughout occupied Palestinian Territory. And perhaps most significant of all is a recommendation "that Israel immediately cease the border closures" to the Gaza Strip and "allow passage of goods necessary and sufficient to meet the needs of the population," including what is required in Gaza to repair the extensive damage done by Operation Cast Lead and to enable the resumption of "meaningful economic activity" in Gaza.[28]

3.5 A Polarized Debate: Liberal Legality and Geopolitical Reality

On one level, the inflamed debate engendered by the release of the Goldstone Report was mindlessly driven by excessive defensiveness on the part of Israel, which was seconded by the United States. The attack on the report as biased and distorted as well as obsessively critical of Israel carried to an extreme "the politics of deflection" consistently practiced by Israel in response to external criticism.[29] Instead of focusing on refuting the substance of any charges by contesting the persuasiveness of the evidence or on the practicality and reasonableness of the conclusions and recommendations, Israeli officials typically do their best to shift international attention to the alleged bias of the auspices or the critics. As argued

---

[27] See especially, the discussion carried on in several issues of the New York Review of Books, anchored in criticism by Michael Walzer and Avishai Margalit of an influential article by two Israelis, Asa Kasher (a retired ethics professor who advises the IDF) and Amos Yadlin (a general, currently head of Israeli military intelligence) who are believed to have altered IDF thinking and policy by their article, "Assassination and Preventive Killing," SAIS Review 25, no. 1 2005 pp. 41–57; Margalit and Walzer change the focus from targeted assassination to the rules of engagement in the Gaza attacks, concentrating on the central question posed by Kasher and Yadlin 2009: "What priority should be given to the duty to minimize casualties among combatants of the state when they are engaged in combat … against terror?" Quoted in Margalit and Walzer 2009; for exchange of views, see Margalit and Walzer 2009.

[28] Goldstone Report, para 1769.

[29] Although at an official level the politics of deflection seems largely tactical, there is some reason to believe that many Israelis believe that Israel is held to higher standards than other nations or that Israel is genuinely in danger of being engulfed by a new surge of global anti-Semitism. See the perceptive article on the tensions between public anxieties and governmental policies, Segev 2010, pp. 47–48.

earlier, here such efforts at deflection, often successful in the past, faced higher hurdles than usual due to the impressive credentials and exceptional credibility of Goldstone as the chair and voice of the mission. As would have been expected, given the composition of the mission and the expectation that any conclusions critical of Israel would be bitterly contested, the report was prepared with scrupulous care, seeking out all available evidence from all viewpoints and giving every benefit of the doubt to Israeli concerns despite their refusal to cooperate with the investigation.

Without the slightest pretense of evidence, the harshest critics of the report even alleged anti-Semitic motivations, insisting that the Human Rights Council was a contaminated sponsoring agency and Goldstone was at best serving its ends by playing the role of useful idiot.[30] Embarrassingly, the US House of Representatives, by a vote of 344–336, condemned the report on November 4, 2009 along the same lines as biased and one-sided, and instructed President Barack Obama and Secretary of State Hillary Rodham Clinton to use the authority of the US government to "oppose unequivocally any endorsement," or even "the further consideration" of the report at the United Nations, and to exert all possible diplomatic influence to block its implementation.[31] Such vitriolic attacks on the Goldstone Report seem completely without merit. Contrary to the criticism, the report is an excellent example of an international inquiry mandated by the UN in adhering to the highest standards of liberal legality given the circumstances of Israeli non-cooperation and the overall problems associated with "the fog of war."[32] The report applies the positive law

---

[30] Among the most extreme statements along these lines was that made by Anne Bayevsky, a researcher at the Hudson Institute as reported by Lazaroff 2009. On numerous occasions, Justice Goldstone has defended the right, even insisting on the duty, of Jews to speak out against injustice as well as violations of human rights and of international law.

[31] "Calling on the President and the Secretary of State to Oppose Unequivocally Any Endorsement or Further Consideration of the 'Report of the United Nations Fact Finding Mission on the Gaza Conflict' in Multilateral Fora," HR 867, 111th Cong., 1st sess., 23 October 2009. The resolution refers to the Goldstone Report in its first operative paragraph as "irredeemably biased and unworthy of further consideration or legitimacy." The long preamble of "whereas" paragraphs in the resolution contained much innuendo and many inaccuracies, which Goldstone attempted to refute point by point in a careful letter to the drafters of the resolution that was completely ignored. See Ackerman 2009. For a general assessment, see Mozgovaya and Ravid 2009. The vituperative language of the resolution in relation to the sobriety and professionalism of the Goldstone Report confirms the impression of the extreme responsiveness of Congress to the Israel lobby, and casts further doubt on the capacity of the US government to play a constructive role as intermediary in the conflict.

[32] The only technical objection with any merit at all is the contention that one of the four members of the mission was already on the public record in the form of a jointly signed published letter to the editor of a British newspaper, and should have been disqualified. For text of the letter, see "Israel's Bombardment of Gaza Is Not Selfdefense—It's a War Crime" Sunday Times 2009, see also Kattan 2009b. Goldstone made the argument that, if the mission had the task of reaching binding judgments adverse to Israel, then Chinkin would have been disqualified. In fact, Chinkin has a deserved reputation of professional integrity, and was particularly qualified to be a member of such a mission by virtue of her familiarity with Israel–Palestine conflict and her expert knowledge of international law.

associated with the Geneva Conventions and international customary law of war with due caution in an exemplary manner.

Indeed, it is the Palestinians who have the stronger case that the report is deficient in failing to take greater account of their legal concerns in the following respects: the report accepts without analysis the Israeli claim that given the relevant circumstances it was fully entitled to use force defensively, thus failing to take any account of the success of the cease-fire that has been in effect and was working well since mid-2008 until disrupted by an Israeli incursion on November 4, 2009. This favorable experience with the cease-fire was further reinforced by a Hamas offer repeated several times prior to the Gaza attacks of an indefinite extension of the cease-fire provided that Israel lift its unlawful blockade. The report also fails to condemn, or even mention, the Israeli refusal to allow Palestinian civilians to leave the Gaza Strip during the attacks, thus depriving all Gazans of a refugee option, which seems to fall afoul of the international customary law prohibition on cruel and inhumane tactics or conduct during wartime, a duty that should be interpreted even more stringently in this case where Israel is an occupying power with obligations to protect the civilian population. The report also neglects to examine whether there was any sufficient connection between the stated belligerent objective of terminating the rocket attacks and the reliance on a generalized onslaught directed at Gaza in the spirit of the Dahiya doctrine; neither does it consider whether Israel as the occupying power is legally entitled to claim a right of self-defense. There are some grounds for claiming an anti-Palestinian bias because the report appropriately expresses its concern about the psychological trauma caused inside Israel by the Hamas rocket attacks, but completely ignores the far more intense and pervasive trauma caused to the whole population of Gaza by the rigors of a coercive occupation that has lasted since 1967 as well as by the blockade, frequent military incursions, nightly sonic booms, and, most dramatically, by Operation Cast Lead.[33] It is a sign of the extent of Israeli and US media dominance that the totality of attention given to criticisms of the report has been discussed exclusively from an Israeli outlook. It is also an indicator of the weakness and co-opted nature of the Palestinian Authority that its officials have limited their responses to an endorsement of the report and, only when pushed from below and without, a call for the immediate implementation of its recommendations.[34]

---

[33] Goldstone Report, Executive Summary, para 105.

[34] On 1 October 2009, the Palestine Liberation Organization announced that it supported a move by the Palestinian Authority, under pressure from Israel and the United States, to defer the vote on a resolution calling for endorsement and implementation until March 2010, suggesting a postponement for several months of any consideration given to the report. Revealingly, there was such a populist backlash that the Palestinian Authority reversed course and led the effort to have the Goldstone Report endorsed and implemented. MacFarquar 2009. For helpful discussion, see Barnette 2010, pp. 48–53. It has been subsequently reported in an Israeli newspaper that the Palestinian president Mahmoud Abbas requested the postponement of any vote in the Human Rights Council on the Goldstone Report only after he was threatened by Yuval Diskin, the head of Shin Bet, with "a second Gaza" in the West Bank along with some other threats. See Eldar 2010.

The more substantive criticisms of the debate by Israeli leaders concerned the argument that its tactics were reasonable and responsible in view of the nature of the security threat posed by Hamas. Here, the argument rests on the double validity of (1) treating Hamas as an illegitimate political actor (a terrorist organization); and (2) regarding the Israeli tactics and rules of engagement as responsive to terror, even if not strictly within the four corners of the international law of war. Such a rationale for Operation Cast Lead resembles the manner in which the Bush administration attempted to justify its approach to detention and interrogation after September 11.[35] The abstractions associated with the supposed need to suspend adherence to the international law of war to be effective in counter-terrorist security are suspect when not connected with the specifics of the situation. In this instance, unless state terrorism is endorsed (i.e., war waged against the civilian population as a means of inhibiting violent resistance to occupation), the case for laxity in interpreting and applying the law is not persuasive. The Goldstone Report characterizes Operation Cast Lead as directed at the population as such and thus does not suspend or qualify the operation of the law of war with respect to the sanctity of civilians and the duty to avoid deliberate attacks on protected targets, although it does give credence to factual conditions in which Israel had some reason to believe that protected targets were harboring Hamas militants or weaponry and ammunition.

If such a legal assessment were not made, and certain operational practices not condemned, it would enable a government to claim a counter-terrorist freedom of action that would be tantamount to the validation of genocidal warfare, even if such counter-terrorist tactics lacked the proof of specific criminal intent needed to establish the crime of genocide in a court of law.[36] In my view, the Goldstone Report is a model of appropriate assessment of contested military operations from the perspective of liberal legality, or what jurists tend to call "legal positivism." It is also fully compatible with the continued validity of legal restrictions on the use force that were reaffirmed by President Obama in his Nobel acceptance speech, seemingly intended in part to legitimize the US-led NATO war in Afghanistan.[37]

---

[35] There is a large literature on this issue. The two sides are clearly articulated by Yoo 2006; Paust 2007; for a sophisticated presentation of a case for departing from strict legalism in addressing terrorist threats, see Wittes 2008.

[36] See an insightful discussion of this delicate issue in the column by Nadia Hijab, Hijab 2009. The word genocide possesses a strong emotive resonance, especially for Israelis, hearkening back to its initial usage by Rafael Lemkin in reaction to the Holocaust. I draw a distinction between moral, political, and legal conceptualizations of the word "genocide." For the most authoritative legal treatment, see judgment of the International Court of Justice in the Bosnian case: *Application of the Convention on the Prevention and Punishment of the Crime of Genocide* (Bosnia Herzegovina v. Serbia and Montenegro) (ICJ Judgment, 11 July 1996).

[37] For text, see White House website, 10 December 2009. The Nobel speech is notable for its incoherence, relying on a vague invocation of justice to uphold counterterrorist uses of force while reaffirming the US dedication to the conduct rules contained in the Geneva Conventions and the law of war. From this perspective, it is hard to grasp the logic, aside from submitting to Israeli pressures, relied on to condemn the Goldstone Report or to back Israel in relation to Operation Cast Lead.

The Goldstone Report is also consistent with *jus in bello* dimensions of the just war doctrine, although less so with the *jus ad bellum* due to its failure to assess whether Israel had a valid underlying claim of "self-defense."[38]

At issue is whether normal notions of self-defense apply to the circumstances of the Gaza Strip. Israel contends that it has not occupied Gaza since its "disengagement" in 2005, which involved withdrawing IDF forces and dismantling the Israeli settlements. This claim has been widely rejected due to the persistence of Israeli effective control in Gaza, including total physical control of entry and exit, air space, sea space, and electromagnetic sphere, as well as ultimate administrative control over Gaza's population registry. Under these circumstances of persisting occupation, Israel has a fiduciary relationship to the Gazan civilian population that imposes more restrictions than if it could be viewed as a foreign political entity. Dean Tom Farer has instructively argued that, at the very least, Israel cannot legally claim defensive force until it tests whether Hamas would cease its violence if Israeli ended its unlawful blockade.[39]

What is less clear is whether the accountability recommendations of the Goldstone Report can be reconciled with the geopolitical realities of world politics and, if not, should these recommendations have been made.[40] I am assuming that these geopolitical realities will short-circuit efforts at implementation by either the UN or intergovernmental action. At the same time, these accountability recommendations of the Goldstone Report are of great importance for carrying on the legitimacy war, giving a foundation of legality to the call for boycott, divestment, and sanctions (the so-called BDS campaign) that has been gathering momentum since Operation Cast Lead was launched. As such, there is a normative dilemma posed: if the United Nations system is likely to be further discredited in the eyes of many governments by its likely unwillingness to implement the accountability recommendations, should it have been more circumspect at the outset and never have authorized the Goldstone fact-finding mission? Or, alternatively, should the Goldstone Report, despite being established by intergovernmental consensus at the Human Rights Council, have regarded its most significant audience to be activist elements in global civil society and, hence, appropriately formulated recommendations that take account of the political limits that exist within the UN system, and called for civil society implementing initiatives? Put differently, is the cost of non-implementation by the UN, as reinforced by the indifference or worse at the governmental level, greater than the gain achieved by giving added strength to the non-violent, yet coercive, legitimacy struggle on behalf of Palestinian rights?

There is no evidence that the authors of the Goldstone Report wrestled with or were even conscious of this dilemma or, if they had been, whether it would have

---

[38] For a critical assessment of the Israeli claim to be acting defensively, see Kattan 2009b, pp. 95–118.

[39] For his views on this rarely analyzed point, see Farer 2009; see also Kattan 2009b.

[40] For a classic argument against pushing international law beyond these geopolitical realities, see Bull 1966, pp. 51–73.

been practicable or advisable to have articulated the difficulties of following the logic of liberal legality all the way to its end point through recommending investigations of allegations followed, as appropriate, by prosecution and possible conviction and punishment. On balance, I am glad that this dilemma was not resolved in favor of deference to geopolitical realities, and that the cause of global justice was promoted by a set of recommendations that stimulate civil society actors to carry on the fight that governments in this sort of political setting cannot do.[41] It was undoubtedly too much to expect that the Goldstone Report would lend support to nonviolent resistance by Palestinians subject to an unlawful and oppressive occupation or encourage civil society actors to mount a legitimacy war seeking justice for the Palestinians.

3.6 International Law and the Peace Process

One of the most significant recommendations of the Goldstone Report that has received virtually no attention is its call to "states involved in peace negotiations between Israel and representatives of the Palestinian people, especially the Quartet" to "ensure that respect for the rule of law, international law and human rights assume a central role in internationally sponsored peace initiatives."[42] This lack of attention is partly due to the general understanding that the mandate of the mission was shaped by the widespread allegations of war crimes associated with the 22-day assault on the Gaza Strip, and not related to the broader relationship of international law to the peace process. Yet such recommended emphasis on international law should be welcome, although it will probably leave an invisible footprint with respect to future efforts at conflict resolution. There is a little known consensus on the part of those supportive of the Palestinian struggle for justice that peace with Israel cannot be achieved unless it becomes responsive to Palestinian rights under international law.[43] Part of this consensus is that past

---

[41] In other settings, accountability for the losing side or vulnerable individuals is consistent with geopolitical realities, even an instrument of the powerful and victorious. From the Nuremberg and Tokyo point of departure, this problem of double standards has haunted the quest for extending criminal responsibility to those who act on behalf of the state. The ebb and flow of support for universal jurisdiction is one theater of this encounter, as was the somewhat unexpected establishment in 2002 of the International Criminal Court. These latter developments are gestures in the direction of extending the rule of law to the domain of accountability, but the pushback on efforts to pursue well-documented allegations against Donald Rumsfeld, Henry Kissinger, and Israeli officials is indicative of the continued robustness of geopolitics. The detention of Augusto Pinochet, the prosecutions of Slobodan Milosevic and Saddam Hussein, and the ICC indictment of President Bashir of the Sudan are not exceptions to the reach of geopolitics, but further illustrations of its continued sway.

[42] Goldstone Report, paras 1772 and 1774.

[43] See Barkan 2005, pp. 441 ff; see also conclusion of Victor Kattan's excellent historical presentation of the conflict in Kattan 2009a, especially p. 261.

unresponsiveness to Palestinian rights under international law has contributed to the failure of past negotiations. Israel has effectively used its diplomatic muscle, with US backing, to exclude from the diplomatic framework of negotiations any consideration of international law on such salient issues as borders, settlements, refugees, water, and the status of Jerusalem.[44] Every initiative since Oslo has been based on a bilateral political bargaining process that treats "facts on the ground," regardless of their legal status, as deserving considerable respect while any reference to the denial of Palestinian rights under international law is dismissed as disruptive of "the peace process."

As with achieving accountability in the face of geopolitical resistance, there exists a seeming dilemma of ignoring international law claims in deference to the geopolitical realities or accentuating these claims so as to lend further legitimacy to the Palestinian struggle for self-determination in accordance with international law. The realist approach believes that history mainly moves forward through the prudent management of power by dominant political actors while a normative approach believes that the march of history depends on resistance from below and popular forces that are guided by a sense of justice. Put differently, the opposite of war is not peace, but justice.

3.7 Conclusion

I argue essentially that the Goldstone Report is not as significant as it seems in relation to either establishing the criminality of Operation Cast Lead or in creating prospects that those Israelis (or Hamas officials) will be held accountable for their gross departures from the law of war, which the report described as war crimes and possibly crimes against humanity.[45] The enduring significance of the Goldstone Report concerns the inability of the state system and the United Nations to uphold basic human rights when their violation accords with geopolitical priorities, the role of global civil society in partially compensating for this inability, and the essential connections between peace and justice. Specifically, the Goldstone Report has stoked a storm of controversy in the United States and Israel while

---

[44] For a focus on this aspect of the relevance of international law, see Falk 2005, pp. 331–348.

[45] The Report implicitly regards the potential criminality of Israel and Hamas as more or less symmetrical. I reject this view. Whether measured in terms of the harm caused or the responsibility for the one-sided violence of the Gaza attacks, Israeli political and military leaders bear the brunt of responsibility. This is consistent with the underlying view that both sides in the encounter should have their activities assessed from the perspective of international criminal law. But it is a mistake to treat the two sides as equally culpable in the Gaza context. It is a still greater mistake to claim, as have both Israeli and US officials, that a deficiency of the Goldstone Report is its tendency to treat a democratic government such as Israel as being subject to the same restraints as are applicable to an alleged terrorist actor. When measured by the death of innocent civilians or by reference to the Dahiya doctrine of deliberate disproportion, the magnitude of responsibility on the side of Israel seems far greater than that of Hamas.

contributing a validating pat on the back to those engaged in the legitimacy war that the Palestinians are winning on a symbolic global battlefield, and increasingly pinning their hopes on. This legitimacy war has become the leading moral struggle of our time, a sequel to the anti-apartheid campaign waged so effectively throughout the world in the late 1980s. Whether it ends in the sort of political victory that unexpectedly and non-violently transformed South Africa from a racist regime to a multiracial constitutional democracy cannot be foretold. Peoples can prevail in legitimacy wars, as have the Tibetans and the democratic forces in Myanmar, and still remain politically frustrated and, to varying degrees, oppressed. It is my central contention that, unless this multifaceted relevance of the Goldstone Report is acknowledged, neither its limits nor its contributions can be properly appreciated, and it is then likely to be misremembered as a failed yet valiant challenge to the impunity of the strong.

My hope is that, through dialog and experience, the Goldstone Report will eventually be appropriately appreciated for its contribution to the struggles of the weak and oppressed, specifically of the Palestinians, and become integrated into a growing confidence in the transformative impact of the theory and practice of non-violence.

References

Ackerman S (2009) Goldstone tells Congress that Resolution Misrepresents his Gaza Report, Washington Independent, 30 October 2009. http://washingtonindependent.com/65926/goldstone-tells-congress-that-resolution-misrepresents-his-gazareport

Arendt H (1964) Eichmann in Jerusalem: A Report on the Banality of Evil (Revised edn). Viking Press, New York

Avnery U (2009) Cast Lead 2, Dissident Voice, 26 December 2009. http://dissidentvoice.org/2009/12/cast-lead-2/

Barkan E (2005) The Mirage of Rights, in the Symposium "Facts, Rights, and Remedies: Implementing International Law in the Israel/Palestine Conflict". Hastings Int Comparat Law Rev 28:441

Barnette J (2010) The Goldstone Report: Combating Israeli Impunity in the International Legal System. Master's Thesis, University of California, Santa Barbara

BBC (2010) Palestinians Urged on Gaza Crimes. http://news.bbc.co.uk/2/hi/middle_east/8465486.stm

Black I, Cobain I (2009) British Court Issued Gaza Arrest Warrant for Former Israeli Minister Tzipi Livni, The Guardian. http://www.guardian.co.uk/world/2009/dec/14/tzipi-livni-israel-gaza-arrest

Bull H (1966) The Grotian Conception of International Society. In: Butterfield H, Wight M (eds) Diplomatic Investigations: Essays in the Theory of International Politics. Harvard University Press, Cambridge, pp 51–73

Bush G (2001) Address to a Joint Session of Congress and the American People, Washington DC, 20 September 2001

Eldar A (2010) Diskin to Abbas: Defer UN Vote on Goldstone or Face 'Second Gaza,' Haaretz, 17 January 2010. http://www.haaretz.com/hasen/spages/1143038.html

Falk R (2005) International Law and the Peace Process, in the Symposium "Facts, Rights, and Remedies": Implementing International Law in the Israel/Palestine Conflict, Hastings. Int Comparat Law Rev 28:331–348

Falk R (2011) Torture War and the Limits of Liberal Legality. In: Cohn M (ed) The United States and Torture. New York University Press, New York

Farer T (2009) A Question of Proportionality: Israel's Excessive Airstrikes, Huffington Post

Goldstone R (2000) For Humanity: Reflections of a War Crimes Investigator. Yale University Press, New Haven

Goldstone R (2009) Justice in Gaza, New York Times, 17 September 2009. http://www.nytimes.com/2009/09/17/opinion/17goldstone.html

Haaretz (2009) Israel Urges World: Reject Goldstone Report on Gaza, 14 October 2009. http://www.haaretz.com/hasen/spages/1121036.html

Hijab N (2009) When Does it Become Genocide? Agence Global, 30 December 2009. http://www.agenceglobal.com/article.asp?id=2225

Hovsepian N (2008) The War of Lebanon: A Reader. Olive Branch Press, New York

Izenberg D (2009) A Real Threat of ICC Prosecution, Jerusalem Post, 1 January 2009. http://www.jpost.com/Home/Article.aspx?id=164912

Kasher A, Yadlin A (2009) Israel & the Rules of War: An Exchange, New York Review of Books. http://www.nybooks.com/articles/archives/2009/jun/11/israel-the-rules-of-war-an-exchange/

Kattan V (2009a) From Coexistence to Conquest: International Law and the Origins of the Arab-Israeli Conflict, Pluto, London

Kattan V (2009b) Israel, Gaza, and Operation Cast Lead: Use of Force Discourse and Jus ad Bellum Controversies, 15 Palestine Yearbook of International Law, pp 95–118

Lazaroff T (2009) UN Report a 21st Century Blood Libel, Scholar says in Geneva, Jerusalem Post, 30 September 2009. http://www.jpost.com/Israel/Article.aspx?id=156240

Macedo S (2004) Universal Jurisdiction. University of Pennsylvania Press, Philadelphia

MacFarquar N (2009) Palestinians Halt Push on War Report, New York Times, 2 October 2009. http://www.nytimes.com/2009/10/02/world/middleeast/02mideast.html

Margalit A, Walzer M (2009) Israel: Civilians & Combatants, New York Review of Books, 14 May 2009. http://www.nybooks.com/articles/archives/2009/may/14/israel-civilians-combatants/

Mozgovaya N, Ravid B (2009) U.S. House Backs Resolution to Condemn Goldstone Gaza Report, Haaretz. http://www.haaretz.com/hasen/spages/1125593.html

Paust J (2007) Beyond the Law: The Bush Administration's Unlawful Responses in the "War" on Terror. Cambridge University Press, Cambridge

Rabinovich A (2009) Israel Savages UN Report on Gaza Attacks, The Australian, 7 May 2009. http://www.theaustralian.com.au/news/israel-savages-un-report-on-gazawar/story-e6frg6tx-1225710427434

Sadeh S (2009) Peres: Goldstone a Small Man, Out to Hurt Israel, Haaretz, 12 November 2009. http://www.haaretz.com/hasen/spages/1127695.html

Segev T (2010) Israel & Palestine: Eternal Enmity, New York Review of Books, 14 January 2010, pp 47–48

Siboni G (2008) Disproportionate Force: Israel's Concept of Response in Light of the Second Lebanon War, INSS Insight No. 74, 2 October 2008. http://www.inss.org.il/publications.php?cat=21&incat=&read=2222

Sunday Times (2009) Israel's Bombardment of Gaza is not Selfdefense—It's a War Crime, 11 January 2009. http://www.timesonline.co.uk/tol/comment/letters/article5488380.ece

Wittes B (2008) Law and the Long War: The Future of Justice in the Age of Terror. Penguin Press, New York

Ynet (2008) Israel Warns Hizbullah War would Invite Destruction, 3 October 2008. http://www.ynet.co.is/english/articles/0,7340,L-3604893,00.html

Yoo J (2006) War by Other Means: An Insider's Account of the War on Terror. Atlantic Monthly Press, New York

Zarchin T (2009) Goldstone to Haaretz: U.S. does not have to Protect Israel Blindly, Haaretz, 13 November 2009. http://www.haaretz.com/hasen/spages/1127942.html

Chapter 4
The Follow up to the Goldstone Report and its Legal Impact in Israel and Beyond

Sharon Weill

Contents

4.1	Introduction	105
4.2	The Recommendations of the FFM Report	107
4.3	The Monitoring of Israeli Investigations	108
	4.3.1 United Nations Monitoring	108
	4.3.2 Israeli Monitoring: The Turkel Commission	110
4.4	The Israeli System of Investigation	111
	4.4.1 Structural Deficiencies	111
	4.4.2 Policy Deficiency	114
4.5	Domestic Investigations and Prosecutions Conducted in the Aftermath of Cast Lead	115
4.6	Conclusion	117
4.7	Annex: Cases Prosecuted by Israel in the Aftermath of Cast Lead	118
References		120

4.1 Introduction

The United Nations Fact-Finding Mission on the Gaza Conflict (FFM) raised serious allegations of war crimes and crimes against humanity committed by Israel in Gaza in December 2008–January 2009, and in order to ensure accountability it is required by international law that these grave allegations be submitted to further

---

PhD Candidate in International Law at Geneva University and lecturer in IHL. Hebrew researcher for the UN Fact Finding Mission on the Gaza conflict.

S. Weill (✉)
University of Geneva, Swiss

investigation, and where appropriate, prosecution.[1] However, since Operation Cast Lead, those responsible for the crimes have yet to be named. At the international level, the United Nations institution in charge of the follow up to the Fact-Finding Mission is still the Human Rights Council, which lacks the authority of the Security Council, and at the national level, liability has to be ascertained by the very party that is alleged to have been responsible for committing the crimes. While Israel officially refused to cooperate with the FFM and the follow-up Expert Committee to the point of physically prohibiting these United Nations bodies from entering Israel, they had a surprising impact on the military and legal institutions in Israel.[2] Never before had a report of an international body generated so much reaction and so many reports, studies, and institutional efforts, all aimed at refuting its allegations. Since the release of the FFM report, the Israeli authorities have published six official reports and mandated the Turkel Commission, an independent inquiry panel, to examine whether the Israeli system for investigating IHL violations is consistent with international law.[3] This measure was directly linked to the FFM follow-up process, as the State report issued in July 2010 says:

> While the State of Israel is confident in the thoroughness, impartiality, and independence of its investigatory system of alleged violations of the Law of Armed Conflict, *in light of criticism raised in certain reports regarding these mechanisms*, the Government of Israel has recently mandated an independent public commission to examine the conformity of Israel's mechanisms for investigating complaints raised in relation to violations of the Law of Armed Conflict with its obligations under international law.[4]

This paper will attempt to describe the legal follow-up process in the aftermath of the FFM report, and its impact on the Israeli judicial authorities—an impact which is far more substantial than might be perceived at first glance. First, I will recall the main legal recommendations of the FFM, which stated that the

---

[1] For more details on the establishment of the Fact-Finding Mission, please see the contribution of Richard Falk, *supra* in this Volume, Chap. 3, and of Jennifer Barnette, *infra* in this Volume, Chap. 5.

[2] On the Committee of Expert, which was mandated to examine the effectiveness of the domestic investigations, please see more in detail the paper of Daragh Murray, *infra* in this Volume, Chap. 6.

[3] The State of Israel issued five reports: (1) "Conclusion of investigations into Central Claims and Issues in Operation Cast Lead", April (2009a) (2) "The Operation in Gaza: Factual and Legal Aspects", July (2009b) (3) "Initial Response to the Fact-Finding Mission on Gaza pursuant to Resolution S-9/1 of the Human Rights Council", September (2009c) (4) "Gaza Operation Investigations: An Update", January (2010a) (5) State of Israel, "Gaza Operation Investigations: Second Update", July (2010b). In addition, in December 2010 the Military Advocate General (MAG) submitted to the Turkel Commission a 100 pages report (in Hebrew) on military investigations and the compliance with the requirements of international law. To this report was annexed a 20 pages analysis in which the findings of the first report of the UN Commission of Experts were specifically addressed.

[4] State of Israel report 2010b, p. 35.

responsibility for investigating violations and prosecute if appropriate "belongs in the first place to domestic authorities"[5] (*infra* 4.2). Then, I will describe the bodies and procedures established with the aim of monitoring Israeli investigations at the international and national levels (*infra* 4.3). In the following section I will examine the Israeli system of investigation and highlight its structural and policy deficiencies (*infra* 4.4). As we shall see, the domestic investigations and prosecutions conducted in the aftermath of Cast Lead serve as an example to show the failure of the domestic legal system to guarantee accountability for grave violations and compliance with the law of armed conflict (*infra* 4.5 and the Annex 4.7). I will conclude by saying that the FFM follow-up process clearly shows that even if Israel has not ignored the demand for accountability, it has been institutionally unwilling to do so. This means that, legally, it is time to search for accountability beyond Israel's boundaries, as Israel is clearly unwilling to do so.

4.2 The Recommendations of the FFM Report

The recommendations of the FFM to ensure accountability encompass the entire enforcement mechanism of the international legal order, which is based on both national and international judicial bodies, consistently with the Geneva Conventions and the Rome Statute of the International Criminal Court. These are: (1) domestic institutions of the forum State, in this case Israel; (2) domestic institutions of third-party States through the exercise of universal jurisdiction; and (3) the International Criminal Court (ICC). The responsibility to investigate and prosecute war crimes allegations was first conferred on Israel, as the forum State. In addition, the FFM report recommended that the international community should investigate and prosecute these allegations on the basis of universal jurisdiction as required by the Geneva Conventions, to which all States are bound (FFM report, §1975). As for the ICC, in addition to the recommendation that the Security Council refer the case to the ICC should Israel be unwilling to investigate and prosecute the war crimes allegations (FMM report, §1963), the FFM also recommended that the ICC Prosecutor determine as expeditiously as possible whether the ICC has jurisdiction in the matter, following the Palestinian government declaration under Article 12(3) of the Rome Statute.[6]

---

[5] The FFM report, para 1963.

[6] For more details, please see the contribution of Michael Kearney, in Part III, Chap. 8, of this Volume.

4.3 The Monitoring of Israeli Investigations

Israel was assigned the primary responsibility to investigate and prosecute the allegations made against it. Under international law, these investigations must be independent, effective, prompt, and impartial.[7] Determining the nature of these domestic investigations and prosecutions is a first stage of the FFM follow-up process. Should these investigations not comply with international standards, and not provide accountability, other international enforcement mechanisms could be triggered—namely, the exercise of universal jurisdiction and the ICC.[8] It is therefore not surprising that in the wake of the Goldstone Report Israeli domestic investigations came under the scrutiny of the international community. Currently, both the United Nations and the domestic follow-up processes are reviewing this issue, through two main organs which have been specifically mandated for that purpose—the United Nations Experts Committee and the Israeli Turkel Commission.[9]

4.3.1 United Nations Monitoring

In September 2009, the Goldstone mission instructed Israel to launch domestic investigations within three months, and to inform the Security Council on the actions taken within the next three months. In parallel, the mission recommended that the Security Council establish an independent committee of experts to monitor

---

[7] See Schmitt 2011, pp. 31–84.

[8] ICC jurisdiction may be exercised when the domestic judiciary system is unwilling or unable to investigate and prosecute. In the case of Israel the ICC may have competence if (quite hypothetically) the case were to be referred to the international court by the Security Council or if the ICC prosecutor recognizes the competence of the Palestinian Authority to recognize *ad hoc* the jurisdiction. As for the exercise of universal jurisdiction, although treaty law does not require this exhaustion of local remedies, in practice most states apply the subsidiary/comity principle, which gives primary jurisdiction to the forum State.

[9] The Turkel Committee (officially The Public Commission to Examine the Maritime Incident of 31 May 2010) is an independent public commission set up by Israeli government in June 2011 in the aftermath of the Flotilla raid. The committee was mandated to examine: (1) "the legality of the naval blockade imposed on the Gaza Strip and the legality of the actions carried out by the IDF in order to enforce the naval blockade"; (2) "whether the investigation and inquiry mechanism that is practiced in Israel in general, and as applied with regard to the current incident, is consistent with the duties of the State of Israel pursuant to the rules of international law". (Summary Report of the Public Commission to Examine the Maritime Incident of 31 May 2010—Part One, pp. 1–2). A 245-page report dealing with the first issue was released on January 23, 2011. The second report is scheduled to be released later in 2011. Although the commission was not originally tasked with examining the FFM allegations, its second mandate is of major importance for the FMM follow up, as it evaluates the domestic military system of investigation and prosecution.

the investigations and report back to the Security Council. "[I]n the absence of good-faith investigations that are independent and in conformity with international standards" when the six-month period expires, the Security Council was to refer the Gaza case to the Prosecutor of the International Criminal Court (FMM report, §1963). As we have witnessed, the Security Council was not to become involved in the follow-up process. Instead, in November 2009, the United Nations General Assembly called upon the United Nations Secretary General to report on the investigations undertaken to date. Three months later, in February 2010, the Secretary General submitted a laconic report to the General Assembly; based on a report submitted a few days before by Israel,[10] Ban Ki Moon stated that Israel had carried out some investigations that were yet to be completed, and that he was therefore not yet able to assess them. The General Assembly responded with a second resolution requiring an independent and transparent investigation to be conducted, and requested the Secretary General to report back by July 2010, and assess whether further action by different United Nations organs, including the Security Council, would be necessary. In the first resolution, the majority of the EU States abstained, none voting in favor and some voting against. In the second resolution, the vote was markedly different: several EU States voted in favor, many abstained, and none voted against.[11] Israel, the United States, and Canada voted against the resolution but these countries were virtually on their own. Finally, in August 2010, the Secretary General published the "Second follow-up to the report of the United Nations Fact-Finding Mission on the Gaza Conflict".[12] But this report simply annexed the July report submitted by Israel for this purpose, without providing any further assessment.

While the GA resolutions were being adopted in New York, the United Nations Human Rights Council, based in Geneva, resolved in a follow-up resolution on March 2010 to establish an independent expert panel, which would monitor the domestic investigations and proceedings undertaken by Israel and assess their conformity with international standards.[13] The United Nations Committee of Experts issued two reports, in which it expressed the view that the Israeli military system of investigation lacked the necessary structural independence to thoroughly

---

[10] See the Israeli Ministry of Foreign Affairs' official statement 2010.

[11] See General Assembly Resolution A/64/10 of 5 November 2009 entitled "Follow-up to the report of the United Nations Fact-Finding Mission on the Gaza Conflict" (see *infra* Document 5 in Part II); General Assembly Resolution 64/254 of 26 February 2010, entitled "Second follow-up to the report of the United Nations Fact-Finding Mission on the Gaza Conflict" (see *infra* Document 7 in Part II).

[12] "Second follow-up to the report of the United Nations Fact-Finding Mission on the Gaza Conflict", 11 August 2010, A/64/890.

[13] "Follow-up to the report of the United Nations Independent International Fact-Finding Mission on the Gaza Conflict", 14 April 2010, A/HRC/RES/13/9 (see *infra* Document 8 in Part II).

investigate the allegations.[14] It further found that the investigations carried out were neither sufficiently transparent nor prompt, which impaired their effectiveness and the prospects of achieving accountability and justice.[15] Finally, it criticized Israel for not investigating those who had designed, planned, ordered, and overseen Operation Cast Lead as the main flaw in the inquiry process.[16]

4.3.2 Israeli Monitoring: The Turkel Commission

An internal independent commission was established by the Israeli State in the aftermath of the Flotilla maritime attack of 31 May 2010.[17] It was mandated, *inter alia*, to examine whether the "mechanism for examining and investigating complaints and claims raised in relation to violations of the laws of armed conflict ... conform with the obligations of the State of Israel under the rules of international law".[18] Currently, the panel consists of four Israeli members (the president, Jakob Turkel, is a former Supreme Court Judge and none of the members are experts in international law) and two international observers, and it is due to submit its report later this year.[19] Unlike the United Nations Experts Committee which was denied entry into Israel, the West Bank and Gaza, the Turkel Commission enjoyed the full collaboration of the State of Israel. During April 2011 it heard the testimonies of the top echelons of the Israeli military and civil authorities, including the Military Advocate General, the State Advocate General, the head of the General Security Services, the head of the military police, as well as representatives of leading

---

[14] "Report of the Committee of Independent Experts in International Humanitarian and Human Rights Laws to monitor and assess any domestic, legal or other proceedings undertaken by both the Government of Israel and the Palestinian side, in the light of General Assembly Resolution 64/254, including the independence, effectiveness, genuineness of these investigations and their conformity with international standards", 23 September 2010, A/HRC/15/50 (hereinafter: 'UN Experts first report'), para 91 (see *infra* Document 9 in Part II); "Report of the Committee of Independent Experts in International Humanitarian and Human Rights Law established pursuant to Council resolution 13/9", A/HRC/16/24, 5 May 2011 (hereinafter: UN Experts second report), para 41 (see *infra* Document 10 in Part II).

[15] UN Experts first report, paras 92–93; Second report at pp. 12–93.

[16] UN Experts first report, para 95, Second report at p. 14, see again the contribution of Daragh Murray to this Volume on this point, *infra* Chap. 6.

[17] See above, n. 9.

[18] Government Resolution of 14.6.2010.

[19] The Israeli members of the commission are former Israeli Supreme Court Justice Jacob Turkel; Maj. Gen (Res.) Amos Horev, the President of the academic institution 'Technion'; Miguel Deutch, Professor of contract law at Tel Aviv University; and Reuven Merhav, former Foreign Ministry director-general. The two international observers are David Trimble (UK)— Nobel Peace Prize winner and former First Minister of Northern Ireland, and Ken Watkin (Canadian)—former head of the Canadian military's judiciary, Judge Advocate General.

Israeli NGOs and distinguished law professors.[20] The Military Advocate General submitted a 100-page report to the commission, inarguably "the most comprehensive document ever written in Israel on the topic of inquiries by military units",[21] in which he reacted in great detail to each of the findings raised in the first report of the United Nations Expert Committee. These testimonies and submissions provide information of major importance for the assessment of the Israeli domestic system of investigation, an assessment which is central for the FFM follow-up process. Other than the submissions by the authorities and the NGOs, most of which already available in the public domain, of special interest are the testimonies of the professors of international law given before the Turkel Committee, which provide the latest analysis of the matter. The following part assesses the Israeli system of investigation in light of these submissions.

4.4 The Israeli System of Investigation

4.4.1 Structural Deficiencies

In Israel, the main body in charge of investigating and prosecuting alleged war crimes committed by the army is the army itself, which raises objective doubts regarding the nature of these investigations. This lack of independence and impartiality cannot be remedied by disqualifying the individual investigators, but has to do with a structural problem with the mechanism in place. The following flaws in the Israeli judicial system of investigation can be mentioned, in particular:

(a) The centralization of all authorities in the hands of the Military Advocate General (MAG)

The MAG is the legal advisor to the army, in charge of enforcing the law and, at the same time, the head of the military prosecution service, which is responsible for investigating and prosecuting cases of violation of the law of armed conflict. It is therefore highly uncertain whether the investigation body can be independent while being subordinate to the MAG, which is the body that lays down the rules and legitimises their execution in real time. This structural difficulty was highlighted by the United Nations Expert Committee, which considered the clash between the role of the MAG as the body that approved the operations conducted in Cast Lead, and his responsibility for prosecuting alleged violations by Israeli soldiers, to be a conflict of interest:

---

[20] The testimonies on the domestic system of investigation given by state authorities, NGOs and international law professors are online (in Hebrew) at http://www.turkel-committee.com/content-153-b.html.

[21] Shany et al. 2011, p. 4.

> "The committee further noted that notwithstanding the built-in structural guarantees to ensure [the MAG's] dual responsibilities as legal advisor to the Chief of Staff and other military authorities, and his role as supervisor of criminal investigations within the military, raise concerns in the present context given allegations in the FFM report that those who designed, planned, ordered, and oversaw the operation in Gaza were complicit in international humanitarian law and international human rights law violations. ... Therefore, the Committee remains of the view that an independent public commission—and not the MAG's office—is the appropriate mechanism for carrying out an independent and impartial analysis, as called for in the FFM report, into allegations that high-level decision-making related to the Gaza conflict violated international law."[22]

In his testimony before the Turkel Commission, Prof. Benvenisti, a distinguished law professor from Tel Aviv University, went beyond the ordinary portrayal of the MAG as wearing a "dual hat", and described him more precisely as centralizing three authorities: legislative (in as much as he defines the army's rules of conduct), executive (in providing legal counseling during warfare), and judicial-like (in deciding on investigations and prosecutions).[23] Under this system, individual soldiers who violated explicit IDF orders (such as looting, the use of human shields, and inhumane treatments of detainees), may be investigated and perhaps prosecuted. However, it is structurally unfeasible to carry out a review on the legality of the orders themselves, as for example in the case of the approval of certain weapons, or assessing an attack as proportional; it is equally unlikely to be able to guarantee accountability at the policy level, as it entails a clear conflict of interests with the different authorities of the MAG. In his own testimony before the Turkel Commission, even the MAG himself admitted that the military investigations system is not a viable mechanism to investigate and assess high-level policy decisions:

> "The mechanism is calibrated for the inspection of individual incidents, complaints of war crimes as individual incidents (...). This is not a mechanism for policy. True, it is not suitable for this."[24]

The Israeli International Law Experts' report submitted to the Turkel Commission raised another specific concern, namely the MAG's inability to order investigations relating to the responsibility of the political echelon.

> "It seems that in the current legal situation in Israel and the practices that exist here, there is no proper solution for verifying suspicions of violations of IHL on the part of the political echelon in Israel. ... The High Court of Justice frequently avoids reviewing the legality of political decisions or specific acts, and the decision of whether to establish a commission of inquiry or open up an investigation is the Government's—the body which, in this case, is the investigated body. In all of these cases, there is no independent, effective verification procedure that can determine whether an international legal norm has been violated or not."[25]

---

[22] Second UN Experts report, para 41; see also the first UN Experts report, para 91.

[23] Benvenisti 2011.

[24] Testimony of the Military Advocate General to the Turkel Commission, Session Number Four, 26 August 2010, cited in the Second UN Experts report, para 41.

[25] Israeli International Law Experts report, p. 39.

(b) Lack of civilian supervision: "a constitutional vacuum"

In any democracy, the army must be subordinate to the civil branch of the State in order to guarantee close supervision over each sphere of the army's actions. But in Israel, the civilian authorities have handed over almost all their responsibilities in the matter of the law of armed conflict to the military system, thus creating a quasi-constitutional vacuum in which the MAG is operating. The State has exclusively mandated the military to define the rules of conduct of hostilities, the guidelines for investigations, and even the criteria for prosecution.[26] The Israeli International Law Experts report equally confirms that the "Israeli military legal system concentrates too much power in the hands of a single body that is only minimally supervised by civilians".[27] To provide an indication of the subordination of the military to civil authorities, the State systematically refers to the competence of the Israeli High Court of Justice to review the decisions of the MAG. Yet, Prof. Benvenisti views it as "too little, too late, and depending on the knowledge available to the public."[28] Indeed, while the judicial review competence of a high court is important, it is an organ that neither can nor should conduct thorough and on-going civil supervision of the army's rules of investigation. Its competence and its rules of procedure are designed to apply in exceptional cases and not for the supervision of military investigations across the board.

(c) Institutional lack of independence and impartiality:

When military investigations are carried out by soldiers, constrained by military discipline, and with promotion prospects measured according to it, it is not at all evident that the investigation at issue will be able to reach the required level of independence and impartiality. Can we seriously expect young officers to independently and impartially assess the legality of their colleagues' orders, who are also subject to supervision by the MAG, and on whom they depend for their future promotion? In this context, the fact that the last two MAGs were promoted by the Chief of the General Staff during their mandate is striking: MAG Menachem Finkelstein was promoted to the rank of Major General a year after his appointment, while the current MAG, Maj. General Avichai Mandelblit, was promoted in September 2009, only five years after taking office.[29]

---

[26] Benvenisti 2011, p. 25. He refers essentially to the State Advocate General, which is the civil body that is supposed to give legal counselling to the State.
[27] See also the submission of the Association for Civil Rights in Israel, para 64.
[28] Benvenisti 2011, p. 24.
[29] Benvenisti 2011, p. 27.

4.4.2 Policy Deficiency

"With military 'operational debriefings' at the core of the system, there is no effective and impartial investigation mechanism ... such investigations, being internal to the Israeli military authority, do not comply with international standards of independence and impartiality." (FFM report, §1959).

The Israeli military judiciary establishes four different investigative mechanisms: (1) disciplinary proceedings, (2) operational debriefings/command investigations, (3) special investigations at the request of the Chief of Staff, and (4) criminal investigations carried out by the military police unit.[30] Generally, most of the investigations undertaken by the army according to one of these options fail to lead to a criminal prosecution, which only occurs in very exceptional cases, such as against soldiers who act wrongly on their own account.[31] The low number of criminal investigations and prosecutions is mostly due to the military's frequent recourse to operational investigations—an inquiry within the concerned military unit, whose principal purpose is to draw operational conclusions, instead of providing criminal accountability.[32] By varying the mechanisms it is possible to avoid criminal accountability and keep the investigations of alleged war crimes as an internal, almost private, matter for the army, to be resolved in that familiar and friendly sphere. Israeli legal experts have observed that "it seems that in the framework of an operational inquiry, soldiers usually tend not to reveal issues that may lead to prosecution of their comrades or that may tarnish their unit's reputation",[33] concluding that "the operational inquiry is not an effective tool for managing criminal investigations. On the contrary, it is a tool whose usage may harm these investigations or even disrupt them completely [...] As a result, the duty to investigate violations of international law during times of combat is not

---

[30] Israel's military judiciary is regulated by the Military Justice Law 5715–1955. For a detailed presentation see State of Israel report 2010a at paras 41–70.

[31] The Israeli NGO Yesh-Din reveals that only 6% of criminal investigations yielded indictments against soldiers. From the beginning of the second Intifada in 2000 until the end of 2009 only 13 investigations into events in which Palestinian civilians were killed led to indictments. In only four cases involving the death of Palestinian civilians were any soldiers convicted. See, Yesh-Din 2008, 2010.

[32] The Military Justice Law (1955) defines a command investigation as "a procedure held by the army, according to the army orders and regulations, with respect to an incident that has taken place during a training or a military operation or with connection to them." They have the following characteristics: (1) All testimonies heard and their conclusions remain confidential and are inadmissible before a court; (2) If the Military Advocate General finds that there is a basis to open a criminal investigation, he can do so only after consulting a Major General. As the materials of the inquiry remain confidential, if the MAG decides to open a criminal investigation, it will start from the beginning.

[33] Israeli International Law Experts report, para 38.

appropriately fulfilled."[34] Still, according the Israeli NGO B'Tselem, "Most complaints of breach of the law committed by soldiers are carried out by operational inquiries [...] Rarely does the Military Police Investigations Unit become involved, and when it does, the investigations only focus on individual soldiers."[35]

4.5 Domestic Investigations and Prosecutions Conducted in the Aftermath of Cast Lead

The deficient pattern described above is well illustrated by the investigations undertaken in the aftermath of Operation Cast Lead. According to the March 2011 United Nations Expert report, more than two years after Cast Lead, the Government of Israel conducted 400 command and 52 criminal investigations. The criminal investigations involve mainly allegations of looting, the use of Palestinian civilians as human shields, and inhumane treatment of detainees—all in violation of explicit army orders. Of these numerous investigations, by June 2011, only three led to a prosecution (see in the annex of this paper). The status of the other investigations remains, in most cases, essentially unknown. For example, the Palestinian Centre for Human Rights (PCHR) pointed out that of 490 criminal complaints that the Centre submitted to the Israeli Military Prosecutor requesting the opening of a criminal investigation, only in 21 of them had any information been communicated, and updates on the ongoing investigations had not been provided.[36] Although Israel has so far produced six long reports, the information on these investigations—such as their current status or the evidence that led to

---

[34] Id., paras 42 and 47. "The combination that exists today, in which there is overly generous use of the operational inquiry tool by the MAG and a high threshold has been set for opening criminal investigations, leads to a situation in which, despite its obvious disadvantages, the operational inquiry is used for the initial filtering of criminal cases—a role that contradicts the original purpose of the inquiry and that is in a state of tension with its principal characteristics. As a result, the duty to investigate violations of international law during times of combat is not appropriately fulfilled. In sum, in our opinion, when the MAG is presented with a credible allegation or a reasonable suspicion that a serious incident has occurred that is unjustified or unexpected, the MAG must open a criminal investigation. ... the MAG must avoid using the operational inquiry as a criminal investigative tool", paras 46–47.
[35] B'Tselem Press release 2011.
[36] PCHR 2011, paras 7–13.

discontinue inquiries—is opaque and inaccessible. This data can be found, sporadically, in the media.[37]

(a) Lack of investigation at policy level

Not a single investigation has been dedicated to policy-making. While International law requires high-ranking political leaders and military officers in the chain of command to be investigated, all the Israeli inquiries have dealt with the behavior of individual soldiers or officers. Israel has not investigated any of the Goldstone Mission's allegations at the command level. Instead it has persistently claimed that the military orders and decisions were made in accordance with international law,[38] while tragically, some mistakes had occurred.[39] As I have demonstrated above, for structural reasons, inquiry into policy-making, or a criminal investigation of a top decision-maker—whether military or political—is not feasible in the current state of affairs.

(b) Consequences for a better observance of the law of armed conflict in the future

While accountability for alleged crimes committed in Gaza during operation Cast Lead has not been achieved, some changes have been introduced that might ensure a better observance of the rules of armed conflict in the future. (1) New orders

---

[37] The UN Expert Committee in its second report was able to report that "nineteen investigations into the serious violations of international humanitarian law and international human rights law reported by the FFM have been completed by the Israeli authorities with findings that no violations were committed. Two inquiries were discontinued for different reasons. Three investigations led to disciplinary action. Six investigations reportedly remain open, including one in which criminal charges have been brought against an Israeli soldier. The status of possible investigations into six additional incidents remains unclear.", p. 21. Israel has since closed another criminal investigation into the death of Mohammed Hajji and the shooting of Shahd Hajji and Ola Masood Arafat http://www.haaretz.co.il/hasite/spages/1224636.html (Hebrew).

[38] See, for example Israel's response to the allegations raised on the legality of the rules of engagement and use of weapons: "While the IDF's rules of engagement were fully consistent with international law, the IDF demonstrated its commitment to protecting civilians by issuing new instructions and orders in the course of the operation designed to further enhance and clarify these protections"; "The IDF uses only weapons and munitions defined as legal under international law and authorized as such by the relevant IDF authorities, including MAG officers," State of Israel report 2009b, paras 222 and 405.

[39] See, for example: "The IDF is examining how the unfortunate operational error occurred, in order to reinforce safeguards and to prevent its recurrence. Israel deeply regrets the tragic outcome. This is the kind of mistake that can occur during intensive fighting in a crowded environment," State of Israel report 2009b, para 387; "Tragic results, including civilian death and damage to property do not necessarily mean that violations of international law have occurred."; "The special investigations revealed some instances of intelligence and operational errors ... The special command investigations also uncovered some instances where IDF soldiers and officers violated the rules of engagement", State of Israel report, 2010a para 4 and paras 99–100.

issued by the Israeli army: the State published that its investigations had "already led to substantial changes in IDF procedures, and other changes are in the process of being implemented" and noted that "the IDF had issued two new orders designed to increase the protection of civilians and civilian objects in urban warfare".[40] (2) Change of investigation policy: The army's official policy since 2000 until very recently was not to open criminal investigation in cases in which Palestinian civilians were killed by its soldiers.[41] In the course of the procedures before the Israeli HCJ challenging this policy, the State announced very recently—on 4th of April 2011—changes to the investigation policy for cases in which Palestinian civilians are killed in the West Bank. "The new policy requires every case in which uninvolved Palestinians are killed by IDF fire to be investigated immediately by the Criminal Investigation Division. This policy applies unless the incident occurred during an activity clearly stated as combat."[42] Yet, this policy is restricted to the West Bank and does not apply to the Gaza Strip.

4.6 Conclusion

Although accountability for alleged crimes committed in Gaza has not been guaranteed, and will probably not be in the near future by either the national or the international judicial body, it may be too soon to fully assess the impact of the FFM report. The calls to conduct domestic investigations were not completely ignored by the Israeli government. Israel's international lawyers produced long reports, and international law discourse was seriously addressed. Yet, one must not be misled by this rhetoric. The structural deficiency, and not only the lack of political will, does not allow for investigations and prosecutions to be conducted in Israel as required by international law. As the military legal system is not independent and impartial, and as it centralizes all the authorities related to

---

[40] State of Israel report 2010b, para 18. These include: safe havens for civilians to take refuge; evacuation routes for civilians to safely escape combat areas; medical treatment for civilians; methods for effectively communicating with and instructing the population; and provisions for humanitarian access during curfews, closures and limitations on movement (paras 150–153). Equally, the New Order Regulating the Destruction of Private Property for Military Purposes was issued.

[41] For a detailed research on the policy and its outcomes see B'Tselem 2010. On 27 October 2003, the Association for Civil Rights in Israel and B'Tselem filed a petition before the Israeli High Court of Justice challenging this policy. HCJ 9594/03, *B'Tselem et al. v. The Military Judge Advocate General et al.*

[42] "New investigation policy regarding Palestinian casualties from IDF fire", Israeli Army Blog 2011b.

investigations and prosecutions, this system established by the State of Israel guarantees that the military and civil authorities will be shielded from scrutiny. This is the important issue that was exposed by the FFM report and its national and international follow-up processes. In legal terms it means that the appropriate judicial forum from now on will have to be beyond Israel's borders. It is suggested that this outcome should be examined beyond the political context of the Israeli-Palestinian conflict, within the more general framework of the enforcement mechanism of international law. If international law is to regulate relations between its subjects according to the principles of the rule of law, it means that it shall be imposed in an equal manner upon all states, as indeed the letter of the law itself provides. In that context, far from being satisfactory, the follow up to the FFM report is another contribution toward a better enforcement of international law, which still remains somewhat utopian. Yet, who could have predicted only 10 years ago that a United Nations fact-finding report would demand the prosecution of Israeli alleged crimes by national and international judicial bodies? Moreover, who could have predicted that Israel would invest so much effort and such resources in an attempt to deny or justify these allegations?

4.7 Annex: Cases Prosecuted by Israel in the Aftermath of Cast Lead[43]

Case no. 1 (August 2009): Theft of credit card. Indictment: looting. Sentence: seven and a half months' imprisonment.

In January 2010, a year after Cast Lead, Israel published the only concrete result it had produced by that time in its efforts to counter the war crimes and crime against humanity allegations that had been raised in the FFM report: one lone soldier had been prosecuted and convicted for stealing a credit card. Sentencing him to seven and a half months, the Court Martial declared:

> The crime of looting is harmful to the moral duty of every IDF soldier to keep human dignity, a dignity 'that does not depend on origin, religion, nationality, sex, status and function.' … The accused harmed the 'combat moral code,' the spirit of the IDF, in using his power and his arms not for the execution of his military mission.[44]

---

[43] By July 2011 only three cases, described below, were followed by a prosecution. Other investigations are still ongoing and may lead to future indictments. However, these will probably have the same characteristics—they will not address the responsibility at command level, but only responsibility of individual soldiers, who violated the army's orders on their own account.

[44] *Military Prosecutor vs. Sergeant A.K.*, S/153/09 12 (11 August 2009) cited in footnote 112, State of Israel report 2010a. It is noted that "the soldier served seven and a half months in prison". Yet, since he was sentenced in August 2009, this information cannot be accurate.

Case no. 2 (November 2010): Use of a Palestinian child as a human shield. Indictment: 'excess of authority' and 'conduct unbecoming'. Sentence: three months on probation and demotion of rank

Two soldiers were convicted of 'excess of authority' and 'conduct unbecoming' for having forced a nine-year-old Palestinian boy to open bags suspected of being booby-trapped.[45] Despite the gravity of the use of children as human shields, both soldiers, who were convicted of these charges, were sentenced to a three-month probation period and a demotion of rank. This sentence is particularly astonishing compared to the prison sentence imposed in the looting case, in which the convict may indeed have "harmed the 'combat moral code' of the IDF", yet he did not endanger life of a nine-year-old child. In an attempt to justify this lenient ruling the Deputy Military Advocate for Operational Affairs said that the court gave weight to "the personal circumstances of the defendants and their contribution to Israel's national security" and that by using a child as a human shield "the defendants did not seek to humiliate or degrade the boy."[46]

It should be noted that on 10 October 2005 the Israeli High Court ruled that the army's use of human shields was illegal.[47] Therefore, from the domestic legal and political point of view, the use of civilians as human shields is an act that can rather easily be prosecuted as failure "to comply with IDF orders prohibiting the use of civilians in carrying out military operations.[48] However, despite the fact that other allegations of this nature were raised, this is the only human shield case brought to justice. It was affirmed by the authorities that sufficient evidence had been found in another case involving a senior IDF commander. While the State of Israel insists that "disciplinary proceedings are reserved for less serious offenses",[49] and the army has explicitly indicated on its website that the use of human shields is a war crime,[50] the senior IDF commander at issue was referred for

---

[45] Israeli Army Blog 2011c; Shany et al 2011.

[46] Israeli Army Blog 2011a.

[47] HCJ 3799/02, Adalah et al. Yitzhak Eitan, Commander of the Israeli Army in the West Bank et al. (6 October 2005). Yet, according to B'Tselem, despite the High Court's decision and army orders preceding and following it, security forces continue to use Palestinians as human shields. http://www.btselem.org/english/human_shields/timeline_of_events.asp See also Adalah 2009.

[48] Israeli Army Blog 2011a. The IDF operational orders during Cast Lead "explicitly prohibited the use of civilians as human shields, as well as the compulsion of civilians to take part in military operations, in accordance with the Law of Armed Conflict and a Supreme Court ruling on the matter." State of Israel report 2010b.

[49] State of Israel report 2010b, footnote 13.

[50] According to the army website "The use of civilians as human shields is a direct violation of the laws of war, violating the basic principle of distinction between combatants and non-combatants" Israeli Army Blog 2011a. Article 51 of the 1977 First Additional Protocol to the 1949 Geneva Conventions, for instance, specifically prohibits the use of human shields. In addition, according to Article 8(2)(xxiii) of the Rome Statute of the International Criminal Court, "[u]tilizing the presence of a civilian or other protected person to render certain points, areas or military forces immune from military operations" constitutes a war crime.

disciplinary proceedings instead of a criminal trial for motives that were not made public.[51]

Case no. 3: Shooting of unarmed civilians holding white flags—pending. Charged with manslaughter.

On 16 June 2010 the daily Haaretz reported[52] that the army would charge a soldier for shooting and killing two Palestinian women, a case that was mentioned in the FMM report; yet, more than a year and a half after the killings, the nature of the charges have not been determined. The soldier was eventually indicted before a military court on charges of manslaughter in relation to the deliberate targeting of an individual waving a white flag, without orders or authorization to do so. The March 2011 United Nations report notes that "the trial was opened on 1 August 2010 but the reading of the indictment was immediately postponed at the request of the defence, which demanded that the trial be suspended while the Military Police pursue allegations that an IDF officer had attempted to block the investigation by not submitting the results of a probe into the incident to his superior officers and to the MAG. The trial is currently in recess while the authorities investigate further".

References

Adalah (2009) Update Report: On the Israeli military's continued use of Palestinian civilians, including minors, as human shields, July 2009, available at http://www.adalah.org/eng/humanshields.php

Benvenisti E (2011) Submission to the Turkel Commission, file with author

B'Tselem (2010) Void of responsibility: Israel Military Policy not to investigate killings of Palestinians by soldiers. http://www.btselem.org/download/201009_void_of_responsibility_eng.pdf

B'Tselem Press Release (2011) B'Tselem to Turkel Commission: Independent investigation apparatus must be appointed to investigate suspected breaches of laws of war 11 April 2011. http://www.btselem.org/press-release/btselem-turkel-commission-independent-investigation-apparatus-must-be-appointed-invest

Israel Army Blog (2011a) Investigating the Gaza operation—an interview with Deputy Military Advocate for Operational Affairs. http://www.mag.idf.il/163-4544-en/patzar.aspx

Israeli Army Blog (2011b) New investigation policy regarding Palestinian casualties from IDF fire. http://dover.idf.il/IDF/English/News/today/2011/04/0604.htm

Israeli Army Blog (2011c) Military Advocate for Operational Affairs, Indictment filed in connection with 'Cast Lead', 11 March 2011, available at http://www.mag.idf.il/164-3952-en/Patzar.aspx?SearchText=human%20shields%20gaza

Israeli Army Blog (2011d) IDF Military Advocate General Takes Disciplinary Action, 6 July 2010 Indicts Soldiers Following Investigations into Incidents during Operation Cast Lead, 6 July 2010 (under "Complaint by Majdi Abed-Rabo), available at http://idfspokesperson.com/

---

[51] Israeli Army Blog 2011d.

[52] http://www.haaretz.com/news/diplomacy-defense/idf-to-charge-soldier-with-killing-two-palestinian-women-during-gaza-war-1.296500

2010/07/06/idf-military-advocate-general-takes-disciplinary-action-6-jul-2010-indicts-soldiers-following-investigations-into-incidents-during-operation-cast-lead

Israeli Ministry of Foreign Affairs', Official Statement Secretary General (2010) Israel responds to UN Secretary-General report on implementing recommendations of the Goldstone report, at http://www.mfa.gov.il/MFA/About+the+Ministry/MFA+Spokesman/2010/Israel_responds_UNSecy-Gen_report_implement_recommendations_Goldstone_report_5-Feb-2010

PCHR (2011) Memorandum on the Status of Domestic Investigations Conducted into Alleged Violations of International Law committed in the Context of Operation 'Cast Lead' Submitted by the Palestinian Centre for Human Rights. http://pchrgaza.org/files/2011/PCHR%20Memorandum.pdf

Schmitt M (2011) Investigating Violations of International Law in Armed Conflict. Harv Natl Sec J 2:31–84

Shany Y et al (2011) Response to the Military Advocate General's Position Paper on the Investigation of Allegations of Violations of International Humanitarian Law. http://www.idi.org.il/sites/english/ResearchAndPrograms/NationalSecurityandDemocracy/Terrorism_and_Democracy/Newsletters/Documents/IDI_Response_for_Turkel_Commission_English.pdf

State of Israel Report (2009a) Conclusion of investigations into Central Claims and Issues in Operation Cast Lead. http://www.mfa.gov.il/MFA/Terrorism+Obstacle+to+Peace/Hamas+war+against+Israel/IDF_Conclusion_of_investigations_Operation_Cast_Lead_Part1_22-Apr-2009.htm.htm

State of Israel Report (2009b) The Operation in Gaza: Factual and Legal Aspects. http://www.mfa.gov.il/NR/rdonlyres/E89E699D-A435-491B-B2D0-017675DAFEF7/0/GazaOperationwLinks.pdf

State of Israel Report (2009c) Initial Response to the Fact-Finding Mission on Gaza pursuant to Resolution S-9/1 of the Human Rights Council. http://www.mfa.gov.il/NR/rdonlyres/FC985702-61C4-41C9-8B72-E3876FEF0ACA/0/GoldstoneReportInitialResponse240909.pdf

State of Israel Report (2010a) Gaza Operation Investigations: An Update. http://www.mfa.gov.il/NR/rdonlyres/8E841A98-1755-413D-A1D2-8B30F64022BE/0/GazaOperationInvestigationsUpdate.pdf

State of Israel Report (2010b) Gaza Operation Investigations: Second Update. http://www.mfa.gov.il/NR/rdonlyres/1483B296-7439-4217-933C-653CD19CE859/0/GazaUpdateJuly2010.pdf

Summary Report of the Public Commission to Examine the Maritime Incident of 31 May 2010. http://www.turkel-committee.com/content-107.html

Yesh-Din (2008) Exceptions—Prosecution of IDF soldiers during and after the second Intifada, 2000–2007. http://yesh-din.org/userfiles/file/Reports-English/Exceptions%20%5BEng%5D%20final.pdf

Yesh-Din (2010) Data Sheet—IDF Investigations of IDF offenses against Palestinians: figures for 2000–2009. http://www.yesh-din.org/sys/images/File/2000-2009%20Investigations%20and%20Indictments%20-%20Datasheet,%20Feb%202010%20%5BEnglish%5D.pdf

Chapter 5
Initial Reactions to the Goldstone Report and Reflections on Israeli Accountability

Jennifer Barnette

> *The Mission concludes that what occurred in just over three weeks at the end of 2008 and the beginning of 2009 was a deliberately disproportionate attack designed to punish, humiliate and terrorize a civilian population, radically diminish its local economic capacity both to work and to provide for itself, and to force upon it an ever increasing sense of dependency and vulnerability.*[1]
>
> Report of the United Nations Fact Finding Mission on the Gaza Conflict

Contents

5.1	Introduction	124
5.2	Initial Reactions to the Goldstone Report	127
5.3	The Legitimacy War	134
5.4	Conclusion	139
References		141

J.D. Candidate at the University of California, Berkeley and Adjunct Professor, Global Studies, California State University San Marcos. Substantial portions of this text first appeared in the article "The Goldstone Report: Challenging Israeli Impunity in the International Legal System?" published in Global Jurist. For a more detailed analysis of the Goldstone Report's findings, you are encouraged to refer to this article: Barnette 2010.

[1] Report of the United Nations Fact Finding Mission on the Gaza Conflict [hereinafter Goldstone Report], September 15, 2009, Article 1690, p. 525.

J. Barnette (✉)
University of California, Berkeley, CA, USA

5.1 Introduction

The legitimacy of Israel's "Operation Cast Lead," the 22-day military offensive in Gaza in December 2008 and January 2009, and of Israeli practices in its occupation of the Palestinian territories of Gaza and the West Bank was called into question by the Report of the United Nations Fact Finding Mission on the Gaza Conflict. The report, more commonly referred to as the Goldstone Report after Justice Richard Goldstone who headed the investigation, sparked an international controversy, the effects of which are still being felt at time of writing.[2] This report was commissioned by the United Nations Human Rights Council on April 3, 2009 with the mandate "to investigate all violations of international human rights law and international humanitarian law that might have been committed at any time in the context of the military operations that were conducted in Gaza during the period from 27 December 2008 and 18 January 2009, whether before, during or after".[3]

This broad mandate endowed the Mission with the responsibility to investigate allegations of violations of international human rights law (IHRL) and international humanitarian law (IHL) by "all parties" of the conflict,[4] enlarging the scope of the investigation to include non-state actors as well as the State of Israel. While some controversy still remains over the wording of the official mandate the Mission was given,[5] the mandate that the Mission used to conduct the investigation (as quoted above) clearly enabled the Mission to investigate potential war crimes committed by Hamas and other Palestinian armed groups in Gaza, thereby preventing an exclusive, one-sided focus on Israel.

True to its mandate, the Mission investigated allegations of IHL and IHRL violations by both Israel and armed Palestinian groups (including Hamas), but chose to limit the investigation to 36 incidents in Gaza that it considered to be "illustrative of the main patterns of violations."[6] In this way, the report "does not purport to be exhaustive in documenting the very high number of relevant incidents that occurred in the period covered by the Mission's mandate."[7] Rather, it

---

[2] At time of writing (May 2011), the Goldstone Report has reappeared in the international spotlight, following an Op-Ed by Richard Goldstone in the Washington Post of April 2011.

[3] Goldstone Report, para 1, p. 5.

[4] Goldstone Report, para 13, p. 7.

[5] Many attempts to discredit the Goldstone Report claim that the official mandate given to the Mission did not allow for investigation of alleged war crimes committed by Hamas, thereby creating a one-sided investigation from the start. Justice Richard Goldstone rejects this position and maintains that the official mandate of the Mission is that which was quoted above, giving the Mission full authority to investigate both Israeli and Hamas violations. This will be discussed more fully later in the paper.

[6] Goldstone Report, para 16, p. 7.

[7] Ibid.

used a relatively small sample of events to represent the larger trends of the war, focusing especially on direct attacks on civilians and civilian infrastructure. The Mission determined that both Israel and Palestinian armed groups in Gaza violated international law and that many of these instances could constitute war crimes and possible crimes against humanity.

The report concluded by recommending that both Hamas and Israel conduct independent investigations into these allegations, and that in the absence of such good faith investigations beginning within 6 months, the UN Security Council refer the situation to the Office of the Prosecutor of the International Criminal Court. The Mission also recommended the use of universal jurisdiction by the international community, encouraging signatories of the Geneva Conventions to open criminal investigations in domestic courts, where there is sufficient evidence of grave breaches of the Geneva Conventions.[8]

Reports drawing the same conclusions about Operation Cast Lead had been published by leading international NGOs, including Human Rights Watch and Amnesty International, as well as Palestinian and Israeli NGOs, months before the Goldstone Report was released. The Arab League had also conducted an investigation, led by a similarly prominent figure in international law, John Dugard, which had likewise concluded that Israel had violated IHRL and IHL during its 22-day assault on the Gaza Strip.[9] However, while much of the substance of these reports was the same, the response from the international community to the reports was anything but.

When the Goldstone Report was delivered to the UN Human Rights Council on September 15, 2009, it was greeted with a controversy and hullabaloo that none of the previous reports had produced. While speculation still persists over why the Goldstone Report touched such an Isreali raw nerve, I understand that it was not just the conclusions reached by the Goldstone Mission that were so upsetting, but who was drawing those conclusions and what they were recommending.

Israel had never before been accused of war crimes at this level, by such an internationally visible and highly credentialed investigation. While there are many reasons to be critical of the United Nations, it does derive some legitimacy from its universality, "from the fact that it can speak and act on behalf of all nations in the world."[10] Because the UN, the greatest example of a global institution,

---

[8] Goldstone Report, para 1772, p. 552.
[9] Report of the Independent Fact Finding Committee on Gaza: No Safe Place, presented to the League of Arab States, April 30, 2009 [hereinafter referred to as Arab League Report] [the Executive Summary of the Report is reprinted in this Volume, see the Annex to Chap. 17—ChM].
[10] Van Staden 2007, p. 107.

commissioned the report, it commanded a sort of international attention that previous reports regarding Operation Cast Lead failed to do.

While there had been a Board of Inquiry established by UN Secretary General Ban Ki-moon into attacks on UN infrastructure during Cast Lead, that investigation, led by the former head of Amnesty International and former UN Special Envoy to East Timor and Nepal, Ian Miller, was limited in scope, only covering cases of death, injury or damage involving UN property and staff, and after its release on May 5, 2009, was largely swept under the rug by Ban Ki-moon himself, who would not release the entire text of the report publicly.[11] Because the Goldstone Mission was sanctioned by the United Nations and covered the entirety of the military assault on the Gaza Strip, the release of the Goldstone Report sparked a much greater controversy than any of the previous reports, including Miller's UN Board of Inquiry Report.

Another reason for the tremendous attention given to the Goldstone Report was the infallible character of Goldstone himself. Richard Goldstone is a former Justice of the Constitutional Court of South Africa, and the former Chief Prosecutor for the International Criminal Tribunals of Rwanda and the Former Yugoslavia. In addition to Goldstone's high regard in the field of international law, he is also Jewish, a self-proclaimed Zionist, and has very strong personal ties to Israel, and therefore cannot credibly be accused of anti-Israel bias.

Nevertheless, the report and even Goldstone himself, received much criticism by pro-Israeli voices in Israel and the United States. The President of Israel, Shimon Peres, went so far as to call the Goldstone Report, "a mockery of history" that "legitimizes terrorist activity, the pursuit of murder and death."[12] The attempts to discredit both Richard Goldstone and the 575-page report that he and his colleagues authored illustrate Israeli panic about the report's findings and recommendations, especially the calls for prosecutions by the ICC and the use of universal jurisdiction.

Until now, Israel has enjoyed virtual impunity in the international system and Israeli attempts to discredit the Goldstone Report highlight the tremendous fear that this immunity from prosecution may be coming to an end. The calls by the report for the Office of the Prosecutor at the ICC and the international community under universal jurisdiction to open investigations into the legitimacy of Israeli actions in Operation Cast Lead threaten Israeli impunity and disturb the commonheld notion that Israel can behave how it likes in the Occupied Territories without facing any legal repercussions or consequences. This chapter examines the significance of the Goldstone Report's findings and recommendations, and offers some insight into what this means for Israeli accountability.

---

[11] McCarthy and Pilkington 2009.

[12] Israeli Ministry of Foreign Affairs 2009.

5.2 Initial Reactions to the Goldstone Report

When the Goldstone Report was released on September 15, 2009, it caused an almost immediate international sensation. Although there had been numerous reports by leading human rights organizations including Human Rights Watch and Amnesty International that came to the same conclusions, the Goldstone Report drew tremendous attention due to the high-profile characteristics of its sponsor organization and the impeccable record of the report's principal author. It also went further than other reports in challenging the legitimacy of many Israeli policies of its occupation, including the blockade on Gaza, military detentions, and restrictions on freedom of movement in the West Bank. The report also did not shy away from using the term "collective punishment" in regards to the situation in Gaza, and goes so far as to state the "the Mission believes [the] primary purpose [of Cast Lead] was to bring about a situation in which the civilian population would find life so intolerable that they would leave (if that were possible) or turn Hamas out of office, as well as to collectively punish the civilian population."[13]

This was the first time a report of such magnitude, sanctioned by the United Nations and authored by one of the most prominent and respected figures in international law, had accused Israel of war crimes, including collective punishment, and called for accountability at the highest levels. At a time when Israel's Prime Minister began calling for the resumption of peace talks with the Palestinians, the report could not have been more of a thorn in Tel Aviv's side.

Israel's primary tactic in dealing with the report's condemning findings and imposing recommendations was to denounce the Human Rights Council as an anti-Israel organization that issued a "clearly one-sided" mandate to the Goldstone Mission and claiming that the biased mandate "prejudged the outcome of any investigation."[14] The mandate of the Mission became the main target of criticism of the report.

The controversy arises over which was the true mandate the Mission received. The original mandate that the Human Rights Council agreed upon January 12, 2009, focuses exclusively on Israeli violations of international law, reading:

> to investigate all violations of international human rights law and international humanitarian law by the occupying Power, Israel, against the Palestinian people throughout the Occupied Palestinian Territory, particularly in the occupied Gaza Strip, due to the current aggression, and calls upon Israel not to obstruct the process of investigation and to fully cooperate with the mission.[15]

---

[13] Goldstone Report, para 1204, p. 333.

[14] Israeli Ministry of Foreign Affairs 2009d. See also Israeli Ministry of Foreign Affairs 2009b.

[15] United Nations Human Rights Council Resolution A/HRC/S-9/L.1, agreed upon January 12, 2009. [see *infra* Document 1 in Part II, ChM]

The broadened mandate that Justice Goldstone sought and agreed upon with the then-president of the HRC and under which the Mission carried out its investigations, reads as follows:

> to investigate all violations of international human rights law and international humanitarian law that might have been committed at any time in the context of the military operations that were conducted in Gaza during the period from 27 December 2008 and 18 January 2009, whether before, during or after.[16]

It is clear that the initial mandate of the Mission was, as Justice Goldstone put in his own words, "stacked against Israel."[17] In an interview with Bill Moyers on PBS, Goldstone acknowledges that had he accepted the initial mandate, it "would have been a one-sided investigation." He then explains how he refused the original mandate issued by the Human Rights Council and got it changed to one that he himself wrote.

> I wasn't prepared, let alone as a Jew, but as a human being, to get involved in investigating under a one-sided mandate. And I refused. And I was then invited by the president of the Human Rights Council to visit with him. And he asked me what I thought would be an even-handed mandate, and I told him, and he said, "Write it out for me." And I wrote it out. And he said, "Well, that's the mandate that I'm giving you, if you're prepared to take it." Well, it was very difficult to refuse, in that situation, to get a mandate that I'd written for myself.[18]

The question of which of these was the official mandate of the Mission has caused significant controversy. Israel claims that the mandate was never officially changed,[19] thereby prejudging the outcome of the investigation. Officials from the United States also spoke out against the mandate of the Mission. Susan Rice, the US Ambassador to the United Nations, speaking in her national capacity said on September 17, 2009 that "we have long expressed our very serious concern with the mandate that was given by the Human Rights Council prior to our joining the Council, which we viewed as unbalanced, one sided and basically unacceptable."[20]

One of the other major criticisms of the report is that one of the members of the Mission, Christine Chinkin, had already predetermined the outcome of the investigation because she had signed an open letter published in The Sunday

---

[16] Goldstone Report, para 1, p. 5.

[17] Goldstone on Bill Moyers Journal 2009.

[18] Ibid.

[19] The Israeli Ministry of Foreign Affairs says that the mandate of the Mission was never legally changed. "Justice Goldstone has claimed that the mandate of the Mission was changed, unilaterally, by the then-President of the Council. However, as a matter of law, the only body with the legal authority to modify the Mandate is the Council itself, and it has never done so." http://www.mfa.gov.il/GazaFacts/Goldstone/israel-gaza-faq-goldstone-mission-3.htm

[20] Remarks by Ambassador Susan Rice 2009.

Times on January 11, 2009 entitled, "Israel's Bombardment of Gaza is Not Self-Defence—It's a War Crime," where Israel is accused of the crime of aggression and prima facie war crimes.[21] In the same letter, however, Hamas is also charged with war crimes. Such tactics that focus criticism on the mandate of the Mission or on previous statements by Mission members enable Israel to avoid having to address the substantial allegations found within the Mission's report.

Richard Falk, the United Nations Special Rapporteur on Human Rights in the Occupied Palestinian Territories, suggests that these diversionary tactics are commonplace for Israel. "The line of response to any criticism of Israel's behavior in occupied Palestine, especially if it comes from the UN or human rights NGOs is to cry "foul play" and avoid any real look at the substance of the charges. It is an example of what I call "the politics of deflection," attempting to shift the attention of an audience away from the message to the messenger."[22]

The other method Israel employed in its initial public relations campaign was to silence calls for an independent investigation by maintaining that the Israeli Defense Force was conducting its own investigations. The Israeli Ministry of Foreign Affairs announced that the IDF had opened its own investigations into "over 100 allegations regarding the conduct of its forces during Operation Cast Lead."[23] On October 15, 2009 Israeli Deputy Foreign Minister reminded the Knesset that "to date, there have been 23 investigations" into IDF operations in Cast Lead.[24]

However, the Goldstone mission looked into Israel's current system of domestic investigations and determined that it is insufficient and does not comply with international standards of independence and impartiality.[25] Based on the evidence it gathered and its analysis, the Goldstone team concluded that there were "serious doubts about the willingness of Israel to carry out genuine investigations in an impartial, independent, prompt and effective way as required by international law"[26] and that "there is little potential for accountability for serious violations of international humanitarian and human rights law through domestic institutions in Israel."[27]

---

[21] The Sunday Times 2009.
[22] Falk 2009a, b.
[23] Israeli Ministry of Foreign Affairs 2009b.
[24] Israeli Ministry of Foreign Affairs 2009a.
[25] Goldstone Report, para 1756, p. 543.
[26] Goldstone Report, para 1758, p. 544.
[27] Goldstone Report, para 1761, p. 544. This is also later reaffirmed by the report of the UN Committee of Independent Experts, headed by Mary McGowan Davis. Please see Chap. 6 in this Volume "Investigating the Investigations: A Comment on the UN Committee of Experts Monitoring of the 'Goldstone Process'" by Daragh Murray.

Justice Goldstone expressed his concern over the reluctance of Israel to open investigations external to the military in his interview with Bill Moyers on October 23, 2009.

> One of the things that disturbs me about the internal military investigation—it's now, what, seven months since the end of the war. There's only been one successful prosecution against a soldier, who stole a credit card, which is really almost fodder for cartoonists, in the plethora of alleged war crimes. But what concerns me is, in those military investigations, as far as I've read, in only one case has the military even approached the victims in Gaza. And obviously, to have a full investigation, one needs, as you say, to hear both sides... And, you know, I always quote Justice Brandeis, who said, "The best disinfectant is sunlight." And this is happening in the dark. And even with the best good faith in the world on the part of the military investigators, the victims are not going to accept decisions that are taken in the dark, and don't involve them.[28]

By delegitimizing the report's findings by focusing on the bias and one-sidedness of the Mission's initial mandate and trying to assuage demands for accountability by emphasizing the IDF's internal investigations, Israel hoped to sweep the report's contents and recommendations under the rug and out of public attention, like it has been able to do with so many reports critical of Israeli policies, including Ian Miller's UN report that found the IDF "involved in varying degrees of negligence or recklessness with regard to United Nations premises."[29] After pressure from Israel, UN Secretary General Ban Ki-moon bluntly rejected the recommendations of the report calling for further investigations of alleged Israeli violations of international law and refused to make the entire 184-page report available to the public, publishing only his own summary of the findings.[30]

Not So Easy to Sweep Under the Rug

A similar fate seemed to await the Goldstone Report when on October 1, 2009, the Palestinian Liberation Organization announced that it supported a decision to defer a vote on the Goldstone Report until March 2010.[31] When Israel's Prime Minister Benjamin Netanyahu warned the international community that any action to advance the report would "strike a fatal blow to the peace process,"[32] the United States Secretary of State Hillary Clinton reportedly phoned PA President Mahmoud Abbas and urged him not to accept the findings of the Goldstone Report, heavily influencing the PA's backing of the move to delay the vote in the Human Rights Council.[33] It has also recently been reported that the head of the Israeli

---

[28] Goldstone on Bill Moyers Journal 2009.
[29] Macintyre 2009.
[30] "UN accuses Israel of Gaza 'negligence or recklessness'", McCarthy and Pilkington 2009.
[31] "Vote on UN Gaza Report Deferred" Al Jazeera English, 2009i.
[32] MacFarquhar 2009a, b.
[33] "US 'Pressured Abbas on UN Report'" Al Jazeera English, 2009g.

Security Agency, Shin Bet chief Yuval Diskin, told Abbas in early October that if he did not ask for a deferral of the vote, Israel would turn the West Bank into a "second Gaza."[34] This is now widely believed to be the reason for Abbas' decision to postpone the vote at the Human Rights Council.

The decision to postpone the vote was heavily criticized by human rights groups, prominent figures in international law and many Arab politicians.[35] Richard Falk, UN Special Rapporteur on Human Rights in the Occupied Palestinian Territories, expressed his dismay at the PA decision to delay the vote at the Human Rights Council in an interview with Al Jazeera.

> I'm certainly not intelligent enough to understand something as perverse as this. The Palestinians have betrayed their own people. This was a moment when finally the international community endorsed the allegations of war crimes and it would have been an opportunity to vindicate the struggle of the Palestinian people for their rights under international law and for the Palestinian representatives in the UN themselves to seem to undermine this report is an astonishing development.[36]

While there was tremendous criticism coming from the international community, especially Arab regimes like Syria and Qatar, it was moderate in comparison to that from Palestinians domestically. While President Abbas maintained that the delay gave the PA time to garner further international support, Palestinians from all factions overwhelmingly disagreed with the action.[37] Palestinian Prime Minister Salam Fayyad "demanded the report's recommendations be implemented in full."[38] Mustafa Barghouti, an independent Palestinian MP, called the decision a "grave and horrible mistake" that had damaged the Palestinian Authority's credibility, and claimed that "the only beneficiary of this postponement was Israel and it happened at a time when there was an opening to hold Israel accountable."[39]

Many Palestinians and Palestinian rights organizations, angry at the PA decision, joined Hamas officials in calling for Mahmoud Abbas to resign from his position as PA President.[40] In Gaza, posters appeared on walls calling Mr. Abbas a traitor and saying he should be consigned to "the trash heap of history."[41] Hundreds of Palestinians in the West Bank and Jerusalem gathered in protest during the week that the decision to delay the vote was announced, calling for an apology from Abbas or for him to step down from office.[42] Director of the PA's media

---

[34] Eldar 2010.
[35] Kershner and MacFarquhar 2009.
[36] "Video: Interview with Richard Falk" Al Jazeera English 2009h.
[37] "Abbas Defends Goldstone Vote Delay" Al Jazeera English 2009a.
[38] "Anger Builds Over Gaza Report Delay" Al Jazeera English 2009b.
[39] McCarthy 2009.
[40] "Pressure Mounts on Abbas to Quit" Al Jazeera English 2009d.
[41] Kershner and MacFarquhar 2009.
[42] Al Jazeera English 2009b.

center, Ghassan Khatib, called the level of public protest "unprecedented."[43] "I do not remember any situation before when the leadership was so unpopular," he told the New York Times from Ramallah.[44]

The pressure on the Abbas regime mounted so high that the Palestinian Authority was forced to reverse its course and call for a formal endorsement of the Goldstone Report,[45] and eventually Mahmoud Abbas announced that he would not seek re-election as PA President.[46]

When Israel realized the vote on the Goldstone Report would take place in the UN Human Rights Council, it upped its anti-Goldstone rhetoric and campaigned for support against the findings and recommendations of the report. On October 12, 2009, Israeli Prime Minister Benjamin Netanyahu spoke to the Israeli Knesset about Israel's "Right to Self-Defense," denouncing the Goldstone Report and reiterating claims that endorsement of the Goldstone Report somehow jeopardizes Israel's right to defend itself, saying "This distorted report, written by this biased committee, undermines the very essence of Israel's right to self-defense. This report encourages terror and endangers peace."[47]

It is interesting to note here that the Goldstone Report does not question Israel's right to self-defense, but actually takes it as a given. In his interview on the Bill Moyers Journal, Justice Goldstone established that the report in no way challenges Israel's right to self-defense, and actually claims that Israel was justified in trying to put an end to the rocket and mortar attacks by Hamas.[48] This acceptance of Israel's claim that Operation Cast Lead was launched in self-defense goes contrary to many other legal assessments, including the Arab League's report authored by John Dugard which claimed that "Israel's actions could not be justified as self-defence,"[49] and the letter published in The Sunday Times on January 11, 2009, entitled "Israel's Bombardment of Gaza is Not Self-Defence—It's a War Crime," which was signed by a number of leading academics in international law including Richard Falk, Christine Chinkin, Victor Kattan, and John Quigley.[50]

Despite being "arguably more sensitive to Israel's contentions that Hamas was guilty of war crimes…than earlier reports had been" and "endorse[ing] the misleading main line of the Israeli narrative by assuming that Israel was acting in self-defense against a terrorist adversary," as Richard Falk has argued,[51] Israel

---

[43] Kershner and MacFarquhar 2009.
[44] Ibid.
[45] Otterman and MacFarquhar 2009.
[46] Bronner and Landler 2009.
[47] Israeli Ministry of Foreign Affairs 2009e.
[48] Goldstone on Bill Moyers Journal 2009.
[49] Arab League Report, p. 4, Article 16(3).
[50] The Sunday Times 2009.
[51] Falk 2009a.

continues to argue that the Goldstone Report questions and undermines its right to self-defense. In his speech to the Knesset on October 12, 2009, Netanyahu reiterated that the attacks on Gaza constitute a "just war" and that Israel will not tolerate anything that questions its ability and right to defend its citizens.

> I want to be very clear here: Israel will not take any risks for peace if it is not able to defend itself. This report brands Israel's leaders and IDF commanders and soldiers as war criminals. But the truth is exactly the opposite: Israel's leaders and soldiers are the ones who defend the citizens of Israel against war criminals ... Israel does not claim that the rules of war don't apply to us. On the contrary: not only does the IDF uphold them, but they do so more than any other army in the world. There are those today who would prosecute Israel's leaders and IDF soldiers who have done nothing but fight a just war using just means against blatant war criminals; we are witnessing a complete reversal of justice and truth. We will not tolerate a situation in which Ehud Olmert, Ehud Barak and Tzipi Livni—who mobilized soldiers to protect our cities and our people—are called to stand trial in The Hague.[52]

A few days later on October 15, the day before the scheduled UNHRC vote, in a similar speech to the Knesset, Deputy Foreign Minister Danny Ayalon called the Goldstone Report a "fraudulent, biased and unprofessional document," claiming "it is one of the things used to censure the State of Israel by its enemies."[53] That same day, after meeting with the Prime Minister of Spain, Israeli Prime Minister Netanyahu urges all nations to vote against the endorsement of the Goldstone Report.

> The IDF is a moral army, and this report accuses us of war crimes. The truth is exactly the opposite. Our just battle was against their war crimes...Israel can only advance peace if it is able to defend itself. Therefore, responsible nations must vote against this decision that encourages terror and undermines peace. Vote against this decision and in favor of peace.[54]

On October 16, 2009 the United Nations Human Rights Council endorsed the Goldstone Report in a resolution passed by 25 votes to 6, with 11 countries abstaining and 5 declining to vote.[55] The resolution *"welcomes* the report of the Independent International Fact-Finding Mission" and *"endorses* the recommendations contained in the report."[56] The resolution also *"recommends that* the

---

[52] Israel Ministry of Foreign Affairs 2009e.

[53] Israeli Ministry of Foreign Affairs 2009a.

[54] Israeli Ministry of Foreign Affairs 2009g.

[55] The countries that voted against the measure were: Hungary, Italy, Netherlands, Slovakia, Ukraine, and the United States. The countries that abstained were: Belgium, Bosnia and Herzegovina, Burkina Faso, Cameroon, Gabon, Japan, Mexico, Norway, Republic of Korea, Slovenia, Uruguay. The five that declined to vote were: France, the United Kingdom, Madagascar, Kyrgyzstan, and Angola. [The text of UNHRC Resolution S-12/1 is reprinted in this Volume as Document 4 in Part II, ChM].

[56] Ibid.

General Assembly consider the report of the Independent International Fact-Finding Mission" in its next session.[57]

What many found problematic about the UNHRC resolution, including Goldstone himself, was its rhetoric; while it endorses the findings and recommendations of the Goldstone Report, it uses very different language than the Goldstone Report itself, referring to Israel as the "occupying Power" and plainly singling out Israel for its violations of IHL and IHRL and not Hamas, which the Goldstone report explicitly does not to do. Justice Goldstone expressed concern about the language of the resolution saying "I hope that the Council can modify the text."[58]

In his explanation of the US vote against the measure, Douglas M. Griffiths, the American chargé d'affaires in Geneva, stated "this resolution goes far beyond even the initial scope of the Goldstone report."[59] U.S. State Department Spokesman Ian Kelly echoed this sentiment, saying the resolution had an "unbalanced focus" and that the U.S. was concerned "it will exacerbate polarization and divisiveness."[60]

Israel's response to the passing of the UNHRC resolution was similar to the United States'. The Israeli Foreign Ministry issued a statement claiming "the adoption of this resolution by the UNHRC impairs both the effort to protect human rights in accordance with international law, and the effort to promote peace in the Middle East. This resolution provides encouragement for terrorist organizations worldwide and undermines global peace."[61]

The UN Human Rights Council's endorsement of the Goldstone Report brought the Goldstone Report back into international spotlight. Both Israel and the United States, recognizing the implications of such a vote in regards to winning what international law expert Richard Falk calls the "legitimacy war," increased their efforts to delegitimize the Goldstone Report and in so doing, began to attack the author of the report himself, Justice Richard Goldstone.

5.3 The Legitimacy War

> "Neither the United States nor Israel has discovered the limits of military power in the contemporary world. The leaders of both countries seem unable to learn the lesson of recent history: that occupation in the postcolonial world rarely produces the desired results at an acceptable cost. It is from this perspective, despite a horrific price in lives and

---

[57] Ibid.
[58] "UN Backs Gaza War Crimes Report" Al Jazeera English 2009f.
[59] MacFarquhar 2009a, b.
[60] Ravid 2009.
[61] Israeli Ministry of Foreign Affairs 2009c.

suffering, that the Palestinians may be slowly winning the "second war," the legitimacy war, whose battlefield has become global."

Richard Falk, UN Special Rapporteur on Human Rights in
the Occupied Palestinian Territories[62]

After the United Nations Human Rights Council endorsed the Goldstone Report on October 16, 2009, Israel and its closest ally and staunch defender, the United States, launched an even more ambitious campaign to discredit the UNHRC, the Goldstone Report, and even Justice Goldstone himself. When it became evident that the Goldstone Report was not just going to be buried under the rug like Israel and the US had initially hoped, that it would instead be going to the United Nations General Assembly for a vote and then potentially on to the UN Security Council, both Israel and the United States upped their public relations campaigns.

H.Res.867

On October 23, 2009, US Representatives Howard Berman and Ileana Ros-Lehtinen of the Committee on Foreign Affairs introduced a bill to the United States House of Representatives "calling on the President and the Secretary of State to oppose unequivocally any endorsement or further consideration of the 'Report of the United Nations Fact Finding Mission on the Gaza Conflict' in multilateral fora."[63] From its outset, the resolution, H.Res.867, was very controversial and received heavy criticism from human rights organizations both in the United States and internationally.[64]

H.Res.867 vehemently attacks the validity of the Goldstone Report but offers no evidence to back up broad, generalized statements like "the report repeatedly made sweeping and unsubstantiated determinations that the Israeli military had deliberately attacked civilians during Operation Cast Lead."[65] Like the majority of the criticism the report has received, the bill heavily focuses on the mandate the Mission was given, purportedly biased and one-sided, and does not get at the substance of the report, the specific violations of international law that Goldstone and his team raise. The text of the resolution also misleads one who has never read the Goldstone Report to believe that it is an unfair, one-sided attack against Israel that denies Israel's right to self-defense.

---

[62] Falk 2009b.

[63] H.Res.867, United States 111th Congress, 1st Session, U.S. House of Representatives, (Introduced October 23, 2009), The Library of Congress.

[64] Organizations that voiced their opposition to H.Res. 867 include: Americans for Peace Now, the US Campaign to End the Israeli Occupation, Jewish Voice for Peace, Codepink, J Street, and the National Lawyers Guild.

[65] H.Res.867.

As with the majority of the anti-Goldstone report criticism, the resolution focuses on the initial mandate the Mission received and suggestive comments of members of the Mission, and not on the actual substance of the findings of the report. The following quotations from H.Res.867 are illustrative of the misleading nature of the bill's text.

> Whereas the mandate of the "fact-finding mission" makes no mention of the relentless rocket and mortar attacks, which numbered in the thousands and spanned a period of eight years, by Hamas and other violent militant groups in Gaza against civilian targets in Israel, that necessitated Israel's defensive measures;
>
> Whereas the "fact-finding mission" included a member who, before joining the mission, had already declared Israel guilty of committing atrocities in Operation Cast Lead by signing a public letter on January 11, 2009, published in the Sunday Times, that called Israel's actions "war crimes"[66];

The first "Whereas clause" deals with the mandate, deceptively leading one to believe that because it failed to mention Hamas rocket attacks, the mandate was biased and one-sided, despite the fact that the mandate called for investigation into both sides of the Gaza attacks and the report devotes several pages to condemning the rocket and mortar attacks launched against Southern Israel, before, during and after Operation Cast Lead. The second "Whereas clause" also illustrates the misleading nature of H.Res.867 by failing to mention that the letter Christine Chinkin signed in The Sunday Times, as noted previously, also accused Hamas of war crimes.

In a letter addressed to Berman and Ros-Lehtinen, Goldstone refuted many of these types of clauses in the resolution, going through point-by-point the factual inaccuracies and comments taken out of context.[67] By taking quotations out of context and wording the text in a misleading way, H.Res.867 represents a clear effort by the United States Congress, urged by AIPAC and the pro-Israel lobby in the US, to undermine and delegitimize the Goldstone Report.

On November 3, 2009, H.Res.867 (slightly modified from its original version to accommodate some of Justice Goldstone's concerns) was passed by the United States House of Representatives by an overwhelming vote of 344 to 36. Many of the 36 who voted against the non-binding resolution spoke out strongly against H.Res.867. Representative William Delahunt criticized how the "resolution came to the floor on suspension without a hearing, despite the willingness of Judge Goldstone to come before the United States Congress and answer any questions that we might pose to him."[68] Representative John Dingell called H.Res.867 a

---

[66] Ibid.
[67] Kampeas 2009.
[68] Ruebner 2009.

"bad resolution. It is unfair. It is unwise. It contributes nothing to peace. It establishes a bad precedent, and it sets up a set of circumstances where we indicate that we're going to just arbitrarily reject a UN finding and a UN resolution and that we're going to have that as a precedent. This is bad."[69] Representative Dennis Kucinich said, tellingly, "Almost as serious as committing war crimes is covering up war crimes, pretending that war crimes were never committed and did not exist."[70]

Attacking Goldstone ... and his report

The passing of H.Res.867 had profound significance in delegitimizing the Goldstone report and, moreover, represents the United States' resolute support for Israel in the 'legitimacy war.' The congressional vote took place two days before the United Nations General Assembly voted on endorsing the Goldstone Report. Recognizing the importance of the General Assembly vote in either giving momentum to the Goldstone Report or stopping it dead in its tracks, Israeli leaders lobbied hard for nations to vote against any measure that would increase the legitimacy of the report. Israel's Ambassador to the United Nations, Gabriela Shalev, exemplified this tactic during her speech to the UN General Assembly on November 4, 2009, where she claimed the report "was conceived in hate and executed in sin."[71]

Despite Israeli efforts to garner support against the Goldstone Report, on November 5, 2009 the United Nations General Assembly by a vote of 114 in favor to 18 against, with 44 abstentions, adopted a resolution endorsing the Goldstone Report and calling on the UN Secretary General, Ban Ki-moon, to send the report to the UN Security Council.[72] The following day, Ban Ki-moon agreed, saying "As requested by the General Assembly, I will transmit the report to the Security Council."[73]

With the overwhelming defeat in the General Assembly, and the Goldstone Report seemingly headed to the UN Security Council, Israeli leaders became more wary of the shifting tide of 'perceived legitimacy'. Some of the most prominent Israeli politicians began attacking Goldstone directly. Shimon Peres, in a meeting with Brazilian President Luis Inacio Lulu da Silva, stooped to the level of name-calling, saying "Goldstone is a small man, devoid of any sense of justice, a technocrat with no real understanding of jurisprudence," who "was on a one-sided mission to hurt Israel."[74]

---

[69] Ibid.
[70] Ibid.
[71] Israeli Ministry of Foreign Affairs 2009f.
[72] United Nations General Assembly 2009.
[73] "Gaza Report to go to Top UN Council" Al Jazeera English 2009c.
[74] Sadeh 2009.

Aside from Goldstone's impeccable record as a judge and international prosecutor, he also happens to be Jewish, a self-proclaimed Zionist and "friend of Israel," a trustee of Hebrew University, and someone who has numerous connections to Israel, including a daughter living there.[75] In the words of Richard Falk, who has himself faced serious criticism and personal attack from members of the Israeli government, "Israel could not find a more sympathetic, internationally credible figure than Goldstone to conduct a Fact Finding Mission and yet they've attacked him in this way that has tried to defame his personal credibility as a trustworthy reporter of the facts and the law."[76]

In responding to the tremendous amount of personal criticism he has faced, Judge Goldstone acknowledges that "there's a knee-jerk reaction to attack the messenger rather than the message. And I think this is typical of that."[77] Falk claims that this tactic of "attacking the messenger" is a typical Israeli response when faced with any criticism of Israel's behavior in occupied Palestine.[78]

> Israel has tended all along to pursue what I call the 'politics of deflection,' trying to focus attention on either the messenger or the auspices whether it's Goldstone or myself or the UN or the Human Rights Council, and not deal with the substance of the allegations, not deal with the criticisms that have been leveled against its tactics and policies from the perspective of international humanitarian law.[79]

As Falk suggests, what the harsh, personalized attacks against Goldstone by Israeli officials represent is Israel's "panicked reaction" that Palestine may in fact be winning the legitimacy war.[80] With two UN resolutions going overwhelmingly in favor of endorsing the Goldstone Report's damning findings and forbidding recommendations, personal attacks on Goldstone and his team prove that Israeli officials will stop at nothing to delegitimize this report.

While the findings of Goldstone Report add nothing new in substantive terms, it is Goldstone's stature, his reputation as a preeminent figure in international law as well as his long-standing ties and support for Israel, and the daunting recommendations that Goldstone encourages that frightened Israel. As discussed earlier, the report recommended that if Israel and Hamas did not conduct their own independent and impartial investigations within 6 months, then the Security Council should consider sending the matter to the Office of the Prosecutor at the International Criminal Court. While the consensus among the international

---

[75] Williams 2009.
[76] Al Jazeera English 2009e.
[77] Goldstone on Bill Moyers Journal 2009.
[78] Falk 2009a.
[79] Al Jazeera English 2009e.
[80] Ibid.

community suggests that there are credible grounds for opening an investigation into Israeli war crimes in Operation Cast Lead, the question lies in whether the ICC has jurisdiction over the matter. The Office of the Prosecutor has opened a preliminary investigation to determine whether the ICC could have jurisdiction over the allegations, but the matter remains legally complicated and politically sensitive.[81] The report also recommended the use of universal jurisdiction, where Israeli officials could face criminal charges abroad for crimes committed domestically or in Gaza. There has been some effort to prosecute Israeli officials who planned and carried out Operation Cast Lead using universal jurisdiction, but these efforts have achieved little success.[82]

5.4 Conclusion

While there are still many obstacles to tackling Israeli impunity in the international legal system, we may be at the cusp of a shifting tide in the legitimacy war. Israeli officials, who have until now enjoyed almost complete impunity, are beginning to be faced with the notions of prosecutions at the ICC or in national courts abroad. The tremendous loss of Palestinian civilian life in Operation Cast Lead, the damning conclusions of the Goldstone Report, and then later the legal murkiness surrounding Israel's assault on the Gaza aid flotilla last May,[83] has caused many in the international community to question the legitimacy of Israel's actions under international law.

---

[81] At time of writing, the Office of the Prosecutor had made no conclusive decision on whether it has jurisdiction to investigate alleged crimes committed during Operation Cast Lead. The Palestinian Minister of Justice submitted a formal declaration recognizing the jurisdiction of the ICC to the Office of the Prosecutor on January 21, 2009. For a discussion of the complexities surrounding the decision before the ICC on whether it can recognize Palestinian statehood for the purposes of jurisdiction, see: Barnette 2010. Also see Part III in this Volume, entitled "Gaza and the International Criminal Court", which includes several legal opinions submitted to the ICC by international legal scholars.

[82] In the wake of Operation Cast Lead, many human rights lawyers and pro-Palestinian activists have been collecting information to develop cases against Israeli officials for their roles in the 22-day offensive in the Gaza Strip. It has yet to be determined whether there is enough political and civil society willpower to overcome political challenges and move forward in prosecuting alleged Israeli war criminals. The most likely scenario is that Israeli leaders will be prevented from traveling to countries where they may face arrests on universal jurisdiction grounds. See: Barnette 2010.

[83] The assault on the Gaza flotilla refers to the Israeli military operation against six humanitarian ships carrying aid bound for Gaza on May 31, 2010. Eight Turkish nationals and one Turkish-American were killed in the raid.

The Israeli government recognizes the importance of this battle for legitimacy in the foreign political arena. Israeli Prime Minister Benjamin Netanyahu has called the "Goldstone threat" one of the top three major issues facing Israel, along with the Iranian nuclear threat and missile and rocket attacks in Southern Israel.[84] "Goldstone is a codeword for an attempt to delegitimize Israel's right to self-defense," Netanyahu has claimed.[85] Israeli Deputy Foreign Minister, Danny Ayalon, has called the greatest challenge for Israeli foreign policy to "counter the delegitimization which is being implemented by UN resolutions, by political attacks and also, in the last two or three years, by legal attacks, by abusing the international legal system."[86] Ayalon invokes imagery of warfare in discussing the legitimacy war, saying "Today the trenches are in Geneva in the Council of Human Rights, or in New York in the General Assembly, or in the Security Council, or in The Hague, the ICJ."[87]

The Goldstone Report has clearly had some success in bringing the legitimacy war to the frontlines of Israeli foreign relations agenda. However, in assessing what can be tangibly measured with regards to the effectiveness of Goldstone's recommendations, it is not clear that the Goldstone Report has had any real impact in successfully challenging what Richard Falk calls the "geopolitics of impunity." Since the release of the Goldstone Report, there has been virtually no challenge to the policies that governed Operation Cast Lead (including the intentional targeting of civilians and civilian infrastructure), nor has it ended its punishing and debilitating blockade that is crippling the population of Gaza. Taking into account this lack of tangible effectiveness, so to speak, it may be that the legacy of the Goldstone Report will not be found in any specific results or actions brought about by it, but rather in being a shining beacon for accountability and justice in international law.

The importance of the Goldstone Report, from this perspective, then lies in delivering the message, loud and clear, that Israel violated international law during its 22-day assault on the Gaza Strip, and that those responsible must be held accountable. The tremendous credibility of the Goldstone Report, as well as the international media hoopla its release generated, serves to bring attention to the injustices and international crimes committed during the Gaza war, as well as to discourage them from happening again.

The brutal attempts to discredit the Goldstone Report highlight the tremendous fear among Israeli leaders that the tide of legitimacy may be shifting toward the Palestinians, that Palestine may be winning the legitimacy war. It is in this respect that the Goldstone Report may prove enormously successful; by commanding

---

[84] "PM: Israel faces the 'Goldstone threat'" The Jerusalem Post 2009.
[85] Ibid.
[86] Israeli Ministry of Foreign Affairs 2010.
[87] Ibid.

world attention to listen to its message that peace can only be built upon a foundation of justice. Only time will tell how effective this message will be heard, both by Israeli leaders and the larger international community who ultimately decides the fate of the legitimacy war.

References

Al Jazeera (2009a) Abbas Defends Goldstone Vote Delay, 12 October 2009. http://english.aljazeera.net/news/middleeast/2009/10/20091011182856246590.html
Al Jazeera (2009b) Anger Builds Over Gaza Report Delay, 5 October 2009. http://english.aljazeera.net/news/middleeast/2009/10/2009105125517543449.html
Al Jazeera (2009c) Gaza Report to go to Top UN Council, 7 November 2009. http://english.aljazeera.net/news/americas/2009/11/200911623050291485.html
Al Jazeera (2009d) Pressure Mounts on Abbas to Quit, 6 October 2009. http://english.aljazeera.net/news/middleeast/2009/10/200910523169821654.html
Al Jazeera (2009e) Talk to Al Jazeera: Richard Falk, 27 December 2009. http://english.aljazeera.net/focus/gazaoneyearon/2009/12/20091222124259758791.html
Al Jazeera (2009f), UN Backs Gaza War Crimes Report, 16 October 2009. http://english.aljazeera.net/news/europe/2009/10/20091016163540814787.html
Al Jazeera (2009g), US Pressured Abbas on UN Report, 4 October 2009. http://english.aljazeera.net/news/middleeast/2009/10/20091039613281857.html
Al Jazeera (2009h) Video: Interview with Richard Falk, 7 October 2009. http://english.aljazeera.net/news/middleeast/2009/10/20091070847949400.html
Al Jazeera (2009i) Vote on UN Gaza Report Deferred, 2 October 2009. http://english.aljazeera.net/news/middleeast/2009/10/200910224162409.html
Barnette J (2010) The Goldstone Report: Challenging Israeli Impunity in the International Legal System? Global Jurist 10:1–28. http://www.bepress.com/gj/vol10/iss3/
Bill Moyers Journal (2009) Interview with Justice Richard Goldstone, 23 October 2009. http://www.pbs.org/moyers/journal/10232009/profile.html
Bronner E, Landler M (2009) Top Palestinian Rules Out Race for Re-election, The New York Times. http://www.nytimes.com/2009/11/06/world/middleeast/06mideast.html
Eldar A (2010) Diskin to Abbas: Defer UN Vote on Goldstone or Face 'Second Gaza', Haaretz. http://www.haaretz.com/hasen/spages/1143038.html
Falk R (2009a) Palestine Winning the Legitimacy War, Al-Arabiya, 29 September 2009. http://www.alarabiya.net/save_pdf.php?cont_id=86478&lang=en
Falk R (2009b) Winning and Losing in Gaza, the Nation, 9 February 2009. http://www.thenation.com/doc/20090209/falk
Goldstone R (2011) Reconsidering the Goldstone Report on Israel and War Crimes, Washington Post, 2 April 2011. http://www.washingtonpost.com/opinions/reconsidering-the-goldstone-report-on-israel-and-war-crimes/2011/04/01/AFg111JC_story.html
Israeli Ministry of Foreign Affairs (2009) President Peres' Reply to the Goldstone Mission Report, 16 September 2009. http://www.mfa.gov.il/MFA/Government/Communiques/2009/President-Peres-Reply-to-the-Goldstone-Commission-Report-16-Sep-2009
Israeli Ministry of Foreign Affairs (2009a) Deputy FM Ayalon Responds in Knesset on Goldstone Report, 15 October 2009. http://www.mfa.gov.il/MFA/Government/Speeches+by+Israeli+leaders/2009/Dep_FM_Ayalon_Knesset_Goldstone_Report_14-Oct-2009
Israeli Ministry of Foreign Affairs (2009b) Israel's Initial Reaction to the Report of the Goldstone Fact Finding Mission, 15 September 2009. http://www.mfa.gov.il/MFA/About+the+Ministry/MFA+Spokesman/2009/Press+releases/Israel_initial_reaction_Goldstone_Mission_15-Sep-2009

Israeli Ministry of Foreign Affairs (2009c) Israel's Reaction to the Decision of the UN Human Rights Council, 16 October 2009. http://www.mfa.gov.il/MFA/About+the+Ministry/MFA+Spokesman/2009/Press+releases/Israel_reaction_decision_UN_Human_Rights_Council_16-Oct-2009

Israeli Ministry of Foreign Affairs (2009d) MFA Briefing to the Foreign Press on the Goldstone Report, 1 October 2009. http://www.mfa.gov.il/MFA/Government/Speeches+by+Israeli+leaders/2009/MFA_briefing_foreign_press_Goldstone_Report_1-Oct-2009.htm

Israeli Ministry of Foreign Affairs (2009e) Policy Statement by PM Netanyahu at Opening of Knesset Winter Session, 12 October 2009. http://www.mfa.gov.il/MFA/Government/Speeches+by+Israeli+leaders/2009/Policy_statement_PM_Netanyahu_Knesset_12-Oct-2009

Israeli Ministry of Foreign Affairs (2009f) Statement by Ambassador Gabriela Shalev to the United Nations General Assembly, 4 November 2009. http://www.mfa.gov.il/MFA/Government/Speeches+by+Israeli+leaders/2009/Statement_Amb_Shalev_UN_General_Assembly_4-Nov-2009

Israeli Ministry of Foreign Affairs (2009g) Statement by PM Netanyahu after Meeting with PM Spain, 15 October 2009. http://www.mfa.gov.il/MFA/Government/Speeches+by+Israeli+leaders/2009/PM_Netanyahu_meeting_PM_Spain_15-Oct-2009

Israeli Ministry of Foreign Affairs (2010) Address by Deputy Foreign Minister Danny Ayalon: 'Challenges for Israeli Foreign Policy', Israel Council on Foreign Relations, 6 January 2010. http://www.mfa.gov.il/MFA/About+the+Ministry/Deputy_Foreign_Minister/Speeches/DepFM_Ayalon_Challenges_Israeli_Foreign_Policy_6-Jan-2010.htm?DisplayMode=print

Kampeas R (2009) Goldstone vs. Ros-Lehtinen and Berman, JTA: The Global News Service of the Jewish People, 30 October 2009. http://blogs.jta.org/politics/article/2009/10/30/1008853/goldstone-v-ros-lehtinen-and-berman

Kershner I, MacFarquhar N (2009) Furor sends Palestinians into Shift on Gaza Report Delay. The New York Times, 7 October 2009. http://www.nytimes.com/2009/10/08/world/middleeast/08mideast.html?_r=1&scp=1&sq=palestinian+report+delay&st=nyt

MacFarquhar N (2009a) U.N. Council Endorses Gaza Report.The New York Times, 16 October 2009. http://www.nytimes.com/2009/10/17/world/middleeast/17nations.html?_r=1

MacFarquhar N (2009b) Palestinians Halt Push on War Report. The New York Times, 1 October 2009. http://www.nytimes.com/2009/10/02/world/middleeast/02mideast.html?scp=3&sq=palestinian+report+delay&st=nyt

Macintyre D (2009) UN Retreats after Israel Hits out at Gaza Report. The Independent, 6 May 2009. http://www.independent.co.uk/news/world/middle-east/un-retreats-after-israel-hits-out-at-gaza-report-1679727.html [broken link, ChM]

McCarthy R, Pilkington E (2009) UN Accuses Israel of Gaza 'Negligence or Recklessness'. The Guardian, 5 May 2009. http://www.guardian.co.uk/world/2009/may/05/israel-gaza-united-nations

McCarthy R (2009) Dropping UN Resolution on Gaza War a Mistake, says Palestinian Official. The Guardian, 7 October 2009. http://www.guardian.co.uk/world/2009/oct/07/un-resolution-gaza-mistake-palestinian

Otterman S, MacFarquhar N (2009) Palestinians, in Reversal, Press U.N. Gaza Report. The New York Times, 14 October 2009. http://www.nytimes.com/2009/10/15/world/middleeast/15nations.html?scp=2&sq=palestinian+report+delay&st=nyt

Ravid B (2009) Delegitimization of Israel must be Delegitimized, Haaretz, 16 October 2009. http://www.haaretz.com/hasen/spages/1121614.html

Report to the Arab League of the Independent Fact Finding Committee on Gaza (2009) No Safe Place. http://www.arableagueonline.org/las/picture_gallery/reportfullFINAL.pdf

Rice S (2009) Remarks on Somalia, the Middle East and the 2009 H1N1 Influenza Pandemic, at the Security Council Stakeout, 17 September 2009. http://usun.state.gov/briefing/statements/2009/september/129303.htm

Ruebner J (2009) Is the "We Love Israel" Consensus on Capitol Hill a Thing of the Past? US Campaign to End the Occupation, 5 November 2009. http://endtheoccupationblog.blogspot.com/2009/11/is-we-love-israel-consensus-on-capitol.html

Sadeh S (2009) Peres: Goldstone a Small Man, Out to Hurt Israel. Haaretz, 12 November 2009. http://www.haaretz.com/hasen/spages/1127695.html

The Jerusalem Post (2009) PM: Israel Faces the 'Goldstone Threat', 23 December 2009. http://www.jpost.com/Israel/Article.aspx?id=164050

The Sunday Times (2009) Israel's Bombardment of Gaza is not Self-defence—It's a War Crime, 11 January 2009. http://www.timesonline.co.uk/tol/comment/letters/article5488380.ece

United Nations General Assembly (2009) By Recorded Vote, General Assembly Urges Israel, Palestinians to Conduct Credible, Independent Investigations into Alleged War Crimes in Gaza, 5 November 2009. http://www.un.org/News/Press/docs/2009/ga10883.doc.htm

Van Staden A (2007) Between the Rule of Power and the Power of Rule: In Search of an Effective World Order. Martinus Nijhoff Publishers, Leiden

Williams I (2009) The NS Interview: Richard Goldstone, The New Statesman, 30 December 2009. http://www.newstatesman.com/middle-east/2010/01/interview-israel-law

Chapter 6
Investigating the Investigations: A Comment on the UN Committee of Experts Monitoring of the 'Goldstone Process'

Daragh Murray

Contents

6.1	Introduction	145
6.2	Background: The Creation of the Committee	146
	6.2.1 Mandate and Methodology	147
	6.2.2 The Committee's Principal Findings	147
6.3	The International Regulation of Domestic War Crimes Investigations	148
6.4	The Committee's Findings	152
	6.4.1 Israel	152
	6.4.2 The Palestinian Side	158
6.5	Concluding Remarks	159
References		160

6.1 Introduction

The Report of the UN Fact-Finding Mission on the Gaza Conflict's ('FFMGC') significance lies in its focus on accountability, and its explicit recommendations to this effect. Of particular importance was the conclusion that:

> ...the responsibility to investigate violations of international human rights and humanitarian law, prosecute if appropriate and try perpetrators *belongs in the first place to domestic authorities and institutions*. This is a legal obligation incumbent on all States and

---

Government of Ireland IRCHSS Scholar, PhD Candidate, Irish Centre for Human Rights, National University of Ireland Galway. International Legal Officer, Palestinian Centre for Human Rights. The views presented in this paper are solely those of the author in his personal capacity.

D. Murray (✉)
National University of Ireland, Galway, Ireland

C. Meloni and G. Tognoni (eds.), *Is There a Court for Gaza?*,
DOI: 10.1007/978-90-6704-820-0_6,
© T.M.C. ASSER PRESS, The Hague, The Netherlands, and the authors/editors 2012

State-like entities. However, *where domestic authorities are unable or unwilling to comply with this obligation, international justice mechanisms must be activated to prevent impunity.*[1]

In light of this emphasis on accountability—which was reflected in the report's specific recommendations to the Security Council[2]—the UN Human Rights Council established a Committee of Independent Experts to monitor and assess domestic investigations and prosecutions conducted in relation to Operation Cast Lead.[3] This article will analyse both the Committee's major findings, and the potential impact of this 'investigation of the investigations' on international law more generally; issues identified herein are presented as talking-points deserving further, in-depth, discussion.

6.2 Background: The Creation of the Committee

Human Rights Council Resolution 13/9 established:

> "a committee of independent experts in international humanitarian and human rights laws to monitor and assess any domestic, legal or other proceedings undertaken by both the Government of Israel and the Palestinian side, in the light of General Assembly resolution 64/254, including the independence, effectiveness, genuineness of these investigations and their conformity with international standards".[4]

The Committee was chaired by Mr. Christian Tomuschat, Professor Emeritus at Humboldt University Berlin, and former member of the UN Human Rights Committee and the International Law Commission. The other two members of the Committee were Judge Mary McGowan Davis, former Justice of the Supreme Court of the State of New York, and Mr. Param Cumaraswamy, jurist and former Special Rapporteur on the independence of judges and lawyers.

Following the submission of this Committee's first report in September 2010,[5] Human Rights Council Resolution 15/6 renewed and resumed the Committees mandate.[6] The second committee was chaired by Judge McGowan Davis, while the other member was Judge Lennart Aspegren, formerly a judge at the Svea Court of Appeal and the International Criminal Tribunal for Rwanda; both Mr. Tomuschat and Mr. Cumaraswamy had resigned following the submission of

---

[1] Report of the UN Fact-Finding Mission on the Gaza Conflict, 25 September 2009, U.N. Doc. A/HRC/12/48, para 1963. Emphasis added.

[2] Id., para 1969.

[3] The mandate of the Committee was renewed in September 2010.

[4] Human Rights Council Resolution 13/9, U.N. Doc. A/HRC/Res/13/9, 14 April 2010, para 9. [See *infra* Document 8 in Part II].

[5] U.N. Doc. A/HRC/15/50, 23 September 2010 ('First Report'). [See *infra* Document 9 in Part II].

[6] Human Rights Council Resolution 15/6, U.N. Doc. A/HRC/Res/15/6, 6 October 2010, para 8.

the first report. The Committee's second and final report was submitted to the 16th session of the Human Rights Council in March 2011.[7]

6.2.1 Mandate and Methodology

The Committee's interpretation of its mandate is of relevance. Appropriately, the Committee understood "domestic, legal or other proceedings"[8] to refer to any "investigations, disciplinary proceedings and prosecutions undertaken by either military or civil justice systems" in the context of Operation Cast Lead.[9] The Committee did not consider its work restricted to those 36 incidents documented in the FFMGC Report, and from a straightforward reading of the above, it is understood that domestic proceedings were to be regarded as formal procedures conducted in accordance with the rules and regulations of either the civil or military justice codes.

In order to give effect to its mandate, the Committee analysed information in the public domain, supplemented by consultations with relevant stakeholders.[10] Thus, a field visit was conducted in the Gaza Strip, consultations were held with governmental representatives and representatives of concerned NGOs, expert submissions were accepted, interviews were conducted with victims, governmental reports were analysed, and so on.

6.2.2 The Committee's Principal Findings

Before proceeding to the substantive component of this paper it is perhaps beneficial to recap the Committee's principal findings, first with respect to Israel, and second for the Palestinian side.

The Committee's work must be analysed in light of the FFMCG Report, and in particular its recommendations regarding criminal accountability, which was to be pursued first at the domestic level; but should these domestic proceedings prove genuinely unwilling or unable, resort was required to mechanisms of international justice. The Committee's monitoring and assessment of domestic proceedings was thus conducted within this framework.

In light of this focus on international justice, it is presented that the Committee's most significant finding was its unequivocal conclusion that: "Israel has *not conducted* investigations into decisions made at the highest levels about the design

---

[7] U.N. Doc. A/HRC/16/24, 18 March 2011 ('Second Report'). [see *infra* Document 10 in Part II].
[8] Human Rights Council Resolution 13/9, U.N. Doc. A/HRC/Res/13/9, 14 April 2010, para 9.
[9] First Report, para 6.
[10] See, First Report paras 8–16, Second Report paras 9–22.

and implementation of the Gaza operations. [...] alleged serious violations go beyond criminal responsibility at the level of combatants and even commanders, and include allegations aimed at decision makers higher up the chain of command."[11] This finding was confirmed and reiterated in the second report.[12] The Committee clearly concluded that those suspected of being the 'most responsible' had been granted impunity.

The Committee also identified serious concerns regarding the impartiality of the Military Advocate General (MAG),[13] the promptness of investigations,[14] and their level of transparency.[15]

On the Palestinian side, the Committee noted that both the government in the West Bank and the government in the Gaza Strip initiated parallel, and distinct, investigative proceedings. These proceedings centred upon the establishment of investigative commissions with international components, mandated to conduct investigations and provide recommendations to the relevant authorities. The report produced by the government in the West Bank was deemed to have independently and impartially engaged with its mandate,[16] while the commission in Gaza comprehensively failed to address the allegations contained in the FFMGC Report.[17]

Ultimately, the Committee found that both the government in Gaza and the government in Ramallah failed to conduct the required criminal investigations and prosecutions.[18] Both Israel and the Palestinian authorities failed to ensure accountability.

6.3 The International Regulation of Domestic War Crimes Investigations

The significance of the UN Committee's reports extends beyond the immediate analysis of Israeli and Palestinian investigations and prosecutions conducted in relation to Operation Cast Lead: the Committee has made a significant contribution with respect to the international regulation of domestic war crimes investigations and prosecutions. These issues are of relevance to future prosecutions conducted by both the International Criminal Court and national courts on the

---

[11] First Report, para 64. Emphasis added.

[12] Second Report, para 79.

[13] Second Report, para 41. This relates specifically to those incidents involving the suspected criminal liability of the MAG.

[14] Second Report, para 82.

[15] Second Report, para 81.

[16] Second Report, para 84. This finding is discussed further below, see Sect. 6.4.2.

[17] Second Report, para 90.

[18] Second Report, paras 87, 90.

basis of universal jurisdiction,[19] and also to the further development of international human rights and international humanitarian law. In effect the Committee has laid out a roadmap for the regulation of such investigations and prosecutions, thereby providing an important basis for future work.

Customary international humanitarian law obliges States to investigate alleged war crimes and, if appropriate, prosecute the suspects.[20] This obligation applies to both international and non-international armed conflicts. However, while the obligation is explicit, international humanitarian law does not specify how such investigations or prosecutions are to be conducted. There are no rules to ascertain whether or not this obligation has been fulfilled.

International human rights law, on the other hand, contains well developed rules regulating investigations, prosecutions, and judicial proceedings.[21] In light of the International Court of Justice's finding that the protections of international human rights law do not cease in times of armed conflict,[22] the question therefore arises as to how the two bodies of law interact with respect to the regulation of domestic war crimes investigations. In this regard, the Committee found that there is no conflict between the duty to investigate under human rights law and humanitarian law,[23] and that "the gap between the expansive standards under IHRL and the less defined standards for investigation under IHL is not so significant."[24] It is noted that, as interpreted, the Committee is here referring to the standards regulating the conduct of investigations under international human rights law or international humanitarian law, and not the duty to open an investigation, which may differ depending on the legal framework applied.

The Committee specified four principal requirements—drawing on both international humanitarian law and international human rights law—which it deemed applicable to domestic war crimes investigations: independence, impartiality, thoroughness and effectiveness, and promptness. These four requirements, as defined by the Committee, are as follows[25]:

> *Independence.* Both the body undertaking the investigation as well as its members should be independent in the sense of being institutionally detached from those implicated in the events. For example, those potentially implicated in violations should have no supervisory role, whether direct or indirect, over those conducting the investigation. Independence goes beyond institutional independence, however: investigatory bodies and their members

---

[19] *Vis-á-vis* complimentarity, the assessment of unwillingness or inability, and so on.

[20] International Committee of the Red Cross 2005, Volume 1: Rules, Rule 158. See further, Article 146 Fourth Geneva Convention, Article 85 Additional Protocol I.

[21] See, for example, Article 14, International Covenant on Civil and Political Rights; Human Rights Committee, General Comment 13, 1984.

[22] *Legality of the Threat or Use of Nuclear Weapons*, International Court of Justice, Advisory Opinion, 8 July 1996, para 25.

[23] First Report, para 29.

[24] First Report, para 30.

[25] Footnotes are omitted.

should not be unduly influenced by powerful social groups, such as the media, industry or political parties.

Impartiality. Impartiality is closely related to independence. While independence relates to the establishment and functioning of an investigative body and its members, impartiality refers to the question of whether an investigator is or is likely to be biased. The Human Rights Committee has stated that "judges must not harbour preconceptions about the matter put before them, and that they must not act in ways that promote the interests of one of the parties". Similar considerations apply to investigators. Indications that investigators uncritically adhere to one interpretation of events without bothering to explore alternatives, including the version of events advanced by the complainant, or fail to acknowledge a lack of evidence to support their interpretation of events, could indicate a lack of impartiality.

Thoroughness and effectiveness. This standard refers to the completeness and comprehensiveness of an investigation. Thorough and effective investigators should: undertake necessary autopsies and medical examinations; collect and record all relevant evidence; conduct site visits as appropriate; identify, question, and take statements from all relevant witnesses; question witnesses comprehensively so that the investigation is able to establish the cause of the alleged violation and those responsible; and provide conclusions based on a comprehensive analysis of all relevant elements. The Committee against Torture has found that inconsistencies in the results of investigations, as well as a lack of qualifications of key experts, such as the doctor undertaking an autopsy, can be evidence of a lack of thoroughness.

Promptness. As a general rule an investigation should commence and progress with reasonable expedition. Determining whether an investigation has met this standard of reasonableness depends on the specific circumstances of the case. Cases of torture and extrajudicial killings—where medical evidence might disappear—and enforced disappearances—where an individual's life might be in imminent danger—require immediate action. The Committee against Torture suggests that the requirement to undertake a prompt investigation means that an investigation should be initiated immediately when there is a suspicion of torture or ill-treatment, namely, within hours or days. It has found delays of 15 months and 10 months between the alleged act and the opening of an investigation to be unreasonable. When examining the progress of investigations, frequent and unexplained adjournments can unacceptably compound delay.[26]

The specification of these requirements, which are derived from international human rights and international humanitarian law jurisprudence, and conventional and soft-law, represents an important contribution and one which should be developed further. However, there is one significant omission which must be addressed.

As noted by the Committee, thoroughness and effectiveness refer to the completeness and comprehensiveness of the investigation.[27] The Inter-American Court of Human Rights has specified that this standard requires that the duty to investigate "must be undertaken in a serious manner and not as a mere formality preordained to be ineffective"[28]; the State must use the means at its disposal

---

[26] First Report, paras 22–25. Emphasis added.

[27] First Report, para 24.

[28] *Velasquez Rodriguez Case*, Inter-American Court of Human Rights, (Series C) No. 4, Judgment of 29 July 1988, para 177.

"to identify those responsible,"[29] and "to impose the appropriate punishment".[30] Clearly, this standard is intrinsically related to the necessity of preventing 'sham' proceedings, such as those designed to shield suspects from justice. As consistently noted by the European Court of Human Rights, investigations must be capable of "leading to the identification and punishment of those responsible."[31]

This requirement must be considered a fundamental component with respect to accountability for international crimes and thus an essential requirement of any genuine investigation. This is particularly evident in light of the customary international humanitarian law rule that individuals are criminally responsible for war crimes they commit,[32] a requirement further reflected in Article 25 of the Rome Statute of the International Criminal Court. Yet this focus on individual responsibility is conspicuously absent from the Committee's reports, and does not appear to have been a feature of their analysis, an issue addressed further below.[33]

A final issue to be addressed relates to the Committee's finding that "the level of transparency expected of human rights investigations is not always achievable in situations of armed conflict, particularly as questions of national security often arise."[34] However, international human rights law's requirement of transparency, or public scrutiny, is regarded as essential in maintaining public confidence in the rule of law, and avoiding any appearance of collusion in, or tolerance of, unlawful acts[35]; as held by the European Court of Human Rights, victims, or their next-of-kin, "must be involved in the procedure to the extent necessary to safeguard his or her legitimate interests."[36] As such, transparency relates to knowledge of the procedures. For example, victims and their legal representatives should be entitled to know the status of their complaint, and if a complaint is closed they must be informed of the reason. It is difficult to see how these requirements are precluded by concerns relating to national security, and furthermore, why any potential difficulties relating to disclosure, for example, could not be resolved in a manner similar to those developed for resolving such issues in non-war crimes related criminal proceedings, such as those involving espionage, terrorism, and so on.

---

[29] Ibid, para 174.

[30] Ibid.

[31] *Hugh Jordan v. the United Kingdom*, European Court of Human Rights, Application No. 24746/94, 4 August 2001, para 107.

[32] International Committee of the Red Cross 2005, Volume 1: Rules, Rule 151.

[33] See, Sect. 6.4.2.

[34] First Report, para 32.

[35] *Bati v. Turkey*, European Court of Human Rights, Application No. 33097/96, 57834/00, 3 September 2004, paras 136–137.

[36] *Finucane v. the United Kingdom*, European Court of Human Rights, Application No. 29178/95, 1 October 2003, para 213.

6.4 The Committee's Findings

This section will analyse the Committee's findings with respect to the investigations and prosecutions conducted by Israel, and the Palestinian authorities in the Gaza Strip and the West Bank. Both reports of the Committee will be addressed concurrently.

6.4.1 Israel

Three principal issues can be identified with respect to the Committee's findings regarding Israel. These relate to: (1) operational debriefings/command investigations, (2) the role of the MAG, and (3) the investigation and prosecution of high-level military and political officials. Following this analysis the investigations actually conducted will be detailed, and the Committee's findings summarised.

6.4.1.1 Operational Debriefings

Operational debriefings—which Israel has recently begun to refer to as 'command investigations'—are defined in Article 539 (A)(a) of the Military Justice Law as:

> "a procedure held in the army, according to the army orders and regulations, with respect to an incident that has taken place during a training or military operation or with connection to them."[37]

Thus, an operational debriefing "normally focuses on examining the performance of the forces and identifying aspects of an operation to preserve and to improve, but may also focus on specific problems that occurred. By undertaking this review, the IDF seeks to reduce further operational errors".[38] These procedures were heavily criticised in the FFMGC Report: "a tool designed for the review of performance and to learn lessons can hardly be an effective and impartial investigation mechanism that should be instituted after every military operation where allegations of serious violations have been made. It does not comply with internationally recognized principles of independence, impartiality, effectiveness, and promptness in investigations."[39]

In its first report the Committee noted that, owing to a lack of cooperation from Israel, it was not in a position to evaluate the role of operational debriefings in the

---

[37] Article 539(A)(a), Military Justice Law 5715-1955.
[38] State of Israel 2010a, para 54.
[39] Report of the UN Fact-Finding Mission on the Gaza Conflict, 25 September 2009, U.N. Doc. A/HRC/12/48, para 1831.

investigative process.[40] While certain reluctance is understandable given the circumstances, it is presented that the Committee's refusal to analyse the role of operational debriefings constitutes a major flaw, and one which prevented the Committee from reaching more definitive, and accurate, overall conclusions. Given that situations of non-cooperation will inevitably arise in the future—both in this and in other contexts—further discussion of this issue is appropriate.

In establishing its methodology, the Committee attached significant importance to governmental sources: "[t]he Committee views the relevant government authorities as among the most important sources of information about the progress of investigations".[41] Indeed, when conducting analysis of this nature, government sources are arguably the most important first port of call. However, the Committee's near exclusive reliance on such sources, given the consequences of such reliance, must be addressed. With respect to the consequences, the following finding of the Committee is highlighted: "[o]wing to a lack of cooperation, the Committee is unable to make a definitive determination as to whether the investigations carried out by Israel meets the criteria in resolution 13/9."[42]

It is presented that while desirable, full cooperation by the State authorities under investigation is not essential, particularly with respect to investigations seeking to analyse issues concerning institutional mechanisms or procedures established in law, the conduct of prosecutorial or judicial organs, and so on. In such circumstances, issues arising consequent to non-cooperation may be effectively overcome by resort to mechanisms such as an analysis of relevant legislation and jurisprudence, expert opinions and memorandums, NGO documentation and analysis, and consultation with lawyers and relevant professionals. Indeed, in this regard it is noted that Article 17 of the Rome Statute of the International Criminal Court requires that domestic investigations and prosecutions be assessed on the basis of a State's willingness or unwillingness to genuinely pursue the interests of justice. Under such circumstances, it is possible that a State may choose not to cooperate with the ICC, but will have initiated some form of domestic proceedings; non-cooperation by the relevant State authorities must be assumed and anticipated. The fact that the State authorities refuse to cooperate with the external investigators should not be regarded as an effective barrier precluding an assessment of the genuineness of domestic proceedings. Furthermore, given that it is the State that is under investigation when assessing '(un)willingness', reliance on non-governmental sources will inevitably be an essential requirement.

Given the serious concerns raised in the FFMGC report, and the central role of operational debriefings in the Israeli investigative systems, it would appear that flaws in this system (which the FFMGC allege render it incompatible with

---

[40] First Report, para 50.
[41] First Report, para 10.
[42] First Report, para 44.

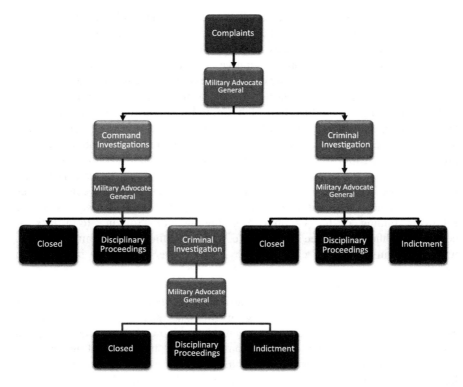

Fig. 6.1 Role of the MAG (The figure is elaborated by the author on the basis of a diagram presented in the report *State of Israel, Gaza Operation Investigations: An Update*, January 2010, §45)

international standards)[43] may have a decisive impact. Israel's lack of cooperation does not appear to constitute sufficient grounds to preclude an assessment of these debriefings given that, *inter alia*, they are established and regulated by the Military Justice Law, have been the subject of Israeli Supreme Court jurisprudence,[44] and in light of the possibility to consult lawyers with experience working with these systems.

6.4.1.2 The Role of the MAG

The MAG serves a dual function: acting as legal advisor to the military,[45] and enforcing penal laws intended to 'represent the rule of law and the public

---

[43] Report of the UN Fact-Finding Mission on the Gaza Conflict, 25 September 2009, U.N. Doc. A/HRC/12/48, para 1831.

[44] See, for example, *Al-Nebari v. The Chief of Staff of the Israeli Army*, HCJ 2366/05 (decision delivered on 29 June 2008).

[45] Military Justice Law para 178(1).

interest'.[46] Consequently, the MAG plays a central role at each stage of the investigative system; he is responsible, *inter alia*, for the decision to open or close an operational debriefing, the decision to open or close a military police investigation, and the decision to press charges.[47] This central and decisive role is perhaps most simply illustrated by Fig. 1.

In analysing the role of the MAG, the Committee noted that, while "the combination of the advisory and supervisory functions in one office does not automatically lead to a conflict of interest or a lack of impartiality,"[48] significant concerns exist given that many of the allegations contained in the FFMGC Report directly link to the advice of the MAG. In order to examine any consequent conflict with the principle of impartiality, the Committee chose to examine the results of the investigations: "Although the Committee does not have access to the full evidence and reasoning behind these decisions, given the seriousness of the allegations, the military investigations thus far appear to have produced very little."[49]

While this conclusion seems valid, if tentative, it is regrettable that the Committee chose only to examine the outcome of the investigations, and not the underlying process or institutional structure involving the office of the MAG. Given the similar role of the MAG in numerous militaries worldwide, clarity regarding the modern requirements of international law would be invaluable with respect to other conflicts. Specifically, can the office of the MAG investigate potential crimes wherein criminal responsibility may rest on advice given by the MAG? As noted by the European Court of Human Rights, "the general rule is that the persons responsible for the injuries and those conducting the investigations *should be independent of anyone implicated in the events.* [...] This means not only that *there should be no hierarchical or institutional connection but also that the investigators should be independent in practice.*"[50] *Prima facie*, this rule appears to be violated in the event that the MAG—having advised that a certain course of action is legal—is then responsible for the decision to open a criminal investigation into the legality of that same action, with potential implications for their own criminal liability. This fact did not receive sufficient attention within the Committee's reports, and is potentially pertinent to other situations worldwide.

---

[46] Military Justice Law para 178(2), (4).
[47] State of Israel 2010a, para 45.
[48] First Report, para 53.
[49] First Report, para 55.
[50] *Bati v. Turkey*, European Court of Human Rights, Application No. 33097/96, 57834/00, 3 September 2004, para 135. Emphasis added.

6.4.1.3 Investigation and Prosecution of High-Level Officials

The Report of the FFMGC concluded that:

> "Whatever violations of international humanitarian and human rights law may have been committed, the systematic and deliberate nature of the activities described in this report leaves the Mission in no doubt that responsibility lies in the first place with those who designed, planned, ordered and oversaw the operations."[51]

The FFMGC thus clearly implicated the individual criminal responsibility of senior political and military officials. This attribution of high-level responsibility with respect to Operation Cast Lead is reflective of a broader historical trend: the commission of international crimes often occurs as a result of government policy or military strategy, thereby implicating the individual criminal responsibility of senior political and military figures. However, States have proven consistently unwilling to investigate and prosecute their own governmental and military commanders, thereby censuring governmental or military policies. As a result, the investigation and prosecution of senior officials has become central to international criminal law, as reflected in the international tribunals' focus on those 'most responsible'. The Committee's findings in this regard are thus relevant to both national and international justice systems, and specifically the activation of international jurisdiction in the event that national jurisdictions prove unable or unwilling to conduct the required investigations and prosecutions.

The first significant issue to arise from the Committee's reports is the unequivocal conclusion that no high-level investigations or prosecutions have occurred. As stated succinctly in the conclusions to the second report: "there is no indication that Israel has opened investigations into the actions of those who designed, planned, ordered and oversaw Operation Cast Lead."[52]

This emphatic conclusion—which applies equally to the Palestinian side[53]—gives rise to an important question relevant to the relationship between national and international courts' jurisdiction over international crimes. Is it possible for national systems to effectively investigate and prosecute alleged international crimes, in which the potential individual criminal responsibility of senior officials arises? In answering this question, other aspects of the Committee's findings will be relevant, in particular those related to institutional structure and performance. Specifically, the finding that "the MAG himself, in his testimony to the Turkel Commission, pointed out that the military investigation system he heads is not a viable mechanism to investigate and assess high-level policy decisions",[54] implies that the answer to this question should perhaps be answered in the negative.

---

[51] Report of the UN Fact-Finding Mission on the Gaza Conflict, 25 September 2009, U.N. Doc. A/HRC/12/48, para 1895.
[52] Second Report, para 79.
[53] Second Report, paras 87, 90.
[54] Second Report, para 41.

6.4.1.4 The Outcomes

As reported by the Committee, Israel investigated approximately "400 allegations of operational misconduct in Gaza reported by the FFM and others."[55] However, details regarding the overwhelming majority of these investigations—including which incidents were actually addressed—are unknown; they have not been communicated to the Committee or the legal representatives of the victims.[56] In total, 4 individuals have been indicted with respect to violations occurring in the context of Operation Cast Lead, three of whom have been tried: one individual was tried and convicted for the theft of a credit card and sentenced to seven and a half months in prison[57]; two individuals were tried in relation to the use of a child as a human shield and received a three month suspended sentence[58]; one individual has been charged in relation to the shooting of a group of civilians carrying white flags, but the trial is currently delayed.[59] It appears that the overwhelming majority of the investigative procedures that were opened have been closed, with findings that no violations were committed.[60]

As noted above, the Committee was reluctant to draw definitive conclusions. However, four principal concerns of the Committee may be summarised. First, the Committee emphatically concluded that no investigations had occurred with respect to those "who designed, planned, ordered and oversaw Operation Cast Lead."[61] Second, the actual operation of Israel's military investigation system raised concern in the present context with respect to the identified requirements of international law,[62] in particular the central role of the MAG.[63] Third, the participation of victims and transparency in reporting progress and results of investigations, raised serious concerns.[64] Finally, the lack of promptness in conducting investigations was addressed, in particular the fact that "[m]ore than one-third of the 36 incidents in Gaza [as reported by the FFMGC] are still unresolved or unclear."[65]

---

[55] Second Report, para 78.
[56] Second Report, para 46.
[57] Second Report, para 32.
[58] Second Report, para 30.
[59] Second Report, para 26.
[60] See, State of Israel 2009, 2010a, b.
[61] Second Report, para 79.
[62] First Report, para 91.
[63] Second Report, para 41.
[64] Second Report, para 81.
[65] Second Report, para 82.

6.4.2 The Palestinian Side

As a result of the political split between the Gaza Strip and the West Bank, two parallel—but distinct—investigative procedures were opened, one by the government in the West Bank, and one by the government in the Gaza Strip. These two procedures were addressed separately in the Committee's Reports, however, they will not be analysed in depth herein. The reason for this is quite simple, both parties established investigative commissions tasked with reporting on alleged violations of international law, however, while the Committee recognized that this task was approached with varying levels of professionalism,[66] ultimately *no* criminal procedures (investigations or prosecutions) were initiated either by the government in Gaza,[67] or the government in the West Bank.[68] On this basis it must be concluded that both parties have unquestionably failed to adhere to the requirements of General Assembly Resolution 64/254.

However, one aspect of the Committee's findings in relation to the government in the West Bank merits further attention.[69] The Committee concluded that the government in the West Bank, through the establishment of an Independent Investigative Committee (the 'PIIC'),[70] had conducted "independent and impartial investigations in a comprehensive manner that squarely addressed the allegations in the FFM Report"[71] and that "the investigations carried out by the PIIC conformed to international standards and could be considered credible and genuine."[72]

Two interrelated issues arise by virtue of this finding. First, the Committee appear to have selectively applied the requirements which they had identified as regulating the conduct of domestic investigations and prosecutions[73]; specifically the requirements of thoroughness and effectiveness, promptness, and transparency did not seem to feature. This is a significant—and dangerous—precedent. It is surely not sufficient for investigations to be independent and impartial if, for example, they are "a mere formality preordained to be ineffective", or if the authorities have not "taken the reasonable steps available to them to secure the evidence concerning the incident, including, *inter alia*, eyewitness testimony, forensic evidence and, where appropriate, an autopsy which provides a complete and accurate record of injury, and an objective analysis of clinical findings,

---

[66] See, *supra* Sect. 6.2.2.

[67] Second Report, para 90.

[68] Second Report, para 87.

[69] Issues arising consequent to the—in this author's view appropriate—attribution of international human rights standards to the Palestinian authorities, as non-State actors, are beyond the scope of this paper.

[70] See the website of the Committee, here: http://www.picigr.ps/.

[71] First Report, para 70.

[72] Second Report, para 84.

[73] See, *supra* Sect. 6.3.

including the cause of death."[74] In order to be considered genuine, investigations must adhere to all of the requirements outlined by the Committee.[75]

The second issue relates to the first and concerns the above-mentioned omission of the requirement that,[76] in order to be considered effective, investigations must be capable of "leading to the identification and punishment of those responsible."[77] By failing to include this standard, investigations—which necessarily form the basis of any prosecution—could potentially be considered genuine *vis-á-vis* the requirements of international law, without having addressed the individual criminal responsibility of suspects, who remain outside the whole process. This would appear to be in conflict with the requirements of customary international law,[78] and the very *raison d'etre* of criminal law, whether national or international.[79]

These two factors constitute a serious, arguably terminal, flaw with respect to the Committee's analysis, and would appear to facilitate, and not frustrate, the occurrence of sham proceedings: following this logic, 'genuine' investigations could be deemed to have occurred without any discussion of individual criminal responsibility; indeed, this seems to be the Committee's view regarding the procedures initiated by the government in the West Bank. As mentioned, this conflicts with the requirements of customary international law, and also has implications with respect to complimentarity and the activation of international jurisdiction.

6.5 Concluding Remarks

The Reports of the UN Committee of Experts were significant on two different levels. First, and most immediately, they provided an analysis of the domestic procedures initiated in relation to alleged violations of international law committed in the context of Operation Cast Lead. Although the Committee exhibited a certain shyness, it is clear that—in their analysis—none of the parties had conducted the necessary criminal investigations and prosecutions as determined by the requirements of international law. Thus, on 25 March 2011, Human Rights Council Resolution 16/32 urged the General Assembly to submit the FFMGC Report to the Security Council "for its consideration and appropriate action, including consideration of referral of the situation in the Occupied Palestinian Territory to the prosecutor of the International Criminal Court, pursuant to Article 13(b) of the

---

[74] *Finucane v. the United Kingdom*, European Court of Human Rights, Application No. 29178/95, 1 October 2003, para 69.

[75] See, *supra* Sect. 6.3.

[76] See, *supra* Sect. 6.3.

[77] *Hugh Jordan v. the United Kingdom*, European Court of Human Rights, Application No. 24746/94, 4 August 2001, para 107.

[78] International Committee of the Red Cross 2005, Volume 1: Rules, Rule 151. See further, Article 146 Fourth Geneva Convention, Article 85 Additional Protocol I.

[79] See, for example, Article 25 Rome Statute of the International Criminal Court.

Rome Statute".[80] At the time of writing it remains to be seen whether the Security Council will pursue accountability in this context with the same enthusiasm recently exhibited with respect to the situation in Libya.[81]

Second, and of more general significance, the Committee specified a framework for monitoring and regulating domestic war crimes investigations. In light of the uncertainties concerning the interaction between international humanitarian law and international human rights law, and the inability of international jurisdictions to prosecute the majority of war crimes, this is an important step and one which should be built on in the future. States must be aware of the international laws regulating their domestic war crimes investigations, and further refinement of the Committee's work will benefit both the International Criminal Court (*vis-á-vis* complimentarity) and national courts exercising universal jurisdiction.

Throughout this paper, however, a number of important issues have also been identified. These include: the question as to whether national courts can be expected to genuinely investigate and prosecute high-level officials; the importance of requiring that investigations be capable of leading to the identification and punishment of suspects; the importance of comprehensively—and not selectively—applying international requirements to an analysis of domestic investigations; and the importance of overcoming State non-compliance. These are serious issues arising from the Committee's reports, and they should be addressed in order both to resolve legal conflicts or inaccuracies, and to ensure that any similar UN Committees in the future learn from the experiences of the past.

References

International Committee of the Red Cross (2005) Customary International Humanitarian Law. Cambridge University Press, Cambridge

State of Israel (2009) The Operation in Gaza 27 December 2008–18 January 2009: Factual and Legal Aspects, July 2009. http://www.mfa.gov.il/MFA/Terrorism-+Obstacle+to+Peace/Hamas+war+against+Israel/Operation_in_Gaza-Factual_and_Legal_Aspects.htm

State of Israel (2010a) Gaza Operation Investigations: An Update, January 2010. http://www.mfa.gov.il/MFA/Terrorism-+Obstacle+to+Peace/Hamas+war+against+Israel/Gaza_Operation_Investigations_Update_Jan_2010.html

State of Israel (2010b) Gaza Operation Investigations: Second Update, July 2010. http://www.mfa.gov.il/MFA/Terrorism-+Obstacle+to+Peace/Hamas+war+against+Israel/Gaza_Operation_Investigations_Second_Update_July_2010.htm

---

[80] Human Rights Council Resolution 16/32, U.N. Doc. A/HRC/Res/16/32, 14 April 2011, para 8. [See *infra* Document 8 in Part II].

[81] Security Council Resolution 1970, U.N. Doc. S/Res/1970, 25 February 2011, para 4.

Chapter 7
The Importance of Fact-Finding Missions Under International Humanitarian Law

Liesbeth Zegveld

Contents

7.1	Inability of IHL to Protect Civilians	161
7.2	Importance of Facts	162
7.3	Goldstone Report and Fact Finding	163
7.4	Evidence Gathering in International Law	164
7.5	Conclusion	166
References		167

7.1 Inability of IHL to Protect Civilians

Legal constraints have often failed to protect civilians from the adverse affects of war. It was no different during the Gaza conflict. IHL proved hardly relevant to the suffering of civilians inside and outside of Gaza a year ago. In order to prevent the rules from becoming even more irrelevant, States should take their obligation to ensure respect for IHL more seriously. The obligation to ensure respect implies that every State ought to take action with regard to any other State which does not respect this law. The duty to ensure respect provides for a system of collective responsibility for compliance with IHL. In the past, the Security Council explicitly called on States

---

Professor of International Humanitarian Law, Leiden University. This paper was presented at the Conference "Politics and International Law after the Gaza War", 25 January 2010, Peace Palace, Den Haag.

L. Zegveld (✉)
Leiden University,
Leiden, The Netherlands

to ensure respect by Israel, as Occupying Power, for its obligations under the Geneva Conventions.[1] The International Court of Justice also stated in its Advisory Opinion on the Wall: "all States Parties to the Fourth Geneva Convention have the obligation to ensure compliance by Israel with IHL".[2] The duty to ensure respect has various dimensions. I have identified one particular measure available to States in order to fulfil their obligation to ensure respect: fact finding.[3]

7.2 Importance of Facts

Part of the problem of IHL, indeed perhaps the main problem, is the facts. I have a standard advice that I repeat in any individual case: take the 'facts' of a case more seriously. The procedure comes after the facts, and only after that follows the 'substantive law' (in particular human rights law, international humanitarian law, and international and domestic criminal law), so cherished by academics. Academic lawyers love the law rather than the facts because they have no experience with the strategic role of the facts and the ways they are collected, weighed, disputed, verified, and determined. But in order to ensure compliance with the law, the facts tend to be decisive. There can be no accountability without facts. There can be no criminal investigation without facts. There can be no sanctions without facts. How can you ensure compliance if you do not know—or do not want to know—what is happening or has happened on the battlefield? The importance of independent establishment of facts is recognised in Additional Protocol I, which provides for the establishment of an International Fact-Finding Commission.[4] Fourteen years after the Protocol, a Fact-Finding Commission was finally set up. Since its establishment, however, the Commission has never had any instructions to investigate facts that have occurred in any armed conflict. There have been a few international *ad hoc* commissions of inquiry, such as the 'Commission of Experts for the former Yugoslavia' and the 'Commission of Inquiry for Darfur'. Prior to those commissions, a UN investigation team looked into the use of chemical weapons by Iraq.[5] In 2009, another fact-finding mission took place: the

---

[1] UN Doc. S/RES/681 (20 December 1990).

[2] International Court of Justice, *Legal Consequences of the Construction of a Wall in the Occupied Palestinian Territories*, Advisory Opinion of 9 July 2004, para 163.

[3] Fact finding means any activity designed to obtain detailed knowledge of the relevant facts of any dispute or situation. See 'Declaration on Fact Finding by the UN in the Field of International Peace and Security', UN Doc. A/RES/46/59 (9 December 1991).

[4] Article 90 of the Additional Protocol I (1977) of the 1949 Geneva Conventions.

[5] One of the findings of the UN investigation team was that chemical weapons had 'without any doubt' been used by Iraq against Iran and that civilians had died as a consequence. See 'Report of the Mission Dispatched by the Secretary-General to Investigate Allegations of the Use of Chemical Weapons in the Conflict Between the Islamic Republic of Iran and Iraq', UN Doc. S/20060 (20 July 1988), p. 9. The importance of international investigation commissions may

Goldstone Mission.[6] The full name of this mission is 'The UN Fact Finding Mission on the Gaza Conflict'.[7] The Goldstone Fact-Finding Mission was a good initiative, since its aim was to obtain full knowledge of all relevant facts inside and outside of Gaza. On the basis of these facts, accountability can be established and implemented.

7.3 Goldstone Report and Fact Finding

How did the Goldstone Mission conduct its fact-finding mission and what was the Mission's impact on fact finding during and after armed conflicts in general? The Mission placed the civilian population in and near Gaza at the centre of its concerns and[8] made victims its first priority regarding violations of IHL.[9] This is a justifiable approach, since the Goldstone Mission—like most fact finding missions—was occasioned by the fact that (in this case) the Gaza war resulted in many victims and rumours about misconduct. The section of the report on the Gaza Strip is based on first-hand information gathered and verified by the Mission. The Mission's preferred option would have been to visit all areas covered by its mandate and undertake on-site investigations in all these areas. The Government of Israel, however, refused to cooperate with the Mission on three levels:

(a) It refused to meet the Mission and provide it with access to Government officials (including military officials) and documentation;
(b) It precluded the Mission from travelling to Israel in order to meet with Israeli victims and witnesses; and

---

(Footnote 5 continued)
proof its worth for many years to come. The UN investigation team's findings in the Iraq/Iran war have gratefully been used in the court case against Dutch businessman Van Anraat.

[6] The name of the report is 'Report of the United Nations Fact Finding Mission on the Gaza Conflict'.

[7] The Goldstone Fact-Finding mission fits into a long tradition of the UN endeavouring to have full knowledge of all relevant facts and to undertake to that end fact-finding activities. See UN Doc. A/RES/46/59.

[8] Human Rights Council, 'Human Rights in Palestine and Other Occupied Arab Territories: Report of the United Nations Fact-Finding Mission on the Gaza Conflict', UN Doc. A/HRC/12/48 (25 September 2009), para 136 [hereinafter Goldstone Report].

[9] For victims, establishment of the facts is also crucial. They may even prefer a correct finding of facts, to an interpretation of these facts, over the application of the law to these facts. Victims want to know what has happened. The 'Basic Principles and Guidelines on the Right to a Remedy and Reparation', which were adopted by the General Assembly of the United Nations in 2005, recognize explicitly "the victim's right to … access to relevant information concerning violations". See UN Doc. A/RES/60/147 (16 December 2005).

(c) It prevented the Mission from travelling to the West Bank, including East Jerusalem, to meet members of the Palestinian Authority and Palestinian victims who were living there.[10]

To assess the situation in Israel and in the West Bank, the Mission therefore had to make comparatively greater use of information produced by others. However, the sections on Israel and the West Bank also include first-hand information directly gathered and verified by the Mission.[11] Israel later qualified many incidents established by the Goldstone report as based on hearsay and unsupported by facts. The witnesses who were heard would not have actually seen the events, according to Israel. Israel Prime Minister Netanyahu said the report was "a perversion of the truth".[12] Israel stated it carried out its own investigations, yet failed to give any details of the cases.[13] The US, for its part, officially called the Goldstone report one-sided and pleaded that its recommendations be rejected.[14] The Netherlands stated that they could not "confirm nor deny the findings" of the Mission. The Netherlands are of the opinion that the parties to the conflict should carry out their own investigation.[15]

7.4 Evidence Gathering in International Law

How did Israel's refusal to cooperate affect the findings of the Goldstone Mission? What are the prospects for the Goldstone report as a factual basis on which to establish justice after the end of the Gaza conflict? Can States use the report as a factual basis for action with a view to ensuring respect for IHL? Can a prosecutor use the report as a factual basis for his investigation? I cannot check the factual findings of the Goldstone report. I was not at the spot of any of these incidents to witness for myself what happened. But what I can do is assess the method adopted by Goldstone to gather and verify information and reach conclusions. This method was guided by best practice methodology developed in the context of United Nations investigations. Goldstone's final conclusions on the reliability of the information received were made:

– taking all of the circumstances into consideration;
– cross-referencing the relevant material and information; and

---

[10] Goldstone Report, para 162.
[11] Id., at para 169.
[12] Falk 2009.
[13] Goldstone Report, para 1583. Israel contends that the vast majority of the casualties resulted from the lawful application of force and that Hamas bears responsibility for allowing armed groups to operate amidst the civilian population.
[14] Falk 2009.
[15] Kamerstukken II 2008/09, 23 432/26 150 nr. 306.

– assessing whether, in all the circumstances, there was sufficient information of a credible and reliable nature for the Mission to make a finding in fact.[16]

In the case of Israel and the West Bank, the Mission made adjustments in view of the Mission's inability to access those areas due to lack of cooperation from Israel.

There are no general rules on the basis of which the reliability of information is to be assessed. Fact-finding missions and courts alike have a broad discretion in assessing the soundness of a given statement or other piece of evidence.[17] For example, it is accepted as a general principle of law that "indirect proof"—that is inferences of fact and circumstantial evidence—is admissible if it can be shown that objective obstacles stand in the way of gathering direct proof.[18] The International Court of Justice found in the *Corfu Channel case* that this is "the more so when such indirect evidence appears to be based 'on a series of facts linked together and leading logically to a single conclusion'."[19] This rule supports the practice of the Goldstone mission regarding its findings with respect to Israel and the West Bank. A part of the report's conclusions about facts that occurred in these areas is based on information produced by others. But this information is supported by first-hand information gathered by the Mission. To assess the method of evidence gathering and evidence examination by Goldstone, the practice of the mass claims procedures may also be taken as a guideline. The mass claims procedures have shown that the burden of proof in situations of armed conflict, in particular for war victims, must be handled flexibly. For example, the United Nations Compensation Commission was prepared to accept, on very thin evidence, that injury or death—following the invasion of Iraq into Kuwait—was an immediate consequence of acts of war committed during that period.[20]

It is not possible to determine in the abstract what evidence may be sufficient to establish certain facts. This must be assessed on a case-by-case basis, taking into account all relevant circumstances. The difficulty of proving facts after the destruction of war is a relevant factor in this regard. The reality of an armed conflict justifies a more relaxed standard of proof, according to the practice of mass claims commissions. Also, the purpose for which the evidence was gathered is important to assess the methods of investigation.

---

[16] Goldstone Report, para 171.

[17] Id., at para 13.

[18] Id., at para 15.

[19] Id., at para 15, referring to the International Court of Justice, *Corfu Channel* Case, ICJ Reports (1949) 4, at 18.

[20] In some cases the Commission thought a personal statement is sufficient unless this was consistent with the injury of the victim. See 'Recommendations Made by the Panel of Commissioners Concerning Individual Claims for Serious Personal Injury or Death' (Category "B" Claims), UN Doc. S/AC.26/1994/1 (26 May 1994), p. 41. See also Singh 2006, p. 73. The UNCC was able to do this because it was handling large groups of claims and was able to distil proof or patterns of proof thereof. See Singh 2006, pp. 76 and 90.

While the Goldstone report may not be a sufficient basis for a criminal conviction, it will be a sufficient basis for a prosecutor to start an investigation. It may also suffice for compensation claims of individual victims. Apart from the circumstances of an armed conflict as a relevant factor to be taken into account when gathering evidence of violations of IHL, the attitude of the parties to the conflict is also relevant. What I mean is that a party cannot simply prevent facts from being established by refusing to cooperate. If a party fails to provide credible counter-evidence, facts will generally be established as presented by the other party. Ultimately, law is not about finding the truth. Law is a reasoned application of rules to presented and substantiated facts. Law is about establishing who is right and who is wrong, on the basis of arguments and counterarguments supported by facts. The other party can question these facts. But without presenting counter-evidence, a party cannot easily discard presented evidence. I find support for this argument in the practice of the human rights organisations. Both the European Court for Human Rights and the Inter-American Court of Human Rights apply the principle that when the State has exclusive power over the evidence, the burden of proof should be reversed. Those cases were often about forced disappearances, or individuals who were imprisoned by the State and had suffered injuries or had died in prison.[21] Similar situations occurred in the Gaza conflict, where Israel has exclusive knowledge of their targets and the way they conducted their military operations. The Goldstone Mission provided the parties concerned with an opportunity to submit additional relevant information, express their position and respond to allegations. It submitted comprehensive lists of questions to the Government of Israel in advance of completing its analysis and findings. The Mission did not receive a reply from Israel.[22] The question is therefore not so much whether the facts in the Goldstone report are true, but more whether Israel and other countries have credible arguments to counter these facts. Without any substantiated counter-evidence presented by Israel, the Goldstone Mission was in a good position to determine the nature and amount of evidence that it deemed necessary and adequate to establish the facts.

7.5 Conclusion

Disputing the facts is a well-tried method of States to ignore or deny violations of IHL. This is true for the parties to the conflict who commit the violations. But it is also true for third States that refuse to take on their duty to ensure respect for the law. IHL in particular is vulnerable to this method of denial of the facts. Because

---

[21] See, among others, European Court of Human Rights, *Salman v. Turkey* (21986/93), 27 June 2000, paras 99–100; Inter-American Court on Human Rights, *Velasquez v. Guatemala*, 25 November 2000, para 152.

[22] Goldstone Report, para 175.

the facts were committed in wartime, States find it easy to argue that the evidence is hidden under the debris of the war. It is often impossible for independent observers to establish facts because they do not have access to the battlefield and are denied access to information. However, international practice shows us that fact-finding missions have a broad discretion in assessing the soundness of a given statement or other piece of evidence. Indirect proof is admissible under certain circumstances. Mass claims commissions have determined that the burden of proof in situations of armed conflict must be handled flexibly. More importantly: Israel cannot simply prevent facts from being established by refusing to cooperate. If a party fails to provide credible counter-evidence, facts will generally be established as presented by the other party. The Goldstone report is therefore a credible source of facts. It provides a *prima facie* case against Israel and the Palestinian Authority for facts listed in that report. Goldstone's conclusions are a sufficient basis for States to impose sanctions on Israel, either through the Security Council or through the European Union. Prosecutors of domestic courts and the ICC (in case it would accept jurisdiction) can start an investigation on the basis of this report, as it creates a reasonable suspicion against certain persons.[23]

References

Falk R (2009) Commentary: The Future of the Goldstone Report: Can the UN Implement International Law? The Berkeley Daily Planet, 1 October 2009. http://www.berkeleydailyplanet.com/issue/2009-10-01/article/33850?headline=Commentary-The-Future-of-the-Goldstone-Report-Can-the-UN-Implement-International-Law-

Singh R (2006) Raising the Stakes: Evidentiary Issues in Individual Claims Before the United Nations Compensation Committee. In: Permanent Court of Arbitration (ed) Redressing Injustices Through Mass Claims Processes. Oxford University Press, Oxford

---

[23] In many cases the Goldstone Mission found that acts entailing individual criminal responsibility have been committed. See Goldstone report, para 172.

Documents Attached to Part II

Document [1] UN Human Rights Council Resolution S-9/1

UNITED
NATIONS

 General Assembly

A/HRC/RES/S-9/1
12 January 2009

S-9/1. **The grave violations of human rights in the Occupied Palestinian Territory, particularly due to the recent Israeli military attacks against the occupied Gaza Strip**

The Human Rights Council,

Guided by the principles and objectives of the Charter of the United Nations and the Universal Declaration of Human Rights,

Acknowledging that peace, security, development and human rights are the pillars of the United Nations system,

Guided by the right to self-determination of the Palestinian people and the inadmissibility of the acquisition of land by the use of force, as enshrined in the Charter of the United Nations,

Recalling General Assembly resolution 60/251 of 15 March 2006,

Affirming the applicability of international human rights law to the Occupied Palestinian Territory, including East Jerusalem,

Affirming also the applicability of international humanitarian law, namely the Fourth Geneva Convention relative to the Protection of Civilian Persons in Time of War, to the Occupied Palestinian Territory, including East Jerusalem,

Emphasizing that international human rights law and international humanitarian law are complementary and mutually reinforcing,

Recalling the obligations of the High Contracting Parties to the Fourth Geneva Convention,

Reaffirming that each High Contracting Party to the Fourth Geneva Convention relative to the Protection of Civilian Persons in Time of War is under the obligation to respect and ensure the respect for the obligations arising from that Convention,

Stressing that the right to life constitutes the most fundamental of all human rights,

Expressing serious concern at the lack of implementation by the occupying Power, Israel, of previously adopted resolutions and recommendations of the Council relating to the human rights situation in the Occupied Palestinian Territory, including East Jerusalem,

Recognizing that the massive ongoing Israeli military operation in the Occupied Palestinian Territory, particularly in the occupied Gaza Strip, has caused grave violations of the human rights of the Palestinian civilians therein, exacerbated the severe humanitarian crisis in the Occupied Palestinian Territory and undermined international efforts towards achieving a just and lasting peace in the region,

Condemning all forms of violence against civilians and deploring the loss of human lives in the context of the current situation,

Recognizing that the Israeli siege imposed on the occupied Gaza Strip, including the closure of border crossings and the cutting of the supply of fuel, food and medicine, constitutes collective punishment of Palestinian civilians and leads to disastrous humanitarian and environmental consequences,

1. *Strongly condemns* the ongoing Israeli military operation carried out in the Occupied Palestinian Territory, particularly in the occupied Gaza Strip, which has resulted in massive violations of the human rights of the Palestinian people and systematic destruction of Palestinian infrastructure;

2. *Calls for* the immediate cessation of Israeli military attacks throughout the Palestinian Occupied Territory, particularly in the occupied Gaza Strip, which to date have resulted in the killing of more than nine hundred and injury to more than four thousand Palestinians, including a large number of women and children, and the end to the launching of crude rockets against Israeli civilians, which have resulted in the loss of four civilian lives and some injuries;

3. *Demands* that the occupying Power, Israel, immediately withdraw its military forces from the occupied Gaza Strip;

4. *Calls upon* the occupying Power, Israel, to end its occupation of all Palestinian lands occupied since 1967 and to respect its commitment within the peace process towards the establishment of the independent sovereign Palestinian State, with East Jerusalem as its capital, living in peace and security with all its neighbors;

5. *Demands* that the occupying Power, Israel, stop the targeting of civilians and medical facilities and staff and the systematic destruction of the cultural heritage of the Palestinian people, in addition to the destruction of public and private properties, as laid down in the Fourth Geneva Convention;

6. *Also demands* that the occupying Power, Israel, lift its siege, open all borders to allow access and free movement of humanitarian aid to the occupied Gaza Strip, including the immediate

establishment of humanitarian corridors, in compliance with its obligations under international humanitarian law, and ensure free access of the media to areas of conflict through media corridors;

7. *Calls upon* the international community to support the current initiative aiming at putting an immediate end to the current military aggression in Gaza;

8. *Calls for* urgent international action to put an immediate end to the grave violations committed by the occupying Power, Israel, in the Occupied Palestinian Territory, particularly in the occupied Gaza Strip;

9. *Also calls for* immediate international protection of the Palestinian people in the Occupied Palestinian Territory, in compliance with international human rights law and international humanitarian law;

10. *Urges* all parties concerned to respect the rules of international human rights law and international humanitarian law and to refrain from violence against the civilian population;

11. *Requests* the United Nations High Commissioner for Human Rights to report on the violations of human rights of the Palestinian people by the occupying Power, Israel, by:

(*a*) Strengthening the field presence of the Office of the High Commission in the Occupied Palestinian Territory, particularly in the occupied Gaza Strip, and deploying the necessary personnel and expertise to monitor and document Israeli violations of the human rights of Palestinians and the destruction of their properties;

(*b*) Submitting periodic reports to the Council on the implementation of the present resolution;

12. *Requests* all relevant special procedures mandate-holders, in particular the Special Rapporteur on the situation of human rights in the Palestinian territories occupied since 1967, the Special Rapporteur on the right of everyone to the enjoyment of the highest attainable standard of physical and mental health, the Special Representative of the Secretary-General for Children and Armed Conflict, the Special Rapporteur on violence against women, its causes and consequences, the Special Representative of the Secretary-General on the human rights of internally displaced persons, the Special Rapporteur on adequate housing as a component of the right to an adequate standard of living, and on the right to non-discrimination in this context, the Special Rapporteur on the right to food, the Special Rapporteur on extrajudicial, arbitrary or summary executions, the Special Rapporteur on the right to education and the independent expert on the question of human rights and extreme poverty, to urgently seek and gather information on violations of the human rights of the Palestinian people and submit their reports to the Council at its next session;

13. *Requests* the occupying Power, Israel, to fully cooperate with all the above-mentioned special procedures mandate-holders and to desist from any further hindrance to the work of the Special Rapporteur on the situation of human rights in the Palestinian territories occupied since 1967;

14. *Decides* to dispatch an urgent, independent international fact-finding mission, to be appointed by the President of the Council, to investigate all violations of international human rights law and international humanitarian law by the occupying Power, Israel, against the Palestinian people throughout the Occupied Palestinian Territory, particularly in the occupied Gaza Strip, due to the current aggression, and calls upon Israel not to obstruct the process of investigation and to fully cooperate with the mission;

15. *Requests* the Secretary-General and the High Commissioner to provide all administrative, technical and logistical assistance required to enable the above-mentioned special procedures mandate-holders and the fact-finding mission to fulfil their mandates promptly and efficiently;

16. *Requests* the Secretary-General to investigate the latest targeting of facilities of the United Nations Relief and Works Agency for Palestine Refugees in the Near East in Gaza, including schools, which resulted in the killing of tens of Palestinian civilians, including women and children, and to submit a report to the General Assembly thereon;

17. *Decides* to follow up on the implementation of the present resolution at its next session.

3rd meeting
12 January 2009

Resolution adopted by a recorded vote of 33 to 1, with 13 abstentions; see Chapter II. The voting was as follows:

In favour: Angola, Argentina, Azerbaijan, Bahrain, Bangladesh, Bolivia, Brazil, Burkina Faso, Chile, China, Cuba, Djibouti, Egypt, Gabon, Ghana, India, Indonesia, Jordan, Madagascar, Malaysia, Mauritius, Mexico, Nicaragua, Nigeria, Pakistan, Philippines, Qatar, Russian Federation, Saudi Arabia, Senegal, South Africa, Uruguay, Zambia.

Against: Canada.

Abstaining: Bosnia and Herzegovina, Cameroon, France, Germany, Italy, Japan, Netherlands, Republic of Korea, Slovakia, Slovenia, Switzerland, Ukraine, United Kingdom of Great Britain and Northern Ireland.

Document [2] Report of the UN Fact Finding Mission - Executive Summary

UNITED NATIONS

 General Assembly

Distr.
GENERAL

A/HRC/12/48 (ADVANCE 1)
23 September 2009

Original: ENGLISH

HUMAN RIGHTS COUNCIL
Twelfth session
Agenda item 7

HUMAN RIGHTS IN PALESTINE AND OTHER OCCUPIED ARAB TERRITORIES

Report of the United Nations Fact Finding Mission on the Gaza Conflict

Executive summary[*]

---

[*] The present document is an advance translation and contains the executive summary only. The full report will be issued as A/HRC/12/48 in all languages according to translation capacity of the United Nations translation services.

GE.09-15795

A/HRC/12/48 (ADVANCE 1)
page 2

A. Introduction

1. On 3 April 2009, the President of the Human Rights Council established the United Nations Fact Finding Mission on the Gaza Conflict with the mandate "to investigate all violations of international human rights law and international humanitarian law that might have been committed at any time in the context of the military operations that were conducted in Gaza during the period from 27 December 2008 and 18 January 2009, whether before, during or after."

2. The President appointed Justice Richard Goldstone, former judge of the Constitutional Court of South Africa and former Prosecutor of the International Criminal Tribunals for the former Yugoslavia and Rwanda, to head the Mission. The other three appointed members were: Professor Christine Chinkin, Professor of International Law at the London School of Economics and Political Science, who was a member of the high-level fact-finding mission to Beit Hanoun (2008); Ms. Hina Jilani, Advocate of the Supreme Court of Pakistan and former Special Representative of the Secretary-General on the situation of human rights defenders, who was a member of the International Commission of Inquiry on Darfur (2004); and Colonel Desmond Travers, a former Officer in Ireland's Defence Forces and member of the Board of Directors of the Institute for International Criminal Investigations.

3. As is usual practice, the Office of the United Nations High Commissioner for Human Rights (OHCHR) established a secretariat to support the Mission.

4. The Mission interpreted the mandate as requiring it to place the civilian population of the region at the centre of its concerns regarding the violations of international law.

5. The Mission convened for the first time in Geneva between 4 and 8 May 2009. Additionally, the Mission met in Geneva on 20 May, on 4 and 5 July, and between 1 and 4 August 2009. The Mission conducted three field visits: two to the Gaza Strip between 30 May and 6 June, and between 25 June and 1 July 2009; and one visit to Amman on 2 and 3 July 2009. Several staff of the Mission's secretariat were deployed in Gaza from 22 May to 4 July 2009 to conduct field investigations.

6. Notes verbales were sent to all Member States of the United Nations and United Nations organs and bodies on 7 May 2009. On 8 June 2009, the Mission issued a call for submissions inviting all interested persons and organizations to submit relevant information and documentation to assist in the implementation of its mandate.

7. Public hearings were held in Gaza on 28 and 29 June and in Geneva on 6 and 7 July 2009.

8. The Mission repeatedly sought to obtain the cooperation of the Government of Israel. After numerous attempts had failed, the Mission sought and obtained the assistance of the Government of Egypt to enable it to enter the Gaza Strip through the Rafah crossing.

9. The Mission has enjoyed the support and cooperation of the Palestinian Authority and of the Permanent Observer Mission of Palestine to the United Nations. Due to the lack of cooperation from the Israeli Government, the Mission was unable to meet members of the Palestinian Authority in the West Bank. The Mission did, however, meet officials of the

A/HRC/12/48 (ADVANCE 1)
page 3

Palestinian Authority, including a cabinet minister, in Amman. During its visits to the Gaza Strip, the Mission held meetings with senior members of the Gaza authorities and they extended their full cooperation and support to the Mission.

10. Subsequent to the public hearings in Geneva, the Mission was informed that a Palestinian participant, Mr. Muhammad Srour, had been detained by Israeli security forces when returning to the West Bank and became concerned that his detention may have been a consequence of his appearance before the Mission. The Mission is in contact with him and continues to monitor developments.

B. Methodology

11. To implement its mandate, the Mission determined that it was required to consider any actions by all parties that might have constituted violations of international human rights law or international humanitarian law. The mandate also required it to review related actions in the entire Occupied Palestinian Territory and Israel.

12. With regard to temporal scope, the Mission decided to focus primarily on events, actions or circumstances occurring since 19 June 2008, when a ceasefire was agreed between the Government of Israel and Hamas. The Mission has also taken into consideration matters occurring after the end of military operations that constitute continuing human rights and international humanitarian law violations related to or as a consequence of the military operations, up to 31 July 2009.

13. The Mission also analysed the historical context of the events that led to the military operations in Gaza between 27 December 2008 and 18 January 2009 and the links between these operations and overarching Israeli policies vis-à-vis the Occupied Palestinian Territory.

14. The Mission considered that the reference in its mandate to violations committed "in the context" of the December–January military operations required it to include restrictions on human rights and fundamental freedoms relating to Israel's strategies and actions in the context of its military operations.

15. The normative framework for the Mission has been general international law, the Charter of the United Nations, international humanitarian law, international human rights law and international criminal law.

16. This report does not purport to be exhaustive in documenting the very high number of relevant incidents that occurred in the period covered by the Mission's mandate. Nevertheless, the Mission considers that the report is illustrative of the main patterns of violations. In Gaza, the Mission investigated 36 incidents.

17. The Mission based its work on an independent and impartial analysis of compliance by the parties with their obligations under international human rights and humanitarian law in the context of the recent conflict in Gaza, and on international investigative standards developed by the United Nations.

18. The Mission adopted an inclusive approach to gathering information and seeking views. Information-gathering methods included: (a) the review of reports from different sources; (b)

A/HRC/12/48 (ADVANCE 1)
page 4

interviews with victims, witnesses and other persons having relevant information; (c) site visits to specific locations in Gaza where incidents had occurred; (d) the analysis of video and photographic images, including satellite imagery; (e) the review of medical reports about injuries to victims; (f) the forensic analysis of weapons and ammunition remnants collected at incident sites; (g) meetings with a variety of interlocutors; (h) invitations to provide information relating to the Mission's investigation requirements; (i) the wide circulation of a public call for written submissions; (j) public hearings in Gaza and in Geneva.

19. The Mission conducted 188 individual interviews. It reviewed more than 300 reports, submissions and other documentation either researched of its own motion, received in reply to its call for submissions and notes verbales or provided during meetings or otherwise, amounting to more than 10,000 pages, over 30 videos and 1,200 photographs.

20. By refusing to cooperate with the Mission, the Government of Israel prevented it from meeting Israeli Government officials, but also from travelling to Israel to meet Israeli victims and to the West Bank to meet Palestinian Authority representatives and Palestinian victims.

21. The Mission conducted field visits, including investigations of incident sites, in the Gaza Strip. This allowed the Mission to observe first-hand the situation on the ground, and speak to many witnesses and other relevant persons.

22. The purpose of the public hearings, which were broadcast live, was to enable victims, witnesses and experts from all sides to the conflict to speak directly to as many people as possible in the region as well as in the international community. The Mission gave priority to the participation of victims and people from the affected communities. The 38 public testimonies covered facts as well as legal and military matters. The Mission had initially intended to hold hearings in Gaza, Israel and the West Bank. However, denial of access to Israel and the West Bank resulted in the decision to hold hearings of participants from Israel and the West Bank in Geneva.

23. In establishing its findings, the Mission sought to rely primarily and whenever possible on information it gathered first-hand. Information produced by others, including reports, affidavits and media reports, was used primarily as corroboration.

24. The Mission's final conclusions on the reliability of the information received were based on its own assessment of the credibility and reliability of the witnesses it met, verifying the sources and the methodology used in the reports and documents produced by others, cross-referencing the relevant material and information, and assessing whether, in all the circumstances, there was sufficient credible and reliable information for the Mission to make a finding in fact.

25. On this basis, the Mission has, to the best of its ability, determined what facts have been established. In many cases it has found that acts entailing individual criminal responsibility have been committed. In all of these cases the Mission has found that there is sufficient information to establish the objective elements of the crimes in question. In almost all of the cases the Mission has also been able to determine whether or not it appears that the acts in question were done deliberately or recklessly or in the knowledge that the consequence that resulted would result in the ordinary course of events. The Mission has thus referred in many cases to the relevant fault

A/HRC/12/48 (ADVANCE 1)
page 5

element (mens rea). The Mission fully appreciates the importance of the presumption of innocence: the findings in the report do not subvert the operation of that principle. The findings do not attempt to identify the individuals responsible for the commission of offences nor do they pretend to reach the standard of proof applicable in criminal trials.

26. In order to provide the parties concerned with an opportunity to submit additional relevant information and express their position and respond to allegations, the Mission also submitted comprehensive lists of questions to the Government of Israel, the Palestinian Authority and the Gaza authorities in advance of completing its analysis and findings. The Mission received replies from the Palestinian Authority and the Gaza authorities but not from Israel.

C. Facts investigated by the Mission, factual and legal findings

The Occupied Palestinian Territory: the Gaza Strip

1. The blockade

27. The Mission focused (chap. V) on the process of economic and political isolation imposed by Israel on the Gaza Strip, generally referred to as a blockade. The blockade comprises measures such as restrictions on the goods that can be imported into Gaza and the closure of border crossings for people, goods and services, sometimes for days, including cuts in the provision of fuel and electricity. Gaza's economy is further severely affected by the reduction of the fishing zone open to Palestinian fishermen and the establishment of a buffer zone along the border between Gaza and Israel, which reduces the land available for agriculture and industry. In addition to creating an emergency situation, the blockade has significantly weakened the capacities of the population and of the health, water and other public sectors to respond to the emergency created by the military operations.

28. The Mission holds the view that Israel continues to be duty-bound under the Fourth Geneva Convention and to the full extent of the means available to it to ensure the supply of foodstuff, medical and hospital items and other goods to meet the humanitarian needs of the population of the Gaza Strip without qualification.

2. Overview of Israel's military operations in the Gaza Strip and casualties

29. Israel deployed its navy, air force and army in the operation it codenamed "Operation Cast Lead". The military operations in the Gaza Strip included two main phases, the air phase and the air-land phase, and lasted from 27 December 2008 to 18 January 2009. The Israeli offensive began with a week-long air attack, from 27 December until 3 January 2009. The air force continued to play an important role in assisting and covering the ground forces from 3 January to 18 January 2009. The army was responsible for the ground invasion, which began on 3 January 2009, when ground troops entered Gaza from the north and the east. The available information indicates that the Golani, Givati and Paratrooper Brigades and five Armoured Corps Brigades were involved. The navy was used in part to shell the Gaza coast during the operations. Chapter VI also locates the incidents investigated by the Mission, described in chapters VII to XV, in the context of the military operations.

A/HRC/12/48 (ADVANCE 1)
page 6

30. Statistics about Palestinians who lost their lives during the military operations vary. Based on extensive field research, non-governmental organizations place the overall number of persons killed between 1,387 and 1,417. The Gaza authorities report 1,444 fatalities. The Government of Israel provides a figure of 1,166. The data provided by non-governmental sources on the percentage of civilians among those killed are generally consistent and raise very serious concerns about the way Israel conducted the military operations in Gaza.

31. According to the Government of Israel, during the military operations there were four Israeli fatalities in southern Israel, of whom three were civilians and one a soldier. They were killed by rocket and mortar attacks by Palestinian armed groups. In addition, nine Israeli soldiers were killed during the fighting inside the Gaza strip, four of whom as a result of friendly fire.

3. Attacks by Israeli forces on government buildings and persons of the Gaza authorities, including police

32. The Israeli armed forces launched numerous attacks against buildings and persons of the Gaza authorities. As far as attacks on buildings are concerned, the Mission examined the Israeli strikes against the Palestinian Legislative Council building and the Gaza main prison (chap. VII). Both buildings were destroyed and can no longer be used. Statements by Israeli Government and armed forces representatives justified the attacks arguing that political and administrative institutions in Gaza are part of the "Hamas terrorist infrastructure". The Mission rejects this position. It finds that there is no evidence that the Legislative Council building and the Gaza main prison made an effective contribution to military action. On the information available to it, the Mission finds that the attacks on these buildings constituted deliberate attacks on civilian objects in violation of the rule of customary international humanitarian law whereby attacks must be strictly limited to military objectives. These facts further indicate the commission of the grave breach of extensive destruction of property, not justified by military necessity and carried out unlawfully and wantonly.

33. The Mission examined the attacks against six police facilities, four of them during the first minutes of the military operations on 27 December 2008, resulting in the death of 99 policemen and nine members of the public. Overall, the approximately 240 policemen killed by Israeli forces constitute more than one sixth of the Palestinian casualties. The circumstances of the attacks seem to indicate, and the Government of Israel's July 2009 report on the military operations confirm, that the policemen were deliberately targeted and killed on the ground that the police, as an institution or a large part of the policemen individually, are, in the Government of Israel's view, part of the Palestinian military forces in Gaza.

34. To examine whether the attacks against the police were compatible with the principle of distinction between civilian and military objects and persons, the Mission analysed the institutional development of the Gaza police since Hamas took complete control of Gaza in July 2007 and merged the Gaza police with the "Executive Force" it had created after its election victory. The Mission finds that, while a great number of the Gaza policemen were recruited among Hamas supporters or members of Palestinian armed groups, the Gaza police were a civilian law-enforcement agency. The Mission also concludes that the policemen killed on 27 December 2008 cannot be said to have been taking a direct part in hostilities and thus did not lose their civilian immunity from direct attack as civilians on this basis. The Mission accepts that there may be individual members of the Gaza police that were at the same time members of

Palestinian armed groups and thus combatants. It concludes, however, that the attacks against the police facilities on the first day of the armed operations failed to strike an acceptable balance between the direct military advantage anticipated (i.e. the killing of those policemen who may have been members of Palestinian armed groups) and the loss of civilian life (i.e. the other policemen killed and members of the public who would inevitably have been present or in the vicinity), and therefore violated international humanitarian law.

4. Obligation on Palestinian armed groups in Gaza to take feasible precautions to protect the civilian population and civilian objects

35. The Mission examined whether and to what extent the Palestinian armed groups violated their obligation to exercise care and take all feasible precautions to protect the civilian population in Gaza from the inherent dangers of the military operations (chap. VIII). The Mission was faced with a certain reluctance by the persons it interviewed in Gaza to discuss the activities of the armed groups. On the basis of the information gathered, the Mission found that Palestinian armed groups were present in urban areas during the military operations and launched rockets from urban areas. It may be that the Palestinian combatants did not at all times adequately distinguish themselves from the civilian population. The Mission found no evidence, however, to suggest that Palestinian armed groups either directed civilians to areas where attacks were being launched or that they forced civilians to remain within the vicinity of the attacks.

36. Although the incidents investigated by the Mission did not establish the use of mosques for military purposes or to shield military activities, it cannot exclude that this might have occurred in other cases. The Mission did not find any evidence to support the allegations that hospital facilities were used by the Gaza authorities or by Palestinian armed groups to shield military activities or that ambulances were used to transport combatants or for other military purposes. On the basis of its own investigations and the statements by United Nations officials, the Mission excludes that Palestinian armed groups engaged in combat activities from United Nations facilities that were used as shelters during the military operations. The Mission cannot, however, discount the possibility that Palestinian armed groups were active in the vicinity of such United Nations facilities and hospitals. While the conduct of hostilities in built-up areas does not, of itself, constitute a violation of international law, Palestinian armed groups, where they launched attacks close to civilian or protected buildings, unnecessarily exposed the civilian population of Gaza to danger.

5. Obligation on Israel to take feasible precautions to protect the civilian population and civilian objects in Gaza

37. The Mission examined how the Israeli armed forces discharged their obligation to take all feasible precautions to protect the civilian population of Gaza, including particularly the obligation to give effective advance warning of attacks (chap. IX). The Mission acknowledges the significant efforts made by Israel to issue warnings through telephone calls, leaflets and radio broadcasts, and accepts that in some cases, particularly when the warnings were sufficiently specific, they encouraged residents to leave an area and get out of harm's way. However, the Mission also notes factors that significantly undermined the effectiveness of the warnings issued. These include the lack of specificity and thus credibility of many pre-recorded phone messages and leaflets. The credibility of instructions to move to city centres for safety was also diminished by the fact that the city centres themselves had been the subject of intense attacks during the air

phase of the military operations. The Mission also examined the practice of dropping lighter explosives on roofs (so-called roof knocking). It concludes that this technique is not effective as a warning and constitutes a form of attack against the civilians inhabiting the building. Finally, the Mission stresses that the fact that a warning was issued does not relieve commanders and their subordinates of taking all other feasible measures to distinguish between civilians and combatants.

38. The Mission also examined the precautions taken by the Israeli armed forces in the context of three specific attacks they launched. On 15 January 2009, the field office compound of the United Nations Relief and Works Agency for Palestine Refugees in the Near East (UNRWA) in Gaza City came under shelling with high explosive and white phosphorous munitions. The Mission notes that the attack was extremely dangerous, as the compound offered shelter to between 600 and 700 civilians and contained a huge fuel depot. The Israeli armed forces continued their attack over several hours despite having been fully alerted to the risks they created. The Mission concludes that the Israeli armed forces violated the requirement under customary international law to take all feasible precautions in the choice of means and method of attack with a view to avoiding and in any event minimizing incidental loss of civilian life, injury to civilians and damage to civilian objects.

39. The Mission also finds that, on the same day, the Israeli armed forces directly and intentionally attacked al-Quds hospital in Gaza City and the adjacent ambulance depot with white phosphorous shells. The attack caused fires which took a whole day to extinguish and caused panic among the sick and wounded who had to be evacuated. The Mission finds that no warning was given at any point of an imminent strike. On the basis of its investigation, the Mission rejects the allegation that fire was directed at the Israeli armed forces from within the hospital.

40. The Mission also examined the intense artillery attacks, again including white phosphorous munitions, on al-Wafa hospital in eastern Gaza City, a facility for patients receiving long-term care and suffering from particularly serious injuries. On the basis of the information gathered, the Mission found a violation of the prohibition of attacks on civilian hospitals in both cases. The Mission also highlights that the warnings given by leaflets and pre-recorded phone messages in the case of al-Wafa hospital demonstrate the complete ineffectiveness of certain kinds of routine and generic warnings.

6. Indiscriminate attacks by Israeli forces resulting in the loss of life and injury to civilians

41. The Mission examined the mortar shelling of al-Fakhura junction in Jabaliyah next to a UNRWA school, which, at the time, was sheltering more than 1,300 people (chap. X). The Israeli armed forces launched at least four mortar shells. One landed in the courtyard of a family home, killing 11 people assembled there. Three other shells landed on al-Fakhura Street, killing at least a further 24 people and injuring as many as 40. The Mission examined in detail statements by Israeli Government representatives alleging that the attack was launched in response to a mortar attack from an armed Palestinian group. While the Mission does not exclude that this may have been the case, it considers the credibility of Israel's position damaged by the series of inconsistencies, contradictions and factual inaccuracies in the statements justifying the attack.

42. In drawing its legal conclusions on the attack on al-Fakhura junction, the Mission recognizes that, for all armies, decisions on proportionality, weighing the military advantage to be gained against the risk of killing civilians, will present very genuine dilemmas in certain cases. The Mission does not consider this to be such a case. The firing of at least four mortar shells to attempt to kill a small number of specified individuals in a setting where large numbers of civilians were going about their daily business and 1,368 people were sheltering nearby cannot meet the test of what a reasonable commander would have determined to be an acceptable loss of civilian life for the military advantage sought. The Mission thus considers the attack to have been indiscriminate, in violation of international law, and to have violated the right to life of the Palestinian civilians killed in these incidents.

7. Deliberate attacks against the civilian population

43. The Mission investigated 11 incidents in which the Israeli armed forces launched direct attacks against civilians with lethal outcome (chap. XI). The facts in all bar one of the attacks indicate no justifiable military objective. The first two are attacks on houses in the al-Samouni neighbourhood south of Gaza City, including the shelling of a house in which Palestinian civilians had been forced to assemble by the Israeli armed forces. The following group of seven incidents concern the shooting of civilians while they were trying to leave their homes to walk to a safer place, waving white flags and, in some of the cases, following an injunction from the Israeli forces to do so. The facts gathered by the Mission indicate that all the attacks occurred under circumstances in which the Israeli armed forces were in control of the area and had previously entered into contact with or had at least observed the persons they subsequently attacked, so that they must have been aware of their civilian status. In the majority of these incidents, the consequences of the Israeli attacks against civilians were aggravated by their subsequent refusal to allow the evacuation of the wounded or to permit access to ambulances.

44. These incidents indicate that the instructions given to the Israeli armed forces moving into Gaza provided for a low threshold for the use of lethal fire against the civilian population. The Mission found strong corroboration of this trend in the testimonies of Israeli soldiers collected in two publications it reviewed.

45. The Mission further examined an incident in which a mosque was targeted with a missile during early evening prayers, resulting in the death of 15 people, and an attack with flechette munitions on a crowd of family and neighbours at a condolence tent, killing five. The Mission finds that both attacks constitute intentional attacks against the civilian population and civilian objects.

46. From the facts ascertained in all the above cases, the Mission finds that the conduct of the Israeli armed forces constitutes grave breaches of the Fourth Geneva Convention in respect of wilful killings and wilfully causing great suffering to protected persons and, as such, give rise to individual criminal responsibility. It also finds that the direct targeting and arbitrary killing of Palestinian civilians is a violation of the right to life.

47. The last incident concerns the bombing of a house resulting in the killing of 22 family members. Israel's position in this case is that there was an "operational error" and that the intended target was a neighbouring house storing weapons. On the basis of its investigation, the Mission expresses significant doubts about the Israeli authorities' account of the incident. The

A/HRC/12/48 (ADVANCE 1)
page 10

Mission concludes that, if a mistake was indeed made, there could not be said to be a case of wilful killing. State responsibility of Israel for an internationally wrongful act would, however, remain.

8. The use of certain weapons

48. Based on its investigation of incidents involving the use of certain weapons such as white phosphorous and flechette missiles, the Mission, while accepting that white phosphorous is not at this stage proscribed under international law, finds that the Israeli armed forces were systematically reckless in determining its use in built-up areas. Moreover, doctors who treated patients with white phosphorous wounds spoke about the severity and sometimes untreatable nature of the burns caused by the substance. The Mission believes that serious consideration should be given to banning the use of white phosphorous in built-up areas. As to flechettes, the Mission notes that they are an area weapon incapable of discriminating between objectives after detonation. They are, therefore, particularly unsuitable for use in urban settings where there is reason to believe civilians may be present.

49. While the Mission is not in a position to state with certainty that so-called dense inert metal explosive (DIME) munitions were used by the Israeli armed forces, it did receive reports from Palestinian and foreign doctors who had operated in Gaza during the military operations of a high percentage of patients with injuries compatible with their impact. DIME weapons and weapons armed with heavy metal are not prohibited under international law as it currently stands, but do raise specific health concerns. Finally, the Mission received allegations that depleted and non-depleted uranium were used by the Israeli armed forces in Gaza. These allegations were not further investigated by the Mission.

9. Attacks on the foundations of civilian life in Gaza: destruction of industrial infrastructure, food production, water installations, sewage treatment plants and housing

50. The Mission investigated several incidents involving the destruction of industrial infrastructure, food production, water installations, sewage treatment plants and housing (chap. XIII). Already at the beginning of the military operations, el-Bader flour mill was the only flour mill in the Gaza Strip still operating. The flour mill was hit by a series of air strikes on 9 January 2009, after several false warnings had been issued on previous days. The Mission finds that its destruction had no military justification. The nature of the strikes, in particular the precise targeting of crucial machinery, suggests that the intention was to disable the factory's productive capacity. From the facts it ascertained, the Mission finds that there has been a violation of the grave breaches provisions of the Fourth Geneva Convention. Unlawful and wanton destruction which is not justified by military necessity amounts to a war crime. The Mission also finds that the destruction of the mill was carried out to deny sustenance to the civilian population, which is a violation of customary international law and may constitute a war crime. The strike on the flour mill furthermore constitutes a violation of the right to adequate food and means of subsistence.

51. The chicken farms of Mr. Sameh Sawafeary in the Zeytoun neighbourhood south of Gaza City reportedly supplied over 10 per cent of the Gaza egg market. Armoured bulldozers of the Israeli armed forces systematically flattened the chicken coops, killing all 31,000 chickens inside, and destroyed the plant and material necessary for the business. The Mission concludes

that this was a deliberate act of wanton destruction not justified by any military necessity and draws the same legal conclusions as in the case of the destruction of the flour mill.

52. The Israeli armed forces also carried out a strike against a wall of one of the raw sewage lagoons of the Gaza wastewater treatment plant, which caused the outflow of more than 200,000 cubic metres of raw sewage onto neighbouring farmland. The circumstances of the strike suggest that it was deliberate and premeditated. The Namar wells complex in Jabaliyah consisted of two water wells, pumping machines, a generator, fuel storage, a reservoir chlorination unit, buildings and related equipment. All were destroyed by multiple air strikes on the first day of the Israeli aerial attack. The Mission considers it unlikely that a target the size of the Namar wells could have been hit by multiple strikes in error. It found no grounds to suggest that there was any military advantage to be had by hitting the wells and noted that there was no suggestion that Palestinian armed groups had used the wells for any purpose. Considering that the right to drinking water is part of the right to adequate food, the Mission makes the same legal findings as in the case of the el-Bader flour mill.

53. During its visits to the Gaza Strip, the Mission witnessed the extent of the destruction of residential housing caused by air strikes, mortar and artillery shelling, missile strikes, the operation of bulldozers and demolition charges. In some cases, residential neighbourhoods were subjected to air-launched bombing and to intensive shelling apparently in the context of the advance of Israeli ground forces. In others, the facts gathered by the Mission strongly suggest that the destruction of housing was carried out in the absence of any link to combat engagements with Palestinian armed groups or any other effective contribution to military action. Combining the results of its own fact-finding on the ground with UNOSAT satellite imagery and the published testimonies of Israeli soldiers, the Mission concludes that, in addition to the extensive destruction of housing for so-called operational necessity during their advance, the Israeli armed forces engaged in another wave of systematic destruction of civilian buildings during the last three days of their presence in Gaza, aware of their imminent withdrawal. The conduct of the Israeli armed forces in this respect violated the principle of distinction between civilian and military objects and amounted to the grave breach of "extensive destruction... of property, not justified by military necessity and carried out unlawfully and wantonly". The Israeli armed forces furthermore violated the right to adequate housing of the families concerned.

54. The attacks on industrial facilities, food production and water infrastructure investigated by the Mission are part of a broader pattern of destruction, which includes the destruction of the only cement-packaging plant in Gaza (the Atta Abu Jubbah plant), the Abu Eida factories for ready-mix concrete, further chicken farms and the al-Wadiyah Group's food and drinks factories. The facts ascertained by the Mission indicate that there was a deliberate and systematic policy on the part of the Israeli armed forces to target industrial sites and water installations.

10. The use of Palestinian civilians as human shields

55. The Mission investigated four incidents in which the Israeli armed forces coerced Palestinian civilian men at gunpoint to take part in house searches during the military operations (chap. XIV). The men were blindfolded and handcuffed as they were forced to enter houses ahead of the Israeli soldiers. In one of the incidents, Israeli soldiers repeatedly forced a man to enter a house in which Palestinian combatants were hiding. Published testimonies of Israeli soldiers who took part in the military operations confirm the continuation of this practice, despite

clear orders from Israel's High Court to the armed forces to put an end to it and repeated public assurances from the armed forces that the practice had been discontinued. The Mission concludes that this practice amounts to the use of Palestinian civilians as human shields and is therefore prohibited by international humanitarian law. It puts the right to life of the civilians at risk in an arbitrary and unlawful manner and constitutes cruel and inhuman treatment. The use of human shields also is a war crime. The Palestinian men used as human shields were questioned under threat of death or injury to extract information about Hamas, Palestinian combatants and tunnels. This constitutes a further violation of international humanitarian law.

11. Deprivation of liberty: Gazans detained during the Israeli military operations of 27 December 2008 to 18 January 2009

56. During the military operations, the Israeli armed forces rounded up large numbers of civilians and detained them in houses and open spaces in Gaza and, in the case of many Palestinian men, also took them to detention facilities in Israel. In the cases investigated by the Mission, the facts gathered indicate that none of the civilians was armed or posed any apparent threat to the Israeli soldiers. Chapter XV of the report is based on the Mission's interviews with Palestinian men who were detained, as well as on its review of other relevant material, including interviews with relatives and statements from other victims submitted to it.

57. From the facts gathered, the Mission finds that numerous violations of international humanitarian law and human rights law were committed in the context of these detentions. Civilians, including women and children, were detained in degrading conditions, deprived of food, water and access to sanitary facilities, and exposed to the elements in January without any shelter. The men were handcuffed, blindfolded and repeatedly made to strip, sometimes naked, at different stages of their detention.

58. In the al-Atatra area in north-western Gaza, Israeli troops had dug out sandpits in which Palestinian men, women and children were detained. Israeli tanks and artillery positions were located inside the sandpits and around them and fired from next to the detainees.

59. The Palestinian men who were taken to detention facilities in Israel were subjected to degrading conditions of detention, harsh interrogation, beatings and other physical and mental abuse. Some of them were charged with being unlawful combatants. Those interviewed by the Mission were released after the proceedings against them had apparently been discontinued.

60. In addition to arbitrary deprivation of liberty and violation of due process rights, the cases of the detained Palestinian civilians highlight a common thread of the interaction between Israeli soldiers and Palestinian civilians which also emerged clearly in many cases discussed elsewhere in the report: continuous and systematic abuse, outrages on personal dignity, humiliating and degrading treatment contrary to fundamental principles of international humanitarian law and human rights law. The Mission concludes that this treatment constitutes the infliction of a collective penalty on these civilians and amounts to measures of intimidation and terror. Such acts are grave breaches of the Geneva Conventions and constitute a war crime.

12. Objectives and strategy of Israel's military operations in Gaza

61. The Mission reviewed available information on the planning of the Israeli military operations in Gaza, on the advanced military technology available to the Israeli armed forces and on their training in international humanitarian law (chap. XVI). According to official Government information, the Israeli armed forces have an elaborate legal advice and training system in place, which seeks to ensure knowledge of the relevant legal obligations and support to commanders for compliance in the field. The Israeli armed forces possess very advanced hardware and are also a market leader in the production of some of the most advanced pieces of military technology available, including unmanned aviation vehicles (UAVs). They have a very significant capacity for precision strikes by a variety of methods, including aerial and ground launches. Taking into account the ability to plan, the means to execute plans with the most developed technology available, and statements by the Israeli military that almost no errors occurred, the Mission finds that the incidents and patterns of events considered in the report are the result of deliberate planning and policy decisions.

62. The tactics used by the Israeli armed forces in the Gaza offensive are consistent with previous practices, most recently during the Lebanon war in 2006. A concept known as the Dahiya doctrine emerged then, involving the application of disproportionate force and the causing of great damage and destruction to civilian property and infrastructure, and suffering to civilian populations. The Mission concludes from a review of the facts on the ground that it witnessed for itself that what was prescribed as the best strategy appears to have been precisely what was put into practice.

63. In the framing of Israeli military objectives with regard to the Gaza operations, the concept of Hamas' "supporting infrastructure" is particularly worrying as it appears to transform civilians and civilian objects into legitimate targets. Statements by Israeli political and military leaders prior to and during the military operations in Gaza indicate that the Israeli military conception of what was necessary in a war with Hamas viewed disproportionate destruction and creating maximum disruption in the lives of many people as a legitimate means to achieve not only military but also political goals.

64. Statements by Israeli leaders to the effect that the destruction of civilian objects would be justified as a response to rocket attacks ("destroy 100 homes for every rocket fired") indicate the possibility of resorting to reprisals. The Mission is of the view that reprisals against civilians in armed hostilities are contrary to international humanitarian law.

13. The impact of the military operations and of the blockade on the people of Gaza and their human rights

65. The Mission examined the combined impact of the military operations and of the blockade on the Gaza population and its enjoyment of human rights. The economy, employment opportunities and family livelihoods were already severely affected by the blockade when the Israeli offensive began. Insufficient supply of fuel for electricity generation had a negative impact on industrial activity, on the operation of hospitals, on water supply to households and on sewage treatment. Import restrictions and the ban on all exports from Gaza affected the industrial sector and agricultural production. Unemployment levels and the percentage of the population living in poverty or deep poverty were rising.

A/HRC/12/48 (ADVANCE 1)
page 14

66. In this precarious situation, the military operations destroyed a substantial part of the economic infrastructure. As many factories were targeted and destroyed or damaged, poverty, unemployment and food insecurity further increased dramatically. The agricultural sector similarly suffered from the destruction of farmland, water wells and fishing boats during the military operations. The continuation of the blockade impedes the reconstruction of the economic infrastructure that was destroyed.

67. The razing of farmland and the destruction of greenhouses are expected to further worsen food insecurity despite the increased quantities of food items allowed into Gaza since the beginning of the military operations. Dependence on food assistance increases. Levels of stunting and thinness in children and of anaemia prevalence in children and pregnant women were worrying even before the military operations. The hardship caused by the extensive destruction of shelter (the United Nations Development Programme reported 3,354 houses completely destroyed and 11,112 partially damaged) and the resulting displacement particularly affects children and women. The destruction of water and sanitation infrastructure (such as the destruction of the Namar wells and the attack against the water treatment plant described in chapter XIII) aggravated the pre-existing situation. Even before the military operations, 80 per cent of the water supplied in Gaza did not meet the World Health Organization's standards for drinking water. The discharge of untreated or partially treated wastewater into the sea is a further health hazard worsened by the military operations.

68. The military operations and resulting casualties subjected the beleaguered Gaza health sector to additional strain. Hospitals and ambulances were targeted by Israeli attacks. Patients with chronic health conditions could not be given priority in hospitals faced with an influx of patients with life-threatening injuries. Patients injured during the hostilities were often discharged quickly to free beds. The long-term health impact of these early discharges, as well as of weapons containing substances such as tungsten and white phosphorous, remains a source of concern. While the exact number of people who will suffer permanent disabilities is still unknown, the Mission understands that many persons who sustained traumatic injuries during the conflict still face the risk of permanent disability owing to complications and inadequate follow-up and physical rehabilitation.

69. The number of persons suffering from mental health problems is also bound to increase. The Mission investigated a number of incidents in which adults and children witnessed the killing of loved ones. Doctors of the Gaza Community Mental Health Programme gave information to the Mission on psychosomatic disorders, on a widespread state of alienation in the population and on "numbness" as a result of severe loss. They told the Mission that these conditions were in turn likely to increase the readiness to embrace violence and extremism. They also told the Mission that 20 per cent of children in the Gaza Strip suffer from post-traumatic stress disorders.

70. Children's psychological learning difficulties are compounded by the impact of the blockade and the military operations on the education infrastructure. Some 280 schools and kindergartens were destroyed in a situation in which restrictions on the importation of construction materials meant that many school buildings were already in serious need of repair.

71. The Mission's attention was also drawn to the particular manner in which women were affected by the military operations. The cases of women interviewed by the Mission in Gaza dramatically illustrate the suffering caused by the feeling of inability to provide children with the care and security they need. Women's responsibility for the household and the children often forces them to conceal their own sufferings, resulting in their issues remaining unaddressed. The number of women who are the sole breadwinners increased, but their employment opportunities remain significantly inferior to men's. The military operations and increased poverty add to the potential for conflicts in the family and between widows and their in-laws.

72. The Mission acknowledges that the supply of humanitarian goods, particularly foodstuffs, allowed into Gaza by Israel temporarily increased during the military operations. The level of goods allowed into Gaza before the military operations was, however, insufficient to meet the needs of the population even before hostilities started, and has again decreased since the end of the military operations. From the facts ascertained by it, the Mission believes that Israel has violated its obligation to allow free passage of all consignments of medical and hospital objects, food and clothing (article 23 of the Fourth Geneva Convention). The Mission also finds that Israel violated specific obligations which it has as the occupying Power and which are spelled out in the Fourth Geneva Convention, such as the duty to maintain medical and hospital establishments and services and to agree to relief schemes if the occupied territory is not well supplied.

73. The Mission also concludes that in the destruction by the Israeli armed forces of private residential houses, water wells, water tanks, agricultural land and greenhouses there was a specific purpose of denying sustenance to the population of the Gaza Strip. The Mission finds that Israel violated its duty to respect the right of the Gaza population to an adequate standard of living, including access to adequate food, water and housing. The Mission, moreover, finds violations of specific human rights provisions protecting children, particularly those who are victims of armed conflict, women and the disabled.

74. The conditions of life in Gaza, resulting from deliberate actions of the Israeli armed forces and the declared policies of the Government of Israel – as they were presented by its authorized and legitimate representatives – with regard to the Gaza Strip before, during and after the military operation, cumulatively indicate the intention to inflict collective punishment on the people of the Gaza Strip in violation of international humanitarian law.

75. Finally, the Mission considered whether the series of acts that deprive Palestinians in the Gaza Strip of their means of sustenance, employment, housing and water, that deny their freedom of movement and their right to leave and enter their own country, that limit their access to courts of law and effective remedies could amount to persecution, a crime against humanity. From the facts available to it, the Mission is of the view that some of the actions of the Government of Israel might justify a competent court finding that crimes against humanity have been committed.

14. The continuing detention of Israeli soldier Gilad Shalit

76. The Mission notes the continued detention of Gilad Shalit, a member of the Israeli armed forces, captured in 2006 by a Palestinian armed group. In reaction to his capture, the Israeli Government ordered a number of attacks against infrastructure in the Gaza Strip and Palestinian

Authority offices as well as the arrest of eight Palestinian Government ministers and 26 members of the Palestinian Legislative Council. The Mission heard testimonies indicating that, during the military operations of December 2008 – January 2009, Israeli soldiers questioned captured Palestinians about the whereabouts of Gilad Shalit. Gilad Shalit's father, Noam Shalit, appeared before the Mission at the public hearing held in Geneva on 6 July 2009.

77. The Mission is of the opinion that, as a soldier who belongs to the Israeli armed forces and who was captured during an enemy incursion into Israel, Gilad Shalit meets the requirements for prisoner-of-war status under the Third Geneva Convention. As such, he should be protected, treated humanely and be allowed external communication as appropriate according to that Convention. The International Committee of the Red Cross (ICRC) should be allowed to visit him without delay. Information about his condition should also be provided promptly to his family.

78. The Mission is concerned by declarations made by various Israeli officials who have indicated the intention of maintaining the blockade of the Gaza Strip until the release of Gilad Shalit. The Mission is of the opinion that this would constitute collective punishment of the civilian population of the Gaza Strip.

15. Internal violence and targeting of Fatah affiliates by security services under the control of the Gaza authorities

79. The Mission obtained information about violence against political opponents by the security services that report to the Gaza authorities. These included the killing of a number of Gaza residents between the beginning of the Israeli military operations and 27 February. Among these were some detainees who had been at al-Saraya detention facility on 28 December and who had fled following the Israeli aerial attack. Not all those killed after escaping detention were Fatah affiliates, detained for political reasons, or charged with collaborating with the enemy. Some of the escapees had been convicted of serious crimes, such as drug-dealing or murder, and had been sentenced to death. The Mission was informed that the movement of many Fatah members was restricted during Israel's military operations in Gaza and that many were put under house arrest. According to the Gaza authorities, arrests were made only after the end of the Israeli military operations and only in relation to criminal acts and to restore public order.

80. The Mission gathered first-hand information on five cases of Fatah affiliates detained, killed or subject to physical abuse by members of the security forces or armed groups in Gaza. In most cases those abducted from their homes or otherwise detained were reportedly not accused of offences related to specific incidents, but rather targeted because of their political affiliation. When charges were laid, these were always linked to suspected political activities. The testimonies of witnesses and the reports provided by international and domestic human rights organizations bear striking similarities and indicate that these attacks were not randomly executed, but constituted part of a pattern of organized violence directed mainly against Fatah affiliates and supporters. The Mission finds that such actions constitute serious violations of human rights and are not consistent with either the Universal Declaration of Human Rights or the Palestinian Basic Law.

A/HRC/12/48 (ADVANCE 1)
page 17

The Occupied Palestinian Territory: the West Bank, including East Jerusalem

81. The Mission considered developments in Gaza and the West Bank as closely interrelated, and analysed both to reach an informed understanding of and to report on issues within its mandate.

82. A consequence of Israel's non-cooperation with the Mission was that the Mission was unable to visit the West Bank to investigate alleged violations of international law there. However, the Mission has received many oral and written reports and other relevant materials from Palestinian, Israeli and international human rights organizations and institutions. In addition, the Mission has met representatives of human rights organizations, members of the Palestinian legislature and community leaders. It heard experts, witnesses and victims at the public hearings, interviewed affected individuals and witnesses, and reviewed video and photographic material.

1. Treatment of Palestinians in the West Bank by Israeli security forces, including use of excessive or lethal force during demonstrations

83. Various witnesses and experts informed the Mission of a sharp rise in the use of force by the Israeli security forces against Palestinians in the West Bank from the beginning of the Israeli operations in Gaza (chap. XX). A number of protestors were killed by Israeli forces during Palestinian demonstrations, including in support of the Gaza population under attack, and scores were injured. The level of violence used in the West Bank during the time of the operation in Gaza was sustained also after the operation.

84. Of particular concern to the Mission were allegations of the use of unnecessary, lethal force by Israeli security forces, the use of live ammunitions, and the provision in the Israeli armed forces "open fire regulations" of different rules to deal with disturbances where only Palestinians are present and those where Israelis are present. This raises serious concern with regard to discriminatory policies vis-à-vis Palestinians. Eyewitnesses also reported to the Mission on the use of sniper fire in the context of crowd control. Witnesses spoke of the markedly different atmosphere they encountered in the confrontation with the soldiers and border police during demonstrations in which all checks and balances had been removed. Several witnesses told the Mission that during the operation in Gaza, the sense in the West Bank was one of a "free for all", where anything was permitted.

85. Little if any action is taken by the Israeli authorities to investigate, prosecute and punish violence against Palestinians, including killings, by settlers and members of the security forces, resulting in a situation of impunity. The Mission concludes that Israel has failed to fulfil its obligations to protect the Palestinians from violence by private individuals under both international human rights law and international humanitarian law.

2. Detention of Palestinians in Israeli prisons

86. It is estimated that, since the beginning of the occupation, approximately 700,000 Palestinian men, women and children have been detained by Israel. According to estimates, as at 1 June 2009, there were approximately 8,100 Palestinian "political prisoners" in detention in Israel, including 60 women and 390 children. Most of these detainees are charged or convicted

A/HRC/12/48 (ADVANCE 1)
page 18

by the Israeli military court system that operates for Palestinians in the West Bank and under which due process rights for Palestinians are severely limited. Many are held in administrative detention and some under the Israeli "Unlawful Combatants Law".

87. The Mission focused on a number of issues in relation to Palestinian detainees that in its view are linked to the December-January Israeli military operations in Gaza or their context.

88. Legal measures since Israel's disengagement from Gaza in 2005 have resulted in differential treatment for Gazan detainees. A 2006 law altered due process guarantees and is applied only to Palestinian suspects, the overwhelming majority of whom are from Gaza, according to Israeli Government sources. The ICRC Family Visits Programme in the Gaza Strip was suspended in 2007, barring all means of communication between Gazan prisoners and the outside world.

89. During the Israeli military operations in Gaza, the number of children detained by Israel was higher than in the same period in 2008. Many children were reportedly arrested on the street and/or during demonstrations in the West Bank. The number of child detainees continued to be high in the months following the end of the operations, accompanied by reports of abuses by Israeli security forces.

90. A feature of Israel's detention practice vis-à-vis the Palestinians since 2005 has been the arrest of Hamas affiliates. A few months before the elections for the Palestinian Legislative Council in 2005, Israel arrested numerous persons who had been involved in municipal or Legislative Council elections. Following the capture by Palestinian armed groups of Israeli soldier Gilad Shalit in June 2006, the Israeli armed forces arrested some 65 members of the Legislative Council, mayors and ministers, mostly Hamas members. All were held at least two years, generally in inadequate conditions. Further arrests of Hamas leaders were conducted during the military operations in Gaza. The detention of members of the Legislative Council has meant that it has been unable to function and exercise its legislative and oversight function over the Palestinian executive.

91. The Mission finds that these practices have resulted in violations of international human rights and humanitarian law, including the prohibition of arbitrary detention, the right to equal protection under the law and not to be discriminated based on political beliefs and the special protections to which children are entitled. The Mission also finds that the detention of members of the Legislative Council may amount to collective punishment contrary to international humanitarian law.

3. Restrictions on freedom of movement in the West Bank

92. In the West Bank, Israel has long imposed a system of restrictions on movement. Movement is restricted by a combination of physical obstacles, such as roadblocks, checkpoints and the Wall, and administrative measures, such as identity cards, permits, assigned residence, laws on family reunification, and policies on the right to enter from abroad and the right of return for refugees. Palestinians are denied access to areas expropriated for the building of the Wall and its infrastructure, for use by settlements, buffer zones, military bases and military training zones, and the roads built to connect these places. Many of these roads are "Israeli only" and forbidden for Palestinian use. Tens of thousands of Palestinians today are subject to a travel ban imposed

by Israel, preventing them from travelling abroad. A number of witnesses and experts invited by the Mission to meet in Amman and participate in the hearings in Geneva could not meet the Mission owing to this travel ban.

93. The Mission has received reports that, during the Israeli offensive in Gaza, restrictions on movement in the West Bank were tightened. Israel imposed a "closure" on the West Bank for several days. In addition, there were more checkpoints in the West Bank, including in East Jerusalem, for the duration of the operation. Most of these were so-called flying checkpoints. In January 2009, several areas of the West Bank between the Wall and the Green Line were declared "closed military areas".

94. During and following the operations in Gaza, Israel tightened its hold on the West Bank by increasing expropriations, house demolitions and demolition orders, granting more permits for homes built in settlements and intensifying the exploitation of the natural resources in the West Bank. Following the operations in Gaza, Israel has amended the regulations which determine the ability of persons with "Gaza ID" to move to the West Bank and vice versa, further entrenching the separation between the people of the West Bank and Gaza.

95. Israel's Ministry of Housing and Planning is planning a further 73,000 settlement homes in the West Bank. The building of 15,000 of these homes has already been approved and, if all the plans are realized, the number of settlers in the Occupied Palestinian Territory will double.

96. The Mission believes that the restrictions on movement and access to which Palestinians in the West Bank are subject, in general, and the tighter restrictions during and, to some extent, after the military operations in Gaza, in particular, are disproportionate to any military objective served . In addition, the Mission is concerned about the steps taken recently to formalize the separation between Gaza and the West Bank, and as such between two parts of the Occupied Palestinian Territory.

4. Internal violence and targeting of Hamas supporters by the Palestinian Authority, restrictions on freedom of expression and assembly

97. The Mission has received allegations of violations relevant to its mandate committed by the Palestinian Authority in the period under inquiry. These include violations related to the treatment of (suspected) Hamas affiliates by the security services, including unlawful arrest and detention. Several Palestinian human rights organizations have reported that practices used by the Palestinian Authority security forces in the West Bank amount to torture and cruel, inhuman and degrading treatment and punishment. There have been a number of deaths in detention to which it is suspected that torture and other ill-treatment may have contributed or which they may have caused. Complaints of such practices have not been investigated.

98. Allegations were also received about the use of excessive force and the suppression of demonstrations by Palestinian security services – particularly those in support of the population of Gaza during the Israeli military operations. On these occasions Palestinian Authority security services have allegedly arrested many individuals and prevented the media from covering the events. The Mission also received allegations of harassment by Palestinian security services of journalists who expressed critical views.

A/HRC/12/48 (ADVANCE 1)
page 20

99. The disabling of the Palestinian Legislative Council following the arrest and detention by Israel of several of its members has effectively curtailed parliamentary oversight over the Palestinian Authority executive. The executive has passed decrees and regulations to enable it to continue its day-to-day operations.

100. Other allegations include the arbitrary closure of charities and associations affiliated with Hamas and other Islamic groups or the revocation and non-renewal of their licences, the forcible replacement of board members of Islamic schools and other institutions, and the dismissal of Hamas-affiliated teachers.

101. The Palestinian Authority continues to discharge a large number of civil and military service employees, or suspend their salaries, under the pretext of "non-adherence to the legitimate authority" or "non-obtainment of security approval" on their appointments, which has become a pre-requirement for enrolment in public service. In effect, this measure excludes Hamas supporters or affiliates from public sector employment.

102. The Mission is of the view that the reported measures are inconsistent with the Palestinian Authority's obligations deriving from the Universal Declaration of Human Rights and the Palestinian Basic Law.

Israel

1. Impact on civilians of rocket and mortar attacks by Palestinian armed groups on southern Israel

103. Palestinian armed groups have launched about 8000 rockets and mortars into southern Israel since 2001 (chap. XXIV). While communities such as Sderot and Nir Am kibbutz have been within the range of rocket and mortar fire since the beginning, the range of rocket fire increased to nearly 40 kilometres from the Gaza border, encompassing towns as far north as Ashdod, during the Israeli military operations in Gaza.

104. Between 18 June 2008 and 18 January 2009, rockets fired by Palestinian armed groups in Gaza have killed three civilians inside Israel and two civilians in Gaza when a rocket landed short of the border on 26 December 2008. Reportedly, over 1000 civilians inside Israel were physically injured as a result of rocket and mortar attacks, 918 of whom were injured during the time of the Israeli military operations in Gaza.

105. The Mission has taken particular note of the high level of psychological trauma suffered by the civilian population inside Israel. Data gathered by an Israeli organization in October 2007 found that 28.4 per cent of adults and 72–94 per cent of children in Sderot suffered from post-traumatic stress disorder. During the military operations in Gaza 1596 people were reportedly treated for stress-related injuries while afterwards over 500 people were treated.

106. Rockets and mortars have damaged houses, schools and cars in southern Israel. On 5 March 2009, a rocket struck a synagogue in Netivot. The rocket and mortar fire has adversely affected the right to education of children and adults living in southern Israel. This is a result of school closures and interruptions to classes by alerts and moving to shelters but also the

diminished ability to learn that is witnessed in individuals experiencing symptoms of psychological trauma.

107. The rocket and mortar fire has also had an adverse impact on the economic and social life of the affected communities. For communities such as Ashdod, Yavne, Beersheba, which experienced rocket strikes for the first time during the Israeli military operations in Gaza, there was a brief interruption to their economic and cultural activities brought about by the temporary displacement of some residents. For towns closer to the Gaza border, which have been under rocket and mortar fire since 2001, the recent escalation has added to the exodus of residents.

108. The Mission has determined that the rockets and, to a lesser extent, the mortars fired by the Palestinian armed groups are incapable of being directed towards specific military objectives and have been fired into areas where civilian populations are based. The Mission has further determined that these attacks constitute indiscriminate attacks upon the civilian population of southern Israel and that, where there is no intended military target and the rockets and mortars are launched into a civilian population, they constitute a deliberate attack against a civilian population. These acts would constitute war crimes and may amount to crimes against humanity. Given the seeming inability of the Palestinian armed groups to direct the rockets and mortars towards specific targets and given that the attacks have caused very little damage to Israeli military assets, the Mission finds that there is significant evidence to suggest that one of the primary purposes of the rocket and mortar attacks is to spread terror among the Israeli civilian population, a violation of international law.

109. Noting that some of the Palestinian armed groups, among them Hamas, have publicly expressed their intention to target civilians in reprisal for the civilian fatalities in Gaza as a result of Israeli military operations, the Mission is of the view that reprisals against civilians in armed hostilities are contrary to international humanitarian law.

110. The Mission notes that the relatively few casualties sustained by civilians inside Israel is due in large part to the precautions put into place by Israel. This includes an early warning system, the provision of public shelters and fortifications of schools and other public buildings at great financial cost – a projected US$ 460 million between 2005 and 2011 – to the Government of Israel. The Mission is greatly concerned, however, about the lack of an early warning system and a lack of public shelters and fortifications for the Palestinian Israeli communities living in unrecognized and in some of the recognized villages that are within the range of rocket and mortars being fired by Palestinian armed groups in Gaza.

2. Repression of dissent in Israel, the right of access to information and treatment of human rights defenders

111. The Mission received reports that individuals and groups, viewed as sources of criticism of Israel's military operations were subjected to repression or attempted repression by the Government of Israel. Amidst a high level of support for the Israeli military operations in Gaza from the Israeli Jewish population, there were also widespread protests against the military operations inside Israel. Hundreds of thousands – mainly, but not exclusively, Palestinian citizens of Israel – protested. While, in the main, the protests were permitted to take place, there were occasions when, reportedly, protesters had difficulty in obtaining permits – particularly in areas populated mainly by Palestinian Israelis. In Israel and in occupied East Jerusalem 715

A/HRC/12/48 (ADVANCE 1)
page 22

people were arrested during the protests. There appear to have been no arrests of counter-protesters and 34 per cent of those arrested were under 18 years of age. The Mission notes that a relatively small proportion of those protesting were arrested. The Mission urges the Government of Israel to ensure that the police authorities respect the rights of all its citizens, without discrimination, including freedom of expression and the right to peaceful assembly, as guaranteed to them by the International Covenant on Civil and Political Rights.

112. The Mission notes with concern the reported instances of physical violence committed by members of the police against protesters, including the beating of protesters and other inappropriate conduct such as subjecting Palestinian citizens of Israel who were arrested to racial abuse and making sexual comments about female members of their families. Article 10 of the Covenant requires that those deprived of their liberty be treated with humanity and respect for the inherent dignity of the human person.

113. Of the protesters brought before the Israeli courts, the Palestinian Israelis were disproportionately held in detention pending trial. The element of discrimination and differential treatment between Palestinian and Jewish citizens of Israel by the judicial authorities, as indicated in the reports received, is a substantial cause for concern.

114. The interviews of political activists by the Israeli General Security Services were cited as the actions contributing most significantly to a climate of repression inside Israel. The Mission is concerned about activists being compelled to attend interviews with Shabak (also known as Shin Bet), without there being any legal obligation on them to do so, and in general at the alleged interrogation of political activists about their political activities.

115. The Mission received reports concerning the investigation by the Government of Israel into New Profile on allegations that it was inciting draft-dodging, a criminal offence, and reports that the Government was seeking to terminate funding from foreign Governments for Breaking the Silence, following its publication of testimonies of Israeli soldiers concerning the conduct of the Israeli armed forces in Gaza in December 2008 and January 2009. The Mission is concerned that the Government of Israel's action with regard to these organizations may have an intimidating effect on other Israeli human rights organizations. The so-called United Nations Declaration on Human Rights Defenders guarantees the right "to solicit, receive and utilize resources for the express purpose of promoting and protecting human rights and fundamental freedoms through peaceful means". If motivated by reaction to the organization's exercise of its freedom of expression, lobbying foreign Governments to terminate funding would be contrary to the spirit of the Declaration.

116. The Government of Israel imposed a ban on media access to Gaza following 5 November 2008. Furthermore, access was denied to human rights organizations and the ban continues for some international and Israeli organizations. The Mission can find no justification for this. The presence of journalists and international human rights monitors aids the investigation and wide public reporting of the conduct of the parties to the conflict, and can inhibit misconduct. The Mission observes that Israel, in its actions against political activists, non-governmental organizations and the media, has attempted to reduce public scrutiny of both its conduct during its military operations in Gaza and the consequences that these operations had for the residents of Gaza, possibly seeking to prevent investigation and public reporting thereon.

A/HRC/12/48 (ADVANCE 1)
page 23

D. Accountability

1. Proceedings and responses by Israel to allegations of violations by its armed forces against Palestinians

117. Investigations and, if appropriate, prosecutions of those suspected of serious violations are necessary if respect for human rights and humanitarian law is to be ensured and to prevent the development of a climate of impunity. States have a duty under international law to investigate allegations of violations.

118. The Mission reviewed public information and reports from the Government of Israel concerning actions taken to discharge its obligation to investigate alleged violations (chap. XXVI). It addressed to Israel a number of questions on this issue, but it did not receive a reply.

119. In response to allegations of serious violations of human rights law and international humanitarian law, the Military Advocate General ordered some criminal investigations that were closed two weeks later concluding that allegations "were based on hearsay". The Israeli armed forces also released the results of five special investigations carried out by high-ranking military officers, which concluded that "throughout the fighting in Gaza, the IDF operated in accordance with international law", but the investigations reportedly revealed a very small number of errors. On 30 July 2009 the media reported that the Military Advocate General had ordered the military police to launch criminal investigations into 14 cases out or nearly 100 complaints of criminal conduct by soldiers. No details were offered.

120. The Mission reviewed the Israeli internal system of investigation and prosecution according to its national legislation and in the light of practice. The system comprises: (a) disciplinary proceedings; (b) operational debriefings (also known as "operational investigations"); (c) special investigations, performed by a senior officer at the request of the chief of staff; and (d) military police investigations, carried out by the Criminal Investigation Division of the military police. At the heart of the system lies the so-called operational debriefing. The debriefings are reviews of incidents and operations conducted by soldiers from the same unit or line of command together with a superior officer. They are meant to serve operational purposes.

121. International human rights law and humanitarian law require States to investigate and, if appropriate, prosecute allegations of serious violations by military personnel. International law has also established that such investigations should comply with standards of impartiality, independence, promptness and effectiveness. The Mission holds that the Israeli system of investigation does not comply with all those principles. In relation to the "operational debriefing" used by the Israeli armed forces as an investigative tool, the Mission holds the view that a tool designed for the review of performance and to learn lessons can hardly be an effective and impartial investigation mechanism that should be instituted after every military operation where allegations of serious violations have been made. It does not comply with internationally recognized principles of impartiality and promptness in investigations. The fact that proper criminal investigations can start only after the "operational debriefing" is over is a major flaw in the Israeli system of investigation.

A/HRC/12/48 (ADVANCE 1)
page 24

122. The Mission concludes that there are serious doubts about the willingness of Israel to carry out genuine investigations in an impartial, independent, prompt and effective way as required by international law. The Mission is also of the view that the Israeli system overall presents inherently discriminatory features that make the pursuit of justice for Palestinian victims very difficult.

2. Proceedings by Palestinian authorities

(a) Proceedings related to actions in the Gaza Strip

123. The Mission found no evidence of any system of public monitoring or accountability for serious violations of international humanitarian law and human rights law set up by the Gaza authorities. The Mission is concerned with the consistent disregard for international humanitarian law with which armed groups in the Gaza Strip conduct their armed activities, through rocket and mortar fire, directed against Israel. Despite some media reports, the Mission remains unconvinced that any genuine and effective initiatives have been taken by the authorities to address the serious issues of violation of international humanitarian law in the conduct of armed activities by militant groups in the Gaza Strip.

124. Notwithstanding statements by the Gaza authorities and any action that they may have taken, of which the Mission is unaware, the Mission also considers that allegations of killings, torture and mistreatment within the Gaza Strip have gone largely without investigation.

(b) Proceedings related to actions in the West Bank

125. With regard to relevant violations identified in the West Bank, it appears that, with few exceptions, there has been a degree of tolerance towards human rights violations against political opponents, which has resulted in a lack of accountability for such actions. The Ministry of Interior has also ignored the High Court's decisions to release a number of detainees or to reopen some associations closed by the administration.

126. In the circumstances, the Mission is unable to consider the measures taken by the Palestinian Authority as meaningful for holding to account perpetrators of serious violations of international law and believes that the responsibility for protecting the rights of the people inherent in the authority assumed by the Palestinian Authority must be fulfilled with greater commitment

3. Universal jurisdiction

127. In the context of increasing unwillingness on the part of Israel to open criminal investigations that comply with international standards, the Mission supports the reliance on universal jurisdiction as an avenue for States to investigate violations of the grave breach provisions of the Geneva Conventions of 1949, prevent impunity and promote international accountability (chap. XXVIII).

4. Reparations

128. International law also establishes that, whenever a violation of an international obligation occurs, an obligation to provide reparation arises. It is the view of the Mission that the current

constitutional structure and legislation in Israel leaves very little room, if any, for Palestinians to seek compensation. The international community needs to provide for an additional or alternative mechanism of compensation for damage or loss incurred by Palestinian civilians during the military operations (chap. XXIX).

E. Conclusions and recommendations

129. The Mission draws general conclusions on its investigations in chapter XXX, which also includes a summary of its legal findings.

130. The Mission then makes recommendations to a number of United Nations bodies, Israel, the responsible Palestinian authorities and the international community on: (a) accountability for serious violations of international humanitarian law; (b) reparations; (c) serious violations of human rights law; (d) the blockade and reconstruction; (e) the use of weapons and military procedures; (f) the protection of human rights organizations and defenders ; (g) follow-up to the Mission's recommendations. The recommendations are detailed in chapter XXXI.

# Document [3] Report of the UN Fact Finding Mission - Conclusions and Recommendations

UNITED
NATIONS

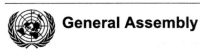 **General Assembly**

Distr.
GENERAL

A/HRC/12/48 (ADVANCE 2)
24 September 2009

Original: ENGLISH

HUMAN RIGHTS COUNCIL
Twelfth session
Agenda item 7

HUMAN RIGHTS IN PALESTINE AND OTHER OCCUPIED ARAB TERRITORIES

Report of the United Nations Fact Finding Mission on the Gaza Conflict

Conclusions and recommendations[*]

---

[*] The present document is an advance translation and contains only the conclusions and recommendations of the Fact-Finding Mission. The full report will be issued as A/HRC/12/48 in all languages according to translation capacity of the United Nations translation services.

GE.09-15836

PART FIVE: CONCLUSIONS AND RECOMMENDATIONS

XXX. CONCLUSIONS

A. Concluding observations

1874. An objective assessment of the events it investigated and their causes and context is crucial for the success of any effort to achieve justice for victims of violations and peace and security in the region, and as such is in the interest of all concerned and affected by this situation, including the parties to the continuing hostilities. It is in this spirit, and with full appreciation of the complexity of its task, that the Mission received and implemented its mandate.

1875. The international community as well as Israel and, to the extent determined by their authority and means, Palestinian authorities, have the responsibility to protect victims of violations and ensure that they do not continue to suffer the scourge of war or the oppression and humiliations of occupation or indiscriminate rocket attacks. People of Palestine have the right to freely determine their own political and economic system, including the right to resist forcible deprivation of their right to self-determination and the right to live, in peace and freedom, in their own State. The people of Israel have the right to live in peace and security. Both peoples are entitled to justice in accordance with international law.

1876. In carrying out its mandate, the Mission had regard, as its only guides, for general international law, international human rights and humanitarian law, and the obligations they place on States, the obligations they place on non-State actors and, above all, the rights and entitlements they bestow on individuals. This in no way implies equating the position of Israel as the occupying Power with that of the occupied Palestinian population or entities representing it. The differences with regard to the power and capacity to inflict harm or to protect, including by securing justice when violations occur, are obvious and a comparison is neither possible nor necessary. What requires equal attention and effort, however, is the protection of all victims in accordance with international law.

B. The Israeli military operations in Gaza: relevance to and links with Israel's policies vis-à-vis the Occupied Palestinian Territory

1877. The Mission is of the view that Israel's military operation in Gaza between 27 December 2008 and 18 January 2009 and its impact cannot be understood or assessed in isolation from developments prior and subsequent to it. The operation fits into a continuum of policies aimed at pursuing Israel's political objectives with regard to Gaza and the Occupied Palestinian Territory as a whole. Many such policies are based on or result in violations of international human rights and humanitarian law. Military objectives as stated by the Government of Israel do not explain the facts ascertained by the Mission, nor are they congruous with the patterns identified by the Mission during the investigation.

1878. The continuum is evident most immediately with the policy of blockade that preceded the operations and that in the Mission's view amounts to collective punishment intentionally inflicted by the Government of Israel on the people of the Gaza Strip. When the operations began, the Gaza Strip had been under a severe regime of closures and restrictions on the movement of people, goods and services for almost three years. This included basic necessities of life, such as food and medical supplies, and products required for the conduct of daily life, such as fuel, electricity, school items, and repair and construction material. These measures were imposed by Israel purportedly to isolate and weaken Hamas after its electoral victory in view of the perceived continuing threat to Israel's security that it represented. Their effect was compounded by the withholding of financial and other assistance by some donors on similar grounds. Adding hardship to the already difficult situation in the Gaza Strip, the effects of the prolonged blockade did not spare any aspect of the life of Gazans. Prior to the military operation, the Gaza economy had been depleted, the health sector beleaguered, the population had been made dependent on humanitarian assistance for survival and the conduct of daily life. Men, women and children were psychologically suffering from long-standing poverty, insecurity and violence, and enforced confinement in a heavily overcrowded territory. The dignity of the people of Gaza had been severely eroded. This was the situation in the Gaza Strip when the Israeli armed forces launched their offensive in December 2008. The military operations and the manner in which they were conducted considerably exacerbated the aforementioned effects of the blockade. The result, in a very short time, was unprecedented long-term damage both to the people and to their development and recovery prospects.

1879. An analysis of the modalities and impact of the December-January military operations also sets them, in the Mission's view, in a continuum with a number of other pre-existing Israeli policies with regard to the Occupied Palestinian Territory. The progressive isolation and separation of the Gaza Strip from the West Bank, a policy that began much earlier and which was consolidated in particular with the imposition of tight closures, restrictions on movement and eventually the blockade, are among the most apparent. Several measures adopted by Israel in the West Bank during and following the military operations in Gaza also further deepen Israel's control over the West Bank, including East Jerusalem, and point to a convergence of objectives with the Gaza military operations. Such measures include increased land expropriation, house demolitions, demolition orders and permits to build homes in settlements, greater and more formalized access and movement restrictions on Palestinians, new and stricter procedures for residents of the Gaza Strip to change their residency to the West Bank. Systematic efforts to hinder and control Palestinian self-determined democratic processes, not least through the detention of elected political representatives and members of Government and the punishment of the Gaza population for its perceived support for Hamas, culminated in the attacks on government buildings during the Gaza offensive, most prominently the Palestinian Legislative Council. The cumulative impact of these policies and actions make prospects for political and economic integration between Gaza and the West Bank more remote.

C. Nature, objectives and targets of the Israeli military operations in Gaza

1880. Both Palestinians and Israelis whom the Mission met repeatedly stressed that the military operations carried out by Israel in Gaza from 27 December 2008 until 18 January 2009 were qualitatively different from any previous military action by Israel in the Occupied Palestinian Territory. Despite the hard conditions that have long been prevailing

A/HRC/12/48 (ADVANCE 2)
page 4

in the Gaza Strip, victims and long-time observers stated that the operations were unprecedented in their severity and that their consequences would be long-lasting.

1881. When the Mission conducted its first visit to the Gaza Strip in early June 2009, almost five months had passed since the end of the Israeli military operations. The devastating effects of the operations on the population were, however, unequivocally manifest. In addition to the visible destruction of houses, factories, wells, schools, hospitals, police stations and other public buildings, the sight of families, including the elderly and children, still living amid the rubble of their former dwellings – no reconstruction possible due to the continuing blockade – was evidence of the protracted impact of the operations on the living conditions of the Gaza population. Reports of the trauma suffered during the attacks, the stress due to the uncertainty about the future, the hardship of life and the fear of further attacks, pointed to less tangible but not less real long-term effects.

1882. Women were affected in significant ways. Their situation must be given specific attention in any effort to address the consequences of the blockade, of the continuing occupation and of the latest Israeli military operations.

1883. The Gaza military operations were, according to the Israeli Government, thoroughly and extensively planned. While the Israeli Government has sought to portray its operations as essentially a response to rocket attacks in the exercise of its right to self-defence, the Mission considers the plan to have been directed, at least in part, at a different target: the people of Gaza as a whole.

1884. In this respect, the operations were in furtherance of an overall policy aimed at punishing the Gaza population for its resilience and for its apparent support for Hamas, and possibly with the intent of forcing a change in such support. The Mission considers this position to be firmly based in fact, bearing in mind what it saw and heard on the ground, what it read in the accounts of soldiers who served in the campaign, and what it heard and read from current and former military officers and political leaders whom the Mission considers to be representative of the thinking that informed the policy and strategy of the military operations.

1885. The Mission recognizes that the principal focus in the aftermath of military operations will often be on the people who have been killed – more than 1,400 in just three weeks. This is rightly so. Part of the functions of reports such as this is to attempt, albeit in a very small way, to restore the dignity of those whose rights have been violated in the most fundamental way of all – the arbitrary deprivation of life. It is important that the international community asserts formally and unequivocally that such violence to the most basic fundamental rights and freedoms of individuals should not be overlooked and should be condemned.

1886. In this respect, the Mission recognizes that not all deaths constitute violations of international humanitarian law. The principle of proportionality acknowledges that, under certain strict conditions, actions resulting in the loss of civilian life may not be unlawful. What makes the application and assessment of proportionality difficult in respect of many of the events investigated by the Mission is that deeds by the Israeli armed forces and words of military and political leaders prior to and during the operations indicate that, as a whole, they were premised on a deliberate policy of disproportionate force aimed not at the enemy but at the "supporting infrastructure." In practice, this appears to have meant the civilian population.

1887. The timing of the first Israeli attack, at 11.30 a.m. on a weekday, when children were returning from school and the streets of Gaza were crowded with people going about their daily business, appears to have been calculated to create the greatest disruption and widespread panic among the civilian population. The treatment of many civilians detained or even killed while trying to surrender is one manifestation of the way in which the effective rules of engagement, standard operating procedures and instructions to the troops on the ground appear to have been framed in order to create an environment in which due regard for civilian lives and basic human dignity was replaced with disregard for basic international humanitarian law and human rights norms.

1888. The Mission recognizes fully that the Israeli armed forces, like any army attempting to act within the parameters of international law, must avoid taking undue risks with their soldiers' lives, but neither can they transfer that risk onto the lives of civilian men, women and children. The fundamental principles of distinction and proportionality apply on the battlefield, whether that battlefield is a built-up urban area or an open field.

1889. The repeated failure to distinguish between combatants and civilians appears to the Mission to have been the result of deliberate guidance issued to soldiers, as described by some of them, and not the result of occasional lapses.

1890. The Mission recognizes that some of those killed were combatants directly engaged in hostilities against Israel, but many were not. The outcome and the modalities of the operations indicate, in the Mission's view, that they were only partially aimed at killing leaders and members of Hamas, al-Qassam Brigades and other armed groups. They were also to a large degree aimed at destroying or incapacitating civilian property and the means of subsistence of the civilian population.

1891. It is clear from evidence gathered by the Mission that the destruction of food supply installations, water sanitation systems, concrete factories and residential houses was the result of a deliberate and systematic policy by the Israeli armed forces. It was not carried out because those objects presented a military threat or opportunity, but to make the daily process of living, and dignified living, more difficult for the civilian population.

1892. Allied to the systematic destruction of the economic capacity of the Gaza Strip, there appears also to have been an assault on the dignity of the people. This was seen not only in the use of human shields and unlawful detentions sometimes in unacceptable conditions, but also in the vandalizing of houses when occupied and the way in which people were treated when their houses were entered. The graffiti on the walls, the obscenities and often racist slogans, all constituted an overall image of humiliation and dehumanization of the Palestinian population.

1893. The operations were carefully planned in all their phases. Legal opinions and advice were given throughout the planning stages and at certain operational levels during the campaign. There were almost no mistakes made according to the Government of Israel. It is in these circumstances that the Mission concludes that what occurred in just over three weeks at the end of 2008 and the beginning of 2009 was a deliberately disproportionate attack designed to punish, humiliate and terrorize a civilian population, radically diminish its local economic capacity both to work and to provide for itself, and to force upon it an ever increasing sense of dependency and vulnerability.

1894. The Mission has noted with concern public statements by Israeli officials, including senior military officials, to the effect that the use of disproportionate force, attacks on civilian population and the destruction of civilian property are legitimate means to achieve Israel's military and political objectives. The Mission believes that such statements not only undermine the entire regime of international law, they are inconsistent with the spirit of the Charter of the United Nations and, therefore, deserve to be categorically denounced.

1895. Whatever violations of international humanitarian and human rights law may have been committed, the systematic and deliberate nature of the activities described in this report leave the Mission in no doubt that responsibility lies in the first place with those who designed, planned, ordered and oversaw the operations.

D. Occupation, resilience and civil society

1896. The accounts of more severe violence during the recent military operations did not obscure the fact that the concept of "normalcy" in the Gaza Strip has long been redefined owing to the protracted situation of abuse and lack of protection deriving from the decades-long occupation.

1897. As the Mission focused on investigating and analysing the specific matters within its mandate, Israel's continuing occupation of the Gaza Strip and the West Bank emerged as the fundamental factor underlying violations of international humanitarian and human rights law against the protected population and undermining prospects for development and peace. Israel's failure to acknowledge and exercise its responsibilities as the occupying Power further exacerbated the effects of occupation on the Palestinian people, and continue to do so. Furthermore, the harsh and unlawful practices of occupation, far from quelling resistance, breed it, including its violent manifestations. The Mission is of the view that ending occupation is a prerequisite for the return of a dignified life for Palestinians, as well as development and a peaceful solution to the conflict.

1898. The Mission was struck by the resilience and dignity shown by people in the face of dire circumstances. UNRWA Director of Operations, John Ging, relayed to the Mission the answer of a Gaza teacher during a discussion after the end of the Israeli military operations about strengthening human rights education in schools. Rather than expressing scepticism at the relevance of teaching human rights in a context of renewed denial of rights, the teacher unhesitantly supported the resumption of human rights education: "This is a war of values, and we are not going to lose it".

1899. The assiduous work of Palestinian non-governmental and civil society organizations in providing support to the population in such extreme circumstances, and in giving voice to the suffering and expectations of victims of violations deserves to be fully acknowledged. Their role in helping to sustain the resilience and dignity of the population cannot be overstated. The Mission heard many accounts of NGO workers, doctors, ambulance drivers, journalists, human rights monitors, who, at the height of the military operations, risked their lives to be of service to people in need. They frequently relayed the anxiety of having to choose between remaining close to their own families or continuing to work to assist others in need, thereby often being cut off from news about the safety or whereabouts of family members. The Mission wishes to pay tribute to the courage and work of the numerous individuals who so contributed to alleviating the suffering of the population and to report on the events in Gaza.

E. Rocket and mortar attacks in Israel

1900. Palestinian armed groups have launched thousands of rockets and mortars into Israel since April 2001. These have succeeded in causing terror within Israel's civilian population, as evidenced by the high rates of psychological trauma within the affected communities. The attacks have also led to an erosion of the social, cultural and economic lives of the communities in southern Israel, and have affected the rights to education of the tens of thousands of children and young adults who attend classes in the affected areas.

1901. Between 27 December 2008 and 18 January 2009, these attacks left four people dead and hundreds injured. That there have not been more casualties is due to a combination of luck and measures taken by the Israeli Government, including the fortification of public buildings, the construction of shelters and, in times of escalated hostilities, the closure of schools.

1902. The Mission notes, with concern, that Israel has not provided the same level of protection from rockets and mortars to affected Palestinian citizens as it has to Jewish citizens. In particular, it has failed to provide public shelters or fortification of schools, for example, to the Palestinian communities living in the unrecognized villages and some of the recognized villages. It ought to go without saying that the thousands of Palestinian Israelis– including a significant number of children – who live within the range of rocket fire, deserve the same protection as the Israeli Government provides to its Jewish citizens.

F. Dissenting voices in Israel

1903. While the Israeli military offensive in Gaza was widely supported by the Israeli public, there were also dissenting voices, which expressed themselves through demonstrations, protests, as well as public reporting on Israel's conduct. The Mission is of the view that actions of the Israeli Government during and following the military operations in the Gaza Strip, including interrogation of political activists, repression of criticism and sources of potential criticism of Israeli military actions, in particular NGOs, have contributed significantly to a political climate in which dissent with the Government and its actions in the Occupied Palestinian Territory is not tolerated. The denial of media access to Gaza and the continuing denial of access to human rights monitors are, in the Mission's view, an attempt both to remove the Government's actions in the Occupied Palestinian Territory from public scrutiny and to impede investigations and reporting of the conduct of the parties to the conflict in the Gaza Strip.

1904. In this context of increased intolerance for dissenting opinions in Israel, the Mission wishes to acknowledge the difficult work of NGOs in Israel, which courageously continue to express criticism of Government action that violates international human rights and humanitarian law. The work of these organizations is essential not only to ensure independent information to the Israeli and international public, but also to encourage a facts-based debate about these issues within Israeli society.

G. The impact of dehumanization

1905. As in many conflicts, one of the features of the Palestinian-Israeli conflict is the dehumanization of the other, and of victims in particular. Palestinian psychiatrist Dr. Iyad al-Sarraj explained the cycle of aggression and victimization through which "the Palestinian in the eyes of the Israeli soldier is not an equal human being. Sometimes [...] even becomes a demon [...]" This "culture of demonization and dehumanization" adds to a state of paranoia. "Paranoia has two sides, the side of victimization, I am a victim of this world, the whole world is against me and on the other side, I am superior to this world and I can oppress it. This leads to what is called the arrogance of power." As Palestinians, "we look in general to the Israelis as demons and that we can hate them, that what we do is a reaction, and we say that the Israelis can only understand the language of power. The same thing that we say about the Israelis they say about us, that we only understand the language of violence or force. There we see the arrogance of power and [the Israeli] uses it without thinking of humanity at all. In my view we are seeing not only a state of war but also a state that is cultural and psychological and I hope, I wish that the Israelis would start, and there are many, many Jews in the world and in Israel that look into themselves, have an insight that would make them, alleviate the fear that they have because there's a state of fear in Israel, in spite of all the power, and that they would start to walk on the road of dealing with the consequences of their own victimization and to start dealing with the Palestinian as a human being, a full human being who's equal in rights with the Israeli and also the other way around, the Palestinian must deal with himself, must respect himself and respect his own differences in order to be able to stand before the Israeli also as a full human being with equal rights and obligations. This is the real road for justice and for peace."

1906. Israeli college teacher Ofer Shinar offered a similar analysis: "Israeli society's problem is that, because of the conflict, Israeli society feels itself to be a victim and to a large extent that's justified and it's very difficult for Israeli society to move and to feel that it can also see the other side and to understand that the other side is also a victim. This I think is the greatest tragedy of the conflict and it's terribly difficult to overcome it [...] I think that the initiative that you've taken in listening to [...] people [...] is very important. The message that you're giving Israeli society is absolutely unambiguous that you are impartial that you should be able to see that the feeling of being a victim is something that characterizes both sides. What requires you to take this responsibility is the fact that you have to understand how difficult it is to get this message through to Israeli society, how closed the Israeli society is, how difficult it is for Israeli society to understand that the other side is not just the party which is infringing our own human rights, but how they are having their human rights infringed, how they are suffering as well."

A/HRC/12/48 (ADVANCE 2)
page 9

1907. The Mission, in fulfilling its mandate to investigate alleged violations of international law that occurred in the context of the December 2008 – January 2009 military operations in Gaza, spoke predominantly to those most affected by the most recent events in a conflict that has spanned decades. As may be expected, the Mission found societies scarred by living in conflict with significant psychological trauma stemming from a life that may rightly seem to those living in more peaceful countries to be unbearable.

1908. Both the Palestinians and the Israelis are legitimately angered at the lives that they are forced to lead. For the Palestinians, the anger about individual events – the civilian casualties, injuries and destruction in Gaza following from military attacks, the blockade, the continued construction of the Wall outside of the 1967 borders – feed into an underlying anger about the continuing Israeli occupation, its daily humiliations and their as-yet-unfulfilled right to self-determination. For the Israelis, the public statements of Palestinian armed groups celebrating rocket and mortar attacks on civilians strengthen a deep-rooted concern that negotiation will yield little and that their nation remains under existential threat from which only it can protect its people. In this way, both the Israelis and the Palestinians share a secret fear – for some, a belief – that each has no intention of accepting the other's right to a country of their own. This anger and fear are unfortunately ably represented by many politicians.

1909. Some Israelis pointed out to the Mission that policies of the Israeli Government relating to the isolation of the Gaza Strip and the tighter restrictions on the movement of Palestinians within the Occupied Palestinian Territory and between the Occupied Palestinian Territory and Israel, have contributed to increasing the distance between Palestinians and Israelis, reducing the opportunities to interact other than in situations of control and coercion such as checkpoints and military posts.

1910. In this context, the Mission was encouraged by reports of exchange and cooperation between Palestinians and Israelis, for example with regard to mental health specialists working with Palestinians from Gaza and southern Israel's communities, and with regard to cooperation between Magen David Adom and the Palestinian Red Crescent Society, especially in the West Bank, as they fulfil a shared commitment to providing humanitarian assistance to the communities in which they work, regardless of the ethnicity of the patient who lies before them.

H. The intra-Palestinian situation

1911. The division and violence between Fatah and Hamas, which culminated in the establishment of parallel governance entities and structures in the Gaza Strip and the West Bank, is having adverse consequences for the human rights of the Palestinian population in both areas, as well as contributing to erode the rule of law in the Occupied Palestinian Territory in addition to the threats already linked to foreign occupation. Even with the narrow focus of the Mission on violations relevant to the context of the December-January military operations, the diminishing protections for Palestinians are evident from the cases of arbitrary deprivation of life, arbitrary detention of political activists or sympathizers, limitations on freedom of expression and association, and abuses by security forces. The situation is compounded by the ever reducing role of the judiciary in ensuring the rule of law and legal remedies for violations. A resolution of the internal divisions based on the free will and decisions of Palestinians and without external interference would strengthen the ability of Palestinian authorities and institutions to protect the rights of the people under their responsibility.

I. The need for protection and the role of the international community

1912. International law sets obligations on States not only to respect but also to ensure respect for international humanitarian law. The International Court of Justice stated in its Advisory Opinion on the *Legal Consequences of the Construction of a Wall in the Occupied Palestinian Territory* that "all States parties to the Fourth Geneva Convention relative to the Protection of Civilian Persons in Time of War of 12 August 1949 have in addition the obligation, while respecting the United Nations Charter and international law, to ensure compliance by Israel with international humanitarian law as embodied in that Convention".

1913. The 2005 World Summit Outcome document recognized that the international community, through the United Nations, also has the responsibility to use appropriate diplomatic, humanitarian and other peaceful means, in accordance with Chapters VI and VIII of the Charter, to help protect populations from, inter alia, war crimes and crimes against humanity. The document stressed that the Members of the United Nations are prepared to take collective action, in a timely and decisive manner, through the Security Council, in accordance with the Charter, including Chapter VII should peaceful means be inadequate and national authorities are manifestly failing to protect their populations from genocide, war crimes, ethnic cleansing and crimes against humanity. In 2009, the Secretary-General, in his report on implementing the responsibility to protect, noted that the enumeration of these crimes did not "detract in any way from the much broader range of obligations existing under international humanitarian law, international human rights law, refugee law and international criminal law."

1914. After decades of sustained conflict, the level of threat to which both Palestinians and Israelis are subjected has not abated, but if anything increased with continued escalations of violence, death and suffering for the civilian population, of which the December-January military operations in Gaza are only the most recent occurrence. Israel is therefore also failing to protect its own citizens by refusing to acknowledge the futility of resorting to violent means and military power.

1915. Israeli incursions and military actions in the Gaza Strip did not stop after the end of the military operations of December – January.

1916. The Security Council has placed the protection of civilian populations on its agenda as a regular item, recognizing it as a matter falling within its responsibility. The Mission notes that the international community has been largely silent and has to date failed to act to ensure the protection of the civilian population in the Gaza Strip and generally the Occupied Palestinian Territory. Suffice it to notice the lack of adequate reaction to the blockade and its consequences, to the Gaza military operations and, in their aftermath, to the continuing obstacles to reconstruction. The Mission also considers that the isolation of the Gaza authorities and the sanctions against the Gaza Strip have had a negative impact on the protection of the population. Immediate action to enable reconstruction in Gaza is no doubt required. However, it also needs to be accompanied by a firmer and principled stance by the international community on violations of international humanitarian and human rights law and long delayed action to end them. Protection of civilian populations requires respect for international law and accountability for violations. When the international community does not live up to its own legal standards, the threat to the international rule of law is obvious and potentially far-reaching in its consequences.

1917. The Mission acknowledges and emphasizes the impressive and essential role played by the staff of the numerous United Nations agencies and bodies working to assist the population of the Occupied Palestinian Territory in all aspects of daily life. An additional disturbing feature of the December-January military operations was the disregard in several incidents, some of which are documented in this report, for the inviolability of United Nations premises, facilities and staff. It ought to go without saying that attacks on the United Nations are unacceptable and undermine its ability to fulfil its protection and assistance role vis-à-vis a population that so badly needs it.

J. Summary of legal findings

1918. Detailed legal findings by the Mission are included in each of the chapters of the report where specific facts and events are analysed. The following is a summary of those findings.

1. Actions by Israel in Gaza in the context of the military operations of 27 December 2008 to 18 January 2009

(a) Precautions in launching attacks

1919. The Mission finds that in a number of cases Israel failed to take feasible precautions required by customary law reflected in article 57 (2) (a) (ii) of Additional Protocol I to avoid or minimize incidental loss of civilian life, injury to civilians and damage to civilian objects. The firing of white phosphorus shells over the UNRWA compound in Gaza City is one of such cases in which precautions were not taken in the choice of weapons and methods in the attack, and these facts were compounded by reckless disregard for the consequences. The intentional strike at al-Quds hospital using high-explosive artillery shells and white phosphorous in and around the hospital also violated articles 18 and 19 of the Fourth Geneva Convention. With regard to the attack against al-Wafa hospital, the Mission found a violation of the same provisions, as well as a violation of the customary law prohibition against attacks which may be expected to cause excessive damage to civilians and civilian objects.

1920. The Mission finds that the different kinds of warnings issued by Israel in Gaza cannot be considered as sufficiently effective in the circumstances to comply with customary law as reflected in Additional Protocol I, article 57 (2) (c). While some of the leaflet warnings were specific in nature, the Mission does not consider that general messages telling people to leave wherever they were and go to city centres, in the particular circumstances of the military campaign, meet the threshold of effectiveness. Firing missiles into or on top of buildings as a "warning" is essentially a dangerous practice and a form of attack rather than a warning.

A/HRC/12/48 (ADVANCE 2)
page 12

(b) Incidents involving the killing of civilians

1921. The Mission found numerous instances of deliberate attacks on civilians and civilian objects (individuals, whole families, houses, mosques) in violation of the fundamental international humanitarian law principle of distinction, resulting in deaths and serious injuries. In these cases the Mission found that the protected status of civilians was not respected and the attacks were intentional, in clear violation of customary law reflected in article 51 (2) and 75 of Additional Protocol I, article 27 of the Fourth Geneva Convention and articles 6 and 7 of the International Covenant on Civil and Political Rights. In some cases the Mission additionally concluded that the attack was also launched with the intention of spreading terror among the civilian population. Moreover, in several of the incidents investigated, the Israeli armed forces not only did not use their best efforts to permit humanitarian organizations access to the wounded and medical relief, as required by customary international law reflected in article 10 (2) of Additional Protocol I, but they arbitrarily withheld such access.

1922. With regard to one incident investigated, involving the death of at least 35 Palestinians, the Mission finds that the Israeli armed forces launched an attack which a reasonable commander would have expected to cause excessive loss of civilian life in relation to the military advantage sought, in violation of customary international humanitarian law as reflected in Additional Protocol I, articles 57 (2) (a) (ii) and (iii). The Mission finds a violation of the right to life (ICCPR, article 6) of the civilians killed in this incident.

1923. The Mission also concludes that Israel, by deliberately attacking police stations and killing large numbers of policemen (99 in the incidents investigated by the Mission) during the first minutes of the military operations, failed to respect the principle of proportionality between the military advantage anticipated by killing some policemen who might have been members of Palestinian armed groups and the loss of civilian life (the majority of policemen and members of the public present in the police stations or nearby during the attack). Therefore, these were disproportionate attacks in violation of customary international law. The Mission finds a violation of the right to life (ICCPR, article 6) of the policemen killed in these attacks who were not members of Palestinian armed groups.

(c) Certain weapons used by the Israeli armed forces

1924. In relation to the weapons used by the Israeli armed forces during military operations, the Mission accepts that white phosphorous, flechettes and heavy metal (such as tungsten) are not currently proscribed under international law. Their use is, however, restricted or even prohibited in certain circumstances by virtue of the principles of proportionality and precautions necessary in the attack. Flechettes, as an area weapon, are particularly unsuitable for use in urban settings, while, in the Mission's view, the use of white phosphorous as an obscurant at least should be banned because of the number and variety of hazards that attach to the use of such a pyrophoric chemical.

A/HRC/12/48 (ADVANCE 2)
page 13

(d) Treatment of Palestinians in the hands of the Israeli armed forces

(i) Use of human shields

1925. The Mission investigated several incidents in which the Israeli armed forces used local Palestinian residents to enter houses which might be booby-trapped or harbour enemy combatants (this practice, known in the West Bank as "neighbour procedure", was called "Johnnie procedure" during the military operations in Gaza). The Mission found that the practice constitutes the use of human shields prohibited by international humanitarian law. It further constitutes a violation of the right to life, protected in article 6 of ICCPR, and of the prohibition against cruel and inhuman treatment in its article 7.

1926. The questioning of Palestinian civilians under threat of death or injury to extract information about Hamas and Palestinian combatants and tunnels constitutes a violation of article 31 of the Fourth Geneva Convention, which prohibits physical or moral coercion against protected persons.

(ii) Detention

1927. The Mission found that the Israeli armed forces in Gaza rounded up and detained large groups of persons protected under the Fourth Geneva Convention. The Mission finds that their detention cannot be justified either as detention of "unlawful combatants" or as internment of civilians for imperative reasons of security. The Mission considers that the severe beatings, constant humiliating and degrading treatment and detention in foul conditions allegedly suffered by individuals in the Gaza Strip under the control of the Israeli armed forces and in detention in Israel, constitute a failure to treat protected persons humanely in violation of article 27 of the Fourth Geneva Convention, as well as violations of articles 7 and 10 of the International Covenant on Civil and Political Rights regarding torture and the treatment of persons in detention, and of its article 14 with regard to due process guarantees. The treatment of women during detention was contrary to the special respect for women required under customary law as reflected in the article 76 of Additional Protocol I. The Mission finds that the rounding-up of large groups of civilians and their prolonged detention under the circumstances described in this report constitute a collective penalty on those persons in violation of article 33 of the Fourth Geneva Convention and article 50 of the Hague Regulations. Such treatment amounts to measures of intimidation or terror prohibited by article 33 of the Fourth Geneva Convention.

(e) Destruction of property

1928. The Mission finds that the attacks against the Palestinian Legislative Council building and the main prison in Gaza constituted deliberate attacks on civilian objects in violation of the rule of customary international humanitarian law whereby attacks must be strictly limited to military objectives.

1929. The Mission also finds that the Israeli armed forces unlawfully and wantonly attacked and destroyed without military necessity a number of food production or food-processing objects and facilities (including mills, land and greenhouses), drinking-water installations, farms and animals in violation of the principle of distinction. From the facts ascertained by it, the Mission finds that this destruction was carried out with the purpose of denying sustenance to the civilian population, in violation of customary law reflected in article 54 (2) of the First Additional Protocol. The Mission further concludes that the Israeli armed forces carried out widespread destruction of private residential houses, water wells and water tanks unlawfully and wantonly.

1930. In addition to being violations of international humanitarian law, these extensive wanton acts of destruction amount to violations of Israel's duties to respect the right to an adequate standard of living of the people in the Gaza Strip, which includes the rights to food, water and housing, as well as the right to the highest attainable standard of health, protected under articles 11 and 12 of the International Covenant on Economic, Social and Cultural Rights.

(f) Impact of the blockade and the military operations on the Gaza population

1931. The Mission concludes that the blockade policies implemented by Israel against the Gaza Strip, in particular the closure of or restrictions imposed on border crossings in the immediate period before the military operations, subjected the local population to extreme hardship and deprivations that amounted to a violation of Israel's obligations as an occupying Power under the Fourth Geneva Convention. These measures led to a severe deterioration and regression in the levels of realization of economic and social rights of Palestinians in the Gaza Strip and weakened its social and economic fabric, leaving health, education, sanitation and other essential services in a very vulnerable position to cope with the immediate effects of the military operations.

1932. The Mission finds that, despite the information circulated by Israel about the humanitarian relief schemes in place during the military operations, Israel has essentially violated its obligation to allow free passage of all consignments of medical and hospital objects, food and clothing that were needed to meet the urgent humanitarian needs of the civilian population in the context of the military operations, which is in violation of article 23 of the Fourth Geneva Convention.

1933. In addition to the above general findings, the Mission also considers that Israel has violated its specific obligations under the Convention on the Rights of the Child and the Convention on the Elimination of All Forms of Discrimination against Women, including the rights to peace and security, free movement, livelihood and health.

1934. The Mission concludes that the conditions resulting from deliberate actions of the Israeli armed forces and the declared policies of the Government with regard to the Gaza Strip before, during and after the military operation cumulatively indicate the intention to inflict collective punishment on the people of the Gaza Strip. The Mission, therefore, finds a violation of the provisions of article 33 of the Fourth Geneva Convention.

(g) Grave breaches of the Geneva Conventions and acts raising individual criminal responsibility under international criminal law

1935. From the facts gathered, the Mission found that the following grave breaches of the Fourth Geneva Convention were committed by the Israeli armed forces in Gaza: wilful killing, torture or inhuman treatment, wilfully causing great suffering or serious injury to body or health, and extensive destruction of property, not justified by military necessity and carried out unlawfully and wantonly. As grave breaches these acts give rise to individual criminal responsibility. The Mission notes that the use of human shields also constitutes a war crime under the Rome Statute of the International Criminal Court.

1936. The Mission further considers that the series of acts that deprive Palestinians in the Gaza Strip of their means of subsistence, employment, housing and water, that deny their freedom of movement and their right to leave and enter their own country, that limit their rights to access a court of law and an effective remedy, could lead a competent court to find that the crime of persecution, a crime against humanity, has been committed.

2. Actions by Israel in the West Bank in the context of the military operations in Gaza from 27 December 2008 to 18 January 2009

(a) Treatment of Palestinians in the West Bank by Israeli security forces, including use of excessive or lethal force during demonstrations

1937. With regard to acts of violence by settlers against Palestinians, the Mission concludes that Israel has failed to fulfil its international obligations to protect the Palestinians from violence by private individuals under both international human rights law and international humanitarian law. In some instances security forces acquiesced to the acts of violence in violation of the prohibition against cruel, inhuman or degrading treatment. When this acquiescence occurs only in respect of violence against Palestinians by settlers and not vice versa, it would amount to discrimination on the basis of national origin, prohibited under ICCPR.

1938. Israel also violated a series of human rights by unlawfully repressing peaceful public demonstrations and using excessive force against demonstrators. The use of firearms, including live ammunitions, and the use of snipers resulting in the death of demonstrators are a violation of article 6 of ICCPR as an arbitrary deprivation of life and, in the circumstances examined by the Mission, appear to indicate an intention or at least a recklessness towards causing harm to civilians which may amount to wilful killing.

1939. Excessive use of force that resulted in injury rather than death constitutes violations of a number of standards, including articles 7 and 9 of ICCPR. These violations are compounded by the seemingly discriminatory "open fire regulations" for security forces dealing with demonstrations, based on the presence of persons with a particular nationality, violating the principle of non-discrimination in ICCPR (art. 2) as well as under article 27 of the Fourth Geneva Convention.

1940. The Mission finds that Israel failed to investigate, and when appropriate prosecute, acts by its agents or by third parties involving serious violations of international humanitarian law and human rights law.

1941. The Mission was alarmed at the reported increase in settler violence in the past year and the failure of the Israeli security forces to prevent settlers' attacks against Palestinian civilians and their property. These are accompanied by a series of violations by Israeli forces or acquiesced by them, including the removal of residential status from Palestinians, which could eventually lead to a situation of virtual deportation and entail additional violations of other rights.

(b) Detention of Palestinians by Israel

1942. The Mission analysed information it received on the detention of Palestinians in Israeli prisons during or in the context of the military operations of December 2008–January 2009 and found those practices generally inconsistent with human rights and international humanitarian law. The military court system to which Palestinians from the Occupied Palestinian Territory are subjected deprives them of due process guarantees in keeping with international law.

1943. The Mission finds that the detention of members of the Palestinian Legislative Council by Israel violates the right not to be arbitrarily detained, as protected by article 9 of ICCPR. Insofar as it is based on political affiliation and prevents those members from participating in the conduct of public affairs, it is also in violation of its articles 25 recognizing the right to take part in public affairs and 26, which provides for the right to equal protection under the law. Insofar as their detention is unrelated to their individual behaviour, it constitutes collective punishment, prohibited by article 33 of the Fourth Geneva Convention. Information on the detention of large numbers of children and their treatment by Israeli security forces point to violations of their rights under ICCPR and the Convention on the Rights of the Child.

(c) Violations of the right to free movement and access

1944. The Mission finds that the extensive restrictions imposed by Israel on the movement and access of Palestinians in the West Bank are disproportionate to any legitimate objective served and in violation of article 27 of the Fourth Geneva Convention and article 12 of ICCPR, guaranteeing freedom of movement.

1945. Where checkpoints become a site of humiliation of the protected population by military or civilian operators, this may entail a violation of the customary law rule reflected in article 75 (2) (b) of Additional Protocol I.

1946. The continued construction of settlements in occupied territory constitutes a violation of article 49 of the Fourth Geneva Convention. The extensive destruction and appropriation of property, including land confiscation and house demolitions in the West Bank, including East Jerusalem, not justified by military necessity and carried out unlawfully and wantonly, amounts to a grave breach under article 147 of the Fourth Geneva Convention.

1947. Insofar as movement and access restrictions, the settlements and their infrastructure, demographic policies vis-à-vis Jerusalem and "Area C" of the West Bank, as well as the separation of Gaza from the West Bank, prevent a viable, contiguous and sovereign Palestinian State from arising, they are in violation of the *jus cogens* right to self-determination.

A/HRC/12/48 (ADVANCE 2)
page 17

3. Actions by Israel in Israel

1948. In relation to alleged violations within Israel, the Mission concludes that, although there does not appear to be a policy in this respect, there were occasions when reportedly the authorities placed obstacles in the way of protesters seeking to exercise their right to peaceful assembly and freedom of speech to criticize Israel's military actions in the Gaza Strip. These rights are protected by the International Covenant on Civil and Political Rights. Instances of physical violence against protesters and other humiliations, not rising to the level of physical violence, of the protesters by the police violated Israel's obligations under article 10 of the Covenant. The Mission is also concerned about activists being compelled to attend interviews with the General Security Services (*Shabak*), which reportedly creates an atmosphere intolerant of dissent within Israel. Hostile retaliatory actions against civil society organizations by the Government of Israel for criticisms of the Israeli authorities and for exposing alleged violations of international human rights law and international humanitarian law during the military operations are inconsistent with the Declaration on the Right and Responsibility of Individuals, Groups and Organs of Society to Promote and Protect Universally Recognized Human Rights and Fundamental Freedoms.

1949. The Mission finds that the imposition of a near blanket exclusion of the media and human rights monitors from Gaza since 5 November 2008 and throughout the operations is inconsistent with Israel's obligations with regard to the right to access to information.

4. Actions by Palestinian armed groups

1950. In relation to the firing of rockets and mortars into southern Israel by Palestinian armed groups operating in the Gaza Strip, the Mission finds that the Palestinian armed groups fail to distinguish between military targets and the civilian population and civilian objects in southern Israel. The launching of rockets and mortars which cannot be aimed with sufficient precisions at military targets breaches the fundamental principle of distinction. Where there is no intended military target and the rockets and mortars are launched into civilian areas, they constitute a deliberate attack against the civilian population. These actions would constitute war crimes and may amount to crimes against humanity.

1951. The Mission concludes that the rocket and mortars attacks, launched by Palestinian armed groups operating from Gaza, have caused terror in the affected communities of southern Israel. The attacks have caused loss of life and physical and mental injury to civilians as well as damaging private houses, religious buildings and property, and eroded the economic and cultural life of the affected communities and severely affected economic and social rights of the population.

1952. With regard to the continuing detention of Israeli soldier Gilad Shalit, the Mission finds that, as a soldier who belongs to the Israeli armed forces and who was captured during an enemy incursion into Israel, Gilad Shalit meets the requirements for prisoner-of-war status under the Third Geneva Convention and should be protected, treated humanely and be allowed external communication as appropriate according to that Convention.

1953. The Mission also examined whether the Palestinian armed groups complied with their obligations under international humanitarian law to take constant care to minimize the risk of harm to the civilian population in Gaza among whom the hostilities were being conducted. The conduct of hostilities in built-up areas does not, of itself, constitute a violation of international law. However, launching attacks – whether of rockets and mortars at the population of southern Israel or at the Israeli armed forces inside Gaza – close to civilian or protected buildings constitutes a failure to take all feasible precautions. In cases where this occurred, the Palestinian armed groups would have unnecessarily exposed the civilian population of Gaza to the inherent dangers of the military operations taking place around them. The Mission found no evidence to suggest that Palestinian armed groups either directed civilians to areas where attacks were being launched or that they forced civilians to remain within the vicinity of the attacks. The Mission also found no evidence that members of Palestinian armed groups engaged in combat in civilian dress. Although in the one incident of an Israeli attack on a mosque it investigated the Mission found that there was no indication that that mosque was used for military purposes or to shield military activities, the Mission cannot exclude that this might have occurred in other cases.

5. Actions by responsible Palestinian authorities

1954. Although the Gaza authorities deny any control over armed groups and responsibility for their acts, in the Mission's view, if they failed to take the necessary measures to prevent the Palestinian armed groups from endangering the civilian population, the Gaza authorities would bear responsibility for the damage arising to the civilians living in Gaza.

1955. The Mission finds that security services under the control of the Gaza authorities carried out extrajudicial executions, arbitrary arrests, detentions and ill-treatment of people, in particular political opponents, which constitute serious violations of the human rights to life, to liberty and security of the person, to freedom from torture or cruel, inhuman or degrading treatment or punishment, to be protected against arbitrary arrest and detention, to a fair and impartial legal proceeding; and to freedom of opinion and expression, including freedom to hold opinions without interference.

1956. The Mission also concludes that the Palestinian Authority's actions against political opponents in the West Bank, which started in January 2006 and intensified during the period between 27 December 2008 and 18 January 2009, constitute violations of human rights and of the Palestinians' own Basic Law. Detentions on political grounds violate the rights to liberty and security of person, to a fair trial and the right not to be discriminated against on the basis of one's political opinion, which are all part of customary international law. Reports of torture and other forms of ill-treatment during arrest and detention and of death in detention require prompt investigation and accountability.

K. The need for accountability

1957. The Mission was struck by the repeated comment of Palestinian victims, human rights defenders, civil society interlocutors and officials that they hoped that this would be the last investigative mission of its kind, because action for justice would follow from it. It was struck, as well, by the comment that every time a report is published and no action follows, this "emboldens Israel and her conviction of being untouchable". To deny modes of accountability reinforces impunity, and tarnishes the credibility of the United Nations and of the international community. The Mission believes these comments ought to be at the forefront in the consideration by Members States and United Nations bodies of its findings and recommendations and action consequent upon them.

1958. The Mission is firmly convinced that justice and respect for the rule of law are the indispensable basis for peace. The prolonged situation of impunity has created a justice crisis in the Occupied Palestinian Territory that warrants action.

1959. After reviewing Israel's system of investigation and prosecution of serious violations of human rights and humanitarian law, in particular of suspected war crimes and crimes against humanity, the Mission found major structural flaws that, in its view, make the system inconsistent with international standards. With military "operational debriefings" at the core of the system, there is no effective and impartial investigation mechanism and victims of such alleged violations are deprived of any effective or prompt remedy. Furthermore, such investigations, being internal to the Israeli military authority, do not comply with international standards of independence and impartiality. The Mission believes that the few investigations conducted by the Israeli authorities on alleged serious violations of international human rights and humanitarian law and, in particular, alleged war crimes, in the context of the military operations in Gaza between 27 December 2008 and 18 January 2009, are affected by the defects in the system, have been unduly delayed despite the gravity of the allegations, and, therefore, lack the required credibility and conformity with international standards. The Mission is concerned that investigations of relatively less serious violations that the Government of Israel claims to be investigating have also been unduly protracted.

1960. The Mission noted the pattern of delays, inaction or otherwise unsatisfactory handling by Israeli authorities of investigations, prosecutions and convictions of military personnel and settlers for violence and offences against Palestinians, including in the West Bank, as well as their discriminatory outcome. Additionally, the current constitutional and legal framework in Israel provides very few possibilities, if any, for Palestinians to seek compensation and reparations.

1961. In the light of the information it reviewed and its analysis, the Mission concludes that there are serious doubts about the willingness of Israel to carry out genuine investigations in an impartial, independent, prompt and effective way as required by international law. The Mission is also of the view that the system presents inherently discriminatory features that make the pursuit of justice for Palestinian victims extremely difficult.

1962. With regard to allegations of violations of international humanitarian law falling within the jurisdiction of responsible Palestinian authorities in Gaza, the Mission finds that these allegations have not been investigated.

1963. The Mission notes that the responsibility to investigate violations of international human rights and humanitarian law, prosecute if appropriate and try perpetrators belongs in the first place to domestic authorities and institutions. This is a legal obligation

A/HRC/12/48 (ADVANCE 2)
page 20

incumbent on States and State-like entities. However, where domestic authorities are unable or unwilling to comply with this obligation, international justice mechanisms must be activated to prevent impunity.

1964. The Mission believes that, in the circumstances, there is little potential for accountability for serious violations of international humanitarian and human rights law through domestic institutions in Israel and even less in Gaza. The Mission is of the view that long-standing impunity has been a key factor in the perpetuation of violence in the region and in the reoccurrence of violations, as well as in the erosion of confidence among Palestinians and many Israelis concerning prospects for justice and a peaceful solution to the conflict.

1965. The Mission considers that several of the violations referred to in this report amount to grave breaches of the Fourth Geneva Convention. It notes that there is a duty imposed by the Geneva Conventions on all high contracting parties to search for and bring before their courts those responsible for the alleged violations.

1966. The Mission considers that the serious violations of international humanitarian law recounted in this report fall within the subject-matter jurisdiction of the International Criminal Court. The Mission notes that the United Nations Security Council has long recognized the impact of the situation in the Middle East, including the Palestinian question, on international peace and security, and that it regularly considers and reviews this situation. The Mission is persuaded that, in the light of the long-standing nature of the conflict, the frequent and consistent allegations of violations of international humanitarian law against all parties, the apparent increase in intensity of such violations in the recent military operations, and the regrettable possibility of a return to further violence, meaningful and practical steps to end impunity for such violations would offer an effective way to deter such violations recurring in the future. The Mission is of the view that the prosecution of persons responsible for serious violations of international humanitarian law would contribute to ending such violations, to the protection of civilians and to the restoration and maintenance of peace.

XXXI. RECOMMENDATIONS

1967. The Mission makes the following recommendations related to:

(a) Accountability for serious violations of international humanitarian law;

(b) Reparations;

(c) Serious violations of human rights law;

(d) The blockade and reconstruction;

(e) The use of weapons and military procedures;

(f) The protection of human rights organizations and defenders;

(g) Follow-up to the Mission's recommendations.

1968. **To the Human Rights Council,**

(a) The Mission recommends that the United Nations Human Rights Council should endorse the recommendations contained in this report, take appropriate action to implement them as recommended by the Mission and through other means as it may deem appropriate, and continue to review their implementation in future sessions;

(b) In view of the gravity of the violations of international human rights and humanitarian law and possible war crimes and crimes against humanity that it has reported, the Mission recommends that the United Nations Human Rights Council should request the United Nations Secretary-General to bring this report to the attention of the United Nations Security Council under Article 99 of the Charter of the United Nations so that the Security Council may consider action according to the Mission's relevant recommendations below;

(c) The Mission further recommends that the United Nations Human Rights Council should formally submit this report to the Prosecutor of the International Criminal Court;

(d) The Mission recommends that the Human Rights Council should submit this report to the General Assembly with a request that it should be considered;

(e) The Mission recommends that the Human Rights Council should bring the Mission's recommendations to the attention of the relevant United Nations human rights treaty bodies so that they may include review of progress in their implementation, as may be relevant to their mandate and procedures, in their periodic review of compliance by Israel with its human rights obligations. The Mission further recommends that the Human Rights Council should consider review of progress as part of its universal periodic review process.

1969. **To the United Nations Security Council,**

(a) The Mission recommends that the Security Council should require the Government of Israel, under Article 40 of the Charter of the United Nations:

(i) To take all appropriate steps, within a period of three months, to launch appropriate investigations that are independent and in conformity with international standards, into the serious violations of international humanitarian and international human rights law reported by the Mission and any other serious allegations that might come to its attention;

(ii) To inform the Security Council, within a further period of three months, of actions taken, or in process of being taken, by the Government of Israel to inquire into, investigate and prosecute such serious violations;

(b) The Mission further recommends that the Security Council should at the same time establish an independent committee of experts in international humanitarian and human rights law to monitor and report on any domestic legal or other proceedings undertaken by the Government of Israel in relation to the aforesaid investigations. Such committee of experts should report at the end of the six-month period to the Security Council on its assessment of relevant domestic proceedings initiated by the Government of Israel, including their progress, effectiveness and genuineness, so that the Security Council may assess whether appropriate action to ensure justice for victims and accountability for perpetrators has been or is being taken at the domestic level. The Security Council should request the committee to report to it at determined intervals, as may be necessary. The committee should be appropriately supported by the Office of the United Nations High Commissioner for Human Rights;

(c) The Mission recommends that, upon receipt of the committee's report, the Security Council should consider the situation and, in the absence of good-faith investigations that are independent and in conformity with international standards having been undertaken or being under way within six months of the date of its resolution under Article 40 by the appropriate authorities of the State of Israel, again acting under Chapter VII of the Charter of the United Nations, refer the situation in Gaza to the Prosecutor of the International Criminal Court pursuant to article 13 (b) of the Rome Statute;

(d) The Mission recommends that the Security Council should require the independent committee of experts referred to in subparagraph (b) to monitor and report on any domestic legal or other proceedings undertaken by the relevant authorities in the Gaza Strip in relation to the aforesaid investigations. The committee should report at the end of the six-month period to the Security Council on its assessment of relevant domestic proceedings initiated by the relevant authorities in Gaza, including their progress, effectiveness and genuineness, so that the Security Council may assess whether appropriate action to ensure justice for victims and accountability for perpetrators has been taken or is being taken at the domestic level. The Security Council should request the committee to report to it at determined intervals, as may be necessary;

(e) The Mission recommends that, upon receipt of the committee's report, the Security Council should consider the situation and, in the absence of good-faith investigations that are independent and in conformity with international standards having been undertaken or being under way within six months of the date of its resolution under Article 40 by the appropriate authorities in Gaza, acting under Chapter VII of the Charter of the United Nations, refer the situation in Gaza to the Prosecutor of the International Criminal Court pursuant to article 13 (b) of the Rome Statute;

(f) The Mission recommends that lack of cooperation by the Government of Israel or the Gaza authorities with the work of the committee should be regarded by the Security Council to be obstruction of the work of the committee.

1970. To the Prosecutor of the International Criminal Court, with reference to the declaration under article 12 (3) received by the Office of the Prosecutor of the International Criminal Court from the Government of Palestine, the Mission considers that accountability for victims and the interests of peace and justice in the region require that the Prosecutor should make the required legal determination as expeditiously as possible.

1971. To the General Assembly,

(a) The Mission recommends that the General Assembly should request the Security Council to report to it on measures taken with regard to ensuring accountability for serious violations of international humanitarian law and human rights in relation to the facts in this report and any other relevant facts in the context of the military operations in Gaza, including the implementation of the Mission's recommendations. The General Assembly may remain appraised of the matter until it is satisfied that appropriate action is taken at the domestic or international level in order to ensure justice for victims and accountability for perpetrators. The General Assembly may consider whether additional action within its powers is required in the interests of justice, including under its resolution 377 (V) on uniting for peace;

(b) The Mission recommends that the General Assembly should establish an escrow fund to be used to pay adequate compensation to Palestinians who have suffered loss and damage as a result of unlawful acts attributable to Israel during the December–January military operation and actions in connection with it, and that the Government of Israel should pay the required amounts into such fund. The Mission further recommends that the General Assembly should ask the Office of the United Nations High Commissioner for Human Rights to provide expert advice on the appropriate modalities to establish the escrow fund;

(c) The Mission recommends that the General Assembly should ask the Government of Switzerland to convene a conference of the high contracting parties to the Fourth Geneva Convention of 1949 on measures to enforce the Convention in the Occupied Palestinian Territory and to ensure its respect in accordance with its article 1;

(d) The Mission recommends that the General Assembly should promote an urgent discussion on the future legality of the use of certain munitions referred to in this report, and in particular white phosphorous, flechettes and heavy metal such as tungsten. In such discussion the General Assembly should draw inter alia on the expertise of the International Committee of the Red Cross (ICRC). The Mission further recommends that the Government of Israel should undertake a moratorium on the use of such weapons in the light of the human suffering and damage they have caused in the Gaza Strip.

1972. To the State of Israel,

(a) The Mission recommends that Israel should immediately cease the border closures and restrictions on passage through border crossings with the Gaza Strip and allow the passage of goods necessary and sufficient to meet the needs of the population, for the recovery and reconstruction of housing and essential services, and for the resumption of meaningful economic activity in the Gaza Strip;

(b) The Mission recommends that Israel should cease the restrictions on access to the sea for fishing purposes imposed on the Gaza Strip and allow such fishing activities within the 20 nautical miles as provided for in the Oslo Accords. It further recommends that Israel should allow the resumption of agricultural activity within the Gaza Strip, including within areas in the vicinity of the borders with Israel;

(c) Israel should initiate a review of the rules of engagement, standard operating procedures, open fire regulations and other guidance for military and security personnel. The Mission recommends that Israel should avail itself of the expertise of the International Committee of the Red Cross, the Office of the United Nations High Commissioner for Human Rights and other relevant bodies, and Israeli experts, civil society organizations with the relevant expertise and specialization, in order to ensure compliance in this respect with international humanitarian law and international human rights law. In particular such rules of engagement should ensure that the principles of proportionality, distinction, precaution and non-discrimination are effectively integrated in all such guidance and in any oral briefings provided to officers, soldiers and security forces, so as to avoid the recurrence of Palestinian civilian deaths, destruction and affronts on human dignity in violation of international law;

(d) The Mission recommends that Israel should allow freedom of movement for Palestinians within the Occupied Palestinian Territory - within the West Bank, including East Jerusalem, between the Gaza Strip and the West Bank, and between the Occupied Palestinian Territory and the outside world - in accordance with international human rights standards and international commitments entered into by Israel and the representatives of the Palestinian people. The Mission further recommends that Israel should forthwith lift travel bans currently placed on Palestinians by reason of their human rights or political activities;

(e) The Mission recommends that Israel should release Palestinians who are detained in Israeli prisons in connection with the occupation. The release of children should be an utmost priority. The Mission further recommends that Israel should cease the discriminatory treatment of Palestinian detainees. Family visits for prisoners from Gaza should resume;

(f) The Mission recommends that Israel should forthwith cease interference with national political processes in the Occupied Palestinian Territory, and as a first step release all members of the Palestinian Legislative Council currently in detention and allow all members of the Council to move between Gaza and the West Bank so that it may resume functioning;

(g) The Mission recommends that the Government of Israel should cease actions aimed at limiting the expression of criticism by civil society and members of the public concerning Israel's policies and conduct during the military operations in the Gaza Strip. The Mission also recommends that Israel should set up an independent inquiry to assess whether the treatment by Israeli judicial authorities of Palestinian and Jewish Israelis expressing dissent in connection with the offensive was discriminatory, in terms of both charges and detention pending trial. The results of the inquiry should be made public and, subject to the findings, appropriate remedial action should be taken;

(h) The Mission recommends that the Government of Israel should refrain from any action of reprisal against Palestinian and Israeli individuals and organizations that have cooperated with the United Nations Fact Finding Mission on the Gaza Conflict, in particular individuals who have appeared at the public hearings held by the Mission in Gaza and Geneva and expressed criticism of actions by Israel;

(i) The Mission recommends that Israel should reiterate its commitment to respecting the inviolability of United Nations premises and personnel and that it should undertake all appropriate measures to ensure that there is no repetition of violations in the future. It further recommends that reparation to the United Nations should be provided fully and without further delay by Israel, and that the General Assembly should consider this matter.

1973. To Palestinian armed groups,

(a) The Mission recommends that Palestinian armed groups should undertake forthwith to respect international humanitarian law, in particular by renouncing attacks on Israeli civilians and civilian objects, and take all feasible precautionary measures to avoid harm to Palestinian civilians during hostilities;

(b) The Mission recommends that Palestinian armed groups who hold Israeli soldier Gilad Shalit in detention should release him on humanitarian grounds. Pending such release they should recognize his status as prisoner of war, treat him as such, and allow him ICRC visits.

1974. To responsible Palestinian authorities,

(a) The Mission recommends that the Palestinian Authority should issue clear instructions to security forces under its command to abide by human rights norms as enshrined in the Palestinian Basic Law and international instruments, ensure prompt and independent investigation of all allegations of serious human rights violations by security forces under its control, and end resort to military justice to deal with cases involving civilians;

(b) The Mission recommends that the Palestinian Authority and the Gaza authorities should release without delay all political detainees currently in their power and refrain from further arrests on political grounds and in violation of international human rights law;

(c) The Mission recommends that the Palestinian Authority and the Gaza authorities should continue to enable the free and independent operation of Palestinian non-governmental organizations, including human rights organizations, and of the Independent Commission for Human Rights.

1975. To the international community,

(a) The Mission recommends that the States parties to the Geneva Conventions of 1949 should start criminal investigations in national courts, using universal jurisdiction, where there is sufficient evidence of the commission of grave breaches of the Geneva Conventions of 1949. Where so warranted following investigation, alleged perpetrators should be arrested and prosecuted in accordance with internationally recognized standards of justice;

(b) International aid providers should step up financial and technical assistance for organizations providing psychological support and mental health services to the Palestinian population;

(c) In view of their crucial function, the Mission recommends that donor countries/assistance providers should continue to support the work of Palestinian and Israeli human rights organizations in documenting and publicly reporting on violations of human rights and international humanitarian law, and advising relevant authorities on their compliance with international law;

(d) The Mission recommends that States involved in peace negotiations between Israel and representatives of the Palestinian people, especially the Quartet, should ensure that respect for the rule of law, international law and human rights assumes a central role in internationally sponsored peace initiatives;

(e) In view of the allegations and reports about long-term environmental damage that may have been created by certain munitions or debris from munitions, the Mission recommends that a programme of environmental monitoring should take place under the auspices of the United Nations, for as long as deemed necessary. The programme should include the Gaza Strip and areas within southern Israel close to impact sites. The environmental monitoring programme should be in accordance with the recommendations of an independent body, and samples and analyses should be analysed by one or more independent expert institutions. Such recommendations, at least at the outset, should include measurement mechanisms which address the fears of the population of Gaza and southern Israel at this time and should at a minimum be in a position to determine the presences of heavy metals of all varieties, white phosphorous, tungsten micro-shrapnel and granules and such other chemicals as may be revealed by the investigation.

1976. To the international community and responsible Palestinian authorities,

(a) The Mission recommends that appropriate mechanisms should be established to ensure that the funds pledged by international donors for reconstruction activities in the Gaza Strip are smoothly and efficiently disbursed, and urgently put to use for the benefit of the population of Gaza;

(b) In view of the consequences of the military operations, the Mission recommends that responsible Palestinian authorities as well as international aid providers should pay special attention to the needs of persons with disabilities. In addition, the Mission recommends that medical follow-up should be ensured by relevant international and Palestinian structures with regard to patients who suffered amputations or were otherwise injured by munitions, the nature of which has not been clarified, in order to monitor any possible long-term impact on their health. Financial and technical assistance should be provided to ensure adequate medical follow-up to Palestinian patients.

1977. To the international community, Israel and Palestinian authorities,

(a) The Mission recommends that Israel and representatives of the Palestinian people, and international actors involved in the peace process, should involve Israeli and

Palestinian civil society in devising sustainable peace agreements based on respect for international law. The participation of women should be ensured in accordance with Security Council resolution 1325 (2000);

(b) The Mission recommends that attention should be given to the position of women and steps be taken to ensure their access to compensation, legal assistance and economic security.

1978. To the United Nations Secretary-General, the Mission recommends that the Secretary-General should develop a policy to integrate human rights in peace initiatives in which the United Nations is involved, especially the Quartet, and request the United Nations High Commissioner for Human Rights to provide the expertise required to implement this recommendation.

1979. To the Office of the United Nations High Commissioner for Human Rights,

(a) The Mission recommends that the Office of the United Nations High Commissioner for Human Rights should monitor the situation of persons who have cooperated with the United Nations Fact Finding Mission on the Gaza Conflict and periodically update the Human Rights Council through its public reports and in other ways as it may deem appropriate;

(b) The Mission recommends that the Office of the High Commissioner for Human Rights should give attention to the Mission's recommendations in its periodic reporting on the Occupied Palestinian Territory to the Human Rights Council.

- - - - -

Document [4] UN Human Rights Council Resolution S-12/1

UNITED NATIONS	

 General Assembly

Distr.
GENERAL

A/HRC/RES/S-12/1
21 October 2009

Original: ENGLISH

HUMAN RIGHTS COUNCIL
Twelfth special session
15 – 16 October 2009

Resolution adopted by the Human Rights Council[*]

S-12/1. The human rights situation in the Occupied Palestinian Territory, including East Jerusalem

A

The Human Rights Council,

Recalling the Universal Declaration of Human Rights, the International Covenant on Civil and Political Rights, and the International Covenant on Economic, Social and Cultural Rights,

Affirming the responsibility of the international community to promote human rights and ensure respect for international law,

Emphasizing the particularity of The Occupied East Jerusalem in its rich religious and cultural heritage,

Recalling all relevant United Nations resolutions including Security Council resolutions on Occupied East Jerusalem,

---

[*] The resolution and decision adopted by the Human Rights Council will be contained in the report of the Council on its twelfth special session (A/HRC/S-12/1), chap. I.

GE.09-16807

A/HRC/RES/S-12/1
page 2

Deeply concerned at the actions by Israel undermining the sanctity and inviolability of religious sites in the Occupied Palestinian Territory including East Jerusalem,

Deeply concerned also at the policy of closure and severe restrictions of Israel, including the permit regime, which continue to be imposed on the movement of Palestinians hindering their free access to their Christian and Muslim holy sites, including Al- Aqsa Mosque,

1. *Strongly condemns* all policies and measures taken by Israel, the occupying Power, including those limiting access of Palestinians to their properties and holy sites particularly in Occupied East Jerusalem, on the basis of national origin, religion, sex, age or any other discriminatory ground, which are in grave violation of the Palestinian People's civil, political, economic, social and cultural rights;

2. *Condemns further* the recent violations of human rights by Israel in Occupied East Jerusalem, particularly the confiscation of lands and properties, the demolishing of houses and private properties, the construction and expansion of settlements, the continuous construction of the separation Wall, changing the demographic and geographic character of East Jerusalem, the restrictions on the freedom of movement of the Palestinian citizens of East Jerusalem, as well as the continuous digging and excavation works in and around Al-Aqsa mosque and its vicinity;

3. *Demands* Israel, the occupying Power, to respect the religious and cultural rights in the Occupied Palestinian Territory as provided for in the Universal Declaration of Human Rights, the core international human rights instruments, the Hague Conventions, and the Geneva Conventions, and to allow Palestinian citizens and worshippers unhindered access to their properties and religious sites therein;

4. *Also demands* that Israel, the occupying Power, immediately cease all digging and excavation works and activities beneath and around Al-Aqsa Mosque and its vicinity, and refrain from any acts or operations that may endanger the structure or foundations or change the nature of holy sites both Christian and Islamic in the Occupied Palestinian Territory, including East Jerusalem;

5. *Requests* the United Nations High Commissioner for Human Rights, pursuant to resolution S-9/1 of 12 January 2009 and in the context of her periodic reports, to monitor,

document and report on the state of implementation by Israel, the occupying Power, of its human rights obligations in and around East Jerusalem;

B

The Human Rights Council,

Guided by the principles and objectives of the Charter of the United Nations and the Universal Declaration of Human Rights,

Considering that the promotion of respect for the obligations arising from the Charter and other instruments and rules of international law is among the basic purposes and principles of the United Nations,

Reaffirming the right of the Palestinian people to self-determination and the inadmissibility of the acquisition of land by the use of force, as enshrined in the Charter of the United Nations,

Acknowledging that peace, security, development and human rights are the pillars of the United Nations system,

Affirming the applicability of international human rights law and the international humanitarian law, namely the Fourth Geneva Convention relative to the Protection of Civilian Persons in Time of War, to the Occupied Palestinian Territory, including East Jerusalem,

Expressing serious concern at the lack of implementation by the occupying Power, Israel, of previously adopted resolutions and recommendations of the Council relating to the human rights situation in the Occupied Palestinian Territory, including East Jerusalem,

Recalling its resolution S-9/1 of 12 January 2009, in which the Council decided to dispatch an urgent, independent international fact-finding mission, and its call upon the occupying Power, Israel, not to obstruct the process of investigation and to fully cooperate with the mission,

Condemning all targeting of civilians and stressing the urgent need to ensure accountability for all violations of international human rights law and international humanitarian law to prevent further violations;

A/HRC/RES/S-12/1
page 4

1. *Condemns* the non-cooperation by the occupying Power, Israel, with the independent international fact-finding mission;

2. *Welcomes* the report of the Independent International Fact-Finding Mission (A/HRC/12/48);

3. *Endorses* the recommendations contained in the report of the Independent International Fact-Finding Mission, and calls upon all concerned parties including United Nations bodies, to ensure their implementation in accordance with their respective mandates;

4. *Recommends that* the General Assembly consider the report of the Independent International Fact-Finding Mission, during the main part of its sixty-fourth session;

5. *Requests* the United Nations Secretary-General to submit to the Council, at its thirteenth session, a report on the status of implementation of paragraph 3. above;

C

The Human Rights Council,

Emphasizing that international human rights law and international humanitarian law are complementary and mutually reinforcing,

Recalling the obligations of the High Contracting Parties to the Fourth Geneva Convention, and *reaffirming* that each High Contracting Party to the Fourth Geneva Convention relative to the Protection of Civilian Persons in Time of War is under the obligation to respect and ensure the respect for the obligations arising from that Convention,

Stressing that the right to life constitutes the most fundamental of all human rights,

Recognizing that the siege by Israel imposed on the occupied Gaza Strip, including its closure of border crossings and the cutting of the supply of fuel, food and medicine, constitutes collective punishment of Palestinian civilians and leads to disastrous humanitarian and environmental consequences,

A/HRC/RES/S-12/1
page 5

1. *Welcomes* the first periodic report of the United Nations High Commissioner for Human Rights on the implementation of the Human Rights Council resolution S-9/1(A/HRC/12/37);

2. *Endorses* the recommendations contained in the first periodic report of the High Commissioner, and calls upon all concerned parties including United Nations bodies to ensure their implementation in accordance with their respective mandates;

3. *Requests* the High Commissioner for Human Rights to submit to the Council, at its thirteenth session, a report on the status of implementation of this resolution;

4. *Decides* to follow up on the implementation of section A, section B and section C of the present resolution at its thirteenth session.

2nd meeting
16 October 2009

[Adopted by a recorded vote of 25 to 6, with 11 abstentions. The voting was as follows:

In favour:	Argentina, Bahrain, Bangladesh, Bolivia, Brazil, Chile, China, Cuba, Djibouti, Egypt, Ghana, India, Indonesia, Jordan, Mauritius, Nicaragua, Nigeria, Pakistan, Philippines, Qatar, Russian Federation, Saudi Arabia, Senegal, South Africa, Zambia;
Against:	Hungary, Italy, Netherlands, Slovakia, Ukraine, United States of America;
Abstaining:	Belgium, Bosnia and Herzegovina, Burkina Faso, Cameroon, Gabon, Japan, Mexico, Norway, Republic of Korea, Slovenia, Uruguay.]

Document [5] UN General Assembly Resolution 64/10 with Official Records

United Nations   A/RES/64/10

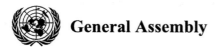 General Assembly

Distr.: General
1 December 2009

Sixty-fourth session
Agenda item 64

Resolution adopted by the General Assembly

[*without reference to a Main Committee (A/64/L.11 and Add.1)*]

64/10. Follow-up to the report of the United Nations Fact-Finding Mission on the Gaza Conflict

The General Assembly,

Guided by the purposes and principles of the Charter of the United Nations,

Recalling the relevant rules and principles of international law, including international humanitarian and human rights law, in particular the Geneva Convention relative to the Protection of Civilian Persons in Time of War, of 12 August 1949,[1] which is applicable to the Occupied Palestinian Territory, including East Jerusalem,

Recalling also the Universal Declaration of Human Rights[2] and the other human rights covenants, including the International Covenant on Civil and Political Rights,[3] the International Covenant on Economic, Social and Cultural Rights[3] and the Convention on the Rights of the Child,[4]

Recalling further its relevant resolutions, including resolution ES-10/18 of 16 January 2009 of its tenth emergency special session,

Recalling the relevant Security Council resolutions, including resolution 1860 (2009) of 8 January 2009,

Recalling also the relevant resolutions of the Human Rights Council, including resolution S-12/1 of 16 October 2009,

Expressing its appreciation to the United Nations Fact-Finding Mission on the Gaza Conflict, led by Justice Richard Goldstone, for its comprehensive report,[5]

Affirming the obligation of all parties to respect international humanitarian law and international human rights law,

---

[1] United Nations, *Treaty Series*, vol. 75, No. 973.
[2] Resolution 217 A (III).
[3] See resolution 2200 A (XXI), annex.
[4] United Nations, *Treaty Series*, vol. 1577, No. 27531.
[5] A/HRC/12/48.

Emphasizing the importance of the safety and well-being of all civilians, and reaffirming the obligation to ensure the protection of civilians in armed conflict,

Gravely concerned by reports regarding serious human rights violations and grave breaches of international humanitarian law committed during the Israeli military operations in the Gaza Strip that were launched on 27 December 2008, including the findings of the Fact-Finding Mission and of the Board of Inquiry convened by the Secretary-General,[6]

Condemning all targeting of civilians and civilian infrastructure and institutions, including United Nations facilities,

Stressing the need to ensure accountability for all violations of international humanitarian law and international human rights law in order to prevent impunity, ensure justice, deter further violations and promote peace,

Convinced that achieving a just, lasting and comprehensive settlement of the question of Palestine, the core of the Arab-Israeli conflict, is imperative for the attainment of a comprehensive, just and lasting peace and stability in the Middle East,

1. *Endorses* the report of the Human Rights Council on its twelfth special session, held on 15 and 16 October 2009;[7]

2. *Requests* the Secretary-General to transmit the report of the United Nations Fact-Finding Mission on the Gaza Conflict[5] to the Security Council;

3. *Calls upon* the Government of Israel to take all appropriate steps, within a period of three months, to undertake investigations that are independent, credible and in conformity with international standards into the serious violations of international humanitarian and international human rights law reported by the Fact-Finding Mission, towards ensuring accountability and justice;

4. *Urges*, in line with the recommendation of the Fact-Finding Mission, the undertaking by the Palestinian side, within a period of three months, of investigations that are independent, credible and in conformity with international standards into the serious violations of international humanitarian and international human rights law reported by the Fact-Finding Mission, towards ensuring accountability and justice;

5. *Recommends* that the Government of Switzerland, in its capacity as depositary of the Geneva Convention relative to the Protection of Civilian Persons in Time of War,[1] undertake as soon as possible the steps necessary to reconvene a Conference of High Contracting Parties to the Fourth Geneva Convention on measures to enforce the Convention in the Occupied Palestinian Territory, including East Jerusalem, and to ensure its respect in accordance with article 1;

6. *Requests* the Secretary-General to report to the General Assembly, within a period of three months, on the implementation of the present resolution, with a view to the consideration of further action, if necessary, by the relevant United Nations organs and bodies, including the Security Council;

---

[6] A/63/855-S/2009/250.
[7] A/64/53/Add.1.

7. *Decides* to remain seized of the matter.

39th plenary meeting
5 November 2009

Document [5] UN General Assembly Resolution 64/10 with Official Records

United Nations   A/64/PV.39

General Assembly
Sixty-fourth session

Official Records

39th plenary meeting
Thursday, 5 November 2009, 3 p.m.
New York

President: Mr. Ali Abdussalam Treki . . . . (Libyan Arab Jamahiriya)

The meeting was called to order at 3.10 p.m.

Agenda item 64 (*continued*)

Report of the Human Rights Council

Report of the Human Rights Council (A/64/53/Add.1)

Note by the President of the General Assembly (A/64/490)

Draft resolution (A/64/L.11)

Mr. Momen (Bangladesh): For more than six decades we have been debating about the peace process in the Middle East. Despite our continuous efforts, we are still far from a lasting peace in the region.

The Bangladesh delegation aligns itself with the statements made by the representative of Egypt on behalf of the Non-Aligned Movement and by the representative of the Syrian Arab Republic on behalf of the Organization of the Islamic Conference. We would, however, like to highlight some points of interest to us.

In that connection, my delegation thanks the United Nations Fact-Finding Mission on the Gaza Conflict for its investigation into documented allegations of criminal activities and for presenting a comprehensive and objective report (A/HRC/12/48) addressing all alleged violations. Our conscience is shaken by the serious violations of international human rights and humanitarian law committed by Israel, as reported in the context of its military operations in Gaza from 27 December 2008 to 18 January 2009.

We believe that the findings and conclusions set out in Judge Goldstone's report will help create an opportunity to put an end to impunity for violations of international law in Israel and in the occupied Palestinian territory and thus to eventually address the dispossession experienced by the people of Gaza. My delegation endorses the findings and recommendations of the Goldstone report and expresses its appreciation for their objectivity and fairness.

The Goldstone report clearly confirms that Israel, whose people themselves had suffered oppression in Europe, committed serious human rights violations and violations of humanitarian law amounting to war crimes and crimes against humanity, while using disproportionate force and deliberately targeting civilian buildings and installations, causing unspeakable losses in terms of property and the lives of civilians, many of them women and children. According to the Goldstone report, all inhabitants of Gaza were targeted, without distinction between military personnel and civilians. The scale of the crimes described in the report should be a wake-up call for the international community. If its findings were to be disregarded, the promotion of human rights would take a step backwards and criticism of others for human rights violations would be a mockery.

The report of the United Nations Fact-Finding Mission on the Gaza Conflict, headed by Judge Richard Goldstone, made a number of recommendations aimed at ensuring accountability for perpetrators and redress for victims. It called on the Government of Israel to resolve to conduct independent and credible

---

This record contains the text of speeches delivered in English and of the interpretation of speeches delivered in the other languages. Corrections should be submitted to the original languages only. They should be incorporated in a copy of the record and sent under the signature of a member of the delegation concerned to the Chief of the Verbatim Reporting Service, room U-506. Corrections will be issued after the end of the session in a consolidated corrigendum.

09-59485 (E)

Please recycle

investigations into the many allegations of serious violations of international humanitarian and human rights law that had taken place during the Gaza conflict at the beginning of the year. The report also called on Hamas to initiate genuine and effective inquiries into and proceedings to deal with the many allegations of violations. In addition, the report called for the cases to be referred to the International Criminal Court in The Hague if Israel and Hamas do not investigate the war crimes allegations against them within six months.

We urge Israel and Hamas to conduct full, neutral and credible investigations into the allegations contained in the report. We call upon the General Assembly to discharge its Charter-mandated responsibilities with respect to the issue. We also look forward to the results of the consideration of the report by the Human Rights Council.

Serious follow-up to the report at all levels is imperative in order to bring an end to this immoral and repugnant impunity and to prevent the recurrence of such crimes against the Palestinians. Israel should allow access to humanitarian goods and freeze settlements. We express our deep concern over the precarious humanitarian situation, and we urge Israel to lift its embargo against the Palestinians and immediately open all border crossings to allow for the free movement of goods, persons and humanitarian aid. Humanitarian access to Gaza must be allowed in order to avoid a humanitarian disaster. An international monitoring mechanism must be established to ensure a ceasefire.

We urge Israel to immediately end settlement activities, including so-called natural growth. If we are to achieve a lasting settlement, it is very important to address the root cause, which is the Israeli occupation of the Arab territories. The solution, therefore, requires Israel's complete withdrawal from the occupied Palestinian territories, including East Jerusalem, and all other occupied Arab lands. We reiterate that the creation of a Palestinian State, coexisting peacefully alongside Israel on the basis of the 1967 borders, with East Jerusalem as its capital, is the only sustainable solution to the conflict. The Road Map, the Arab Peace Initiative and relevant resolutions are the best parameters for achieving a two-State solution. Thus, Israelis and Palestinians could live in peace and harmony. I am hopeful that that dream will come true.

We would like to restate that it is only through negotiations that a fair and lasting peace can be established in the Middle East. Intensive and sincere work is needed to ensure a resumption of negotiations.

Let me conclude by echoing the words of Judge Goldstone:

"Now is the time for action. A culture of impunity in the region has existed for too long. The lack of accountability for war crimes and possible crimes against humanity has reached a crisis point; the ongoing lack of justice is undermining any hope for a successful peace process and reinforcing an environment that fosters violence. Time and again, experience has taught us that overlooking justice only leads to increased conflict and violence."

Mr. Al Nafisee (Saudi Arabia) (*spoke in Arabic*): On behalf of the Kingdom of Saudi Arabia, Mr. President, I have the honour to thank you for your efforts in convening this urgent meeting to discuss the Goldstone report (A/HRC/12/48), prepared for the Human Rights Council by the United Nations Fact-Finding Mission on the Gaza Conflict, which investigated violations perpetrated during the Israeli war against Gaza last December and the human rights situation in Palestine and the occupied Arab territories.

My country associates itself with the statements made, respectively, by the representative of the Arab Republic of Egypt on behalf of the Non-Aligned Movement, the representative of the Syrian Arab Republic on behalf of the Arab Group, and the representative of the Republic of Sudan on behalf of the Group of 77 and China.

In the view of the Kingdom of Saudi Arabia, the Goldstone report is clear and transparent and demands appropriate action by the General Assembly, in view of its condemnation of Israel for war crimes committed during its recent aggression in Gaza. The Assembly is now in the process of discussing the report and will soon be voting on endorsing it.

The investigation conducted in Gaza by Judge Goldstone and his international team shows that Israel committed war crimes and crimes against humanity in a war that caused the death of more than 1,400 Palestinians, most of them civilian women and children, and the wounding of thousands more. Furthermore, Israel committed deliberate acts of aggression against United Nations facilities in Gaza and used bombs and rockets that increased the toll of death or injury of unarmed Palestinians who had sought shelter there.

On 12 January the Human Rights Council adopted its resolution S-9/1, condemning Israel for its attacks on Gaza and its serious violations of human rights, and requesting that a fact-finding mission be established to investigate violations against unarmed civilians in the area. We support the Mission's findings in Gaza and the occupied territories, and its condemnation of the violations of human rights and international humanitarian law.

Judge Goldstone described fairly and objectively the scale of destruction committed by Israel in a war in which it used weapons of every kind. He met with injured and displaced Palestinians, was shown pictures of the burned bodies of dead women, children and old people and saw for himself how Israel had deliberately targeted them. At a press conference Judge Goldstone said,

> "The aim of holding these public hearings ... was to show the human side of the suffering; to give a voice to the victims so they are not lost among statistics. No written words can by themselves convey human stories the way people can do it in their own voice and words".

He has also said that the Mission wanted to show the effect of violence on communities, especially the psychological effects on children.

We endorse Judge Goldstone's words when he presented the report to the Human Rights Council:

> "A culture of impunity in the region has existed for too long ... the ongoing lack of justice is undermining any hope for a successful peace process and reinforcing an environment that fosters violence."

We reiterate that the Goldstone report aims to strengthen a culture of accountability and to draw attention to disturbing violations of international principles of human rights and international humanitarian law. With the publication of the report, a growing culture of accountability is becoming more apparent.

The international community must shoulder its responsibility and take action to achieve justice, for no country or military organization should be above the law. A failure to achieve justice in the face of the serious violations committed in the war on Gaza would have disastrous consequences for international justice.

The Arab world, including the State of Palestine, has made every possible effort to achieve a genuine and lasting peace. The Arab Peace Initiative is still on the table; it offers a comprehensive route to ending the Arab-Israeli conflict and reaching an agreement on reciprocal recognition, normal relations and peaceful coexistence for all States in the region. It is completely in line with the peace process and embodies the commitment of the Arab side to peace as a strategic option, in accordance with the Charter of the United Nations.

If everyone recognizes such a solution, they should also recognize why peace has still not been achieved. That is because of Israel's perpetration of massacres, arbitrary bombardments and attacks against the Palestinians in the occupied territories. Israel has deliberately prevaricated and procrastinated in order to avoid any commitment to peace. Peace cannot be achieved by imposing punishment and preconditions on a people whose country has been occupied and whose rights have been violated in contravention of all the principles and norms of international law. No conditions should be imposed before a peace settlement is reached. The aggressor cannot be rewarded before negotiations even begin. All the international initiatives and efforts in this context have consistently faced a blank refusal from the Israeli side, embodied in its unilateral measures. This is contrary to international law and Security Council resolutions.

Instead of seeking genuine peace, Israel continues its daily humiliation of the Palestinian people and its building of settlements, the separation wall and bypass roads. These are all actions that violate international law and attempt to change reality on the ground, to change the geographic and demographic makeup of Palestinian land, especially in Jerusalem and its environs, in grave violation of international law and the relevant Security Council resolutions. Settlements encircle most Palestinian cities in the West Bank, and also use more than half of its water resources.

Saudi Arabia is deeply concerned about the ongoing Israeli blockade of Gaza, resulting in the continued deterioration of Palestinian living conditions in the face of restricted access to services, goods, food, fuel and building materials. In addition, Israel has blockaded East Jerusalem and prevented people from getting to their homes and houses of worship. Israeli acts against Islamic sites represent daily aggression against unarmed Palestinians, provoking distress among Muslims all over the world. Israel's grave assaults on the Al-Aqsa mosque can only have a direct and serious impact on international peace and security.

In this regard, my Government calls upon the international community, through the General Assembly, to take a stand against this wanton aggression, act together and vote to adopt the draft resolution (A/64/L.11) concerning the Goldstone report in order to prevent any future repetition of these crimes.

Mr. Pálsson (Iceland): The comprehensive report of the United Nations Fact-Finding Mission on the Gaza Conflict (A/HRC/12/48) has concluded that there is evidence indicating serious violations of international human rights and humanitarian law, committed both by Israel during Operation Cast Lead and in the West Bank, as well as by Palestinian armed groups and their repeated launching of rockets into southern Israel. The report deserves serious consideration and follow-up. The conclusions drawn require concrete action, including the establishment of a credible system of investigation into the alleged violations. We reiterate our shared principle that every Member State must commit itself to full cooperation with the United Nations.

My delegation fully recognizes Israel's legitimate security concerns, including concerns over weapons smuggling and the unacceptable firing of rockets from Gaza, which destroy and endanger the lives of innocent civilians. At the same time, we take the view that such violations do not justify the disproportionate use of force or the breaching of international humanitarian and human rights law. The conflict continues to threaten stability far beyond the region and the situation in the occupied Palestinian territory remains of grave concern. The people of Gaza continue to be besieged through limited freedom of movement, import and export restrictions and the worsening economic situation. The situation remains unacceptable by international standards.

Meanwhile, the closure regime is still operating in the West Bank. Here also the situation, including violence and evictions in East Jerusalem, gives cause for deep concern. Settlement activities must be ended. The prolonged climate of impunity has created a crisis of justice in the occupied Palestinian territory that needs to be addressed. In that regard, the system of investigation recommended by the report of the Fact-Finding Mission would be a welcome step in the right direction.

In line with the report, my delegation urges both the Israeli and the Palestinian parties to launch independent investigations, in conformity with international standards, into the allegations of serious violations of international human rights and humanitarian law. We also support the requests to the High Commissioner for Human Rights to report to the next session of the Human Rights Council on the situation in the occupied Territory and to the Secretary-General to report to the Assembly on further developments.

Mr. Heller (Mexico) (*spoke in Spanish*): We welcome the convening of this meeting on the report of the Human Rights Council pertaining to the United Nations Fact-Finding Mission on the Gaza Conflict (A/64/53/Add.1). The information contained in that report deserves the General Assembly's full attention given not only the seriousness and the implications of the conflict in Gaza, but also on the grounds that respect for international law and international humanitarian law should be upheld at all times and under any circumstance.

The report of the Fact-Finding Mission (A/HRC/12/48), headed by Judge Richard Goldstone, is a document that cannot be disregarded and whose recommendations should be responsibly and seriously considered by all parties, since impartial and credible investigations in conformity with international standards were carried out with regard to the accusations of serious violations of international humanitarian law and human rights committed during the conflict in Gaza. Its greatest merit is that it seeks a balanced approach, taking into account the actions of all parties involved.

The civilian populations affected by that conflict, both Palestinians and Israelis, deserve to know that those kinds of acts will not go unpunished and that their rights will be respected under any circumstance, in accordance with international humanitarian law. That guarantees them a better future.

Justice should always go hand in hand with the pursuit of peace. Furthermore, justice, accountability and the fight against impunity are essential elements in any settlement of conflict, since they facilitate the end of hostilities and, at the same time, lay the foundations for stability and reconciliation.

The main conclusion of the report of the Fact-Finding Mission is that both the Government of Israel and the Palestinian factions should establish investigation mechanisms that will make it possible to obtain a better understanding of the alleged serious violations of international law and international humanitarian law committed during that conflict. We are not going to debate the composition of the Fact-Finding Mission. Rather, we wish to focus on the fact that those acts should be investigated and, if need be, duly punished.

The Government of Israel, like any democratic State, has the resources and the institutional and legal means to act in conformity with its international obligations. Mexico recognizes the right of legitimate self-defence of Member States of the United Nations, in accordance with Article 51 of the United Nations Charter. However, that right does not in any circumstance exempt the parties to a conflict from fulfilling their obligations under international humanitarian law. Israel has the right and the obligation to protect its population. However, it also has the obligation to comply with international humanitarian law.

With respect to the Palestinian side, taking into account the responsibility of the factions involved in that conflict as non-State entities, we believe that innovative mechanisms should be put in place that provide an institutional approach ensuring credibility and trust in accountability and in establishing responsibilities, with the active contribution of the international community.

In any case, the investigations of both sides should begin as soon as possible and should have a set deadline for submitting their results in order to bring about the necessary trust to overcome that tragic chapter of the conflict in the Middle East. Mexico believes that the international community should ensure that that process takes place in the best possible conditions and, for that, considerable effort and commitment on the part of the sides involved is needed.

Consideration of the Mission's report reminds us that Middle East peace talks must not be postponed yet again, nor should they be subject to preconditions. The goal, as everyone knows, is clear: to achieve a comprehensive and definitive solution to the Middle East conflict that reasserts the recognition of Israel's right to exist and allows the establishment of an economically and politically viable Palestinian State, living side by side in peace with Israel, within secure, internationally recognized borders, in compliance with the relevant Security Council resolutions, the Road Map, the Madrid Principles and the Arab Peace Initiative.

Today we have an opportunity to serve both peace and international justice. Let us not let this unique opportunity pass.

Mr. Ould Hadrami (Mauritania) (*spoke in Arabic*): Mr. President, I would like at the outset to thank you for organizing this important meeting so quickly at the request of the Group of Arab States to study the war of 27 December 2008 to 18 January 2009 and the report on that war. The report of the United Nations Fact-Finding Mission on the Gaza Conflict (A/HRC/12/48) that was prepared pursuant to Human Rights Council resolution S-12/1 is our topic today. That report consists of more than 450 pages and it looks at the impact of the catastrophic Israeli war on the Gaza Strip that took place over a three-week period.

The international community must organize a comprehensive inquiry into the suffering of the Palestinian people over the past 60 years. The report has shown some conclusive facts and findings that have demonstrated the terrible nature of the Israeli crimes. More than 1,400 people died in a three-week period. The initial act of aggression took place at 11.30 in the morning. That shows that it was a deliberate attack, as it targeted children who were going to school — because children have to go to school — and came at a time when the streets are crowded with people. The Israeli army killed Palestinians, not distinguishing between civilians and combatants. There is proof that shows that United Nations facilities were also the victims of that aggression. The report shows the terrible impact of the unfair blockade of the Gaza Strip that is still in place today and that has a direct impact on the vulnerable segments of society, be they elderly people, women or children. The report also shows that at the end of this past June — that is, six months after the end of the war — the catastrophic consequences were still clearly in evidence. We could see the destruction of buildings, industries, wells, schools, hospitals, police stations and the only flour mill in Gaza. International assistance and construction materials are not reaching civilians, because of the closure of crossing points. That is extremely important because winter is coming and the suffering will only continue.

Since the United Nations was founded, resolutions and legislation have been adopted to promote international law and international humanitarian law. Unfortunately we are facing various sorts of difficulties in implementing those resolutions, which requires more political resolve. The last Israeli war against Gaza, which also caused a great deal of killing and destruction, proved the existence of a climate of legal impunity and the lack of legal responsibility. The suffering of the Palestinian people is as old as the United Nations itself — 60 years. The Palestinian people are still suffering from injustice, unfair treatment and displacement. We call on the international community to put an end to their suffering and tragedy.

The State of Israel, which is the occupying Power, must accept the Arab Peace Initiative, which is based on the principles of land for peace and an independent, sovereign and secure Palestinian State, with East Jerusalem as its capital, peacefully coexisting with the Israeli State. The State of Israel must withdraw from all occupied Arab land, including the Golan Heights and the Lebanese Shab'a farms. The Goldstone report is extremely comprehensive and objective and gives new hope for implementing its recommendations. We call on all relevant United Nations bodies, in particular the Security Council, to take the measures necessary to implement those recommendations and enforce justice in order to promote accountability and to punish the perpetrators of the crimes.

Finally, my delegation supports draft resolution A/64/L.11 and calls on the General Assembly to adopt it. It will promote peace, strengthen the purposes and principles of the United Nations and promote international justice. Such crimes and their origins must not be repeated in the future. Furthermore, those crimes are not subject to any statute of limitations.

Mr. Ali (Malaysia): My delegation wishes to align itself with the statements delivered by the representatives of Egypt and Syria on behalf of the Non-Aligned Movement and the Organization of the Islamic Conference, respectively. We would like to thank the Human Rights Council and the United Nations Fact-Finding Mission on the Gaza Conflict for their reports (A/64/53/Add.1 and A/HRC/12/48).

The report of the United Nations Fact-Finding Mission on the Gaza Conflict, also known as the Goldstone report, has clearly shown the brutality of Israeli actions in the execution of Operation Cast Lead, unleashed in Gaza for more than three weeks, from 27 December 2008 until 18 January 2009. Therefore, while the purpose of our meeting is ostensibly to discuss and take action on the two reports before us, its real purpose is much greater. It is to ensure that Israel can no longer shed Palestinian blood with impunity.

I say this because the Goldstone report makes for grim reading. The report, which speaks for itself, highlights Israel's record of unbridled barbarity towards the people in Gaza. Due to the paucity of time, I would like to point out just some of its most salient points. First, the military operation in question is not an aberration. Rather, it fits into a continuum of policies, based on or resulting in violations of international human rights and humanitarian law.

Secondly, Operation Cast Lead was qualitatively different from any previous military action by Israel in the occupied Palestinian territory by dint of its unprecedented severity and its long-lasting consequences. The visible destruction of houses, factories, wells, schools, hospitals, police stations and other public buildings proves that it was the deliberate aim of Israel to inflict as much damage and suffering as possible.

Thirdly, Israeli military actions, premised on a deliberate policy of disproportionate force, were aimed not at a specific enemy, but at the supporting infrastructure. In practice, that meant the civilian population in Gaza.

Fourthly, this operation, which led to killings and destruction, was carefully planned and executed. That also indicated that all aspects of the operation were deliberate. Therefore, all killings must have been conducted in cold blood.

However, despite the gruesome situation, we were struck by the courage of the Palestinian people. The assiduous work of Palestinian non-governmental and civil society organizations in providing support to the population in such extreme circumstances, and in giving voice to the suffering and expectations of victims of violations, deserves to be fully acknowledged.

We note with interest that there were also dissenting voices in Israel against the operation, expressed through demonstrations and protests, as well as public reporting on Israel's conduct. Those voices understood that Israel could not purchase peace and security for itself with the blood and suffering of the Palestinian people.

We, the international community, have thus far failed to act to ensure the protection of the civilian population in the Gaza Strip and the occupied Palestinian territory. Hence, we must break this inertia by undertaking concrete actions in order to ensure that justice for the people of Palestine is neither delayed nor denied.

The Goldstone report provides us with two options: either take action to achieve justice for the Palestinians or allow the abhorrent, illegal actions of Israel to remain unpunished. In that regard, as a responsible member of the international community, we choose the former. Accordingly, we urge all Member States to work together in implementing all the recommendations stipulated in the report of the United Nations Fact-Finding Mission on the Gaza Conflict.

Mr. Sial (Pakistan): My delegation would like to thank you, Mr. President, for convening today's meeting to consider the report of the United Nations Fact-Finding Mission on the Gaza Conflict, also known as the Goldstone report (A/HRC/12/48).

Early this year, the international community was horrified by the events surrounding three weeks of Israeli aggression in the occupied Gaza Strip. The report of the Human Rights Council on its twelfth special session (A/64/53/Add.1) and periodic reports of the High Commissioner for Human Rights corroborated other independent reports on those events. The Goldstone report only authenticated those reports with evidence.

The Human Rights Council, after detailed discussions at its twelfth special session, referred the Goldstone report to the General Assembly. The Council also requested the Secretary-General to submit at its thirteenth session a report on the status of the implementation of the Goldstone recommendations. I believe that, against that backdrop, the present session of the General Assembly has three-faceted significance.

First, the General Assembly must actively and constructively consider the Goldstone report, in terms of implications and future follow-up action. It is our hope that the Assembly will discharge that responsibility in an efficient and just manner.

Secondly, pursuant to the request of the Human Rights Council, the Secretary-General has been asked to submit a report on the status of the implementation of the Goldstone recommendations to the Council. We may rightfully expect him to keep the General Assembly informed on the subject. Therefore, the Assembly's present session can give him requisite inputs and guidelines for the preparation of his report.

Thirdly, the General Assembly, through this session, has an opportunity to position itself behind the growing concern of the international community at the stalled peace process in the Middle East. In the absence of a meaningful and durable peace process, violence will continue and respect for human rights will remain a distant dream. We sincerely believe that our meaningful deliberations on the issue will help to revive the peace process.

From the discussions in the Human Rights Council, it is evident that many Member States have greatly appreciated the Goldstone report for being objective, impartial and comprehensive. We see the deliberations on the report as an opportunity for the international community to address the suffering of the Palestinian people and for Israel to rectify its past actions and policies.

Achieving lasting peace in the Middle East is a long-held common objective of the international community. This meeting should bring us closer to that objective. Thus, the overarching message of the need for a revival of the peace process with firm commitment to a two-State solution must resonate from our deliberations.

During last month's debate in the Security Council, Pakistan outlined four parameters for international engagement with a view to achieving a sustained peace process in the Middle East. We called upon the Security Council and the Middle East Quartet to utilize their full potential in support of the peace process through transparent and objective engagement. They must prevail upon Israel to cease all settlement activity and illegal excavation in East Jerusalem, as the two actions have so far proved the largest stumbling blocks on the road to peace. We will reiterate that message. There is also a pressing need to address the plight and suffering of the Palestinian population and to rebuild Palestinian institutions battered by conflict and violence.

The foregoing measures must be supplemented by addressing the root cause of all trouble — that is, by ending the Israeli occupation of Arab territories. Such a framework for peace is not new. It has already been determined in the relevant resolutions of the Security Council, as well as in the Madrid terms of reference, the Road Map, the Arab Peace Initiative and the understanding reached in Annapolis in 2007.

I wish to conclude by expressing Pakistan's sincere hope that the Goldstone report will ultimately strengthen the initiative for peace in the region and that the General Assembly will be able to utilize that important document to find a meaningful basis for lasting peace and security in the Middle East.

Mr. Mohamed (Maldives): The Maldives would like to welcome the report of the United Nations Fact-Finding Mission on the Gaza Conflict (A/HRC/12/48), headed by Judge Richard Goldstone, that was presented to the Assembly today. It is regrettable that the Government of Israel, as the occupying Power, decided not to cooperate with the Fact-Finding Mission in its compilation of the report.

As a firm believer in the principles enshrined in the Charter of the United Nations, the Maldives is disheartened by the continued suffering of the people of Palestine, who have been denied their very basic right to self-determination and the right to live in peace and freedom in their own State, their own homeland. The Maldives also supports the inalienable right of the people of Israel to live in peace and security alongside a sovereign and independent State of Palestine.

The protection of civilians, especially women and children, is one of the most sacred obligations resting upon the parties to a conflict under international law. Thus, the onus rests with us, as responsible members of the international community, to ensure that we uphold the legal standards and norms that we have prescribed for ourselves. For any hope of peace and stability in the Middle East, it is crucial that accountability be established for the clear and manifest violations of human rights and humanitarian law that have been highlighted in the report. Justice must be pursued independently for the violations by both sides to the conflict. It is also essential that such investigations and subsequent prosecutions be monitored by the Security Council.

The Maldives strongly believes that a negotiated outcome based on the relevant Security Council resolutions is the only way to ensure long-term peace, security and stability in the region. To this end, we support the current efforts by the United States to revive the peace talks between the two parties. The Maldives therefore calls for a final, just and comprehensive settlement with the realization of two States, Israel and Palestine, living side by side in peace and within secure and recognized borders.

Mr. Valero Briceño (Bolivarian Republic of Venezuela) (*spoke in Spanish*): The Government of Israel must be brought to justice for crimes committed against the Palestinian people. Those responsible for that operation of terror and death, known as Cast Lead, and for the criminal blockade against the people of Gaza, must not go unpunished. How many more genocides will be necessary before the United Nations decides to act? How long will the occupying Power continue to flout the resolutions adopted by this forum?

We have heard the answers from the representative of Israel. In her speech, she lashed out against the findings and recommendations of the Goldstone report, claiming that it was "conceived in hate and executed in sin" (*A/64/PV.36*), and that its consideration by the General Assembly was in response to cynical political manoeuvres and not principles.

The Human Rights Council is clear and unambiguous in its resolution when it strongly condemns all policies adopted by Israel, the occupying Power. It also condemns the recent violations of human rights committed by Israel in East Jerusalem. For Venezuela, the report of the United Nations Fact-Finding Mission on the Gaza Conflict and the Human Rights Council resolution are worthy of recognition.

The recommendation of the Goldstone report is commendable in that it seeks to create a fund to guarantee compensation to the Palestinian victims of Israel's criminal acts, with the understanding that the funding should come entirely from the Government of that country.

The aforementioned report conclusively demonstrates the organization, planning and implementation of the policy of extermination carried out by the Israeli State against the Palestinian nation. According to the report, these acts of violence generate individual criminal responsibility. Those on the Israeli side responsible for the thousands of dead and wounded should be brought to justice.

In its conclusion, the report emphasizes the multiple and massive violations of the Fourth Geneva Convention, which are considered to be war crimes committed by the Israeli occupying forces. The report concludes that the prolonged blockade of Gaza by the Israeli Government, which includes the deprivation of the basic means of sustenance, could be considered crimes against humanity.

Israel's military operations in Gaza are a lamentable example of the disastrous Dahiya doctrine, put into practice by Israel during its invasion of Lebanon in 2006 and which is characterized by the use of disproportionate force, the mass destruction of civilian property and infrastructure and the suffering inflicted on civilians. Indeed, the Israel Government itself has declared that the Gaza invasion was planned in a comprehensive manner and on a large scale.

The international community must acknowledge the willingness of the Palestinian authorities to cooperate with the work of the Fact-Finding Mission, which is in stark contrast to the position of the Israeli leaders, who repeatedly have ignored all resolutions of the main organs of the United Nations on the Palestinian issue. They have also refused to cooperate with the 23 United Nations-appointed fact-finding missions since 1947. That clearly demonstrates the gross violation of international law by the Israeli regime.

The report we are discussing today reinforces the need for the General Assembly to continue to review regularly all those topics in the area of international peace and security that the Security Council cannot or will not resolve.

The complicit tolerance shown by some members of the Security Council with respect to the systematic aggression and crimes under international law committed by Israel against the Palestinian people, nation and State is alarming.

Venezuela is concerned that some members of the Security Council, in exercising their right of veto, could block an initiative that could be conducive to prosecuting Israeli genocide. Our concern further increases when a super-Power and permanent member of the Security Council is the main ally of the country responsible for genocide and is the chief architect of the irrational and disproportionate arms build-up developed by Israel and which has turned this nation into a nuclear Power.

The financial and military resources provided by the United States to the Government of Israel, as well as the protection that is afforded it in international forums, further support the genocide against the Palestinian people. The ineffectiveness of the United Nations in the face of a history of Israeli aggressiveness must cease. Those responsible for the genocide of the Palestinian people should be promptly punished for their crimes and brought before the International Criminal Court.

The policies and practices of the Israeli Government violate the inalienable right of the Palestinians to self-determination. It is unjust and absurd to place on the same level the genocidal Government of Israel and the Palestinian forces which, under the protection of their inalienable historical rights and in the exercise of legitimate self-defence, resist the criminal aggression against their nation and their people.

We wish to recall that the revolutionary Government of President Hugo Chávez Frías suspended diplomatic relations with the Government of Israel as a result of the brutal invasion of Gaza by its armed forces, and is not willing to resume its relations until the inhuman treatment of the Palestinian people ceases.

The Bolivarian Republic of Venezuela reaffirms its unequivocal support for the Palestinian people's right to self-determination. We support their struggle against the occupying Power, as well as their historical claims. The Palestinian people have a right to resist the occupying Power. Their heroism is worthy of admiration and respect. This is why we wish to recall the words of the great poet of the Palestinian resistance, Ali Ahmad Said, better known as Adonis, who wrote that darkness is born kneeling whereas, light is born standing up.

Venezuela hopes that the resolution that we adopt will reflects the expectations of the Palestinian people who demand justice, without delay, for the perpetrators of war crimes and crimes against humanity who repeatedly violate international law, in particular, international humanitarian law.

Israel does not deserve another opportunity to continue flouting United Nations resolutions. It should be brought without delay before the International Criminal Court. Israel has committed enough crimes. It is time for it to be held accountable under international law. The resolution to be adopted by the General Assembly, therefore, must accept the spirit of the resolution of the Human Rights Council. It is time for this Assembly to be the official voice of the Palestinian State.

The President (*spoke in Arabic*): In accordance with General Assembly resolution 477 (V) of 1 November 1950, I now give the floor to the observer of the League of Arab States.

Mr. Mahmassani (League of Arab States) (*spoke in Arabic*): I would like to thank you, Mr. President, for affording us the opportunity to participate in the General Assembly's debate on the report of the United Nations Fact-Finding Mission on the Gaza Conflict (A/HRC/12/48).

The seriousness of the military campaign against Gaza, the blockade imposed by Israel against its inhabitants and the deprivation of their most basic needs has prompted the international community to dispatch a Fact-Finding Mission, under the leadership of Justice Richard Goldstone, to look into alleged war crimes and crimes against humanity perpetuated by Israel during its military campaign in the Gaza Strip from 27 December, 2008 to 18 January 2009. The conclusions reached by the Mission were identical with those reached by the independent fact-finding mission of the League of Arab States.

In the preparation of its report, the Mission took into account the provisions of international humanitarian law and human rights law, as well as the responsibility and obligations of States, particularly of occupying Powers, towards civilian inhabitants. It reached certain factual and legal conclusions to the effect that Israel, in its aggression against Gaza, deliberately killed civilians and used them as human shields.

Israel's use of disproportionate force and its attacks against civilian inhabitants, as well as its destruction of civilian property and infrastructure, are all illegitimate means to realize military and political objectives. Such actions undermine international law and run counter to the United Nations Charter. Israel continues to act as if it were above the law; not holding it accountable or responsible encourages impunity and casts a shadow over the credibility of the United Nations and that of international law.

The time has come for the international community to put an end to the culture of impunity and to Israel's immunity to the consequences of its aggression against the region. The time has also come to hold the perpetuators of violations of international law and human rights law accountable and to implement the machinery of international justice.

The objective of the Goldstone report is to salvage justice and to hold those accused of perpetuating war crimes accountable for those crimes. Respect for international humanitarian law and its application does not impede the peace process; peace does not run counter to respect of the rights of the Palestinian people in the occupied territories.

The draft resolution before us (A/64/L.11) was prepared in a balanced and objective manner and represents the absolute acceptable minimum for the implementation of the recommendations of the Goldstone report. We would like to urge all Member States to vote in favour of the draft resolution for the sake of accountability and justice.

We express our deep concern over the serious humanitarian crisis faced by the Palestinian people in the Gaza Strip and the other occupied Palestinian territories due to the Israeli blockade and aggression, as well as over the continued closing of crossing points and the prevention of access to humanitarian assistance. We therefore call upon the international community to compel Israel to lift its blockade and to ensure access of humanitarian assistance to the Gaza Strip.

Israel continues its actions in East Jerusalem in an attempt to judaize the city and confiscate its land

and to isolate it from the remaining Palestinian territories through intensified settlement activities within and outside the city. Its blockade, the policy of house demolitions and its attempts to bring down Al-Aqsa mosque through continued excavations and tunnel-digging, all seek to change the features of the Arab and Islamic Old City.

We would like to call attention to the fact that Jerusalem and the Al-Aqsa mosque are in imminent danger. We call upon the international community to put an end to Israel's flouting of the heritage of the city and its desecration of the city's sanctity. We call upon the international community to oblige Israel to respect international law, international resolutions and the Fourth Geneva Convention.

The Israeli occupation of Palestinian and Arab territories is the root cause of the suffering in our region and of so many wars and tragedies. All attempts and negotiations to put an end to that occupation have failed due to Israel's intransigence and its continued building of settlements in the occupied Palestinian territories.

At present, the Middle East question is going through an extremely delicate stage and current efforts to establish peace through negotiations seem to have regressed in an alarming way. The continued faltering of those efforts will only lead to further deterioration and instability in the region. The international community considers Israeli settlements in the occupied Palestinian territories illegitimate and an obstacle to negotiations, as stated by the United Kingdom's Minister for Foreign Affairs, Mr. Miliband, a few days ago.

Working to put an end to the building of settlements — all settlements — and ensuring the re-launching of negotiations on a clear and sound basis in a serious and credible manner is the only way to find a permanent and just solution to the Palestinian question and to establishing peace in the region.

The President (*spoke in Arabic*): We shall now proceed to consider draft resolution A/64/L.11.

(*spoke in English*)

I call on the representative of Israel who wishes to speak on a point of order.

Mr. Carmon (Israel): I would like to take this opportunity before the Assembly proceeds to the vote to seek clarification on an element contained in operative paragraph 4 of draft resolution A/64/L.11, which is a matter of concern to us and I suspect to other delegations as well.

More specifically, we would like to ask, who exactly would be the accountable "Palestinian side", that would be responsible for undertaking investigations that are independent, credible and in conformity with international standards? Would it be the Palestinian Authority that was ousted from Gaza in a violent coup and is not effectively present there? Or would it be the Hamas terrorist organization, terrorist entity, which violates every international standard, promotes terrorism, rejects the recognition of Israel and tries to derail the region from the track of the peace process?

Israel, through you, Sir, would like to ask the sponsors of the draft resolution to clarify this critical aspect so that Member States of the General Assembly will know better what they will be voting for.

The President: I give the floor to the representative of Egypt, who presented the draft resolution on behalf of the Arab Group and the Non-Aligned Movement.

Mr. Abdelaziz (Egypt): With regard to operative paragraph 4 of the draft resolution, the Palestinian Authority itself declared that it is going to conduct its own investigation which is independent, credible and in conformity with international standards. And Hamas, which may be considered in Israel as a terrorist organization but is considered the legitimately elected representative of the Palestinian people, has already expressed its willingness to cooperate and to investigate and to prosecute those that are responsible for such crimes.

We would like to hear the same from the representative of Israel. If he can confirm today that Israel is willing to undertake investigations that are independent, credible and in conformity with international standards, international law and international humanitarian law, I think this would be very happy news to the General Assembly before voting on this draft resolution.

The President: I give the floor to the representative of Israel.

Mr. Carmon (Israel): I thank the representative of Egypt and will refer to his question later in my explanation of vote before the vote.

The President (*spoke in Arabic*): The Assembly will now proceed to take action on draft resolution A/64/L.11. Before giving the floor to those representatives who wish to speak in explanation of vote before the voting, may I remind delegations that explanations of vote are limited to 10 minutes and should be made by delegations from their seats.

Mr. Wolff (United States of America): The United States remains deeply concerned about the human suffering of the Palestinian and Israeli peoples that results from the ongoing Arab-Israeli conflict. The best way to end that suffering is to bring about a comprehensive peace in the region, including two States, Israel and Palestine, living side by side in peace and security. The United States is firmly committed to pursuing that goal.

As we urge the parties to restart permanent status negotiations leading to the creation of a Palestinian State, we should all be seeking to advance the cause of peace, and doing nothing to hinder it. The United States strongly supports accountability for human rights and humanitarian law violations in relation to the Gaza conflict. Our goal is to achieve genuine accountability in a way that respects internal processes and the ongoing efforts to restart permanent status negotiations between Israel and the Palestinians.

As the United States made clear in Geneva, we believe that the Goldstone report is deeply flawed, including its unbalanced focus on Israel, its sweeping conclusions of law, the excessively negative inferences it draws about Israel's intentions and actions, its failure to deal adequately with the asymmetrical nature of the Gaza conflict, its failure to assign appropriate responsibility to Hamas for its decision to base itself and its operations in heavily civilian-populated urban areas and its many overreaching recommendations.

First, let me point out that we appreciate that the draft resolution under consideration calls on both Israel and the Palestinians, although it does not name Hamas, to pursue investigations of the allegations that pertain to each of them in the report. This is an advance over the original one-sided mandate provided by the Human Rights Council to the Goldstone Commission.

We will continue to call for all parties to meet their responsibilities and pursue credible, domestic investigations. Nevertheless, we also have real concerns about this draft resolution. Given the far-reaching legal conclusions and recommendations of the 575-page Goldstone report, including findings that have serious implications for conflicts in other parts of the world, we do not think it appropriate to endorse the report in its entirety.

Attempting as this draft resolution does to press the Security Council to take this matter up is equally unconstructive. The Security Council is already seized of the situation in the Middle East and holds monthly meetings on the topic — the only subject on the Council's entire agenda that is discussed with such frequency. As many Member States have made clear, the appropriate forum for discussion of this report is the Human Rights Council.

The draft resolution also unhelpfully introduces international supervision of the investigations to be undertaken by the parties that would interfere with the parties' ability to conduct their own processes. The proposed convocation of the High Contracting Parties to the Fourth Geneva Convention is also unnecessary and unproductive. Convening a conference of the Contracting Parties to the Geneva Convention for the purpose of spotlighting one country would only heighten divisions and could set back the process of restarting permanent status negotiations. That and other imbalanced references to the parties throughout the text, including the failure to mention Hamas by name, convey the impression that the Assembly is once again handling Arab-Israeli issues in an unbalanced manner.

For those reasons, we will vote against the draft resolution, but we believe that life-saving progress can be made if we can lift our sights and look towards a more hopeful future. The United States will continue to work resolutely in pursuit of a just and lasting peace.

Mr. Carmon (Israel): Two days after the revelation of Hamas's newly improved Iranian-made rockets and one day after the interception of a ship, the *Francop*, loaded with hundreds of tons of rockets and ammunition destined to be launched at Israeli population centres, which is a grave event — we have just submitted our complaint an hour ago to the Security Council — this draft resolution (A/64/L.11) mocks the reality faced by democratic States, such as Israel, that face relentless terrorist threats.

The draft resolution before us endorses and legitimizes a deeply flawed, one-sided and prejudiced report of the discredited Human Rights Council and its politicized work that bends both facts and the law. It disregards Israel's inherent right to defend its citizens in the face of ongoing terrorist attacks. It represents yet another pretext to bash Israel at the United Nations and is detrimental to any positive diplomatic engagement in the region. It attempts to export from Geneva to New York a campaign of de-legitimization.

While Israel has been conducting professional, credible and thorough investigations, as part of its standard operating procedures and irrespective of any United Nations report, the report before the Assembly (A/64/53/Add.1) attempts to draw an implausible equivalence between Israel, a democracy exercising its inherent right to defend itself from terrorist attacks, and those who target Israeli civilians and operate from behind Palestinian mosques, hospitals, schools and human shields or, alternatively, those who effectively are absent from Gaza at this point.

The draft resolution, in paragraph 4, refers to the "Palestinian side". Yet, although we have received some clarification that does not resolve the issue, I will still put the question before the Assembly as to who precisely that accountable Palestinian side is. Is that the Palestinian Authority that was ousted from power in the Gaza Strip in a bloody coup? Is it the Hamas terrorist organization that violently seized control of Gaza, an organization that rejects the recognition of Israel and any peaceful solution of the conflict?

For those and other reasons, Israel has called for a recorded vote on this draft resolution and will vote against the draft resolution. And we urge all other Member States to do the same.

The President (*spoke in Arabic*): We have thus heard the last speaker in explanation of vote before the vote.

The Assembly will now take action on draft resolution A/64/L.11, entitled "Follow-up to the report of the United Nations Fact-Finding Mission on the Gaza Conflict". A recorded vote has been requested.

Before proceeding to take action on the draft resolution, I should like to announce that, since the introduction of draft resolution A/64/L.11, the following countries have become sponsors: Algeria, Senegal, Somalia, South Africa and the Sudan.

A recorded vote was taken.

In favour:
Afghanistan, Albania, Algeria, Angola, Antigua and Barbuda, Argentina, Armenia, Azerbaijan, Bahamas, Bahrain, Bangladesh, Barbados, Belarus, Belize, Benin, Bolivia (Plurinational State of), Bosnia and Herzegovina, Botswana, Brazil, Brunei Darussalam, Cambodia, Central African Republic, Chad, Chile, China, Comoros, Congo, Cuba, Cyprus, Democratic People's Republic of Korea, Democratic Republic of the Congo, Djibouti, Dominica, Dominican Republic, Ecuador, Egypt, El Salvador, Eritrea, Gabon, Gambia, Ghana, Grenada, Guatemala, Guinea, Guinea-Bissau, Guyana, Haiti, India, Indonesia, Iran (Islamic Republic of), Iraq, Ireland, Jamaica, Jordan, Kazakhstan, Kuwait, Lao People's Democratic Republic, Lebanon, Lesotho, Libyan Arab Jamahiriya, Malawi, Malaysia, Maldives, Mali, Malta, Mauritania, Mauritius, Mexico, Mongolia, Morocco, Mozambique, Myanmar, Namibia, Nepal, Nicaragua, Niger, Nigeria, Oman, Pakistan, Paraguay, Peru, Philippines, Portugal, Qatar, Saint Lucia, Saint Vincent and the Grenadines, Saudi Arabia, Senegal, Serbia, Sierra Leone, Singapore, Slovenia, Solomon Islands, Somalia, South Africa, Sri Lanka, Sudan, Suriname, Switzerland, Syrian Arab Republic, Tajikistan, Thailand, Timor-Leste, Trinidad and Tobago, Tunisia, Turkey, United Arab Emirates, United Republic of Tanzania, Uzbekistan, Venezuela (Bolivarian Republic of), Viet Nam, Yemen, Zambia, Zimbabwe.

Against:
Australia, Canada, Czech Republic, Germany, Hungary, Israel, Italy, Marshall Islands, Micronesia (Federated States of), Nauru, Netherlands, Palau, Panama, Poland, Slovakia, the former Yugoslav Republic of Macedonia, Ukraine, United States of America.

Abstaining:
Andorra, Austria, Belgium, Bulgaria, Burkina Faso, Burundi, Cameroon, Colombia, Costa Rica, Croatia, Denmark, Estonia, Ethiopia, Fiji, Finland, France, Georgia, Greece, Iceland, Japan, Kenya, Latvia, Liberia, Liechtenstein, Lithuania, Luxembourg, Monaco, Montenegro, New Zealand, Norway, Papua New Guinea, Republic of Korea, Republic of Moldova, Romania, Russian Federation, Samoa, San Marino, Spain, Swaziland, Sweden, Tonga, Uganda, United Kingdom of Great Britain and Northern Ireland, Uruguay.

Document [6] Follow-up to the Report of the UN Fact Finding Mission

United Nations A/64/651

 General Assembly

Distr.: General
4 February 2010

Original: English

Sixty-fourth session
Agenda item 64
Report of the Human Rights Council

Follow-up to the report of the United Nations Fact-Finding Mission on the Gaza Conflict

Report of the Secretary-General

Summary

The present report is submitted pursuant to General Assembly resolution 64/10 of 5 November 2009. On 3 December 2009, the Secretary-General sent notes verbales to the Permanent Mission of Israel to the United Nations, the Permanent Observer Mission of Palestine to the United Nations and the Permanent Mission of Switzerland to the United Nations, drawing their attention to the relevant provisions of resolution 64/10, and requesting written information by 29 January 2010 concerning any steps that may have been taken or were in the process of being taken in relation to their implementation. The full text of the materials received by the Secretariat in reply to those requests is attached as annexes. The report also contains the observations of the Secretary-General.

10-22583 (E) 040210

Please recycle

A/64/651

I. Introduction

1. The present report is submitted in pursuance of paragraph 6 of General Assembly resolution 64/10 of 5 November 2009 on the follow-up to the report of the United Nations Fact-Finding Mission on the Gaza Conflict, in which the Secretary-General was requested to report to the General Assembly, within a period of three months, on the implementation of the resolution. To fulfil this request, it was therefore necessary to ascertain what steps the parties named in paragraphs 3, 4 and 5 had taken.

2. On 3 December 2009, the Secretary-General drew the attention of the Permanent Mission of Israel to the United Nations to resolution 64/10, with the request that the Permanent Mission provide the Secretariat with written information by 29 January 2010 of any steps that the Government of Israel may have taken or was in the process of taking further to the call of the General Assembly in paragraph 3 of the resolution.

3. On 29 January 2010, the Secretariat received a document from the State of Israel entitled "Gaza operation investigations: an update". The full text of the document is attached as annex I to the present report.

4. On 3 December 2009, the Secretary-General drew the attention of the Permanent Observer Mission of Palestine to the United Nations to resolution 64/10, with the request that the Permanent Observer Mission provide the Secretariat with written information by 29 January 2010 of any steps that the Palestinian side may have taken or was in the process of taking further to the exhortation of the General Assembly in paragraph 4 of the resolution.

5. On 29 January 2010, the Secretary-General received a letter of the same date from the Permanent Observer Mission of Palestine to the United Nations conveying a letter dated 27 January 2010 from the Prime Minister of the Palestinian Authority, Salam Fayyad. The full text of the letters is attached as annex II to the present report.

6. On 3 December 2009, the Secretary-General drew the attention of the Permanent Mission of Switzerland to the United Nations to resolution 64/10, with the request that the Permanent Mission provide the Secretariat with written information by 29 January 2010 of any steps that the Government of Switzerland may have taken or was in the process of taking further to the recommendation of the General Assembly in paragraph 5 of the resolution.

7. On 29 January 2010, the Secretary-General received a letter of the same date from the Permanent Mission of Switzerland concerning the steps taken in connection with General Assembly resolution 64/10 on the follow-up to the report of the United Nations Fact-Finding Mission on the Gaza Conflict. The full text of the letter is attached as annex III to the present report.

II. Observations

8. At the beginning of 2009, I visited both Gaza and southern Israel in order to help to end the fighting and to show my respect and concern for the deaths and injuries of so many people during the conflict in and around Gaza. I was, and remain, deeply affected by the widespread death, destruction and suffering in the

Gaza Strip, as well as moved by the plight of civilians in southern Israel who have been subject to indiscriminate rocket and mortar fire.

9. I believe that, as a matter of principle, international humanitarian law needs to be fully respected and civilians must be protected in all situations and circumstances. Accordingly, on several occasions, I have called upon all of the parties to carry out credible domestic investigations into the conduct of the Gaza conflict. I hope that such steps will be taken wherever there are credible allegations of human rights abuses.

10. It is my sincere hope that General Assembly resolution 64/10 has served to encourage investigations by the Government of Israel and the Palestinian side that are independent, credible and in conformity with international standards.

11. I note from the materials received that the processes initiated by the Government of Israel and the Government of Switzerland are ongoing, and that the Palestinian side initiated its process on 25 January 2010. As such, no determination can be made on the implementation of the resolution by the parties concerned.

Annex I

[Original: English]

Gaza operation investigations: an update

January 2010

Contents

		Page
EXECUTIVE SUMMARY		6
I. INTRODUCTION		9
II. OVERVIEW OF ISRAEL'S SYSTEM FOR REVIEWING MISCONDUCT ALLEGATIONS		11
A. The Military Justice System		12
(1) The Military Advocate General's Corps		12
(2) The Military Police Criminal Investigation Division (MPCID)		14
(3) The Military Courts		15
B. Civilian Supervision Over the Military Justice System		17
(1) Attorney General of Israel		17
(2) Supreme Court of Israel		17
III. THE INVESTIGATION OF ALLEGED VIOLATIONS OF THE LAW OF ARMED CONFLICT		21
A. Sources of Complaints		23
B. Military Advocate General Screening and Referral		24
C. Command Investigations		26
D. Criminal Investigations and Prosecutions		29
E. The Similar Investigatory Systems of Other States		31
(1) United Kingdom		32
(2) United States		33
(3) Australia		35
(4) Canada		36
(5) Summary		37
IV. COMPLAINTS ALLEGING VIOLATIONS OF THE LAW OF ARMED CONFLICT DURING THE GAZA OPERATION		38
A. Command Investigations		40

(1) Five Special Command Investigations Opened Upon the
Conclusion of the Gaza Operation 40

  (i) Claims regarding incidents in which a large number of
  civilians not directly participating in the hostilities were
  harmed.. 43

  (ii) Claims regarding incidents where U.N. and international
  facilities were fired upon and damaged during the Gaza
  Operation 43

  (iii) Incidents involving shooting at medical facilities, buildings,
  vehicles and crews 44

  (iv) Destruction of private property and infrastructure by
  ground forces 45

  (v) The use of weaponry containing phosphorous..................... 45

  (vi) Concluding observations 46

(2) Additional Special Command Investigation............................ 47

(3) Other Command Investigations 48

B. Criminal Investigations... 48

C. Incidents Discussed in Human Rights Council Fact-Finding Report 50

(1) Namar wells group, Salah ad-Din Street, Jabaliyah refugee camp...... 51

(2) The Gaza wastewater treatment plant, Road No. 10, al-Sheikh
Ejlin, Gaza City 53

  (i) The date of the incident...................................... 53

  (ii) The possibility of an aerial strike 54

  (iii) The possibility of a ground attack........................... 55

  (iv) The possible causes of damage to the basin.................... 55

(3) El-Bader flour mill 56

(4) The house of Abu-Askar family...................................... 60

V. CONCLUSION 61

EXECUTIVE SUMMARY

1. This Paper describes Israel's process for investigating alleged violations of the Law of Armed Conflict. It focuses in particular on investigations, legal proceedings, and lessons learned in relation to the actions of the Israeli Defence Forces (IDF) in Gaza from 27 December 2008 through 18 January 2009 (the "Gaza Operation," also known as "Operation Cast Lead").

2. The Paper supplements and updates a paper Israel released in July 2009, *The Operation in Gaza: Factual and Legal Aspects*,[1] which addressed a range of factual and legal issues related to the Gaza Operation. The earlier paper included detailed accounts of Hamas's incessant mortar and rocket attacks on Israel's civilians (some 12,000 such attacks in the 8 years prior to the Operation) and the steadily increasing range of such attacks; Hamas's suicide bomb attacks; and Hamas's smuggling of weaponry and ammunition through tunnels under the Egyptian-Gaza border, as well as Israel's attempts to address these threats through non-military means, including diplomatic overtures and urgent appeals to the United Nations.

3. *The Operation in Gaza* also set out the legal framework governing the use of force and the principles – including the principles of distinction and proportionality – that apply in such a conflict. It also described the IDF's efforts to ensure compliance with these principles during the Gaza Operation and the *modus operandi* of Hamas, in particular its abuses of civilian protections that created such acute operational dilemmas.

4. *The Operation in Gaza* also included preliminary findings of a number of the investigations established following the operation, although such investigations were, and remain, works in progress. For this reason, six months after the publication of the original paper, it is appropriate once again to take stock publicly regarding the progress made and the current findings of the investigative process. While many of these investigations are still underway, this Paper aims to present a clear and up-to-date picture of the current status of Israel's investigations.

5. Israel's system for investigating alleged violations of the Law of Armed Conflict is comparable to the systems adopted by other democratic nations, including the United Kingdom, the United States, Australia, and Canada. The Paper notes that Israel has demonstrated its ability and its commitment to pursue serious criminal charges to uphold

---

[1] *The Operation in Gaza: Factual and Legal Aspects*, available at http://www.mfa.gov.il/MFA/Terrorism-+Obstacle+to+Peace/Hamas+war+against+Israel/Operation_in_Gaza-Factual_and_Legal_Aspects.htm.

the Law of Armed Conflict, a commitment which has been confirmed by outside observers and foreign legal systems.

6. Israel's investigative system has multiple layers of review to ensure impartiality and independence. These include the Military Advocate General's Corps (MAG), which determines whether to initiate criminal investigations and file charges against IDF soldiers. The Military Advocate General is legally independent from the military chain of command. Israel's Attorney General provides civilian oversight, as any decision of the Military Advocate General on whether or not to investigate or indict may be subject to his review. Further review is available through Israel's Supreme Court either as an appeals court, or exercising judicial review over any decision of the Military Advocate General or the civilian Attorney General. Such review can be – and frequently is – initiated by a petition of any interested party, including non-governmental organisations, Palestinians, and other non-citizens.

7. The Paper describes the structure and process of operation of these various elements of Israel's investigative system in some detail, particularly in order to correct misrepresentations and inaccuracies in recent reports describing these mechanisms.[2]

8. Describing the application of these mechanisms to the Gaza Operation, the Paper notes that the IDF to date has launched investigations of 150 separate incidents arising from the Gaza Operation. A number of these were opened at the IDF's own initiative. Others were opened in response to complaints and reports from Palestinian civilians, local and international non-governmental organisations, and U.N. and media reports.

9. Of the 150 incidents, so far 36 have been referred for criminal investigation. To date, criminal investigators have taken evidence from almost 100 Palestinian complainants and witnesses, along with approximately 500 IDF soldiers and commanders. The Paper describes some of the challenges encountered in the conduct of the investigations, including accessing evidence from battlefield situations and the need to make arrangements, together with non-governmental organisations such as B'Tselem, to locate and interview Palestinian witnesses. To address these challenges, special investigative teams have been appointed and are currently investigating complaints arising from the Gaza Operation.

---

[2] Numerous assertions made by the Human Rights Council's Report of the U.N. Fact-Finding Mission on the Gaza Conflict – for example, that criminal investigations must await the completion of a military command investigation or that all command investigators are within the direct chain of command – are incorrect.

10. The Paper relates to all investigations initiated following the Gaza Operation and does not limit itself to those incidents in the Human Rights Council's Report of the U.N. Fact-Finding Mission on the Gaza Conflict, chaired by Justice Richard Goldstone (the "Human Rights Council Fact-Finding Report" or "Report"). As Israel has clarified before, Israel disagrees with the findings and recommendations of the Report, which reflect many misunderstandings and fundamental mistakes with regard to the Gaza Operation, its purposes, and Israel's legal system. This Paper, however, is not intended as a comprehensive response to the Report or a catalogue of the Report's serious inaccuracies and misstatements.

11. With respect to the incidents described in the Human Rights Council Fact-Finding Report, the Paper notes that, prior to the publication of the Report, Israel was investigating 22 of the 34 incidents it addresses. The remaining 12 incidents, none of which had previously been brought to the attention of the Israeli authorities, were promptly referred for investigation upon the Report's publication. The Paper details the various stages of investigation of these incidents. It also notes that in some cases, after reviewing all the evidence available, the Military Advocate General has concluded that there was no basis for criminal investigations. The Paper gives detailed accounts of a number of these incidents.

12. The Paper also provides updated information regarding the special command investigations initiated by the IDF Chief of General Staff after the conclusion of hostilities in Gaza. As noted in *The Operation in Gaza*, shortly after the close of the Operation, the Chief of General Staff appointed five senior field commanders to investigate the most serious allegations of wrongdoing. The Chief of General Staff recently adopted a recommendation by the Military Advocate General and initiated a sixth special investigation, to consider additional allegations and to re-examine a complaint that a command investigator could not substantiate.

13. The Paper provides updates regarding the findings of these investigations, which have, in addition to prompting criminal inquiries, further command investigations, and disciplinary proceedings, also yielded operational lessons resulting in changes already made or underway.

14. The Paper concludes by recognizing the importance of conducting the investigative process in a timely manner. At the same time, it notes the need to ensure that legal processes are conducted thoroughly and with full due process, and in a manner comparable with that of other states guided by a respect for the rule of law.

I. INTRODUCTION

1. This Paper describes Israel's process for investigating alleged violations of the Law of Armed Conflict.[1] It focuses in particular on investigations, legal proceedings, and lessons learned in relation to the actions of the Israeli Defence Forces (IDF) in Gaza from 27 December 2008 through 18 January 2009 (the "Gaza Operation," also known as "Operation Cast Lead").

2. The Gaza Operation represented a striking example of the complex and challenging asymmetric conflicts in which states are increasingly finding themselves. In such conflicts, states are forced to confront non-state actors which do not regard themselves as bound by legal or humanitarian obligations. Such actors frequently abuse these principles as a deliberate strategy, placing both their own civilian population and that of the defending state at greater risk.

3. Faced with such challenges, and the acute real-time dilemmas created by militants operating from within and behind civilian areas, the importance of legal guidance and full compliance with legal and humanitarian obligations is paramount. At the international level, this requires close dialogue and consultation between states confronting similar threats in order to share experience and to consider how established principles of law can best be applied in such complex circumstances. At the national level, it requires continuous efforts to ensure that the principles of the Law of Armed Conflict are an integral part of the training of soldiers and commanders, and that these principles guide planning and operational decisions.

4. Beyond these measures, which are generally taken prior to and during operations, extreme importance must also be given to reviewing the operation after the fact. This should include the thorough investigation of all incidents that raise questions regarding the appropriateness or lawfulness of measures used or decisions made. The complexity and scale of such operations means that inevitably there are tragic instances, mistakes, and errors of judgment.[2] Tragic results, including civilian death and damage to property do not necessarily mean that violations of international law have occurred. At the same time, in

---

[1] This Paper uses the term "Law of Armed Conflict" in its ordinary sense – describing the legal obligations of parties to an armed conflict in the course of their military operations. The term "International Humanitarian Law" is used by many commentators and countries as an interchangeable term. Israel, like many other countries, prefers the term Law of Armed Conflict.

[2] A harsh reminder for Israel of this reality is the fact that nearly half of its soldiers killed during the Gaza Operation were killed by IDF fire mistakenly directed towards them.

instances in which evidence indicates that violations have taken place, this must be fully investigated and prosecuted.

5. Israel is committed to ensuring that every such incident is fully and fairly investigated, to ensure that lessons can be learned and that, if justified, criminal or disciplinary proceedings initiated. To this end the IDF policy requires that every allegation of wrongdoing be investigated, irrespective of its source. The 150 separate incidents investigated following the Gaza Operation include, as detailed later in this Paper, not only investigations opened as a result of Israel's own concerns about certain incidents but also investigations in response to complaints and reports from Palestinian residents, local and international non-governmental organisations and UN and media reports.

6. Parts II and III of this Paper provide an overview of Israel's mechanisms for investigating alleged violations of the Law of Armed Conflict. These include mechanisms operating within the IDF, but independently of the military chain of command as well as civilian oversight mechanisms including the Attorney General and the Supreme Court sitting as the High Court of Justice, with power of judicial review over every decision to prosecute or not prosecute alleged offenders. Israel's system of investigation and prosecution is comparable to that of many democratic states confronting similar challenges, and in the course of Part III reference is made to the systems other states have developed in this regard.

7. Part IV focuses specifically on the investigation of complaints alleging violations of the Law of Armed Conflict during the Gaza Operation and sets out where the investigations opened currently stand. It also addresses some of the lessons that have already been learned, including changes to operational procedures, as a result of the findings of the investigations conducted so far.

II. OVERVIEW OF ISRAEL'S SYSTEM FOR REVIEWING MISCONDUCT ALLEGATIONS

8. Israel is a democracy, with a well-developed legal system. Even though it has confronted constant and existential threats from neighbouring states and non-state actors, Israel stands committed to the rule of law. As Israel's Supreme Court has recognized:

> "This is the destiny of a democracy – it does not see all means as acceptable, and the ways of its enemies are not always open before it. A democracy must sometimes fight with one hand tied behind its back. Even so, a democracy has the upper hand. The rule of law and the liberty of an individual constitute important components in its understanding of security. At the end of the day, they strengthen its spirit and this strength allows it to overcome its difficulties."[3]

9. Under Israel's Basic Law for the Military, the IDF is subordinate and accountable to the civilian Government. Like any other governmental authority, it is subject to the rule of law, including the applicable rules of international law. The Israeli system of justice holds the Government, including the IDF, to its legal obligations.

10. First and foremost, Israel is committed to educating state agents – in this case, IDF commanders and soldiers – of their duties and restrictions. This includes the widespread dissemination of relevant Law of Armed Conflict principles across the ranks of the IDF.[4] When violations of those principles are suspected, the Israeli justice system is designed not only to mete out punishment and deter future violations but also to provide the opportunity for redress to parties injured by state offences. The lawlessness of an adversary, or the severity of the threat they pose, is not and cannot be an excuse for unlawful or improper conduct.

11. To ensure compliance with the rule of law, including international law and the Law of Armed Conflict, the IDF has established a system to investigate and pursue allegations of misconduct. This system, like its counterparts in many states, includes multiple components and layers of review – an internal military disciplinary procedure, a network of military police, prosecutors, and courts, and a process for oversight by civilian authorities and the judiciary. While individual components of this system – like any

---

[3] *Public Committee Against Torture in Israel v. State of Israel*, HCJ 5100/94 ¶ 39 (6 September 1999).
[4] This dissemination is particularly important since Israeli law forbids a soldier from complying with an order that is manifestly unlawful.

governmental organisation – may not always work as intended, numerous checks and balances ensure that the rule of law is upheld.

A. The Military Justice System

12. Israel's military justice system, like those of many other democracies, is part of the state's military forces but is professionally independent. Israel's Military Justice Law of 1955 established the Court Martial system and governs the investigation, indictment, and prosecution of those accused of misconduct. This military justice system deals with all allegations of offences or violations of law committed by IDF personnel, including allegations of improper conduct on the battlefield.

13. The military justice system includes three main components: the Military Advocate General's Corps, the Military Police Criminal Investigation Division (MPCID), and the Military Courts.

(1) The Military Advocate General's Corps

14. The Military Advocate General's Corps is comprised of highly professional and trained lawyers, and is responsible for enforcing the rule of law throughout the IDF.[5] It also provides advice on military, domestic, and international law to the Chief of General Staff and all divisions of the IDF.[6] The decisions and legal opinions of the Military Advocate General are binding on all components of the military.[7]

15. Although he serves on the General Staff of the IDF, the Military Advocate General is legally independent. IDF Supreme Command Orders state that in executing his powers and authority, the Military Advocate General is "subject to no authority but the law."[8] Thus, the Chief of General Staff has no authority over him regarding legal matters. The Military Advocate General is not subject to direct orders of any superior officers, excluding the Chief of Staff in non-legal matters. As a former Military Advocate General has explained, the Military Advocate General has a unique status in the military:

---

[5] Military Justice Law, § 178(2), (4); IDF Supreme Command Order 2.0613(2)(a).
[6] Military Justice Law, § 178(1); IDF Supreme Command Order 2.0613(2)(b)(4).
[7] See Avivit Atiyah v. Attorney General, HCJ 4723/96 ¶ 11 (29 July 1997).
[8] IDF Supreme Command Order 2.0613(9)(A).

"Members of the Military Advocate are not subject to the functional command orders of the command ranks that they serve, and the decisions that they make are in their exclusive discretion. The MAG is not subordinate to the Chief of Staff in respect of the exercise of his powers and is not under any command whatsoever – de jure or de facto."[9]

16. The independence of the Military Advocate General extends to every officer within the Military Advocate General's Corps. Each is subordinate only to the Military Advocate General and is not subject to direct orders by commanders outside the Corps.

17. The manner in which the Military Advocate General is appointed further evidences his independence. Under the Military Justice Law, the Minister of Defence appoints the Military Advocate General, upon a recommendation of the Chief of General Staff of the IDF.[10] Most other senior officers in the IDF are appointed directly by the Chief of General Staff.

18. The Military Advocate General's dual enforcement and advisory responsibilities parallel those of chief military lawyers in other countries, such as the United Kingdom.[11] The units within the Military Advocate General's Corps that issue legal guidance to the IDF and that examine and prosecute alleged crimes by IDF forces are separate from one another. The latter function of the Military Advocate General's Corps is conducted by the Chief Military Prosecutor, Military Advocates (who head regional and other prosecution units), and military prosecutors (collectively, "the military prosecution").

19. The military justice system empowers the Military Advocate General, the Chief Military Prosecutor, and the Military Advocates to direct the prosecution of soldiers for military offences identified in the Military Justice Law (such as absence without leave, conduct unbecoming an officer, and pillage), as well as criminal offences under Israel's general Penal Law.[12] When the evidence establishes a reasonable likelihood that a crime or infraction has been committed, a Military Advocate may order a prosecutor to file an indictment in the Military Courts or order a commander to hold a disciplinary hearing.

---

[9] Menachem Finkelstein and Yifat Tomer, *The Israeli Military Legal System – An Overview of the Current Situation and a Glimpse Into the Future*, 52 AIR FORCE L. REV. 137, 140 (2002) (footnotes omitted), *available at* http://findarticles.com/p/articles/mi_m6007/is_2002_Wntr/ai_103136516/?tag=content;col1.

[10] Military Justice Law, § 177(a).

[11] *See* Part III.E below.

[12] Military Justice Law, § 280.

Like any criminal proceeding, this process requires military prosecutors to examine the evidence carefully and to file an indictment only if there is sufficient evidence.[13]

20. In 2007, the Military Advocate General established a specialized unit within the military prosecution, the Office of the Military Advocate for Operational Affairs, to oversee all investigations and to conduct all prosecutions of alleged operational misconduct – particularly, alleged misconduct by IDF soldiers against Palestinian civilians during military operations. The mandate of the Office includes investigation and prosecution of alleged violations of the Law of Armed Conflict. The prosecutors assigned specifically to the Office have special training and expertise to address the unique difficulties in investigating and trying these kinds of cases. When necessary, prosecutors from other units supplement this unit.

(2) The Military Police Criminal Investigation Division (MPCID)

21. The MPCID is the primary entity within the IDF for investigating alleged crimes committed by soldiers. It has hundreds of trained investigators, including reservists, who are posted in different regional and specialized units. The training course of each investigator lasts about six months, including legal studies at the IDF's School of Military Law, which is under the authority of the Military Advocate General. After concluding this training, each soldier is required to pass an examination conducted by a Military Advocate before he or she is authorized to serve as an MPCID investigator.[14]

22. The scope of the MPCID's activities is substantial. In the last five years, the unit opened almost 3,300 investigations on average each year and collected more than 11,000 testimonies. The MPCID investigates an average of 5,500 suspects and arrests an average of 1,400 people per year. In 2009, seven percent of these investigations involved Palestinian complainants.

23. Criminal investigators who handle complaints by Palestinians undergo specialized training, including training in international law. Some of these investigators are Arabic speakers, while others use Arabic interpreters, who participate in interviews with Palestinian complainants and witnesses.

---

[13] Under Israeli Supreme Court precedent, a criminal indictment may only be filed where a "reasonable chance to convict" exists in light of all evidence collected, including exculpatory evidence. *See, e.g., Yahav v. State Attorney*, HCJ 2534/97 (30 June 1997).

[14] Military Justice Law, § 252(A)(3).

24. As necessary, MPCID investigators consult with prosecutors from the Military Advocate General's Corps regarding the proper handling of an investigation. In addition, the Military Advocate General appointed a legal officer from the Military Advocate General's Corps to serve as the legal adviser of the MPCID. The legal adviser works to ensure that legal policy is assimilated in MPCID standing orders and regulations.

25. At the conclusion of an investigation, the MPCID reports to the military prosecution and transfers the file for review by a prosecutor. In many cases, the military prosecution returns the file to MPCID with concrete instructions to conduct a supplemental investigation. If no supplement is needed, a Military Advocate or the Chief Military Prosecutor decides whether to initiate criminal or disciplinary proceedings, based on the evidence available and the nature of the alleged misconduct. In cases of heightened complexity or sensitivity, this decision is made in consultation with the Military Advocate General.

(3) The Military Courts

26. The Military Courts adjudicate charges against IDF soldiers for military and other criminal offences through a Court Martial. The Courts, which include the Military Court of Appeals and several regional courts, are composed of both professional military judges and regular officers (who must have no connection to the cases they hear). Every Court Martial must include at least one professional military judge, and professionals must comprise a majority of any appellate panel.[15] The Military Justice Law provides that "[i]n judicial matters, a military judge is not subject to any authority save that of the law, and is not subject in any way to the authority of his commanders."[16]

27. Military commanders do not appoint professional military judges. Rather, an independent commission comprised of the Minister of Defence, the Minister of Justice, members of the Israeli Supreme Court and the Military Court of Appeals, and a representative of the Israeli Bar Association (among others), makes the appointments.[17] Professional military judges serve in a separate military courts unit, headed by the President of the Military Court of Appeals. The cadre of professional military judges includes many civilian judges, who

---

[15] Military Justice Law, §§ 202, 216.

[16] Military Justice Law, § 184. The Israeli Supreme Court has noted that the participation of regular officers in Courts Martial serves "to emphasize the common responsibility of all of those who serve in the military regarding what happens in the military." *Katz v. President of the Court Martial, Central Jurisdictional District*, HCJ 142/79 ¶ 6 (10 June 1979).

[17] *See* Military Justice Law, § 187(a).

may preside over military proceedings as part of their military reservist duties.[18] Professional military judges can be removed only for gross misconduct, under a special procedure.

28. Even though the Military Courts are located within military bases, their proceedings are generally open to the public. Military Courts may conduct proceedings *in camera* only in limited circumstances, such as when an open proceeding would jeopardize the security of the state.[19] The news media can and does cover Military Court proceedings, and many judgments of the Military Courts are published on the official website of the Israeli judiciary, as well as on various public online databases. In general, the rules of evidence in the Military Courts are practically identical to the rules applicable in civilian criminal proceedings.[20]

29. Prosecutors have the right to appeal a sentence they regard as too lenient. Traditionally, the Military Courts have dealt sternly with soldiers convicted of offences against civilians. For example, in *Military Prosecutor v. Sgt Ilin*, the Military Court of Appeals increased the sentence of a soldier convicted of looting. The court observed:

> "A soldier committing prohibited acts during armed conflict inflicts injury upon the human dignity of the conquered as well as upon the humanity of the conqueror. . . . It is clear therefore that the thunder of war and the heat of the battle actually demand reinforcement and amplification of the voice of morality . . . ."[21]

30. Likewise, in *Military Prosecutor v. Corp. Lior and Corp. Roi*, the Military Court of Appeals raised the sentences of two soldiers serving in the Military Police who were convicted of assaulting Palestinian detainees. The court concluded:

> "The respondents grossly violated their obligations as human beings, citizens of the State of Israel, as soldiers and as police officers. The respondents are part of the Israeli society, soldiers in the IDF and members of the Military Police. In their actions, they harmed each and every person who is a part of these groups. The damage of their actions

---

[18] *See* Military Justice Law, §§ 185(b), 187C.

[19] *See* Military Justice Law, § 324.

[20] *See* Military Justice Law, § 476 (establishing that evidence law applicable to criminal proceedings in civilian courts shall apply in Military Courts unless a specific provision states differently). Rules of evidence that are unique to the Military Courts must be interpreted in light of similar provisions and the principles of general evidence law. *See Isascharov v. Military Prosecutor General*, Cr.A. 5121/98 (4 May 2006).

[21] *Military Prosecutor v. Sgt. Ilin*, C/62/03 ¶ E (23 May 2003).

is not limited to the ugly act they committed. It radiates in a circular pattern – similar to a rock thrown down a well – on its entire surrounding."[22]

B. Civilian Supervision Over the Military Justice System

(1) Attorney General of Israel

31. The decision of the Military Advocate General whether or not to open a criminal investigation, as well as his decision whether or not to file an indictment, may be subject to further review by the Attorney General of the State of Israel, an independent figure of high authority.

32. For example, in *Avivit Atiyah v. Attorney General*, the Israeli Supreme Court ruled that the Attorney General could order the Military Advocate General's Corps to change its position concerning whether to file a criminal indictment. The Court ruling has been interpreted as follows:

> "[T]he power of the Attorney General to impose his opinion on the MAG will, in those cases, include the cancellation of and the filing of a charge in a court-martial. In other words, even if the MAG thinks, in these cases, that a charge ought not be filed, and the matter is brought before the Attorney General ... the Attorney General shall be authorized to decide that a charge should be filed, and his decision shall prevail."[23]

33. A complainant or non-governmental organisation may trigger the review of the Attorney General by simply sending a letter to the Attorney General, requesting further review of the matter.

(2) Supreme Court of Israel

34. Civilian judicial review of the military system occurs in two ways. First, the Supreme Court of Israel has discretion to hear direct appeals from judgments of the Military Court of Appeals "concerning an important, difficult, or innovative legal question."[24] Second, the

---

[22] *Military Prosecutor v. Corp. Lior and Corp. Roi*, C/128/03 and C/146/03 ¶ 17 (21 August 2003).

[23] Finkelstein and Tomer, *supra*, at 163 (referring to precedent set in *Avivit Atiyah v. Attorney General*, HCJ 4723/96 (29 July 1997)).

[24] Military Justice Law, § 440I(a),(b).

Supreme Court, sitting as the High Court of Justice, can review and reverse a decision of the Military Advocate General, the military prosecution, and/or the Attorney General whether to investigate or file a criminal indictment concerning alleged misconduct by soldiers.

35. Any interested party (including non-governmental organisations) or any person (including non-citizens and non-residents) affected or potentially affected by a government action can petition the Supreme Court, residing as the High Court of Justice, on a claim that the action is *ultra vires,* unlawful, or substantially unreasonable. When warranted, the Supreme Court can enjoin the Government or grant other relief. Under Israel's legal system, a ruling of the Supreme Court against the IDF or another government agency is final and binding.

36. Palestinian residents, as well as non-governmental organisations or persons representing their interests, have filed successful petitions challenging the Military Advocate General's exercise of prosecutorial discretion. Some examples include:

    o The Supreme Court reversed the Military Advocate General's decision not to file criminal charges against a high-ranking field commander, and the commander ultimately was convicted on those charges.[25]

    o During a Supreme Court hearing, the Military Advocate General's Corps consented to opening a military criminal investigation into an incident that had only previously been examined by a command investigation.[26]

    o The Supreme Court intervened in the Military Advocate General's decision to indict a soldier and a commander for "unbecoming conduct" (rather than more serious offences), in connection with the alleged firing of a rubber bullet at the feet of a detainee.[27] Following the judgment, the Military Advocate General's Corps amended the indictment, charging the commander and the soldier with more serious offences.[28]

---

[25] *See Jamal Abed al Kader Mahmoud Zofnan v. Military Advocate General,* HCJ 425/89 (27 December 1989).

[26] *See Brian Avery v. Military Advocate General,* HCJ 11343/04 (1 March 2005).

[27] *Ashraf Abu Rahma v. Military Advocate General,* HCJ 7195/08 (1 July 2009) ("The military justice system, which is in charge of implementing the IDF's values of conduct, must send out a determined message of consistent and decisive defence of the basic values of the society and the army, and of uncompromising enforcement in all levels – educational, commanding authority and punitive – of the fundamental principles that are shared by the Israeli society and the Israeli army and give them their ethical and humane character.").

[28] The amended indictment charged the commander with the offence of threats under Section 192 of Israel's Penal Law and the soldier with the crime of illegal use of a firearm in accordance with Section 85

[Footnote continued on next page]

Document [6] Follow-up to the Report of the UN Fact Finding Mission

37. In other cases, the Supreme Court has affirmed the Military Advocate General's decisions not to file charges, corroborating the Court's authority to approve, as well as disapprove, those decisions.[29]

38. As noted above, the Court has enforced the obligation of the state and the IDF to abide by applicable law (including international law) and humanitarian standards, notwithstanding the reality and constant threat of terrorist attacks.[30] For example, the Court held in 2006:

> "'Israel is not an isolated island. It is a member of an international system.' ... The combat activities of the IDF are not conducted in a legal void. There are legal norms – some from customary international law, some from international law entrenched in conventions to which Israel is party, and some in the fundamental principles of Israeli law – which determine rules about how combat activities should be conducted."[31]

39. The Israeli Supreme Court has demonstrated that it can and will intercede in actual hostilities between the IDF and Palestinian terrorist organisations – including the Gaza Operation. In January 2009, while IDF forces were still fighting Hamas in Gaza, the Court reviewed two petitions by human rights groups challenging the IDF's efforts to satisfy humanitarian obligations to Palestinian civilians.[32] The Court "endeavour[ed] to examine the claims in real time, so that it may grant effective relief or arrive at an agreed settlement."[33] In doing

---

[Footnote continued from previous page]
of the Military Justice Law. Both were also charged with the offence of conduct unbecoming an officer. The case is pending in Military Court.

[29] *See, e.g., Iman Atrash v. Military Advocate General*, HCJ 10682/06 (18 June 2007).

[30] Official English translations of over 25 cases that address this issue are available at the website of Israel's Supreme Court, http://elyon1.court.gov.il/VerdictsSearch/EnglishStaticVerdicts.html. *See, e.g., Public Committee Against Torture in Israel v. State of Israel*, HCJ 5100/94 (6 September 1999); *Iad Ashak Mahmud Marab v. IDF Commander in West Bank*, HCJ 3239/02 (6 February 2003); *Beit Sourik Village Council v. State of Israel*, HCJ 2056/04 (30 June 2004); *Zaharan Yunis Muhammad Mara'aba v. Prime Minister of Israel*, HCJ 7957/04 (15 September 2005); *Ahmad Issa Abdalla Yassin, Bil'in Village Council Chairman v. State of Israel*, HCJ 8414/05 (15 December 2008); *Public Committee Against Torture in Israel v. State of Israel*, HCJ 769/02 (14 December 2006); *Adalah - The Legal Center for Arab Minority Rights in Israel v. GOC Central Command, IDF*, HCJ 3799/02 (6 October 2005).

[31] *Public Committee Against Torture in Israel v. State of Israel*, HCJ 769/02 ¶ 17 (14 December 2006) (quoting *Physicians for Human Rights v. Commander of IDF Forces in Gaza*, HCJ 4764/04 (30 May 2004)).

[32] *Physicians for Human Rights v. Prime Minister of Israel*, HCJ 201/09 and 248/09 (19 January 2009). After examining the steps taken by the IDF and high command authorities, the Court determined that they had indeed complied with international law.

[33] *Id.* ¶ 13.

so, the President of the Court affirmed the Court's jurisdiction to hear such petitions even in the midst of combat:

> "Cases in which the court examines the legality of military operations while they are happening are not uncommon occurrences, in view of the reality of our lives in which we are constantly confronting terrorism that is directed against the civilian population of Israel, and in view of the need to respond to it while discharging the duties imposed by law even in times of combat. . . . [I]t is the role of the court, even in times of combat, to determine whether within the framework of the combat operations the obligation to act in accordance with legal guidelines – both within the context of Israeli law and within the context of international humanitarian law – is being upheld."[34]

40. Israel's Supreme Court has earned international respect for its jurisprudence and its independence in enforcing international law. Its rulings balancing security and individual rights are highly regarded by jurists and academic scholars of international law, and have been cited favourably by foreign courts, including the Supreme Court of Canada, the House of Lords in the United Kingdom, and the European Court of Justice.[35]

---

[34] *Id.* ¶ 12. Also during the Gaza Operation, the Supreme Court considered a petition from foreign journalists seeking to enter Gaza at military checkpoints. *Foreign Press Association in Israel v. OC Southern Command*, HCJ 9910/08 (2 January 2009). The Court affirmed that "the freedom of speech and the freedom of the press . . . have an all the more special importance" during armed hostilities, *id.* ¶ 5, but the Gaza Operation ended before the dispute was completely resolved. *Foreign Press Association in Israel v. OC Southern Command*, HCJ 643/09 (25 January 2009).

[35] *See, e.g., Application Under S. 83.28 of Criminal Code*, 2004 SCC 42 ¶ 7 (Supreme Court of Canada 2004) (citing the "eloquent" statements of Israel's Supreme Court on the importance of responding to terrorism within the rule of law); *Suresh v. Canada*, [2002] 1 S.C.R. 3, 2002 SCC ("we note that the Supreme Court of Israel sitting as the High Court of Justice and the House of Lords have rejected torture as a legitimate tool to use in combating terrorism and protecting national security"); *A and Others v. Secretary of State for Home Department*, 2 A.C. 221 ¶ 150 (U.K. House of Lords 2005) (emphasizing importance of the United Kingdom "retain[ing] the moral high ground which an open democratic society enjoys," and thereby "uphold[ing] the values encapsulated in the judgment of the Supreme Court of Israel in *Public Committee Against Torture in Israel v. Israel* . . . [that] '[a]lthough a democracy must often fight with one hand tied behind its back, it nonetheless has the upper hand'") (citation omitted); *Kadi v. Council of European Union*, 3 C.M.L.R. 41 ¶ AG 45 (European Court of Justice 2008) (quoting former President of Supreme Court of Israel regarding importance of judicial oversight of political decisions: "It is when the cannons roar that we especially need the laws . . . . It is an expression of the difference between a democratic state fighting for its life and the fighting of terrorists rising up against it. The state fights in the name of the law and in the name of upholding the law. The terrorists fight against the law, while violating it. The war against terrorism is also law's war against those who rise up against it.").

III. THE INVESTIGATION OF ALLEGED VIOLATIONS OF THE LAW OF ARMED CONFLICT

41. The consistent policy of the IDF has been to investigate alleged violations of the Law of Armed Conflict, regardless of the source of the allegations, and to prosecute where there is credible evidence that a violation has occurred. This policy reflects a commitment to resolve complaints against IDF personnel fairly, impartially, and effectively. Israel's Attorney General has affirmed this policy and it has been presented to the High Court of Justice for review.

42. The effectiveness of Israel's justice system has been acknowledged by international bodies. For example, the Criminal Chamber of the National Court of Spain (Audiencia Nacional) decided by a wide margin last year to discontinue a Spanish investigation into alleged IDF war crimes in the Gaza Strip. The proceedings concerned a 2002 incident during which the IDF killed the head of Hamas's military wing but also a number of civilians during an air strike. A Spanish judge had opened an inquiry into the matter pursuant to Spain's universal jurisdiction statute.

43. In closing the investigation, the Criminal Chamber of the National Court of Spain emphasised Israel's ability fully and fairly to investigate the charges itself. Contrary to the allegations raised in the Human Rights Council Fact-Finding Report, the Court held that Israeli procedures and precedents with regard to defensive strikes, and the military, civilian, and judicial review in Israel of the incident, comport with principles of international law. The court stated:

> "[D]isputing the impartiality and organic and functional separation from the Executive of the Israeli Military Advocate General, the Attorney General of the State of Israel and the Investigation Commission appointed by the Israeli Government involves ignoring the existence of a social and democratic state with rule of law, where the members of the Executive and the Judiciary in question are subject to the rule of law. On the basis of those premises, there can be no doubt whatsoever with regard to the exercise of pertinent criminal actions in the event that the existence of any criminally relevant conduct on the part of the

individuals who ordered, planned and carried out the bomb attack should come to light in the course of the investigations performed."[36]

44. In general, the investigation policy of the IDF regarding alleged violations of the Law of Armed Conflict is as follows:

- o The Military Advocate General reviews complaints from a variety of sources.

- o The Military Advocate General refers individual complaints for a command investigation or, when there is an allegation of *per se* criminal behaviour, for a criminal investigation.

- o For those complaints referred for a command investigation, the Military Advocate General reviews the record and findings of the command investigation, along with other available material, to determine whether to recommend disciplinary proceedings and whether there is a suspicion of a criminal act – in which case the complaint is referred for a criminal investigation.

- o Following a criminal investigation, the Military Advocate General reviews the entire evidentiary record to determine whether or not to file an indictment or to recommend disciplinary proceedings.

45. This process is illustrated in the following diagram:

---

[36] Unofficial translation of Decision no. 1/2009, 17 July 2009 (plenary), of the National Criminal Court of Appeals ("Sala de lo Penal de la Audiencia Nacional"), at 24, regarding Preliminary Criminal Proceedings no. 154/2008 of the Central Investigation Court no. 4. *See also* Appeal of the Coordinating Prosecutor (Pedro Martinez Torrijos), 6 May 2009, from the Order of the Audiencia Nacional de Madrid, 4 May 2009, in Preliminary Proceedings Case No. 157/2008 (emphasizing that Israel's investigatory system, with review by Military Advocate General, Attorney General, and Supreme Court, "fully satisfy" the requirements of "an independent and impartial system of justice").

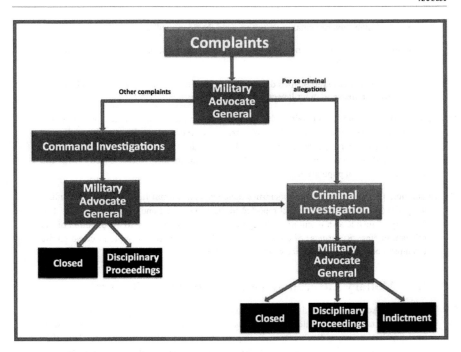

A. Sources of Complaints

46. The IDF investigates alleged violations of the Law of Armed Conflict in essentially the same way it investigates other allegations of criminal misconduct. When a complaint raises a reasonable suspicion that a crime has been committed, the IDF opens a criminal investigation. If the investigation yields sufficient evidence to support the complaint, the IDF initiates either criminal or disciplinary proceedings, depending on the severity of the findings.

47. Information on alleged misconduct of soldiers reaches the IDF authorities in various ways, including:

   o formal or informal complaints by alleged victims themselves or family members;

   o complaints by commanders or soldiers who witnessed an incident;

- reports by non-governmental organisations and the news media;
- complaints or letters by non-governmental organisations, journalists, embassies, or international bodies; and
- complaints forwarded to or filed directly with the Military Advocate General's Corps by the Israeli Police and other law enforcement agencies.

48. Any person may file a complaint with the Military Police at any civilian police station regarding alleged misconduct by IDF soldiers. Gaza residents can file complaints directly in writing (in Hebrew, Arabic, and English), through a non-governmental organisation acting on their behalf, or through the Military Liaison that works directly with the Palestinian civilian population.

49. In addition, the IDF independently identifies incidents that warrant further inquiry, including allegations of military misconduct reported in the news media and by other sources. The Ministry of Justice also monitors such reports and brings allegations to the attention of the relevant bodies. Regardless of the source, the IDF evaluates each complaint based on the circumstances of the case and the evidence available.

B. Military Advocate General Screening and Referral

50. The Military Advocate General and the military prosecution play a major role in the IDF's system of investigating alleged violations of the Law of Armed Conflict. Such investigations are considered extremely important, and the Military Advocate General is personally involved in the examination of many cases. The military prosecution receives all complaints of IDF misconduct for screening and review, and directly refers any complaint that alleges *per se* criminal behaviour – including allegations of maltreatment of detainees, the use of civilians as human shields, intentional targeting of civilians and looting – to the MPCID for criminal investigation.

51. Other complaints – for example, allegations of civilian deaths due to artillery shelling or the destruction of civilian property on the battlefield – may or may not constitute a criminal offence, depending on the specific circumstances. Where hostilities occur in a heavily populated area, and where enemy combatants deliberately seek to blend in with the populace, civilian casualties, unfortunately, are inevitable. Under the Law of Armed Conflict, the occurrence of damage to civilian property, and of injury, or even death of civilians, during an operational activity does not necessarily indicate nor even imply

criminal misconduct.³⁷ Rather, criminal responsibility for violation of the Law of Armed Conflict requires evidence that military personnel *intended* to harm civilians or clearly foresaw that excessive harm to civilians would result, when balanced against the anticipated military advantage.³⁸

52. Therefore, as to this second class of complaints, before initiating a criminal investigation, the Military Advocate General must first determine whether the evidence raises a suspicion of criminal activity and warrants a referral to MPCID. As discussed below, in making his decision, the Military Advocate General evaluates the complaint itself, which may include first-hand accounts from complainants and witnesses, along with the record of evidence developed during military command investigations (also known as operational debriefings) and other materials.

53. Some of Israel's critics have misunderstood the nature of these dual investigative tracks and incorrectly assumed that all complaints first must proceed through the command investigation stage, thereby delaying criminal proceedings for months. This premise – a

---

³⁷ *See, e.g.*, Open Letter from Luis Moreno-Ocampo, Chief Prosecutor of International Criminal Court, "Allegations concerning War Crimes" at 4-5 (9 February 2006), *available at* http://www2.icc-cpi.int/NR/rdonlyres/F596D08D-D810-43A2-99BB-B899B9C5BCD2/277422/OTP_letter_to_senders_re_Iraq_9_February_2006.pdf ("Under international humanitarian law and the Rome Statute, the death of civilians during an armed conflict, no matter how grave and regrettable, does not in itself constitute a war crime."); Kenneth Watkin, *Assessing Proportionality: Moral Complexity and Legal Rules*, *in* YEARBOOK OF INTERNATIONAL HUMANITARIAN LAW 3, 9 (Timothy L.H. McCormack ed., 2005) ("[A]lthough civilians are not to be directly made the object of an attack, humanitarian law accepts that they may be killed or civilian property may be damaged as a result of an attack on a military objective."); W. Hays Parks, *Air War and the Law of War*, 32 A.F. L. REV. 1, 4 (1990) ("Within both the Just War Tradition and the law of war, it has always been permissible to attack combatants even though some noncombatants may be injured or killed . . . ."); Michael N. Schmitt, *The Principle of Discrimination in 21st Century Warfare*, 2 YALE HUM. RTS & DEV. L.J. 143, 150 (1999) (noting that international legal doctrine of proportionality "operates in scenarios in which incidental injury and collateral damage are the foreseeable, albeit undesired, result of attack on a legitimate target"); *see also* NATO BOMBINGS: FINAL REPORT TO THE ICTY PROSECUTOR ¶ 51 ("Collateral casualties to civilians and collateral damage to civilian objects can occur for a variety of reasons.").

³⁸ *See, e.g.*, Yves Sandoz, Christophe Swinarski & Bruno Zimmermann, Commentary on the Additional Protocols of 8 June 1977 to the Geneva Conventions 12 June 1949 (International Committee of the Red Cross, 1987), art. 51(2), ¶ 1934 ("[I]n relation to criminal law the Protocol requires intent and, moreover, with regard to indiscriminate attacks, the element of prior knowledge of the predictable result."); Rüdiger Wolfrum & Dieter Fleck, *Enforcement of International Humanitarian Law*, in THE HANDBOOK OF INTERNATIONAL HUMANITARIAN LAW 675, 697 (Dieter Fleck ed., 2d ed. 2008) ("The prerequisite for a grave breach is intent; the attack must be intentionally directed at the civilian population or individual civilians, and the intent must embrace physical consequences."). The ICTY has found that for an attack to qualify as a war crime, it "must have been conducted *intentionally* in the *knowledge*, or when it was impossible not to know, that civilians or civilian property were being targeted." *Prosecutor v. Galić*, Case No. IT-98-29-T, Judgment and Opinion ¶ 42 (5 December 2003), *quoted in* Watkin, *supra*, at 38.

central premise of the Human Rights Council Fact-Finding Report[39] – is wrong. The Military Advocate General and the military prosecution have full authority to initiate, and do initiate, direct criminal investigations of those complaints alleging conduct that is clearly criminal in nature. For example, in the case of the alleged firing of a rubber bullets at the feet of a detainee, the Military Advocate General conducted a direct criminal investigation immediately after the incident was published in the media, and filed an indictment within two weeks.[40] With respect to other complaints, those that are first subject to command investigations, there is no requirement that the Military Advocate General or military prosecution await a final report from the command investigator before making a criminal referral. At any point when there is a reasonable suspicion of criminal misconduct, the military prosecution may launch a criminal investigation.[41]

C. Command Investigations

54. Under the Military Justice Law, a command investigation is an "inquiry held in the army, in accordance with IDF orders, regarding an event which occurred during training or operational activity, or in relation to them."[42] The longstanding practice of the IDF, and many other militaries, is to conduct a command investigation in the field following any kind of military action. Such an investigation normally focuses on examining the performance of the forces and identifying aspects of an operation to preserve and to improve, but may also focus on specific problems that occurred. By undertaking this review, the IDF seeks to reduce future operational errors, including those potentially resulting in civilian casualties.

---

[39] *See, e.g.*, Human Rights Council Fact-Finding Report ¶¶ 1820, 1831 (criticizing Israel's investigative process for "undue delay" because "proper criminal investigations can start only after the 'operational debriefing' is over"); *see also id.* ¶¶ 121, 1798, 1830.

[40] *Ashraf Abu Rahma v. Military Advocate General*, HCJ 7195/08 (1 July 2009). This case was discussed in Part II.B.2.

[41] The Human Rights Council Fact-Finding Report wrongly concluded that "in practice criminal investigations do not begin before six months after the events in question." Human Rights Council Fact-Finding Report ¶ 1830. As discussed below, the Military Advocate General directly initiated more than two dozen criminal investigations related to the Gaza Operation – all within six months. In fact, the Human Rights Council Fact-Finding Report discusses one of these investigations, which was completed less than two months after the Gaza Operation ended. *Id.* ¶ 1780; *see* "Military Police Investigation Concerning Statements Made at the Rabin Center: Based on Hearsay," IDF Press Release (30 March 2009), *available at* http://dover.idf.il/IDF/English/Press+Releases/09/03/3001.htm.

[42] Military Justice Law, § 539A(A).

55. But routine post-operation investigations are not the only inquiries conducted by the IDF. In addition to these inquiries, when a complaint is filed with the Military Advocate General which does not allege *per se* criminal behaviour, the Military Advocate General requests a command investigation, to compile an evidentiary record and make a preliminary assessment of the complaint. If warranted, the command investigation will also recommend remedial measures, such as disciplinary action (which can result in prison sentences).[43]

56. Under IDF Supreme Command Order 2.0702, the command investigator must transmit the complete record of a command investigation to the Military Advocate General's Corps upon request or automatically in certain types of cases – for example, whenever a civilian has been killed or seriously injured. The investigation of specific complaints as part of a command investigation thus serves not merely as a means to improve military performance but also as a preliminary inquiry on behalf of the Military Advocate General into potential military misconduct.

57. Further, the IDF's Chief of General Staff has the authority to initiate special (sometimes called "expert") command investigations for exceptional or complex cases. This type of investigation is conducted by a commanding officer who is outside the relevant chain of command. As with other command investigations, the results of a special command investigation must be transmitted to the Military Advocate General's Corps in appropriate circumstances – for example, whenever a civilian has been killed or seriously injured.

58. IDF Supreme Command Order 2.0702 provides requirements for command investigations, including:

   o "The command investigator shall not be limited by the rules of evidence."

   o "A soldier who is inquired in the course of a command investigation shall not be represented by a lawyer."

---

[43] The process of internal disciplinary action in the IDF is limited to less serious offenses (those with a maximum sentence of three years or less). The Military Advocate General's Corps may approve, change, or cancel a disciplinary judgment or punishment. Notwithstanding a disciplinary judgment, the Military Advocate General has the authority to approve a military indictment for the same offense. *See* Military Justice Law, § 171(B).

- "A soldier cannot refuse a demand by a command investigator to provide information, by testimony of other manner, even if he is entitled not to provide it to an investigating entity, since it might incriminate him."[44]

59. IDF Supreme Command Order 2.0702 further requires that all evidence obtained during a command investigation must be preserved. Specifically, "[m]aterials of a command investigation, including exhibits, maps, photos, and so on, shall be preserved by the commanding headquarters superior to the investigator." Thus, the Military Advocate General has the benefit of the entire record of a command investigation in those cases that are subject to review.[45]

60. Contrary to some criticisms – including those of the Human Rights Council Fact-Finding Report – command investigations do not substitute *de jure* or *de facto* for criminal investigations conducted by trained investigators.[46] They serve as a means of compiling an evidentiary record for the Military Advocate General, and enabling him, from his central vantage point, to determine whether there is a factual basis to open a criminal investigation. The Military Advocate General's review, not the command investigation, lies at the heart of the system. Many military systems rely on preliminary reviews, similar to command investigations, to assess complaints of soldier misconduct and to identify those that actually raise suspicions of criminal behaviour.[47]

---

[44] A statement made by a soldier during a command investigation, like all the evidence gathered, is preserved as part of the record. The Military Advocate General may use such a statement as a reason to launch a criminal investigation. A statement may also form the basis for a disciplinary proceeding. However, as in other countries that recognize the right against self-incrimination, compulsory soldier statements during a command investigation are not admissible in court except when a soldier is charged with presenting false information or obstructing an investigation.

[45] Ignoring these IDF regulations and without citing any evidence, the Human Rights Council Fact-Finding Report falsely claims that command investigations "destroy the scene of the crime," making criminal investigations "nearly impossible." Human Rights Council Fact-Finding Report ¶ 1817; *see also id.* ¶ 1830 (noting that "evidence may be corrupted" by the time a criminal investigation is launched). While some investigations have experienced delays, due to the large number of complaints submitted after the Gaza Operation, the suggestion that evidence has been lost or destroyed as a result of the process of command investigations has no basis in fact.

[46] *See, e.g.*, Human Rights Council Fact-Finding Report ¶ 1819 (faulting command investigations for falling short of "established methods of criminal investigations such as visits to the crime scene, interviews with witnesses and victims, and assessment by reference to established legal standards").

[47] *See* Part III.E below.

61. The Israeli Supreme Court has recognized that command investigations are "usually the most appropriate way to investigate an event that occurred during the course of an operational activity."[48] Specifically, the Court observed that a command investigation is:

> "usually conducted close to the time of the event, when it is still fresh in the memory of those that take part in it. It is performed in a direct and non-cumbersome manner. It is an integral part of the whole operational activity and it is well rooted into the operational experience in the IDF since its very beginning."[49]

62. At the conclusion of a command investigation, the investigator submits a written report of the findings, along with any recommendations, to the commander who commissioned the investigation and up the chain of command. As noted, the final report, along with any evidence collected, must also be transmitted to the Military Advocate General's Corps upon request or automatically in certain instances – for example, whenever a civilian has been killed or seriously injured.

D. Criminal Investigations and Prosecutions

63. The MPCID conducts criminal investigations, including investigations of complaints alleging that soldiers violated the Law of Armed Conflict. As noted above, the Military Prosecution automatically refers any complaint alleging *per se* criminal conduct to the MPCID for direct criminal investigation. With respect to other complaints, the Military Advocate General initiates a criminal investigation once he finds a reasonable suspicion of criminal activity.[50]

64. To make this determination, the Military Prosecution generally relies on the complaint itself (including any statements submitted by the complainant or witnesses) together with the report and record of a command investigation. In many cases, the Military Prosecution reviews additional materials, such as reports by non-governmental organisations and media accounts. The Military Prosecution can – and in many instances does – request additional information from the command investigator, including a supplemental investigation.

---

[48] *Mor Haim v. Israeli Defence Forces*, HCJ 6208/96 (16 September 1996). This case dealt with the appropriate manner for investigating the circumstances of the death of a soldier during an IDF operation.

[49] *Id.*

[50] When a command investigation precedes a criminal investigation, the Military Advocate General has to consult with an officer ranked Major or above. Nevertheless, the Military Advocate General alone has the authority to decide whether to initiate a criminal investigation and no officer has the authority to veto his decision.

65. The Military Prosecution notifies the complainant of his decision whether to open a criminal investigation, including an explanation of the reasons. As noted, the complainant can appeal the decision both to the Attorney General and the Supreme Court.

66. When a criminal investigation is opened, the MPCID consults as needed with the relevant Military Advocate (in cases involving alleged operational misconduct against Palestinians, the Military Advocate for Operational Affairs) regarding professional and legal questions.

67. When the MPCID completes its criminal investigation, the military prosecution reviews the evidence and decides whether to file an indictment. The military prosecution exercises prosecutorial discretion according to Israeli law – similar to any prosecutor in Israel or other common law states. For example, the military prosecution will file an indictment only if it determines that there is sufficient evidence to obtain a conviction. A complainant retains the right to appeal a decision of the military prosecution. The military prosecution's exercise of prosecutorial discretion in individual cases is subject to review by both the Attorney General and the Supreme Court.

68. From January 2002 through December 2008, there were 1,467 criminal investigations into alleged misconduct by IDF soldiers, leading to 140 indictments against soldiers for alleged crimes committed against the Palestinian population. Of these indictments, as of December 2008, 103 defendants were convicted and ten cases are still pending. During 2009, 236 criminal investigations were opened, and 14 indictments were filed against officers and soldiers.

69. Historically, the Military Advocate General's Corps has aggressively prosecuted cases of soldier misconduct toward Palestinian civilians. For example, last year the military prosecution indicted a Lieutenant and a Sergeant for the improper use of force while questioning civilians during a military operation in the West Bank. A military Court Martial convicted the Lieutenant of aggravated assault, for both his own use of force as well as the use of force by his subordinate.[51]

70. In *Lt. Col. Geva v. Chief Military Prosecutor*, the Military Advocate General's Corps filed an appeal to seek a harsher sentence for a senior officer convicted of threatening the child of a suspected terrorist and using a civilian as a human shield. The Military Court of Appeals sided with the prosecution:

---

[51] *Military Prosecutor v. Lt. A.M. and Sgt. A.G.*, C/125+126/09. The Lieutenant is awaiting his sentencing hearing.

"The requirement of 'personal example' by IDF commanders has been, from time immemorial, at the heart of military leadership which adopted the heritage of Gideon: 'Look on me and do likewise.' (Judges 7). The example given by the respondent to his subordinates, to the IDF and to society in general has been negative and the harm caused – both at home and abroad – is probably irretrievable. Given the seriousness of the failure, . . . a clear and distinct statement is warranted."[52]

E. The Similar Investigatory Systems of Other States

71. Under international law, the responsibility to investigate and prosecute alleged violations of the Law of Armed Conflict by a state's military forces falls first and foremost to that state.[53]

72. International law does not indicate the precise manner or pace at which a state should investigate alleged violations of the Law of Armed Conflict. As commentators have noted, "states do seem to enjoy broad discretion (subject to good faith requirements) in conducting ex post investigations in situations where human rights or IHL [international humanitarian law] had been allegedly breached."[54]

73. Nonetheless, the investigative systems in Israel and other democratic states (in particular, those based on the Common Law tradition) appear to have several similarities. Like Israel, countries such as the United Kingdom, the United States, Australia, and Canada have processes to screen for Law of Armed Conflict and other complaints that warrant criminal investigation, including the use of preliminary military reviews (comparable to command investigations), to assist in that determination.[55] These countries also use a courts-martial

---

[52] *Lt. Col. Geva v. Chief Military Prosecutor*, A/153/03 ¶ 50 (5 August 2004).

[53] *See* Informal Expert Paper, *The Principle of Complementarity In Practice*, at 3, *available at* http://www.icc-cpi.int/iccdocs/doc/doc654724.pdf ("States have the first responsibility and right to prosecute international crimes.").

[54] Amichai Cohen and Yuval Shany, *A Development of Modest Proportions: The Application of the Principle of Proportionality in the Targeted Killing Case*, 5 J. INT'L CRIM. JUS. 310, 318 (2007). The Human Rights Council Fact-Finding Report recognizes these principles. The Report notes that "the responsibility to investigate violations of international human rights and humanitarian law, prosecute if appropriate and try perpetrators belongs in the first place to domestic authorities and institutions"; and that "international justice mechanisms" should only intercede "where domestic authorities are unable or unwilling to comply with this obligation." Human Rights Council Fact-Finding Report ¶ 1760.

[55] *See, e.g.*, Aitken Report, *An Investigation into Cases of Deliberate Abuse and Unlawful Killing in Iraq in 2003 and 2004*, 25 January 2008, *available at* http://mod.uk/NR/rdonlyres/7AC894D3-1430-4AD1-911F-8210C3342CC5/0/aitken_rep.pdf (hereafter "Aitken Report") (describing the procedures for investigating

[Footnote continued on next page]

system based within the military justice framework to adjudicate criminal indictments alleging violations of the Law of Armed Conflict.[56]

74. When investigating high profile or other alleged incidents of soldier misconduct, these countries, like Israel, have sometimes encountered criticism concerning the pace at which their investigations or prosecutions have proceeded.

75. While there is no question that investigators should move expeditiously, the key imperative is that they take the time necessary to conduct a thorough and professional inquiry and to uncover the truth. Investigators should not sacrifice careful, complete examination of the facts nor adherence to the principles of due process.

(1) United Kingdom

76. The United Kingdom uses both criminal investigations and independent investigations within the military to examine alleged violations of the Law of Armed Conflict.[57] The Army Prosecuting Authority (APA) (which has recently been consolidated into a service-wide Prosecution Authority) traditionally has dealt with cases referred to it by the army chain of command.[58] "Legal advice is available for commanding officers and higher authorities to assist with decisions on referring appropriate cases to the APA."[59] The Director of Army Legal Services (ALS), who is appointed by the Queen as the APA, "has responsibility for decisions on whether to direct trial for all cases referred by the military chain of command, and for the prosecution of all cases tried before courts-martial, the Standing Civilian Court and the Summary Appeal Court and for Appeals before the Courts-Martial Appeal Court and the House of Lords."[60]

[Footnote continued from previous page]
violations of the Law of Armed Conflict in the United Kingdom); Dept. of Defense Directive No. 2311.01E, *Dept. of Defense Law of War Program*, 9 May 2006 (setting forth the procedures for the investigation of "reportable incidents" regarding of the Law of Armed Conflict in the United States).

[56] *See, e.g.*, Victor Hansen, *Changes Made in Modern Military Codes and the Role of the Military Commander: What Should the United States Learn From this Revolution*, 16 TUL. J. INT'L & COMP. L. 419 (2008) (describing U.S., Canadian, and United Kingdom court martial systems).

[57] *See generally* Aitken Report.

[58] *See* HM Crown Prosecution Inspectorate's Follow-Up Report on the Army Prosecuting Authority, February 2009, at 1.

[59] Aitken Report ¶ 28.

[60] *Id.*

77. The Director of ALS delegates these decision-making functions to "ALS officers appointed as prosecutors in the APA."[61] As in Israel, "[t]he APA is under the general superintendence of the Attorney-General and is, rightly, independent of the Army Chain of Command."[62] The APA (and new consolidated Prosecuting Authority) can decide not to institute court martial proceedings, refer the case back to the commanding officer to address, or direct a trial by court martial.[63] Like the Military Advocate General, the Director General of ALS is responsible both for providing legal advice to the army chain of command and for prosecution of offenders.[64]

78. For those incidents that do not warrant direct referral to the APA, the United Kingdom military investigates allegations of misconduct within its military justice framework through administrative actions, informal investigations, or formal investigations ordered by a Board of Inquiry.[65]

(2) United States

79. To respond to alleged violations of the Law of Armed Conflict, the United States grants multiple actors within the Department of Defense and the military branches independent authority to order an investigation.[66] Specifically, the investigatory procedures in the United States follow the same general practice as in Israel. When a "reportable incident"[67] involving the Law of Armed Conflict occurs, the appropriate field commander has the duty to report the incident up the chain of command immediately.[68] Commanders receiving information about an alleged Law of Armed Conflict violation conduct a formal, or more often informal, investigation to collect evidence and assess the credibility of the

---

[61] *Id.*

[62] *Id.*

[63] *See* HM Crown Prosecution Inspectorate's Follow-Up Report, *supra*, at 1.

[64] *See* British Army Website, *Army Legal Services, available at* http://www.army.mod.uk/agc/9935.aspx.

[65] Aitkin Report ¶ 36. Formal and informal investigations can be independent of the chain of the command but are conducted within the military.

[66] *See* Dept. of Defense Directive No. 2311.01E, *Dept. of Defense Law of War Program* (9 May 2006). Although the Defense Department Law of War Program Directive establishes comprehensive procedures for investigating incidents related to the Law of Armed Conflict, as developed below, investigations are typically ordered by military commanders or military investigation agencies.

[67] A "reportable incident" is defined as "[a] possible, suspected, or alleged violation of the law of war, for which there is credible information, or conduct during military operations other than war that would constitute a violation of the law of war if it occurred during an armed conflict." *See* CJCSI 5810.01C ¶ 5(b).

[68] *See* Dept. of Defense Directive No. 2311.01E ¶¶ 6.3-6.8; CJCSI 5810.01C ¶ 7(a)-(b).

allegations to determine whether a crime has been committed.[69] The report then both moves up the chain of command to the relevant Commander of the Combatant Command, and goes to the appropriate military investigation agency to determine whether to initiate a criminal investigation, as well as to the General Counsel of the Department of Defense.[70]

80. One recent example of this process is the investigation of a U.S. military engagement with Taliban insurgents in Afghanistan, which resulted in civilian casualties. There, "U.S. military elements in Afghanistan began a preliminary inquiry" of the incident.[71] After the preliminary inquiry, the Commander of U.S. Central Command "directed a U.S. Army General from outside Afghanistan to conduct a full investigation" who later presented his final report to the Commander and key leaders. The investigating officer's findings and recommendations, which found no violation of the Law of Armed Conflict but suggested operational improvements, were approved by the Commander.

81. Criminal investigations of soldier misconduct in the United States are conducted by, among others, the United States Army Criminal Investigation Command (USACIDC).[72] The USACIDC's investigative responsibilities include alleged war crimes and in some cases crimes against coalition forces and host nation personnel.[73] The USACIDC does not impose time tables for investigations. Rather, like Israel, it takes the time needed to conduct a professional inquiry:

> "Criminal investigations take as long as required to get to the truth and determine exactly what transpired in a particular circumstance. Although time is very important, criminal investigations are conducted to a standard not necessarily to a timetable. CID is dedicated to conducting thorough and professional criminal investigations no matter how long it takes."[74]

---

[69] See U.S. Dept. of Navy, JAG Inst. 5800.7D, Manual of the Judge Advocate General, ch 11 (15 March 2004); U.S. Dept. of Army, Reg. 15-6, Procedures for Investigating Officers and Boards of Officers (2 November 2006).

[70] See Dept. of Defense Directive No. 2311.01E ¶ 6.5.1-2; CJCSI 5810.01C ¶ 7(c).

[71] UNCENTCOM's Unclassified Executive Summary, *U.S. Central Command Investigation into Civilian Casualties in Farah Province, Afghanistan on 4 May 2009*.

[72] U.S. Army Criminal Investigation Command website, *available at* http://www.cid.army.mil/mission.html.

[73] *Id.*

[74] U.S. Army Criminal Investigation Command frequently asked questions website, *available at* http://www.cid.army.mil/faqs.html.

82. If an investigation reveals evidence of criminal wrongdoing, the ensuing criminal proceeding in the American system is a court-martial similar to the proceedings in Israel. Military prosecutors, known as Judge Advocates, are free from command influence, although as a matter of organizational structure they are subordinate to the command authority. Judge Advocates advise the "Convening Authority"[75] whether to refer cases to a court martial for trial and to approve, modify, or disapprove the findings and sentences in court martial proceedings.[76] Unlike in Israel, Judge Advocates in the United States do not file cases on their own[77] and the U.S. system does not provide for independent judicial review of the decision to commence or not commence a criminal proceeding.

(3) Australia

83. Under the Australian legal system, upon receipt of a complaint alleging soldier misconduct, a commander or supervisor may direct what is called a Quick Assessment (QA) of the incident. A QA has a similar purpose to the Israeli initial command investigation as it is conducted to determine whether there is any substance to allegations that may warrant further investigation or inquiry.[78]

84. The Quick Assessment Officer (QAO) conducts informal interviews, collects evidence, and issues a report and recommendation. The QAO can recommend no further inquiry if he or she finds insufficient evidence of a violation of the Law of Armed Conflict or other law. Alternatively, depending on the nature of the alleged violation, the QAO can recommend a Military Commission Board of Inquiry, an Inquiry Officer inquiry, or a Routine Inquiry (all of which are conducted within the military).

85. When the QA indicates a concern regarding criminal wrongdoing, the QA Officer will recommend a criminal investigation by the Australian Defence Force Inquiry Services

---

[75] "Convening Authority" is defined to include "a commissioned officer in command for the time being and successors in command." Manual for Courts-Martial United States (2008 ed.), Rules for Courts-Martial ("R.C.M.") 103(6), *available at* http://www.jag.navy.mil/documents/mcm2008.pdf.

[76] Uniform Code of Military Justice, Art. 34, Art. 64, *available at* http://www.army.mil/references/UCMJ/. As with the Military Advocate General, Judge Advocates are responsible both to provide legal advice to the military chain of command and to prosecute UCMJ offenders. *See* U.S. Army JAG website, *available at* http://www.goarmy.com/JobDetail.do?id=318 (providing that JAG officers "[p]rosecute criminal cases under [UCMJ]" and "[a]dvise commanders of all levels on all legal issues as they arise"); U.S. Air Force JAG website, *available at* http://www.afjag.af.mil/shared/media/document/AFD-080502-052.pdf (similar).

[77] *See* R.C.M. 401, 504, 505, 601, 1107, *available at* http://www.jag.navy.mil/documents/mcm2008.pdf.

[78] *See* The Defence Instructions (General) - Quick Assessment (Defence Instructions), Admin 67-2 (7 August 2007), *available at* http://www.defence.gov.au/fr/Policy/ga67_02.pdf.

(ADFIS). The recommendation is referred and reviewed up the chain of command. If the matter is referred to the ADFIS, it in turn may investigate and send the matter to a hearing before a Defence Force Magistrate or a Commanding Officer or may refer the incident to the civilian police.

(4) Canada

86. Under Canada's system, complaints alleging a *prima facie* violation of the Law of Armed Conflict during an operational activity generally are referred to the National Investigation Service (NIS).[79] The NIS is accountable to the Canadian Forces Provost Marshal.[80] The NIS's mandate is to investigate "serious and sensitive matters," including alleged violations of the Law of Armed Conflict, concerning Canadian Forces serving in Canada and abroad.[81] If NIS becomes aware of allegations of a potential criminal offence (through regular military police or through complaints from members of the Canadian forces or other sources), it reviews the information to determine whether a NIS investigation should be conducted.[82] If the allegation does not appear to meet the "serious or sensitive" standard, it can be investigated by non-NIS military police or by the command unit. Prosecutions for serious charges are carried out by the Canadian Military Prosecution Service (CMPS), which is answerable to the Director of Military Prosecutions (DMP). The DMP reports to the Judge Advocate General (JAG) but exercises his or her duties and functions independently.[83] The CMPS provides legal advice to NIS military police, reviews charge for court martial (including on grounds of sufficiency of evidence) and conducts prosecution of trials by court martial.[84]

87. Matters that do not initially indicate criminal wrongdoing go to either Summary Investigations (SI) if they are minor or uncomplicated, or to a military Board of Inquiry

---

[79] *See* Canadian Forces National Investigation Service, Annual Report 2007, dated 11 March 2008, at 11, *available at* http://www.vcds.forces.gc.ca/cfpm-gpfc/cfp-ggp/nis-sne/ar-ra/2007/doc/nisar-snera-2007-eng.pdf.

[80] The Canadian Forces National Investigation Service, CFNIS 2009-02, 1 May 2009, *available at* http://news.gc.ca/web/article-eng.do?m=/index&nid=446989.

[81] The Investigation and Charging Process in the Military Justice System (National Defence Canada), *available at* http://www.forces.gc.ca/jag/publications/Training-formation/ChargInves-EnqueAccu-eng.pdf.

[82] The Canadian Forces National Investigation Service, CFNIS 2009-02, 1 May 2009.

[83] Abridged Annual Report of the Director of Military Prosecutions, 2006-7, *available at* http://www.forces.gc.ca/jag/publications/DMP-DPM/DMP-DPM-AR0607-eng.pdf.

[84] Abridged Annual Report of the Director of Military Prosecutions, 2006-7.

(BOI) if they are more complex.[85] If either an SI or BOI receives evidence that reasonably relates to an allegation of criminal conduct, the proceedings must be suspended for potential criminal investigations.[86] In a BOI, a soldier can be compelled to testify, but as in Israel's command investigations, any self-incriminatory statements are inadmissible as evidence against the soldier in a court martial or trial.[87]

(5) Summary

88. In sum, these military justice systems share similarities with the system in Israel. They rely on a combination of field reviews, informal and formal military investigations, and prosecutions by courts martial or their equivalent. While these other systems differ in some respects from each other and from the Israeli system, all of them nonetheless have been accepted worldwide as sufficient for investigating alleged violations of the Law of Armed Conflict. The comparisons also reflect that investigations into alleged violations of the Law of Armed Conflict can take several weeks, months, or even years. The length of time is contingent on a variety of factors and customary international law does not reflect a standard pace for conducting such investigations, much less a deadline that Israel has exceeded.

---

[85] *See* National Defence and the Canadian Forces, Defence Administration Orders and Directives ("DAOD") 7002-1, 8 February 2002 (as modified 7 May 2007), *available at* http://www.admfincs.forces.gc.ca/dao-doa/7000/7002-1-eng.asp (purpose of BOI is "to investigate and report on matters of unusual significance or complexity"); DAOD 7002-2 8 February 2002 (as modified 7 May 2007), *available at* http://www.admfincs.forces.gc.ca/dao-doa/7000/7002-2-eng.asp (purpose of SI is "to investigate and report on matters of a minor, straightforward and uncomplicated nature").

[86] DAOD 7002-1; 7002-2 (providing that terms of reference for both SI and BOI must contain paragraphs stating "Should the BOI receive evidence that it reasonably believes relates to an allegation of a criminal act or a breach of the Code of Service Discipline, the BOI shall adjourn, the convening authority shall be notified, and the matter shall be referred to the nearest JAG representative for advice."). Like the Military Advocate General, the Canadian Judge Advocate General is responsible both to provide legal advice to the military chain of command and to prosecute criminal offenders. *See* National Defence and the Canadian Forces JAG website, *available at* http://www.forces.gc.ca/jag/office-cabinet/law-droit-eng.asp (providing that the JAG is responsible for being "legal advisor . . . to the Canadian Forces" on a number of issues, including "international and operational law" and "criminal law and military justice policy," and for "[p]referral of charges for tr[ia]l at courts martial" and "[p]rosecutions at courts martial").

[87] *Meade v. Her Majesty the Queen in Right of Canada* [1991] 3 F.C. 365 ¶ 9.

IV. COMPLAINTS ALLEGING VIOLATIONS OF THE LAW OF ARMED CONFLICT DURING THE GAZA OPERATION

89. Israel is aware of concerns raised regarding the Gaza Operation. As discussed in detail in *The Operation in Gaza*, and as outlined above, the deliberate strategy of Hamas to blend in with the civilian population made it difficult for the IDF to achieve the objective of the Gaza Operation – reducing the threat of deliberate attacks against Israeli civilians – while also avoiding harm to Palestinian civilians. To be sure, the IDF undertook strenuous efforts to minimise such harm. It intensively trained its personnel on the requirements of the Law of Armed Conflict. It delayed, diverted, or refrained from attacks to spare civilian life. It provided numerous and varied types of concrete warnings before launching attacks.[88] Nevertheless, Israel's efforts to comply with the Law of Armed Conflict do not lessen its regret for the loss of innocent lives and damage to civilian property.

90. Following the Gaza Operation, Israel took several concrete steps to reaffirm its commitment to thoroughly investigating, and where appropriate, prosecuting, alleged violations of the Law of Armed Conflict:

   o Israel undertook to investigate every specific complaint of alleged violations during the Gaza Operation, regardless of the credibility of the source.

   o The Military Advocate General personally reviewed each complaint submitted and, when available, the record of each command investigation before deciding whether to initiate a criminal investigation.

   o The Chief of General Staff initiated six special command investigations to examine some of the most serious allegations, in addition to the other command investigations conducted.[89]

   o The Military Advocate General ordered the Office of the Military Advocate for Operational Affairs to work closely with the MPCID on every criminal investigation, even before any decision on whether to file charges.

91. At the time of this Report, the IDF has investigated or is currently investigating more than 150 separate incidents that allegedly occurred during the Gaza Operation involving violations of the Law of Armed Conflict. The IDF initiated many of these investigations based on its own sources of information. Others came to the attention of the Israeli

---

[88] *See The Operation in Gaza: Factual and Legal Aspects* ¶¶ 262-65.

[89] Five special command investigations were initiated immediately after the conclusion of the Operation, and an additional special command investigation was initiated on 10 November 2009.

authorities through a variety of channels, either directly via complaints submitted by Palestinians and non-governmental organisations, or indirectly through media accounts and reports published by non-governmental organisations and other sources (among them, the Human Rights Council Fact-Finding Report).

92. The pace of these investigations reflects an orderly approach to uncovering the facts while at the same time safeguarding the rights of civilians and military personnel. Ideally, investigations would begin earlier, end sooner, and yield irrefutable results. But the combat and immediate post-combat environment is not ideal, and it complicates the gathering of evidence and the conduct of investigations. While the Gaza Operation concluded only one year ago, a thorough investigation takes time.

93. The unique difficulties involved in the investigation of alleged violations of the Law of Armed Conflict in the battlefield should not be ignored. They include: the inability to secure the scene for forensic and physical evidence, either during a battle or after, when the territory is under enemy control; the possible destruction of evidence during fighting and the possible manipulation of the scene by the enemy; the need to recall reserve soldiers back for questioning; the difficulty of accurately identifying the location of an incident, when it is described in local and unofficial terms and slang; and the need to locate the adversary's civilians as witnesses and overcome their natural suspicion and fear of reprisals by their authorities.[90]

94. Despite these complexities, the IDF has made significant progress with the investigations and concluded many of them. To date, some investigations have resulted in prosecutions for disciplinary and criminal violations. In others, the preliminary command investigations have been concluded and the Military Advocate General is undertaking his own review to determine whether the record warrants further investigation. In some cases, the Military Advocate General found no evidence of wrongdoing and closed the investigation. As many of the investigations are subject to further review by the Military Advocate General, the Attorney General, and the Supreme Court, it is possible that different conclusions will emerge as these cases advance through Israel's justice system.

---

[90] As discussed below, the MPCID has interviewed almost 100 Palestinians at the Erez border crossing point principally by working with non-governmental organisations acting as liaisons with the civilian population of Gaza.

95. Israel has periodically released detailed information concerning the status of its investigations into the Gaza Operation.[91] Current information about these investigations is provided in the following sections.

A. Command Investigations

(1) Five Special Command Investigations Opened Upon the Conclusion of the Gaza Operation

96. On 20 January 2009 – just two days after the conclusion of the Gaza Operation – IDF Chief of General Staff Lt. Gen. Ashkenazi ordered five special command investigations into a range of allegations raised by international and non-governmental organisations and various news media. To head the investigations, he appointed five Colonels with substantial field and command expertise who were not directly involved with the incidents investigated or in the direct chain of command. These investigations were not routine field reviews. Rather, the mandates focused on five types of alleged violations of the Law of Armed Conflict, encompassing 30 individual incidents:

o Claims regarding incidents in which a large number of civilians not directly participating in the hostilities were harmed;[92]

o Claims regarding incidents where U.N. and international facilities were fired upon and damaged during the Gaza Operation;[93]

---

[91] See, e.g., *The Operation in Gaza: Factual and Legal Aspects*. Israel also posts information concerning the investigations at the Ministry of Foreign Affairs website, *available at* http://www.mfa.gov.il/MFA.

[92] The Chief of General Staff's mandate was very specific about the allegations to be investigated, requiring review of, for example, the "Attack of a senior Hamas operative Nizar Rian, allegedly resulting in the death of 15 other individuals (4 January)," "Attack of the mosque in Beit Lahia, allegedly resulting in the death of 8 individuals (3 January)," and "Attack of the mosque of Imad Aq'al, allegedly resulting in the death of 7 individuals, 4 of them minors (29 December)." The mandate provided details, when available, such as dates, location, family names and relationships, and the number and gender of individuals allegedly killed. The mandate also required an investigation into the "[d]etails regarding the orders and instructions given in the IDF (on different levels of command before and during the operation) and regarding avoidance of disproportional harm to civilians not taking active part in the hostilities, regarding safety ranges from such civilians in different circumstances and using different weapons."

[93] The Chief of General Staff's mandate identified with specificity four alleged incidents to be investigated – for example, the "Shooting towards Fakhura school in Jabaliyah (6 January)," and "Damage to the UNRA school as a result of a strike by the air force, allegedly resulting in the death of 3 individuals." The mandate also required investigators to gather "information regarding intentional use by Hamas of UN premises or facilities for cover or as cover for shooting" and the "information regarding the orders and

[Footnote continued on next page]

o Incidents involving shooting at medical facilities, buildings, vehicles and crews;[94]

o Destruction of private property and infrastructure by ground forces;[95] and

o The use of weaponry containing phosphorous.[96]

97. The investigations focused not merely on improving operational performance, but rather on assessing specific incidents of harm to civilians and protected persons or facilities. The

---

[Footnote continued from previous page]
instructions given in the IDF (by different command levels, before and during the operation) regarding avoidance of harm to UN and international organizations' premises, facilities, vehicles and teams." This mandate was later extended to include other incidents investigated by the United Nations Headquarters Board of Inquiry in the Gaza Strip between 27 December 2008 and 19 January 2009.

[94] The Chief of General Staff's mandate required investigations into seven specific alleged incidents, such as the "Hitting of a medical team on its way to aid a wounded bleeding person in the area of Jabel Kashef, in the north-eastern area of the Gaza Strip, resulted in the death of a doctor, Dr. Ihmad Madhoun, the paramedic Abu Hesri, and the 1 wounded person (31 December)," and "Shelling of Dababish family residence in Sheikh Raduan, during a time when the medical team was at the location in order to evacuate the wounded, as a result of which one member of the medical team was killed (3 January)." With regard to each of these incidents, the mandate directed that the investigations seek "information regarding shooting incidents from within or nearby medical premises, facilities or vehicles, and regarding intentional use by Hamas of medical premises, facilities and vehicles for the purpose of fighting, cover for shooting, movement of weapons and combatants" and the "[d]etails regarding the orders and instructions given in the IDF (on different command levels, before and during the operation) regarding avoidance of harm to medical premises, facilities, vehicles and medical teams."

[95] The Chief of General Staff's mandate required investigations into the following issues: "a. Orders and instructions given and determined by different command levels (from the headquarters to the ground forces, before and during the operation), regarding the destruction of buildings and infrastructure. b. Extent of destruction of buildings and infrastructure in the different areas, divided in accordance to: stages of the operation, operating units, types of buildings or infrastructure that were damaged, purposes of destruction, the manner in which the destruction was carried out (via engineers/method of destruction/verification of evacuation of residents) and whether the destruction was planned or spontaneous by decisions which were taken in the field in 'real time'. c. Intelligence and operational information regarding the nature of the enemy's offensive and defensive methods, and with regard to infrastructure of the enemy that was identified and documented by our forces, which support the operational necessity of destruction."

[96] The Chief of General Staff's mandate required investigations into the following issues: "a. Kinds and amount of weapons containing phosphorous, allocated to the forces before and during the operation. b. Kinds and amount of weapons containing phosphorous, actually used during the operation. c. Purpose and military needs for the use of weapons which contain phosphorous (for example – smoke screening, marking), the targets at which these weapons were fired (for example – open areas, sources of fire in built up areas), all this divided in accordance with the type of weapon. d. Professional instructions which exist with regard to every kind of these weapons. e. Rules of engagement relevant to every type of these weapons, including safety ranges which apply with regard to the firing of weapons which contain phosphorous (specifically, the existence of limitations of any kind on the firing of these weapons to populated areas). f. Deviations (if there were) from the instructions and orders with regard to the use of weapons which contain phosphorous, and the core reasons behind such exceptions."

mandates directed the command investigators to conduct detailed inquiries into, among other things, "the orders and instructions given in the IDF (at different levels, before and during the operation) regarding the avoidance of harm" – including instructions regarding "avoidance of disproportional harm to civilians not taking active part in the hostilities, regarding safety ranges for the use of different weapons from such civilians in different circumstances."

98. In accordance with standard IDF procedures for command investigations, the investigators operated independently and had access to all available materials as well as the freedom to question any relevant IDF personnel. They interviewed numerous soldiers and officers, and gathered relevant documents and other materials from external sources. They reviewed operational logs, video footage and photographs from aerial vehicles, fragment analysis reports, internal military debriefings, intelligence documents, relevant rules of engagement and operational plans, and volumes of other relevant materials. Each soldier interviewed was required to cooperate with the investigation, and each did so.

99. The special investigations revealed some instances of intelligence and operational errors. For example, one special command investigation determined that the IDF mistakenly targeted the home of the Al-Daya family rather than a neighbouring weapons storage facility, resulting in civilian deaths. In another instance, where the lead car of a UNRWA convoy was fired upon, the investigation revealed communication errors in coordinating the movement of the convoy. To avoid these types of errors in the future, IDF Chief of General Staff Lt. Gen. Gabi Ashkenazi directed that certain standing orders be highlighted or clarified and ordered improvements in certain command operations.

100. The special command investigations also uncovered some instances where IDF soldiers and officers violated the rules of engagement. For example, in one case, a Brigadier General and a Colonel had authorized the firing of explosive shells which landed in a populated area, in violation of IDF orders limiting the use of artillery fire near populated areas. The Commander of the Southern Command disciplined the two officers for exceeding their authority in a manner that jeopardized the lives of others.

101. Upon completion of the special command investigations, the investigators presented their findings to the IDF Chief of General Staff, Lt. Gen. Gabi Ashkenazi, who adopted their recommendations.[97] The Chief of General Staff ordered the IDF to implement lessons

---

[97] See IDF Spokesperson Announcement, *Conclusion of Investigations into Central Claims and Issues in Operation Case Lead* (22 April 2009), available at http://idfspokesperson.com/2009/04/22/idf-announcement-findings-from-cast-lead-investigations/.

learned on a broad range of matters, directing that certain standing orders be highlighted or clarified, establishing further guidelines on the use of various munitions, and instructing that steps be taken to improve coordination with humanitarian organisations and entities.

102. The Military Advocate General received the findings and evidentiary record of each special command investigation as a source of factual information to assist in the analysis of the relevant allegations. On 19 January 2010, the Military Advocate General issued his opinion, which addressed each of the five special command investigations.

    (i)   Claims regarding incidents in which a large number of civilians not directly participating in the hostilities were harmed

103. The investigation into these allegations included 7 separate incidents. Some of the findings of the special command investigation are detailed in *The Operation in Gaza*.[98]

104. As to 4 of the incidents, the Military Advocate General completed his investigation and review, finding no grounds to open a criminal inquiry.[99] The investigations with regard to three incidents are still underway.[100] In 2 instances, due to the complexity of the circumstances, the special command investigation is still ongoing. The third incident involved the alleged strike on the Al Maquadme Mosque, which the Chief of General Staff had remanded for a new special command investigation (as discussed below).

    (ii)   Claims regarding incidents where U.N. and international facilities were fired upon and damaged during the Gaza Operation

105. The investigation into these allegations included 13 separate incidents. Some of the findings of the special command investigation are detailed in *The Operation in Gaza*.[101]

106. The Military Advocate General reviewed the findings and entire record of this special command investigation. He also reviewed additional materials, including information in the Human Rights Council Fact-Finding Report and the Report of the United Nations Headquarters Board of Inquiry into certain incidents in the Gaza Strip Between 27 December 2008 and 19 January 2009.

---

[98] *The Operation in Gaza: Factual and Legal Aspects* ¶¶ 381-403.

[99] The four incidents are: the attack resulting in the death of Hamas senior operative Nizar Ri'an and allegedly 15 other individuals; alleged attack of the mosque of Al Rabat; attack of a truck carrying oxygen tanks; and attack of Dr. Abu El Eish family residence.

[100] The three incidents are: the alleged attack of the Mosque of Imad Aq'al; the strike of the Al Daiya family residence; and the alleged attack of Al Maquadme Mosque.

[101] *The Operation in Gaza: Factual and Legal Aspects* ¶¶ 330-69.

107. The Military Advocate General found no basis to order criminal investigations of the thirteen incidents under review. With regard to two of these incidents, the Military Advocate General affirmed the decisions to pursue disciplinary proceedings against IDF personnel.

108. One of these incidents involved alleged damage to the UNRWA field office compound in Tel El Hawa.[102] The special command investigation revealed that, during the course of a military operation in Tel El Hawa, IDF forces fired several artillery shells in violation of the rules of engagement prohibiting use of such artillery near populated areas. Based on these findings, the Commander of the Southern Command disciplined a Brigadier General and a Colonel for exceeding their authority in a manner that jeopardized the lives of others.

109. As noted in *The Operation in Gaza*, the United Nations Secretary General established a Board of Inquiry to examine a number of incidents involving damage to U.N. facilities, independent of the ongoing investigations in Israel. Israel cooperated fully with U.N. Board of Inquiry, sharing the results of its internal investigations and providing detailed information about the incidents in question. The Secretary General commended Israel for its extensive cooperation.[103]

110. Following the U.N. Board of Inquiry's examination, and notwithstanding certain reservations it had with some aspects of the Board's report, Israel entered into a dialogue with the United Nations to address all issues arising from the incidents examined. On 22 January 2010, the Secretary General thanked Israel for its "cooperative approach" in these discussions and confirmed that all financial issues relating to these incidents had been satisfactorily concluded.[104]

  (iii) *Incidents involving shooting at medical facilities, buildings, vehicles and crews*

111. The investigation into these allegations included 10 separate incidents. Some of the findings of the special command investigation are detailed in *The Operation in Gaza*.[105]

---

[102] *Id.* ¶¶ 341-47.

[103] *See* Letter from the Secretary General to the President of the Security Council (4 May 2009), *available at* http://www.unhcr.org/refworld/docid/4a292c8dd.html (expressing "appreciation for the cooperation provided by Israel to the Board").

[104] U.N. Spokesperson Briefing (22 January 2010), *available at* http://www.unmultimedia.org/radio/english/detail/89687.html.

[105] *The Operation in Gaza: Factual and Legal Aspects* ¶¶ 370-80.

112. The Military Advocate General found no basis to order criminal investigations of the 10 incidents under review.

(iv) Destruction of private property and infrastructure by ground forces

113. This investigation dealt with the general allegations that the IDF intentionally destroyed private property and civilian infrastructure during the Gaza operation. The investigation did not deal with specific incidents alleged in complaints or reports. Some of the findings of the special command investigation are detailed in *The Operation in Gaza*.[106]

114. The Military Advocate General reviewed the findings and the entire record of the investigation. The Military Advocate General noted that according to the Law of Armed Conflict, the destruction of private property is prohibited, except where such a destruction is justified by military necessity. He also emphasised that the findings of the special investigation are consistent with Israel's obligations under the Law of Armed Conflict. In this regard, the Military Advocate General noted that the extent of destruction, by itself, cannot establish a violation of the Law of Armed Conflict.

115. Because this investigation was limited in scope and dealt with overall issues, specific incidents reported after the conclusion of the special command investigation have been referred to individual command investigations. The Military Advocate General stressed the importance of a thorough investigation of each such incident.

116. The Military Advocate General further emphasised the importance of clear regulations and orders, as well as clear combat doctrine, regarding the demolition of structures and infrastructure. The IDF has already adopted such regulations and combat doctrine.

(v) The use of weaponry containing phosphorous

117. This investigation dealt with the use of weapons containing phosphorous by IDF forces during the Gaza Operation. The investigation focused on the different types and number of weapons containing phosphorous used during the Operation, the purposes for which they were used, the applicable professional instructions and rules of engagement, and the extent of compliance with those instructions and rules. Some of the findings of the special command investigation are detailed in *The Operation in Gaza*.[107]

---

[106] *Id.* ¶¶ 436-45.
[107] *Id.* ¶¶ 405-35.

118. The Military Advocate General reviewed the entire record of the special command investigation. With respect to exploding munitions containing white phosphorous, the Military Advocate General concluded that the use of this weapon in the operation was consistent with Israel's obligations under international law.

119. With respect to smoke projectiles, the Military Advocate General found that international law does not prohibit use of smoke projectiles containing phosphorous. Specifically, such projectiles are not "incendiary weapons," within the meaning of the Protocol on Prohibitions or Restrictions on the Use of Incendiary Weapons,[108] because they are not primarily designed to set fire or to burn. The Military Advocate General further determined that during the Gaza Operation, the IDF used such smoke projectiles for military purposes only, for instance to camouflage IDF armor forces from Hamas's anti-tank units by creating smoke screens.

120. The Military Advocate General found no grounds to take disciplinary or other measures for the IDF's use of weapons containing phosphorous, which involved no violation of the Law of Armed Conflict. Nevertheless, the Military Advocate General's opinion did not address a number of specific complaints that were received after the investigation concluded and which are being investigated separately.

(vi) Concluding observations

121. The Military Advocate General ended his opinion on the five special command investigations by underlining the IDF's commitment to compliance with the Law of Armed Conflict, as well as its intention to investigate thoroughly every alleged violation by IDF forces. He noted that the evidence gathered by the special investigations reflected great effort by the IDF to ensure such compliance and to minimize harm to civilians.

122. The Military Advocate General acknowledged that the investigations had found operational lapses and errors in the exercise of discretion. However, given the complexities of decision making under pressure, particularly when the adversary has entrenched itself within the civilian population, such mistakes do not in themselves establish a violation of the Law of Armed Conflict.

123. The Military Advocate General further emphasised the importance of implementing the operational lessons learned from the special command investigations.

---

[108] Protocol III of the Convention on Prohibitions or Restrictions on the Use of Certain Weapons Which May Be Deemed to Be Excessively Injurious or to Have Indiscriminate Effects (CCW). Israel is not a party to CCW Protocol III.

(2) Additional Special Command Investigation

124. In addition to the original five special command investigations, the Military Advocate General recommended that the Chief of General Staff establish an additional special command investigation to assess certain allegations discussed in the Human Rights Council Fact-Finding Report. The Chief of General Staff agreed and, on 10 November 2009, appointed another Colonel with substantial field and command experience who was not directly involved with the incidents in question to conduct that investigation.

125. The additional special command investigation focuses on three sets of allegations from the Human Rights Council Fact-Finding Report. One set relates to the Al-Samouni residence, where an IDF attack allegedly caused the injury and death of several dozen civilians who were seeking shelter there.[109] Another set of allegations under review relates to claims that the IDF mistreated Palestinians detainees.[110] A third set of allegations under review relates to an alleged attack on the Al-Maquadme Mosque.[111]

126. The alleged attack of the Al-Maquadme Mosque was first examined during one of the original five special command investigations. At that time, the special command investigator concluded that the mosque had not been struck during a military operation. After reviewing the findings of the investigation, along with media accounts and reports of non-governmental organisations (some of which were published after the investigation had concluded), the Military Advocate General recommended that a new special command investigation examine the allegations again.

127. Upon conclusion of his investigation, the special command investigator will present his findings to the Military Advocate General, who will then determine whether there is suspicion of a violation of the Law of Armed Conflict warranting further investigation.

---

[109] *See* Human Rights Council Fact-Finding Report ¶¶ 712-22. The mandate required an investigation of allegations that "IDF deliberately shot civilians in the Al-Samouni residential compound in Zeitoun, and prevented the access of medical teams, as well as evacuation of the wounded," resulting in the death of more than 20 civilians. The Military Advocate General had previously referred additional allegations related to the alleged shooting of members of the Al-Samouni family for a criminal investigation. *See* Human Rights Council Fact-Finding Report ¶¶ 709-11.

[110] *See* Human Rights Council Fact-Finding Report ¶¶ 1107-26. The mandate required an investigation of allegations that "IDF forces held the detainees in cruel, inhumane and degrading conditions," such "in pits, exposed to cold and bad weather conditions, handcuffed and with their eyes covered, without food or ability to relieve themselves" and "during the night in trucks, while they are handcuffed, without having enough blankets."

[111] *See* Human Rights Council Fact-Finding Report ¶¶ 822-30. The mandate directed the command investigator to "examine the allegations . . . that during prayer time (between 17:00 and 18:00), an explosion had happened in the entrance to the mosque, resulting in the death of 15 civilians."

(3) Other Command Investigations

128. In addition to the special command investigations discussed above, the Military Advocate General referred complaints regarding approximately 90 incidents for command investigations. These incidents generally involve allegations of civilian injuries or deaths and destruction of civilian property during the Gaza Operation.

129. As explained above, injuries to civilians and damage to civilian property during hostilities do not, in themselves, provide grounds for opening a criminal investigation into potential violations of the Law of Armed Conflict. There must be additional circumstances to warrant a reasonable suspicion of such a violation. As also explained above, after reviewing the findings and record of a command investigation, along with the complaint and other relevant information, the Military Advocate General will decide whether to order a criminal investigation into each incident.

130. To date, the IDF has completed 45 of the approximately 90 command investigations referred by the Military Advocate General. As discussed below, after reviewing the findings and records of command investigations along with other relevant materials, the Military Advocate General has referred 7 incidents for criminal investigations. The Military Advocate General has found that other incidents investigated raised no reasonable suspicion of a violation of the Law of Armed Conflict. Investigations into the remaining 45 incidents continue.

B. Criminal Investigations

131. To date, the Military Advocate General has already referred 36 separate incidents for criminal investigation. The Military Advocate General determined that the nature of the alleged incidents and/or the evidentiary record raised a reasonable suspicion that allegedly criminal behaviour occurred.

132. Special investigative teams of the MPCID were appointed solely for the purpose of investigating complaints stemming from the Gaza Operation. The Commander of the MPCID supervises the professional investigative teams, with involvement by the Office of the Military Advocate for Operational Matters. The teams included 16 investigators, as well as Arabic interpreters.

133. The MPCID has sought assistance from non-governmental organisations (such as B'Tselem) to help locate Palestinian complainants and witnesses and to coordinate their arrival at the Erez crossing point to Gaza, to allow interviews and questioning. To date, MPCID

investigators have taken testimony from almost 100 Palestinian complainants and witnesses, along with approximately 500 IDF soldiers and commanders. They have devoted thousands of working hours to the investigations thus far.

134. Of the 36 incidents referred thus far for criminal investigation, 19 incidents involved alleged shootings towards civilians. The Military Advocate General referred most of these incidents (12) directly for criminal investigation (without requesting a command investigation or awaiting the results of one), while some of them (7) were referred after the Military Advocate General reviewed the findings and records gathered during command investigations and concluded that there was a reasonable suspicion of criminal activity by IDF forces.

135. The remaining 17 incidents involved allegations of using civilians as human shields, mistreatment of detainees and civilians, and pillage and theft. In these instances, the Military Advocate General determined that the allegations, if true, concerned events that were clearly beyond any legitimate operational activity, and therefore directly referred all of the cases to criminal investigation.

136. The allegations referred for criminal investigation came from a variety of sources, including: local and international media reports and inquiries; letters from Palestinians or their attorneys; and letters and reports from non-governmental organisations (e.g., Public Committee against Torture in Israel, Human Rights Watch, Amnesty International, Médecins Sans Frontières). Some of these incidents are also described in the Human Rights Council Fact-Finding Report. The Military Advocate General opened a number of direct criminal investigations after hearing reports alleging that IDF soldiers had described conduct by themselves or fellow soldiers that would violate the Law of Armed Conflict.

137. Of these 36 criminal investigations, 1 investigation has already led to an indictment and conviction of an IDF soldier.[112] The Military Advocate General has exercised his discretion to close 7 criminal investigations without charges because the complainants

---

[112] During a search of a Palestinian residence, the soldier stole a credit card belonging to one of the occupants and subsequently used the card to withdraw the equivalent of more than $400. Following his confession, the soldier served seven and a half months in prison. The Court Martial declared: "The crime of looting is harmful to the moral duty of every IDF soldier to keep human dignity, a dignity 'that does not depend on origin, religion, nationality, sex, status and function.' Besides, with the commission of the crime of looting, the accused harmed the 'combat moral code,' the spirit of the IDF, in using his power and his arms not for the execution of his military mission." *Military Prosecutor v. Sergeant A.K.*, S/153/09 ¶ 12 (11 August 2009).

refused to give testimony and/or there was insufficient evidence of a criminal violation.[113] The remaining 28 investigations are ongoing.

C. Incidents Discussed in Human Rights Council Fact-Finding Report

138. The incidents subject to command and criminal investigations discussed above include the 34 incidents addressed at length in the Human Rights Council Fact-Finding Report.[114]

139. As of 15 September 2009, when the Human Rights Council Fact-Finding Report was released, Israel was already investigating 22 of these 34 incidents. The Report brought the remaining 12 incidents to the IDF's attention for the first time – 10 of which involved alleged damage to property and 2 of which involved alleged harm to civilians. The Military Advocate General promptly referred these 12 additional incidents for investigation.[115]

140. The current status of the investigations of incidents discussed in the Human Rights Council Fact-Finding Report is as follows:

- o 11 incidents are the subject of on-going criminal investigations by the MPCID (Part IV.B above). Two of these investigations were concluded, with no suspicion for criminal behaviour.

- o 7 incidents were investigated as part of the special command investigations (Part IV.A.1 and Part IV.A.2 above). The Military Advocate General has requested further review of 2 of these incidents.

- o The remaining incidents were subject to regular command investigations (Part IV.A.3 above). Some of these investigations are still ongoing.

---

[113] As noted above, the Military Advocate General's decision to close these investigations is subject to review by the Attorney General and the Supreme Court.

[114] The exact number of incidents addressed in the Human Rights Council Fact-Finding Report is unclear. The Report itself indicates that the Fact-Finding Mission investigated 36 incidents in Gaza. *See* Human Rights Council Fact-Finding Report ¶ 16. However, the State of Israel has been able to identify 34 separate incidents in Gaza that are discussed in the Report.

[115] As noted earlier, the Military Advocate General recommended a sixth special command investigation to consider certain incidents discussed in the Human Rights Council Fact-Finding Report. In addition, the Military Advocate General referred one incident discussed in the Report – alleging the use of a Palestinian as a human shield – directly for criminal investigation.

141. Regarding certain incidents discussed in the Human Rights Council Fact-Finding Report, the Military Advocate General has reviewed the entire record and concluded that there was no basis for a criminal investigation. Some examples are detailed below.

(1) Namar wells group, Salah ad-Din Street, Jabaliyah refugee camp[116]

142. When the IDF first learned about the allegations relating to the Namar wells from the Human Rights Council Fact-Finding Report, it tried to locate the wells (since the Report does not provide any coordinates). For this purpose, the Israeli Coordination and Liaison Administration (CLA) asked the Gaza Coastal Municipalities Water Utility (CMWU) to provide the exact coordinates of the facility.

143. According to the findings of the command investigation, the CMWU provided coordinates located within a closed military compound of Hamas. This compound served as a regional command and control center and was used for military training and weapons storage. Guards manned the entry to the compound and prohibited entry by unauthorized civilians. The coordinates provided for the wells and the manned entry point to the compound are illustrated in the following photograph, taken prior to the alleged incident.

▶ Hamas military compound, with coordinates provided for the Namar wells circled in red (Source: IDF)

---

[116] *See* Human Rights Council Fact-Finding Report ¶¶ 975-83.

144. The IDF attacked the compound on 27 December 2008, at 11:30. All strikes were accurate. The command investigation further determined that pre-planned attacks, such as this one, took into account the existence of sensitive sites, including water facilities, inside or near the intended target, in the decisions whether to attack the target and what precautions to use. When planning the attack on this specific military target, the IDF knew of no water facility inside the compound. The IDF did identify a water well 195 metres from the compound and took precautionary measures, which ensured that the well was not hit or damaged.

145. The command investigation revealed that although the Israeli CLA requests and receives updates from different sources on sensitive sites inside Gaza, it had no information about the Namar water wells before the operation. After the Gaza Operation, the CMWU provided the CLA information about the location of 143 water wells. According to IDF procedures and practices, had the CLA received such information before the operation, it would have been immediately reported to all relevant IDF units.

146. The Military Advocate General reviewed the findings of the command investigation, together with the additional information contained in the Human Rights Council Fact-Finding Report.

147. The Military Advocate General concluded that the Hamas military compound, where the Namar wells were located, was a legitimate military target. The Military Advocate General found that the IDF did not know of the existence of the water wells within the Hamas military compound and did not direct the strike against the water facilities.

148. The Military Advocate General took note of the fact that standing orders issued throughout the Gaza Operation strictly forbade any acts damaging water installations. Moreover, the Military Advocate General found no credible basis for the allegation that the strike was intended to deprive the civilian population of Gaza of water. To the contrary, the IDF made significant efforts to ensure that the population of Gaza had a sufficient and continuous water supply.[117]

149. Accordingly, the Military Advocate General found no basis to order a criminal investigation regarding the case.

---

[117] During the actual fighting, in several instances, the IDF coordinated the movement of the Palestinian Water Authority (CMWU) maintenance teams to repair water infrastructure (beyond the repairs permitted during humanitarian windows). Additionally, five trucks of infrastructure supplies, including pumps, generators, spare parts, and purification kits, were brought into Gaza at the request of the CMWU.

Document [6] Follow-up to the Report of the UN Fact Finding Mission   303

A/64/651

(2) The Gaza wastewater treatment plant, Road No. 10, al-Sheikh Ejlin, Gaza City[118]

150. The IDF first learned of allegations of deliberate attacks of the Gaza wastewater treatment plant in Sheikh Ejlin from the Human Rights Council Fact-Finding.

151. The command investigation of this incident included the gathering of information from relevant commanders and officers and from ground and aerial forces. In addition, investigators received information from the Israeli CLA, which was in direct contact with Mr. Munther Shublaq, the Director of the CMWU.

152. Initial findings from the investigation were presented to the Military Advocate General, who asked for several clarifications before reaching his conclusions. The main findings of the command investigation are as follows.

(i) The date of the incident

153. Based on an analysis of aerial photographs of the wastewater treatment plant from the relevant days, it was determined that the damage to the facility occurred on 10 January 2009. In an aerial photograph taken that day, the damage to the wall of one of the basins, as well as the flow of sewage to nearby fields, can be seen for the first time.

▶ Aerial photograph of wastewater treatment plant in Sheikh Ejlin, 9 January 2009, with no damage visible (Source: IDF)

---

[118] See Human Rights Council Fact-Finding Report ¶¶ 962-72.

▶ Aerial photograph of wastewater treatment plant in Sheikh Ejlin, 10 January 2009, with breach of upper basin marked in red (Source: IDF)

154. The ICRC presented a preliminary report about the basin breach to the Israeli CLA on 12 January 2009. During the following days, the CLA tried to coordinate the arrival of Gaza's CMWU teams to address the situation, but these efforts did not succeed due to the fighting in the area.

155. The Director of Gaza's CMWU reported to the CLA that 50,000 cubic meters of sewage leaked from the treatment plant; and that the direction of the leak was towards the southwest, an agricultural area.

   (ii)   *The possibility of an aerial strike*

156. The wastewater treatment plant was not defined, prior to or during the operation, as a target for an aerial strike. The nearest aerial strike on the relevant dates was 1.3 kilometres away from the plant.

(iii) The possibility of a ground attack

157. Given the characteristics of the damage caused to the basin, it is unlikely that it resulted from flat-trajectory fire of the IDF. The IDF executed no high-trajectory fire towards the plant, and the operations logs identify no such target point.

158. When the armoured forces passed near the plant, during the operation, the basin wall was already breached and the area surrounding it was flooded, thus limiting the movement of the forces in that area.

(iv) The possible causes of damage to the basin

159. The Military Advocate General reviewed the findings of the command investigation, in light of the details provided in the Human Rights Council Fact-Finding Report and the CMWU report of January 2009, entitled "Damage Assessment Report: Water and Waste Water Infrastructure and Facilities."

160. Taking into account all available information, the Military Advocate General could not definitively rule out the possibility that IDF activity had caused the damage to the wall of the third basin of the wastewater treatment plant (which probably occurred on 10 January). At the same time, he could also not dismiss the possibility that the damage to the basin might have resulted from a deliberate action by Hamas as part of a defensive plan to hamper the movement of IDF forces in the area.

161. The Military Advocate General was able to determine that this damage did not result from an intentional and pre-planned IDF attack. In this regard, the Military Advocate General endorsed the conclusions of the command investigation that the wastewater treatment plant was not a pre-planned target and that the breaching of the basin wall and the flooding of the area with sewage significantly limited the maneuverability of IDF ground forces, especially armoured vehicles, in that area. Moreover, the Military Advocate General noted that there was no physical evidence or eyewitness testimony to support the conclusion of the Human Rights Council Fact-Finding Report.

162. Accordingly, the Military Advocate General found no reason to order a criminal investigation regarding the case.

(3) El-Bader flour mill[119]

163. With respect to the allegation of deliberate targeting of the el-Bader flour mill, the IDF conducted a command investigation, which gathered evidence from numerous sources, including relevant commanders and officers and ground and aerial forces. In addition, the investigator received information from the Israeli CLA, which was in direct contact with the owner of el-Bader flour mill, Mr. Rashad Hamada. The command investigation included several findings, which are delineated below.

164. From the outset of the Gaza Operation, the immediate area in which the flour mill was located was used by enemy armed forces as a defensive zone, due to its proximity to Hamas's stronghold in the Shati refugee camp. Hamas had fortified this area with tunnels and booby-trapped houses, and deployed its forces to attack IDF troops operating there. For example, 200 meters south of the flour mill an IDF squad was ambushed by five Hamas operatives in a booby-trapped house; 500 meters east of the flour mill another squad engaged enemy forces in a house that was also used for weapons storage; and adjacent to the flour mill, two booby-trapped houses exploded.

165. The IDF ground operation in this area began on 9 January 2009, during night time. Before the ground operation, the IDF issued early warnings to the residents of the area, included recorded telephone calls, urging them to evacuate. Such telephone calls were made to the flour mill as well.

166. While preparing for the operation, the commanders identified the flour mill as a "strategic high point" in the area, due to its height and clear line of sight. Nevertheless, in the planning stage, it was decided not to pre-emptively attack the flour mill, in order to prevent damage to civilian infrastructure as much as possible.

---

[119] *See* Human Rights Council Fact-Finding Report ¶¶ 913-21.

A/64/651

▶ El-Bader flour mill, 9 January 2009, prior to alleged incident (Source: IDF)

167. In the course of the operation, IDF troops came under intense fire from different Hamas positions in the vicinity of the flour mill. The IDF forces fired back towards the sources of fire and threatening locations. As the IDF returned fire, the upper floor of the flour mill was hit by tank shells. A phone call warning was not made to the flour mill immediately before the strike, as the mill was not a pre-planned target.

168. Several hours after the incident, and following a report about fire in the flour mill, the IDF coordinated the arrival of several fire engines to fight the fire.

▶ El-Bader flour mill, 10 January 2009, following alleged incident. Fire trucks are visible on the scene. (Source: IDF)

169. The Military Advocate General reviewed the findings and the records of the command investigation and other materials. In addition, the Military Advocate General reviewed the information included in the Human Rights Council Fact-Finding Report, as well as the transcript of the public testimony of Mr. Hamada to the Fact-Finding Mission.

170. Taking into account all available information, the Military Advocate General determined that the flour mill was struck by tank shells during combat. The Military Advocate General did not find any evidence to support the assertion that the mill was attacked from the air using precise munitions, as alleged in the Human Rights Council Fact-Finding Report. The Military Advocate General determined that the allegation was not supported in the Report itself, nor in the testimony to the Fact-Finding Mission by Rashad Hamada, who had left the area prior to the incident in response to the IDF's early warnings. Photographs of the mill following the incident do not show structural damage consistent with an air attack.

Document [6] Follow-up to the Report of the UN Fact Finding Mission

A/64/651

▶ El-Bader flour mill, 11 January 2009, following alleged incident (Source: IDF)

171. The Military Advocate General found that, in the specific circumstances of combat, and given its location, the flour mill was a legitimate military target in accordance with the Law of Armed Conflict. The purpose of the attack was to neutralize immediate threats to IDF forces.

172. The Military Advocate General did not accept the allegation in the Human Rights Council Fact-Finding Report that the purpose of the strike was to deprive the civilian population of Gaza of food. In this regard, he noted the fact that shortly after the incident, the IDF allowed Palestinian fire trucks to reach the area and extinguish the flames, as well as the extensive amount of food and flour that entered Gaza through Israel during the Gaza Operation.[120]

173. Although the Military Advocate General could not conclusively determine that the flour mill was in fact used by Hamas's military operatives, there was some evidence of such use. The Military Advocate General noted that Mr. Hamada testified before the Fact-Finding Mission that after the operation he found empty bullets on the roof of the flour mill. This could not have been the result of IDF fire, since – as was evident from the findings of the command investigation – the IDF forces which occupied the mill's compound three days

---

[120] See *The Operation in Gaza: Factual and Legal Aspects* ¶¶ 266-82.

after the incident did not occupy the roof of the mill, where they would have been exposed to enemy fire.

174. Accordingly, the Military Advocate General found no reason to order a criminal investigation regarding the case.

(4) The house of Abu-Askar family[121]

175. The IDF conducted a command investigation into allegations concerning a deliberate strike of the residence of Muhammad Abu-Askar. The command investigation gathered evidence from numerous sources, including relevant commanders and officers, ground and aerial forces, and aerial photos.

176. According to the findings of the command investigation, the cellar and other parts of Mr. Abu-Askar's house were used to store weapons and ammunitions, including Grad rockets. Furthermore, the area where the house was located was frequently used as a launch area for rockets aimed at Israeli towns.

177. Before the strike, the IDF made a telephone call to Mr. Abu-Askar's house warning of the strike. The call was received by Muhammad Abu-Askar. Following this warning, all occupants immediately evacuated the premises. Moreover, the attack took place at night, when fewer civilians were likely to be in the area. There were no civilian casualties from the strike.

178. Shortly after the strike, two sons of Mr. Abu-Askar, both Hamas military operatives, were killed while they were involved in launching mortars at IDF forces.[122]

179. The Military Advocate General reviewed the findings and the entire record of the command investigation, together with other information on the incident included in the Human Rights Council Fact-Finding Report. He also reviewed the public testimony given by Mr. Abu-Askar before the Fact-Finding Mission.

180. The Military Advocate General concluded that due to its use as a large storage facility for weapons and ammunition, including Grad missiles, the house of Muhammad Abu-Askar

---

[121] *See* Human Rights Council Fact-Finding Report ¶¶ 975-85.

[122] The circumstances of this incident were detailed in *The Operation in Gaza: Factual and Legal Aspects* ¶¶ 336-40.

was a legitimate military target. The strike was not directed against the residents of the house, but rather against the weapons stored in it.[123]

181. The Military Advocate General further determined that the attack adhered to the IDF's obligation to take precautions to minimise incidental loss of civilian life. The effectiveness of certain precautions – the timing of the attack and the use of warnings – was evident in the fact that there were no civilian casualties in the incident. The intended military advantage of eliminating a large stockpile of weapons, including long-range rockets, exceeded the anticipated harm to civilians.

182. Accordingly, the Military Advocate General found no reason to order a criminal investigation regarding the case.

V. CONCLUSION

183. The Gaza Operation presented complex challenges to Israel and the IDF. While the need and obligation to respond effectively to the thousands of Hamas rockets and mortars that had terrorized Israeli civilians for years was clear and acute, the strategies adopted by Hamas, and in particular its systematic entrenchment in the heart of civilian areas, created profound operational dilemmas.

184. These challenges did not end with the close of operations. A key element of respecting the Law of Armed Conflict is a commitment genuinely to review military operations after the fact, and thoroughly investigate allegations of unlawful activity. Fulfilling this commitment in the context of Gaza is demanding, and requires serious efforts to obtain evidence from battleground situations and to make arrangements to enable residents of Gaza to give their accounts. It also requires an awareness that, in complex combat situations, errors of judgment, even with tragic results, do not necessarily mean that violations of the Law of Armed Conflict have occurred.

185. A further challenge is presented by the scale of the investigations. Because Israel followed up on every allegation, regardless of whether the source was neutral, hostile, or friendly, it launched investigations into 150 separate incidents, including 36 criminal investigations opened thus far. More broadly, the six special command investigations initiated by the IDF addressed more general concerns that arose in the course of the fighting. Beyond the

---

[123] The sole basis for the claim in the Human Rights Council Fact-Finding Report that the house was a civilian target was Mr. Abu-Askar's testimony before the Fact-Finding Mission. The Mission, however, did not ask Mr. Abu-Askar any questions about the potential use of his house for military purposes.

disciplinary and criminal proceedings that have been initiated, operational lessons from these investigations have been incorporated in IDF practice.

186. In this Paper, Israel has sought to share its investigative procedures, and has described the various mechanisms involved, including those operating independently within the military system as well as the civilian oversight provided by the Attorney General and the Supreme Court.

187. Israel recognizes the importance of engaging in dialogue and sharing best practices on the conduct of investigative proceedings with other democratic states facing similar challenges and committed to upholding the rule of law.

A/64/651

Annex II

Letter dated 29 January 2010 from the Permanent Observer of Palestine to the United Nations addressed to the Secretary-General

[Original: English]

Pursuant to the note of 3 December 2009, in which the United Nations Secretariat, on your behalf, requested the Permanent Observer Mission of Palestine to the United Nations to provide written information with regard to the steps that the Palestinian side may have taken in connection with paragraph 4 of General Assembly resolution 64/10 of 5 November 2009, entitled "Follow-up to the report of the United Nations Fact-Finding Mission on the Gaza Conflict", I have the honour to convey to you a letter, dated 27 January 2010, from Prime Minister Salam Fayyad transmitting the following documents submitted by the Palestinian leadership:

- A Presidential Decree establishing an Independent Investigative Commission in Follow-up of the Goldstone Report

- A preliminary report by the Independent Investigative Commission in Follow-up of the Goldstone Report

As Prime Minister Fayyad has indicated in his letter, we will continue to provide you with updates and further reports regarding future developments and progress of the work of the Investigative Commission in Follow-up of the Goldstone Report. In this regard, I wish to assure you that the Commission, as evident in its mandate, its composition and its programme of work, will strive to carry out in the most efficient and timely manner an independent and credible investigation that is in conformity with international standards into the allegations of violations of international humanitarian and human rights law contained in the report of the United Nations Fact-Finding Mission on the Gaza Conflict, as urged by the General Assembly in paragraph 4 of resolution 64/10.

In this regard, I wish to reiterate Palestine's firm position that there is absolutely no symmetry or proportionality between the occupying Power and the occupied people and thus our rejection of any equating of the military aggression and crimes committed by Israel, the occupying Power, against the Palestinian people with actions that may have been committed by the Palestinian side.

Nevertheless, Palestine does take seriously the allegations contained in the Goldstone report regarding possible Palestinian violations, and we have thus, in accordance with General Assembly resolution 64/10, launched this Independent Investigative Commission. We do so on the basis of our utmost respect for and conviction in the rule of law and United Nations resolutions. Moreover, we are upholding our responsibilities in this regard based upon our strong belief that the genuine pursuit of accountability by all members of the international community will ultimately bring an end to the impunity that Israel, the occupying Power, has for too long acted with and benefited from. Such accountability will in the long term unquestionably serve the cause of peace, which cannot be attained without justice.

(*Signed*) Riyad **Mansour**
Ambassador
Permanent Observer of Palestine to the United Nations

Enclosure

[Original: Arabic]

27 January 2010

I have the honour to deposit with you a copy of the Presidential Decree issued by President Mahmoud Abbas on 25 January 2010 concerning the formation of an independent commission to follow up the Goldstone report. That commission will undertake its mandated duties and responsibilities, including investigation and production of a preliminary report on its work.

The attachments to the present letter constitute a response to the demands made on us in General Assembly resolution 64/10, paragraph 4, dated 5 November 2009. That paragraph states as follows:

> [*The General Assembly*]
>
> *Urges*, in line with the recommendation of the Fact-Finding Mission, the undertaking by the Palestinian side, within a period of three months, of investigations that are independent, credible and in conformity with international standards into the serious violations of international humanitarian and international human rights law reported by the Fact-Finding Mission, towards ensuring accountability and justice.

The attached documents also constitute a response to the letter dated 3 December 2009 from the United Nations Secretariat which requested the Permanent Observer Mission of Palestine, by 29 January 2010, to provide the Secretary-General with written information on the steps taken or currently being taken by the Palestinian side in response to the request of the General Assembly in its resolution 64/10, paragraph 4.

(*Signed*) Salam **Fayyad**
Prime Minister
Palestinian National Authority

Attachment I

[Original: Arabic]

Decree No. ( ) 2010

Concerning the formation of an independent commission to follow up the Goldstone report

The President of the State of Palestine,

President of the Palestine Liberation Organization Executive Committee,

President of the Palestinian National Authority,

On the basis of the provisions of the Amended Basic Law of 2003 and its amendments,

Having considered the Decision of the Prime Minister dated 14 January 2010,

Having considered also the Goldstone report,

By virtue of the powers with which he is invested, and in the interests of the public, has decided as follows:

Article 1

To form an independent commission to follow up implementation of the recommendations made in the Goldstone report with respect to the Palestinian National Authority, composed of the following:

1. Issa Abu Sharar, Chairman
2. Zuhair al-Surani, member
3. Ghassan Farmand, member
4. Yasser al-Amuri, member
5. Nasser Rayyes, member

Article 2

1. To authorize that Commission to undertake the investigative duties and responsibilities required of it pursuant to the Goldstone report, and to work in accordance with the timetable provided for in that report.

2. The Commission shall submit its recommendations and the outcome of its work to the relevant authorities.

Article 3

The Commission shall appoint the experts and specialists it considers most appropriate to assist it in performing its duties.

Article 4

All relevant official and unofficial parties shall cooperate with the Commission and provide it with all the facilities and information necessary for it to perform its duties.

Article 5

All the relevant parties shall implement the provisions of this Decree with effect from its publication. The Decree shall be published in the Official Gazette.

Ramallah, 25 January 2010

(*Signed*) Mahmoud **Abbas**
President of the State of Palestine
President of the Palestine Liberation Organization Executive Committee
President of the Palestinian National Authority

Attachment II

[Original: Arabic]

I have the honour to transmit to you herewith the preliminary report on the work of the Independent Commission to follow up implementation of the recommendations made in the Goldstone report, for transmission to the Permanent Observer of Palestine to the United Nations by the date specified, namely, 29 January 2010.

(*Signed*) Issa **Abu Sharar**
Chairman
Independent Commission to follow up implementation
of the recommendations made in the Goldstone report

Ramallah, 28 January 2010

Report of meeting of the Independent Investigation Commission that was established pursuant to General Assembly resolution 64/10

On 25 January 2010, Presidential Decree No. 0105 of 2010 was issued by the President of the State of Palestine, President of the Palestine Liberation Organization Executive Committee and President of the Palestinian National Authority, H.E. President Mahmoud Abbas. The Decree concerned the formation of an independent investigative commission, in accordance with the recommendation of the Fact-Finding Mission and pursuant to General Assembly resolution 64/10, paragraph 4, dated 5 November 2009. That paragraph states as follows:

> [*The General Assembly*]
>
> *Urges*, in line with the recommendation of the Fact-Finding Mission, the undertaking by the Palestinian side, within a period of three months, of investigations that are independent, credible and in conformity with international standards into the serious violations of international humanitarian and international human rights law reported by the Fact-Finding Mission, towards ensuring accountability and justice.

The Commission was constituted as follows:

1. Judge Issa Abu Sharar, Chairman: 1963-1970 Public Prosecutor and subsequently Assistant Prosecutor General of Jordan; 1971-1996 lawyer, Jordan; 1998 President of the Court of Appeal; 2002 Judge of the Palestinian High Court; 2005 President of the High Court and President of the Palestinian High Judicial Council. Retired on 29 November 2009.

2. Judge Zuhair al-Surani, member: 1958-1964 representative of the Public Prosecutor's Office, Gaza; 1964 Judge, Court of First Instance; 1967 Judge, Supreme Court; 1999 Public Prosecutor; 2002 Palestinian Minister of Justice; 2003 President of the High Court and President of the Palestinian High Judicial Council. Retired in 2005.

3. Ghassan Farmand, member. Awarded doctorate of law in France in 1981. 1982 Professor of Law at Birzeit University; 1993 established and directed Institute of Law at Birzeit University. President of Palestinian Red Crescent Society, Ramallah, and member of numerous non-governmental legal institutions. Participated in numerous international conferences, including Yale conferences.

4. Yasser al-Amuri, member. Awarded doctorate of public international law in Spain in 2003. 2003 Professor of Public International Law at Al-Quds University; 2005 Professor of Public International Law at Birzeit University; 2006-2009 Head of Institute of Law and Dean of Masters of Law Programme at Birzeit University. Member of many non-governmental legal institutions. Participated in numerous international conferences and contributed to various studies on human rights.

5. Professor Nasser Rayyes, member. Practitioner of law since 1997. 1998 researcher and legal consultant to Al-Haq, a branch of the International Commission of Jurists; 2002 President of the Committee on Human Rights of the Palestine Academy for Science and Technology; 2003 established Palestinian National Committee for International Humanitarian Law. Member of and contributor to many non-governmental legal institutions. Participated in numerous international

conferences and contributed to various studies on human rights. Head of International Humanitarian Law Team responsible for producing a training guide to the provisions of international law; specialized trainer in human rights law and documentation of crimes and violations.

The Commission held its first meeting in Ramallah on 28 January 2010, with a view to undertaking its mandated duties and responsibilities, pursuant to the above-mentioned Presidential Decree. In accordance with General Assembly resolution 64/10, paragraph 4, dated 5 November 2009, the Commission adopted a working methodology based on the principles and standards laid down in public international law, the Charter of the United Nations, international humanitarian law, international human rights law, international criminal law and the relevant United Nations human rights decisions and declarations, in addition to the precepts of the Palestinian Basic Law and the provisions of national legislation. The Commission considered the Goldstone report and the demands it had made of the Palestinian National Authority, and decided to devise a plan of action and a series of measures for implementation of the mandated duties, including the procedural rules and principles that would ensure that the Commission undertook its investigation in accordance with the principles of justice, equity and impartiality. It would also establish the conditions for the selection of experts, give specifications for investigators and devise witness and informer protection mechanisms. The Commission decided to enlist the help of experts, specialists and appropriate civil society organizations in carrying out its duties, and in due course will inform the relevant parties of all pertinent developments and reports.

Annex III

Letter dated 29 January 2010 from the Chargé d'affaires a.i. of the Permanent Mission of Switzerland to the United Nations addressed to the Secretary-General

[Original: French]

I have the honour to transmit to you the attached summary of the steps that Switzerland has taken to date to implement paragraph 5 of General Assembly resolution 64/10 on the follow-up to the report of the United Nations Fact-Finding Mission on the Gaza Conflict.

(*Signed*) Heidi **Grau**
Chargé d'affaires a.i.

A/64/651

Enclosure

Progress of consultations regarding action pursuant to paragraph 5 of General Assembly resolution 64/10

On 5 November 2009, the United Nations General Assembly adopted resolution 64/10, entitled "Follow-up to the report of the United Nations Fact-Finding Mission on the Gaza Conflict", in paragraph 5 of which the General Assembly "Recommends that the Government of Switzerland, in its capacity as depositary of the Geneva Convention relative to the Protection of Civilian Persons in Time of War, undertake as soon as possible the steps necessary to reconvene a Conference of High Contracting Parties to the Fourth Geneva Convention on measures to enforce the Convention in the Occupied Palestinian Territory, including East Jerusalem, and to ensure its respect in accordance with common article 1".

In accordance with this recommendation, Switzerland, in its capacity as depositary of the Geneva Conventions, and through its Permanent Mission to the United Nations in Geneva, undertook preliminary consultations between 9 and 17 December 2009. Because of time pressure, the preliminary consultations could be held only with a limited number of parties.

Switzerland consulted Israel and Palestine, as parties directly involved; Egypt, Saudi Arabia, Syria, Pakistan (as coordinator on human rights and humanitarian issues in Geneva of the Organization of the Islamic Conference) and Algeria (as the Chair of the Council of Arab Ambassadors in Geneva), as interested parties from the region; China, the United States of America, France, the United Kingdom and Russia, as permanent members of the United Nations Security Council; and Sweden and Spain, as outgoing and incoming holders of the Presidency of the European Union.

The League of Arab States, the International Committee of the Red Cross, the Office of the High Commissioner for Human Rights, the human rights coordinators of the five regional groups in Geneva, the United Nations Relief and Works Agency for Palestine Refugees in the Near East and the Department of Political Affairs of the United Nations Secretariat were informed of these steps.

In addition, Switzerland was notified of the positions of Australia and Canada on the matter, and was approached by a number of delegations from various regional groups, which expressed their desire to be informed of the process under way.

The preliminary consultations were oral and informal. The responses followed the same pattern, with the exception of the two written contributions. Switzerland began each meeting by emphasizing its view that a Conference of High Contracting Parties must be inclusive and be conducive to a concrete result, rather than being used as a platform to air recriminations connected with any party to the conflict. Switzerland accordingly requested the parties it approached to give their views on the content, timing and level of representation at a Conference, and to make concrete suggestions. The reactions can be divided into three categories:

(1) The first group favoured the holding of a conference, preferably at high level, aimed at identifying individual and collective steps to ensure respect for and implementation of the Fourth Geneva Convention on measures to enforce the Convention in the Occupied Palestinian Territory, including East Jerusalem. The

States in question took the view that a Conference of High Contracting Parties should be held in April 2010, in order to avoid a clash with other major conferences or events in Geneva, while still acknowledging the importance of proper and appropriate preparation. They emphasized the need to focus on legal issues. Some States were reflecting on concrete steps, including proposed mechanisms, which they intended to submit for consideration at a later stage.

(2) The second group firmly opposed the holding of a Conference of High Contracting Parties. The States in question were concerned that such a conference could be a needless distraction from, or a damaging obstacle to, the resumption of bilateral negotiations between the Government of Israel and the Palestinian Authority. A politicization of the discussions was regarded as inevitable. Some States also voiced their opposition on grounds of substance. They pointed to the lack of specific provision for such a conference in the Geneva Conventions. They also underlined that paragraph 5 of General Assembly resolution 64/10 took the form of a recommendation.

(3) The third group, while not formally opposing the convening of a Conference of High Contracting Parties, was unenthusiastic at that prospect. Those States regarded such an event as neither useful nor urgent. They were sceptical about the added value of a reconvened conference, indicating that the experience of the Conference of High Contracting Parties of 5 December 2001 had shown no discernible tangible impact on the ground. They could not support a conference that would be used to criticize one particular country.

In conclusion, these consultations, which were limited in number, did not reveal a dominant trend for or against the holding of a Conference of High Contracting Parties, or a view on the contribution to the civilian population affected of a reconvened Conference of High Contracting Parties to the Fourth Geneva Convention; in other words, it was uncertain what results could be expected for what issues.

Switzerland has been encouraged to hold its own discussions on the matter and to share their outcome at the appropriate time. Such discussions will focus on the environment and aims of a reconvened Conference of High Contracting Parties. They will be an integral part of a second round of consultations, open to all the High Contracting Parties and other interested parties, that Switzerland intends to conduct in the near future. In that task, Switzerland will be guided by the desire to protect civilians and to ensure that their humanitarian needs are met.

Document [7] UN General Assembly Resolution 64/254

United Nations   A/RES/64/254

General Assembly

Distr.: General
25 March 2010

Sixty-fourth session
Agenda item 64

Resolution adopted by the General Assembly

[*without reference to a Main Committee (A/64/L.48 and Add.1)*]

64/254. Second follow-up to the report of the United Nations Fact-Finding Mission on the Gaza Conflict

The General Assembly,

Recalling its relevant resolutions, including resolution 64/10, adopted on 5 November 2009, in follow-up to the report of the United Nations Fact-Finding Mission on the Gaza Conflict,[1]

Recalling also the relevant rules and principles of international law, including international humanitarian and human rights law, in particular the Geneva Convention relative to the Protection of Civilian Persons in Time of War, of 12 August 1949,[2] which is applicable to the Occupied Palestinian Territory, including East Jerusalem,

Recalling further the Universal Declaration of Human Rights[3] and the other human rights covenants, including the International Covenant on Civil and Political Rights,[4] the International Covenant on Economic, Social and Cultural Rights[4] and the Convention on the Rights of the Child,[5]

Reaffirming the obligation of all parties to respect international humanitarian law and international human rights law,

Reiterating the importance of the safety and well-being of all civilians, and reaffirming the obligations under international law regarding the protection of civilians in armed conflict,

Stressing the need to ensure accountability for all violations of international humanitarian law and international human rights law in order to prevent impunity, ensure justice, deter further violations and promote peace,

---

[1] A/HRC/12/48.
[2] United Nations, *Treaty Series*, vol. 75, No. 973.
[3] Resolution 217 A (III).
[4] See resolution 2200 A (XXI), annex.
[5] United Nations, *Treaty Series*, vol. 1577, No. 27531.

09-47707

Please recycle ♻

A/RES/64/254

Convinced that achieving a just, lasting and comprehensive settlement of the question of Palestine, the core of the Arab-Israeli conflict, is imperative for the attainment of a comprehensive, just and lasting peace and stability in the Middle East,

1. *Takes note* of the report of the Secretary-General of 4 February 2010,[6] submitted pursuant to paragraph 6 of its resolution 64/10;

2. *Reiterates its call upon* the Government of Israel to conduct investigations that are independent, credible and in conformity with international standards into the serious violations of international humanitarian and international human rights law reported by the United Nations Fact-Finding Mission on the Gaza Conflict, towards ensuring accountability and justice;

3. *Reiterates its urging* for the conduct by the Palestinian side of investigations that are independent, credible and in conformity with international standards into the serious violations of international humanitarian and international human rights law reported by the Fact-Finding Mission, towards ensuring accountability and justice;

4. *Reiterates its recommendation* to the Government of Switzerland, in its capacity as depositary of the Geneva Convention relative to the Protection of Civilian Persons in Time of War,[2] to reconvene as soon as possible a Conference of High Contracting Parties to the Fourth Geneva Convention on measures to enforce the Convention in the Occupied Palestinian Territory, including East Jerusalem, and to ensure its respect in accordance with article 1, bearing in mind the convening of such a Conference and the statement adopted on 15 July 1999 as well as the reconvening of the Conference and the declaration adopted on 5 December 2001;

5. *Requests* the Secretary-General to report to the General Assembly, within a period of five months, on the implementation of the present resolution, with a view to the consideration of further action, if necessary, by the relevant United Nations organs and bodies, including the Security Council;

6. *Decides* to remain seized of the matter.

72nd plenary meeting
26 February 2010

---

[6] A/64/651.

Document [8] UN Human Rights Council Resolution 13/9

United Nations　　　　　　　　　　　　　　　　A/HRC/RES/13/9

 General Assembly　　　　Distr.: General
14 April 2010

Original: English

Human Rights Council
Thirteenth session
Agenda item 7
**Human rights situation in Palestine
and other occupied Arab territories**

Resolution adopted by the Human Rights Council*

**13/9
Follow-up to the report of the United Nations Independent International Fact-Finding Mission on the Gaza Conflict**

The Human Rights Council,

Recalling its relevant resolutions, including resolution S-9/1, adopted on 12 January 2009, and resolution S-12/1, adopted on 16 October 2010, in follow-up to the human rights situation in the Occupied Palestinian Territory, including East Jerusalem, and the report of the United Nations Independent International Fact-Finding Mission on the Gaza Conflict,

Recalling also relevant General Assembly resolutions, including resolution 64/10, adopted on 5 November 2009, and resolution 64/254, adopted on 26 February 2010, in follow-up to the report of the Fact-Finding Mission,

Recalling further the relevant rules and principles of international law, including international humanitarian and human rights law, in particular the Geneva Convention relative to the Protection of Civilian Persons in Time of War, of 12 August 1949, which is applicable to the Occupied Palestinian Territory, including East Jerusalem,

Recalling the Universal Declaration of Human Rights and other international human rights instruments, including the International Covenant on Civil and Political Rights, the International Covenant on Economic, Social and Cultural Rights and the Convention on the Rights of the Child,

Reaffirming the obligation of all parties to respect international humanitarian law and international human rights law,

Reiterating the importance of the safety and well-being of all civilians, and reaffirming the obligation to ensure the protection of civilians in armed conflict,

---

* The resolutions and decisions of the Human Rights Council will be contained in the report of the Council on its thirteenth session (A/HRC/13/56), chap. I.

GE.10-12838　　　　　　　　　　　　　　　　　　　　　　Please recycle

Stressing the need to ensure accountability for all violations of international humanitarian law and international human rights law in order to prevent impunity, ensure justice, deter further violations and promote peace,

Convinced that achieving a just, lasting and comprehensive settlement of the question of Palestine, the core of the Arab-Israeli conflict, is imperative for the attainment of comprehensive, just and lasting peace and stability in the Middle East,

1. *Takes note* of the report of the Secretary-General (A/64/651), submitted pursuant to paragraph 6 of General Assembly resolution 64/10;

2. *Welcomes* the report of the Secretary-General on the status of implementation of paragraph 3 of section B of Council resolution S-12/1 (A/HRC/13/55);

3. *Also welcomes* the report of the United Nations High Commissioner for Human Rights on the implementation of Council resolutions S-9/1 and S-12/1 (A/HRC/13/54) and endorses the recommendations contained therein;

4. *Also reiterates* its call upon all concerned parties, including United Nations bodies, to ensure their implementation of the recommendations contained in the report of the United Nations Independent International Fact-Finding Mission on the Gaza Conflict, in accordance with their respective mandates;

5. *Further reiterates* the call by the General Assembly upon the Government of Israel to conduct investigations that are independent, credible and in conformity with international standards into the serious violations of international humanitarian and international human rights law reported by the Fact-Finding Mission, with a view to ensuring accountability and justice;

6. *Reiterates* the urging by the General Assembly for the conduct by the Palestinian side of investigations that are independent, credible and in conformity with international standards into the serious violations of international humanitarian and international human rights law reported by the Fact-Finding Mission, with a view to ensuring accountability and justice;

7. *Welcomes* the recommendation made by the General Assembly to the Government of Switzerland, in its capacity as depositary of the Geneva Convention relative to the Protection of Civilian Persons in Time of War, to reconvene, as soon as possible, a conference of High-Contracting Parties to the Fourth Geneva Convention on measures to enforce the Convention in the Occupied Palestinian Territory, including East Jerusalem, and to ensure its respect in accordance with common article 1, bearing in mind the statement adopted on 15 July 1999 as well as the reconvening of the conference and the declaration adopted on 5 December 2001, and recommends that the Government of Switzerland reconvene the above-mentioned conference before the end of 2010;

8. *Calls upon* the High Commissioner to explore and determine the appropriate modalities for the establishment of an escrow fund for the provision of reparations to the Palestinians who suffered loss and damage as a result of unlawful acts attributable to the State of Israel during the military operations conducted from December 2008 to January 2009;

9. *Decides*, in the context of the follow-up to the report of the Independent International Fact-Finding Mission, to establish a committee of independent experts in international humanitarian and human rights laws to monitor and assess any domestic, legal or other proceedings undertaken by both the Government of Israel and the Palestinian side, in the light of General Assembly resolution 64/254, including the independence, effectiveness, genuineness of these investigations and their conformity with international standards;

10. *Requests* the High Commissioner to appoint the members of the committee of independent experts and to provide them with all the administrative, technical and logistic assistance required to enable them to fulfil their mandate promptly and efficiently;

11. *Requests* the Secretary-General to transmit all the information submitted by the Government of Israel and the Palestinian side pursuant to paragraphs 2 and 3 of General Assembly resolution 64/254 to the committee of independent experts;

12. *Requests* the committee of independent experts to present its report to the Council at its fifteenth session;

13. *Calls upon* the General Assembly to promote an urgent discussion on the future legality of the use of certain munitions as referred to in the report of the United Nations Independent International Fact-Finding Mission on the Gaza conflict, drawing, inter alia, on the expertise of the International Committee of the Red Cross;

14. *Requests* the Secretary-General to present a comprehensive report on the progress made in the implementation of the recommendations of the Fact-Finding Mission by all concerned parties, including United Nations bodies, in accordance with paragraph 3 of section B of resolution S-12/1, to the Council at its fifteenth session;

15. *Requests* the High Commissioner to present a report on the implementation of the present resolution to the Council at its fifteenth session;

16. *Also requests* the High Commissioner to submit to the Council, at its fourteenth session, a progress report on the implementation of the present resolution;

17. *Decides* to follow up on the implementation of the present resolution at its fifteenth session.

42nd meeting
25 March 2010

[Adopted by a recorded vote of 29 to 6, with 11 abstentions. The voting was as follows:

In favour:
Angola, Argentina, Bahrain, Bangladesh, Bolivia (Plurinational State of), Bosnia and Herzegovina, Brazil, China, Cuba, Djibouti, Egypt, Ghana, India, Indonesia, Jordan, Kyrgyzstan, Mauritius, Nicaragua, Nigeria, Pakistan, Philippines, Qatar, Russian Federation, Saudi Arabia, Senegal, Slovenia, South Africa, Uruguay, Zambia;

Against:
Hungary, Italy, Netherlands, Slovakia, Ukraine, United States of America;

Abstaining:
Belgium, Burkina Faso, Cameroon, Chile, France, Japan, Madagascar, Mexico, Norway, Republic of Korea, United Kingdom of Great Britain and Northern Ireland.]

Document [9] Report of the Committee of Experts

United Nations   A/HRC/15/50

 General Assembly

Distr.: General
23 September 2010

Original: English

Human Rights Council
Fifteenth session
Agenda item 7
Human rights situation in Palestine and other occupied Arab territories

Report of the Committee of independent experts in international humanitarian and human rights laws to monitor and assess any domestic, legal or other proceedings undertaken by both the Government of Israel and the Palestinian side, in the light of General Assembly resolution 64/254, including the independence, effectiveness, genuineness of these investigations and their conformity with international standards*

Summary

> This report is submitted to the Human Rights Council pursuant to its resolution 13/9. The Committee reviewed numerous reports, including the official reports submitted to the United Nations Secretary-General by the Government of Israel and the Palestinian side pursuant to General Assembly resolution 64/254, as well as other documents, reports and articles by non-governmental organizations and military justice experts. The Committee undertook two field missions, to Amman and to the Gaza Strip, to interview victims and witnesses, Government officials and human rights organizations. The Committee was not granted access to Israel and the West Bank.
>
> The Committee sought to assess investigations for compliance with international standards of independence, impartiality, effectiveness, thoroughness and promptness.

---

* Late submission.

GE.10-16225

A/HRC/15/50

Contents

		Paragraphs	Page
I.	Introduction	1–4	3
II.	Mandate and approach	5–16	3
	A. Mandate	5–7	3
	B. Methods of work	8–16	4
III.	Applicable law and standards	17–34	6
IV.	The Government of Israel	35–64	11
	A. Investigations conducted	35–41	11
	B. Assessment	42–64	12
V.	The Palestinian side	65–88	18
	A. The Palestinian Authority	65–75	18
	B. The de facto Gaza authorities	76–88	20
VI.	Conclusions	89–101	22
	A. Israel	89–95	22
	B. The Palestinian side	96–101	23

Annexes

I.	List of stakeholders consulted	25
II.	Table: Incidents in the report of the United Nations Fact-Finding Mission on the Gaza Conflict	27

I. Introduction

1. By its resolution 13/9, the Human Rights Council decided, in the context of the follow-up to the report of the International Independent Fact-Finding Mission (hereinafter FFM report),[1] "to establish a committee of independent experts in international humanitarian and human rights laws to monitor and assess any domestic, legal or other proceedings undertaken by both the Government of Israel and the Palestinian side, in the light of General Assembly resolution 64/254, including the independence, effectiveness, genuineness of these investigations and their conformity with international standards".

2. On 14 June 2010, the High Commissioner for Human Rights announced the appointment of Mr. Christian Tomuschat, Professor Emeritus at Humboldt University Berlin, former member of the United Nations Human Rights Committee and the International Law Commission (President in 1992), as Chair of the Committee. The other two members were: Judge Mary McGowan Davis, former Justice of the Supreme Court of the State of New York and former federal prosecutor, who has advised widely on international justice issues, including for the International Criminal Tribunal for Rwanda and the International Criminal Court; and Mr. Param Cumaraswamy, jurist and former Special Rapporteur of the Commission on Human Rights on the independence of judges and lawyers.

3. The Office of the United Nations High Commissioner for Human Rights (OHCHR) established a secretariat to support the Committee.

4. The present report is submitted to the Human Rights Council pursuant to its resolution 13/9.

II. Mandate and approach

A. Mandate

5. The Committee interpreted its mandate by reading Human Rights Council resolution 13/9 in conjunction with General Assembly resolution 64/254, in which the General Assembly reiterated its call upon the Government of Israel and the Palestinian side to conduct investigations "that are independent, credible and in conformity with international standards into the serious violations of international humanitarian and international human rights law reported by the [United Nations] Fact-Finding Mission [on the Gaza Conflict], towards ensuring accountability and justice".

6. The Committee understood "domestic, legal or other proceedings" to refer to investigations, disciplinary proceedings and prosecutions undertaken by either military or civil justice systems. In accordance with the General Assembly's resolution, the Committee's primary focus was on those proceedings related to the serious violations alleged in the FFM report. However, the reference to "any" proceedings in the Human Rights Council's resolution meant that the Committee was not restricted to the allegations in the FFM report but could review proceedings pertaining to any incident connected to the military operations in Gaza. Additionally, the Committee looked into specific legal issues of institutional responsibility and reform processes relating to the legal regime of armed

---

[1] A/HRC/12/48.

conflict in the aftermath of these operations, which Israel codenamed "Operation Cast Lead".

7. Regarding the temporal scope of the mandate, the Committee considered that any proceedings initiated by Israel or the Palestinian side which commenced on or after 18 December 2008 were relevant to its task.

B. Methods of work

8. The Committee sought to discharge its mandate by analysing information in the public domain and supplementing this information through consultations with stakeholders. It relied primarily on the FFM report, the three reports on the Gaza conflict prepared by the Government of Israel,[2] the report of the Independent Investigation Commission of the Palestinian Authority,[3] and the reports of the Government Committee and the subsequent Independent Legal Committee established by the de facto Gaza authorities in response to the recommendations set forth in the FFM report.[4]

9. The Committee also consulted Governments, witnesses and victims, non-governmental organizations (NGOs), a national human rights institution, and experts in international law and military justice (see annex I). The Committee held three consultations in Geneva on 28-30 June, 11-12 August and 1-3 September 2010, and one in Brussels on 1 July 2010. They included meetings with civil society organizations and military justice and international law experts. The Committee undertook a mission to Amman on 26-30 July 2010 and another to Gaza on 15-16 August 2010 to meet representatives from Governments and NGOs as well as witnesses and victims of the incidents mentioned in the FFM report.

10. The Committee views the relevant government authorities as among the most important sources of information about the progress of investigations mandated by the General Assembly and so sought their cooperation from the initial stages of its work. On 22 June 2010, its Chair wrote to the Permanent Representative of the Permanent Observer Mission of Palestine, on behalf of the Committee, seeking a meeting and on 30 June 2010 the Committee met a representative of the Permanent Observer Mission. With the assistance of the Permanent Observer Mission, the Committee was able to meet three members of the Independent Investigation Commission Established Pursuant to the Goldstone Report on 28 July 2010. The Committee met the representative of the Permanent Observer Mission again on 12 August 2010 and the Permanent Representative himself on 1 September 2010. The Committee is grateful to the Palestinian Authority for the cooperation extended to it throughout its term.

11. To access the fullest information available on investigations undertaken by the Palestinian side, the Committee met the Chair of the Government Committee for Follow-up

---

[2] "The operation in Gaza: factual and legal aspects—27 December 2008 – 18 January 2009", July 2009 (hereinafter "The operation in Gaza"); "Gaza operation investigations: an update", January 2010 (hereinafter "January update") (A/64/651, annex I); "Gaza operation investigations: second update", July 2010 (hereinafter "Second update") (A/64/890, annex I).

[3] "Report of the Palestinian Independent Investigation Commission established pursuant to the Goldstone Report", August 2010 (A/64/890, annex II).

[4] "Case of applying recommendations of the United Nations Fact-Finding Mission report in relation to the Israeli aggression against Gaza (December 2008 to January 2009)" prepared by the Government Committee for Follow-up to the Implementation of the United Nations Fact-Finding Mission Report of the de facto Gaza authorities; "Report of the Independent Legal Committee to Monitor Implementation of the United Nations Fact-Finding Report Recommendation on Gaza Conflict", presented to the Committee in Gaza on 15 August 2010.

to the Implementation of the United Nations Fact-Finding Mission Report in Gaza. In addition, it met the three national members of a second investigation committee, the Independent Legal Committee to Monitor Implementation of the United Nations Fact-Finding Report Recommendation on Gaza Conflict, as well as the Prosecutor-General. The Committee is grateful for the assistance extended to it while in Gaza.

12. The Committee also sought the cooperation of the Government of Israel. On 22 June 2010, its Chair wrote to the Permanent Representative of Israel requesting a meeting and they met, on 30 June 2010. As the possibility of cooperation between Israel and the Committee was left open at that meeting, the Chair wrote again to the Permanent Representative on 30 June seeking Israel's cooperation, including by providing access to Israel, the Gaza Strip, the West Bank and East Jerusalem. The Chair requested a response by 6 July 2010. On 8 July 2010, the Chair wrote to the Permanent Representative inviting the Government of Israel to make official submissions to the Committee describing the domestic, legal and other proceedings it had undertaken in response to the FFM report. The Chair wrote again to the Permanent Representative on 12 July 2010 reiterating his request for cooperation and asking for a response to the letter of 30 June by 15 July 2010. The Committee did not receive a response. On 3 August 2010, the Chair wrote to the Permanent Representative noting the Committee's intention to travel to the Gaza Strip through an alternative route, given its inability to enter Gaza through Israel. On 5 August 2010, the Chair sent a letter to the Permanent Representative requesting a meeting and, on 12 August 2010, they met to discuss the Committee's work. On 24 August 2010, the Chair wrote to the Permanent Representative requesting a telephone conference with the Military Advocate General to discuss matters related to the Committee's mandate. On 31 August 2010, the Permanent Representative of Israel contacted the Chair to suggest that governmental legal representatives might meet the Committee. The Committee spoke with the Permanent Representative on 1 September to express its great interest in this possibility. The Committee received no further communication from the Permanent Representative and in fact never received any official responses to its efforts to reach out to the Government of Israel. The Committee deeply regrets the lack of cooperation from the Government of Israel.

13. The Committee met many witnesses and victims. In its view, their experience in accessing investigatory bodies provides an important perspective on the operation of such bodies. Given the restricted time available in the Gaza Strip, the Committee met a representative group of victims and witnesses concerning the following incidents: the attack on al-Quds hospital; attacks on the houses of Ateya al-Samouni and Wa'el al-Samouni in Zeytoun; the killing of Majda and Rayya Hajaj; the shooting of Amal, Souad, Samar and Hajja Souad Abd Rabbo; the shooting of Rouhiyah al-Najjar; the attack on the al-Daya family house; the destruction of el-Bader flour mill; the alleged use of Abbas Ahmad Ibrahim Halawa and Mahmoud Abd Rabbo al-Ajrami as human shields; and deprivation of liberty and ill-treatment in the al-Atatra sandpits.[5]

14. Finally, the Committee consulted experts in various fields related to its mandate, principally those with knowledge about military justice systems and the international standards relevant to investigations during armed conflict. The discussions were informal in nature and provided a means for the Committee to deepen its understanding of the legal and military issues underlying the mandate and to supplement the available written materials.

15. The totality of this information has provided the basis for the Committee's efforts to implement its mandate "to assess" domestic, legal or other proceedings undertaken by

---

[5] A/HRC/12/48, paras. 596–629, 706–735, 764–769, 770–779, 780–787, 844–866, 913–941, 1064–1075, 1076–1085, 1112–1126.

Israel and the Palestinian side. The Committee has faced considerable constraints in discharging the other part of its mandate, namely "to monitor" relevant proceedings. Owing to the lack of access to Israel and the West Bank, the Committee was able to visit only the Gaza Strip. While in Gaza, the Committee did not receive any detailed information substantiating claims that criminal or other proceedings had been initiated by the de facto Gaza authorities.

16. The Committee has laboured under strict time limitations.

III. Applicable law and standards

17. The General Assembly called upon Israel and the Palestinian side to conduct independent and credible investigations that conform with international standards. The Human Rights Council added to these criteria the requirements of effectiveness and genuineness. Initially, the Committee must identify the standards by which the Israeli and the Palestinian investigations should be evaluated.

18. International standards are derived from the duty to investigate under international humanitarian law (IHL) and international human rights law (IHRL). Because of the intensity of the clashes between the Israeli Defense Forces (IDF) and the armed Palestinian groups, "Operation Cast Lead" in the Gaza Strip constitutes an armed conflict governed by IHL. The Committee views this conflict as being of an international character, as do both Israel and the Palestinian side.[6] Consequently, IHL was applicable to the conduct of hostilities in the Gaza Strip. The other violations alleged in the FFM report, such as those in the West Bank, did not take place within the context of an armed conflict. They must, therefore, be assessed by the yardstick of IHRL.

19. IHL imposes the duty to investigate and prosecute grave breaches of all four Geneva Conventions on High Contracting Parties.[7] The duty to investigate and prosecute allegations of war crimes arises also under customary international law.[8] Article 146 of the Fourth Geneva Convention requires each High Contracting Party "to search for persons alleged to have committed, or to have ordered to be committed, such grave breaches and bring such persons, regardless of their nationality, before its own courts."[9] The article requires legal safeguards for the accused in prosecutions, but beyond that, the treaty offers little guidance as to the relevant standards an investigation must satisfy. The ICRC Commentary provides some direction, specifying that the Parties must actively search for and prosecute the accused with speed and that the necessary police action should be taken spontaneously and not merely at the request of another State. The Commentary further provides that court proceedings should be carried out in a uniform manner and that "nationals, friends, enemies, all should be subject to the same rules of procedure and judged by the same courts".[10]

---

[6] See discussion in the FFM report (A/HRC/12/48, paras. 281–285).

[7] First Geneva Convention, art. 49; Second Geneva Convention, art. 50; Third Geneva Convention, art. 129; Fourth Geneva Convention, art. 146.

[8] International Committee of the Red Cross (ICRC), *Customary International Humanitarian Law*, vol. I, Jean-Marie Henckaerts and Louise Doswald-Beck, eds. (Cambridge University Press, 2005), rule 158.

[9] The Committee follows the position of the FFM report that the substantive rules applicable to either international or non-international armed conflicts are broadly converging in this area (A/HRC/12/48, para. 281).

[10] Jean Pictet (ed.), *Commentary: Fourth Geneva Convention Relative to the Protection of Civilian Persons in Time of War* (Geneva, ICRC, 1958), pp. 592–593.

20. In contrast, international human rights law sets out more elaborate standards with respect to the duty to investigate. The Convention against Torture and Other Cruel, Inhuman or Degrading Treatment or Punishment requires "prompt" and "impartial" investigations by competent authorities into allegations of torture (art. 12). The International Covenant on Civil and Political Rights does not refer explicitly to a duty to investigate; however, the Human Rights Committee has consistently urged States parties to undertake full criminal investigations in cases of serious violations of human rights so as to bring the perpetrators to justice.[11] Despite the Covenant's silence on this point, the Human Rights Committee has held that a failure to investigate alleged human rights violations, such as violations of the right to life and enforced disappearances, itself constitutes a violation of the Covenant.[12]

21. The human rights treaties and soft law instruments rely on a range of criteria or standards, at times overlapping, to guide investigations. Most of the relevant pronouncements stem from the Human Rights Committee. Its jurisprudence runs largely parallel to the jurisprudence of the European Court of Human Rights and the Inter-American Court of Human Rights. The most common criteria – referred to in the FFM report as "universal principles"[13] – are independence, impartiality, thoroughness, promptness and effectiveness. In addition, soft law standards specify that investigative bodies should have adequate powers to carry out their duties; soft law standards also provide direction with respect to collecting and analysing evidence, undertaking autopsies, reporting by medical experts, calling and protecting witnesses, involving victims and family members, providing budgetary and technical resources, as well as establishing independent commissions of inquiry.[14] Transparency is also a key element, both as to the manner in which the inquiry is conducted and in ensuring there is public scrutiny of the results.[15] Human rights bodies have defined the most common criteria as follows:

22. Independence. Both the body undertaking the investigation as well as its members should be independent in the sense of being institutionally detached from those implicated in the events. For example, those potentially implicated in violations should have no supervisory role, whether direct or indirect, over those conducting the investigation.[16] Independence goes beyond institutional independence, however: investigatory bodies and

---

[11] See, e.g., its general comment No. 31 (2004) on the nature of the legal obligation on States parties to the Covenant, para. 15.
[12] See, e.g., A/HRC/12/48, footnote 1153; *Umetaliev et al.* v. *Kyrgyztan*, communication No. 1275/2004, views of 30 October 2008, paras. 9.4–9.6; *Amirov* v. *Russian Federation*, communication No. 1447/2006, views of 2 April 2009, paras. 11.2–11.4.
[13] A/HRC/12/48, para. 1814.
[14] Principles on the Effective Prevention and Investigation of Extra-legal, Arbitrary and Summary Executions (Economic and Social Council resolution 1989/65, annex, principles 9–17); Principles on the Effective Investigation and Documentation of Torture and Other Cruel, Inhuman or Degrading Treatment or Punishment (General Assembly resolution 55/89, annex).
[15] Principles on the Effective Prevention and Investigation of Extra-legal, Arbitrary and Summary Executions, principles 10, 16 and 17; Principles on the Effective Investigation and Documentation of Torture, principles 2, 3, 4 and 5 (*b*). See also Committee against Torture, *Danilo Dimitrijevic* v. *Serbia and Montenegro*, communication No. 172/2000, views of 16 November 2005, para. 7.3, and *Osmani* v. *Serbia*, case 261/2005, 8 May 2009, para. 10.7; and Inter-American Court of Human Rights, case of the *"Las Dos Erres" Massacre*, No. 211, Judgement, 24 November 2009, para. 236.
[16] European Court of Human Rights, *Davydov and Others* v. *Ukraine*, application Nos. 17674/02 and 39081/02, Judgement, 1 July 2010, para. 277; Principles on the Effective Prevention and Investigation of Extra-legal, Arbitrary and Summary Executions, principle 15; Principles on the Effective Investigation and Documentation of Torture, principle 3 (*b*).

their members should not be unduly influenced by powerful social groups, such as the media, industry or political parties.[17]

23. Impartiality. Impartiality is closely related to independence. While independence relates to the establishment and functioning of an investigative body and its members, impartiality refers to the question of whether an investigator is or is likely to be biased. The Human Rights Committee has stated that "judges must not harbour preconceptions about the matter put before them, and that they must not act in ways that promote the interests of one of the parties".[18] Similar considerations apply to investigators. Indications that investigators uncritically adhere to one interpretation of events without bothering to explore alternatives, including the version of events advanced by the complainant, or fail to acknowledge a lack of evidence to support their interpretation of events, could indicate a lack of impartiality.[19]

24. Thoroughness and effectiveness. This standard refers to the completeness and comprehensiveness of an investigation. Thorough and effective investigators should: undertake necessary autopsies and medical examinations; collect and record all relevant evidence; conduct site visits as appropriate; identify, question and take statements from all relevant witnesses; question witnesses comprehensively so that the investigation is able to establish the cause of the alleged violation and those responsible; and provide conclusions based on a comprehensive analysis of all relevant elements.[20] The Committee against Torture has found that inconsistencies in the results of investigations, as well as a lack of qualifications of key experts, such as the doctor undertaking an autopsy, can be evidence of a lack of thoroughness.[21]

25. Promptness. As a general rule an investigation should commence and progress with reasonable expedition.[22] Determining whether an investigation has met this standard of reasonableness depends on the specific circumstances of the case. Cases of torture and extrajudicial killings – where medical evidence might disappear – and enforced disappearances – where an individual's life might be in imminent danger – require immediate action. The Committee against Torture suggests that the requirement to undertake a prompt investigation means that an investigation should be initiated immediately when there is a suspicion of torture or ill-treatment, namely, within hours or days.[23] It has found delays of 15 months and 10 months between the alleged act and the

---

[17] Manfred Nowak, *U.N. Covenant on Civil and Political Rights: CCPR Commentary*, 2nd rev. ed. (N.P. Engel, 2005), pp. 320–321.
[18] *Karttunen v. Finland*, communication No. 387/1989, views of 23 October 1992, para. 7.2.
[19] European Court of Human Rights, *Assenov and Others v. Bulgaria*, Judgement, 28 October 1998, para. 103.
[20] European Court of Human Rights, *Musayev and Others v. Russia*, application Nos. 57941/00, 58699/00 and 60403/00, Judgement, 26 July 2007, para. 162; *Gül v. Turkey*, Case 22676/93, Judgement, 14 December 2000, para. 89–90; *Cennet Ayhan and Mehmet Salih Ayhan v. Turkey*, application No. 41964/98, Judgement, 27 June 2006, para. 88; *Nachova and Others v. Bulgaria*, application Nos. 43577/98 and 43579/98, Judgement, 6 July 2005, para. 113.
[21] *Ristic v. Yugoslavia*, communication No. 113/1998, views of 11 May 2001, para. 8.6. See also European Court of Human Rights, *Kopylov v. Russia*, application No. 3933/04, Judgement, 29 July 2010, para. 169; *Akulinin and Babich v. Russia*, application No. 5742/02, Judgement, 2 October 2008, para. 51.
[22] European Court of Human Rights, *Isayeva, Yusupova and Bazayeva v. Russia*, application Nos. 57947/00, 57948/00, 57949/00), Judgement, 24 February 2005, paras. 209–213; *Benuyeva and Others v. Russia*, application No.8347/05, Judgement, 22 July 2010, para. 112.
[23] *Blanco Abad v. Spain*, communication No. 59/1996, views of 14 May 1998, para. 8.5.

opening of an investigation to be unreasonable.[24] When examining the progress of investigations, frequent and unexplained adjournments can unacceptably compound delay.[25]

26. The Committee must determine what standards are applicable to investigations in the present context. Both Israel and the Palestinian side have a duty to investigate alleged serious violations of IHL and IHRL. This duty arises as a result of international law and is further imposed by General Assembly resolution 64/254.

27. As extensively explained in the FFM report,[26] all parties to the armed conflict are bound by the relevant rules of IHL. Israel is a party to the Fourth Geneva Convention and is, moreover, bound by the rules of customary international law reflected in the 1907 Hague Regulations concerning the Laws and Customs of War on Land and Additional Protocol I of 1977. Palestine is not a party to any of the relevant international instruments. However, in June 1989, the Palestinian Authority submitted a unilateral written undertaking to Switzerland, the depositary of the Geneva Conventions, to be bound by the four Geneva Conventions of 1949 and the two Additional Protocols of 1977.[27] This declaration established a binding commitment under international law.[28] Additionally, both the Palestinian Authority and the de facto Gaza authorities are subject to the IHL rules of customary international law that apply to non-State actors.

28. With regard to inquiries into alleged violations of IHRL, Israel has accepted legal responsibility to investigate by ratifying the International Covenant on Civil and Political Rights and the Convention against Torture. As clarified by the International Court of Justice, the Covenant is applicable also to actions by Israel in the occupied Palestinian territory.[29] The Palestinian Authority has pledged to respect international human rights law by several declarations addressed to the international community[30] and by enshrining that commitment in its Basic Law (arts. 9–33). Lastly, the de facto Gaza authorities have made a series of unilateral declarations of respect for human rights and have acknowledged that the Palestinian Basic Law applies to the Gaza Strip.[31]

29. The question remains whether the more elaborate IHRL standards on investigations also govern inquiries into violations of IHL. In principle, IHRL continues to apply during armed conflict alongside IHL, subject to the possible derogation of certain civil and political rights in states of emergency. IHL may prevail as *lex specialis*.[32] There is no

---

[24] See *Halimi-Nedzibi* v. *Austria*, application No. 8/1991, 18 November 1993, para. 13.5; *M'Barek* v. *Tunisia*, case 60/1996, 10 November 1999, paras. 11.5–11.7.
[25] *Musayev and Others* v. *Russia*, para. 160.
[26] A/HRC/12/48 paras. 270–285, 304.
[27] On 13 September 1989, the Swiss Federal Council informed the States parties that it was not in a position to decide whether the letter constituted an instrument of accession "due to the uncertainty within the international community as to the existence or non-existence of a State of Palestine".
[28] See *Nuclear Tests (Australia* v. *France), Judgment, I.C.J. Reports 1974*, p. 253 (p. 267, para. 43).
[29] Legal *Consequences of the Construction of a Wall in the Occupied Palestinian Territory, Advisory Opinion, I.C.J. Reports 2004*, p. 136 (pp. 179–180, paras. 109–111).
[30] See, for instance, the Barcelona Declaration of the Euro-Mediterranean Ministerial Conference, 27–28 November 1995.
[31] A/HRC/12/48, para. 307.
[32] Legality *of the Threat or Use of Nuclear Weapons, Advisory Opinion, I.C.J. Reports 1996*, p. 226 (p. 240, para. 25); *Legal Consequences of the Construction of a Wall in the Occupied Palestinian Territories, Advisory Opinion, I.C.J. Reports 2004*, p. 136 (p. 178, para. 106); *Case concerning Armed Activity on the Territory of the Congo (Democratic Republic of Congo* v. *Uganda), Judgment, I.C.J. Reports 2005*, p. 168 (p. 243, para. 216); *Application of the International Convention on the*

conflict as such between the duty to investigate under IHL and IHRL. Accepting that the IHRL standards apply in the current situation of armed conflict, the question arises as to how to interpret the more elaborate IHRL standards of investigation in the light of the pre-eminent position of IHL as the specialized body of law designed for armed conflict.

30. The Committee believes that the gap between the expansive standards under IHRL and the less defined standards for investigations under IHL is not so significant. Several criteria under human rights law can be met within the context of armed conflict. Above all, investigators must be impartial, thorough, effective and prompt; otherwise, an investigation would be no more than a manoeuvre of artful deceit. Any investigations that meet these criteria may be called credible and genuine. Credibility presupposes also that the investigating bodies enjoy some measure of independence. The standard of promptness is alluded to in the ICRC Commentary, which refers to the duty to search for and prosecute the perpetrator with speed.

31. It is important to note the growing trend towards requiring comparable standards for investigations under IHL and IHRL. The Basic Principles and Guidelines on the Right to a Remedy and Reparation for Victims of Gross Violations of International Human Rights Law and Serious Violations of International Humanitarian Law, adopted by the General Assembly on 16 December 2005 as a set of rules designed to develop the law, state that the "obligation to respect, ensure respect for and implement international human rights law and international humanitarian law as provided for under the respective bodies of law, includes, inter alia, the duty to: ... (*b*) Investigate violations effectively, promptly, thoroughly and impartially and, where appropriate, take action against those allegedly responsible in accordance with domestic and international law".[33]

32. Nonetheless, there are constraints during armed conflict that do impede investigations. For example, not every death during an armed conflict can be effectively investigated. Similarly, the level of transparency expected of human rights investigations is not always achievable in situations of armed conflict, particularly as questions of national security often arise. The nature of hostilities might obstruct on-site investigations or make prompt medical examinations impossible. The conflict might have led to the destruction of evidence, and witnesses might be hard to locate or be engaged in conflict elsewhere. When the fighting is over, some of these constraints tend to lose their relevance. As summarized by the Special Rapporteur on extrajudicial, summary or arbitrary executions: "On a case-by-case basis a State might utilize less effective measures of investigation in response to concrete constraints. For example, when hostile forces control the scene of a shooting, conducting an autopsy may prove impossible. Regardless of the circumstances, however, investigations must always be conducted as effectively as possible and never be reduced to mere formality."[34]

33. The purpose and objectives of IHL also affect the legal significance of some IHRL standards of investigation beyond the common criteria of independence, impartiality, thoroughness, effectiveness and promptness mentioned above. The overriding concern of IHRL to protect the rights and freedoms of individuals from the abuse of State power is not the primary focus of IHL. The latter seeks first to balance the lawful use of force with the protection of individuals. Consequently, some human rights standards, such as the involvement of victims in investigations, while desirable, are not requisite for evaluating the inquiries into alleged IHL violations. However, the Committee acknowledges that, in

---

Elimination of All Forms of Racial Discrimination (Georgia v. Russian Federation), Provisional Measures, Order of 15 October 2008, I.C.J. Reports 2008, p. 353 (p. 387, para. 112).

[33] Resolution 60/147, annex, para. 3.
[34] E/CN.4/2006/53, para. 36.

the light of the Basic Principles and Guidelines on the Right to a Remedy and Reparations, victims' access to justice is increasingly being accepted as a relevant criterion applicable to investigations into alleged war crimes.

34. Finally, international humanitarian law and human rights standards do not require any specific body to undertake investigations. Military justice systems usually take the lead in inquiring into alleged violations of IHL. This is consistent with Additional Protocol I to the Geneva Conventions reflecting customary law principles, which places a duty on High Contracting Parties to require military commanders "to prevent and, where necessary, to suppress and to report to competent authorities breaches of the Conventions and of this Protocol" as well as "to initiate disciplinary or penal action against violators" (art. 87). Military investigators have the specialized knowledge of combat conditions and munitions that are important to such investigations. However, the use of military courts for prosecution of alleged human rights violations has been controversial and has been found to lack the independence and impartiality required under IHRL.[35] Nonetheless, both military and civilian justice systems may properly undertake investigations of incidents occurring in armed conflict, the only requirement being that the mechanisms employed conform to the various standards discussed above.

IV. The Government of Israel

A. Investigations conducted

35. Israel has issued three reports detailing the proceedings it has undertaken, including investigations into some of the allegations raised in the FFM report (see footnote 2 above). At the centre of Israel's investigation system is the Military Advocate General (MAG). He supervises the rule of law in the military, acts as legal adviser to the Chief of Staff and to other military authorities in respect of law and justice, and provides legal supervision of disciplinary law in the military.[36]

36. The MAG relied on three mechanisms for examining and investigating allegations related to the Gaza conflict. The first is the operational debriefing or command investigation: an "inquiry held in the army, in accordance with IDF orders, regarding an event which occurred during training or operational activity, or in relation to them".[37] The command investigation forwards its findings to the MAG, who decides whether or not to order a criminal investigation. Ordinary command investigations examined 90 allegations, including civilian injuries and deaths, and destruction of civilian property.

37. Second, the Minister of Defense and the Chief of General Staff may appoint an officer or group of officers, often high-ranking, to investigate in confidence high-profile or sensitive matters and then submit their findings and recommendations to the MAG. These investigations are known as special command investigations. On 20 January 2009, the Chief of General Staff ordered five special command investigations headed by Colonels not personally related to the incidents. The investigations covered 30 alleged violations of IHL grouped as follows: harm to a large number of civilians not directly participating in the hostilities; damage to United Nations and international facilities; shooting at medical facilities, buildings, vehicles and crews; destruction of private property and infrastructure

---

[35] See, e.g., E/CN.4/1995/61, para. 93.
[36] Military Justice Law, sect. 178.
[37] Ibid., sect. 539A (a).

by ground forces; and use of weaponry containing phosphorous.[38] A sixth command investigation was established in November 2009 to investigate the allegations relating to the al-Samouni residence, the mistreatment of Palestinian detainees by IDF and the attack on the al-Maqadmah mosque.[39]

38. Third, the MAG may order the Military Police Criminal Investigation Division (MPCID) to open a criminal investigation into allegations of criminal behaviour.[40] He does so either directly upon receipt of a complaint from any source or on the basis of the results of a command investigation. A team of 16 investigators was designated to undertake investigations stemming from the Gaza conflict.[41] By July 2010, the MAG had launched 47 such criminal investigations, of which he had referred 34 directly for criminal investigation while the remaining 13 cases had previously been the subject of command or special command investigations.

39. Once the review is concluded, MPCID reports to the military prosecution and transfers the file for review by a prosecutor. The MAG or Chief Military Prosecutor then decides whether to initiate disciplinary or criminal proceedings or to undertake further investigations. The military prosecution files an indictment before a military court if it determines that there is sufficient evidence to obtain a conviction.[42]

40. In total, Israel has launched more than 150 investigations into allegations of misconduct or violations of IHL during "Operation Cast Lead". As previously noted, this has led to 47 criminal investigations and 4 criminal indictments, one of which led to a conviction for the crime of looting.[43] In addition, investigations have examined operational procedures and the use of certain munitions, such as white phosphorous.[44]

41. The FFM report set out 36 incidents alleging serious violations of IHL and IHRL. Annex II below illustrates the status of investigations into these incidents based on available information. While most have been investigated, the Committee does not have information on whether inquiries into certain matters have been launched and these are discussed below.

B. Assessment

Positive developments

42. The Committee welcomes certain positive steps that have resulted from Israel's investigations into complaints raised in relation to the Gaza conflict. The adoption of new written procedures for the protection of civilians in urban warfare should help to increase that protection in armed conflict and ensure that IDF places more emphasis on civilian safety. The establishment of a "humanitarian officer" for every fighting battalion with responsibility for handling the civilian population should be highlighted as an innovative means to educate soldiers and advise commanders on the protection of civilians and civilian property and the planning and coordination of humanitarian assistance. Likewise, the New Order Regulating the Destruction of Private Property for Military Purposes should help to minimize such destruction in the future. The establishment of a clear doctrine and strict

---

[38] "January update", para. 96.
[39] Ibid., paras. 124–126.
[40] Ibid., para. 50.
[41] Ibid., para. 132.
[42] Ibid., para. 67.
[43] "Second update", para. 10.
[44] "January update", paras. 117–120.

orders on the use of munitions containing white phosphorous is a step forward. In addition, the Committee notes the establishment of the Turkel Commission, which includes two international observers.[45] Part of its mandate is to examine "the question of whether the mechanism for examining and investigating complaints and claims raised in relation to violations of the laws of armed conflict, as conducted in Israel generally,... conform with the obligations of the State of Israel under the rules of international law".[46]

43. In spite of the many investigations undertaken and the sophisticated nature of Israel's military justice system, the Committee has concerns about the investigations conducted into the Gaza conflict thus far.

Lack of cooperation

44. As a result of the lack of cooperation from Israel, the Committee could rely only on three public reports of the Government, supplemented by information from NGOs and witnesses. The information in the three reports is inadequate as a basis for a reliable evaluation of the independence, effectiveness and genuineness of investigations into such serious allegations. The available information is extensive, providing detail on many investigations although not on all. The Committee would have preferred to speak directly with investigators to assess the thoroughness and effectiveness of their work. Instead, the Committee is left with many questions. The fact that it had difficulty verifying whether Israel had investigated all 36 incidents in the FFM report illustrates the opacity of the information available. Owing to the lack of cooperation, the Committee is unable to make a definitive determination as to whether the investigations carried out by Israel meet the criteria in resolution 13/9.

45. First, in some cases, the Committee could not ascertain whether Israel had met its duty to investigate in relation to all 36 incidents. For example, the Committee was unable to find any information as to whether or not an investigation into the death of Muhammad Hajji and the shooting of Shahd Hajji and Ola Masood Arafat[47] was launched. This incident might have been the subject of one of the 90 command investigations or the first special command investigation that considered harm to civilians not directly participating in the hostilities. No reference is made to any investigations into the alleged deprivation of liberty of AD/02.[48] Likewise, the Committee was unable to find information on whether inquires were made into the allegations of indiscriminate killing of members of the Abu Halima family[49] and instead had to rely on NGO material.[50] Cooperation with Israel would have enabled the Committee to verify that information.

46. In other cases, it is evident that investigators compiled a good deal of information. A case in point is the incident at the el-Bader flour mill, destroyed by an air attack.[51] The MAG reopened the investigation upon receiving new evidence and provided further explanations to support his conclusion that the mill had not been intentionally targeted. The example illustrates a serious attempt on the part of Israeli investigators to explain what happened at the flour mill.

---

[45] "Second update", paras. 158–163.
[46] Ibid., para. 160.
[47] A/HRC/12/48, paras. 745–754.
[48] Ibid., paras. 1127–1142.
[49] Ibid., paras. 788–801.
[50] Human Rights Watch, *Turning a Blind Eye: Impunity for Laws-of-War Violations during the Gaza War* (April 2010), p. 40, footnote 132.
[51] A/HRC/12/48, paras. 913–941.

47. A second category of cases raises questions about the extent of the inquiries undertaken. For example, the Committee would have benefited from clarification from Israeli investigators with respect to the shooting of Majda and Rayya Hajaj at Juhr ad-Dik on 4 January 2009.[52] The Israeli report of the investigation into this incident notes the indictment of a soldier on the charge of manslaughter for shooting a civilian at the time and place where the Hajaj women – one of whom was carrying a white flag – were killed.[53] Yet, the press release announcing the soldier's indictment appeared to concern an incident where a man, rather than two women, was shot, suggesting that the indictment may relate to an entirely different incident.[54] The admitted confusion as to the identity and number of the victims at Juhr ad-Dik that day calls into serious question whether a full and prompt investigation was undertaken into the shooting of the Hajaj women.

48. Another case concerned the Abd al-Dayem condolence tents incident.[55] The Fact-Finding Mission alleged that Israeli soldiers had launched a deliberate attack on civilians, killing 5 and injuring 20. The results of the command and criminal investigations suggest instead that soldiers were firing on combatants launching a Grad rocket and that soldiers "did not identify any civilians in the vicinity" of "the terrorist squad".[56] The Committee notes the discrepancy in the two versions of the incident. Owing to the lack of cooperation from Israel, it is unable to confirm that extensive efforts were taken by investigators to reconcile these conflicting accounts.

49. In the al-Quds hospital case,[57] there is insufficient information to determine with any accuracy what the results of the inquiry demonstrate. Israel has communicated very little with respect to this incident. The first Israeli report indicated that an inquiry was ongoing into attacks on medical facilities.[58] The second report noted that the third special command investigation examined incidents of shootings at medical facilities, buildings, vehicles and crews.[59] The third report reflected that disciplinary action was taken against some officers as a result of these attacks,[60] but it is unclear whether that disciplinary action corresponded to the attack on al-Quds hospital or to attacks on other medical centres. The Committee has no basis for assessing whether this investigation was, in fact, effective and thorough.

50. Third, owing to a lack of cooperation from Israel, the Committee is not in a position to evaluate a range of allegations in the FFM report about the way in which the Israeli system of military investigations actually functions. For example, it is alleged that: the system of command investigations was not effective owing to the failure of investigators to comply with regulations and orders;[61] command investigations obstructed criminal investigations by destroying the scene of the crime and obstructing and delaying the process of identifying and collecting evidence;[62] penalties imposed on Israeli offenders had been noticeably more lenient than those imposed on Palestinians;[63] command investigations had

---

[52] Ibid., paras. 764–769.
[53] "Second update", paras. 99–102.
[54] See IDF Military Advocate General takes disciplinary action, indicts soldiers following investigations into incidents during Operation Cast Lead, 6 July 2010. Available from http://dover.idf.il/IDF/English/Press+Releases/10/07/0601.htm.
[55] A/HRC/12/48, paras. 867–885.
[56] "Second update", paras. 113–117.
[57] A/HRC/12/48, paras. 596–629 (al-Quds hospital) and paras. 630–652 (al-Wafa hospital).
[58] "The operation in Gaza", para. 376.
[59] "January update", paras. 111–112.
[60] "Second update", para. 60.
[61] A/HRC/12/48, para. 1816.
[62] Ibid., para. 1817.
[63] Ibid., paras. 1818 and 1825.

no established methods of criminal investigations "such as visits to the crime scene, interviews with witnesses and victims, and assessment by reference to established legal standards";[64] the delay of six months to start some 13 criminal investigations constituted undue delay;[65] criminal investigations had been conducted in an unprofessional way, making it virtually impossible to prove charges beyond reasonable doubt;[66] and command investigations were generally a tool to review performance and learn lessons, which can hardly be an effective and impartial investigation mechanism to respond to allegations of serious violations.[67]

Promptness

51. The Committee has reservations as to whether investigations were sufficiently prompt. Promptness requires investigations to commence and progress with reasonable expedition. The Committee notes that many Palestinian witnesses were interviewed only at the very end of 2009, while many allegations of IHL and IHRL violations were reported almost immediately at the end of "Operation Cast Lead" in January 2009 and at the latest in September 2009 with the publication of the FFM report. Such delays can result in evidence being lost or compromised, and in the kind of confusing and conflicting testimony that affected the results of the inquiries into the shooting of Majda and Rayya Hajaj and the attack on the el-Bader flour mill referred to above. Without additional information on when specific investigations actually got under way, the Committee is not in a position to make a definitive finding on the expeditiousness with which Israel conducted the relevant proceedings.

Independence and impartiality

52. In general terms, it appears that Israel's military justice system has certain built-in mechanisms to preserve its independence. At the heart of the system is the MAG, whose hierarchical independence rests on a number of factors. Specifically, the Minister of Defense, rather than the Chief of General Staff, is responsible for his appointment and decisions of the MAG are subject to review by the Attorney-General and by the Supreme Court sitting as the High Court of Justice, including through petition by individuals and civil society. Israeli jurisprudence illustrates the careful attention paid to ensuring the independent functioning of the MAG within the rule of law.[68]

53. In spite of the structural guarantees of independence built into the military justice system, the dual responsibilities of the MAG, in the specific context of these investigations, raise concerns of a lack of impartiality. The MAG is legal adviser to the Chief of Staff and other military authorities. Yet, at the same time, he is the supervisor of disciplinary law in the military. Although the combination of the advisory and supervisory functions in one office does not automatically lead to a conflict of interest or a lack of impartiality, the situation is complicated in the present case by the fact that many of the allegations of

---

[64] Ibid., para. 1819.
[65] Ibid., para. 1820.
[66] Ibid., para. 1829.
[67] Ibid., para. 1831.
[68] See, e.g., HCJ 4723/96, *Avivit Atiyah* v. *Attorney-General* 51(3) P.D. 714; HCJ 425/89, *Jamal Abdel Kader Mahmoud* v. *the Chief Military Prosecutor*, 43(4) P.D. 718; HCJ 372/88, *Fuchs* v. *the Military Advocate General*, 42(3) P.D. 154; HCJ 425/89, *Zofan* v. *the Military Advocate General* 43(4) P.D. 718; Cr.A. 6009/94, *Shafran & Ors* v. *the Chief Military Prosecutor*, 48(5) P.D. 573; HCJ 442/87, *Shaul* v. *the Military Advocate General*, 42(2) P.D. 749; HCJ 4550/94, *Isha* v. *the Attorney-General*, 49(5) P.D. 849.

serious violations of IHL and IHRL in the FFM report directly link to the advice he provided.

54. Indeed, Israel publicly stated that the MAG gave legal advice on IHL to commanders at all levels leading up to and during the Gaza conflict and that "the lawyers examined the legality of planned targets, participated in the operational planning process, helped direct humanitarian efforts and took part in situation assessments, exercises and simulations".[69] However, as noted above, the Fact-Finding Mission strongly criticized the objectives, strategy and policy underlying the entire Gaza operation.[70] The link between the advice given and the allegations in the FFM report underlines the importance of the MAG not only acting impartially, but also being seen to act impartially.

55. One way to dispel any suspicion of a lack of impartiality is to examine the results of the investigations. Of the 36 incidents in the FFM report, the Committee notes the following findings: no violation or discontinuation of proceedings for various reasons (20); unclear results (7); disciplinary action taken (3); indictments (1); ongoing criminal investigations (5). Although the Committee does not have access to the full evidence and reasoning behind these decisions, given the seriousness of the allegations, the military investigations thus far appear to have produced very little.

56. The Committee notes that civilian oversight of the MAG decisions provides a commendable mechanism to protect against arbitrariness. However, the Committee is not aware of any requests for judicial review of a decision of the MAG related to investigations connected to the Gaza conflict. While any interested party, including NGOs, can seek a High Court judicial review, even in the course of armed conflict, Palestinians in Gaza face significant hurdles.

Treatment of Palestinian complainants and witnesses

57. Palestinian complainants and their legal representatives stated that they were not systematically informed of the progress of their cases. While the military has a standard practice of acknowledging receipt of a complaint, the vast majority of complainants received no further information whatsoever about the status of their cases. Two organizations which filed complaints on behalf of Palestinians told the Committee that they had learned about the dismissal of their complaints only through the Israeli media.[71] The lack of any standard process of informing complainants about the progress and results of investigations affects the perception of justice. Not surprisingly, the Committee learned that the complainants and witnesses affected by investigations had little confidence in the system.

58. The same lack of transparency was also reported in civil cases. In addition to lodging a complaint with the MAG, complainants can initiate a proceeding to seek compensation with the Ministry of Defense. The claimant must lodge a form within 60 days of incurring damage, followed by a civil claim within two years. The Palestinian Centre for Human Rights (PCHR) submitted 1,028 compensation claims to the Israeli Ministry of Defense, of which, by 11 February 2010, only 7 on behalf of 20 individuals had been acknowledged. The Israeli Military Police notified PCHR that it had opened investigations in 15 cases and summoned 35 witnesses to the Erez crossing. According to PCHR, none of the interviewed witnesses received any information following their appearance before the investigation panel in Erez. In the case of the attack on the al-Daya family residence –

---

[69] "The operation in Gaza", para. 216.
[70] A/HRC/48/12, para. 1895.
[71] Consultation with Adalah, Amman, 29 July 2010; consultation with the Palestinian Centre for Human Rights, Gaza City, 15 August 2010.

where Israel admitted it had made an operational error leading to the deaths of 23 civilians – PCHR filed the compensation form on 11 February 2009 and a criminal petition on 18 May 2009, only to receive a formal letter acknowledging receipt of its petition on 13 September 2009 and requesting a power of attorney (which PCHR had already filed). PCHR has received no further information on the progress of this compensation claim.[72] Furthermore, Palestinian witnesses in Gaza are not always granted a permit to travel out of Gaza and so cannot reach courts in Israel, particularly since the closure of the Gaza Strip in June 2007.[73] Consequently, access to justice is rarely guaranteed in practice to Palestinian complainants.

59. The experience of victims and witnesses when giving testimony at the border and in accessing Israeli justice more broadly helps to explain why Palestinians have little confidence in the Israeli investigations. The Committee interviewed 28 witnesses, of whom 19 had given evidence at the Erez border. Witnesses had had to wait long hours at the border. One of the witnesses in the al-Samouni case reported having to wait 13 hours and being refused access to sanitary facilities for hours, finally being allowed to use a toilet, but only in the company of soldiers.[74] Another witness to the Halawa incident had to wait four hours without water or food; the witness was forced to wait an hour and a half to use a toilet.[75] Another person related to the Abd Rabbo incident had to wait six hours at the border and was sent home without being interviewed.[76]

60. In the view of the Palestinians residing in Gaza, the Israeli military justice system is simply the extension of the same military system that organized and carried out "Operation Cast Lead". Most distrust its ability to deliver justice. For this reason, many potential witnesses declined to appear in Erez. Perhaps this is not surprising since victims of military operations naturally perceive a deep bias and predisposition towards self-preservation and national interests among those representing the adversary State. However, in the interests of performing effective and impartial investigations, the Committee emphasizes the importance of treating all victims and witnesses, whether Israeli or Palestinian, with dignity and courtesy.

Allegations not investigated

61. The information available suggests that Israel has not investigated all the allegations of serious violations of IHL and IHRL set out in the FFM report.

62. First, Israel has not conducted investigations into the allegations of human rights violations with respect to its actions in the West Bank at the time of the military operations in Gaza.[77] The allegations of violations of the right to life, as well as claims of torture and unlawful conditions of detention, give rise to the duty to investigate under the International Covenant on Civil and Political Rights and the Convention against Torture. There is no evidence that Israel has met this duty.

63. Furthermore, the information available suggests that Israel has not conducted a general review of the military doctrine regarding legitimate military targets. The Fact-Finding Mission rejected the Israeli viewpoint that the entire governmental infrastructure in

---

[72] Discussions with PCHR, Gaza, 15 August 2010.
[73] PCHR, "Memorandum for the United Nations Committee of Experts", annex I, August 2010.
[74] Interviews, Gaza, 15 August 2010.
[75] Interviews, Gaza, 16 August 2010.
[76] Interviews, Gaza, 15 August 2010.
[77] A/HRC/12/48, paras. 1394–1404 (use of force during demonstrations in the West Bank); paras. 1411–1418 (violence by settlers against Palestinians in the West Bank).

the Gaza Strip, including the Legislative Council building, was a legitimate target, warning that it was incompatible with the principle of distinction.[78]

64. Finally, Israel has not conducted investigations into decisions made at the highest levels about the design and implementation of the Gaza operations.[79] A core allegation in the FFM report was that the systematic and deliberate nature of the destruction in Gaza left the Mission "in no doubt that responsibility lies in the first place with those who designed, planned, ordered and oversaw the operations".[80] Those alleged serious violations go beyond individual criminal responsibility at the level of combatants and even commanders, and include allegations aimed at decision makers higher up the chain of command. The official inquiry must be conducted by a truly independent body, given the obvious conflict inherent in the military's examining its own role in designing and executing "Operation Cast Lead".

V. The Palestinian side

A. The Palestinian Authority

65. On 25 January 2010, the Palestinian Authority established a four-member Independent Investigation Commission by Presidential Decree to follow up on the implementation of the recommendations of the FFM report.[81] The Commission was authorized to undertake investigative duties pursuant to that report, work in accordance with the timetable provided in it, and submit its conclusions and recommendations to the relevant authorities.[82]

66. The Committee received the report of the Independent Investigation Commission (see footnote 3 above) from the High Commissioner for Human Rights on 19 August 2010. It set out in detail the Commission's methodology and scope of investigations. The Commission's mandate was to investigate the alleged violations committed by the Palestinian side both before and after the Gaza conflict that were described in the FFM report.[83] The Commission had powers to collect information, evidence and data relevant to its activities; to receive complaints of human rights violations falling within its mandate; and to hear testimony from complainants, including victims, witnesses, human rights organizations and official agencies.[84]

---

[78] A/HRC/12/48, para. 392.
[79] In this regard, the FFM report names particular individuals, including the Deputy Prime Minister, Eli Yishai, and the Foreign Minister, Tzipi Livni, as well as Major-General Dan Harel, whose statements during "Operation Cast Lead" support its contentions that the Operation was indeed intended to cause disproportionate destruction and violence against civilians as part of a deliberate policy. The Fact-Finding Mission also charges that Israel's strategic goals demonstrated a qualitative shift from relatively focused operations to massive and deliberate destruction. See A/HRC/12/48, paras. 1177–1216.
[80] Ibid., para. 1895.
[81] Issa Abu Sharar, Chair and former Head of the Supreme Court and former President of the Supreme Judicial Council; Judge Zuhair al-Surani, former Head of the Supreme Court and former President of the Supreme Judicial Council; Ghassan Farmand, Professor of Law at Birzeit University; Yasser al-Amuri, Professor of International Law at Birzeit University.
[82] See Decree concerning the formation of an independent commission to follow up on the Goldstone report, article 2 (A/64/651, annex II, attachment I).
[83] A/64/890, annex II, chap. II, para. 60.
[84] Ibid., para. 62.

Document [9] Report of the Committee of Experts

A/HRC/15/50

67. The Commission sought the expertise of independent international scholars,[85] human rights organizations and officials in the West Bank. The Commission also collected and analysed data from the reports of national and international human rights organizations. It placed notices in local newspapers in the West Bank and Gaza Strip, organized a press conference to introduce itself to its constituents and encourage individuals to bring complaints before it,[86] and held public hearings.

68. The Commission made a series of findings, including allegations of torture and ill-treatment by security forces in the West Bank and Gaza; extrajudicial killings by law enforcement agencies and armed groups connected to the de facto Gaza authorities; failure by these Gaza authorities to protect against extrajudicial killings and to prosecute those responsible; and various violations by the West Bank and de facto Gaza authorities in relation to the right to form associations, press freedoms and the right to take part in public affairs.

69. The Commission addressed recommendations to the Palestinian Authority, including the Office of the Public Prosecutor, the Office of the Military Prosecutor, the security services, the Preventive Security Service, the General Intelligence Service and the Military Intelligence Service. In addition, it addressed findings to the de facto Gaza authorities and their security services, as well as to the United Nations.

70. The Committee notes that the Independent Investigation Commission undertook independent and impartial investigations in a comprehensive manner that squarely addressed the allegations in the FFM report.[87]

71. The Commission was established as an independent investigatory body and its members were not directly linked to the Palestinian Authority hierarchy being investigated. Two of the four members were retired judges of high standing in the occupied Palestinian territories; the other two were university professors. The Commission established in its statute the principle of complete independence of its members. It claimed that "no party was allowed to interfere with or influence the course of the investigation".[88] The conclusions tend to support this claim, particularly given the Commission's allegations of violations committed by the Palestinian Authority, including at high levels, as well as by the de facto Gaza authorities. Furthermore, the Commission's investigatory powers were sufficient to support its investigations and are reflected in its statute.

72. Moreover, its report demonstrates that it was thorough. In the elaboration of its methods of work, the Commission set out in detail the process it had followed to arrive at its conclusions. The fact that the Commission was able to undertake some 100 hearings in relation to each of the alleged violations illustrates the comprehensiveness of its work. The Commission met governmental representatives accused of violations, including high-level officials. The steps taken to protect witnesses and safeguard the information it obtained demonstrate its professionalism.

---

[85] Ibid., para. 63.
[86] Ibid., paras. 68–70.
[87] The Commission covered allegations in the FFM report as follows: arrest and detention by security forces (A/HRC/12/48, paras. 1555–1558); torture and ill-treatment (paras. 1559–1560); freedom of association (para. 1561); freedom of the press; freedom of expression and opinion (paras. 1564–1570); freedom of assembly (paras. 1571–1575). The Commission also attempted to cover allegations of violations by armed groups and security services in the Gaza Strip including: launching of attacks within civilian areas (paras. 446–460); detention of Gilad Shalit (paras. 1336–1344); killings, torture and other human rights violations (paras. 1345–1372); and rocket and mortar attacks by Palestinian armed groups on Israel (paras. 1594–1691).
[88] A/64/890, annex II, chap. II, para. 62.

73. The Commission set out the limitations impeding its work, including the fact that it was unable to travel to the Gaza Strip. While these limitations affected the thoroughness of its work, the Commission was able to interview victims, witnesses and representatives of human rights organizations in the Gaza Strip by videoconference.[89] However, it is unclear to what extent its report will lead to criminal investigations and prosecutions there.

74. The Committee also has some concerns about the promptness of the investigations. The FFM report published allegations of violations in September 2009. Yet the Commission was established only in January 2010, presumably in response to General Assembly resolution 64/10 (para. 4) rather than to the FFM report itself. This delays the start of criminal investigations and prosecutions. That said, the Committee observes that the Commission undertook a task of significant proportions with reasonable expedition so that it was able to submit its results to the Secretary-General in a timely manner.

75. Finally, the Committee emphasizes that investigations are only the first step to achieving accountability for alleged human rights violations and that the prosecution of perpetrators, as well as the provision of an effective remedy to those whose rights have been violated, should follow promptly. At the time of writing, the Committee had not received any information to indicate that criminal investigations or prosecutions were actually under way in the West Bank. On 6 September 2010, the Committee received a copy of a letter sent by the Prime Minister, Mr. Sallam Fayyad, to the Chair of the Commission, Mr. Issa Abu-Sharar, reiterating the commitment of the Council of Ministers "to the full implementation of the recommendations contained [in the Commission's report] towards respecting and ensuring respect of human rights and public freedoms in Palestine". The Committee strongly encourages the Palestinian Authority to live up to this commitment through prompt and effective prosecutions where appropriate.

B. The de facto Gaza authorities

76. The de facto Gaza authorities established two committees in response to General Assembly resolution 64/254. The United Nations received the report of the first Committee in January 2010 and the report of the second in August 2010 (see footnote 4 above).

77. The first Committee was an entirely governmental body headed by the Minister of Justice of the de facto Gaza authorities. The other Committee members were members of the Prime Minister's Legal Council, the Under-Secretary of the Ministry of Foreign Affairs, the Under-Secretary of the Ministry of Justice, the Chair of the Military Jurisdiction Authority, the Public Prosecutor, the Head of the Central Documentation Committee, a Judge of the Court of Appeal, the Director-General of Legal Affairs at the Ministry of Justice, the Director-General of Fatwa and Legislation, the Director-General of the Legislative Council, and the General Controller of the Ministry of the Interior. Its report focused entirely on Israeli Government policy vis-à-vis the Gaza Strip and the conduct of Israeli military troops during the Gaza conflict.

78. It did not carefully consider the violations allegedly perpetrated by the de facto Gaza authorities or associated armed groups. However, in its report, it stated that all claims concerning the conduct of the de facto Gaza authorities and armed groups should be directed to the Office of the Prosecutor-General.

79. The report, while submitted as a response to the FFM report, did not discuss the Fact-Finding Mission's recommendations in detail, nor did it propose measures to address alleged violations committed by the de facto Gaza authorities or the armed groups under its

---

[89] Ibid., para. 66.

control. The report is not an investigative report, but simply a description of what, in the view of the de facto Gaza authorities, the situation currently is in the Gaza Strip. It primarily reiterated the allegations of the FFM report against Israel.

80. However, the report did announce the establishment of a follow-up Independent Legal Committee (hereinafter "second Gaza Committee"), composed of three national and three international experts, to implement the Fact-Finding Mission's recommendations "in accordance with international standards."

81. This second Gaza Committee[90] presented its report to this Committee in Gaza on 15 August 2010. Its national experts were introduced as Gaza-based lawyers with many years' experience in international law practice. Its three international experts were international lawyers from Egypt and Saudi Arabia. They were unable to enter the Gaza Strip and were limited to communicating with the national members by telephone. The Committee accepts that the de facto Gaza authorities sought to establish an independent body to undertake investigations.

82. The second Gaza Committee made field visits, interviewed victims and officials, and reviewed criminal investigation files. However, its report did not include sufficient information to demonstrate systematically the steps it took to collect and evaluate evidence. More details would have shed light on the thoroughness of its investigations.

83. The second Gaza Committee's report did give examples of criminal proceedings related to alleged violations of IHL and IHRL, including a case where a number of defendants were convicted and imprisoned, while others were given suspended prison sentences. Some cases were settled out of court between the families involved. While in the Gaza Strip, the Committee requested the Prosecutor-General to provide it with specific information about the number and progress of the investigations his Office had undertaken. His Office subsequently responded in writing, but its submission contained no statistics or other data substantiating the report's reference to investigations or prosecutions undertaken by the de facto Gaza authorities.

84. The second Gaza Committee's report stated in addition that all persons detained on political grounds had been released; Palestinian groups had not deliberately violated the principle of distinction; there was no credible testimony to support the charge that Palestinian armed groups had intentionally targeted Israeli civilians when launching rockets against Israeli targets; mosques and civilian buildings had not been used as storage space or bases for weapons; and there was no evidence that Palestinians had used civilians as human shields.

85. The Committee is not in a position to ascertain the veracity of any of these assertions.

86. The Committee also has concerns related to the impartiality of the second Gaza Committee's investigations. The report did not seriously address the recommendations by the Fact-Finding Mission to the de facto Gaza authorities. This is in stark contrast to the report of the Palestinian Authority's Commission, which demonstrated a sincere effort on its part to investigate and expose the culpability of the government authorities. Instead, the second Gaza Committee – like the first – addressed recommendations to the United Nations and the international community, while its conclusions concentrated on criticizing Israel's policies and actions towards Gaza, rather than on addressing those of the de facto Gaza authorities. This gives the impression that the investigations sought to deflect attention from

---

[90] Mr. Abdollah Alasha'al (Chair, Egypt); Mr. Basem A'alem (Saudi Arabia); Mr. Mahmood Almobarak (Saudi Arabia); Mr. Muhammad No'man Elnahhal (Gaza); Mr. Salem Elsaqqa (Gaza); Mr. Nazem Owaida (Gaza).

the alleged violations of IHL and IHRL by the de facto Gaza authorities and raises concerns about their credibility and genuineness.

87. Moreover, some aspects of the report sought to explain away allegations of serious violations of IHL. For example, the second Gaza Committee suggested that the unavailability of modern military technology could not preclude armed groups from defending themselves. This implicitly acknowledges the truth of the allegations in the FFM report that armed groups violated IHL by launching weapons at Israel that were incapable of striking precise targets, while seeking to justify the violation and absolve the perpetrators.

88. The investigations of the second Gaza Committee, which began more than a year after the Gaza conflict, also raise questions as to the promptness of its inquiry. The report set out reasons for the delay, noting the difficulties inherent in undertaking effective investigations in the wake of the destruction caused by the conflict. This Committee understands that the chaos resulting from armed conflict had an impact on the second Gaza Committee's capacity to undertake investigations. In this sense, the strict application of the standard of promptness might not be appropriate.

VI. Conclusions

A. Israel

89. **A lack of cooperation hampered the Committee's assessment of Israel's response to the call by the General Assembly to conduct investigations that are independent, credible and in conformity with international standards into the serious violations of IHL and IHRL reported by the United Nations Fact-Finding Mission on the Gaza Conflict. The Committee's bases of information are insufficient for a definitive assessment. Consequently, the Committee is not in a position to establish whether the investigations carried out by Israel met international standards of independence, impartiality, thoroughness, effectiveness and promptness.**

90. **The Committee acknowledges that there are mechanisms in place within the Israeli legal order to investigate allegations of war crimes. It accepts that military as well as civilian investigative bodies may inquire into such crimes so long as the investigations conform to international standards. Investigations into allegations of violations of either IHL or IHRL should meet the universal criteria of independence, impartiality, thoroughness, effectiveness and promptness, subject to the constraints of armed conflict.**

91. **The actual operation of Israel's military investigations system raises concern in the present context. Specifically, the Committee concludes that the dual role of the Military Advocate General (MAG) to provide legal advice to IDF with respect to the planning and execution of "Operation Cast Lead" and to conduct all prosecutions of alleged misconduct by IDF soldiers during the operations in Gaza raises a conflict of interest, given the Fact-Finding Mission's allegation that those who designed, planned, ordered and oversaw the operation were complicit in IHL and IHRL violations. This bears on whether the MAG can be truly impartial – and, equally important, be seen to be truly impartial – in investigating these serious allegations.**

92. **The Israeli investigators did not always undertake steps to inform victims, witnesses and their legal representatives of the progress of their inquiries, nor did they consistently treat victims with dignity and courtesy. Transparency in reporting progress and results of investigations and access to justice for victims are**

requirements for investigations under IHRL, although they are not strictly applicable to investigations under IHL, owing to the differing objectives of investigations under these two bodies of law.

93. Nonetheless, without the full participation of victims and witnesses in investigations, their effectiveness and thoroughness suffer. The Committee notes that international standards are evolving in this area, with ever stronger emphasis on affording access to justice for victims even with respect to investigations into alleged violations of IHL.

94. The Committee does not have any information on whether Israel has undertaken investigations into the allegations raised in the FFM report concerning IHRL violations in the West Bank. In this regard, Israel has not met its duty, under the International Covenant or under the Convention against Torture, to investigate these claims.

95. Similarly, there is no indication that Israel has opened investigations into the actions of those who designed, planned, ordered and oversaw "Operation Cast Lead". The FFM report contained serious allegations that officials at the highest levels were complicit in violations of IHL and IHRL. Israel has not met its duty to investigate this charge. The Committee observes that the military justice system would not be the appropriate mechanism to undertake such an investigation, given the military's inherent conflict of interest.

B. The Palestinian side

1. The Palestinian Authority

96. The Palestinian Authority established an independent commission of investigation, which carried out a careful and detailed inquiry into the allegations addressed to the Palestinian Authority. On the basis of the Commission's report and its meeting with the Commission's Chair and members, the Committee concludes that the Commission was not only independent in form, according to its legal statute, but also in fact. Its report alleges that serious violations of IHRL were committed by public officials in the West Bank. The Committee concludes that the investigation conforms with international standards and can be considered credible and genuine.

97. However, the Committee observes that the Commission's work was hampered by difficulties in accessing the Gaza Strip. While the Commission took all appropriate steps to investigate the allegations of serious violations of IHL and IHRL in Gaza, the Committee concludes that the Commission was unable to do so.

98. The Commission has laid the groundwork for the commencement of proceedings against the perpetrators and other measures suited to provide redress to the victims. Its Chair has received written assurances from the Prime Minister concerning the implementation of all its recommendations, but the Committee is unaware of any criminal proceedings that may have been initiated since the Commission filed its report.

2. The de facto Gaza authorities

99. The de facto authorities in Gaza established two committees of inquiry.

100. The report of the first Committee, made up of officials of the de facto Gaza authorities, makes no serious effort to address the allegations detailed in the FFM report against the de facto authorities in Gaza; it focuses primarily on the allegations directed against Israel.

101. The second report, prepared by three national and three international legal experts, provides some information about the actual measures taken to redress the violations that were alleged, but fails to substantiate assertions that all political prisoners have been released and criminal prosecutions have taken place in response to the FFM report. On the basis of the information before it, the Committee cannot conclude that credible and genuine investigations have been carried out by the de facto authorities in the Gaza Strip.

Document [9] Report of the Committee of Experts

A/HRC/15/50

Annex I

[English only]

List of stakeholders consulted

Diplomatic missions

Permanent Mission of the Arab Republic of Egypt to the United Nations in Geneva

Permanent Mission of Israel to the United Nations in Geneva

Permanent Mission of the Hashemite Kingdom of Jordan to the United Nations in Geneva

Permanent Observer Mission of Palestine to the United Nations in Geneva

Domestic authorities

Muhammad Abed	Prosecutor General, Gaza
Dhiya al-Madhoun	Central Documentation Committee, Gaza

Investigative bodies

Judge Issa Abu Sharar	Chair, Independent Investigation Commission of the Palestinian Authority
Ghassan Farmand	Member, Independent Investigation Commission of the Palestinian Authority
Yasser al-Amuri	Member, Independent Investigation Commission of the Palestinian Authority
Muhammad Faraj al-Ghoul	Chair of the Government Committee for Follow-up to the Implementation of the United Nations Fact-Finding Mission Report
Muhammad No'man Elnahhal	Member, Independent Legal Committee to Monitor Implementation of the United Nations Fact-Finding Report
Salem Elsaqqa	Member, Independent Legal Committee to Monitor Implementation of the United Nations Fact-Finding Report
Nazem Owaida	Member, Independent Legal Committee to Monitor Implementation of the United Nations Fact-Finding Report

Non-governmental organizations

Addameer, al-Haq, Badil, Cairo Institute for Human Rights, Christian Aid, Defence National (Israel), Geneva for Human Rights, Human Rights Watch, International Federation for Human Rights (FIDH), Save the Children, UN Watch, the Women's

International League for Peace and Freedom, the World Council of Churches. In addition, the Committee received submissions from: Adalah, al-Mezan, B'Tselem, Hamoked, the Palestinian Centre for Human Rights, the Euro-Mediterranean Human Rights Network (EMHRN).

National human rights institutions

The Palestinian Independent Commission for Human Rights

Independent experts

Philip Alston, Professor	Former Special Rapporteur on extrajudicial, arbitrary and summary executions
Abraham Bell, Professor	Bar Ilan University Israel
Richard Falk	Special Rapporteur on the Occupied Palestinian Territories
William Fenrick	Schulich School of Law, Dalhousie University, Canada; former Senior Legal Adviser, Office of the Prosecutor, International Criminal Tribunal for the former Yugoslavia
Eugene Fidell	President of the National Institute of Military Justice, United States of America, and Florence Rogatz Lecturer in Law, Yale Law School
Jim Goldston	Open Society Institute – Justice Initiative
Col. Daniel Reisner (ret.)	Former head of the IDF international law department.
Marco Sassoli, Professor	University of Geneva
Michael Schmitt	Professor Durham University and ex-Advocate-General, United States of America
Rupert Skilbeck	Open Society Institute – Justice Initiative
Canadian military law expert	

International organizations

United Nations Special Coordinator Office for the Middle East

Office of the United Nations High Commissioner for Human Rights

International Committee of the Red Cross

Document [9] Report of the Committee of Experts 355

A/HRC/15/50

Annex II

[English only]

Table: Incidents in the report of the United Nations Fact-Finding Mission on the Gaza Conflict

Indiscriminate or deliberate killings

Incident	Paragraphs FFM report	Investigation body	Status
1. Killing of Ateya Samouni and his son Ahmad	706-735	Sixth special command investigation; MPCID	Ongoing
2. Attack on the Wa'el al-Samouni house	706-735	Sixth special command investigation; MPCID	Ongoing
3. Al-Fakhura Street massacre/al-Deeb family	653-703	Special command investigation	No violation
4. Shooting of Iyad al-Samouni	736-744	Sixth special command investigation; MPCID	Ongoing
5. Death of Mohammed Hajji and shooting of Shahd Hajji and Ola Masood Arafat	745-754	Unclear	Unclear
6. Shooting of Ibrahim Juha	755-763	MPCID	Ongoing
7. Killing of Majda and Rayya Hajaj	764-769	MPCID; military court	Ongoing but unclear if same case
8. Khalid Abd Rabbo's daughters	770-779	MPCID	No violation
9. Shooting of Rouhiyah al-Najjar	780-787	Command investigation; MPCID	No violation
10. Abu Halima family	788-801	MPCID	Unclear
11. Attack on al-Maqadmah mosque	822-843	Two special command investigations (January 2009 and November 2009)	Disciplinary action
12. Attack on al-Daya family	844-866	Special command investigation	No violation
13. Attack on the Abd al-Dayem condolence tents	867-885	Command investigation; MPCID	No violation

Attacks on government infrastructure

Incident	Paragraphs FFM report	Investigation body	Status
14. Israeli air strikes on the Gaza main prison	366-392	Command investigation	No violation
15. Strikes on the Palestinian Legislative Council building	366-392	Unclear	Unclear
16. Arafat City police HQ	393-438	Command investigation	No violation
17. Deir al-Balah police attacks	393-438	Command investigation	No violation
18. Abbas police station	393-438	Command investigation	No violation
19. Zeytoun police stations	393-438	Command investigation	No violation
20. Al-Shujaeiyah and al-Tuffah police station	393-438	Command investigation	No violation

Use of Palestinians as human shields

Incident		Paragraphs FFM report	Investigation body	Status
21.	Abbas Ahmed Ibrahim Halawa	1064-1075	MPCID	No violation
22.	Majdi Abd Rabbo	1033-1063	MPCID	Disciplinary action
23.	Mahmoud Abd Rabbo al-Ajrami	1076-1085	MPCID	No violation
24.	AD/03	1086-1088	MPCID	Discontinued insufficient evidence

Arbitrary detention

Incident		Paragraphs FFM report	Investigation body	Status
25.	Al-Atatra incident	1112-1126	Sixth special command investigation	Ongoing
26.	AD/02	1127-1142	MPCID	Unclear
27.	AD/03	1143-1164	MPCID	Discontinued insufficient evidence
28.	AD/06	1107	Unclear	Unclear

Use of harmful weapons

Incident		Paragraphs FFM report	Investigation body	Status
29.	Al-Quds hospital	596-629	Special command investigation	Unclear Possible disciplinary action
30.	Al-Wafa hospital	630-652	Special command investigation	Unclear Possible disciplinary action
31.	UNRWA	543-595	Special command investigation	Apology, disciplinary action, compensation

Attacks on infrastructure and food production

Incident		Paragraphs FFM report	Investigation body	Status
32.	El-Bader flour mill	913-941	Command investigation	No violation
33.	Sawafeary chicken farm	942-961	Command investigation	No violation
34.	Abu Jubba cement company	1012-1017	Command investigation	No violation

Attacks on water and sewage installations

Incident		Paragraphs FFM report	Investigation body	Status
35.	Gaza wastewater treatment plant	962-974	Command investigation	No violation
36.	Namar wells group	975-986	Command investigation	No violation

Document [10] Second Report of the Committee of Experts

A/HRC/16/24

Advance Unedited Version

Distr.: General
18 March 2011

Original: English

Human Rights Council
Sixteenth session
Agenda item 7
Human rights situation in Palestine and other occupied Arab territories

Report of the Committee of independent experts in international humanitarian and human rights law established pursuant to Council resolution 13/9*

> *Summary*
>
> This report is submitted to the Human Rights Council pursuant to its resolution 15/6, which "renews and resumes" the mandate of the Committee established in Human Rights Council resolution 13/9. The Committee sought to assess investigations for compliance with international standards of independence, impartiality, effectiveness, thoroughness and promptness. In attempting to fulfill its renewed mandate, the Committee reviewed numerous documents, reports and articles submitted by non-governmental organizations, and held interviews with representatives of governmental and non-governmental organizations, as well as with Israeli and Palestinian victims and witnesses. The Committee undertook one field mission to Amman to interview relevant actors, including Government officials and human rights advocates. The Committee was not granted access to Israel, the West Bank, or Gaza.

---

* Late submission.

GE.11-

Contents

		Paragraphs	Page
I.	Introduction	1–5	
II.	Mandate and methodology of work	6–22	
	A. Mandate	6–8	
	B. Methodology	9–22	
III.	Applicable law and standards	23	
IV.	The Government of Israel	24–48	
	A. Investigations conducted	24–39	
	B. Assessment	40–46	
	C. Allegations not investigated	47–48	
V.	The Palestinian side	49–63	
	A. The Palestinian Authority	49–59	
	B. The de facto Gaza authorities	60–63	
VI.	Other issues of concern	64–76	
VII.	Conclusions	77–90	

I. Introduction

1. The Human Rights Council, in resolution 13/9, decided, in the context of the follow-up to the report of the International Independent Fact-Finding Mission (hereinafter FFM report),[1] "to establish a committee of independent experts in international humanitarian and human rights laws to monitor and assess any domestic, legal or other proceedings undertaken by both the Government of Israel and the Palestinian side, in the light of General Assembly resolution 64/254, including the independence, effectiveness, genuineness of these investigations and their conformity with international standards". In accordance with this directive, the Committee of Independent Experts (hereinafter the Committee) submitted its first report to the Council on 23 September 2010.

2. Thereafter, in resolution 15/6, the Human Rights Council determined "to renew and resume the mandate of the Committee of independent experts, established pursuant to Council resolution 13/9". The Council requested that the Committee submit its updated report to the Council at its sixteenth session.

3. The High Commissioner for Human Rights appointed Judge Mary McGowan Davis, former Justice of the Supreme Court of the State of New York and former federal prosecutor, as Chair of the Committee. The other member was Judge Lennart Aspegren, formerly a Judge at the Svea Court of Appeal, Director-General for Legal and International Affairs at different Swedish Ministries, Justice at the Supreme Social Insurance Court, and Judge at the United Nations International Criminal Tribunal for Rwanda.

4. The Office of the High Commissioner for Human Rights (OHCHR) established a Secretariat to support the Committee.

5. The present report is submitted to the Human Rights Council pursuant to its resolution 15/6.

II. Mandate and methodology

A. Mandate

6. The Committee, in its initial report to the Human Rights Council of 23 September 2010,[2] interpreted its mandate by reading Human Rights Council resolution 13/9 in conjunction with General Assembly resolution 64/254, in which the General Assembly reiterated its call upon the Government of Israel and the Palestinian side to conduct investigations "that are independent, credible and in conformity with international standards into the serious violations of international humanitarian and international human rights law reported by the [United Nations] Fact Finding Mission [on the Gaza conflict] towards assuring accountability and justice". As set forth in that report, the Committee understood "domestic, legal or other proceedings" to refer to investigations, disciplinary proceedings and prosecutions undertaken by either military or civil justice systems in Israel and on the Palestinian side. Although the Committee's primary focus was on proceedings related to the serious violations alleged in the FFM report, it determined that its mandate was not restricted to these events and that it could review proceedings pertaining to "any incident connected to the military operations in Gaza". Thus, the Committee also looked into

---

[1] A/HRC/12/48 of 25 September 2009.
[2] A/HRC/15/50 of 23 September 2010.

specific legal issues of institutional responsibility and reform processes relative to the legal regime of armed conflict in the aftermath of these operations, which Israel codenamed "Operation Cast Lead".

7. Regarding the temporal scope of the mandate, the Committee considered that any proceedings initiated by Israel or the Palestinian side that commenced on or after 18 December 2008 were relevant to its task. For the current phase of its work, the Committee has focused in particular on identifying and analyzing relevant information issued or released since the filing of its first report in September 2010.

8. Taking into account that Human Rights Council resolution 15/6 "renews and resumes" the mandate of the Committee, the Committee understands its current mandate to be exactly as previously defined and reported to the Council.

B. Methodology

9. Following the renewal of its mandate, the Committee updated its Terms of Reference in order to reflect its approach to the assignment given to it by the Council. The Committee further established its working methodology.

10. Specifically, the Committee sought to discharge its mandate by analyzing information in the public domain and by supplementing this information through consultations with identified stakeholders. As detailed below, the Committee consulted with relevant authorities, including diplomatic representatives from Israel and the Palestinian Authority, as well as with officials of the Palestinian Authority and the de facto authorities in Gaza.

11. The Committee also undertook a mission to Amman on 20-21 February 2011 to meet with Palestinian officials and NGOs. While the Committee had planned to carry out a separate mission to Gaza, it was unable to gain access to Gaza through Israel, due to the lack of authorization from the Government of Israel, or through Egypt, in view of the security situation prevailing there during the weeks preceding preparation of the present report.

12. The Committee continues to view the relevant government authorities as among the most important sources of information about the progress of investigations called for by the General Assembly and sought their cooperation from the initial stages of its work.

13. On 13 January 2011, the Committee wrote to the Permanent Representative of Israel seeking a meeting and met with him on 26 January 2011. Although the Permanent Representative received the Committee members most cordially, he explained that it was the Government of Israel's policy to refuse to cooperate with any aspect of the "Goldstone process". Further, he relayed his Government's denial of the Committee's request for permission to enter Israel in order to speak to government officials and victims of rocket attacks launched from Gaza, and to access the West Bank and Gaza through Israel to interview victims and relevant authorities with respect to the operations in Gaza. The Committee sent another letter to the Permanent Representative on 27 January 2010, expressing the hope that Israel would reconsider its stated policy of non-cooperation, including by providing access to official information related to ongoing and completed investigations undertaken by Israel in relation to the events described in the FFM report.

14. On 13 January 2011, the Committee wrote to the Permanent Representative of the Permanent Observer Mission of Palestine seeking a meeting and on 26 January 2011 the Committee met with him. With the assistance of the Permanent Observer Mission, the Committee held discussions in Amman with the Minister of Justice, the General Prosecutor, and the Chairman and two members of the Palestinian Independent Investigation

Commission (PIIC) established pursuant to the FFM report. As a follow-up to these discussions, on 3 March 2011, the Committee wrote to the General Prosecutor and the Minister of Justice requesting additional information. On 10 March 2011, the Minister of Justice submitted supplemental materials. Likewise, the General Prosecutor forwarded documents on 10 March 2011 related to criminal investigations undertaken by his office. The Committee also held a teleconference on 10 March 2011 with members of the Palestinian Independent Commission for Human Rights (hereinafter PICHR).

15. The Committee is grateful to the Palestinian Authority for the extensive cooperation provided throughout its term.

16. Finally, to obtain the fullest information available on investigations undertaken by the Palestinian side, the Committee contacted the de facto authorities in Gaza on 24 February 2011 requesting specific information on investigations undertaken in response to the FFM report. On 8 March 2011, the de facto authorities asked the Committee for additional time in which to submit the information and the Committee agreed to extend the deadline. The de facto Gaza authorities sent a document on 13 March, with two annexes, in response to the Committee's detailed list of questions.

17. The experience of NGOs that have filed complaints and lawsuits on behalf of victims or have defended clients in Palestinian and Israeli civil, criminal and military courts offers an important perspective on the operation of investigative mechanisms. The Committee, therefore, met with a number of NGO representatives in Geneva on 27 January 2011 and in Amman on 20-21 February 2011. NGOs also made written submissions to the Committee and during teleconferences with the Committee members further documented incidents they had brought to the attention of authorities in Israel and on the Palestinian side.

18. The Committee also interviewed Israeli and Palestinian victims and witnesses. On 9 March 2011, the Committee held a video-teleconference with Israeli victims and witnesses, who provided information on the human and material damage suffered as a direct consequence of rocket attacks launched from the Gaza Strip. These individuals described their injuries and the continuing physical and psychological effects of living near the border in constant apprehension of further attacks. They also noted their complete inability to gain redress for these crimes. On 14 March, another Israeli victim spoke to members of the Committee by teleconference.

19. On 15 March 2011, the Committee held video-teleconferences with Palestinian victims, who recounted their first-hand experience with Israeli criminal investigations into incidents reported by the FFM. These witnesses detailed their frustration with the Israeli investigating authorities and gave articulate voice to their perception that Israeli justice mechanisms were completely ineffective and non-existent. Although these victims and witnesses had suffered serious injuries during Operation Cast Lead and had cooperated fully with investigators, after two years they have heard absolutely nothing with respect to the status of their cases – apart from one family that had learned in an official government report that the criminal investigation into the killing of their young children had been closed without elucidation of the circumstances that led to such a tragedy.

20. On 25 February 2011, the Committee held a teleconference with Mr. Noam Shalit, who reminded the Committee of the continuing isolation and captivity of his son, Gilad Shalit, who has had no communication with his family, nor has he been allowed visits by the International Committee of the Red Cross to monitor his detention conditions since he was captured and detained during an incursion into Israel in June 2006. Mr. Shalit expressed concern about the psychological and physical well-being of his son after five years in detention and appealed for his immediate release.

21. The totality of this information has provided the basis for the Committee's efforts to implement its mandate "to assess domestic, legal or other proceedings undertaken by Israel and the Palestinian side."

22. The Committee carried out its work under considerable challenges and constraints. In particular, given that the Committee did not travel to Israel, the West Bank or Gaza, it was unable to meet with a number of persons who could have supplied first-hand, updated information as to the status and impact of investigations and legal proceedings undertaken by the respective parties into the violations alleged in the FFM report. Moreover, the Committee worked under strict time limitations in order to meet the timeframe imposed on it by the Human Rights Council.

III. Applicable law and standards

23. In its previous report to the Human Rights Council,[3] the Committee extensively analyzed the legal framework and standards applicable in the context of the Committee's mandate. In the Committee's view, that legal analysis remains valid and does not require further elaboration.

IV. The Government of Israel

A. Investigations conducted

1. Military Operations in Gaza

24. According to available information, the Government of Israel has conducted some 400 command investigations in relation to Operation Cast Lead. Reports indicate that the Israeli Military Advocate General (MAG) has opened 52 criminal investigations into allegations of wrongdoing.[4] Of these 52 investigations, thus far three cases have been submitted to prosecution; two have resulted in convictions, while the trial of one case is still ongoing.

25. Focusing on incidents discussed in the previous report, the Committee could ascertain significant changes in the status of only two cases since September 2010. The first change concerns the completed inquiry into the alleged shooting and killing of Matar Abu Halima Muhammad (aged 17) and Hekmat Abu Halima (aged 16), and the wounding of Omar Abu Halima, on 4 January 2009.[5] The incident reportedly occurred as the young men were transporting wounded family members to the hospital and after they had complied with soldiers' orders to stop.[6] Notwithstanding difficulties created by discrepancies in testimonies given by IDF soldiers, the MAG ultimately concluded that the soldiers "acted lawfully in light of a perceived threat".[7] In addition, an apparently extensive investigation into allegations that earlier on the same day the family home had been hit by a white phosphorous shell, killing five and injuring four – which included interviews with family members present at the time of the alleged shelling, consultations with technical experts,

---

[3] A/HRC/15/50 of 23 September 2010.
[4] IDF, Interview with the Deputy Military Advocate for Operational Affairs, article dated 9 March 2011, available at http://www.mag.idf.il/163-4544-en/patzar.aspx, accessed on 14 March 2011.
[5] FFM report, paras. 788-801.
[6] FFM report, para. 800.
[7] IDF, Interview with the Deputy Military Advocate for Operational Affairs, article dated 9 March 2011, available at http://www.mag.idf.il/163-4544-en/patzar.aspx, accessed on 14 March 2011.

and review of medical records – ended with the determination that "it was unclear what ammunition had hit the house and who had launched it."[8]

26. The second case refers to the killing of Majda and Rayya Hajaj.[9] The Committee learned that a soldier was indicted before a military court on charges of manslaughter in relation to the deliberate targeting of an individual waving a white flag, without orders or authorization to do so.[10] The indictment reportedly refers to the death of an unknown person, as the evidence gathered did not establish sufficient connections[11] between the information provided in Palestinian testimonies – that the shooting victims at Juhr ad Dik on January 4, 2009 were the two Hajaj women – and the admissions made by the soldier – which referred to the killing of a single man. According to media reports, the trial was opened on 1 August 2010 but the reading of the indictment was immediately postponed at the request of the defense,[12] which demanded that the trial be suspended while the Military Police pursue allegations that an IDF officer had attempted to block the investigation by not submitting the results of a probe into the incident to his superior officers and to the MAG.[13] The trial is currently in recess while the authorities investigate further.

27. The Committee does not have sufficient information to establish the current status of the on-going criminal investigations into the killings of Ateya and Ahmad Samouni, the attack on the Wa'el al-Samouni house and the shooting of Iyad Samouni. This is of considerable concern: reportedly 24 civilians were killed and 19 were injured in the related incidents on 4 and 5 January 2009.[14] Furthermore, the events may relate both to the actions and decisions of soldiers on the ground and of senior officers located in a war room, as well as to broader issues implicating the rules of engagement and the use of drones. There are also reports indicating that the MAG's decision to investigate was opposed by the then Head of the IDF Southern Command.[15] Media reports further inform that a senior officer, who was questioned "under caution"[16] and had his promotion put on hold,[17] told investigators that he was not warned that civilians were at the location.[18] However, some of those civilians had been ordered there by IDF soldiers from that same officer's' unit and air

---

[8] FFM paras. 791 and 792. The FFM concluded that it could not "make any determination as to whether the shelling of the Abu Halima house was a direct attack against a civilian objective, an indiscriminate attack or a justifiable part of the broader military operation."

[9] Killing of Majda and Rayya Hajaj, FFM report, paras. 764-769. This case relates to the alleged killing of two women, who were reportedly part of a group of people seeking to evacuate. The group was walking down a road with two white flags when they came under fire from soldiers approximately 120 metres away. The Hajaj family found the bodies of Majda and Rayya Hajaj under the rubble when they were able to return to Juhr ad-Dik on the evening of 18 January 2009.

[10] The Official Blog of the IDF, http://idfspokesperson.com, posted on 6 July 2010, accessed on 13 March 2011.

[11] The Official Blog of the IDF, http://idfspokesperson.com, posted on 6 July 2010, accessed on 13 March 2011.

[12] YNET, 1 August 2010, available at http://www.ynetnews.com, accessed on 13 March 2011.

[13] The Jerusalem Post, 18 Nov 2010, available at http://www.jpost.com, accessed on 13 March 2011.

[14] FFM report, paras. 706 to 744

[15] Israel colonel 'quizzed over deadly raid', 22 October 2010, available at http://www.google.com/hostednews/afp/article/ALeqM5gZ9FAI2Hq2nuE7K0oapiunq-5Y5Q?docId=CNG.2f057538640f1e680daa7203d3609eff.521, accessed on 17 March 2011.

[16] Ynet, 22 October 2010, IDF Commander questioned over Gaza killing, available at http://www.ynetnews.com/articles/0,7340,L-3973310,00.html, accessed on 20 January 2011.

[17] Ynet, 22 October, IDF Commander questioned over Gaza killing, available at http://www.ynetnews.com/articles/0,7340,L-3973310,00.html, accessed on 20 January 2011.

[18] Haaretz, 22 October 2010, IDF probes top officers on Gaza war strike that killed 21 family members, available at http://www.haaretz.com/print-edition/news/idf-probes-top-officers-on-gaza-war-strike-that-killed-21-family-members-1.320505, accessed on 14 March 2011.

force officers reportedly informed him of the possible presence of civilians.[19] Despite allegedly being made aware of this information, the officer apparently approved air strikes[20] that killed 21 people and injured 19 gathered in the al-Samouni house. Media sources also report that the incident has been described as a legitimate interpretation of drone photographs portrayed on a screen[21] and that the special command investigation, initiated ten months after the incidents,[22] did not conclude that there had been anything out of the ordinary in the strike.[23] As of 24 October 2010, according to media reports, no decision had been made as to whether or not the officer would stand trial.[24] The same officer who assertedly called in the strike reportedly insisted that ambulances not enter the sector under his control, fearing attempts to kidnap soldiers.[25]

28. The Committee notes that the MAG is apparently reviewing the completed special command investigation into the treatment of Palestinian detainees and is evaluating whether criminal or disciplinary measures are necessary. The Committee understands that this command investigation examined broad issues related to the treatment of Palestinian detainees,[26] including those related to the Al-Atatra sandpit,[27] and that specific allegations of torture and ill-treatment remain under investigation by the Military Police.[28]

29. The Committee has discovered no information relating to four incidents referred to in the FFM report: incident AD/02;[29] incident AD/06;[30] the attack on the Al-Quds

---

[19] Haaretz, 22 October 2010, IDF probes top officers on Gaza war strike that killed 21 family members, available at http://www.haaretz.com/print-edition/news/idf-probes-top-officers-on-gaza-war-strike-that-killed-21-family-members-1.320505, accessed on 14 March 2011.
[20] Ynet, 22 October 2010, IDF Commander questioned over Gaza killing, available at http://www.ynetnews.com/articles/0,7340,L-3973310,00.html, accessed on 20 January 2011.
[21] Haaretz, 24 October 2010, What led to IDF bombing of house full of civilians during the Gaza war?, available at http://www.haaretz.com/news/diplomacy-defense/what-led-to-idf-bombing-house-full-of-civilians-during-gaza-war-1.320816, accessed on 14 March 2010
[22] "Gaza operations investigations: an update, January 2010" (A/64/651, annex I), paragraph 124, page 26. This command investigation was initiated to assess certain allegations in the FFM report.
[23] Haaretz, 22 October 2010, IDF probes top officers on Gaza war strike that killed 21 family members, available at http://www.haaretz.com/print-edition/news/idf-probes-top-officers-on-gaza-war-strike-that-killed-21-family-members-1.320505, accessed on 14 March 2011.
[24] Haaretz, 24 October 2010, What led to IDF bombing of house full of civilians during the Gaza war?, available at http://www.haaretz.com/news/diplomacy-defense/what-led-to-idf-bombing-house-full-of-civilians-during-gaza-war-1.320816, accessed on 14 March 2010
[25] Haaretz, 24 October 2010, What led to IDF bombing of house full of civilians during the Gaza war?, available at http://www.haaretz.com/news/diplomacy-defense/what-led-to-idf-bombing-house-full-of-civilians-during-gaza-war-1.320816, accessed on 14 March 2010
[26] The command investigation reportedly makes recommendations to improve the way the IDF manages issues related to detainees including detention conditions, questioning of detainees and the documentation of related operations.
[27] FFM report, paras. 1112-1176. This incident refers to a series of alleged violations related to the detention of a group of Palestinians in Gaza and Israel, including torture, cruel, inhuman and degrading treatment and denial of due process. The FFM reports that a group men, women and children people were detained in Al-Atatra on 5 January and held in three trenches dug in a pit surrounded by barbed wire and sand about three metres high. Tanks were inside the pit, one firing occasionally. On 8 January 2009 the women and children were released and the men taken to a pit at Izokim barracks. On 9 January 2009, the detainees from Al-Atatra, possibly as many as 65, were taken to prison in Israel. Reportedly all were eventually released.
[28] IDF, Interview with the Deputy Military Advocate for Operational Affairs, 9 March 2011, available at http://www.mag.idf.il/163-4544-en/patzar.aspx, accessed on 14 March 2011.
[29] FFM report, paras. 1127-1142.
[30] FFM report, para. 1107.

hospital;[31] and the attack on the Al-Wafa hospital.[32] Nor has the Committee uncovered updated information concerning the status of the criminal investigations into the death of Mohammed Hajji and the shooting of Shahd Hajji and Ola Masood Arafat;[33] and the shooting of Ibrahim Juha.[34] Accordingly, the Committee remains unable to determine whether any investigation has been carried out in relation to those incidents.

30. The Committee also conducted an assessment of specific inquiries into the use of human shields that were not explicitly mentioned in the FFM report. The Committee recalls that the Government of Israel reported that the MAG has directly referred for criminal investigation all allegations that civilians were used as human shields or compelled to take part in military operations.[35] In his April 2010 report on children and armed conflict, the Secretary-General noted that the MAG was investigating reports of seven Palestinian children used by Israeli soldiers as human shields in three separate incidents during the Gaza conflict.[36] The outcome of the investigations into two of these incidents is unknown. The other investigation was opened in June 2009 on the instructions of the MAG following a complaint by Defence for Children International.[37] According to media reports, two soldiers forced a boy to search bags suspected of being booby trapped and were convicted of offenses including inappropriate behavior and overstepping authority.[38] Both soldiers were demoted and received suspended sentences of three months each.[39]

31. It should be noted that while some media reports described the conviction as a credit to the IDF, a former IDF deputy chief of staff reportedly said that the soldiers' criminal records should be cleared and that such events should be probed inside the units and not in interrogation rooms.[40] The boy's mother apparently indicated her disappointment over the decision to suspend the prison terms and expressed concern at the message that such a lenient sentence would send to IDF soldiers.[41] Reportedly, in the ruling, the actions of the soldiers were condemned by the judges, but they also gave weight to issues such as the contribution of the soldiers to Israel's security and their personal circumstances, as well as to their fatigue at the time, the unprecedented nature of the case, and that the soldiers did not seek to degrade or humiliate the boy. Evidently the court also indicated that any future such incidents would be dealt with more severely.[42]

32. The Committee does not have sufficient information to comment definitively on this judgment, although it is hard to square the apparent finding that the soldiers "did not seek to degrade or humiliate the boy" with evidence that they intended to put him directly in

---

[31] FFM report, paras. 596-629.
[32] FFM report, paras. 630-652.
[33] FFM report, paras. 745-754.
[34] FFM report, paras. 755-763. According to the report, Ibrahim Juha, 15 years old, was allegedly shot in the chest on 5 January 2009 by soldiers and died 6 hours later, whilst trying to walk to safety with his family and others, a group of approximately 70 people waving a white flag.
[35] Government of Israel, July 2010, para. 37, page 9.
[36] Report of the Secretary General on Children and Armed Conflict, A/64/742S/2010/181, para. 101.
[37] Press Release posted on the official blog of the IDF on 11 March 2010.
[38] Haaretz, Soldiers convicted of using boy, 11, as human shield during Cast Lead, 4 October 2010, available at http://www.haaretz.com/print-edition/news/soldiers-convicted-of-using-boy-11-as-human-shield-during-cast-lead-1.317008, accessed on 13 March 2011.
[39] Haaretz, IDF soldiers demoted after convicted of Gaza war misconduct, 21 November 2010, available at http://www.haaretz.com/news/diplomacy-defense/idf-soldiers-demoted-after-convicted-of-gaza-war-misconduct-1.325850, accessed on 13 March 2011.
[40] Available at www.ynetnews.com, 21 November 2010, accessed on 13 March 2011.
[41] Available at www.ynetnews.com, 21 November 2010, accessed on 13 March 2011.
[42] IDF, Interview with the Deputy Military Advocate for Operational Affairs, 9 March 2011, available at http://www.mag.idf.il/163-4544-en/patzar.aspx, accessed on 14 March 2011.

harm's way at grave risk to his life. The Committee is likewise mindful of other judicial decisions, such as the case of the soldier who was sentenced to a prison term of seven and a half months for stealing a credit card during the operation in Gaza, where a harsher penalty was imposed for acts that did not entail danger to the life or physical integrity of a civilian, much less to a nine year old child.

2. **West Bank**

33. The FFM analyzed the general situation in the West Bank and pointed to a series of incidents that were not directly related to the military operations in Gaza but nonetheless required investigation by Israel.[43] In its previous report, the Committee indicated that the record before it was silent as to whether or not Israel had conducted investigations into allegations of human rights violations in the West Bank, including in relation to the alleged use of force during demonstrations and violence by settlers at the time of the events in Gaza. Recent information indicates that Israel has in fact investigated fourteen such incidents, eleven of which were referred to in the FFM report.[44] Of those fourteen investigations, two criminal indictments have been filed, six investigations are ongoing, and six cases were closed without charges.

34. The first indictment refers to the alleged killing of ten year old Ahmed Husam Yusef Mousa in Ni'lin on 29 July 2008 by a member of the Israeli Border Police.[45] A second criminal indictment was filed in relation to an incident in which three members of the al-Matariyeh family were allegedly shot and injured by an Israeli settler in Hebron in December 2008.[46] However, the indictment was withdrawn in light of a Supreme Court decision requiring that the Prosecutor disclose information classified for national security reasons. The Prosecutor reportedly decided to withdraw the case after the defendant's attorney requested that the Court order that the information be revealed.

35. Concerning ongoing investigations, the Military Police and the Israeli police are carrying out parallel criminal investigations into the killing of Basam Abu Rahma on 17 April 2009 in Bi'lin.[47] He was allegedly killed by a high velocity tear gas canister shot at his chest during a peaceful demonstration against the Wall.[48] This incident was filmed and Mr. Rahma is reportedly seen standing on a small hill, clearly visible and not armed or otherwise posing a threat.[49] The Committee learned that the MAG ordered a criminal investigation after representations from the family's attorney that the issue would be raised with the Supreme Court and taking into account expert opinion based on viewing a film of the incident. An earlier decision not to launch a criminal investigation was apparently based on statements given by soldiers in the operational de-briefing.[50] According to media

---

[43] FFM report, paras. 1381-1440.
[44] Israel Ministry of Foreign Affairs, Israel's investigations of alleged incidents of misconduct in the West Bank, available at http://www.mfa.gov.il/NR/rdonlyres/0FA91C66-9A2D-4149-9B99-8D346442E697/0/IsraelsinvestigationsofallegedincidentsofmisconductintheWestBank.pdf, accessed on 14 March 2011.
[45] See FFM report, para. 1388.
[46] See FFM report, para. 1385.
[47] Israel Ministry of Foreign Affairs, Israel's investigations of alleged incidents of misconduct in the West Bank, available at http://www.mfa.gov.il/NR/rdonlyres/0FA91C66-9A2D-4149-9B99-8D346442E697/0/IsraelsinvestigationsofallegedincidentsofmisconductintheWestBank.pdf, accessed on 14 March 2011.
[48] See FFM report, para. 1395
[49] Ibid.
[50] B'tselem Press Release, 12 July 2010, available at http://www.btselem.org/english/press_releases/20100712.asp, accessed on 13 March 2011.

reports the decision to open a criminal investigation was announced in July 2010, more than one year after the incident.[51]

36. A criminal investigation is also reportedly being conducted into the killing of 'Iz a-Din Radwan Radwan al-Jamal on 13 February 2009 in Hebron. He was allegedly shot by soldiers as he was throwing stones at soldiers at a checkpoint from the roof of a house.[52] According to reports, the criminal investigation was opened following the finalization of a command investigation.[53]

37. Finally, an investigation by the military police was conducted into the alleged killing of Yasser Tmeizi by the IDF at Tarqumiyah checkpoint on 13 January 2009. The results of the investigation were apparently sent to the MAG in August 2009.[54] Reports indicate that, after almost two years, the results of the investigation are still under review by the MAG.

3. Other investigations

38. As the Committee indicated in its previous report,[55] the Government of Israel established a public commission – known as the Turkel Commission – to examine the maritime incident of 31 May 2010. The Commission – which includes two international observers – was mandated, inter alia, to examine the question whether the "mechanism for examining and investigating complaints and claims raised in relation to violations of the laws of armed conflict, as conducted in Israel generally, (…) conform with the obligations of the State of Israel under the rules of international law".[56]

39. The Committee considers that the work of the Turkel Commission is relevant to its own mandate, because it is evidence that Israel does have a mechanism for carrying out inquiries into decisions and policies adopted by high-level officials. The Committee has focused on the process and methodology adopted by the Turkel Commission, not on the substance of its analysis and conclusions. It notes that Commission members interviewed and actively questioned the Prime Minister, the Defense Minister, the Chief of General Staff, the Chief Military Advocate, members of Parliament, the Director General of the Ministry of Foreign Affairs, the Coordinator of Government Activities in the Territories, as well as representatives of human rights organizations. An analysis of the transcripts of the public hearings demonstrates that the Commission members – with active participation from the international observers – thoroughly examined the controversial legal and political issues presented for their consideration. The Turkel Commission issued Part I of its report, which dealt with the investigation into the flotilla incident, on 21 January 2011. Part II of the report, which will address the effectiveness of Israel's mechanism for investigations, will be issued later this year.

---

[51] Haaretz, IDF to probe death of Palestinian protester at West Bank rally, 12 July 2010, available at http://www.haaretz.com/news/diplomacy-defense/idf-to-probe-death-of-palestinian-protester-at-west-bank-rally-1.301484, accessed on 13 March 2011.

[52] Report available at http://www.btselem.org, accessed on 13 March 2011.

[53] Israel Ministry of Foreign Affairs, Israel's investigations of alleged incidents of misconduct in the West Bank, available at http://www.mfa.gov.il/NR/rdonlyres/0FA91C66-9A2D-4149-9B99-8D346442E697/0/IsraelsinvestigationsofallegedincidentsofmisconductintheWestBank.pdf, accessed on 14 March 2011.

[54] B'Tselem, "Void of Responsibility Israeli military policy not to investigate killings of Palestinians by soldiers", October 2010, p. 20.

[55] Paras. 36-38.

[56] Government Resolution of 14.6.2010, quoted in the Report of the Public Commission to Examine the Maritime Incident of 31 May 2010 (The Turkel Commission), part one, January 2011, p. 17.

B. Assessment

1. Independence and impartiality

40. The Committee noted in its previous report that Israel's military justice system provides for mechanisms to ensure its independence, in particular the fact that the MAG is not hierarchically subordinate to the Chief of General Staff and that his decisions are subject to review by the Attorney General and by the Supreme Court. The Committee has not received any new evidence that challenges this finding.

41. The Committee further noted that notwithstanding the built-in structural guarantees to ensure the MAG's independence, his dual responsibilities as legal advisor to the Chief of Staff and other military authorities, and his role as supervisor of criminal investigations within the military, raise concerns in the present context given allegations in the FFM report that those who designed, planned, ordered, and oversaw the operation in Gaza were complicit in international humanitarian law and international human rights law violations. It is notable that the MAG himself, in his testimony to the Turkel Commission, pointed out that the military investigations system he heads is not a viable mechanism to investigate and assess high-level policy decisions. When questioned by commission members about his "dual hat" and whether his position at the apex of legal advisory and prosecutorial power can present a conflict of interest under certain circumstances, he stated that "the mechanism is calibrated for the inspection of individual incidents, complaints of war crimes in individual incidents (…). This is not a mechanism for policy. True, it is not suitable for this."[57] Therefore, the Committee remains of the view that an independent public commission – and not the MAG's office – is the appropriate mechanism for carrying out an independent and impartial analysis, as called for in the FFM report, into allegations that high-level decision-making related to the Gaza conflict violated international law.

2. Promptness[58]

42. In its report of 23 September 2010, the Committee expressed strong reservations as to whether Israel's investigations into allegations of misconduct were sufficiently prompt. In particular, the Committee expressed concern about the fact that unnecessary delays in carrying out such investigations may have resulted in evidence being lost or compromised, or have led to the type of conflicting testimony that characterizes the investigations into the killings of Majda and Raayya Hajaj[59] and the inconclusive findings reported with respect to the tragic deaths of Souad and Amal Abd Rabbo and the grave wounding of Samar Abd Rabbo and their grandmother Souad.[60]

43. The Committee is fully aware of the difficulties involved in investigating alleged violations that occurred in a situation of combat, in particular when it comes to the collection of evidence, interviewing witnesses and victims, and the accurate establishment of the facts, often in the absence of sufficient forensic tools. Yet, while acknowledging the

---

[57] Testimony of the Chief Military Advocate General, Avichai Mandelblit, to the Turkel Commission, Session Number Four, 26 August 2010.
[58] In its previous report the Committee noted that as a general rule an investigation should commence and progress with reasonable expedition. Determining whether an investigation has met this standard of reasonableness depends on the specific circumstances of the case. The Committee against Torture suggests that the requirement to undertake a prompt investigation means that an investigation should be initiated immediately when there is a suspicion of torture or ill-treatment, namely, within hours or days. When examining the progress of investigations, frequent and unexplained adjournments can unacceptably compound delay. A/HRC/15/50 of 23 September 2010, para. 25.
[59] A/HRC/15/50 of 23 September 2010, para. 51.
[60] FFM report, paras. 770-779.

complexity and difficulty of the challenges presented to investigators in the wake of the numerous allegations of wrongdoing by IDF soldiers during the Gaza conflict, it is worth noting that out of 36 incidents related to Gaza referred to in the Committee's previous report, more than one-third remain unresolved or with an unclear status two years after the events took place. That situation raises serious concern as to whether the existing mechanisms are capable of insuring that investigations are conducted in a prompt manner. Presumably this is an issue that is under careful review by the Turkel Commission and will be addressed in Part II of its report.

44. The promptness of an investigation is closely linked to the notion of effectiveness. An effective investigation is one in which all the relevant evidence is identified and collected, is analyzed, and leads to conclusions establishing the cause of the alleged violation and identifying those responsible. In that respect, the Committee is concerned about the fact that the duration of the ongoing investigations into the allegations contained in the FFM report – over two years since the end of the Gaza operation – may seriously impair their effectiveness and, therefore, the prospects of achieving accountability and justice.

3. Transparency

45. The issue of the transparency of Israel's investigations is a concern that has been highlighted by a number of different sources and appears to be a matter of some dispute. Thus, in his testimony to the Turkel Commission, the MAG indicated that his office, as a matter of practice, regularly informs claimants and their attorneys about its decisions with respect to the outcome of an investigation. He emphasized that his office advises the complainants and their lawyers of the reasons why his office determines not to pursue a criminal investigation and makes available relevant evidence for their examination in case they wish to file a petition with the Supreme Court. The MAG concluded that from the standpoint of transparency, "despite the fact that there is no obligation according to the rules of warfare we in practice update, both the families as well as the applicants, the attorneys without superfluous delays."[61]

46. The Committee notes, however, that consistent reports from NGOs, victims and their legal representatives reflect that only on rare occasions do they actually receive information from the MAG concerning the status of investigations into their complaints. A number of organizations have informed the Committee that they often found out about the results of inquiries into cases they have filed on behalf of alleged victims either through the press or in the public reports issued by the Government of Israel. Indeed, the Committee received detailed, case-specific information concerning requests for information by different organizations – the great majority of which have gone unanswered. This situation raises serious questions concerning the effective implementation of the MAG's reported policy to assure transparency into the investigation process. Indeed, as pointed out by the MAG himself, such transparency is important to insure that victims have effective access to existing judicial mechanisms, in the form of petitions to the Supreme Court.

C. Allegations not investigated

47. The information available to the Committee suggests that not all allegations of violations identified in the FFM report have been adequately investigated. These include allegations related to higher level decisions about the design and implementation of the

---

[61] Testimony of the Chief Military Advocate General, Avichai Mandelblit, to the Turkel Commission, Session Number Four, 26 August 2010.

Gaza operation, including those related to the nature, objectives and targets of the Israeli military in that conflict.[62] The Committee has no new information leading it to change its view that Israel does not appear to have conducted a general review of doctrine regarding military targets. However, it has been informed of media reports suggesting that if criminal charges are brought as a result of the investigation into the al-Samouni case, it is possible that there will be deliberations on the broader question of the rules of engagement that obtained during Operation Cast Lead.[63]

48. Nor has the Committee uncovered information concerning investigations into certain alleged human rights violations committed in the West Bank, including allegations of torture, discrimination, lack of access to effective remedies, unlawful detention, violations of the rights to freedom of expression and to peaceful assembly, or alleged violations related to the removal of residency status from Palestinians.

V. The Palestinian side

A. The Palestinian authority

1. Investigations conducted

49. The Committee noted in its previous report that the Palestinian Authority established the Palestinian Independent Investigation Commission (PIIC) to follow-up on the implementation of the recommendations of the FFM report. The PIIC submitted its report to the Secretary-General in July 2010.[64] On 13 February 2011, the PIIC made a written submission to the Committee, in which it explained the measures taken since September 2010 to follow-up on its July 2010 report. In particular, the PIIC referred to its efforts to establish contacts with the Government of Israel and the de facto authorities in Gaza so as to have access to witnesses and victims and to inspect the sites of rocket attacks on Israeli territory. The PIIC indicated that it had not received a positive response either from Israel or from the de facto Gaza authorities. The PIIC, therefore, concluded that in light of the lack of access it was not in a position to provide any further update to its July 2010 report with respect to the rocket attacks on Israel launched from Gaza.

50. The Committee was advised that on 18 October 2010, the Council of Ministers of the Palestinian Authority established a Ministerial Committee to follow-up on the PIIC recommendations. The Ministerial Committee was mandated to issue recommendations to the Council of Ministers for the implementation of the PIIC report and submitted its report – a copy of which was made available to this Committee – to the Council of Ministers in February 2011.

51. The Ministerial Committee recommended a number of short-term strategies – which are to be implemented within two months of the adoption of the report. In particular, it called on the General Prosecutor to investigate any allegation of torture or ill-treatment in detention centers;[65] it recommended the immediate abolition of the protocol of cooperation between the Office of the Public Prosecutor and the Office of the Military Prosecutor,

---

[62] FFM report, Section C, paras. 1880-1895.
[63] Haaretz, IDF probes top officers on Gaza war strike that killed 21 family members, 21 October 2010, available at http://www.haaretz.com/print-edition/news/idf-probes-top-officers-on-gaza-war-strike-that-killed-21-family-members-1.320505, accessed on 14 March 2011.
[64] A/64/890 of 11 August 2010.
[65] The report further refers to decision 149 (2009) of the Ministry of Interior prohibiting the use of torture or ill-treatment by security services.

which authorizes the Military Prosecutor to conduct criminal investigations into offenses provided for in the Penal Code; it specified that civilians should not be subject to detention by the military justice system, but that all civilian detainees should be transferred to the ordinary civilian justice system; it urged the General Prosecutor to prosecute any official who refuses to implement a court decision, and that any such official should be dismissed from his functions; and it recommended that the Prime Minister issue clear directives instructing all relevant officials that clearance by security services is not a legal requirement for employment in the civil service. Instead, applicants may be requested to certify only that they have no criminal record.

52. With respect to long-term strategies, the Ministerial Committee proposed six recommendations: a) to establish a Constitutional Court to address issues related to conflicts of jurisdiction; b) to adopt an administrative courts act creating first and second instance administrative courts, with a view to insuring adequate access to justice and an effective remedy; c) to amend the prisons act to allow systematic oversight and monitoring by the Ministry of Justice; d) to enact the Palestinian criminal code; e) to amend the Palestinian code of criminal procedures to separate investigating functions from prosecution functions; and f) to adopt legislation to regulate the functioning of the military justice system, criminal offenses, criminal procedure and other issues related to jurisdictional scope of military justice.

2. **Assessment**

53. In its previous report, the Committee noted that the PIIC had undertaken independent and impartial investigations in a comprehensive manner. The Committee has received no new evidence to challenge this finding. Rather, to the contrary, the PIIC has persevered in attempting to investigate the rocket attacks on Israeli territory, as well as other violations allegedly committed in the Gaza Strip, but has not been provided access to interview the victims or to inspect the scene. Such limitation seriously hampers the adequate fulfillment of its mandate.

54. The Committee finds that since the adoption of the PIIC's report, implementation of the PIIC'S recommendations, in particular those related to the obligation to investigate and prosecute allegations of arbitrary detention, torture and ill-treatment, and extra-judicial killings,[66] has been limited. The General Prosecutor informed the Committee of specific examples of criminal investigations dating from 2008 and 2009 into suspected deaths of individuals detained by Palestinian security forces. He provided documentary evidence of one case in particular, in which five security officers were charged with the murder of an individual detained by the Palestinian security services. In the judgment, the military court acquitted the defendants of all charges in view of the fact that it could not clearly identify the actual perpetrator, but it determined that, at a minimum, the death had resulted from negligence on the part of the security services and, therefore, ordered the payment of compensation to the family of the deceased.

55. Despite this example, the Committee has received no information respecting the opening of criminal investigations or of prosecutions underway relating to incidents outlined in the FFM or in the PIIC report, since January 2010. For instance, the General Prosecutor provided a list of 326 criminal investigations carried out between 7 January 2010 and 7 March 2011. While this list reflects commendable efforts on the part of the Palestinian Authority to investigate criminal cases, these inquiries appear to be unrelated to the allegations in the FFM report. Accordingly, further efforts should be expended to systematically investigate allegations of extra-judicial killings, of torture and ill-treatment,

---

[66] See A/64/890 of 11 August 2010, paras. 464-465, at p. 173.

of unlawful detention, and re-arrests, and of the lack of implementation of Court orders directing the release of unlawfully detained individuals.

56. Notwithstanding the problems listed above, the Committee underscores that the establishment of the Ministerial Committee is a very welcome development. The Ministerial Committee's report lays down a road-map of short-term and long-term strategies that go squarely in the direction of implementing the PIIC's recommendations. Indeed, some positive developments have already taken place. For instance, information provided by the Minister of Justice indicates that on 15 January, 2011 a decision was made by the General Prosecutor, the Military Prosecutor and Palestinian security services to transfer all cases of civilians being tried before military courts to domestic criminal courts for prosecution. This change in policy was confirmed by the Palestinian Independent Human Rights Commission (PIHRC). The PIHRC represented to the Committee on 10 March 2011, that since 15 January 2011, no new cases against civilians have been brought before military courts, but it noted that the transfer of existing cases before military courts to civilian courts has still not been fully implemented.

57. Moreover, the General Prosecutor has adopted new rules relating to the monitoring of places of detention by his office.[67]

58. To underscore the importance of these changes and assure that they are implemented throughout the West Bank, the Ministerial Committee recommended that the Palestinian President and the Prime Minister should issue timely and clearly defined instructions to all security, judicial and executive services ordering the strict observance of the existing legal framework so that changes that have been accomplished at the policy level actually have consequences in practice. The Committee notes with concern that, according to the PIHRC monthly reports, allegations of torture and ill-treatment remained at the same level in the West Bank throughout 2010 and the beginning of 2011. Therefore, much more needs to be done to effectively implement the necessary measures indicated above.

59. Finally, the Committee is of the view that the strengthening of the PIHRC proposed by the Ministerial Committee could indeed contribute to insuring the effective monitoring and implementation of the PIIC's and the Ministerial Committee's recommendations within the established timeframe.

B. The de facto Gaza authorities

60. The Committee requested updated information from the de facto Gaza authorities with respect to measures they have taken in response to the FFM report since September 2010.

61. In their response, the de facto authorities informed the Committee that their officials did not have access to persons involved in the launching of rockets and mortars into Israel, nor to the sites and victims that had been affected by the rockets. The de facto authorities also indicated that since 30 October 2008 all political prisoners have been released. In an annex, the de facto authorities provided a list of 32 names of political prisoners that have reportedly been liberated. The de facto authorities stated that all persons currently under detention are under criminal investigation or have been sentenced to prison terms.

---

[67] The Committee was informed by the General Prosecutor that his office now conducts regular visits to both civilian and military detention facilities to monitor the treatment of detainees and the conditions of detention.

Document [10] Second Report of the Committee of Experts

A/HRC/16/24

62. Finally, the de facto authorities provided a list of seven cases related to investigations into allegations of torture, injuries or extra-judicial killings. According to the information, four out of those seven cases were discontinued at the request of the victim.[68] Of the remaining three cases, one investigation into ill-treatment is still ongoing and two prison sentences were imposed in relation to killings. The de facto authorities provided a detailed list of those cases, including each victim's name, the name of the alleged perpetrator, the description of the charges, the date of commencement of the inquiry, the status of the investigation, and the description of the penalties imposed.

63. The Committee acknowledges the de facto authorities' effort to provide specific information related to criminal investigations into alleged human rights violations committed by their security forces. The Committee is aware of the fact that it is not uncommon for such cases to be resolved to the satisfaction of the families through out-of-court settlements. Nevertheless, the Committee remains concerned that no investigations have been carried out into the launching of rocket attacks against Israel. It considers that the de facto authorities should make genuine efforts to conduct criminal inquiries and to hold accountable those who have allegedly engaged in serious violations of international humanitarian law by firing these rockets.

VI. Other issues of concern

64. After nine months of working with the question of the implementation of the FFM report by Israel and the Palestinian side, the Committee considers it opportune to discuss several issues of concern that it has encountered in the implementation of its mandate and that directly relate to the FFM report's allegation that there is a "justice crisis" that warrants action.[69]

The current context

65. First, it should be noted that the current situation in Israel and the West Bank and Gaza remains tense. The Committee was informed that during the period between 10 December 2010 and 10 March 2011, 78 rockets and 96 mortars were launched against southern Israel, with the vast majority of these attacks taking place during the afternoon hours.[70] While this report was being prepared, a ship bound for the Gaza Strip bearing arms was intercepted by Israel[71] and a family in the West Bank was brutally murdered while asleep.[72] Palestinian civilians continue to be injured and killed by Israeli soldiers, and a 66 year old Palestinian man was killed "by mistake" as he slept in his bed in Hebron in January.[73] Meanwhile, Palestinian children are routinely arrested in the middle of the night

---

[68] Of those four cases, two referred to alleged ill-treatment and two to shooting incidents.
[69] FFM report, Chapter XXX, paras. 1874-1966.
[70] Letter to the Committee by the International Association of Jewish Lawyers and Jurists, dated 15 March 2011.
[71] Haaretz, Commandos stop boatload of arms headed for Gaza, 16 March 2011, available at http://www.haaretz.com/print-edition/news/commandos-stop-boatload-of-arms-headed-for-gaza-1.349438, accessed 17 March 2011.
[72] Human Rights Watch, West Bank: No excuse for murder of settler family, 12 March 2011, available at http://www.hrw.org/en/news/2011/03/12/west-bank-no-excuse-murder-settler-family
[73] Haaretz, IDF kills 65-year-old Palestinian man during raid on Hamas cell in Hebron, 7 January 2011, available at http://www.haaretz.com/news/diplomacy-defense/idf-kills-65-year-old-palestinian-man-during-raid-on-hamas-cell-in-hebron-1.335713

and taken off to military detention.[74] Settler violence against Palestinians and Palestinian violence against Israeli civilians continues in the West Bank. The harsh conditions imposed on Palestinians at checkpoints and border controls, often in humiliating circumstances, feeds the feeling of injustice among the civilian population.[75] As recently reported by the High Commissioner for Human Rights in her report covering the period 4 February to 30 November 2010, the situation is of profound concern and serious violations "occur on a widespread and persistent basis".[76] As stressed by the General Assembly in its resolution 64/254, there is a "need to ensure accountability for all violations of international humanitarian law and international human rights law in order to prevent impunity, ensure justice, deter further violations and promote peace".[77] The Committee believes that significant and sustained efforts from the parties concerned are required to insure accountability and justice.

Human rights defenders

66. Second, the Committee is keenly aware that human rights organizations play a vital role in any system of investigating and prosecuting allegations of violations of international law. The Government of Israel has acknowledged that the MAG himself considers the information provided by human rights defenders as an important part of his deliberations about incidents. It has further represented that the Military Police actively seek the help of human rights organizations and Israeli lawyers representing complainants in order to facilitate meetings between Israeli investigators and Gaza residents.[78] Other investigation mechanisms, such as the Turkel Commission, have also sought to obtain information from human rights organizations with respect to evaluating the humanitarian situation in the Gaza Strip. Similarly, both the PIIC and the de facto Gaza authorities report receiving valuable information from human rights organizations. The PIIC engages consultations with human rights and other civil society organizations and national figures in relation to its methods of work, potential difficulties, and how to resolve them.[79] The Committee itself has obtained invaluable information from NGOs in Israel, the West Bank, Gaza, Geneva, London and New York.

67. The FFM expressed concerns about allegations of hostile retaliatory actions directed at civil society organizations for criticism of the Israeli authorities and for exposing alleged violations of international human rights and humanitarian law during the military operations – concerns that appear to be increasingly valid.[80] The Committee has heard a constant refrain from NGOs about the deteriorating climate for human rights defenders in Israel and that this has had a negative impact on their ability to pursue their work. Specifically, the Committee has been informed about an initiative in the Knesset to launch a parliamentary inquiry probing human rights organizations, notwithstanding the Attorney

---

[74] In their own Words: A report on the situation facing Palestinian children detained in occupied East Jerusalem", Defence for Children International – Palestine Section, 3 February 2011.
[75] Haaretz, Machsom Watch activist: removing checkpoints doesn't remove the occupation, 15 February 2011, available at http://www.haaretz.com/print-edition/features/machsom-watch-activist-removing-checkpoints-doesn-t-remove-the-occupation-1.343471#send-friend-popup, accessed on 15 March 2011.
[76] A/HRC/16/71 of 3 March 2011, para. 55.
[77] A/RES/64/254 25 March 2010.
[78] Government of Israel, Gaza Operation Investigations: Second Update, July 2010.
[79] A/64/890, Annex II
[80] FFM report, para. 1767.

General's warning that such an inquiry could violate fundamental human rights.[81] Similarly, a bill to punish individuals who call for academic or economic boycotts against Israel was reportedly adopted in its first reading by the Knesset,[82] and there are efforts underway as well to discourage organizations that seek to hold IDF soldiers accountable for war crimes in international courts.[83]

68. The FFM also reported allegations that the security services of the Palestinian Authority had interfered with the work of journalists.[84] Further, the Committee has received information that the de facto authorities in Gaza, while generally tolerant of local human rights organizations,[85] have recently stated that the PIHRC is not legally qualified to work in Gaza.

69. Equally distressing are reports that victims who travel to Erez to meet with Israeli military investigators have been summoned for questioning about these contacts by the de facto authorities in Gaza.

70. Given this situation, the Committee wishes to remind all parties that the ability of human rights organizations to function freely and independently is crucial for the improvement of the domestic human rights situation in general, and for the effective functioning of accountability mechanisms in particular. Indeed, a democratic society based on the rule of law relies to some extent on the independent contribution that human rights defenders make.

The victims' right to justice and accountability

71. Third, and most importantly, the Committee recalls that General Assembly resolution 64/254 reiterates its call upon the Government of Israel and the Palestinian side to conduct investigations that are independent, credible and in conformity with international standards towards insuring accountability and justice.[86] During its work, the Committee was struck by the testimony of victims on both sides that justice has not been done, and their lack of confidence that it is ever likely to be done. For example, a Palestinian resident in Gaza told the Committee that investigations into Cast Lead Operation incidents "were superficial, not significant, and misleading to the international community. Despite our belief that the investigation was not serious we decided to appear and deliver testimony, out of a belief that we are civilians and innocent. But we also believed that in the end, we will end up with nothing. We were correct; the investigation carried out by Israel is just a game, nothing more."[87]

---

[81] Haaretz, Israel's Attorney General: Probing leftist NGOs infringes on human rights, 21 February 2011, available at http://www.haaretz.com/print-edition/news/israel-s-attorney-general-probing-leftist-ngos-infringes-on-human-rights-1.344684, accessed on 15 March 2011.

[82] Jerusalem Post, Anti-Boycott bill passes first reading in Knesset, 7 March 2011, available at http://www.jpost.com/DiplomacyAndPolitics/Article.aspx?ID=211188&R=R1, accessed on 15 March 2011; Haaretz, Israel's Attorney General: Probing leftist NGOs infringes on human rights, 7 March 2011, available at http://www.haaretz.com/news/national/bill-to-punish-anti-israel-boycotters-passes-first-knesset-hurdle-1.347734, accessed on 15 March 2011.

[83] See for example information available at http://www.acri.org.il/en/?p=1639, accessed on 17 March 2011.

[84] FFM report, para 1551.

[85] The Committee has also received information that the de facto authorities have taken measures against a broad range of civil society organizations, allegedly for involvement in Fatah affiliated political activities or immoral conduct.

[86] A/RES/64/254 of 25 March 2010.

[87] Video-conference of 15 March 2011.

72. One Israeli victim of rocket attacks expressed her frustration at the lack of justice and said, "I have no Court, no one to represent me, no one to sue. Is that real justice?"[88] She also articulated her disappointment with the international community: "I was disappointed [by the FFM] and found myself feeling more humiliated than ever before in my life because it seemed to me there was no mention of Israeli victims who, like me, have suffered for more than eight years the rockets and mortars, it seemed to me that no one wanted to issue a strong condemnation of terror coming from Gaza. Since that time I have lost faith in the international committees, especially the United Nations, as it seems no one is asking if I have a right to live."[89]

73. The Committee heard the respective parties' claims that their systems have established mechanisms to ensure accountability and justice. Yet, after listening to victims, witnesses and human rights organizations, it is clear that the needs of victims are not being adequately addressed. For example, while the Israeli system allows for Palestinian victims to file civil claims with the Supreme Court, the reality for Gaza residents is that, given existing restrictions preventing entry into Israel, their right to a remedy and reparation is limited in such a way as to render it virtually ineffective. A petition filed by a human rights organization points out that the existing two-year statute of limitations, and the number of obstacles to accessing Israel, effectively undermine any real prospect of obtaining justice.[90]

74. Similarly, victims on both sides continue to raise the question whether their right to obtain reparation will be adequately respected. This is not just a matter of law; this is, in the view of the Committee, a matter of the most basic principles of justice. When harm has been done, irrespective of the reasons and justifications for it, victims should be given the opportunity to be compensated for the damages suffered, whether physical, psychological, or patrimonial. The Committee notes the increasing practice of Member States carrying out military operations in different parts of the world to offer ex-gratia payments when direct or indirect damage is caused to civilians. Such practice is commendable and should, in the near future, constitute the norm rather than the exception.[91]

75. But above all, listening to the testimony, the Committee apprehended that many people continue to feel insecure, they carry the burden of injuries and disabilities, and struggle to live in difficult conditions. The Committee heard testimonies from mothers on both sides who are raising children suffering from post-traumatic stress disorder and who have to consider where they can run for shelter to protect their families.[92] The Committee

---

[88] Teleconference of 14 March 2011.
[89] Teleconference of 14 March 2011.
[90] See Palestinian Centre for Human Rights, Israel Effectively Denies Palestinian Victims of Operation Cast Lead Access to Justice: PCHR files petition to Israeli High Court of Justice, 12 December 2010, available at
http://www.pchrgaza.org/portal/en/index.php?option=com_content&view=article&id=7167:israel-effectively-denies-palestinian-victims-of-operation-cast-lead-access-to-justice-pchr-files-petition-to-israeli-supreme-court&catid=36:pchrpressreleases&Itemid=194, accessed on 16 March 2011.
[91] According to reports, for example, between 1 April 2009 and 31 March 2010 the Canadian military issued 272 ex-gratia payments - more than five per week. See the Canadian Encyclopedia, Canadian military payments for death and destruction in Afghanistan, 17 January 2011, available at http://www.thecanadianencyclopedia.com/index.cfm?PgNm=TCE&Params=M1ARTM0013580, accessed on 16 March 2011. See also reports that Germany has made ex-gratia payments to victims in Afghanistan, at http://freeinternetpress.com/story.php?sid=26575, accessed on 16 March 2011. For the United States' use of solatia and condolence payments see "The Department of Defense Use of Solatia and Condolence Payments in Iraq and Afghanistan", available at http://www.gao.gov/new.items/d07699.pdf, accessed on 16 March 2011.
[92] Teleconference Palestinian victims, 15 March 2011; teleconference with Israeli victims, 14 March 2011.

also received requests to assist people to rebuild in Gaza and is mindful of submissions it received about the destruction of environmental health related infrastructure there and the need for material to be allowed in to enable the civilian population to repair damage to wells and household water and sanitation systems.[93] The Committee considers that, for as long as victims – in Israel and in Gaza -- continue to lack confidence in the investigative processes, and continue to live in difficult and unsafe conditions, without remedy, there will be no genuine accountability and no justice.

VII. Conclusions

A. General conclusion

76. The Committee, in the course of its work since the adoption of Human Rights Council resolution 13/9, has monitored and assessed the different proceedings undertaken by the Government of Israel and the Palestinian side on the basis of available public information, contributions from government authorities, NGOs and other actors, and accounts from victims and witnesses. It considers that the analysis presented in this report completes and concludes its examination of the issues it was requested to address in resolution 13/9.

B. Israel

77. Although the Committee was able to access official information detailing the progress of some investigations by the Israeli authorities since September 2010, it relied largely on media reports and other secondary sources to inform its deliberations. The Israeli authorities' refusal to allow the Committee access to Israel and the West Bank, and access to Gaza through Israel, significantly constrained the Committee's ability to engage with key interlocutors.

78. That said, the Committee finds that Israel has dedicated significant resources to investigate over 400 allegations of operational misconduct in Gaza reported by the FFM and others. Given the scale of this undertaking, it is unsurprising that in 2011, much remains to be accomplished. The Committee is able to report that, to the best of its knowledge, nineteen investigations into the serious violations of international humanitarian law and international human rights law reported by the FFM have been completed by the Israeli authorities with findings that no violations were committed. Two inquiries were discontinued for different reasons. Three investigations led to disciplinary action. Six investigations reportedly remain open, including one in which criminal charges have been brought against an Israeli soldier. The status of possible investigations into six additional incidents remains unclear.

78. Furthermore, Israel has launched fourteen investigations into incidents related to alleged violations in the West Bank. Of those, two criminal indictments have been filed, six investigations are ongoing and six cases were closed without charges. The Committee did not receive any information concerning any other investigation of alleged violations committed in the West Bank, nor to investigations related to persons detained in Israel.

---

[93] Written submission by the Emergency Water, Sanitation and Hygiene group (EWASH) for the Occupied Palestinian Territory (OPT), March 2011.

79. The Committee reiterates the conclusion of its previous report that there is no indication that Israel has opened investigations into the actions of those who designed, planned, ordered and oversaw Operation Cast Lead.

80. However, the Committee notes the work of the Turkel Commission and its probing of some decisions and policies adopted by high-level officials in Israel. The Commission was able to interview and actively question high-level officials, including the Prime Minister, the Defense Minister, the Chief of General Staff, and the Chief Military Advocate, and examined questions related to the legality and the enforcement of the blockade on Gaza, as well as the question of whether the impact of the land crossings policy constitutes collective punishment. The Committee concludes that a public commission constitutes one of the mechanisms that Israel could use to assess high-level operational and legal decisions concerning the execution of the military operation in Gaza.

81. Concerns related to transparency and the participation of victims and witnesses in investigations reported by the Committee in its previous report continue to be relevant. NGOs, victims and their legal representatives have difficulty accessing information about progress in investigations. They report that the majority of their requests for information go unanswered. The Committee is of the view that transparency and participation help build the confidence of victims and other interested parties in the investigation process, including fostering a sense that credible and genuine investigations are taking place.

82. The Committee has strong reservations respecting the promptness of some investigations of individual incidents referred to by the FFM. More than one-third of the 36 incidents in Gaza are still unresolved or unclear. The status of investigations into incidents in Israel and the West Bank is also unclear. Presumably this serious issue respecting the ability of the military justice system promptly to investigate allegations of wrongdoing during military operations is under careful review by the Turkel Commission.

83. Finally, the Committee is concerned about the fact that the duration of the ongoing investigations into the allegations contained in the FFM report -- over two years since the end of the Gaza operation – could seriously impair their effectiveness and, therefore, the prospects of ultimately achieving accountability and justice.

C. The Palestinian side

1. The Palestinian Authority

84. In September the Committee reported that the investigation carried out by the PIIC conformed to international standards and could be considered credible and genuine. More recently the PIIC has sought to complete its mandate by investigating rocket and mortar attacks against Israel and other human rights violations in the Gaza Strip. The Committee was informed that the PIIC had been unable to do so, as it had not received positive responses to requests for access from either Israel or the de facto authorities in Gaza.

85. Nonetheless, the work of the PIIC did provide a solid basis for proceeding against perpetrators and developing other measures. In October 2010, the Council of Ministers of the Palestinian Authority established a Ministerial Committee with a mandate to issue recommendations to the Council of Ministers about implementation of the PIIC report. The report of the Ministerial Committee details strategies for significant institutional change over the next nine months, including the establishment of a Constitutional Court. The report also urges that the Prime Minister issue a directive that employment in the civil service not be dependent on security clearances, and that an ad hoc committee review past administrative decisions that led to dismissals. The Ministerial Committee further recommended that the General Prosecutor conduct criminal investigations into allegations

of extra-judicial killings in Gaza, and of incidents in which officials allegedly refuse to implement court decisions.

86. The Committee was also informed that a decision has been taken to transfer cases from military to civilian courts and that the office of the General Prosecutor now conducts regular monitoring visits to military and civilian detention facilities.

87. These proposals and changes are important developments. Nonetheless, the Committee is concerned that criminal accountability mechanisms have not yet been duly activated in relation to many of the allegations of serious violations in the FFM report.

2. **The de facto Gaza authorities**

88. In September 2010, the Committee stated it had been unable to substantiate reports that the de facto Gaza authorities had released all political prisoners or conducted criminal prosecutions, in response to the FFM report. The Committee also reported that two committees of inquiry had been established. However, one committee focused on allegations directed at Israel rather than on allegations directed at the de facto authorities. The other reported on measures to redress alleged violations but the information presented was not substantiated.

89. The Committee acknowledges that the de facto authorities have now made efforts to provide specific information concerning criminal investigations into alleged human rights violations committed by their security forces. The Committee is aware of the fact that it is not uncommon for such cases to be resolved to the satisfaction of the families through out-of-court settlements.

90. Nevertheless, the Committee remains extremely concerned by the fact that the de facto authorities have not conducted any investigations into the launching of rocket and mortar attacks against Israel. It considers that the de facto authorities should make serious efforts to conduct criminal inquiries into all the allegations of grave violations of international law implicated by these attacks.

Annex I

List of stakeholders consulted[94]

Diplomatic missions

Permanent Mission of the Arab Republic of Egypt to the United Nations in Geneva

Permanent Mission of Israel to the United Nations in Geneva

Permanent Mission of the Hashemite Kingdom of Jordan to the United Nations in Geneva

Permanent Observer Mission of Palestine to the United Nations in Geneva

Domestic authorities

Mr. Muhammad Abed	De facto authorities, Gaza
Judge Issa Abu Sharar	Palestinian Independent Investigation Commission
Dr. Mamdouh Aker	Palestinian Independent Human Rights Commission
Mr. Gandhi Aldube	Palestinian Independent Human Rights Commission
Mr. Muhammad Faraj al-Ghoul	De facto authorities, Gaza
Dr. Ali Kashan	Minister of Justice, Palestinian National Authority
Mr. Ahmed Mughani	General Prosecutor, Palestinian National Authority
Ms. Randa Siniora	Palestinian Independent Human Rights Commission

Non-governmental organizations

Adalah, Al-Haq, Al-Mezan, Amnesty International, Badil, B'Tselem, Cairo Institute for Human Rights, Defense for Children International, EWASH, Human Rights Watch, International Association of Jewish Lawyers and Jurists, Public Committee against Torture in Israel, Palestinian Centre for Human Rights, Physicians for Human Rights, UN Watch.

In addition, the Committee received submissions from: Al-Haq, Adalah, B'Tselem, EWASH, Hamoked, the Palestinian Centre for Human Rights, NGO Monitor.

International organizations

Office of the United Nations High Commissioner for Human Rights

---

[94] In light of the Committee's confidentiality policy, it should be noted that inclusion in this list was done on the basis of explicit authorization by the relevant party. Therefore, the list is not exhaustive and includes only those persons and organizations that authorized the Committee to be mentioned in the report.

Annex II

Table: Incidents in the report of the UN Fact-Finding Mission on the Gaza Conflict

Indiscriminate or deliberate killings

Incident	Paragraphs FFM report	Investigation body	Status
1. The killing of Ateya Samouni and his son Ahmad	706-735	Sixth special command investigation; MPCID	Ongoing
2. Attack on the Wa'el al-Samouni house	706-735	Sixth special command investigation; MPCID	Ongoing
3. Al Faqura Street massacre/al Deeb family	653-703	Special command investigation	No violation
4. Shooting of Iyad Samouni	736-744	Sixth special command investigation; MPCID	Ongoing
5. Death of Mohammed Hajji and shooting of Shahd Hajji and Ola Masood Arafat	745-754	MPCID	Ongoing
6. Shooting of Ibrahim Juha	755-763	MPCID	Ongoing
7. Killing of Majda and Rayya Hajaj	764-769	MPCID; military court	Ongoing
8. Khalid Abed Rabbo's daughters	770-779	MPCID	No violation
9. Shooting of Rouhiya al-Najjar	780-787	Command investigation; MPCID	No violation
10. Abu Halima family	788-801	MPCID	No violation
11. Attack on Al Maqadmah Mosque	822-843	Two special command investigations (January 2009 and November 2009)	Disciplinary action
12. Attack on Al Daya Family	844-866	Special command investigation	No violation
13. Attack on the Abd al-Dayem condolence tents	867-885	Command investigation; MPCID	No violation

Attacks on government infrastructure

Incident	Paragraphs FFM report	Investigation body	Status
14. Israeli air strikes on the Gaza main prison	366-392	Command investigation	No violation
15. Strikes on the Palestinian Legislative Council building	366-392	Unclear	Unclear
16. Arafat City police HQ	393-438	Command investigation	No violation
17. Deir Al Balah police attacks	393-438	Command investigation	No violation
18. Abbas police Station	393-438	Command investigation	No violation
19. Zeytoun police Stations	393-438	Command investigation	No violation
20. Al Shejaeiyah and al-Tuffah police station	393-438	Command investigation	No violation

Use of Palestinians as human shields

Incident	Paragraphs FFM report	Investigation body	Status
21. Abbas Ahmed Ibrahim Halawa	1064-1075	MPCID	No violation
22. Majdi Abed Rabbo	1033-1063	MPCID	Disciplinary action
22. Mahmoud Abd Rabbo Al-Ajrami	1076-1085	MPCID	No violation
24. AD/03	1086-1088	MPCID	Discontinued insufficient evidence

Arbitrary detention

Incident	Paragraphs FFM report	Investigation body	Status
25. Al Atatra incident	1112-1126	Sixth special command investigation	Under review by MAG
26. AD/02	1127-1142	MPCID	Unclear
27. AD/03	1143-1164	MPCID	Discontinued insufficient evidence
28. AD/06	1107	Unclear	Unclear

Use of harmful weapons			
Incident	Paragraphs FFM report	Investigation body	Status
29. Al Quds Hospital	596-629	Special command investigation	Unclear Possible disciplinary action
30. Al Wafa hospital	630-652	Special command investigation	Unclear Possible disciplinary action
31. UNRWA	543-595	Special command investigation	Apology, disciplinary action, compensation

Attacks on infrastructure and food production			
Incident	Paragraphs FFM report	Investigation body	Status
32. El Bader flour mill	913-941	Command investigation	No violation
33. Sawafeary chicken farm	942-961	Command investigation	No violation
34. Abu Jubba cement company	1012-1017	Command investigation	No violation

Attacks on water and sewage installations			
Incident	Paragraphs FFM report	Investigation body	Status
35. Gaza wastewater treatment plant	962-974	Command investigation	No violation
36. Namar wells group	975-986	Command investigation	No violation

Document [11] UN Human Rights Council Resolution 16/32

United Nations   A/HRC/RES/16/32

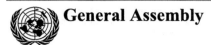

General Assembly

Distr.: General
13 April 2011

Original: English

Human Rights Council
Sixteenth session
Agenda item 7
Human rights situation in Palestine and other
occupied Arab territories

Resolution adopted by the Human Rights Council*

16/32
Follow-up to the report of the United Nations Fact-Finding Mission on the Gaza Conflict

The Human Rights Council,

Recalling its relevant resolutions, including resolution S-9/1, adopted on 12 January 2009, and resolution S-12/1, adopted on 16 October 2009, in follow-up to the human rights situation in the Occupied Palestinian Territory, including East Jerusalem, and the report of the United Nations Fact-Finding Mission on the Gaza Conflict,

Recalling also relevant General Assembly resolutions, including resolution 64/10, adopted on 5 November 2009, and resolution 64/254, adopted on 26 February 2010, in follow-up to the report of the Fact-Finding Mission,

Recalling further the relevant rules and principles of international law, including international humanitarian law and human rights law, in particular the Geneva Convention relative to the Protection of Civilian Persons in Time of War, of 12 August 1949, which is applicable to the Occupied Palestinian Territory, including East Jerusalem,

Recalling the Universal Declaration of Human Rights and other international human rights instruments, including the International Covenant on Civil and Political Rights, the International Covenant on Economic, Social and Cultural Rights and the Convention on the Rights of the Child,

Reaffirming the obligation of all parties to respect international humanitarian law and international human rights law,

Reiterating the importance of the safety and well-being of all civilians, and reaffirming the obligation to ensure the protection of civilians in armed conflict,

---

* The resolutions and decisions adopted by the Human Rights Council will be contained in the report of the Council on its sixteenth session (A/HRC/16/2), chap. I.

Stressing the need to ensure accountability for all violations of international humanitarian law and international human rights law in order to prevent impunity, ensure justice, deter further violations and promote peace,

Convinced that achieving a just, lasting and comprehensive settlement of the question of Palestine, the core of the Arab-Israeli conflict, is imperative for the attainment of comprehensive, just and lasting peace and stability in the Middle East,

Recalling the report of the Secretary-General submitted to the General Assembly pursuant to paragraph 6 of Assembly resolution 64/10,[1]

Recalling also the report of the Secretary-General on the status of implementation of paragraph 3 of section B of Human Rights Council resolution S-12/1,[2]

1. *Takes note* of the reports of the United Nations High Commissioner for Human Rights on the implementation of Human Rights Council resolutions S-9/1 and S-12/1,[3] and endorses the recommendations contained therein;

2. *Also takes note* of the reports of the committee of independent experts in international humanitarian and human rights law to monitor and assess any domestic, legal or other proceedings undertaken by both the Government of Israel and the Palestinian side, in the light of General Assembly resolution 64/254,[4] and calls for the implementation of its conclusions;

3. *Reiterates its call* upon all concerned parties, including United Nations bodies, to ensure the full and immediate implementation of the recommendations contained in the report of the United Nations Fact-Finding Mission on the Gaza Conflict, in accordance with their respective mandates;

4. *Regrets* the non-cooperation by the occupying power, Israel, with the members of the committee of independent experts, and its failure to comply with the calls of the Human Rights Council and the General Assembly to conduct investigations that are independent, credible and in conformity with international standards into the serious violations of international humanitarian and international human rights law reported by the Fact-Finding Mission, and calls on all the parties to the conflict including the Palestinian side, to take into account the conclusions of the committee;

5. *Welcomes* the efforts made by the Government of Switzerland, in its capacity as depositary of the Geneva Convention relative to the Protection of Civilian Persons in Time of War, to reconvene, as soon as possible, a conference of High Contracting Parties to the Fourth Geneva Convention on measures to enforce the Convention in the Occupied Palestinian Territory, including East Jerusalem, and to ensure its respect in accordance with common article 1, bearing in mind the statement adopted on 15 July 1999, as well as the reconvening of the conference and the declaration adopted on 5 December 2001, and recommends that the Government of Switzerland continue to pursue its efforts with the aim of resuming the above-mentioned conference before September 2011;

6. *Calls upon* the High Commissioner to follow up on the determination of the appropriate modalities for the establishment of an escrow fund for the provision of reparations to Palestinians who suffered loss and damage as a result of unlawful acts attributable to the State of Israel during the military operations conducted from December

---

[1] A/64/651.
[2] A/HRC/13/55.
[3] A/HRC/13/54 and A/HRC/16/71.
[4] A/HRC/15/50 and A/HRC/16/24.

2008 to January 2009, also taking into consideration Israelis who suffered loss and damage as a result of unlawful acts attributable to the Palestinian side;

7. *Reiterates its call* to the General Assembly to promote an urgent discussion on the future legality of the use of certain munitions, as referred to in the report of the United Nations Independent International Fact-Finding Mission on the Gaza Conflict, drawing on, inter alia, the expertise of the International Committee of the Red Cross;

8. *Recommends* that the General Assembly reconsider the report of the United Nations Fact-Finding Mission on the Gaza Conflict at its sixty-sixth session, and urges the Assembly to submit that report to the Security Council for its consideration and appropriate action, including consideration of referral of the situation in the Occupied Palestinian Territory to the prosecutor of the International Criminal Court, pursuant to article 13 (b) of the Rome Statute;

9. *Also recommends* that the General Assembly remain apprised of the matter until it is satisfied that appropriate action has been taken at the domestic or international level to ensure justice for victims and accountability for perpetrators, and also remain ready to consider whether additional action within its powers is required in the interests of justice;

10. *Requests* the Secretary-General to present a comprehensive report on the progress made in the implementation of the recommendations of the Fact-Finding Mission by all concerned parties, including United Nations bodies, in accordance with paragraph 3 of section B of Human Rights Council resolution S-12/1, to the Council at its eighteenth session;

11. *Requests* the High Commissioner to submit a progress report on the implementation of the present resolution to the Human Rights Council at its eighteenth session;

12. *Decides* to follow up on the implementation of the present resolution at its nineteenth session.

48th meeting
25 March 2011

[Adopted by a recorded vote of 27 to 3, with 16 abstentions. The voting was as follows:

In favour:
Angola, Argentina, Bahrain, Bangladesh, Brazil, Chile, China, Cuba, Djibouti, Ecuador, Gabon, Ghana, Jordan, Kyrgyzstan, Malaysia, Maldives, Mauritania, Mauritius, Nigeria, Pakistan, Qatar, Russian Federation, Saudi Arabia, Senegal, Thailand, Uganda, Uruguay

Against:
Slovakia, United Kingdom of Great Britain and Northern Ireland, United States of America

Abstaining:
Belgium, Burkina Faso, Cameroon, France, Guatemala, Hungary, Japan, Mexico, Norway, Poland, Republic of Korea, Republic of Moldova, Spain, Switzerland, Ukraine, Zambia]

Part III
Gaza and the International Criminal Court: The Legal Debate on the Admissibility of the Palestinian Declaration pursuant to Article 12(3) of the Rome Statute

Chapter 8
Why Statehood Now: A Reflection on the ICC's Impact on Palestine's Engagement with International Law

Michael G. Kearney

Contents

8.1	Introduction	391
8.2	De-Politicization and Human Rights Advocacy	393
8.3	From the Partition Resolution to the ICC	396
	8.3.1 The 1988 Declaration of Independence and Engagement with International Law	398
	8.3.2 The Palestinian Declaration to the ICC	401
8.4	The Fact-Finding Mission Report and the Pressures on the PA to Defer the Vote at the UN	403
8.5	Summary	405
References		407

8.1 Introduction

In 1947, a sub-committee of the General Assembly of the United Nations, by a majority of one, voted not to submit a request for an Advisory Opinion to the International Court of Justice. The question under consideration was as follows: 'Whether the United Nations, or any of its Member States, is competent to enforce or recommend the enforcement of any proposal concerning the constitution and future government of Palestine, in particular, any plan of partition which is contrary to the wishes, or adopted without the consent of, the inhabitants of Palestine.'[1]

Research Fellow in Law, London School of Economics, London.

---

[1] Elaraby 1968, p. 97.

M. G. Kearney (✉)
London School of Economics, London, UK

C. Meloni and G. Tognoni (eds.), *Is There a Court for Gaza?*,
DOI: 10.1007/978-90-6704-820-0_8,
© T.M.C. ASSER PRESS, The Hague, The Netherlands, and the authors/editors 2012

Since that decision, international law has orbited Palestine to varying degrees, and controversies of legal interpretation are increasingly seized upon by various parties to the conflict to stake or break claims.[2] Nonetheless, and despite a substantial and growing engagement by all parties to the conflict, both governmental and civil society, with the international legal framework, the conflict already underway in 1947 remains unresolved. Palestine continues to be subject to violence and occupation, denied a positive status in international law, and relegated to the periphery of the international legal framework. The wishes and consent of Palestinians continue to be ridden roughshod by an international community whose policy preference may be the emergence of a Palestinian state, but whose actions have consistently been to exclude Palestinians and Palestine from public international law.

The situation that has persisted since UN General Assembly Resolution 181 of 1947 allowed for the partition of Mandate Palestine may be summarized as one whereby Palestine—and Palestinians—are recognized as having legitimate claims underpinned by international law, but that given the particulars of the establishment of the state of Israel and its relationship with the great powers, if Palestinians wish to secure their independence then they must forfeit such claims and pursue political negotiations with Israel. These negotiations are premised on an assumption that Palestinians will compromise on their fundamental rights, accept the situation on the ground as dictated by Israel, and be grateful for whatever package the international community concludes is suitable for them.

Such an attitude has been most readily visible in the refusal of influential western nations to recognize the state of Palestine that declared independence and recognized the state of Israel in 1988. Refusing recognition has facilitated the continued exclusion of Palestine, despite the near unanimity that the emergence of a Palestinian state is a global policy priority, from the international legal framework, thereby radically diminishing the possibility that Palestine can seek redress through the legal institutions available to all other states.

The subsequent essays in this Volume will discuss the various legal arguments that have arisen in the wake of Palestine's submission of a declaration to the International Criminal Court in January 2009 [see *infra* Chapters 9 to 15—ChM]. The declaration sought to empower the Court to commence investigations into crimes within its jurisdiction that may have occurred on the territory of Palestine since 2002. Rather than discuss these arguments in any detail, this essay seeks to reflect on the sudden emergence in the international law discourse of a sustained debate on the question of statehood since, after all, the question of Palestinian statehood has been an issue of concern even before 1947.

It is stating the obvious to note that it was the declaration to the ICC that prompted the joining of a debate that for many decades was the concern of just a few scholars, but if the fundamental question of the legal status of Palestine has for so long being largely neglected in the advocacy of activists, diplomats, and

---

[2] For example, McHugo 2002, p. 851; Darcy and Reynolds 2010, p. 211; Shaw 2011, p. 301.

lawyers, one might ask why this has been so. The impact of 'Operation Cast Lead', the Report of the UN Fact-Finding Mission on the Gaza Conflict, and the declaration to the ICC, need to be considered in the context of undeniable increase in the 'legalization' of the diplomatic, cultural, political, and military aspects of the conflict.[3] Since the beginning of the second *intifada* in 2000, the emphasis in legal analysis of the conflict has moved from one primarily focused on individual violations of international human rights and humanitarian law to consideration of broader questions of public international law.

This paper aims to reflect, generally, on this development, by touching upon why a legal analysis fitted into a framework largely restricted to human rights and humanitarian law in the Palestinian territory occupied since 1967 is being expanded temporally and normatively to engage with the overarching politico-legal questions around statehood, colonialism, and self-determination that have for the most part remained in the background of legal analysis since Palestine's first encounters with the international legal framework under the aegis of the League of Nations.

8.2 De-Politicization and Human Rights Advocacy

Since the *Al Aqsa intifada* began in 2000, international law has come to play an ever more significant role in the Palestinian struggle for self-determination, to a point where senior Israeli politicians have asserted the necessity of confronting Palestinian engagement with the framework of international law as being one of Israel's foreign policy priorities 'over the coming decade.'[4] While Palestinian claims against Israel have long been rooted in the language of international law, the emphasis has tended to focus on securing the rights of individuals as set forth in the international bill of human rights. The collective right of Palestinians to self-determination as guaranteed under the bill of rights and the UN Charter has nonetheless been a fixed reference point, one continually reasserted as the underpinning collective right of the Palestinian people, whether in Israel, the territory occupied in 1967, or as refugees outside historic Palestine. Often, however, it can appear that this collective right, that encompasses the key issues in the so-called final status political negotiations, has been ceded by legal activists—scholars and NGOs—to the exclusive domain of historians and politicians.

Palestinian civil society, along with Israeli and international colleagues, emerged in large part to become the community it is today as the Cold War drew to a close. Advocacy based on human rights law steadily increased thereafter, struggling to inform the world of the violations and crimes that have characterized

---

[3] For example: Strawson 2010; D'Aspremont 2011; Kearney 2010a; Kattan 2009; Diamond 2010.

[4] Ayalon 2010.

the occupation, giving a face to the Palestinian people to an outside world that often blamed them for their own suffering. This civil society often—but not always as there does exist a significant diversity of NGO tactics and strategies—sought to establish itself as non-political, seeking to monitor, record, and document human rights violations in order to advocate for respect for human rights. It was a civil society that operated on mandates which limited advocacy to the particular jurisdiction within which various organizations operated. Thus in Israel civil society groups advocated before the Israeli courts for the rights of Palestinians in Israel within the realm of Israeli law and international human rights law. In the Palestinian territory occupied in 1967 Palestinian NGOs drew on the laws applicable under a regime of belligerent occupation, while in the Palestinian diaspora and refugee camps civil society groups were slower to formulate their claims in the language of international human rights law. This fragmentation of Palestinian engagement with the framework of international law is understandable given the myriad authorities, *de facto* and *de jure*, under which various elements of the Palestinian nation live, and the walls, fences, and borders that continue to divide them.

As part of the international human rights movement, Palestinian civil society often tended to avoid certain overarching questions of public international law which may have been implicitly understood as exclusively political, a tendency that was followed by legal scholars whose work can be regarded as having been shaped by the themes emerging from Palestine itself. The literature can be criticized as having overlooked questions such as the legal status of Palestine, the legality of the partition resolution, the status of territory declared by the same resolution to be part of the Palestinian state, yet which was on the Israeli side of the 1949 armistice lines, and the question of whether the occupation of the territory taken by Israel in 1967 is lawful or not.

Civil society as a mass force structured around NGOs emerged in Palestine at the 'end of history', within the context of the first intifada that had led to the negotiations between Israel and the PLO, and which in turn led to the establishment of the Palestinian Authority, whose *raison d'être* was to build the institutions of an independent state. In many respects this civil society came of age in the shadow of, and following the example set by the likes of Amnesty International and Helsinki Watch (today's Human Rights Watch), western liberal organizations that had championed human rights through the Cold War, whose emergence as influential and effective human rights advocates was built on their non-political stance. In this context overarching questions of public international law such as those cited above were ceded to the political elite of the PLO, which for the most part failed to engage as matters of international law, as opposed to politics, with the right to self-determination, the legality of prolonged occupation, continued transfer of settlers into occupied territory, charges of apartheid and colonialism, status of statehood, and so forth.

A critique did emerge warning that the switch from the mass mobilization and grassroots struggle of the first *intifada* to a liberal, depoliticized, and foreign-funded NGO-based civil society would result in the disempowerment of the

Palestinian masses,[5] insofar as a focus on the details of the occupation regime would necessarily overlook the fundamental questions of colonialism, the nature of Zionism, and the national liberation struggle as a whole. A contemporary example that may illustrate the limitation of human rights advocacy underpinned by an attempt to sharply distinguish between what is 'political' or what is 'human rights' can be seen in the ongoing refusal of Amnesty International or Human Rights Watch to engage in advocacy around the ongoing efforts to have the crime of aggression triggered in the Rome Statute of the ICC.[6] We may consider that Palestinian civil society's traditional reluctance—and by extension that of international lawyers writing on the application of international law to Palestine—to engage actively with legal questions pertaining to the partition resolution or the question of statehood, to be the result of seeking to fit within this established framework, leading to a wariness of losing their hard built reputations by appearing overtly politicized and partisan, and thereby losing the ability to have their objectivity respected.

The year 1967 is by most accounts the departure point for any examination of Israel and Palestine from the perspective of international law, with detailed commentary on the legal status of the territory on the Israeli side of the Green Line and of the refugees in surrounding states, for the most part absent. A significant example of this fitted approach may be found in what otherwise was a highly significant departure for Palestinian civil society in legal advocacy, namely the South African Human Sciences Research Council (HRSC) funded 2009 Report *Occupation, Colonialism, Apartheid?*[7] The Report (to which this author was a contributor) is notable in that it was one of the first substantial Palestinian civil society efforts to undertake legal analysis of the prevailing situation in Palestine that went beyond violations of international human rights and humanitarian law to question the very nature of the occupation regime itself, drawing as it did on the international law prohibitions of colonialism and apartheid. Such a discourse was already common in political analyses of the situation so in a sense the lawyers were playing catch up.[8] While otherwise including a fairly comprehensive review of legal questions applicable to Palestine, the HSRC Report limited itself temporally to post-June 1967, and geographically to the territory occupied in 1967. Such a limitation was in essence determined by logistics and resources, but nonetheless serves to demonstrate, how a study to which civil society gave a crucial input, and which moved the discourse from consideration of individual violations of human rights and humanitarian law, by seeking to present the occupation in light of highly political norms of international law that were otherwise very undeveloped, remained within the stock legal framework of the Green Line without pronouncing on the legality or otherwise of the occupation as a

---

[5] See for example Samara 2002 and Said 2001.
[6] See for example Schabas 2011.
[7] Tilley 2009, p. 57 (revised edition to be published by Pluto Press 2012).
[8] Although such themes do arise for example in Greenwood 1992.

whole. The HSRC Report also noted with respect to the question of Palestinian statehood that 'Examination of this topic is tangential to this study, however, because it is clear that the Palestinian territories are occupied and consequently that the Palestinian population is not effectively exercising sovereign rights or its right to self-determination.'[9]

In a similar vein, the Report of the UN Fact-Finding Mission on the Gaza Conflict, in seeking to provide an historical context to 'Operation Cast Lead', takes 1967 as its departure point explaining that: 'A review of the historical, political and military developments between the Six-Day War in 1967 and the announcement of the "period of calm" (Tahdiyah) in June 2008, and of Israeli policies towards the Occupied Palestinian Territory is necessary to consider and understand the events that fall more directly within the scope of the Mission's mandate.'[10] The limitations of the established legal discourse had been identified by Orna Ben-Naftali et al., who criticized the formula whereby analyses of Israel's occupation of the Palestinian territories tended toward a 'habitual focus on specific actions undertaken within the occupation, as distinct from the nature of the occupation as a normative regime'.[11]

8.3 From the Partition Resolution to the ICC

This essay proposes the need for further reflection on whether legal activists and civil society have refrained from revisiting significant political developments, from the partition resolution on, in a sort of deference to a political and legal orthodoxy, essentially seeing their role as to be understood as objective and forward looking, and thereby necessarily eschewing 'political' matters. The correctness of such a tendency was questioned by Nabil Elaraby (appointed Secretary-General of the Arab League in May 2011) in a 1968 essay entitled *Some Legal Implications of the 1947 Partition Resolution and the 1949 Armistice Agreements*. The essay began by noting that 'The legal aspects of the 1947 partition resolution may today appear merely academic, outdated events of the past, fit for oblivion and without relevance to the future. The future, however, is determined by the accumulation of past events, and no reasonable concern for the future can possibly exclude a firm grasp of past events.'[12]

Elaraby described the fate of the Palestinians as having been 'decided for them by the United Nations, to their detriment, without reference to the rule of law',[13] a situation which continues to prevail, as he noted as a judge at the ICJ: 'Decisions

---

[9] Tilley 2009, p. 57.
[10] Goldstone et al. 2009, para 176.
[11] Ben-Naftali et al. 2005, p. 552.
[12] Elaraby 1968, p. 97.
[13] Elaraby 1968, p. 97.

with far-reaching consequences were taken on the basis of political expediency, without due regard for the legal requirements.'[14] Of the various developments Elaraby's essay considers, perhaps the most salient to note is the vote on submitting the question of partition to the International Court of Justice for an Advisory Opinion highlighted at the outset. In 1947 the UN General Assembly established the Special Committee on Palestine (UNSCOP)[15] to prepare a Report that was studied by the Assembly's Ad Hoc Committee on the Palestinian Question. The UNSCOP Report made three recommendations, one of which was the submission of eight questions to the International Court of Justice for advisory opinions in accordance with Article 96 of the Charter and Chapter 4 of the Statute of the Court. Elaraby noted that 'The questions called for interpretations of commitments, obligations, and responsibilities growing out of the administration of Palestine under the League of Nations, and the competence of the United Nations to recommend partition or trusteeship for Palestine without obtaining the consent of the inhabitants.'[16] It was proposed specifically that the Court be asked to decide "Whether the United Nations, or any of its Member States, is competent to enforce or recommend the enforcement of any proposal concerning the constitution and future government of Palestine, in particular, any plan of partition which is contrary to the wishes, or adopted without the consent of, the inhabitants of Palestine." Elaraby considered the vote on these questions to be of considerable significance since they indicated that the legal aspects of the issues at hand 'were not clear in the minds of a substantial number of states'. Seven of the questions were defeated by 25 countries voting against while eighteen voted in favor and eleven abstained. The eighth question, pertaining to the power of the General Assembly to partition Palestine and quoted above, was defeated by twenty-one votes to twenty, with thirteen abstentions.[17]

Also in 1968, the PLO revised the Palestine Charter of 1964, though retaining its single reference to international law which provided that 'The partition of Palestine in 1947 and the establishment of the state of Israel are entirely illegal, regardless of the passage of time, because they were contrary to the will of the Palestinian people and to their natural right in their homeland, and inconsistent with the principles embodied in the Charter of the United Nations, particularly the right to self-determination.'[18]

---

[14] *Legal Consequences of the Construction of a Wall in Occupied Palestinian Territory*, Advisory Opinion, 9 July 2004, ICJ Rep 2004. Separate Opinion of Judge Elaraby para 1.
[15] UNGA Res I06, UN GAOR, 1st Spec Sess, Resolutions 6, UN Doc. A/3I0 (1947).
[16] Elaraby 1968, p. 101.
[17] Elaraby 1968, p. 97. 2 UN GAOR Ad Hoc Comm. on the Palestinian Question, Annex 25, at 300-01, UN Doc. A/AC.I4/32 and Add. I (1947).
[18] The Palestinian National Charter 1968.

8.3.1 The 1988 Declaration of Independence and Engagement with International Law

This position was radically altered in the PLO's 1988 Declaration of Independence, where Resolution 181, which provided for the partition of Mandate Palestine into a Jewish and a Palestinian state, while described as an 'historical injustice', is cited as providing 'those conditions of international legitimacy that ensure the right of the Palestinian Arab people to sovereignty' in the territory occupied in 1967.[19] The 1988 Declaration, building on the emergent grassroots movement for democracy in the refugee camps of the occupied West Bank and Gaza—the *intifada*—constituted not just the declaration of an independent Palestinian state, but recognition by the PLO of the state of Israel in the territory it held on the eve of the 1967 war.

It was from this point that the question of Palestine's legal status and the matter of statehood became of concern as Palestine emerged as an autonomous international entity. The General Assembly in 1974 had invited the PLO to participate as an observer at the Assembly.[20] In reaction to the 1988 Declaration and recognition of Israel, the General Assembly moved that the designation Palestine be accepted as a replacement for PLO.[21] The Security Council admitted the Palestinian delegation to sessions of concern to Palestine,[22] prompting some to argue that it thereby 'treated Palestine as a state'.[23] Attempting to seize the opportunity to assert Palestinian rights and duties by sharing in the obligations adhering to all states, in June 1989 the PLO made its first significant move of engagement with international law, submitting to Switzerland ratification documents for the Geneva Conventions and their Additional Protocols. This attempted accession was thwarted by the Swiss government which stated that it was not in a position to decide whether it could accept the ratification 'due to the uncertainty [sic] within the international community as to the existence or the non-existence of a State of Palestine'.[24]

The strategy of attempting to accede to international treaties was accompanied by a move to elicit membership of UN specialized agencies and the PLO applied for membership of the World Health Organisation and UNESCO at this time, both of whom similarly deferred decisions on the basis that the status of Palestine as a

---

[19] Palestinian Declaration of Independence 1988.

[20] General Assembly Resolution 3237 (XXIX), 22 November 1974.

[21] General Assembly Resolution 43/177, 15 December 1988.

[22] UN SCOR 44th Session, 2841st meeting, U.N. Doc. S/PV.2841 (1989).

[23] Quigley 1997, p. 722. According to the Security Council's rules of procedure, only states are permitted to participate in such session. See Security Council, *Provisional Rules of Procedure*, Rule 14, U.N. Doc. S/96/Rev.4 (1946).

[24] Embassy of Switzerland, Note of Information sent to the High Contracting Parties to the Geneva Conventions, 13 September 1989. See also Boyle 1990, p. 301; Crawford 1990, p. 307; Crawford 2006, pp. 435–442; Lapidoth and Calvo-Goller 1992, p. 777.

state remained unclear.[25] Palestine, as a nation rather than a state presumably, was admitted into the International Olympic Committee in 1995 and as a member of the *Fédération Internationale de Football Association* (FIFA) in 1998. Subsequently, the Internet Corporation for Assigned Names and Numbers (ICANN) provided Palestine with an internet suffix and Palestinian phones received a national prefix. As the Oslo Accords process labored through the 1990s, Palestinian statehood remained far from formal realization, and at the 1998 United Nations Diplomatic Conference of Plenipotentiaries on the Establishment of an International Criminal Court, Palestine's attendance was recorded in a category specifically devised for it alone, under the heading 'other organisations', confirming Palestine's isolation on the periphery of international law and community.[26]

If the PLO had failed to effectively press for the rights of Palestinians through the framework of the international legal system, they took a landmark step toward remedying this in 2003 by impressing upon the General Assembly the need to take action against the Wall that Israel had began to construct in the West Bank the previous year. In 2004 the International Court of Justice delivered its Advisory Opinion on the question posed to it by a General Assembly Resolution concerning the legality of Israel's construction of a Wall in occupied Palestinian territory. The Court treated Palestine's statehood as having not yet been established, and the Opinion sought:

> 'to draw the attention of the General Assembly, to which the present Opinion is addressed, to the need for these efforts to be encouraged with a view to achieving as soon as possible, on the basis of international law, a negotiated solution to the outstanding problems and the establishment of a Palestinian State, existing side by side with Israel and its other neighbours, with peace and security for all in the region.'[27]

The entire ICJ process had been opposed by the Quartet (UN, EU, USA and Russia), the European Union,[28] the United States, and many other liberal democracies that claim a direct stake in the mechanisms of the Oslo Accords. It is said that Palestinian engagement with international law will wreck the opportunity for a sustainable political settlement with Israel. Britain stated that, 'the United Kingdom and the other States involved in the Quartet have made it clear that they consider that for the Court to give an opinion on this matter would be likely to hinder, rather than assist, the peace process.'[29] Switzerland opposed the referral to

---

[25] See WHO A42/VR/10, 12 May 1989, and UNESCO 132 EX/31, 29 September 1989, respectively. See generally Kearney and Reynolds 2012.

[26] Volume II: Summary records of the plenary meetings and of the meetings of the Committee of the Whole. A/CONF.183/13 (Vol. 11) 44.

[27] *Legal Consequences of the Construction of a Wall in Occupied Palestinian Territory*, Advisory Opinion, 9 July 2004, ICJ Rep 2004, para 162.

[28] Statement of Ireland on behalf of the European Union, January 2004. Available at: http://www.icj-cij.org/docket/files/131/1615.pdf.

[29] Written Statement of the United Kingdom of Great Britain and Northern Ireland, January 2004, para 1.6. Available at: http://www.icj-cij.org/docket/files/131/1605.pdf.

the Court since: 'We do not judge it to be appropriate in the current circumstances to bring before a legal body a subject in which highly political implications predominate.'[30]

Israel shared this view, but further asserted that it was inappropriate for the Court to take a decision 'that accords "Palestine" a status that has been highly contentious amongst UN Members for many years'. Palestine's participation in the Court's proceedings reinforced Israel's wider concerns, since 'the Order itself is already being viewed as an additional substantive factor in the political debate about Palestinian statehood.'[31] The inconsistent position of Palestine as a subject of international law was noted by Judge Higgins in a separate opinion attached to the Advisory Opinion. Critical of the majority position that Israel could not rely upon Article 51 of the UN Charter to justify construction of the Wall, Judge Higgins stated that 'Palestine cannot be sufficiently an international entity to be invited to these proceedings and to benefit from international humanitarian law but not sufficiently an international entity for the prohibition of armed attack on others to be applicable'.[32]

For all its clear assertions of the legal obligations owed to Palestinians by third states, Israel, and international institutions, the Advisory Opinion had no effect on Israel's policy or practices. It did however signal a threat to Israel, one outlined in a 2005 article by Gerald Steinberg of NGO Monitor, entitled *War by Other Means*, in which he claimed of the ICJ proceedings that the "pseudo legal system, referred to as international law," lacked necessary "legitimacy based on the consent of the governed'.[33] The Wall Opinion, and the increased efforts of Palestinian civil society in third states in engaging the principle of universal jurisdiction, as well as through advocacy at the Human Rights Council, Brussels and New York, was denigrated as 'lawfare'. Lawfare is understood as a strategy 'of the weak using international fora, judicial processes, and terrorism'[34] and 'of using—or misusing—law as a substitute for traditional military means to achieve an operational objective.'[35] Considered from such a perspective, Palestinian recourse to the principles and institutions of international law should be understood as little more than a subversive tactic by which antidemocrats can sabotage the western liberal project of human rights.[36]

---

[30] Written statement addressed to the ICJ by the Swiss Confederation pursuant to the Order of the Court of 19 December 2003, para 7. Available at: http://www.icj-cij.org/docket/files/131/1577.pdf.

[31] Letter dated 29 January 2004 from the Deputy Director General and Legal Advisor of the Ministry of Foreign Affairs, together with the Written Statement of the Government of Israel, para 2.16.

[32] *Legal Consequences of the Construction of a Wall in Occupied Palestinian Territory*, Advisory Opinion, 9 July 2004, ICJ Rep 2004. Separate Opinion of Judge Higgins para 34.

[33] Steinberg 2005, p. 331.

[34] Lin 2008–2009, p. 865.

[35] Dunlap 2009, p. 35.

[36] Kearney 2011.

8.3.2 The Palestinian Declaration to the ICC

When the PA submitted the Article 12(3) declaration to the ICC in January 2009 as Israeli sea, air, and ground forces attacked Gaza, the question of Palestine's status, for the first time since the UNSCOP proposal was defeated in 1947, was taken from the exclusive domain of the politicians and placed before an independent international legal institution. The Palestinian declaration was a surprise move in many ways. It was not a position on which Palestinian advocacy groups had been actively lobbying, and given the persistent opposition to Palestinian engagement with international law by the Quartet and the liberal democracies—the very states and institutions on which the PA relied for its very existence—it seems inconceivable that they would have approved in advance the Palestinian declaration.

During 'Operation Cast Lead' the Fatah led PA in the West Bank was an onlooker to events, unable or unwilling to take any action to protect the civilians they purported to represent. Protests against the Israeli assault that were held in Ramallah and elsewhere were broken up by PA security forces.[37] It was in such an environment that PA Justice Minister Ali Al-Khashan sought approval to approach the ICC. This avenue may have been assumed to allow the PA to assert its relevance by taking action on the international plane to deter or hold to account Israelis responsible for the war crimes underway in Gaza, while not actually impinging on Israeli actions in a direct manner which would have incurred the displeasure of the PA's foreign backers. The extent to which the PA leadership had given consideration to the matter of the ICC ruling on the status of Palestine as a state is uncertain, but subsequent inaction suggests it does not appear to have been fully appreciated at the time.

The FFM Report, published in September 2009,[38] did not address the question of Palestinian statehood but it did emphasize the role which the International Criminal Court should play in giving effect to the international community's responsibility for ensuring accountability for the victims of 'Operation Cast Lead'. The Fact-Finding Mission recommended that the Human Rights Council formally submit the report to the Prosecutor of the International Criminal Court,[39] and that in the absence of good faith investigations by the parties to the conflict, the Security Council, acting under Chapter VII of the UN Charter, should refer the situation in Gaza to the Office of the Prosecutor pursuant to Article 13(b) of the Rome Statute.[40] Addressing the Prosecutor directly the Report recommended that 'With reference to the declaration under Article 12(3) received by the Office of the Prosecutor of the ICC from the Government of Palestine, the Mission considers that accountability for victims and the interests of peace and justice in the region

---

[37] Goldstone et al. 2009, paras 1604–08.
[38] See the contributions in this Volume under Part II.
[39] Goldstone et al. 2009, para 1765.
[40] Goldstone et al. 2009, para 1766.

require that the legal determination should be made by the Prosecutor as expeditiously as possible.'[41]

The subsequent Chapters of this Volume shall consider in detail the varied legal and political issues that have arose with respect to the Palestinian declaration to the ICC, so at this juncture it is useful to reflect in some general terms on the implications of the declaration being either accepted or rejected. First though, it could be that neither course of action will be followed and that the declaration is allowed to drift unresolved, a scenario with precedent given that the declaration submitted in accordance with Article 12(3) by Cote d'Ivoire in 2003 has at the time of going to press yet to be formally acknowledged as other than having been received by the ICC.[42] A lack of PA advocacy toward ensuring full acceptance of the declaration suggests that the legal question of the status of Palestine that the declaration has prompted jars with the politico-diplomatic approach to negotiations that the PA favors, and is best left unanswered in the short to medium term.

Al-Haq,[43] as with Alain Pellet,[44] John Dugard[45] and other commentators, have suggested that in considering the Palestinian declaration, the Prosecutor of the ICC should accept Palestine's transfer of jurisdiction to the Court on the basis that the role of the Court is not to recognize a Palestinian state, but rather to identify whether Palestine can be considered a state for the purposes of the Rome Statute only. In adopting a functional approach to this question the Court should have reference to the context, object, and purpose of the Rome Statute, acknowledge the consistent legal and political assertions by bodies such as the ICJ and the Security Council that the Palestinians have the right to self-determination and that Israel holds no sovereignty over any of the territory occupied in the 1967 war, and promptly accept that Palestine meets the requirements to be considered a state for the purpose of the Statute. Such a move would allow international criminal law to begin to play the role for which it is designed, acting as a deterrent against any further military actions such as 'Operation Cast Lead'.

Rejection of the Palestinian declaration would not be justified given the factual and legal situation. Were it to be rejected, it is likely that either through third state referral, or perhaps even through a UN body, if not by Palestine itself again, that the ICC—whether the OTP or the Assembly of States Parties—would at some future date be once more faced with a Palestinian request to transfer jurisdiction. Various critiques of the declaration have been made,[46] but there are few genuine legal obstacles to acknowledging that Palestine can be considered a state for the purposes of the Rome Statute. Given the strong legal arguments that have been made to demonstrate the validity of the declaration, its rejection would undermine

---

[41] Goldstone et al. 2009, para 1767.
[42] Republic of Côte D'Ivoire 2003.
[43] Al Haq 2009.
[44] Pellet 2010.
[45] Dugard 2009.
[46] Shaw 2011.

the role that the ICC can play in the promotion of peace and in ensuring accountability for the victims of war crimes everywhere. Such a move does appear unlikely, since the stalling of the process, by whatsoever party, provides a less contentious opportunity to avoid immediate controversy.

8.4 The Fact-Finding Mission Report and the Pressures on the PA to Defer the Vote at the UN

Despite intense international media coverage, and a broad welcome to the FFM Report by Palestinian authorities, armed factions,[47] and civil society, on 1 October 2009 the Human Rights Council deferred consideration of the Report until March 2010. This decision, taken the evening before a scheduled vote on a draft resolution endorsing the Report, was the result of pressure from the US and European states on the Palestinian leadership in the West Bank. Palestinian civil society reacted immediately, with public meetings and demonstrations condemning the move. Popular despair hardened underlying anger and frustration with the political leadership, causing the PA to rapidly request that a Special Session of the Human Rights Council be convened to debate the Report. This was held in Geneva on 15 and 16 October 2009, with a Resolution ultimately adopted that endorsed the Report, condemned Israel's blockade of Gaza on the basis that it constitutes collective punishment, and condemned Israel's unlawful policies and practices in East Jerusalem.[48]

In the weeks before the Report was to be considered at the General Assembly, Palestinian NGOs criticized the Palestinian negotiating strategy: 'Too often have the rights of Palestinians been negotiated away in order to provide the appearance of political progress, and too often has progress manifested itself as mere maintenance of the *status quo*, which for decades has denied Palestinians their fundamental rights.'[49] At the General Assembly the Report was adopted by a majority vote in a Resolution calling upon the parties to the conflict to conduct proper investigations, calling upon Switzerland to undertake the necessary steps to reconvene a Conference of High Contracting Parties to the Fourth Geneva Convention on measures to enforce the Convention in the occupied Palestinian territory, and requesting the UN Secretary-General to report to the General

---

[47] Ma'an News 2009.

[48] Resolution A/HRC/RES/S-12/1, The human rights situation in the Occupied Palestinian Territory, including East Jerusalem. Adopted at the 12th Special Session on 16 October 2009 by a recorded vote of 25 in favour, 6 Against, and 11 abstentions.

[49] Joint Press Release 2009. Co-signatories included: Adalah—Legal Center for Arab Minority Rights in Israel, Addameer, Al Dameer Association for Human Rights, Al-Haq—Law in the Service of Man, Al Mezan Centre for Human Rights, Arab Association for Human Rights, Badil Resource Center for Palestinian Residency and Refugee Rights, Defence for Children International-Palestine Section, Ensan Center for Human Rights and Democracy, Jerusalem Legal Aid Center, Palestinian Centre for Human Rights, Ramallah Center for Human Rights Studies, Women's Center for Legal Aid and Counselling.

Assembly within a period of 3 months on the implementation of the Resolution with a view to considering further action.[50]

According to an internal commission of inquiry, on 28 September 2009, Mahmoud Abbas, President of both the PA and the PLO, attended General Assembly meetings where he was told he should deal with the Report very carefully because of the way it dealt with Palestinian resistance groups and due to 'larger issues with the international standing of the report.'[51] It found that on 1 October the US representative to the PA spoke with Prime Minister Salam Fayyad asking him to delay the vote. Fayyad testified that he refused the request but nonetheless Abbas made the directive to delay that evening. The Commission found near unanimous and stunned agreement between the leadership over the magnitude of the political fallout: 'According to the Commission chairman, and PA legislator Azmi Shu'aybi, none of the Palestinian officials involved properly estimated the reaction of Palestinians to the postponement. The only thing on the minds of the leaders influencing the decision, the Commission found, were the final days in Geneva and Ramallah when the United States began applying pressure on the issue.'[52] A Ha'aretz report then claimed that the decision came after a meeting between Abbas and Shin Bet chief Yuval Diskin, who threatened Abbas that unless he deferred the vote Israel would revoke promises to lift movement restrictions, withdraw the operational capacity for a second Palestinian mobile phone network, and turn the West Bank into a 'second Gaza.'[53]

In November 2009, and following on from their criticism of the PA, Palestinian and Israeli NGOs released a public letter expressing concern 'regarding the EU's apparent inconsistent position on the protection of human rights, justice and the rule of law in the Occupied Palestinian Territory.' The letter criticized the EU for the majority of its member states having failed to support the recommendations of the Report, either at the UN Human Rights Council or General Assembly, and stated that since some of the signatory NGOs were recipients of EU aid under the European Instrument for Democracy and Human Rights (EIDHR), donor inaction on accountability placed them in an 'untenable position *vis-à-vis* Palestinian society on whose behalf we receive assistance.' They requested 'an explanation of the EU's intended action on the matter of war crimes allegedly committed in the course of 'Operation Cast Lead' in Gaza.'[54]

---

[50] UNGA Res A/64/L.11, Follow-up to the report of the United Nations Fact-Finding Mission on the Gaza Conflict. Adopted by a recorded vote of 114 in favor, 18 against, 44 abstentions.

[51] Ma'an News 2010.

[52] Ma'an News 2010.

[53] Eldar 2010.

[54] Letter Re: EU Position on respect for human rights, justice and the rule of law in the OPT. Addameer, Al Dameer Association for Human Rights, Al-Haq, Al Mezan Centre for Human Rights, Badil Resource Center for Palestinian Residency and Refugee Rights, Defence for Children International-Palestine Section, Arab Association for Human Rights, Ensan Center for Human Rights and Democracy, Jerusalem Legal Aid Center, Physicians for Human Rights-Israel, Public Committee Against Torture in Israel, Ramallah Center for Human Rights Studies, Women's Center for Legal Aid and Counseling. Available at: http://www.alhaq.org/pdfs/presidency_goldstone_12_nov_2009.pdf.

Two key developments were highlighted in the manner by which the Report worked its way through the UN bodies. In the first instance was the blatant political pressure on the Palestinian leadership to refrain and desist from pursuing Palestinian rights through the international legal framework. The second may be regarded as the determination of Palestinian civil society to engage in lobbying (diplomacy) on behalf of their community in Geneva and New York in order to ensure the enforcement of international human rights and humanitarian law. This was combined with forthright *political* criticism of the failure of the European Union and the Palestinian leadership (not just the US and Israel) to act to support the rights they claimed to uphold. To suggest such is not to deny that civil society had not been shifting its advocacy practices in such a direction previously. The impact of the 'Goldstone Report' was to bring the scale and terror of 'Operation Cast Lead' to the world's attention, and to suggest the possibility of accountability and enforcement through international law of respect for Palestinians' human rights.[55] The necessity for civil society to shift to engaging openly in the political sphere, domestically and internationally, did not mean the abandonment of objectivity and nonpartisanship, nor reduction to lawfare, but rather demonstrated that in the light of the politicians' weakness it became civil society to ensure that their monitoring, field work, and reporting, undertaken in traumatic conditions, was not permitted to be continually ignored or dismissed, even by those who provide the funding for this crucial work.

The General Assembly Resolution that endorsed the Report of the FFM was notable in one regard with respect the question of the status of Palestine that remains before the consideration of the ICC. The Resolution asserted that Palestinian and Israeli authorities investigate and prosecute any individuals alleged to be responsible for the war crimes and crimes against humanity as documented in the Report. I have argued elsewhere that this assertion represented a clear acknowledgment that even without formal recognition of the state of Palestine, the General Assembly considered that Palestine was obliged to share in the obligations of other states as established in customary international law to investigate and prosecute grave breaches of international humanitarian law.[56] Such a situation presented a situation converse to that outlined by Judge Higgins in the Wall Advisory Opinion, and the question of the Palestinian declaration and the ICC is discussed in depth in the subsequent essays of this volume.

8.5 Summary

Whether by design or accident, the PA declaration to the ICC did contribute to setting in motion a train of events that led to a statement by Mahmoud Abbas in May 2011 (when writing in the *New York Times* following a significant step

---

[55] Horowitz et al. 2011.
[56] Kearney 2010.

toward a Palestinian national unity government including both Fatah and Hamas), that: 'Palestine's admission to the United Nations would pave the way for the internationalization of the conflict as a legal matter, not only a political one. It would also pave the way for us to pursue claims against Israel at the United Nations, human rights treaty bodies and the International Court of Justice.'[57]

The international response to 'Operation Cast Lead', manifesting as the Report of the FFM and the controversy it raised, may easily have been buried in the stalling politics of the UN. The declaration to the ICC, and the activism of Palestinian civil society, has served to ensure that accountability for the victims of the occupation, and the question of the legal status of Palestine, cannot be bargained away by politicians without significant political cost. Nonetheless, the absence of any reference to the ICC in Abbas's NYT article does lend credence to concerns that PA engagement with the ICC has been stalled so that political, rather than legal, considerations continue to dominate.

The majority of states have already recognized the state of Palestine and been supportive of Palestinian engagement with the international legal framework, while many others treat Palestine as a *de facto* state. Others have threatened and cajoled the PA into dropping all claims to legal remedy or resolution. When considering forcing predetermined negotiations on Palestine, the US, the European Union, and above all the United Nations, would do well to recall the fallout from the further violation of Palestinian rights that the Oslo process facilitated.

The Report of the Fact-Finding Mission and the declaration to the ICC have served to provide an institutional frame to which Palestinian civil society, and legal scholars, can turn in order to seek accountability for the violations of human rights that have been documented in so many reports and advocacy documents, and discussed and analyzed in so many academic papers. Christopher Greenwood has pointed out the necessity of realizing the limitations of international law in its attempts to regulate belligerent occupations. Noting that 'alien rule for a prolonged period is inherently unsatisfactory', he emphasized that the framework of international law should be developed toward 'bringing about an end to the conflict which produced the occupation, not in trying to turn a body of law designed to ensure that a military regime observes basic standards of humanity into a device for establishing a liberal democracy or other long-term solution.'[58]

International law will not, in isolation, provide a resolution to the conflict. Its inherent weakness is all too clear in the lack of formal criteria or precedent around the question of what constitutes a state, one of the key building blocks of the international legal framework. Nonetheless, the trend toward a legal analysis that considers occupation as a normative regime, rather than a series of individual violations of international human rights and humanitarian law, is to be welcomed and encouraged. The ICJ's Wall Opinion asserted that the UN's responsibility toward Palestine 'also has its origin in the Mandate and the Partition Resolution

---

[57] Abbas 2011.
[58] Greenwood 1992, p. 266.

concerning Palestine'.[59] Keeping this in mind, the response of civil society and of legal scholars to developments such as the ICC declaration and the potential role of the General Assembly in acknowledging Palestinian statehood, must continue to develop so as to incorporate a temporal and normative framework that takes into consideration the full spectrum of Palestinian rights and the history of Palestine on the periphery of international law.

References

Abbas M (2011) The Long Overdue Palestinian State. New York Times, 16 May 2011. http://www.nytimes.com/2011/05/17/opinion/17abbas.html?_r=2&ref=opinion

Al Haq (2009) Position Paper on Issues Arising from the Palestinian Authority's Submission of a Declaration to the Prosecutor of the International Criminal Court under Article 12(3) of the Rome Statute. http://www.alhaq.org/etemplate.php?id=494

Ayalon D (2010) Ayalon: "Challenges for Israeli Foreign Policy", 6 January 2010. http://www.mfa.gov.il/MFA/About+the+Ministry/Deputy_Foreign_Minister/Speeches/DepFM_Ayalon_Challenges_Israeli_Foreign_Policy_6-Jan-2010.htm

Ben-Naftali O, Gross A, Michaeli K (2005) Illegal Occupation: Framing the Occupied Palestinian Territory. BJIL 23:551

Boyle F (1990) Creation of the State of Palestine. EJIL 1:301

Crawford J (1990) The Creation of the State of Palestine: Too much Too soon? EJIL 1:307

Crawford J (2006) The Creation of States in International Law, 2nd edn. Clarendon Press, Oxford

D'Aspremont J (2011) The International Legal Scholar in Palestine: Hurling Stones Under the Guise of Legal Forms? A talk with Martti Koskenniemi and Mudar Kassis. Working paper. http://papers.ssrn.com/sol3/papers.cfm?abstract_id=1846867

Darcy S, Reynolds J (2010) An Enduring Occupation: The Status of the Gaza Strip from the Perspective of International Humanitarian Law. JC & SL 15(2):211–243

Diamond E (2010) Before the Abyss: Reshaping International Humanitarian Law to Suit the Ends of Power. ILR 43:414

Dugard J (2009) Take the Case. The New York Times, 22 July 2009. http://www.nytimes.com/2009/07/23/opinion/23iht-eddugard.html

Dunlap C (2009) Lawfare: A Decisive Element of 21st-Century Conflicts? JFQ 54:35

Elaraby N (1968) Some Legal Implications of the 1947 Partition Resolution and the 1949 Armistice Agreements. LCP 33:97

Eldar A (2010) Diskin to Abbas: Defer UN Vote on Goldstone or Face 'Second Gaza', Ha'artez, 17 January 2010. http://www.haaretz.com/hasen/spages/1143038.html

Goldstone R et al. (2009) Report of the United Nations Fact-Finding Mission on the Gaza Conflict, A/HRC/12/48. http://www2.ohchr.org/english/bodies/hrcouncil/specialsession/9/docs/UNFFMGC_Report.PDF

Greenwood C (1992) The Administration of Occupied Territory in International Law. In: Playfair E (ed) International Law and the Administration of Occupied Territories: Two Decades of Israeli Occupation of the West Bank and Gaza Strip. Clarendon Press, Oxford

Horowitz A, Ratner L, Weiss P (eds) (2011) The Goldstone Report: The Legacy of the Landmark Investigation of the Gaza Conflict. Nations Books, New York

---

[59] *Legal consequences of the construction of a wall in occupied Palestinian territory*, Advisory Opinion, 9 July 2004, ICJ Rep 2004 para 49.

Joint Press Release (2009) The Goldstone Report at the UN General Assembly: States must Ensure Victim's Rights and not Compromise the Rule of Law. http://www.alhaq.org/etemplate.php?id=486

Kattan V (2009) From Coexistence to Conquest: International Law and the Origins of the Arab-Israeli Conflict 1891–1949. Pluto Press, London

Kearney M (2011) Lawfare, Legitimacy & Resistance: The Weak and the Law. 16 Palestinian Yearbook of International Law (forthcoming)

Kearney M (2010) Palestine and the International Criminal Court: Asking the Right Question. UCLA HR & ICL 1

Kearney M, Reynolds J (2012) Palestine, Politics, and the International Criminal Court. In: Schabas W (ed) Ashgate Research Companion to International Criminal Law: Critical Perspectives. Ashgate, London (forthcoming)

Lapidoth R, Calvo-Goller N (1992) Les Éléments Constitutives de l'État et la Déclaration du Conseil National Palestinien du 15 Novembre 1988. RGDIP 96:777

Lin T (2008–2009) Boumediene and Lawfare. U Rich L Rev 43:865

Ma'an News (2009) Islamic Jihad: UN Probe into Gaza Factions will not Criminalize them, Ma'an News, 10 October 2009. http://www.maannews.net/eng/ViewDetails.aspx?ID=231204

Ma'an News (2010) Abbas takes Blame for Goldstone Delay, Commission says, Ma'an News, 9 January 2010. http://www.maannews.net/eng/ViewDetails.aspx?ID=253025

McHugo J (2002) Resolution 242: A Legal Reappraisal of the Rightwing Israeli Interpretation of the Withdrawal Phrase with Reference to the Conflict between Israel and the Palestinians. ICLQ 51:851–882

Palestinian Declaration of Independence, Algiers, Algeria, 15 November 1988. http://www.nad-plo.org/userfiles/file/Document/Declaration%20of%20Independence.pdf

Pellet J (2010) The Palestinian Declaration and the Jurisdiction of the International Criminal Court. J Int Crim Justice 8:4

Quigley J (1997) The Israel-PLO Agreements: Are they Treaties? CILJ 30:717

Republic of Côte D'Ivoire (2003) Declaration to the ICC, 1 October 2003, No. 481/ACI/BNL/CE-2/dd. http://www.icc-cpi.int/NR/rdonlyres/74EEE201-0FED-4481-95D4-C8071087102C/279843/ICDENG.pdf

Said E (2001) The End of the Peace Process: Oslo and After. Vintage, New York

Samara A (2002) Epidemic of Globalization: Ventures in World Order, Arab Nationlism and Zionism. Palestine Research and Publishing Foundation, California

Schabas W (2011) Déjà Vu All Over Again. http://humanrightsdoctorate.blogspot.com/2011/05/deja-vu-all-over-again.html

Shaw M (2011) The Article 12(3) Declaration of the Palestinian Authority, the International Criminal Court and International Law. JICJ 9(2):301

Steinberg G (2005) The UN, the ICJ, and the Separation Barrier: War by Other Means. ILR 38:331

Strawson J (2010) Partitioning Palestine: Legal Fundamentalism in the Palestinian-Israeli Conflict. Pluto Press, London

The Palestinian National Charter (1968) Resolutions of the Palestine National Council, 1–17 July 1968. http://avalon.law.yale.edu/20th_century/plocov.asp

Tilley V (ed) (2009) Occupation, Colonialism, Apartheid? A Re-assessment of Israel's Practices in the Occupied Palestinian Territories Under International Law. Human Sciences Research Council, Cape Town

Chapter 9
The Effects of Palestine's Recognition of the International Criminal Court's Jurisdiction

Allain Pellet

Contents

9.1	Introduction..	409
9.2	The Relevance of a Functional Approach..	410
9.3	The Validity of the Palestinian Declaration of 21 January 2009.........................	415
9.4	Postscript..	425
References..		428

9.1 Introduction

1. This opinion has been written on the request of Maître William Bourdon, Barrister at law before the Court of Paris. It attempts to determine whether the Palestinian Authority's recognition of the International Criminal Court's (hereinafter "the ICC" or "the Court") jurisdiction in a statement dated January 21, 2009, can have any effect for the purpose of Article 12 of the ICC Statute. It therefore limits itself to a purely legal point of view, in spite of the obvious political aspect permeating the background it applies to.

Professor of International Law, University Paris-Ouest; former Member and Chairperson, United Nations International Law Commission; Associé de l'Institut de Droit international. The Opinion, originally submitted in French to the Office of the Prosecutor of the ICC, was also published in English, slightly modified, in Journal of International Criminal Justice 8 (2010), 981–999.

A. Pellet (✉)
University of Paris Ouest, Nanterre-La Défense, France

2. Article 12 of the Rome Statute is worded as follows:

> Preconditions to the exercise of jurisdiction
>
> 1. A State which becomes a Party to this Statute thereby accepts the jurisdiction of the Court with respect to the crimes referred to in Article 5.
> 2. In the case of Article 13, para (a) or (c),[1] the Court may exercise its jurisdiction if one or more of the following States are Parties to this Statute or have accepted the jurisdiction of the Court in accordance with para 3:
>
>> (a) The State on the territory of which the conduct in question occurred or, if the crime was committed on board a vessel or aircraft, the State of registration of that vessel or aircraft;
>> (b) The State of which the person accused of the crime is a national.
>
> 3. If the acceptance of a State which is not a Party to this Statute is required under para 2, that State may, by declaration lodged with the Registrar, accept the exercise of jurisdiction by the Court with respect to the crime in question. The accepting State shall cooperate with the Court without any delay or exception in accordance with Part 9.

3. The Palestinian declaration dated January 21, 2009 is worded as follows:

> The Government of Palestine hereby recognizes the jurisdiction of the Court for the purpose of identifying, prosecuting and judging the authors and accomplices of crimes committed on the territory of Palestine since July 1, 2002.

4. It is clear from the start that the issue is whether such recognition may produce effects considering the terms of Article 12 of the ICC Statute and the controversial nature of the Palestinian entity. The answer to such a question must rely on a teleological and functional approach.

---

[1] Article 13: *Exercise of jurisdiction*: "The Court may exercise its jurisdiction with respect to a crime referred to in Article 5 in accordance with the provisions of this Statute if: (a) A situation in which one or more of such crimes appears to have been committed is referred to the Prosecutor by a State Party in accordance with Article 14; (b) A situation in which one or more of such crimes appears to have been committed is referred to the Prosecutor by the Security Council acting under Chapter VII of the Charter of the United Nations; or (c) The Prosecutor has initiated an investigation in respect of such a crime in accordance with Article 15."

Article 14: *Referral of a situation by a State Party*: "1. A State Party may refer to the Prosecutor a situation in which one or more crimes within the jurisdiction of the Court appear to have been committed requesting the Prosecutor to investigate the situation for the purpose of determining whether one or more specific persons should be charged with the commission of such crimes. 2. As far as possible, a referral shall specify the relevant circumstances and be accompanied by such supporting documentation as is available to the State referring the situation."

Article 15: *Prosecutor*: "1. The Prosecutor may initiate investigations *proprio motu* on the basis of information on crimes within the jurisdiction of the Court. 2. The Prosecutor shall analyse the seriousness of the information received. For this purpose, he or she may seek additional information from States, organs of the United Nations, intergovernmental or non-governmental organizations, or other reliable sources that he or she deems appropriate, and may receive written or oral testimony at the seat of the Court." (paras 3–6 not reproduced).

9.2 The Relevance of a Functional Approach

5. Although it could make sense to consider that Palestine is a State in the general and usual meaning of the word and the present Opinion has been drafted notwithstanding the solution to be given to that issue,[2] it seems pointless to have a categorical stand on that issue to answer the question raised which is not formulated in a general and abstract way, but in the specific and precise context of Article 12 of the ICC Statute.

6. It is important to stress that though the Court itself has to consider the scope of the recognition dated January 21, 2009, it should not attempt to determine the nature of the Palestine State in the abstract; it should only wonder whether, under Article 12 of its Statute, the Palestinian declaration can be effective. It does not belong to the Court to substitute itself to States in recognising Palestine as a State[3]; it is only called to pronounce on whether the conditions for exercising its statutory jurisdiction are fulfilled.

7. With regard thereto, the problem is rather similar to the question posed in view of an Advisory Opinion by the General Assembly of the United Nations to the International Court of Justice with its resolution A/RES/63/3 of 8 October 2008, and currently under deliberation. In that case, the General Assembly was careful not to ask the ICJ about the State status of Kosovo in general; it asked whether "the unilateral declaration of independence by the Provisional Institutions of Self-Government of Kosovo [is] in accordance with international law?" Likewise in this instance, the ICC is not called for to "recognise" the State of Palestine, but only to ensure that the conditions necessary for the exercise of its jurisdiction are fulfilled.

8. To this end, it is necessary and sufficient for the Court to interpret the provisions of its Statute relating to jurisdiction. It is in light of these provisions that the Court must judge the admissibility of the declaration of the Palestinian government: for that purpose, but for that one only, it has to determine whether Palestine is a State *in the meaning of Article* 12, *para* 3, *of the Statute*, which comes to wondering whether Palestine could usefully make the declaration specified in that provision. In other words, the idea is not for the Court to rely on a general and "ready made" definition of the concept of State in international law, but to adopt a functional approach allowing it to finally determine whether the

---

[2] For my stand on that issue, see Pellet 1998, pp. 51–52; in essence, I show there that the statehood of the Palestinian Authority is doubtful to the extent *it* does not consider *itself* as a State; I have not changed my mind on this matter, even though it can be argued that the fact that it behaves like a State in some circumstances (for instance when it formulated the declaration reviewed) should lead to put this position in perspective; see also: Daillier et al. 2009, pp. 509–512.

[3] Currently more than one hundred States have recognised Palestine as a State, though figures vary rather significantly from one source to the other—see http://en.wikipedia.org/wiki/state-of-palestineStates_recongising_the_state_of_palestine.

Palestinian declaration fulfils the conditions set out in Article 12, para 3, enabling the Court to exercise its statutory jurisdiction.

9. A functional approach to concepts is extremely frequent in international law. Just refer, in this regard, to the very many conventions that define the concepts they refer to "for the purpose of this convention…" or "of the present treaty…"[4]; Such is also the approach followed by the ICJ to grasp the concept of international organisation: in order to answer the question of whether the United Nations Organisation has international personality—which issue, it noted, "is not settled by the actual terms of the Charter"—the World Court considers that "we must consider what characteristics it was intended thereby to give to the Organization".[5] When commenting on that "praetorian revolution" [*"révolution prétrorienne"*]— which is nowadays generally accepted, Professor Pierre-Marie Dupuy stressed in his General Course to the Hague Academy of International Law that "[t]hough the legal personality can vary, in scope and content, depending on the 'needs of the community', there is no reason for the number of subjects not to increase following the development of the international legal order, which itself reflects the extension of the social needs that "hunger for law" is intended to meet. Thanks to that opinion of the Court, various entities can be granted a personality without this constituting a crime of against sovereignty"[6]; and the author continues by giving numerous examples of recognition of a functional legal personality to individuals before international criminal courts,[7] to companies in investment laws,[8] to non-State armed entities,[9] to micro States whose dependence on their neighbours leaves one to wonder about their true sovereignty.[10]

---

[4] See among the numerous examples: the Vienna Conventions on Diplomatic Relations of 1961 and on Consular Relations of 1963 (Article 1), the Vienna Conventions on the Law of Treaties of 1969 and 1986 (Article 2), the Convention against Torture of 1984 (Article 1), the United Nations Convention on the Law of the Sea of 1982 (Article 1), the 1992 United Nations Framework Convention on Climate Changes (Article 1), the 1997 Convention on the Law of Non-Navigational Uses of International Watercourses (Article 2) or the 1998 Aarhus Convention Access to Information, Public Participation in Decision-making and Access to Justice in Environmental Matters (Article 2).

[5] ICJ, Advisory Opinion, 11 April 1949, *Reparation for Injuries Suffered in the Service of the United Nations*, Rep. 178. See also below, para 19.

[6] Dupuy 2002, pp. 108–109. My translation [« [s]*i la personnalité peut varier, en extension comme en contenu, eu égard aux 'besoins de la communauté', il n'y a pas de raison pour que le nombre des sujets ne s'accroisse pas en fonction du développement normatif de l'ordre juridique international, reflétant lui-même l'extension des nécessités sociales auxquelles cette 'faim de droit' est destinée à répondre. Grâce à cet avis de la Cour, des entités diverses peuvent se voir conférer une personnalité sans pour autant qu'il s'agisse d'un crime de lèse-souveraineté* »].

[7] Ibid., 111.

[8] Ibid., 112.

[9] Ibid., 112.

[10] The example of Monaco is given on p. 111; one can also think of the example of Andorra, before its 1993 constitution.

10. Besides, some conventional definitions of the State itself pertain to this functional approach. Such is the case, for instance, in Article 44 of the Convention on the Rights of Persons with Disabilities (on "Regional Integration Organisations") under which:

1. Regional integration organization' shall mean an organization constituted by sovereign States of a given region, to which its member States have transferred competence in respect of matters governed by this Convention. (...)
2. References to 'States Parties' in the present Convention shall apply to such organizations within the limits of their competence.

In the same way, according to Article XXII of the 1972 Convention on International Liability for Damage Caused by Space Objects:

1. In this Convention, with the exception of Articles XXIV–XXVII , references to States shall be deemed to apply to any international intergovernmental organisation which conducts space activities if the organisation declares its acceptance of the rights and obligations provided for in this Convention and if a majority of the States members of the organisation are State Parties to this Convention and to the Treaty on Principles Governing the Activities of States in the Exploration and Use of Outer Space, including the Moon and Other Celestial Bodies.[11]

11. As stated by Advocate General Sir Francis Geoffrey Jacobs in the ECJ *Stardust* case:

The concept of the State has to be understood in the sense most appropriate to the provisions in question and to their objectives; the Court rightly follows a functional approach, basing its interpretation on the scheme and objective of the provisions within which the concept features.[12]

This functional view of the State and its subdivisions is omnipresent, for instance, in the ECJ case-law relating to the direct effect of the directives:

... it should be noted that a directive cannot be relied on against individuals, whereas it may be relied on as against a State, regardless of the capacity in which the latter is acting, that is to say, whether as employer or as public authority. The entities against which the provisions of a directive that are capable of having direct effect may be relied upon include a body, whatever its legal form, which has been made responsible, pursuant to a measure adopted by the State, for providing a public service under the control of the State and has for that purpose special powers beyond those which result from the normal rules applicable in relations between individuals.[13]

---

[11] See also the definition of a "country" in the Explanatory Notes of the Agreement Establishing the WTO dated April 15, 1994: "The terms 'country' or 'countries' as used in this Agreement and the Multilateral Trade Agreements are to be understood to include any separate customs territory Member of the WTO."

[12] ECJ, *French Republic v Commission*, Case C-482/99, Rep. p. I-04397, Opinion of the Advocate General, December 13, 2001, ibid., para 56. See the Court's ruling in this case (dated May 16, 2002, para 55).

[13] ECJ, *Farell*, case C-356/05, ruling dated April 19, 2007, Rep. p. I-03067, para 40. See also Case C-188/89 *Foster and Others* [1990] ECR I-3313, para 20; Case C-343/98 *Collino and Chiappero* [2000] ECR I-6659, para 23; and Case C-157/02 *Rieser Internationale Transporte* [2004] ECR I-1477, para 24.

12. It is also this idea that supports the principle applied by the European Court of Human Rights in the *Drozd and Janousek* case. Although in that instance it admitted the preliminary objection relating to its lack of jurisdiction *ratione loci*, it specified that it was only because it had not received from Andorra a declaration establishing its consent to the application of the Convention on its territory; but it acknowledged that the Principality could have formulated such a declaration based on Article 5 of the Statute of the Council of Europe,[14] despite its *sui generis* nature that the Court stresses robustly.[15] It is noteworthy that the Strasbourg Court, guided by the concern of ensuring a broad implementation of the Convention and thereby of an improved human rights protection, as wanted by its authors, does not doubt that its jurisdiction can extend to *sui generis* entities such as the Principality was supposed to be.

13. Similarly, an ICSID tribunal noted that:

> 74 Under the ICSID Convention, the Centre's jurisdiction extends only to legal disputes arising directly out of an investment between a Contracting state and a national of another Contracting State. Just as the Centre has no jurisdiction to arbitrate disputes between two states, it also lacks jurisdiction to arbitrate disputes between two private entities. Their main jurisdictional feature is to decide disputes between a private investor and a State. However neither the term 'national of another Contracting State' nor the term 'Contracting State' are defined in the Convention. (...).
>
> 75 Accordingly the Tribunal has to answer the following two questions: first, whether or not SODIGA is a State entity for the purpose of determining the jurisdiction of the Centre and the competence of the Tribunal, and second, whether the actions and missions complained of by the Claimant are imputable to the State. While the first issue is one that can be decided at the jurisdictional state of these proceedings, the second issue bears on the merits of the dispute and can be finally resolved only at that state.[16]

It is interesting to note that, in this case, the Tribunal sought to determine the nature of the State entity at the phase of the appreciation of its jurisdiction (and not of the merits), considering that the difficulty concerned its jurisdiction *ratione personae*. Therefore it handled it "from a point of view different of that of attribution in the meaning of responsibility law, since 'State' can have a specific meaning in the context of the dispute".[17]

14. As has been stressed in doctrine, "following actually a 'functional approach' ultimately called for by the World Court in its 1949 Opinion in the *Reparation for Injuries* case, modern international law conceives the State under the form of a variable geometry shape, whose outline depends on the subject at issue, and it relegates it to the rank of general 'notion' whose interpretation depends 'on the

---

[14] Which provides for the possibility that a European 'country' become an associate member.

[15] ECHR, Plenary, req n° 12747/87, *Drozd and Janousek v France and Spain*, ruling dated June 26, 1992, paras 67 and 86.

[16] *Maffezini v. Spain*, Case N° ARB/97/7, Decision of the Tribunal on Objections to Jurisdiction, 25 January 2000, ICSID Rev.—For. Investment L. Jl., pp. 27–28, paras 74–75.

[17] Forteau 2007, pp. 762–763. My translation [« *sous un angle distinct de celui de l'attribution au sens du droit de la responsabilité, car 'l'État' peut avoir un sens particulier dans le contexte du litige* »].

economy and the aims of the provisions' within which it finds itself (…). The boundaries of the concept of the State are nonetheless in movement, its 'perimeter' is not an intangible and physically marked limit. International law apprehends the State as an entity that it can itself reshape (as witnesses by the use of conventional definitions of the State[18] or the jurisprudential formula whereby international or foreign courts decide that such an entity 'must be considered as an emanation of the State'), and the latter is, in contemporary international law, increasingly understood differently depending on the norm being applied".[19]

15. Therefore it is by taking into account the general scheme of the provisions of the Rome Statute and the object and purpose of Article 12 that the Court is called upon to give a meaning to the term 'State' within the framework of this provision.

9.3 The Validity of the Palestinian Declaration of 21 January 2009

16. It is for the ICC to define its jurisdiction and the limits imposed on its exercise of jurisdiction, based on its interpretation of the provisions of the Statute, in accordance with the principle of the *kompetent kompetenz*, according to which it is judge of its own jurisdiction. This is a general principle of international dispute settlement[20] whose specific conditions of implementation by the ICC are specified in Articles 18 and 19 of the Statute.

---

[18] [Footnote 118]: "Of which for the rest, one of the most obvious expressions is Article 3 of the United Nations Charter on the basis of which original UN member states have been considered to include the federated entities of Ukraine and Belarus (…)." My translation [« *Dont, d'ailleurs, une des plus évidentes manifestations est l'article 3 de la Charte des Nations Unies sur la base duquel ont été considérées comme des États membres originaires de l'ONU les entités fédérées de l'Ukraine et de la Biélorussie (…)* »].

[19] Forteau 2007, p. 768—my translation [« [s]uivant effectivement une 'approche fonctionnelle', au demeurant déjà sollicitée par la Cour de La Haye dans son avis de 1949 rendu dans l'affaire de la *Réparation des dommages*, le droit international contemporain dessine l'État sous la forme d'une figure à géométrie variable, dont le tracé des contours dépend de la matière impliquée, et il le relègue au simple rang d'une 'notion' dont l'interprétation dépend de 'l'économie et de l'objectif des dispositions au sein desquelles' elle figure (…). Les confins de l'État n'en sont pas moins mouvants, son 'périmètre' n'a rien d'une frontière intangible et physiquement bornée. Le droit international appréhende l'État comme une entité qu'il peut lui-même modeler (en témoigne le recours à des définitions conventionnelles de l'État [fn.18] ou la formule jurisprudentielle par laquelle les juridictions internationales ou étrangères décident que telle entité 'doit être considérée comme' une émanation de l'Etat), et ce dernier est, dans le droit international contemporain, de plus en plus souvent appréhendé différemment selon la norme appliquée. »]. See also Higgins 2001, pp. 547–562.

[20] See ICJ, Judgment, 21 March 1953, *Nottebohm (Liechtenstein v Guatemala), Preliminary Objection*, Rep. 1953, p. 7, para 119 or ICTY, Appeal Chamber, *Decision on the Defence Motion for Interlocutory Appeal on Jurisdiction*, 2 October 1995, IT-94-1-T, *Prosecutor v. Dusko Tadić*, para 17.

17. That appreciation must be made in accordance with the "general rule of interpretation" codified in Article 31, para 1, of the Vienna Convention on the Law of Treaties of 23 May 1969:

> 1. A treaty shall be interpreted in good faith in accordance with the ordinary meaning to be given to the terms of the treaty in their context and in the light of its object and purpose.

18. In this instance, the context and the object and purpose of the Statute and of its Article 12 are of particular importance due to the "variable geometry"[21] of the very concept of the State, which makes it difficult to keep to a single unambiguous meaning, and, therefore to an 'ordinary meaning'. In addition, the determination of the jurisdiction of international bodies (organisations and courts—the ICC being both) is a privileged area of teleological treaty interpretation.

19. The *Comte Bernadotte* case is a remarkable illustration of the use of such reasoning. The ICJ justifies therein the use of the UN's implied powers doctrine:

> It must be acknowledged that its Members, by entrusting certain functions to it, with the attendant duties and responsibilities, have clothed it with the competence required to enable those functions to be effectively discharged.[22]

And, regarding more precisely the capacity to submit an international claim with a view to seeking compensation for damages caused to its agents, the Court noted:

> Under international law, the Organization must be deemed to have those powers which, though not expressly provided in the Charter, are conferred upon it by necessary implication as being essential to the performance of its duties.[23]

20. Regarding more specifically the assessment of their own jurisdiction, international courts and tribunals usually opt for a teleological interpretation of the statutory provisions that support it. As noted by the ICTY in its founding ruling:

> 10. [J]urisdiction is not merely an ambit or sphere (better described in this case as 'competence'); it is basically—as is visible from the Latin origin of the word itself, *jurisdictio*—a legal power, hence necessarily a legitimate power, 'to state the law' (*dire le droit*) within this ambit, in an authoritative and final manner. [...]
> 11. A narrow concept of jurisdiction may, perhaps, be warranted in a national context but not in international law. International law, because it lacks a centralized structure, does not provide for an integrated judicial system operating an orderly division of labour among a number of tribunals, where certain aspects or components of jurisdiction as a power could be centralized or vested in one of them but not the others. In international law, every tribunal is a self-contained system (unless otherwise provided). This is incompatible with a narrow concept of jurisdiction, which presupposes a certain division of labour. Of course, the constitutive instrument of an international tribunal can limit some of its jurisdictional powers, but only to the extent to which such limitation does not jeopardize its "judicial character", as shall be discussed later

---

[21] Above, n. 17.
[22] Advisory Opinion, above, n. 5, p. 179.
[23] Ibid., p. 182. See also PCIJ, Advisory Opinion n° 13, 23 July 1926, *Competence of the ILO to Regulate Incidentally the Personal Work of the Employer*, Series B, N° 13, p. 18.

on. Such limitations cannot, however, be presumed and, in any case, they cannot be deduced from the concept of jurisdiction itself.[24]

21. The ICJ has faced similar issues in the *Genocide* and *Legality of the Use of Force* cases brought before it in the framework of the Yugoslav crisis.[25] Without entering into the meandering (and contradictions) of the Court's successive argument in those emotionally-charged and extraordinarily politically delicate cases, one can note that, except in those cases where the Claimant itself had in fact disputed the jurisdiction of the World Court,[26] in the end, the ICJ always retained its competence. It is quite apparent that in doing so, despite the legal "difficulties" of which it was aware and that it constantly tried to minimise,[27] the ICJ recognized full effect to the provisions regarding its jurisdiction—in cases involving unquestionably the most serious of international crimes: the crime of genocide.

22. Likewise, there cannot be any question for the ICC to go beyond the mission that the State Parties to the Rome Statute have given it, or to substitute its will to theirs, thus making itself a law maker, which it certainly is not. Nor can the problem be posed either in terms of "extensive" or "restrictive" interpretation of the Statute.[28] The idea is only to interpret a provision thereof in its context and in the framework of the specific issue on which the ICC might be called to pronounce itself for the purpose of determining the scope (and the limits) of its jurisdiction in the circumstances in question. For that purpose, the sensible guideline appearing in

---

[24] Decision, above, n. 20, paras 10–11. For another illustration of that approach, see for instance: ICJ, Advisory Opinion, 16 October 1975, *Western Sahara*: "the references to 'any legal question' in the abovementioned provisions of the Charter and Statute are not to be interpreted restrictively" (Rep 1975, p. 20, para 18).

[25] Application of the Convention on the Prevention and Punishment of the Crime of Genocide (*Bosnia and Herzegovina v. Serbia and Montenegro*), Provisional Measures, Order of 8 April 1993, Preliminary Objections, Judgment of 11 July 1996, Merits, Judgment of 26 February 2007; Application for Revision of the Judgment of 11 July 1996 in the Case concerning Application of the Convention on the Prevention and Punishment of the Crime of Genocide (*Bosnia and Herzegovina v. Yugoslavia*), Preliminary Objections (*Yugoslavia v. Bosnia and Herzegovina*), Judgment of 3 February 2003. Legality of Use of Force (*Serbia and Montenegro v. Belgium*), Provisional Measures, Order of 2 June 1999, Preliminary Objections, Judgment of 15 December 2004 (and seven other similar cases); Application of the Convention on the Prevention and Punishment of the Crime of Genocide (*Croatia v. Serbia*), Preliminary Objections, Judgment of 18 November 2008.

[26] Although it had not formally given notice of the discontinuance of the proceedings (*Rep* 2004, pp. 293–295, paras 31–36)—see also the ruling dated November 28, 2008, para 89; for the Preliminary Objections, see pp. 327–328, paras 129–172: in its ruling on the merits of 2007, in the *Genocide* case (Bosnia Herzegovina), the Court also comments that "No finding was made in those [eight similar] judgments on the question whether or not the Respondent was a party to the Genocide Convention at the relevant time" (Rep 2007, para 83).

[27] See in particular Rep 1993, p. 14, para 18; see also the 2007 Judgment, para 130 or the 2008 Judgment, para 75.

[28] On all these matters, see Charles de Visscher 1963, p. 263 or Denys Simon 1981, *passim*—in particular pp. 319–466.

the International Law Commission's Report on its final Draft Articles on the Law of Treaties should be kept in mind:

> When a treaty is open to two interpretations one of which does and the other does not enable the treaty to have appropriate effects, good faith and the objects and purposes of the treaty demand that the former interpretation should be adopted.[29]

23. Article 12 of the Statute,[30] according to its very title, establishes the "Preconditions to the Exercise of Jurisdiction" by the ICC. Participation in the Statute (para 1) or the declaration provided for in para 3 are therefore conditional acts whose non-existence would prevent the Court from exercising its jurisdiction. It is indeed only if this declaration is made[31] that the Court can carry out its mission (to which para 1 of Article 12 formally refers, mentioning "the crimes specified in Article 5"[32]): the judgment of persons accused of the crime of genocide, of a crime against humanity or of a war crime. This involves, to quote the terms of the Preamble, crimes of such gravity that they "threaten the peace, security and well-being of the world", which, being "of concern to the international community as a whole, must not go unpunished" and whose "effective prosecution must be ensured by taking measures at the national level and by enhancing international cooperation."

24. It is also telling that according to the terms of Article 12, para 3, the jurisdiction of the Court is established whenever a State that can claim a territorial title *or* a personal title has agreed to its jurisdiction.[33] As a result, the Court may exercise its jurisdiction for events that took place under the jurisdiction of States that have not ratified the Statute nor made the declaration specified in para 3 of Article 12, or with regard to nationals of States that are not parties nor have formulated a declaration.[34] Consequently, mutual consent, which is a crucial condition for the jurisdiction of most international courts (including the ICJ), is not a condition for the exercise by the

---

[29] ILC, Yearbook 1966, vol. II, p. 218, para (6) of the Commentaries under Draft Article 28.

[30] Above, para 1.

[31] The question of Palestine ratifying the Statute does not arise for now, but it is not forbidden that it might appear in the future.

[32] Article 5, para 1: "The jurisdiction of the Court shall be limited to the most serious crimes of concern to the international community as a whole. The Court has jurisdiction in accordance with this Statute with respect to the following crimes:

(a) The crime of genocide;
(b) Crimes against humanity;
(c) War crimes;
(d) The crime of aggression.

See also the introduction to Article 13, referring to para 2 of Article 12: "The Court may exercise its jurisdiction with respect to a crime referred to in Article 5 in accordance with the provisions of this Statute".

[33] For a clear description of the drafting history that led to the adoption of that principle in spite of the determined opposition of some States, including the United States, see Kaul 2002, pp. 593–605.

[34] See in particular Condorelli 1999, p. 18.

ICC of its jurisdiction. The possibility open to the Security Council acting under Chapter VII of the UN Charter by Article 13(b) of the Statute, to refer to the Prosecutor "a situation in which one or more of such crimes appears to have been committed" confirms this conclusion. In this regard, the ICC can be compared to regional courts dedicated to human rights protection. The finding made, for example, by the European Court of Human Rights in the *Loizidou v Turkey* case, in which the Court strongly stressed that the non-recognition, by one of the parties to the dispute, of the Government of the other does not prevent the exercise of its jurisdiction, can, in its principle, be transposed to the problem under review:

> 41. In any event recognition of an applicant Government by a respondent Government is not a precondition for either the institution of proceedings under Article 24 (Article 24[*sic*] [*sic*]) of the Convention or the referral of cases to the Court under Article 48 (Article 48) (see application no. 8007/77, *loc. cit.*, pp. 147–148). If it were otherwise, the system of collective enforcement which is a central element in the Convention system could be effectively neutralised by the interplay of recognition between individual Governments and States.[35]

25. Far from governing only relations between States "[t]he Statute deals with the collective reaction of its State Parties to the breach by an individual of its obligation *erga omnes*".[36] This puts into perspective the importance not that a consent be given by the holder of a territorial or personal title, but that of the legal qualification of the entity providing this consent: whether it is a State, as believed by a majority of the existing States in the world, that have recognised Palestine as such[37]—or not as considered by a minority of other countries, the fact is that only the Palestinian authority possesses, under international law, an exclusive territorial title over the Palestinian territory and the population established therein.

26. Besides, it is indeed in its capacity as territorial sovereign that Palestine made the declaration under Article 12, para 3, on January 21, 2009:

> The Government of Palestine hereby recognizes the jurisdiction of the Court for the (…) crimes committed *on the territory* of Palestine since 1 July 2002.[38]

27. There is no doubt that the West Bank and Gaza are occupied territories and are internationally recognised as such. Like the ICJ observed in its Advisory Opinion of 9 July 2004:

> The territories situated between the Green Line (…) and the former eastern boundary of Palestine under the Mandate were occupied by Israel in 1967 during the armed conflict between Israel and Jordan. Under customary international law, these were therefore occupied territories in which Israel had the status of occupying Power. Subsequent events in these territories (…) have done nothing to alter this situation. All these territories

---

[35] ECHR, *Loizidou v. Turkey, Preliminary Objections*, 23 March 1995, n°. 15318/89, para 41. My emphasis.

[36] Kaul 2002, p. 609.

[37] See above, n. 3.

[38] For the full text of the declaration, see above para 3.

(including East Jerusalem) remain occupied territories and Israel has continued to have the status of occupying Power.[39]

28. This Opinion is not an appropriate framework for drawing all the consequences of this hard to challenge position. It suffices to note that:

- In no way does the occupation of a territory grant the occupying power sovereignty thereupon: "Whatever the effects of the occupation of a territory by the opponent before peace is re-established, it is certain that such occupation alone does not cause the sovereignty to be transferred".[40]
- Conversely, the *de facto* annexation of Palestinian territories infringes territorial sovereignty and the rights of the Palestinians to self-determination.[41] And it is untenable to consider the Oslo–Washington Interim Agreement as a renunciation from their part to the right to self-determination: not only is this right imprescriptible, but also Article 1 of the Declaration of Principles on Interim Self-Government Arrangements (Washington, 13 September 1993—"Aim of the Negotiations") emphasises that the suspension of the effects of the 1988 Algiers Declaration, in view of « a permanent settlement based on Security Council Resolutions 242 and 338 » , was only intended for a maximal period of five years;
- Besides, Israel does not claim the exercise of territorial sovereignty over the occupied territories[42]: thus for instance, in its report to the Committee on Economic and Social Rights, dated October 19, 2001, it argued that: "Israel has consistently maintained that the Covenant does not apply to areas that are not

---

[39] ICJ, Advisory Opinion, 9 July 2004, *Legal Consequences of the Construction of a Wall in the Occupied Palestinian Territory*, Rep 167, para 78.

[40] Eugène Borel's Arbitral Award in the case of the *Dette publique ottomane*, RIAA, vol. I, p. 535, my translation [« *Quels que soient les effets de l'occupation d'un territoire par l'adversaire avant le rétablissement de la paix, il est certain qu'à elle seule cette occupation ne pouvait opérer le transfert de souveraineté* »]; see Pellet 1992, pp. 174–180; in French: "*La destruction de Troie n'aura pas lieu—Il n'y a qu'un critère de mise en œuvre du droit de l'occupation de guerre: le respect des droits souverains du peuple soumis à occupation*" (Pal YBIL, 1987–1988, pp. 51–58) and the case-law and doctrine cited.

[41] See above n. 39, the ICJ's Advisory Opinion, pp. 181–182, para 115 and p. 184, para 122.

[42] Even though it denies,—wrongly in my opinion—the occupied territory status of some portions of the territory annexed following the 1967 armed conflict (Golan Heights, East Jerusalem). Among the numerous resolutions of the General Assembly condemning the occupation, one can mention: A/RES/63/29 26 November 2008, A/RES/61/25, 1st December 2006, A/RES/58/21, 3 December 2003 (Peaceful settlement of the question of Palestine), A/RES/43/58, 6 December 1988 (Report of the Special Committee to Investigate Israeli Practices Affecting the Human Rights of the Population of the Occupied Territories). A great number of resolutions of the Security Council also remind Israel of the duties of an occupying country; see en particular 446 (1979), 22 March 1979, 452 (1979), 20 July 1979, 465 (1980), 1st March 1980 or 904 (1994), 18 March 1994.

subject to its sovereign territory and jurisdiction"[43] (i.e. the West Bank and Gaza).[44]

- On many occasions the United Nations General Assembly[45] and the Security Council[46] recalled the enforceability, in all occupied territories, of the law of war occupation, and in particular of the Fourth Geneva Convention, as the ICJ recalled in its *Wall* Opinion of 2004.[47]
- In the Cairo Agreement of 4 May, 1994, on Gaza and Jericho, and in the Israeli–Palestinian Interim Agreement on the West Bank and the Gaza Strip signed in Washington DC on 25 September 1995, Israel recognises[48] the Palestinian jurisdiction in judicial (including criminal)[49] and human rights[50] matters. By accepting the ICC's jurisdiction with regard to the crimes specified in Article 5 of the Rome Statute, Palestine partly discharges this responsibility.[51]

29. It is additionally noteworthy that, in its 2004 Opinion, the World Court stressed that Section III of the Regulation appended to the 1907 Hague Regulations that "concerns 'Military authority over the territory *of the hostile State*', is particularly pertinent in the present case".[52] In doing so, the ICJ clearly considers that the Fourth 1949 Geneva Convention "is applicable in the Palestinian territories

---

[43] E/1990/6/Add.32, para 5; see also the Advisory Opinion, above, n. 39, Rep 2004, pp. 173–174, para 93 and the ruling of the Supreme Court of Israel dated May 30, 2004, mentioned, same pp. 175–176, para 100.

[44] Such is the stand constantly maintained by Israel before the universal human rights conventions monitoring bodies. See CERD/C/ISR/CO/13, para 3. CEDAW, Report by the Committee for the elimination of discrimination against women, August 31, 2005, doc A/60/38, p. 143, para 243, Human Rights Committee, Final Observations of the Human Rights Committee, Israel, August 21, 2003, doc CCPR/CO/78/ISR, para 1.

[45] See the General Assembly resolution A/ES–10/2 dated April 23, 1997: "Also convinced, in this context, that the repeated violation by Israel, the occupying Power, of international law and its failure to comply with relevant Security Council and General Assembly resolutions and the agreements reached between the parties undermine the Middle East peace process and constitute a threat to international peace and security". See also A/RES/63/29 dated November 26, 2008, above n. 42.

[46] See resolution 242 (1967) dated November 22, 1967, which stresses the inadmissibility of the acquisition of territories by means of war and calls for the "withdrawal of Israel armed forces from territories occupied in the recent conflict" and "termination of all claims or states of belligerency"; see also resolution 446 (1979) dated March 22, 1979 and more recent resolutions cited above, n. 42.

[47] Above, n. 39, Rep 2004, p. 176, paras 98–99.

[48] It cannot be a transfer of jurisdiction: the occupying party is certainly not the original holder; see, for instance, on that matter: Bastid-Burdeau 2006, p. 169.

[49] See Articles IV and XVII of the Interim Agreement and annex IV, Article I (see also Article VII, para 2, de Oslo Agreement of 13 September 1993).

[50] See Article XIX ibid.

[51] It is a fact that the Israel Palestinian agreements exclude Israeli citizens from the jurisdiction of Palestinian courts. See Article XVII 4(ii) of the 1995 interim agreement and Article 13(ii) of Appendix IV. But it is doubtful that bilateral agreements prevail over the ICC's jurisdiction such as specified in its Statute.

[52] Above-mentioned Advisory Opinion, note 39, Rep 2004, p. 171, para 89, emphasis added.

which before the conflict lay to the east of the Green Line and which, during that conflict, were occupied by Israel, *there being no need for any enquiry into the precise prior status of those territories*".[53]

30. The same reasoning can be transposed, *mutatis mutandis*, to this instance:

- The general interpretation rule reflected in Article 31 of the 1969 Vienna Convention should be applied to Article 12 of the Rome Statute[54];
- That provisions applies whenever a State (holding a territorial or personal title) makes the declaration planned in para 3[55];
- It reflects the intention of the authors of the Statute not to permit a State to unilaterally block the exercise of its jurisdiction by the ICC and to give as broad an extent as possible to the fight against impunity of the crimes listed in Article 5, which is the basic object of the treaty[56];
- While encompassing both the territorial sovereignty and the jurisdiction of the flag or registration State within the spaces submitted to an international legal regime, Article 12, para 2(a), of the ICC Statute is worded in such a way as to cover all the world spaces; in the contemporary world, there exists no more '*terra nullius*' (namely spaces free of any State or inter-State hold): they are either submitted to a State sovereignty or to an international legal regime according to which States may exercise police powers, by virtue of their 'personal' jurisdiction, over ships, aircrafts and space objects; the consequence thus entailed by Article 12, para 2(a), is consistent with the overall philosophy of the Statute: universal jurisdiction calls for an universal field of application.
- It can be inferred from the above that one or more contracting Parties could not prevent the Palestinian declaration of January 21, 2009 from producing its effects on the Palestinian territory; by making it ineffective, the Court would give its blessing to the constitution of a zone of impunity in the territories occupied by Israel, which is contrary to the intentions of the authors of the Rome Statute, and to is very purpose and object, since, in this case, *no* State could grant the Court jurisdiction within these territories.

31. The situation which would ensue from the ICC's refusal to give effect to the 2009 Palestinian declaration accepting its jurisdiction would be far more shocking and would have far more serious consequences than the one resulting from the position—moreover quite open to criticism[57]—of Switzerland following

---

[53] Ibid., p. 177, para 101.

[54] See above, para 17.

[55] See above, para 23.

[56] Ibid.

[57] For a few examples of those justified criticisms, see for instance: Vera Gowlland-Debbas "Collective response to the Unilateral Declarations of Independence of Southern Rhodesia and Palestine: an application of the Legitimizing Function of the United Nations", BYBIL, Vol. LXI (1990), in particular p. 141 or Fatsah Ouguergouz 2001.

Palestine's 1989 ratification of the Fourth 1949 Red Cross Conventions. Indeed, as explained by the ICJ:

> Palestine gave a unilateral undertaking, by declaration of 7 June 1982, to apply the Fourth Geneva Convention. Switzerland, as depositary State, considered that unilateral undertaking valid. It concluded, however, that it '[was] not—as a depositary—in a position to decide whether' 'the request [dated 14 June 1989] from the Palestine Liberation Movement in the name of the 'State of Palestine' to accede' *inter alia* to the Fourth Geneva Convention 'can be considered as an instrument of accession.[58]

In other words, the unilateral undertaking by Palestine (which certainly binds it)[59] overcame most[60] of the disadvantages resulting from Switzerland's undeniable failure to perform its duties as depository[61]: under its 1982 Declaration Palestine was (and is) bound to comply with the rules of the Fourth 1949 Convention. However, the implementation of the Rome Statute is not Palestine's responsibility, it is the Court's[62]: if the latter declares the Palestinian declaration to be invalid, it will remain irreversibly (except if the Security Council takes action) ineffective in the Palestinian occupied territories.

31. This situation would be all the more intolerable that by its very nature, the purpose of the Statute is to protect the basic interests of the international community as a whole and is reminiscent of the 1948 Genocide Convention of which the ICJ observed that:

> In such a convention the contracting States do not have any interests of their own; they merely have, one and all, a common interest, namely, the accomplishment of those high purposes which are the raison d'être of the convention. Consequently, in a convention of

---

[58] Advisory Opinion, above, n. 39, Rep 2004, p. 173, para 91.

[59] See ICJ, Judgment, 20 December 1974, *Nuclear Tests*, Rep 1974, p. 267, para 43 and p. 472, para 46; see also Principles relating to Guiding Principles Applicable to Unilateral Declarations of States Capable of Creating Legal Obligations, in particular principles n° 1 and 3 (see ILC's Report on its fifty-eighth session (May 1–June 9–July 3–August 11, 2006) General Assembly, Official Documents, 61st session, Supplement n° 10, (A/61/10) p. 370.

[60] This situation could however be unfair to Palestine if it were found that its undertaking was made without any condition of reciprocity—for reasons that do not need to be developed here, it is not my opinion.

[61] See Article 77 of the 1969 Vienna Convention on Law of Treaties, which indisputably shows that Switzerland—which was indeed not responsible for pronouncing on the nature of the PLO's application—should have informed the Parties to the 1949 Conventions as well as the States eligible to become such Parties.

[62] In addition, the Swiss government relied on the fact that "in its capacity as depository of the Geneva Conventions and their additional protocols, it was not in a position to settle the point of knowing whether that communication has to be considered as a membership instrument in the meaning of the relevant contractual provisions of the Conventions and their additional protocols" (*Note d'information du Gouvernement suisse*, Berne, 13 September1989, para 2). The Court, which has the *kompetenz kompetenz*, (see above para 16), could not rely on such reasoning.

this type one cannot speak of individual advantages or disadvantages to States, or of the maintenance of a perfect contractual balance between rights and duties.[63]

As the World Court found in the same Advisory Opinion (and as is true in the present case):

> The object and purpose of the Genocide Convention [here the Rome Statute] imply that it was the intention of the General Assembly [here the State Parties Conference] and of the States which adopted it that as many States as possible should participate. The complete exclusion from the Convention of one or more States would not only restrict the scope of its application, but would detract from the authority of the moral and humanitarian principles which are its basis. It is inconceivable that the contracting parties readily contemplated that an objection to a minor reservation should produce such a result.[64]

33. As a result, and based on this review, I am led to conclude that the Palestinian Declaration of 21 January 2009, accepting the ICC's jurisdiction for the purpose of identifying, prosecuting and judging the authors of crimes listed in Article 5 of the Rome Statute committed in the territory of Palestine since 1st July 2002 and their accomplices, can be effective in accordance with the provisions of Article 12 of the Statute, and specifically that all conditions for the Court to exercise its jurisdiction in pursuance of Article 13 are met:

- *Ratione materiae*, the Goldstone Report—to mention only it—allows to reasonably believe that crimes that could fall under the Court's jurisdiction may have been committed by both sides[65] during the "Operation Cast Lead"[66];

---

[63] ICJ, Advisory Opinion, 28 May 1951, *Reservations to the Convention on the Prevention and Punishment of the Crime of Genocide*, Rep 1951, p. 24. See also *Application of the Convention on the Prevention and Punishment of the Crime of Genocide, Preliminary Objections*, Rep. 1996, p. 611, para 22 and, in the same case, Judgment of 26 February 2007, para 161 and the Advisory Opinion, 8 July 1996, *Legality of the Threat or Use of Nuclear Weapons*, Rep. 1996, p. 257.

[64] Rep. 1951, p. 24; see also Rep. 1996, p. 612, para 22.

[65] It is not uninteresting to note that Palestine intends to follow up on the recommendations of the Goldstone Report, by setting up an independent investigating committee in its territory (see Letter dated 29 January 2010 from the Permanent Observer of Palestine to the United Nations addressed to the Secretary-General, Appendix II, document A/64/651, Report of the Secretary-General, Follow-up to the report of the United Nations Fact-Finding Mission on the Gaza Conflict. The undertaking, which can only be based on the territorial sovereignty of the Palestinian Authority in the occupied territories, is part of the same process than the one that led to the January 21, 2009 declaration.

[66] Other international reports lead to believe that war crimes and/or crimes against humanity may have been committed in the territory of Palestine since July 1, 2002; see in particular Amnesty International 2009 dated July 2, 2009, and Human Rights Watch 2009 dated March 25, 2009.

- *Ratione temporis*, by retrospectively recognising the jurisdiction of the ICC for actions posterior to 1st July 2002 (the date on which the Rome Statute came into force), the Declaration complies with the terms of Article 11[67];
- *Ratione loci* (and as a result *ratione personae*), it extends the jurisdiction of the Court to crimes committed on the territory of Palestine, upon which only the Palestinian Authority has territorial sovereignty[68] (and to the persons having committed them) in accordance with the provisions of Article 12, para 2(b), which provides for the Court's jurisdiction over a State "on the territory of which the conduct in question occurred"; and
- "*Ratione conventionis*" so to speak, these mechanisms can be set into motion, in pursuance of the statement made by a relevant Palestinian authority[69] on 21 January 2009.

34. On this last point, which is central to the issues discussed in this Opinion, it appears to me that the Court does not, for the reasons developed above, need to pronounce, in theory, on the issue of whether, "in absolute", Palestine is or not a State. This would necessitate for it to decide between the sovereign assessments of the States that constitute the international society (and that have a power of appreciation for that purpose) whereas they are deeply divided. Rather, it just has to acknowledge that, whatever the situation in other cases, for the purpose of the Rome Statute, this Declaration could be made in accordance with the provisions of Article 12 and that it can have the effects specified by Article 13.

9.4 Postscript

This legal opinion has been co-signed by the following authorities:

Georges ABI-SAAB, Honorary Professor of International Law at the Graduate Institute of International and Development Studies, Geneva, Honorary

---

[67] "Article 11, Jurisdiction *ratione temporis*:

1. The Court has jurisdiction only with respect to crimes committed after the entry into force of this Statute.
2. If a State becomes a Party to this Statute after its entry into force, the Court may exercise its jurisdiction only with respect to crimes committed after the entry into force of this Statute for that State, unless that State has made a declaration under Article 12, para 3."

[68] See above paras 25–28.

[69] The declaration is signed by the Minister for Justice, but as noted by the ICJ, "with increasing frequency in modern international relations other persons [other than the Head of State, the Head of Government and the Minister for Foreign Affairs] representing a State in specific fields may be authorized by that State to bind it by their statements in respect of matters falling within their purview. This may be true, for example, of holders of technical ministerial portfolios exercising powers in their field of competence in the area of foreign relations, and even of certain officials" (ICJ, Judgment, 3 February 2006, *Armed Activities on the Territory of the Congo* (*New Application*: 2002) (*Democratic Republic of the Congo v. Rwanda*), para 47.

Professor at the Law Faculty of the University of Cairo, Member of the Institut de Droit international

M. Cherif BASSIOUNI, Distinguished Research Professor of Law Emeritus at DePaul University College of Law, President Emeritus of the Law School's International Human Rights Law Institute, President of the International Institute of Higher Studies in Criminal Sciences (Siracusa) and Honorary President of the International Association of Penal Law (Paris)

Rafaâ BEN ACHOUR, Professor of Law, Director of the International Law and International Tribunals Research Unit, Faculty of Social, Political and Juridical Studies, Tunis

Phon van den BIESEN, Attorney at Law, Amsterdam

Michael BOHLANDER, Professor of International Law, Durham Law School, Director of the Centre for Criminal Law and Criminal Justice

Laurence BOISSON DE CHAZOURNES, Professor of International Law, Director of the Department of Public International Law and International Organization, Faculty of Law, University of Geneva

Jorge CARDONA LLORENS, Professor of International Law at Jaume I University (Castellón), Director of the International Law Department of the Bancaja International Center for Peace and Development

Monique CHEMILLIER-GENDREAU, Professor emeritus at the University Denis Diderot (Paris VII); Honorary President of the European Association of Lawyers for Democracy and Human Rights in the World

Luigi CONDORELLI, Professor of Law, University of Florence

Benedetto CONFORTI, Professeur of International Law at the University of Naples; Former Judge of the European Court of Human Rights, Member of the Institut de Droit international

Vojin DIMITRIJEVIC, Professor of Public International Law, Union University School of Law (Belgrade); Director, Belgrade Centre for Human Rights; Member of the Institut de Droit international

John DUGARD, Professor of Public International Law, University of Leiden, Member of the UN International Law Commission, Member of the Institut de Droit international

Paula ESCARAMEIA, Professor of International Law at the Higher Institute of Social and Political Sciences, Technical University of Lisbon; Member of the UN International Law Commission

Marina EUDES, Assistant Professor at the University Paris Ouest Nanterre/La Défense

Ahmed S. El KOSHERI, Professor of Law and Former President of Senghor University in Alexandria, Member of the Institut de Droit International

Salifou FOMBA, Professor of International Law, University of Mali, Member of the UN International Law Commission

Mathias FORTEAU, Professor of International Law, University of Paris Ouest, Nanterre-La Défense, Secretary-General of the Société française pour le Droit international

Francesco FRANCIONI, Professor of International Law and Human Rights, Director of the European Law Academy, European University Institute, Florence, Associate Member of the Institut de Droit international

Zdzislaw W. GALICKI, Professor and Director of the Institute of International Law, University of Warsaw, Member and former Chairman of the UN International Law Commission

Habib GHÉRARI, Professor of International Law, University Paul Cézanne Aix-Marseille III

Vera GOWLLAND-DEBBAS, Honorary Professor of International Law at the Graduate Institute of International and Development Studies, Geneva

Emmanuel JOS, Professor of Public International Law, University of the Antilles and Guyane, Dean of the Faculty of Law (Fort-de-France)

Franck LATTY, Professor of International Law, University of Auvergne (Clermont-Ferrand)

Ahmed MAHIOU, Professor of Law, Emeritus Director of Researches at the CNRS, Former Member and Former President of the International Law Commission, Member of the Institut de Droit international

Djamchid MOMTAZ, Professor of International Law at the University of Law, Tehran, Former Member and Former President of the International Law Commission, Member of the Institut de Droit international

Daniel MÜLLER, Researcher at the Centre de droit international de Nanterre (CEDIN), University of Paris Ouest, Nanterre-La Défense

Jordan PAUST, Mike & Teresa Baker Law Center Professor, University of Houston

Paolo PICONE, Professor of International Law at the University of Rome La Sapienza, Member of the Institut de Droit international

Antonio REMIRO BROTONS, Professor of Public International Law, Autonomous University of Madrid, Associate Member of the Institut de Droit international

François RIGAUX, Professor Emeritus at the Catholic University of Louvain, Member of the Institut de Droit international

Hélène RUIZ-FABRI, Professor of International Law at the University of Paris I—Panthéon Sorbonne, Director of the UMR de Droit comparé de Paris, President of the European Society of International Law

Jean SALMON, Professor Emeritus of the Université libre de Bruxelles, Member of the Institut de droit international, Member of the Permanent Court of Arbitration

William A. SCHABAS, Professor of International Law and Director, Irish Centre for Human Rights, National University of Ireland, Galway

Nico SCHRIJVER, Professor of International Law and Academic Director, Grotius Centre for International Legal Studies, Leiden University, Associate Member of the Institut de Droit international

Linos-Alexander SICILIANOS, Professor at the University of Athens, Rapporteur of the Committee on the Elimination of Racial Discrimination

Habib SLIM, Emeritus Professor of Public International Law, Law and Political Sciences Faculty, Tunis

Jean-Marc SOREL, Professor of International Law, University Paris I Panthéon-Sorbonne, Director, CERDIN

Sandra SZUREK, Professor of International Law, University of Paris Ouest, Nanterre-La Défense

Paul TAVERNIER, Emeritus Professor at the University Paris Sud (Paris XI)

Bérangère TAXIL, Professor of International Law at the University of Angers

References

Amnesty International (2009) Report: Israel/Gaza: operation "Cast Lead": 22 days of death and destruction. http://www.amnesty.org/en/library/info/MDE15/015/2009/en

Bastid-Burdeau G (2006) Les Références au Droit International dans la Question des Titres de Compétence dans les Territoires de L'ancienne Palestine sous mandat: Incertitudes et Confusion. In: SFDI, Colloque de Rennes, Les compétences de l'Etat en Droit international, Pedone

Condorelli L (1999) La Cour Internationale en débat. RGDIP 1:18

Daillier P, Forteau M, Pellet A (2009) Droit International Public, 8th edn. LGDJ, Paris

de Visscher (1963) Problèmes D'interprétation Judiciaire en Droit International Public, Pedone, Paris

Dupuy P (2002) L'unité de l'Ordre Juridique International, RCADI 297(1):108–109

Forteau M (2007) L'État selon le Droit International: une Figure à Géométrie Variable? RGDIP 4:762–763

Higgins R (2001) The Concept of the 'State': Variable Geometry and Dualist Perceptions. In: de Chazournes LB, Gowlland-Debbas V (eds) The International Legal System in Quest of Equity and Universality. Kluwer, The Hague, pp 547–562

Human Rights Watch (2009) Report: Rain of Fire, Israel, Unlawful Use of White Phosphorus in Gaza. http://www.hrw.org/fr/reports/2009/03/25/rain-fire

Kaul H (2002) Preconditions to the Exercise of Jurisdiction. In: Cassese A, Gaeta P, Jones J (eds) The Rome Statute of the International Criminal Court: A Commentary. Oxford University Press, Oxford, pp 593–605

Ouguergouz F (2001) Palestine and the August 12, 1949 Geneva Conventions or the History of an Aborted Membership. In: de Chazournes LB, Gowlland-Debbas V (eds) The International Legal System in Quest of Equity and Universality. Kluwer, The Hague, pp 507–543

Pellet A (1992) The Destruction of Troy Will Not Take Place. In: Playfair E (ed) The Administration of Occupied Territories: The West Bank. Clarendon Press, Oxford, pp 174–180

Pellet A (1998) Le Droit International à L'aube du XXIème Siècle (La Société Internationale Contemporaine—Permanence et Tendances Nouvelles). In: Cours Euro-méditerranéens Bancaja de Droit International, vol 1, 1997, Aranzadi, Pampelune, pp 51–52

Simon D (1981) L'interprétation Judiciaire des Traités D'organisations Internationales—Morphologie des Conventions et Fonction Juridictionnelle, Pedone, Paris

Chapter 10
The Palestine Declaration to the International Criminal Court: The Statehood Issue

John Quigley

Contents

10.1	Prior Episodes that Raised the Issue of Palestine Statehood	431
10.2	Palestine's Declaration of Statehood	432
10.3	Possible Claimants to Palestine Territory	434
10.4	Entitlement to Self-Determination	435
10.5	Reaction of States	435
10.6	A Continuing Statehood	436
10.7	Conclusion	439
References		439

In the wake of Israel's military incursion into Gaza from December 2008 to January 2009, the Palestinian National Authority filed in the International Criminal Court (ICC) a declaration accepting the jurisdiction of the ICC in the territory of Palestine. The Declaration, submitted on the letterhead of the Palestinian National Authority, Ministry of Justice, Office of Minister, reads:

Declaration recognizing the Jurisdiction of the International Criminal Court
In conformity with Article 12, para 3 of the Statute of the International Criminal Court, the Government of Palestine hereby recognizes the jurisdiction of the Court for the purpose of identifying, prosecuting and judging the authors and accomplices of acts committed on the territory of Palestine since 1 July 2002. As a consequence, the Government of Palestine will cooperate with the Court without delay or exception, in conformity with Chapter IX of the Statute. This declaration, made for an indeterminate duration, will enter into force

---

President's Club Professor in Law, Moritz College of Law, The Ohio State University. This article was first published in 35 Rutgers Law Records (2009), 1–10.

J. Quigley (✉)
Moritz College of Law, The Ohio State University, USA

upon its signature. Material supplementary to and supporting this declaration will be provided shortly in a separate communication.

Signed in The Hague, The Netherlands, 21 January 2009. For the Government of Palestine Minister of Justice s/Ali Khashan[1]

The declaration references the ICC Statute, which gives the ICC jurisdiction over aggression, genocide, crimes against humanity, and war crimes.[2] Article 13 specifies the circumstances in which the ICC has jurisdiction over the crimes listed in the Statute.[3] Article 12 provides that if a state party refers a case to the Prosecutor, or if the Prosecutor initiates an investigation on the basis of information received, the ICC has jurisdiction if either (1) the state in whose territory the conduct occurred is a party to the ICC Statute, or (2) the state of nationality of a particular accused person is a party.[4] Article 12 goes on to say that if the state in whose territory the conduct occurred, or the state of nationality of a named person, is not a party to the ICC Statute, that state may accept ICC jurisdiction "with respect to the crime in question" by filing a declaration with the Registrar of the Court.[5] It was under that provision that the Minister of Justice filed.

The Palestine declaration was not limited to a particular crime but accepted ICC jurisdiction over any crimes committed in Palestine territory from the date on which the ICC Statute entered into force, July 1, 2002.[6] The declaration did not further identify the "territory of Palestine" but such territory would presumably include at least Gaza and the West Bank of the Jordan River.

The ICC Prosecutor received the Minister of Justice's declaration and indicated that the filing would be analyzed before a decision was made on whether to pursue an investigation. In a press statement, his office indicated:

The ICC Prosecutor received the Minister of Justice's declaration and indicated that the filing would be analyzed before a decision was made on whether to pursue an investigation. In a press statement, his office indicated:

> Since 27 December 2008, the Office of the Prosecutor (OTP) has also received 326 communications under Article 15 by individuals and NGOs, related to the situation context of Israel and the Palestinian Territories; some of them were made public by the senders. As per normal practice, the Office is considering all information, including open sources. The Office will carefully examine all relevant issues related to the jurisdiction of the Court, including whether the declaration by the Palestinian National Authority accepting the exercise of jurisdiction by the ICC meets statutory requirements; whether the

---

[1] Declaration recognizing the Jurisdiction of the International Criminal Court, available at http://www.icc-cpi.int/NR/rdonlyres/74EEE201-0FED-4481-95D4-C8071087102C/279777/20090122PalestinianDeclaration2.pdf.

[2] Rome Statute of the International Criminal Court, July 17, 1998, Article 5, para 1 [hereinafter ICC Statute], available at http://untreaty.un.org/cod/icc/statute/english/rome_statute(e).pdf.

[3] Id. Article 13.

[4] Id. Article 12.

[5] Id. Article 12, para 3.

[6] See ICC Statute, *supra* n. 2. The ICC has jurisdiction "only with respect to crimes committed after the entry into force of this Statute." Article 11, para 1.

10   The Palestine Declaration to the International Criminal Court   431

alleged crimes fall within the category of crimes defined in the Statute, and whether there are national proceedings in relation to those crimes.[7]

A few days earlier, Bolivia called on the UN Security Council to refer the Gaza situation to the ICC so that the responsibility of Israeli officials could be investigated.[8] Under the ICC Statute, the ICC gains jurisdiction over a situation if the Security Council refers it to the ICC.[9]

As indicated in the press statement of the OTP, an investigation can be opened only if the ICC has jurisdiction.[10] The Palestine declaration may provide that jurisdiction. A key element in that determination is whether Palestine qualifies as a "state," since only a state that is sovereign in a particular territory can confer jurisdiction on the ICC in that territory.[11] This Article will argue that Palestine is a state, therefore satisfying a required element of the preconditions for ICC jurisdiction in Article 12(3) of the ICC Statute.

10.1 Prior Episodes that Raised the Issue of Palestine Statehood

Palestinian officials had twice before sought a status that required Palestine to be a state. In 1989, the Palestine Liberation Organization (PLO) applied for membership in the World Health Organization (WHO).[12] This effort floundered, however, after the United States informed the WHO that if Palestine were admitted as a member state, the United States would withhold funding.[13] At the time, the United States contributed one fourth of the WHO budget.[14] PLO Chairperson Yasser Arafat called the US statement "blackmail."[15] The WHO director general asked the PLO to withdraw the application.[16] The WHO then voted to postpone action on

---

[7] Press Release, ICC Office of the Prosecutor, Visit of the Palestinian National Authority Minister of Foreign Affairs, Mr. Riad al-Malki, and Minister of Justice, Mr. Ali Khashan, to the Prosecutor of the ICC (Feb. 13, 2009), available at http://www.icc-cpi.int/NR/rdonlyres/A3B77241-DEC1-4E14-9EE5-A850086A7F70/280140/ICCOTP20090213Palestinerev.pdf. The ICC Statute allows the ICC Prosecutor to "initiate investigations *proprio motu* on the basis of information on crimes within the jurisdiction of the Court." ICC Statute, Article 15. para 1.

[8] See Press Release, General Assembly, General Assembly Demands Full Respect For Security Council Resolution 1860, UN Doc. GA/10809/Rev. 1 (Jan. 16, 2009) (statement of Hugo Siles Alvarado, Bolivia) available at http://un.org/News/Press/docs/2009/ga10809.doc.htm

[9] ICC Statute, Article 13(b).

[10] See ICC Statute, Article 15, para 1.

[11] Id., Article 12, para 3.

[12] Lewis 1989c.

[13] Lewis 1989b.

[14] Pertman 1989.

[15] Randal 1989.

[16] Kempster 1989.

the application.[17] Thus, the WHO came to no conclusion on the issue of Palestine statehood.

A few weeks later, in June 1989, the PLO submitted to the Government of Switzerland ratification documents for the Geneva Conventions of 1949. The validity of this ratification depended on Palestine being a state, since ratification of these four treaties is open only to "powers".[18] The Swiss Government replied to the PLO three months later:

> Due to the uncertainty [sic] within the international community as to the existence or the non-existence of a State of Palestine and as long as the issue has not been settled in an appropriate framework, the Swiss Government, in its capacity as depositary of the Geneva Conventions and their additional Protocols, is not in a position to decide whether this communication can be considered as an instrument of accession in the sense of the relevant provisions of the Conventions and their additional Protocols.[19]

Thus, like the WHO, Switzerland took no position on Palestine statehood. Switzerland did not regard it as proper, as a single state, to make a determination that would have implications for the international community.

10.2 Palestine's Declaration of Statehood

In 1988, statehood was declared for Palestine by its representative body, the Palestine National Council. It was that declaration that provided the basis for the approaches both to the WHO and to the Government of Switzerland. The 1988 statehood declaration proclaimed "the establishment of the State of Palestine in the land of Palestine with its capital at Jerusalem."[20] As a result of the declaration, PLO Chairman Yasser Arafat was invited to address the UN General Assembly.[21] The General Assembly then adopted a resolution in which it "acknowledg[ed] the proclamation of the State of Palestine by the Palestine National Council on 15 November 1988," and, further, decided that "the designation 'Palestine' should be used in place of the designation 'Palestine Liberation Organization' in the

---

[17] Randal 1989; Bollag 1989.

[18] Convention for the Amelioration of the Condition of the Wounded and Sick in Armed Forces in the Field Article 60, Aug. 12, 1949, 75 UNTS; Convention for the Amelioration of the Condition of Wounded, Sick and Shipwrecked Members of Armed Forces at Sea Article 59, Aug. 12, 1949, 75 UNTS 85; Convention Relative to the Treatment of Prisoners of War Article 139, Aug. 12, 1949, 75 UNTS 135; Convention Relative to the Protection of Civilian Persons in Time of War Article 155, Aug. 12, 1949, 75 UNTS 287.

[19] *Note of Information*, Government of Switzerland, Berne, Sept. 13, 1989.

[20] Palestine National Council: Political Communique and Declaration of Independence, Nov. 15, 1988, UN Doc. A/43/827, S/20278, Annex III, Nov. 18, 1988, reprinted in 27 ILM 1668 (1988).

[21] Pear 1988.

United Nations system."[22] One hundred and four states voted for this resolution, forty four abstained; only the United States and Israel voted against.[23]

That strong vote indicates that Palestine was regarded as a state. Had there been opposition, it would have been expressed. One may contrast in this regard the UN reaction in 1983 to a declaration of statehood for a Turkish Republic of Northern Cyprus. The international community found this declaration invalid on the grounds that Turkey had occupied Cypriot territory militarily and that the putative state was an infringement on Cypriot sovereignty. The UN Security Council pronounced the independence declaration illegal: "Concerned at the declaration by the Turkish Cypriot authorities issued on 15 November 1983 which purports to create an independent State in northern Cyprus, … [c]onsidering … that the attempt to create a 'Turkish Republic of Northern Cyprus' is invalid," the Security Council said that it "[c]onsiders the declaration referred to above as legally invalid and calls for its withdrawal [...]."[24]

Had the international community viewed the 1988 Palestine declaration as invalid, it would have said so loudly and clearly, given the volatility of the situation in the Middle East. It did not.

The United Nations, as indicated, was already referring to Palestine as a state for purposes of its participation in the Organization.[25] In 1989, a resolution was drafted in the UN General Assembly to construe "Palestine" as a "State" in UN documents.[26] The United States threatened to withhold its UN dues, and the draft was not put to a vote.[27]

All of this UN action came against a background of support for the proposition that the Palestinians enjoyed a right of self-determination. In 1974, the UN General Assembly had resolved in favor of the self-determination rights of the Palestinian people.[28] In a companion resolution, it accepted the Palestine Liberation Organization as an observer at the United Nations.[29]

The UN dealt with Palestine as a state. The UN Security Council let it participate routinely in Security Council sessions when relevant issues were on its agenda.[30] Under Security Council rules, only a "state" is entitled to participate.[31]

---

[22] GA Res. 43/177, UN GAOR, 43d Sess., UN Doc. A/RES/43/177 (Dec. 15, 1988); Lewis 1988.

[23] GA Res. 43/177.

[24] SC Res. 541, UN Doc. S/INF/39 (Nov. 18, 1983).

[25] See GA Res. 43/177.

[26] L.A. Times 1989.

[27] Lewis 1989a.

[28] GA Res. 3236, UN GAOR, 29th Sess., Supp. No. 31 at 4, UN Doc. A/9631 (Nov. 22, 1974).

[29] GA Res. 3237, UN GAOR, 29th Sess., Supp. No. 31 at 4, UN Doc. A/9631 (Nov. 22, 1974).

[30] Letter dated May 21, 2008 from the Permanent Observer of Palestine to the United Nations addressed to the President of the Security Council, UN Doc. S/2008/335 (2008) (referring to the Security Council's "past practice" in requesting participation at a Security Council discussion of the protection of civilians in armed conflict).

[31] Security Council, *Provisional Rules of Procedure*, Rule 14, UN Doc. S/96/Rev.4 (1946).

Following the 1988 Palestine declaration, Palestine was shortly thereafter recognized by 89 states.[32] Others hesitated, but their hesitation did not necessarily mean that they did not regard Palestine as a state. French President François Mitterand characterized the European view: "Many European countries are not ready to recognize a Palestine state. Others think that between recognition and non-recognition there are significant degrees; I am among these."[33]

10.3 Possible Claimants to Palestine Territory

At the time of the 1988 Palestine declaration, Israel controlled Gaza and the West Bank. That fact, however, is not fatal to Palestine statehood. The normal requirement of effective control over territory is applied less strictly if no competing entity claims title.[34] With Gaza and the West Bank, there were no competing claimants. Gaza was controlled by Egypt from 1948 to 1967, but Egypt never claimed sovereignty. Egypt regarded Gaza as part of Palestine.[35] A Constitution adopted for Gaza by Egypt in 1962 stated, "[t]he Gaza Strip is an indivisible part of the land of Palestine...."[36] Egypt regarded itself as protecting Gaza from Israel until the Palestine state could assume control. The 1962 Constitution proclaimed in this regard, "[t]his constitution shall continue to be observed in the Gaza Strip until a permanent constitution for the state of Palestine is issued."[37]

Jordan controlled the West Bank from 1948 to 1967. Jordan did assert sovereignty, but did so subject to Palestine's overriding claim to the territory. Jordan's parliament clarified in 1950 that Jordan acted "without prejudicing the final settlement of Palestine's just case within the sphere of national aspirations, inter-Arab co-operation and international justice."[38] One analyst characterized Jordan's arrangement: "One might thus conclude, it seems, that the Palestinians are only *provisionally* placed under Jordanian sovereignty."[39] In 1988, Jordan renounced its claim.[40]

Israel was in control of Gaza and the West Bank as a belligerent occupant but did not claim sovereignty. When territory is taken via belligerent occupation, sovereignty is not affected.[41] Upon entry of a belligerent occupant, "[t]he legal

---

[32] Lewis 1989a.

[33] Flory 1989, pp. 385 ff (translation by author).

[34] See Crawford 2006, p. 59.

[35] Farhi 1982, pp. 61 ff.

[36] *Republican Decree Announcing Constitutional System of Gaza Sector*, Mar. 9, 1962, Article 1, 17 Middle E.J. 156 (1963).

[37] Id., Article 73.

[38] Ross 1950.

[39] Feuer 1970 (translation by author).

[40] Kifner 1988a; Kifner 1988b; Times 1988.

[41] Crawford 2006, p. 73.

(*de jure*) sovereignty still remains vested where it was before the territory was occupied, although obviously the legal sovereign is unable to exercise his ruling powers in the occupied territory."[42] "[T]he occupant does not in any way acquire sovereign rights in the occupied territory but exercises a temporary right of administration on a trustee basis."[43] According to the *Restatement of Foreign Relations Law of the United States*, "[a]n entity does not necessarily cease to be a state even if all of its territory has been occupied by a foreign power or if it has otherwise lost control of its territory temporarily."[44] Kuwait, for example, was a state in 1990–1991, even as it was under Iraq's occupation.[45] Israel's control poses no impediment to a conclusion that Palestine is sovereign in Gaza and the West Bank.[46]

10.4 Entitlement to Self-Determination

Palestine's solid self-determination claim provides a further reason why the international community accepted Palestine as a state even though it did not control territory. As Africa was being decolonized, the issue arose of recognition of colonies as states when the colonial power remained in control. Congo was accepted as a UN member state while Belgium was still in control but had granted independence.[47] Congolese authorities were in no sense the effective government, yet Congo was regarded as a state.[48] Guinea-Bissau was accepted as a UN member state at a time when Portugal, similarly, remained in control[49] but had agreed to withdraw.[50]

10.5 Reaction of States

The attitude of other states is a key ingredient in regard to statehood. If an entity is accepted as a state, then it is a state. Palestine was regarded as a state even by states that did not formally recognize it. In 1991, the United States and the USSR

---

[42] Greenspan 1959, pp. 223–227.
[43] Von Glahn 1957, p. 350.
[44] 1 Restatement of the Foreign Relations Law of the United States (1987), §201 comment b.
[45] See Henkin 1993, p. 247; Benvenisti 1993.
[46] Cotran 1996, pp. 67–73.
[47] Crawford 2006, p. 57.
[48] Id.
[49] GA Res. 3205, UN GAOR, 29th Sess., Supp. No. 31, at 2, UN Doc. A/9631 (Sept. 17, 1974).
[50] Joint Declaration (Guinea-Bissau, Portugal) signed at Algiers, Aug. 26, 1974, reprinted in 78 Revue Générale de Droit International Public 1252–1253 (1974).

initiated a process of dialogue between Palestine and Israel, starting with a conference in Madrid.[51] That dialogue was aimed at settling the conflict between the two parties, particularly in regard to territory.[52] This process was forwarded by a bilateral Declaration of Principles in 1993 that envisaged negotiations over territory.[53] Israeli Prime Minister Yitzhak Rabin recognized the PLO "as the representative of the Palestinian people."[54] He demanded that the PLO recognize Israel, and in response Chairman Arafat wrote him a letter, stating, "[t]he PLO recognizes the right of the State of Israel to exist in peace and security."[55] Recognition is an act done by states.[56] If Israel did not regard Palestine as a state, there would have been no point in asking for recognition. Israel was clearly dealing with Palestine as a state.

Recognition need not be expressed in a formal document. If states treat an entity as a state, then they are considered to recognize it. "[R]ecognition," writes one analyst, "need not necessarily be express; it may be implied from the circumstances."[57] "[I]nformal relations, without intent to recognize in the political sense, especially if these persist," writes another, "have probative value on the issue of statehood."[58] That has been the case with Palestine. The international community deals with it on the assumption that it is sovereign in at least some of the territory that was Palestine in the mandate period. Recognition does not require that there be certainty about the precise borders of a state. Israel, for example, is recognized by many states even though Israel's borders are not defined.[59]

This manner in which the international community has dealt with Palestine in recent decades is central to resolving the issue of Palestine statehood. The international community regards Palestine as a state. Otherwise, the international community would not encourage Palestine to recognize Israel and negotiate with respect to territory.

10.6 A Continuing Statehood

The statehood declared by the Palestine National Council in 1988 was not of a new statehood. Rather, it was a declaration of an existing statehood. That fact strengthens the Palestine claim to statehood, as requirements for an existing state

---

[51] Curtius 1991, p. 1.
[52] N.Y. Times 1991.
[53] Declaration of Principles on Interim Self-Government Arrangements (Israel-PLO), Sept. 13, 1993, reprinted in 32 ILM 1525 (1993).
[54] Rabin 1993.
[55] Arafat 1993.
[56] Lauterpacht 1947, p. 6.
[57] Wallace-Bruce 1994, p. 74.
[58] Brownlie 1999.
[59] Kumaraswamy 2002.

are less rigorous than those for an entity purporting to be a new state. Palestine became an international entity upon the demise of the Ottoman Empire in the wake of World War I. As the Ottoman Empire lost sovereignty, a Palestine emerged. Great Britain administered Palestine under an arrangement devised by the League of Nations called "mandates."[60] This arrangement, as provided in Article 22 of the League Covenant, was based on the concept that certain peoples were "not yet able to stand by themselves under the strenuous conditions of the modern world [...]"[61] France and Britain were to administer various sectors of the former Ottoman Empire, and to do so for the benefit of the people.[62] The people, in their collectivity, were recognized as the ultimate holder of sovereignty.[63] As the International Court of Justice explained, the "ultimate objective" of the mandate system was the "self-determination and independence of the peoples concerned."[64] It would be only a matter of time until those peoples would control their territories.

The 1988 declaration in fact referred expressly to the League Covenant, stating that "the international community, in Article 22 of the Covenant of the League of Nations of 1919 [...] recognized that the Palestinian Arab people was no different from the other Arab peoples detached form the Ottoman State and was a free and independent people."[65] Thus, the 1988 declaration read as a reaffirmation of an existing status of Palestine statehood.

Under the mandate system, a mandatory power, as Britain was in Palestine, was forbidden to claim title to the territory, the operative principle being "no annexation."[66] It was that principle that distinguished the mandate system from the colonial system.[67] Thus, Britain did not hold sovereignty. The role of the mandatory power was to promote self-governing institutions, after which it would cease its administration. The Attorney-General of the Government of Palestine, Norman Bentwich, explained the relationship as follows: "[A]mong the leading doctrines of international law in its extended sphere, is the right of nationalities, great and small, in the East as in the West, to live their national life, and the duty of the greater States to train them to that end."[68]

---

[60] League of Nations Covenant Article 22.

[61] Id. at para 1.

[62] Id.; Stoyanovsky 1928, p. 262.

[63] Id.

[64] *Legal Consequences for States of the Continued Presence of South Africa in Namibia (South West Africa) Notwithstanding Security Council Resolution 276 (1970)*, Advisory Opinion, 1971 ICJ 16, 31 (June 21).

[65] Palestine National Council, *supra* n. 20 (preamble paragraph of declaration).

[66] Legal Consequences, *supra* n. 64 at 30. See also Crawford 2006, p. 566.

[67] Margalith 1930, p. 46.

[68] Bentwich 1921–1922.

The governments of mandate territories concluded treaties with the governments of other states. The "Class A" mandates, which included Palestine, were the most active in concluding treaties.[69] Palestine was party to treaties that were published in the *League of Nations Treaty Series* like the treaties of other states. Palestine was party to a multilateral treaty, for example, that established an international agency to deal with locust plagues.[70] The International Agreement for the Establishment of an International Bureau of Intelligence on Locusts, concluded at Damascus in 1926, referred in its text to the contracting parties as the "contracting states."[71]

Palestine was party to an Agreement with Egypt Regarding the Reciprocal Enforcement of Judgments.[72] It was party to bilateral treaties on the exchange of postal parcels with Switzerland,[73] Italy,[74] Greece,[75] and France.[76] Most indicative is a treaty with the mandatory power, Great Britain. The Agreement between the Post Office of the United Kingdom of Great Britain and Ireland and the Post Office of Palestine for the Exchange of Money Orders, signed at London, January 10, 1922, and at Jerusalem, January 23, 1922, provided for a regular exchange of money orders.[77] This treaty was registered with the League of Nations and was published in the *League of Nations Treaty Series*.[78] Had Britain and Palestine constituted a single sovereignty, there would have been no point to a treaty between them. Sovereignty resided with Palestine.

The sovereignty of Palestine was reflected as well in the arrangement for citizenship. The inhabitants of Palestine lost their Ottoman nationality when the Ottoman Empire fell but gained a new nationality, namely, that of Palestine. They were not British nationals, even though it was Britain who represented individual Palestinians abroad. An Order in Council adopted by Britain in its capacity as administering power dealt with Palestine nationality and referred to "Palestinian citizenship."[79]

---

[69] Lissitzyn 1968, pp. 55–56.

[70] International Agreement for the Establishment of an International Bureau of Intelligence on Locusts, May 20, 1926, 109 LNTS 121.

[71] Id.

[72] Agreement with Egypt, Jan. 12, 1929, 9 LNTS 96.

[73] Agreement concerning the Exchange of Postal Parcels, May 5 & 16, 1929, 95 LNTS 395.

[74] Agreement concerning the Exchange of Postal Parcels, Dec. 6 & 16, 1931, 139 LNTS 59.

[75] Agreement on the Exchange of Parcels by Parcel Post, Mar. 13 & 28, 1936, 170 LNTS 145.

[76] Agreement on the Exchange of Parcels by Parcel Post, Mar. 31 & June 19, 1936, 172 LNTS 17.

[77] 13 LNTS 9.

[78] Id.

[79] Palestinian Citizenship Order in Council, 1925, Stat. R. & O., no. 777, at 474, (UK); see also Bentwich 1926.

10.7 Conclusion

For the ICC Prosecutor, the question of Palestine statehood has a particular twist. Only states can give consent to ICC jurisdiction over acts committed in their territory. The consent of the territorial state is the primary means by which the ICC gains jurisdiction. If Palestine is not a state, then there is no state that has the capacity to grant the ICC jurisdiction in Gaza. Gaza would be a virtual dead zone from the perspective of the ICC. The only remaining potential bases of jurisdiction would be the nationality of a particular offender, or a referral by the UN Security Council.

References

Arafat Y (1993) Letter to Prime Minister Yitzhak Rabin, reprinted in 7 Palestine Yearbook of International Law (1992), p 230
Benvenisti E (1993) International Law of Occupation, vol 18. Princeton University Press, Princeton
Bentwich N (1921–1922) Mandated Territories: Palestine and Mesopotamia (Iraq). British Yearbook of International Law 2:48–56
Bentwich N (1926) Nationality in Mandated Territories Detached from Turkey. British Yearbook of International Law 7:97–102
Bollag B (1989) UN Health Agency Defers PLO Application to 1990. N.Y. Times, 13 May 1988
Brownlie I (1999) Principles of Public International Law, 5th edn. Oxford University Press, Oxford
Cotran E (1996) Some Legal Aspects of the Declaration of Principles: A Palestinian View. In: Cotran E, Mallat C (eds) The Arab-Israeli Accords: Legal Perspectives, pp 67–73
Crawford J (2006) The Creation of the States in International Law, 2nd edn. Oxford University Press, Oxford
Curtius M (1991) US, Soviets invite Sides to Mideast Peace Talks. Boston Globe, 18 October 1991
Farhi C (1982) On the Legal Status of the Gaza Strip, In Shamgar M (ed), Military Government in the Territories Administered by Israel 1967–1980, Hebrew University, Jerusalem
Feuer G (1970) Les Accords Passés par les Gouvernements Jordanien et Libanais Avec les Organisations Palestiniennes (1968–1970), 16 Annuaire Français de droit International, pp 177–189
Flory M (1989) La Naissance D'un État Palestinien. 93 Revue Generale de Droit International Public, pp 385–401
Greenspan M (1959) The Modern Law of Land Warfare. University of California Press, Berkeley
Henkin L et al. (1993) International Law: Cases and Materials, 3rd edn. St. Paul Minnesota West Publishing Co.
Kempster N (1989) PLO Urged to Drop Bid to U.N. Unit; US Warns it would Withhold Money for Health Agency. L.A. Times, 3 May 1989
Kifner J (1988a) Hussein Surrenders Claims on West Bank to the PLO. N.Y. Times, 1 August 1988
Kifner J (1988b) Excerpts from Hussein's Address on Abandoning Claims to the West Bank, N.Y. Times, 1 August 1988
Kumaraswamy P (2002) The Legacy of Undefined Borders. 40 Tel Aviv Notes
L.A. Times (1989) PLO Delays Bid for Higher U.N. Status, 5 December 1989

Lauterpacht H (1947) Recognition in International Law, Cambridge University Press
Lewis P (1988) U.N. Ends its Session in Geneva, Approving 2 Mideast Resolutions. N.Y. Times, 16 December 1988
Lewis P (1989a) Arabs at U.N. Relax Stand on PLO. N.Y. Times, 6 December 1989
Lewis P (1989b) U.N. Health Agency Seeks Compromise on PLO. L.A Times, 1 May 1989
Lewis P (1989c) Health Organization asks US Tolerance on PLO. N.Y. Times, 30 April 1989
Lissitzyn O (1968) Territorial Entities other than Independent States in the Law of Treaties. 125 Recueil des Cours
Margalith A (1930) The International Mandates
N.Y. Times (1991) In the Dispute Over Land: 3 Leaders Trade Accusations and Offer Answers, 2 November 1991
Pear R (1988) US Won't Oppose UN Geneva Session. N.Y. Times, 29 November 1988
Pertman A (1989) US Vows Cutoff in WHO Funds if PLO Joins. Boston Globe
Rabin Y (1993) Letter to PLO Chairman Arafat. In 7 Palestine Yearbook of International Law (1992), pp 231
Randal J (1989) PLO Defeated in Bid to Join World Health Organization. Washington Post, 13 May 1989
Ross A (1950) Amman Parliament Vote Unites Arab Palastine and Transjordan, N.Y. Times, 25 April 1950
Stoyanovsky J (1928) The Mandate for Palestine. Longmans, Green and Co., London
Von Glahn G (1957) The Occupation of Enemy Territory, vol 67. University of Minnesota Press, Minneapolis
Wallace-Bruce N (1994) Claims to Statehood in International Law. Carlton Press, New York

Chapter 11
Is Palestine a "State"? A Response to Professor John Quigley's Article, "The Palestine Declaration to the International Criminal Court: The Statehood Issue"

Robert Weston Ash

Contents

11.1 Introduction.. 441
11.2 That Palestinian Officials Repeatedly and Openly Admit that Palestine is not a "State" Conclusively Establishes that Palestine Does not Meet the Conditions Required to Accede to ICC Jurisdiction 443
11.3 That Palestine is not Recognized as a "State" by Key International Institutions is Additional Indication that the International Community Does not Recognize Palestine as a "State" 449
11.4 That no Arab Palestinian State Currently Exercises Sovereign Control Over Claimed Palestinian "Territory" Also Confirms that Palestine is not a "State"... 455
11.5 Conclusion 458
References.. 459

11.1 Introduction

On December 19, 2008, the six-month ceasefire mediated by Egypt between Israel and leaders of Hamas in the Gaza Strip expired.[1] Shortly thereafter, Hamas and other Palestinian groups resumed indiscriminate rocket and mortar attacks from

---

Senior Litigation Counsel for National Security Law, American Center for Law and Justice (ACLJ). This article was first published in 36 Rutgers Law Record (2009), 186–201.

---

[1] Reuters 2009.

R. W. Ash (✉)
American Center for Law and Justice, USA

the Gaza Strip against Israeli settlements and territory.[2] In response, Israel launched 'Operation Cast Lead', a military incursion into the Gaza Strip, which lasted approximately three weeks.[3] In the wake of Cast Lead, the Palestine Authority (PA) lodged a declaration (Declaration) with the Registrar of the International Criminal Court (ICC) accepting ICC jurisdiction in the "territory of Palestine," retroactive to July 1, 2002.[4] The PA cited Article 12(3) of the ICC Statute as the legal basis for its Declaration.[5] Article 12(3) reads as follows: "If the acceptance of a *State* which is not a Party to this Statute is required under paragraph 2, that *State* may, by declaration lodged with the Registrar, accept the exercise of jurisdiction by the Court with respect to the crime in question..."[6]

As Professor John Quigley correctly noted in his article, "The Palestine Declaration to the International Criminal Court: The Statehood Issue,"[7] the ICC will have jurisdiction pursuant to Article 12(3) *only if* "Palestine qualifies as a 'state,' since only a *state* that is *sovereign* in a particular territory can confer jurisdiction on the ICC in that territory."[8] Having stated the ICC Statute's requirement correctly, Professor Quigley then set out to show that Palestine, in fact, meets the requirements under international law to be a "State".

Professor Quigley raised five basic arguments to demonstrate that Palestine qualifies as a "State" under international law. His arguments can generally be summarized as follows: (1) that Palestine had officially declared its statehood in 1988;[9] (2) that the UN, responding to that declaration of statehood, regards Palestine as a "State";[10] (3) that many states have recognized Palestine as a "State";[11] (4) that there are no competing claimants to the Gaza Strip and the West Bank[12]; and (5) that sovereignty devolved upon the Palestinian people when the

---

[2] Id.

[3] Makovsky 2009.

[4] Ali Khashan, Minister of Justice, Palestinian National Authority, Declaration Recognizing the Jurisdiction of the International Criminal Court (Jan. 21, 2009), available at http://www2.icc-cpi.int/NR/rdonlyres/74EEE201-0FED-4481-95D4-C8071087102C/279777/20090122Palestinian Declaration2.pdf.

[5] Id. Note that Article 11 of the Rome Statute limits ICC jurisdiction to *States* that become Parties after the Rome Statute came into force (i.e., July 1, 2002) to those crimes committed *after* entry of the new State Party, "unless that *State* has made a declaration under Article 12, para 3". Rome Statute of the International Criminal Court, Conference of Plenipotentiaries on the Establishment of an International Criminal Court, Article 11(2), U.N. Doc. A/CONF.183/9 (17 July 1998) [hereinafter "Statute" or "Rome Statute"] (emphasis added).

[6] Rome Statute Article 12(3) (emphasis added).

[7] Quigley 2009 [also in this Volume, see *supra* Chap. 10—ChM].

[8] Id. p. 3 (emphasis added) [citing Rome Statute Article 12(3)].

[9] Id. p. 4 [citing Palestine National Council: Political Communique and Declaration of Independence, Nov. 15, 1988, U.N. Doc. A/43/827, S/20278, Annex III, Nov. 18, 1988, reprinted in 27 I.L.M. 1668 (1988)].

[10] Id. pp. 4–5 (citations omitted).

[11] Id. p. 5 (citing Lewis 1989), 7.

[12] Id. p. 5 (citations omitted).

British Mandate ended, thereby establishing a "continual statehood" for the Palestinians.[13]

This Response will show that Professor Quigley's case for Palestinian statehood is not as clear-cut and convincing as he apparently believes. First and foremost, Professor Quigley utterly failed to consider a long series of official statements (including very recent ones) by top Palestinian officials openly and repeatedly disclaiming that Palestine is currently a "State". Additionally, he seriously overstated or misinterpreted much of the other evidence he cited. This Response will argue, contrary to Professor Quigley's conclusion, that readily available evidence overwhelmingly establishes that "Palestine" is not currently a "State"—and never has been one. As such, the PA Declaration lodged with the ICC Registrar is of no legal effect whatsoever and cannot convey jurisdiction over any territory or persons to the International Criminal Court.

11.2 That Palestinian Officials Repeatedly and Openly Admit that Palestine is not a "State" Conclusively Establishes that Palestine Does not Meet the Conditions Required to Accede to ICC Jurisdiction

11.2.1 Statements by PLO and PA Leaders Consistently Declare that Palestinian Statehood Remains a Future Event

Of prime importance concerning whether Palestine is currently a "State" is the position consistently espoused by Palestine Liberation Organization (PLO) and PA officials themselves—something that Professor Quigley simply neglects to mention at all. As shown below, PLO and PA leaders repeatedly admit that Palestine is not currently a "State"—*a fact which by itself should put the issue to rest*. If Palestinian leaders themselves admit that no Palestinian State currently exists—a clear admission against PA interests—there is no reason to reject their position and ponder the issue further.

Professor Quigley places great importance on the 1988 Palestinian declaration of statehood, which he claims has led to broad recognition of Palestinian statehood by the world community.[14] Yet, he ignores repeated statements made by Palestinian leaders *since 1988* (i.e., *after* the 1988 declaration) about Palestinian statehood. Even PLO Chairman Yasser Arafat, during his tenure in office *after* the 1988 declaration of statehood (which Mr. Arafat helped champion), publicly recognized

---

[13] See Id. pp. 8–9 (citations omitted).

[14] See Id. pp. 4–5 (citations omitted).

that Palestinian statehood remained a *future* goal. At the Arab Summit in Beirut in March 2002, for example, Mr. Arafat said the following:

> We are all confident in the inevitability of victory, as well as in the inevitability of achieving our national and Pan-Arab goals ... including the right of return, the right to self-determination and the *establishment of the independent state of Palestine*, with holy Jerusalem as its capital [...]
>
> Beloved brothers, I would like to tell you in frank and precise terms that we want our national, firm and inalienable rights, the rights that are supported by international legality, the rights of our refugees, our right to self-determination and to the *establishment of our independent state*, on the whole territory which was occupied in 1967, with holy Jerusalem as its capital.[15]

Moreover, the position currently espoused by PA President Mahmoud Abbas that Palestinians are *looking forward* to achieving statehood is consistent with a long line of speeches made by Mr. Abbas and others. For example, Mr. Abbas said the following in his inaugural speech as PA President in 2005: "The greatest challenge before us, and the fundamental task facing us[,] is national liberation. The task of ending the occupation [and] *establishing the Palestinian State*..."[16]

In February 2005, shortly after his inauguration as PA President, Mr. Abbas said the following at an Egyptian summit meeting in Sharm el-Sheikh:

> [J]ust less than one month ago the Palestinian people went to the ballot boxes for the presidential elections, which were held after the departure of President Yasser Arafat. In this remarkable democratic practice, the Palestinian people embodied through this election[] their [decision for a] just peace that will put an[] end to dictates of war, violence and occupation. *Peace that means the establishment of a Palestinian state*, or the state of—the democratic state of independent Palestine along[side] the State of Israel, as mentioned in the road map plan.[17]

Further, on November 24, 2008, President Abbas addressed the General Assembly of the United Nations in observance of the International Day of Solidarity with the Palestinian People.[18] In that speech, Mr. Abbas clearly confirmed the *aspirational* nature of the current drive for an independent Palestinian state:

> We highly appreciate your significant role in supporting our efforts to enable our people to realize their goals. We are certain that your role contributes in [a] clear and effective way in enhancing international solidarity with our just cause and enlarges the circle of

---

[15] Yasser Arafat 2002 (emphasis added). Note that Mr. Arafat did not speak as if Palestine were already an independent state, despite the Palestine National Council's 1988 publicly announced Declaration of Independence for Palestine—a declaration made while the PLO was in exile in Tunisia. See Arafat 1988. Hence, even Mr. Arafat discounted the importance and effect of the 1988 Declaration.

[16] Abbas 2005a (emphasis added).

[17] Abbas 2005b (emphasis added).

[18] Abbas 2008 (emphasis added).

11 Is Palestine a "State"?

international support for the aspirations of our people for *freedom and independence and the establishment of their State...* .[19]

Continuing his UN speech, Mr. Abbas referred to Jerusalem as "the capital *of our future independent State.*"[20]

Regarding the January 2009 PA Declaration to the ICC, because Article 12(3) of the ICC Statute requires that a "State" lodge such a declaration, it would have been in the PA's interest to explicitly claim statehood if PA officials believed Palestine to be a state; yet, Palestinian officials failed to do so. Moreover, on February 4, 2009, (i.e., *after* the January 22, 2009, lodging of the PA Declaration with the ICC Registrar), PA President Abbas, in a speech before the European Parliament concerning the then-recently concluded Israeli military operation in the Gaza Strip, accused Israel of "preventing [the Palestinian] people from attaining their *ultimate goal*: an end to occupation, gaining freedom and the right to self-determination and the *establishment of an independent Palestinian state...* ."[21]

One day later, on February 5, 2009, President Abbas appeared with British Prime Minister Gordon Brown at a press conference at Number 10 Downing Street in London. In answering one of the questions put to him, President Abbas emphasized the need for international support for "the Arab peace initiative which calls for *the two state solution.*"[22] Prime Minister Brown stated in support: "I believe the Arab peace initiative does point the way forward. I believe that the general terms of an agreement are well known to everyone: an Israel that is secure within its own borders, [and] *a Palestinian state that is viable ... .*"[23] Taken together, President Abbas's and Prime Minister Brown's statements refute any notion that an independent Palestinian state currently exists (or existed when the PA Declaration was lodged with the ICC Registrar in January 2009). Yet, there is more.

On June 22, 2009, Palestinian Prime Minister Salam Fayyad "called for the *establishment of a Palestinian state within two years.*"[24] In the same speech, he called on all Palestinians to "help create the institutions that will 'embody' *the future state.*"[25]

---

[19] Id. Admittedly, in his UN address, President Abbas does refer to 1988, when the Palestine National Council issued a Declaration of Independence while in exile in Tunisia. Nevertheless, when taken in context with his repeated statements concerning a *future* independent state made in that same speech, it is apparent that even current Palestinian officials do not take the 1988 Declaration seriously.

[20] Id. (emphasis added).

[21] See Abbas 2009b (emphasis added).

[22] See Abbas 2009a (emphasis added).

[23] Id. (emphasis added).

[24] Schneider 2009 (emphasis added). It is obvious that one does not call for establishing a State "within two years" (or any other time limit) when such a State already exists.

[25] Id. (emphasis added).

One final example should suffice to demonstrate that President Abbas (representing the PA in general) has no illusions that a state of Palestine currently exists. At the August 2009 Fatah conference in Bethlehem, Mr. Abbas continued to express his vision and hope for a *future* Palestinian state: "Our people are committed to the peace option ... and to reach its objectives of freedom, independence and the *creation of a Palestinian state.*"[26] Further, "[President Abbas] insisted that he still believed in the peace talks which began in the early 1990s, *even though they have failed to create a Palestinian state.*"[27]

As shown above, even after the 1988 declaration of statehood, Palestinian leaders have consistently expressed—and continue to express—the view that no Palestinian state has yet come into existence. Such evidence conclusively refutes Professor Quigley's contrary conclusion. It also lessens the actual significance of the 1988 declaration to both the Palestinians and the international community.

11.2.2 Information on the Official Website of the PLO Negotiations Affairs Department Also States that Palestinian Statehood Remains a Future Event

In addition to the many public admissions by Palestinian leaders that no Palestinian state currently exists, there are a number of similar admissions on the official website of the PLO Negotiations Affairs Department,[28] confirming that Palestinian statehood remains a future prospect as well. For example, The PLO Negotiations Affairs Department has published a "Negotiations Primer" that describes the purpose of Palestinian negotiations as a means "to realize Palestinian national rights of self-determination *and statehood*"[29] as well as to achieve "the end of Israeli occupation and the *establishment of a sovereign and independent Palestinian state.*"[30]

---

[26] See AGI News 2009. Abu Mazen is an alias of Mahmoud Abbas. See Biography of Abu Mazen, available at http://www.answers.com/topic/abu-mazen. In the portion of the quotation replaced by the ellipsis, Mr. Abbas discussed using resistance to achieve Palestinian independence. Since that was a possible *means* to the end sought, it did not refute the fact that Palestinian statehood has not yet been achieved.

[27] McCarthy 2009 (emphasis added). In a letter addressed to the same conference, Saudi King Abdullah likewise acknowledged the absence of a Palestinian state: "I can honestly tell you, brothers, that even if the whole world joins to found a Palestinian independent state, and if we have full support for that, this state would not be established as long as the Palestinians are divided." Toameh 2009. Such a statement clearly shows that the Saudi King (a prominent figure in the greater Arab community) also acknowledges that Palestine is not a State.

[28] See PLO Negotiations Affairs Department http://www.nad-plo.org/

[29] PLO Negotiations Affairs Department 2009 (emphasis added).

[30] Id. at 12 (emphasis added).

11 Is Palestine a "State"?

In its introduction to the section on Frequently Asked Questions (FAQ), the PLO Negotiations Affairs Department wrote the following:

> The 15th of November 2008 marks the twentieth anniversary of the Palestinian Declaration of Independence. The Declaration was made at the 19th Session of the Palestinian National Council (PNC), the highest Palestinian legislative authority, and provided the first official Palestinian endorsement of a two-state solution to the Israeli-Palestinian conflict.
>
> *Twenty years later, Palestinians are still waiting for Israel to respond in kind* to this historic compromise by ending its 41-year-old occupation of Palestinian territory and *supporting the establishment of an independent, viable, sovereign Palestinian state* living side-by-side with Israel in peace and security.[31]

These are unequivocal admissions that Palestine is not yet a State. Moreover, Question 5 of the FAQ asks: "Why have the Palestinians *failed to attain statehood*, twenty years after their Declaration of Independence?"[32] The answer provided to that question, though laying sole blame on Israel, openly admits that all efforts to attain statehood in the intervening period failed.[33] If the Palestinians admit this, surely Professor Quigley should do so as well.

11.2.3 PLO/PA Participation in the Ongoing Peace Process, One of Whose Goals is the Establishment of a Palestinian State, Provides Further Proof that no Palestinian "State" Currently Exists

Since the early 1990s, Palestinians have been engaged in a peace process with Israelis in an effort to resolve the ongoing conflict between them and to establish a viable Palestinian State neighboring the State of Israel. This process was agreed to by Israel and the PLO and involves a series of arrangements which established the Palestinian Authority[34] and which defined the legal situation between the parties until such time as a final settlement is concluded. The International Court of Justice (ICJ) described the situation between Israel and the PLO as follows:

> [A] number of agreements have been signed since 1993 between Israel and the Palestine Liberation Organi[z]ation imposing various obligations on each party. Those agreements *inter alia* required Israel to transfer to Palestinian authorities certain powers and

---

[31] PLO Negotiations Affairs Department 2008 (emphasis added).

[32] Id. at 3 (emphasis added).

[33] Id.

[34] Note that the PA was *not* created by Palestinians acting independently; rather, the PA was established by virtue of a series of Israeli-Palestinian agreements (the Oslo Peace Process) as an initial step to an eventual two-state solution. Palestine Facts, Israel 1991 to Present: PA Origins, What is the Palestinian Authority and How Did it Originate? http://www.palestinefacts.org/pf_1991to_now_pa_origin.php.

responsibilities exercised in the Occupied Palestinian Territory by its military authorities and civil administration. Such transfers have taken place, but, as a result of subsequent events, they remained partial and limited.[35]

The terms of the 1995 Interim Agreement, to which the Palestinian authorities have agreed to be bound, explicitly withhold from the PA authority to engage in foreign relations (specifically limiting the PA ability to establish embassies or other types of diplomatic missions abroad or to permit their establishment in the West Bank or Gaza Strip, as well as limiting the exercise of other diplomatic functions that normally attend statehood).[36] Foreign relations responsibilities are to be retained by Israel under the Interim Agreement. That is significant because the ability to enter into relations with foreign states is one of the four criteria generally recognized as being indispensable to statehood.[37]

Israel also retained control over external defense of the West Bank and Gaza Strip:

> Israel shall continue to carry responsibility for defen[s]e against external threats, including the responsibility for protecting the Egyptian and Jordanian borders, and for defen[s]e against external threats from the sea and from the air, as well as the responsibility for overall security of Israelis and settlements, for the purpose of safeguarding their internal security and public order, and will have all the powers to take steps necessary to meet this responsibility.[38]

Israel's retention of these responsibilities is also significant in which it indicates that the PA was not able to freely govern any territory in the West Bank or Gaza Strip without the express warrant of Israel. Moreover, even when the PA began to exercise a modicum of governmental authority, that authority did not include external security, control of airspace, or control of Israeli civilians and settlements. This fact is crucial because the ability to govern one's territory is also an indispensable requirement to establish statehood.[39]

---

[35] *Legal Consequences of the Construction of a Wall in the Occupied Palestinian Territory*, Advisory Opinion, 2004 I.C.J. 136, 167 (July 9). Among the agreements signed between the two parties are the following: Declaration of Principles on Interim Self-Government Arrangements, Isr.-PLO, Sept. 13, 1993, 32 I.L.M. 1525; Agreement on the Gaza Strip and Jericho Area ("Cairo Agreement"), Isr.-PLO, May 4, 1994, 33 I.L.M. 622; Interim Agreement on the West Bank and Gaza Strip, Isr.-PLO, Sept. 28, 1995, 36 I.L.M. 551 [hereinafter "Interim Agreement"].

[36] Interim Agreement, Article 9(5). The Palestinians were permitted, however, to interact internationally with respect to "economic agreements," "agreements with donor countries," "cultural, scientific and educational agreements," and the like. Id. Article 9(5)(a)–(b).

[37] Convention on the Rights and Duties of States Article 1, Dec. 26, 1933, 49 Stat. 3097 [hereinafter "Montevideo Convention"], available at http://avalon.yale.edu/20th_century/intam03.asp. Article 1 of the Montevideo Convention established four prerequisites to statehood: a permanent population; a defined territory; a government; and a capacity to enter relations with other States. Id.

[38] Interim Agreement, *supra* n. 35, Article 12.

[39] Montevideo Convention, Article 1.

Finally, the terms of the Interim Agreement prohibit both Israel and the PA from "initiat[ing] or tak[ing] any step that will change the status of the West Bank and the Gaza Strip pending the outcome of the permanent negotiations."[40] Such negotiations promise to be the most difficult, since they include highly contentious issues such as "Jerusalem, refugees, settlements, security arrangements, borders, relations and cooperation with other neighbours [sic]..."[41]

Even the brief recitation above demonstrates that Palestinian officials agreed to abide by measures during the ongoing peace process that clearly left in Israeli hands sovereign responsibilities that normally would inhere in an independent state. Such agreement further demonstrates that no sovereign Palestinian "State" currently exists and that Palestine does not exercise "sovereign" authority over any territory in the West Bank or the Gaza Strip.

* * * * *

In sum, there can be no doubt that there is no "State" of Palestine in existence at this particular point in history, as even Palestinian officials readily admit. If the Palestinians themselves recognize that no state of Palestine currently exists, as indicated by their repeated public admissions and their ongoing participation in negotiations aimed at creating just such a state, then surely Professor Quigley's conclusions to the contrary must be incorrect.

11.3 That Palestine is not Recognized as a "State" by Key International Institutions is Additional Indication that the International Community Does not Recognize Palestine as a "State"

Professor Quigley noted that "[t]he attitude of other states is a key ingredient in regard to statehood."[42] He concluded that "[i]f an entity is accepted as a state, then it is a state."[43] This begs the question: Accepted as a state *by whom*? Surely, Professor Quigley's assertion is subject to some limitations. For example, Turkey "accepts" the Turkish Republic of Northern Cyprus as a "State". Does that make it one? Professor Quigley (correctly, in my view) argues "no" in that case.[44] So, mere "accept[ance] as a state" cannot be the sole standard. In fact, recognition or nonrecognition of an entity as a "State" is a sovereign political decision made by individual states that is not always (at least, on the surface) rational—*or*

---

[40] Interim Agreement, n. 35, Article 31(7).
[41] Id. Articles 17(1)(a), 31(5).
[42] Quigley 2009, p. 7.
[43] Id.
[44] Id. p. 4.

conclusive (as Professor Quigley's example regarding Northern Cyprus attests). Actions by international bodies often suffer from the same or similar defects. Consider, for example, how important international bodies treat "Palestine" *in practice* (despite multiple recognitions of Palestinian statehood by individual Member States of those same international bodies[45]).

11.3.1 In the United Nations, Palestine is Credentialed, not as a "State," But as an "Entit[y] Having Received a Standing Invitation to Participate as Observer in the Sessions and the Work of the General Assembly and Maintaining Permanent Observer Mission at Headquarters"[46]

As noted earlier, Professor Quigley placed great significance on the Palestine National Council's (PNC) 1988 declaration of statehood.[47] He noted that PLO Chairman Yasser Arafat was invited to address the UN General Assembly as a direct result of that declaration.[48] He further noted that the General Assembly—by an overwhelming vote—decided to adopt the designation, "Palestine", to replace the prior designation, "Palestine Liberation Organization," in the UN system.[49] Professor Quigley then concluded from such a strong showing of General Assembly support "that Palestine was regarded as a *State*".[50] In support of his argument, he also cited the fact that both the former Belgian Congo and Guinea-Bissau were accepted as UN member states *before* their respective colonial powers relinquished actual control over their territories.[51] Yet, how Palestinian officials have been (and are currently) treated at the UN strongly suggests that Professor Quigley's assertions *vis-à-vis* the UN and Palestine are, at best, questionable and, in fact, wrong.

---

[45] Id. p. 5 (citing Lewis 1989).

[46] Executive Office of the Secretary General, Protocol & Liaison Serv., *Publication of Permanent Missions to the United Nations*, at 311, U.N. Doc. ST/SG/SER.A/299 (emphasis added).

[47] *Supra* n. 14 and accompanying text.

[48] Quigley 2009, p. 4 (citing Pear 1988).

[49] Id. (citations omitted).

[50] Id. (emphasis added). *But see* Crawford 2006 ["Applying the Montevideo Convention in accordance with its terms, *Palestine before 1993 could not possibly have constituted a State*. Its whole territory was occupied by Israel which functioned as a government there and claimed the right to do so until further agreement. The PLO had never functioned as a government there and lacked the means to do so, given strong Israeli opposition." (emphasis added)].

[51] Quigley 2009, pp. 6–7 (citations omitted).

Although it is true that Palestinian officials actively participate in activities at the UN in New York and elsewhere, Palestine nonetheless enjoys only observer status. It is not a member of the UN General Assembly, and, hence, its representatives are not permitted to vote. Only *States* may become UN members.[52] And, unlike the Holy See, which, though not a UN member, is an internationally recognized State, Palestine is not included or seated in the category "[n]on-member *State* having received a standing invitation to participate as observer in the sessions and the work of the General Assembly and maintaining permanent observer mission at Headquarters".[53] Instead, Palestine is listed under "[e]*ntities* having received a standing invitation to participate as observers in the sessions and the work of the General Assembly and maintaining permanent observer mission at Headquarters".[54] Palestine has been listed as an "entity" with observer status (not as a "non-member *State*" with observer status) since 1988.[55] Such a long-standing practice seriously undermines Professor Quigley's contention that Palestine "was regarded as a state"[56] by the General Assembly.

11.3.2 At the 1998 Rome Conference and at Subsequent Meetings Concerning the International Criminal Court and its Implementation, Palestine has not Been Listed as a Participating "State"

Palestine was also not credentialed as a participating "State" at the Rome Conference in 1998 that resulted in the creation of the ICC. The official roster of "Participating States" at the Conference included the names of 163 States; it did not include the PA or Palestine as a "State". Rather, Palestine was placed under the category of "Other Organizations" in the diplomatic roster of the

---

[52] U.N. Charter Article 4, para 1 (noting that membership is available to "peace-loving *States*" (emphasis added)).

[53] *Publication of Permanent Missions to the United Nations*, supra n. 46, p. 310.

[54] Id. at 311 (emphasis added).

[55] As noted above, Professor Quigley was correct in stating that the UN adopted "Palestine" to replace the prior designation "Palestine Liberation Organization" in 1988. "Palestine" has thus enjoyed observer status since that time. However, the *PLO* began enjoying observer status in 1974. Observer Status for the Palestine Liberation Organization, G.A. Res. 3237 (XXIX), U.N. Doc A/RES/3237 (Nov. 22, 1974). The important thing to note is that, throughout its history, the PLO and "Palestine" have never been regarded as anything but 'entities' by the UN.

[56] Quigley 2009, p. 4. At best, Palestine can be considered an 'incipient' or 'emerging' State—not a full-fledged State—whose ultimate statehood depends on the outcome of the ongoing Israeli-Palestinian peace process, one of the goals of which is the eventual establishment of a Palestinian State.

Conference.⁵⁷ Moreover, the two Palestinian delegates accredited to the Conference, Mr. Nimer Hammad, the PA General Delegate to Italy, and Mr. Marwan Jilani, the Counselor of the Permanent Observer Mission of Palestine to the United Nations, were listed as representing an "Organization" *not* a "State".⁵⁸ In subsequent meetings of the ICC Preparatory Commission, Palestine was present in the category of "Entities, intergovernmental organizations and other bodies having received a standing invitation to participate as *observers* in the sessions and the work of the General Assembly,"⁵⁹ once again, not as a "State".

The ICC has consistently treated (and continues to treat) Palestine as an organization and not as a "State". A prominent example of this took place in February 2009, at the ICC States Parties meeting in New York City, where Palestine was grouped with "Entities, intergovernmental organizations, and other entities".⁶⁰ Given its consistent treatment by the ICC as a non-state entity, it is somewhat ironic that Palestine sought to accede to ICC jurisdiction via Article 12(3) without some explicit claim of statehood, since an action brought under Article 12(3) is limited to "States".⁶¹

11.3.3 *In its 2004 Advisory Opinion Regarding the Security Barrier Being Built by Israel in Portions of the West Bank, the International Court of Justice Advisory Opinion was Predicated on the Court's Conclusion that Palestine was not a "State"*

Not only does the UN General Assembly not officially recognize Palestine as a State, but the International Court of Justice (ICJ) has also concluded that Palestine has not yet attained statehood. The ICJ, in its advisory opinion on the *Legal Consequences of the Construction of a Wall in the Occupied Palestinian*

---

⁵⁷ United Nations Diplomatic Conference of Plenipotentiaries on the Establishment of an International Criminal Court, June 15 to July 17, 1998, *Official Records*, at 5, 44, U.N. Doc. A/CONF.183/13 (vol. II) (2002), available at http://untreaty.un.org/cod/icc/rome/proceedings/E/Rome%20Proceedings_v2_e.pdf.

⁵⁸ Id. p. 44.

⁵⁹ United Nations Preparatory Commission for the International Criminal Court, New York, Apr. 8–19, 2002, *List of Delegations*, at 10, U.N. Doc. PCNICC/2002/INF/6 (Apr. 30, 2002) (emphasis added), available at http://daccessdds.un.org/doc/UNDOC/GEN/N02/401/72/IMG/N0240172.pdf?OpenElement.

⁶⁰ International Criminal Court, Assembly of States Parties, New York, Feb. 9–13, 2009, *Delegations to the Second Resumption of the Seventh Session of the Assembly of States Parties to the Rome Statute of the International Criminal Court*, at 50, U.N. Doc. ICC-ASP/7/INF.1/Add.2 (Mar. 26, 2009), available at http://www.icc-cpi.int/iccdocs/asp_docs/ICC-ASP-7-INF.1-Add.2.pdf.

⁶¹ Rome Statute Article 12(3).

Territories (Advisory Opinion),⁶² confirmed that the Palestinian territories have not achieved statehood. The Court held that Israel could not justify the building of its security barrier by invoking the right to self-defense under Article 51 of the UN Charter.⁶³ The specific reason for the ICJ holding was that Israel claimed the barrier was necessary to defend against Palestinian attacks. The ICJ rejected the Israeli rationale because Israel "d[id] not claim that the attacks against it [we]re imputable to a foreign *State*."⁶⁴ The Court opined that because Article 51 only recognizes "the existence of an inherent right of self-defense in the case of an armed attack by one State against another State," the right did not apply to attacks launched at Israel from Palestinian territory.⁶⁵

This conclusion was buttressed by Judge Elaraby (whose separate opinion in the *Legal Consequences* case articulated Palestinian rights at their highest). Judge Elaraby gave a history of Palestine and concluded that no sovereign Palestinian State existed: "On 14 May 1948, the independence of the Jewish State was declared. The Israeli declaration was 'by virtue of [Israel's] natural and historic right' and based 'on the strength of the resolution of the United Nations General Assembly.' *The independence of the Palestinian Arab State has not yet materialized.*"⁶⁶

11.3.4 The Government of Switzerland, as Custodian of the Geneva Conventions, Concluded that it Could Not Accept Palestinian Accession to the 1949 Geneva Conventions Because Palestine Could not be Determined to be a "Power" (i.e., a "State") Permitted to Accede to the Conventions

Professor Quigley also mentioned the June 1989 Palestinian attempt to accede to the 1949 Geneva Conventions as evidence of Palestinian statehood.⁶⁷ He correctly noted that the validity of the Palestinian attempt "depended on Palestine being a

---

⁶² 2004 I.C.J. 136. This opinion is quite controversial and has been extensively criticized. Nevertheless, it is noteworthy for confirming that no Palestinian State existed in 2004, despite the 1988 declaration of statehood by the Palestinian National Council.

⁶³ Id. p. 194.

⁶⁴ Id. (emphasis added).

⁶⁵ Id.

⁶⁶ Id. p. 251, Elaraby, separate opinion (citations omitted) (emphasis added). Judge Elaraby's concurrence is especially significant for noting that no Palestinian state has existed since 1948, when the British Mandate ended and British troops departed Palestine. That conclusion also contradicts Professor Quigley's assertions about the importance and impact of the 1988 declaration of statehood. See Quigley 2009, pp. 4–5.

⁶⁷ See Quigley 2009, p. 3.

state, since ratification of these four treaties is open only to 'powers.'"[68] The Swiss Government declined to accept the Palestinian attempt because it could not determine whether Palestine was a state, a prerequisite to being able to accede to the 1949 Conventions.[69] From this, Professor Quigley concluded that "Switzerland took no position on Palestinian statehood."[70] Professor Quigley's final observation about the Swiss action was that "Switzerland did not regard it as proper, as a single state, to make a determination that would have implications for the international community."[71] The observation concerning the Swiss action *in 1989* seems to contradict Professor Quigley's assertion that the 1988 UN General Assembly vote was a strong indication "that Palestine was regarded as a state"[72] as well as his assertion that "[i]f an entity is accepted as a state, then it is a state."[73]

By declining to affirm Palestine's right to accede to the Conventions, Switzerland did, in fact, take a position on Palestinian statehood—*albeit indirectly*. The Swiss Government determined that Palestinian statehood was not a settled issue in the international community.[74] On that basis, the Swiss Government concluded that it was incapable of recognizing Palestine as a "Power" that could accede to the Conventions. Yet, if Palestine was not a power that could accede to the conventions, it had to be something less than a "State", since States could accede to the Conventions. The Swiss conclusion comports fully with the UN's consistent designation of Palestine—as a recognizable political entity, but not a "State".[75]

* * * * *

As indicated above, key international bodies have consistently recognized—and continue to recognize—Palestine as a political entity that has yet to attain statehood. The determinations by these international bodies comport fully with what Palestinian officials themselves readily and repeatedly concede: Palestine is not currently a "State".

---

[68] Id. (quoting Convention for the Amelioration of the Condition of the Wounded and Sick in Armed Forces in the Field Article 60, Aug. 12, 1949, 75 U.N.T.S. 31; Convention for the Amelioration of the Condition of Wounded, Sick and Shipwrecked Members of Armed Forces at Sea Article 59, Aug. 12, 1949, 75 U.N.T.S. 85; Convention Relative to the Treatment of Prisoners of War Article 139, Aug. 12, 1949, 75 U.N.T.S. 135; Convention Relative to the Protection of Civilian Persons in Time of War Article 155, Aug. 12, 1949, 75 U.N.T.S. 287).

[69] Quigley 2009, pp. 3–4 (quoting *Note of Information*, Government of Switzerland, Berne, Sept. 13, 1989).

[70] Id. p. 4.

[71] Id.

[72] Id.

[73] Id. p. 7.

[74] *Supra* n. 69 and accompanying text.

[75] E.g., *supra* nn. 46–56 and accompanying text.

11.4 That no Arab Palestinian State Currently Exercises Sovereign Control Over Claimed Palestinian "Territory" Also Confirms that Palestine is not a "State"

Professor Quigley correctly pointed out that "only a state that is *sovereign in a particular territory*" can accede to ICC jurisdiction.[76] Hence, Professor Quigley had to find a way to argue that "Palestine" is, in fact, sovereign over particular territory.[77] He bases his argument of Palestinian sovereignty over the West Bank and the Gaza Strip (to wit, "Palestinian territory") on the fact that the British, during the Mandate, were merely holding Palestinian sovereignty in trust for the Palestinian people. Thus, when the British departed, sovereignty over Palestine reverted to the Palestinian people.[78] Yet, Professor Quigley's analysis fails to explain a number of key issues. First, the "Palestinian people" to whom sovereignty reverted upon the departure of the British would have included both Jews and Arabs.[79] So, under Professor Quigley's reversion theory, sovereignty over Palestine reverted to both its Jewish and Arab inhabitants (thereby establishing a colorable *Jewish*—as well as Arab—claim to all of Palestine, including the West Bank and Gaza Strip,[80] and tending to refute Professor Quigley's contention that there are no other claimants to that territory[81]).

---

[76] Quigley 2009, p. 3 (emphasis added); see also Crawford 2006, p. 62 ("Independence is the central criterion for statehood").

[77] Professor Quigley fails to mention the fact that the PA has acceded to the terms set forth in the various arrangements which form the centerpiece of the ongoing peace process; terms by which Israel retains the key indicia of sovereignty over the West Bank and the Gaza Strip. See *supra* Sect. 11.2.3.

[78] Quigley 2009, pp. 8–9.

[79] E.g., Mandate for Palestine Article 7, League of Nations Doc. C.529 M.314 1922 VI (1922), available at http://www.mfa.gov.il/MFA/Peace+Process/Guide+to+the+Peace+Process/The+Mandate+for+Palestine.htm.

[80] If one were to argue that the Palestinian Jews' acceptance of the partition plan constituted the waiving of any future legal claim of sovereignty over any remaining portions of Palestine, it would logically follow that the Palestinian Arabs' rejection of sovereignty over the portions allocated to them by the plan would likewise have a legal effect on their sovereign rights over such territory.

[81] Quigley 2009, p. 5 ("The normal requirement of effective control over territory is applied less strictly if no competing entity claims title. With Gaza and the West Bank, there were no competing claimants." [citing Crawford 2006, p. 59)]. Professor Quigley's assertion that there were no competing claimants is simply incorrect. Recall that Israel (the Jewish *Palestinian successor State* to the British Mandate) claims the City of Jerusalem (including East Jerusalem, which is part of the West Bank) as its historic capital, see Friedland and Hecht 2000, and that UN Security Council Resolution 242 foresees that final territorial questions (including the issue of establishing defensible boundaries) will be resolved as part of the final negotiations to resolve the Israeli-Palestinian conflict, including acquisitions of land by Israel on the West Bank. See Rostow 1990 (responding to Roberts 1990) ("The right of the Jewish people to settle in Palestine has

Second, the UN partition plan had designated specified territory within Palestine for an Arab state, but the Arabs rejected that plan—and, concomitantly, control over such territories. That rejection strongly suggests that Arab Palestinians rejected the UN grant of sovereignty over those portions of land designated for the Arab state.[82] Yet, whatever one concludes in that regard, one thing is clear—following that rejection, the Palestinian Arabs have never had the opportunity to exercise full sovereign control over any Palestinian territory.[83]

Third, once the 1948–1949 Arab-Israeli war was concluded, Arab states in control of Palestinian territory at the time of signing the various armistice agreements with Israel declined to relinquish to Palestinian Arab authorities control over Palestinian territory remaining in Arab hands.[84] Thus, it was not Israel that kept Arab Palestinians from establishing a state in either 1948 or 1949; it was the neighboring Arab states. The Gaza Strip remained under Egyptian occupation, and the West Bank remained occupied by Jordanian forces. In fact, Jordan even went so far as to claim Jordanian sovereignty over the entire West Bank.[85] Hence, even if the Arab Palestinians did not reject sovereignty (which their rejection of the lands allotted to Palestinian Arabs by the UN partition plan certainly suggests), they were nonetheless precluded by their putative Arab allies from exercising sovereignty over any portion of Palestine from 1948 to the 1967 Arab-Israeli War.

Fourth, as a result of the 1967 Arab-Israeli War, both the West Bank and the Gaza Strip came under Israeli control, once again *without any intervening period of Arab Palestinian rule whatsoever*. Hence, Israel never took over territory over which Palestinian Arabs had ever exercised sovereignty. Rather, Israel seized territory which had been under continuous military occupation by neighboring Arab states since the departure of the British in 1948. Because no independent (Arab or Jewish) *Palestinian state* had, prior to 1967, ever existed in the West Bank and Gaza Strip, the last people in whom sovereignty over those territories resided—consistent with Professor Quigley's reversion theory—included both Arab *and Jewish* Palestinians. As such, in 1967, Israel captured territory to which

---

(Footnote 81 continued)
never been terminated for the West Bank."). See generally Rosenne 2008, http://www.defensibleborders.org/db_rosenneb.pdf. Further, there have been—and continue to be—segments of Israeli society that continue to view "Judea and Samaria" as areas promised to the Jews by the Balfour Declaration (which was, in turn, made part of the World War I peace treaties as well as part of the British Mandate). See, e.g., Arens 2009 ("[A] reading of that convention and an acquaintance with the history of Palestine since the Balfour Declaration and the League of Nations Mandate for Palestine, as well as with the circumstances of the occupation of Judea and Samaria by the Jordanian army in the years between 1948 and 1967, make it clear that that Geneva Convention is not applicable to Israel's presence in these territories.").

[82] See *supra* n. 80.

[83] Even noted Palestinian supporter, Professor Avi Shlaim, admitted as much. See, Attapatu 2004 ("[T]he Palestinians have never exercised sovereignty over the land in which they lived…"). For further support, see *supra* nn. 34–35 and 38–39, and accompanying text.

[84] Sayigh 1999.

[85] Id. p. 16.

it has an arguable claim of sovereignty as the only existing, sovereign successor state to the British Mandate[86] (especially since the Arab Palestinians had explicitly rejected accepting sovereignty in 1947 or 1948). In that light, it is questionable whether Israel can legitimately be viewed as an occupying power.[87] That position was also made clear to the international community by the Israeli Government when Israel announced its intention to implement Fourth Geneva Convention humanitarian measures, *despite having no legal duty to do so*,[88] since a State cannot "occupy" territory (in the sense of the Fourth Geneva Convention) over which it has colorable "sovereign" claims and which had no legitimate prior sovereign.

Fifth, although Israel understands and agrees that an Arab Palestinian state must be established to fulfill the national aspirations of Arab Palestinians, the establishment of such an Arab state must result from mutual negotiations between the parties. To that end, both Israelis and Palestinians have freely entered into an ongoing process to resolve the outstanding issues between them, one of which is the eventual establishment of a viable, independent Palestinian state.[89] The fact that the Arab Palestinians have entered into such a process is proof positive that no

---

[86] See, e.g., Sharon 2009 (noting that "saying that the territories were occupied by Israel 'could conceivably be interpreted as a renunciation of sovereign rights by Israel to the areas [since] one does not "occupy" one's own territory'"). An additional Israeli concern is that saying that the territories were occupied by Israel "could be construed as acceptance of the 1949 ceasefire lines as international borders." Id. at 155. This latter point, once again, refutes Professor Quigley's assertion that there is no other claimant to "Palestinian territory," since Israel will doubtless seek to negotiate "defensible boundaries" (meaning boundary adjustments that will modify the 1949 ceasefire line in Israel's favor) pursuant to UN Security Council Resolution 242. See *also* Arens 2009.

[87] For an interesting, in-depth discussion of this topic, see generally Sharon 2009.

[88] Sharon 2009, pp. 153–54. Sharon continues:

"Upon assumption of control of the territories, Israel had to make a decision as to the applicable law. There were several reasons for Israel not to wish to view the captured territories as occupied, and therefore subject to the provisions of the Fourth Geneva Convention. From a legal standpoint, Israel took the view that in the absence of a prior sovereign, Israel's control of the West Bank and Gaza did not fall within the definition of "occupation" inasmuch as a fundamental premise of the law of occupation—a prior legitimate sovereign—was lacking.

Israel's argument concerning de jure application of the law of occupation did not, however, deter it from declaring its intention to act in accordance with customary international law and the humanitarian provisions of the Fourth Geneva Convention... This intention seems consistent with the view of [Yehuda Z.] Blum:

The conclusion to be drawn from all this is that whenever, for one reason or another, there is no concurrence of a normal "legitimate sovereign" with that of a "belligerent occupant" of the territory, only that part of the law of occupation applies which is intended to safeguard the humanitarian rights of the population". Id. (citations omitted).

[89] *Supra* Sect. 11.2.3.

current Palestinian "State" exists (because one does not negotiate to obtain what one already possesses).

And finally, given the current degree of Israeli military and economic control and influence over the West Bank and the Gaza Strip, it remains highly problematic to assert that an Arab Palestinian entity (such as the PLO or PA) is "sovereign" over any Palestinian territory at all.[90] Hence, to date, since the departure of the British in 1948, there has been no Arab Palestinian control equivalent to sovereign control over any portion of Palestine. Even the Hamas-controlled Gaza Strip (where one might plausibly argue that Arab Palestinians exercise the most control over their own affairs) does not control its land borders, coastline, or airspace and remains dependent on Israel for electricity, fuel, and other basic necessities of life.[91]

11.5 Conclusion

In light of the foregoing, it is difficult to fathom how anyone could argue that there is a state of Palestine currently in existence. Even the Palestinian leaders themselves, through both their frequent statements and their voluntary participation in a process whose goal is to establish a Palestinian "State", testify that *what they hope to achieve in the future* is the creation of a viable Palestinian state. If creation of a viable Palestinian state is the goal Palestinian leaders continue to pursue, that is proof positive that no such "State" currently exists, despite Professor Quigley's contrary conclusion. Absent Palestinian statehood, the PA Declaration to the ICC is *ipso facto* invalid and incapable of conveying jurisdiction to the ICC over the West Bank and the Gaza Strip. As such, the Declaration must be rejected.

---

[90] A specific example that is included under the Interim Agreement should serve to illustrate this point. The West Bank is divided into three types of Areas, designated A, B, and C. Interim Agreement, *supra* n. 35, Articles 3(1), 9(2). The degree of PA control varies in each area, with the most control in Areas A and the least control in Areas C. See Id. Even in Areas A, where the PA exercises the most control, the PA still does not control individual Israelis in such areas, and it does not control the airspace or external security. Id. Articles 5(2)(a), 8(1)(a), 13(4). In Areas B, the PA controls public order and civilian affairs of Palestinian residents, but Israel retains control of Israelis and all airspace, security, and so on. Id. Article 5(3). In Areas C, Israel continues to exercise control over most governmental fields. Id. Taken together, Areas A and B constitute approximately 40% of the entire West Bank; Areas C constitute the remainder, which remains under virtually total Israeli control. The Gaza Strip is currently under total Hamas (not PA) control, and the Hamas leaders who govern Gaza openly oppose the PA and its authority. Erlanger 2007; see *also* BBC News 2009 (detailing Hamas's restoration of order following an insurrection in southern Gaza).

[91] See Erlanger 2009; see also Human Rights Watch 2008.

References

Abbas M (2005a) Inauguration Speech, 15 January 2005. http://electronicintifada.net/bytopic/historicalspeeches/338.shtml

Abbas M (2005b) Speech at Egypt Summit, 8 February 2005. http://edition.cnn.com/2005/WORLD/meast/02/08/transcript.abbas

Abbas M (2008) Speech on the Occasion of the International Day of Solidarity with the Palestinian People, 24 November 2008. http://www.un.int/palestine/AbbasSolidarity08.shtml

Abbas M (2009a) Press Conference with British Prime Minister Gordon Brown and Palestinian National Authority President Mahmoud Abbas, 5 February 2009. http://www.number10.gov.uk/Page18253

Abbas M (2009b) Press Release: Mahmoud Abbas at the European Parliament, 4 February 2009. http://www.europarl.europa.eu/news/expert/infopress_page/030-48165-033-02-06-903-20090203IPR48164-02-02-2009-2009-true/default_en.htm

AGI News (2009) On Mideast: Abu Mazen, Resisting Israel is a Right. http://www.agi.it/world/news/200908131547-pol-ren0034-mideast_abu_mazen_resisting_israel_is_a_right

Arafat Y (1988) Speech at UN General Assembly, 13 December 1988. http://mondediplo.com/focus/mideast/arafat88-en

Arafat Y (2002) Address at the Arab summit in Beirut, 27 March 2002. http://www.al-bab.com/arab/docs/league/arafat02.htm

Arens M (2009) A Matter we must Solve Ourselves, Haaretz, 28 July 2009. http://www.haaretz.com/hasen/spages/1103397.html

Attapatu D (2004) Interview with Middle East Scholar Avi Shlaim: America, Israel and the Middle East, The Nation, 28 June 2004. http://www.thenation.com/doc/20040628/attapatu

BBC News (2009) Hamas says Gaza now Under Control, BBC News, 15 August 2009. http://news.bbc.co.uk/2/hi/middle_east/8203713.stm

Crawford J (2006) The Creation of States in International Law. Oxford University Press, Oxford

Erlanger S (2007) Hamas Seizes Broad Control in Gaza Strip. New York Times, 14 June 2007. http://www.nytimes.com/2007/06/14/world/middleeast/14mideast.html

Erlanger S (2009) An Egyptian Border Town's Commerce, Conducted via Tunnels, Comes to a Halt. New York Times, 31 December 2008. http://www.nytimes.com/2009/01/01/world/middleeast/01rafah.html

Friedland R, Hecht R (2000) To rule Jerusalem, 2nd revised edn. University of California Press

Human Rights Watch (2008) Q&A on Hostilities between Israel and Hamas, What International Humanitarian Law Applies to the Current Conflict between Israel and Hamas? http://www.hrw.org/en/news/2008/12/31/q-hostilities-between-israel-and-hamas#_What_international_humanitarian

Lewis P (1989) Arabs at U.N. Relax Stand on P.L.O., New York Times, New York

Makovsky D (2009) Preliminary Assessment of Israel's Operation Cast Lead, Policy Watch No. 1462, 23 January 2009. http://www.washingtoninstitute.org/templateC05.php?CID=2997

Mandate for Palestine. http://www.mfa.gov.il/MFA/Peace+Process/Guide+to+the+Peace+Process/The+Mandate+for+Palestine.htm

McCarthy R (2009) Fatah holds first Party Conference for 20 Years, The Guardian, 4 August 2009. http://www.guardian.co.uk/world/2009/aug/04/fatah-conference-abbas-west-bank

Pear R (1988) U.S. Won't Oppose U.N. Geneva Session. New York Times, 29 November 1988. http://www.nytimes.com/1988/11/29/world/us-won-t-oppose-un-geneva-session.html

PLO Negotiations Affairs Department (2008) The Historic Compromise: The Palestinian Declaration of Independence and the Twenty-Year Struggle for a Two-State Solution. http://www.nad-plo.org/news-updates/Historic%20Compromise%20FAQs%20FINAL.pdf

PLO Negotiations Affairs Department (2009) Negotiations Primer. http://www.nad-plo.org/news-updates/magazine.pdf

Quigley J (2009) The Palestine Declaration to the International Criminal Court: The Statehood Issue, 35 Rutgers Law Record: 1–10. http://www.lawrecord.com/files/35-rutgers-l-rec-1.pdf, [and in this Volume, Chapter 10]

Reuters (2009) Israel–Hamas Violence Since Ceasfire Ended, 13 January 2009. http://www.reuters.com/article/topNews/idUSTRE50B6CL20090113

Robert A (1990) Prolonged Military Operations: The Israeli-Occupied Territories Since 1967. Am J Int Law 84:44

Rosenne M (2008) Understanding UN Security Council Resolution 242 of November 22, 1967, on the Middle East, in Defensible Borders for a Lasting Peace 45. http://www.defensibleborders.org/db_rosenneb.pdf

Rostow E (1990) Correspondence. Am J Int Law 84:717–718

Sayigh Y (1999) Armed Struggle and the Search for State: The Palestinian National Movement, 1949–1993. http://www.questia.com/PM.qst?a=o&d=10156112

Schneider H (2009) Palestinian Premier Sets 2-Year Statehood Target. Washington Post. http://www.washingtonpost.com/wp-dyn/content/article/2009/06/22/AR2009062202962.html

Sharon A (2009) Keeping Occupied: The Evolving Law of Occupation. Regent J. L. & Pub. Pol'y 1:145–155

Toameh K (2009) Palestinian Rift Worse than Israel. Jerusalem Post, 8 May 2009. http://www.jpost.com/MiddleEast/Article.aspx?id=150914

Chapter 12
Palestine Statehood: A Rejoinder to Professor Robert Weston Ash

John Quigley

Contents

12.1 Professor Ash's Sect. 11.2: Statements by Palestinian Officials and Palestinian Participation in the Peace Process 462
12.2 Professor Ash's Sect. 11.3: The International Community 463
12.3 Professor Ash's Sect. 11.4: The Attributes of Statehood 466
12.4 Conclusion 467
References 468

Professor Robert Weston Ash, in his response to my article The Palestine Declaration to the International Criminal Court: The Statehood Issue [*supra* in this Volume, Chap. 10—ChM], takes issue with my position that Palestine is a state.[1] He thinks it is not. Professor Ash argues that Palestinian officialdom itself understands that Palestine is not a state, that the international community does not treat Palestine as a state, and that Palestine lacks the attributes of statehood.[2] On none of these points is Professor Ash's argument persuasive. Palestinian officialdom does regard Palestine as a state. The international community does as well. And the asserted lack of attributes involves a misunderstanding by Professor Ash of what is required for statehood in the specific situation in which a state's

---

President's Club Professor in Law, Moritz College of Law, The Ohio State University. This article was first published in 36 Rutgers Law Record (2009), 257–263.

[1] *Supra*, Chap. 11 in this Volume, previously published as Ash 2009.
[2] See *supra* Chap. 11, respectively at Sects. 11.2, 11.3, and 11.4. [Ash 2009 at 188, 193, 197].

J. Quigley (✉)
The Ohio State University, Columbus, OH, USA

territory has come under belligerent occupation. This rejoinder follows Professor Ash's scheme, including his sub-categories.

12.1 Professor Ash's Sect. 11.2: Statements by Palestinian Officials and Palestinian Participation in the Peace Process

Statements by Palestinian Officials

In Sects. 11.2.1 and 11.2.2 [see *supra*, Chap. 11 in this Volume–ChM], Professor Ash cites statements by Palestine Liberation Organization (PLO) and Palestinian Authority (PA) officials, and by the PLO Negotiations Affairs Department, that, in his view, reflect Palestine statehood as a "future event", and to that extent a negation of a claim to present statehood.[3] Here Professor Ash misconstrues a series of statements by Palestinian officials. He takes statements in which they speak of establishing an "independent state" as proof that they do not regard Palestine presently as a state. These statements focus on independence, namely, on having control over their territory by ending Israel's belligerent occupation of it. These statements are not inconsistent with a claim of present statehood. Palestine lacks independence but does not lack statehood. What these officials are calling for is an end to the occupation of the territory of Palestine. They are not saying that Palestine is not presently a state.

The Peace Process

In Sect. 11.2.3 [see *supra*, Chap. 11—ChM], Professor Ash argues that Palestinian participation in the peace process that began in Oslo in 1993 proves that no Palestine state currently exists.[4] Professor Ash here repeats the argument that the Government of Israel has made, based on the 1995 Interim Agreement between Israel and the PLO.[5] He refers to a provision in which the PLO agreed that the PA would not engage in foreign relations, and specifically that it would not establish embassies abroad.[6]

Engaging in foreign relations is an attribute of a state, so Professor Ash argues that what he sees as a lack of a capacity to do so negates a claim to statehood. The provision to which Professor Ash refers indeed is found in the 1995 Interim Agreement, but that provision has no relevance to the conduct of foreign relations by the PLO. The 1995 Interim Agreement in fact specifically provides that "Neither Party shall be deemed, by virtue of having entered into this Agreement, to have renounced or waived any of its existing rights, claims or positions."[7]

---

[3] Id. at Sect. 11.2.

[4] Id.

[5] Israeli–Palestinian Interim Agreement on the West Bank and the Gaza Strip, Sept. 28, 1995, UN Doc. A/51/889, S/1997/357, reprinted in 8 PAL. Y.B. INT'L L. 353 (1994–1995).

[6] Id., Article IV(5), at 360.

[7] Id., Article XXXI(6), at 371.

As of 1995, the PLO already maintained an extensive network of embassies abroad and routinely engaged in diplomacy.[8]

Professor Ash finds a negation of Palestine statehood in Article 31(7) of the 1995 Interim Agreement, which states that neither party will change the status of the West Bank or Gaza pending the outcome of negotiations with the other. But that provision is irrelevant to Palestine statehood, which had been declared already in 1988.[9] An assertion of Palestine statehood post-1995 involves no change in status for the West Bank or Gaza.

Additionally, Professor Ash argues that under the 1995 Interim Agreement Israel retains control over external defense, hence that there is a lack of exercise of control over territory from the standpoint of Palestine.[10] Control of territory is, to be sure, a normal requirement for statehood.[11] What Ash omits is the fact that the West Bank and Gaza, even after the 1995 Interim Agreement, remained under Israel's belligerent occupation.[12] A state whose territory is occupied is obviously unable to exercise control, but that circumstance does not negate its statehood.[13]

12.2 Professor Ash's Sect. 11.3: The International Community

UN Protocol

In Sect. 11.3.1 [see *supra*, Chap. 11—ChM] Professor Ash argues that Palestine is not a state because at the United Nations it is not credentialed as a state.[14] He writes, correctly, that Palestine "enjoys only observer status" at the United Nations but has not been admitted as a member state.[15] He takes the lack of admission to membership as a negation of Palestine statehood. Professor Ash is correct that, in UN protocol documents, Palestine is not listed in the category "state." His argument, however, elevates form over substance. He omits the many indications that Palestine is treated as a state at the UN, even though it has not admitted it as a member state.[16] What is key to whether an entity is a state is the attitude of the international community towards it. Formal recognition—an act that

---

[8] Talmon 1998.
[9] Palestine National Council, Declaration of Independence, Nov. 15, 1988, UN Doc. A/43/827, S/20278, Annex III, 18 November 1988, reprinted in 27 ILM 1668 (1988).
[10] See *supra* Chap. 11 at Sect. 11.2.
[11] See Kelsen 1941.
[12] *Legal Consequences of the Construction of a Wall in the Occupied Palestinian Territory*, Advisory Opinion, 2004 ICJ 136, at 167 (July 9) [hereinafter "Legal Consequences"].
[13] Quigley, *supra* Chap. 10 [previously published as Quigley 2009].
[14] See supra Chap. 11, at Sect. 11.3.
[15] Id.
[16] See *supra* Chap. 10, at Sects. 10.5, 10.6.

by tradition is discretionary and that may involve political considerations—is not required.[17]

The United Nations first admitted the PLO as an observer, then changed the designation of the observer from "PLO" to "Palestine".[18] The obvious implication of changing the reference to "Palestine" is that it is a state. One only calls states by such names as they themselves use to refer to themselves. When an effort was made in 1989 to make the implication more explicit, however, the United States used its clout to stop the effort.[19] In that year, a group of Arab states proposed a draft resolution for the UN General Assembly that would have said "that the designation Palestine shall be construed, within the United Nations, as the State of Palestine."[20] The proponents withdrew the draft resolution a week later, however, after the United States threatened to stop paying its UN dues if the draft resolution was adopted.[21]

The fact that the UN did not take this step, and beyond it an admission of Palestine to the UN as a member state, was a result of fear that the US might carry through with its threats. These threats were openly discussed at the UN. The same was true for Palestine's efforts to gain admission in 1989 to the World Health Organization (WHO) and the UN Economic and Social Organization (UNESCO). WHO's director pled with member states to reject Palestine's application for admission because he feared that the organization would collapse without the US contribution.[22]

The failure of the United Nations, or its related organizations, to go farther in a formal recognition of Palestine cannot be attributed to a lack of understanding that Palestine is a state. When it has come to very practical issues, like the right of reply in the General Assembly, a right that attaches only to states,[23] or participation in Security Council debate,[24] a right that similarly attaches only to states, the UN organs have treated Palestine as a state.

The Rome meeting for an International Criminal Court

In Sect. 11.3.2 [see *supra*, Chap. 11 in this Volume—ChM] Professor Ash says that Palestine was treated as less than a state when it was represented at the 1998

---

[17] Convention on Rights and Duties of States, Dec. 26, 1933, Article. 7, 165 LNTS 19 (stating, "The recognition of a state may be express or tacit").

[18] GA Res. 43/177, UN Doc. A/RES/43/177 (1988), available at http://unispal.un.org/UNISPAL. nsf/181c4bf00c44e5fd85256cef0073c426/146e6838d505833f852560d600471e25?OpenDocument.

[19] See Paul Lewis 1989.

[20] UN Doc. A/44/L.50 (Nov. 29, 1989).

[21] Lewis 1989.

[22] Kempster 1989.

[23] UN General Assembly, 32d session, 27th plen. mtg. at 513, UN Doc. A/32/PV.27 (Oct. 10, 1977).

[24] UN SCOR, 31st sess., 1870th mtg. at 2–3, 12–13, UN Doc. S/PV.1870 (Jan. 12, 1976). See also Suy 1978, pp. 138–139.

meeting organized in Rome by the United Nations that led to the adoption of the Rome Statute of the International Criminal Court. He is correct that Palestine was listed not with "states." However, except for several NGOs involved in humanitarian law, only states or organizations of states were invited to participate. What is important about this episode, and this Professor Ash fails to mention, is that Palestine was invited to that meeting. Not being a humanitarian law organization, but rather an entity representing a territory, the only rationale for Palestine's participation was that it was a state.

The International Court of Justice

In Sect. 11.3.3 [see *supra*, Chap. 11—ChM] Professor Ash says that the International Court of Justice (ICJ) determined that Palestine is not a foreign state by rejecting Israel's claim of self-defense as a rationale for building a security barrier in the West Bank.[25] Professor Ash says that the ICJ rejected the Israeli rationale because Israel did not claim that the attacks were imputable to a foreign state. The ICJ passage on which Professor Ash relies reads:

> Article 51 of the Charter thus recognizes the existence of an inherent right of self-defense in the case of armed attack by one State against another State. However, Israel does not claim that the attacks against it are imputable to a foreign State.[26]

It does not flow from the Court's recitation of Israel's position that the ICJ was saying anything about Palestine statehood. The ICJ simply said that Israel did not claim that Palestine was a state. The ICJ could, perhaps, have gone on to state its own view, but contented itself with rejecting Israel's argument based on the manner in which Israel asserted it and left the matter there.

Elsewhere in its advisory opinion—and this Professor Ash does not mention—the ICJ strongly implied that Palestine is a state. In addressing the potential long-term consequences of the barrier, the ICJ noted Israel's assurances of the structure's temporary character but said that it, the Court, "nevertheless cannot remain indifferent to certain fears expressed to it that the route of the wall will prejudge the future frontier between Israel and Palestine...."[27] The ICJ did not elaborate on its statement about the "future frontier between Israel and Palestine," but the question of a border between two territorial entities makes little sense unless each of them is a state. The question of a border remained, to be sure, in the future, but in speaking about the frontier, the Court referred to "Palestine", not to a "future Palestine". The ICJ, moreover, treated Palestine as a state in the way it treated Palestine as a participant in the advisory opinion litigation. Palestine submitted a written statement and made oral argument.[28] Under the rules applicable to such proceedings, UN member states are invited to submit statements in the nature of

---

[25] Legal Consequences, at 194.
[26] Id.
[27] Id. at 184.
[28] Id. at 141.

legal briefs and to argue before the Court, but it is only states, or inter-governmental organizations, that are so entitled.[29] Finally, Professor Ash claims that Judge Elaraby, in his separate opinion in the advisory opinion, "concluded that no sovereign Palestinian state existed." The language of Judge Elaraby cited by Ash reads:

On 14 May 1948, the independence of the Jewish State was declared. The Israeli declaration was "by virtue of [Israel's] natural and historic right" and based "on the strength of the resolution of the United Nations General Assembly". The independence of the Palestinian Arab State has not yet materialized.[30]

Judge Elaraby was saying precisely the opposite of what Professor Ash claims. Judge Elaraby said that the "independence" of the "Palestinian Arab State" has not materialized. He was not saying that Palestine is not a state. Judge Elaraby in fact there refers to Palestine as a state, albeit one whose independence remained in the future. Judge Elaraby was distinguishing statehood from the effectuation of a state's independence.

Switzerland and the Palestine Ratification of the Geneva Conventions

In Sect. 11.3.4 [see *supra*, Chap. 11—ChM], Professor Ash says that Switzerland indirectly took a position against Palestine statehood when it declined in 1989 to accept Palestine's attempted ratification of the four 1949 Geneva conventions relating to the law of war. The Government of Switzerland is the depositary of these conventions. Professor Ash concedes that Switzerland, in declining to accept Palestine's ratification, did not determine that Palestine was not a state. He argues instead that Switzerland indirectly took a position that Palestine was not a state when it said, as it did, that the issue of Palestine statehood was not settled in the international community.

Switzerland's view, as reflected in its statement declining ratification, was that the issue was being handled by the U.N. General Assembly. That body had recently voted its approbation of the 1988 Palestine declaration of independence.[31] Switzerland's position was that it did not regard it as its function as depositary of the Geneva conventions to usurp the role of the UN General Assembly in determining Palestine's status. Switzerland's action thus reflected no position on Palestine statehood, direct or indirect.

12.3 Professor Ash's Sect. 11.4: The Attributes of Statehood

Professor Ash argues that Palestine is not a state because of a lack of exercise of control over the territory claimed for it. His error here is that he regards it as required for statehood that a state maintain control of its territory even when

---

[29] Statute of the International Court of Justice, Article 66.
[30] Legal Consequences, at 251.
[31] GA Res. 43/177.

another state has entered militarily and has taken control, as Israel did in 1967 in the West Bank and Gaza. Were Professor Ash's proposition true, Kuwait would not have existed as a state once Iraqi military units forced the Kuwaiti leadership to flee in 1990. Yet Kuwait continued to be regarded as a state during this period, while the international community engaged in efforts to restore control to its government.[32]

Additionally, Professor Ash asserts that Israel may have a valid claim to the West Bank and Gaza, and that this may call Palestine statehood into question. Here, he overlooks the fact that Israel has not asserted such a claim, and that the Supreme Court of Israel has ruled repeatedly that the West Bank and Gaza are under Israel's belligerent occupation—a status that is at variance with a claim to sovereignty.[33]

The entry by the PLO into the peace process that began in 1993, says Professor Ash, is "proof positive that no current Palestinian 'State' exists (because one does not negotiate to obtain what one already possesses)."[34] This assertion is groundless. The Palestinians are negotiating not for statehood, but for a withdrawal of Israel from the territory of their state. The fact that Israel has shown itself willing to enter into negotiations that would set Israel's borders reflects an Israeli understanding that the Palestinian negotiators have the capacity to conclude an agreement that would give Israel internationally recognized borders.[35] The acknowledgment of a border has significance only if it comes from a state. If Palestine were not a state, there would be no point, from Israel's side, in gaining agreement to a border. The peace process reflects the understanding not only of Israel, but of the international community in general, that Palestine is a state.

12.4 Conclusion

Professor Ash's attempted refutation of my thesis that Palestine is a state only serves to reinforce the validity of my position. Palestine statehood was declared in 1988 on the basis of a prior existing statehood dating from the interwar period.[36] Palestine functions as a state, albeit under the considerable constraints imposed by the belligerent occupation of its territory.

---

[32] SC Res. 662, UN Doc. S/RES/662 (1990) (seeking restoration of the "sovereignty, independence and territorial integrity of Kuwait."), available at http://www.unhcr.org/refworld/category,,,LEGAL,,,KWT,3b00f13750,0.html.

[33] See, e.g., *Tamimi v. Minister of Defence*, H.C. 507/85, 41(4) Piskei 1988; accord Dinstein 2009, pp. 277–279.

[34] See *supra* Chap. 11, Sect. 11.4.

[35] See Declaration of Principles on Interim Self-Government Arrangements (Israel-PLO), Sept. 13, 1993, reprinted in 32 ILM 1525 (1993).

[36] See Palestine National Council: Political Communique and Declaration of Independence, Nov. 15, 1988, UN Doc.A/43/827, S/20278, Annex III, Nov. 18, 1988, reprinted in 27 ILM 1668 (1988).

The fundamental error made by Professor Ash is one that is made by other scholars, and by courts, namely, that they regard statehood as present only if the state enjoys independence, and in particular they ignore the fact that a state whose territory is occupied is unable to exert control over it.[37] On this basis, Palestine statehood is said not to exist. The fact that Professor Ash is not alone in his view makes it all the more significant to show the deficiencies of his approach.

Conclusions on international legal issues must be made on the basis of the practice of states. This proposition is particularly true in regard to the question of whether a particular entity is a state. Those who deny Palestine statehood base their position on abstract concepts relating to the definition of statehood. They ignore the practice of the international community in relation to Palestine. As indicated in my piece to which Professor Ash has responded, Palestine has been regarded as a state since it was set up as a Class A mandate under the supervision of the League of Nations. That statehood was never extinguished, despite a variety of control arrangements that have intervened in regard to segments of its territory, and despite the fact that independence remains elusive.

References

Ash R (2009) Is Palestine A "State"? A Response to Professor John Quigley's Article, "The Palestine Declaration to The International Criminal Court: The Statehood Issue. Rutgers Law Record 36:186–201. http://www.lawrecord.com/files/36-Rutgers-L-Rec-186.pdf [also in this Volume, Chapter 11]

Dinstein Y (2009) The International Law of Belligerent Occupation. Cambridge University Press, Cambridge

Kelsen H (1941) Recognition in International Law: Theoretical Observations. Am J Int Law 35:605

Kempster N (1989) PLO Urged to Drop Bid to UN Unit; U.S. Warns it would Withhold Money for Health Agency, 3 May 1989. L.A. Times

Lewis P (1989) Arabs at UN Relax Stand on PLO, 6 December 1989. N.Y. Times

Quigley J (2009) The Palestine Declaration to the International Criminal Court: The Statehood Issue. Rutgers Law Record 35:1–10. http://www.lawrecord.com/files/35-rutgers-l-rec-1.pdf [also in this Volume, Chapter 10]

Suy E (1978) The Status of Observers in International Organizations. 160 Rec. Des Cours (Hague Acad Int Law) 75:138–139

Talmon S (1998) Recognition of Governments in International Law: With Particular Reference to Governments in Exile. Oxford University Press, Oxford

---

[37] See Ash 2009 [and *supra* Chap. 11].

Chapter 13
ICC Jurisdiction Over Acts Committed in the Gaza Strip: Article 12(3) of the ICC Statute and Non-State Entities

Yaël Ronen

Contents

13.1 Introduction.. 469
13.2 Preconditions for ICC Jurisdiction.. 473
13.3 Admission of the Palestinian Declaration as that of a Full-Fledged State.... 476
13.4 Admission Under Article 12(3) of a Declaration by a Quasi-State.............. 481
13.5 Institutional Considerations.. 485
13.6 Conclusion.. 491
References... 492

13.1 Introduction

On 27 December 2008, Israel opened a three-week long military offensive in the Gaza Strip ('Operation Cast Lead').[1] During that period, Israel carried out over 2,360 air strikes over Gaza,[2] as well as ground assaults. These attacks left 1,300

Senior Lecturer, Sha'arei Mishpat College, and Hebrew University, Faculty of Law. This article was published in Journal of International Criminal Justice (2010) 8(1), 8–27. The editors wish to thanks OUP for kindly granting permission to republish the article. [For author's acknowledgments, please refer to J Int Crim. Justice].

[1] The applicability of Article 12(3) ICCSt to the Palestinians has been discussed previously as a theoretical question: Schabas 2007, p. 81.
[2] Macintyre and Sengupta 2009.

Y. Ronen (✉)
Sha'arei Mishpat College, Hod HaSharon, Israel

Palestinians dead and more than 5,000 wounded, a third of them children.[3] At the same time, Hamas and its associates bombed Israeli territory with 617 rockets and 178 mortar shells,[4] causing a total of three civilian fatalities, 182 wounded and 584 persons suffering from shock and anxiety syndrome.[5] Nine Israeli soldiers were killed inside the Gaza Strip.[6]

The conflict was followed by numerous allegations of violations of the laws of armed conflict on the part of both Israel and Hamas,[7] and by calls to determine and enforce the responsibility for these violations, of state actors, non-state entities and individuals.[8] Most prominently, a United Nations Fact Finding Mission on the Gaza Conflict appointed by the Human Rights Council[9] concluded in a September 2009 report (the 'Goldstone Report') that both the Israeli military and Palestinian armed groups had violated international humanitarian law by indiscriminately and intentionally targeting civilians.[10] Of the various enforcement mechanisms capable of responding to violations of the laws of war, international criminal law and recourse to the ICC specifically have been most forcefully advocated.

---

[3] Briefing to the UN Security Council based on data from Palestinian Ministry of Health, by Under-Secretary-General Holmes, UN Doc. S/PV. 6077, 27 January 2009, at 2.

[4] Israel Ministry of Foreign Affairs, The Operation in Gaza—Factual and Legal Aspects, July 2009.

[5] Data provided by the Israeli Ministry of Foreign Affairs, 2008, Israel justifies its action by reference to the continuous attacks from the Gaza Strip on civilian communities in Israel. In 2008 alone, nearly 3,000 rockets and mortars were fired at Israeli civilian targets, Israel Ministry of Foreign Affairs, 2009, para 3.

[6] Id.

[7] E.g. UN Doc. S/PV.6061, 6 January 2009, and UN Doc. S/PV.6061 (Resumption 1), 7 January 2009; Statement by 31 international lawyers, 'Israel's bombardment of Gaza is not self-defence— it's a war crime', The Sunday Times 2009; Israel Ministry of Foreign Affairs 2009, 52–76; Human Rights Watch 2009b; Amnesty International, 2009b.

[8] General Assembly Demands Full Respect For Security Council Resolution 1860, UN Doc. GA/10809/Rev. 1, 16 January 2009 (Statement of Bolivia), available online at http://un.org/News/Press/docs/2009/ga10809.doc.htm; Human Rights Watch, 2009a; Amnesty International 2009c, Amnesty International 2009a; ACRI and Organizations 2009; The ICC Prosecutor has received over 210 appeals from Palestinians and NGOs to investigate the Israeli–Palestinian conflict, Interview with Luis Moreno-Ocampo, Al Jazeera 2009. These include complaints predating the Gaza Conflict, RNW International Justice, 'ICC starts analysis of Gaza war crimes allegations', 3 February 2009, available online at http://www.rnw.nl.

[9] Human Rights Council Resolution S-9/1 on the Grave Violations of Human Rights in the Occupied Palestinian Territory, Particularly due to the Recent Israeli Military Attacks Against the Occupied Gaza Strip, UN Doc. A/HRC/S-9/L.1, 12 January 2009.

[10] Report of the United Nations Fact Finding Mission on the Gaza Conflict, UN Doc. A/HRC/12/48, 25 September 2009 (hereafter 'Goldstone Report'), paras 1886, 1891, 1921, 1950.

The Goldstone Report called on the Security Council to demand of both Israel and the relevant authorities in the Gaza Strip to conduct good faith investigations that are independent and in conformity with international standards, and, if those are not undertaken, to refer the situation in Gaza to the ICC Prosecutor.[11] It also recommended invocation of state responsibility pursuant to the Fourth Geneva Convention. The Human Rights Council has endorsed the Mission's recommendations and called upon all concerned parties, including United Nations bodies, to ensure their implementation.[12]

On 21 January 2008, the Palestinian Minister of Justice lodged with the ICC Registrar a 'Declaration Recognizing the Jurisdiction of the International Criminal Court'.[13] The declaration, signed by the 'Government of Palestine' on 'Palestinian National Authority' (PNA) letterhead,[14] provides:

> In conformity with Article 12, para 3 of the Statute of the International Criminal Court, the Government of Palestine hereby recognizes the jurisdiction of the Court for the purpose of identifying, prosecuting and judging the authors and accomplices of acts committed on the territory of Palestine since 1 July 2002.

The present article examines the capacity of the Palestinian declaration to provide the ICC with jurisdiction based on a territorial nexus, focusing on three issues regarding the admissibility of the Palestinian declaration under Article 12(3), all of which are linked to the question of statehood. Following a brief review in part 2 of the need to rely on territorial jurisdiction, part 3 addresses the question whether the Palestinian declaration can be admitted[15] as that of a state. There is already a wealth of scholarly literature on the question whether a state of Palestine merits recognition, in particular by reference to the factual requisites for

---

[11] Goldstone Report, para 1969.

[12] Human Rights Resolution S-12/1 The human rights situation in the Occupied Palestinian Territory, including East Jerusalem, UN Doc. A/HRC/RES/S-12/1 B, 16 October 2009, para 3.

[13] Declaration recognizing the Jurisdiction of the International Criminal Court, available online at http://www.icc-cpi.int/NR/rdonlyres/4F8D4963-EBE6-489D-9F6F-1B3C1057EA0A/279764/20090122PalestinianDeclaration.pdf.

[14] The Independent Fact Finding Committee appointed by the League of Arab States (hereafter 'Arab League Committee') criticized the ICC for exceeding its authority by 'changing the Government of Palestine into the PNA' in its response to the declaration. Given the fact that the declaration was submitted on PNA letter head, this assertion is puzzling. Report of the Independent Fact Finding Committee on Gaza: No Safe Place, Presented to the League of Arab States, 30 April 2009, para 594, available online at http://www.arableagueonline.org/las/picture_gallery/reportfullFINAL.pdf [the Executive Summary in included in this Volume, *infra* Annex to Chap. 17—ChM].

[15] The present article uses the term 'admission' to distinguish admissibility of the declaration from acceptance of jurisdiction within the declaration.

statehood and to the right to self-determination.[16] This article does not purport to arbitrate among the various views; it argues that regardless of the normative arguments regarding the existence and recognition of a Palestinian state,[17] the ICC Prosecutor may not assume the existence of a Palestinian state because the Palestinians themselves do not make a claim to that effect. Part 4 examines a more nuanced question: whether under a purposive interpretation of Article 12(3), declarations should also be admitted from quasi-states such as the PNA. Part 5 focuses on institutional considerations, examining the consequences of the ICC Prosecutor engaging in questions concerning statehood and recognition. A separate issue, not analyzed here, is the geographical areas which are covered by the declaration, and specifically whether the territory of 'Palestine' that is governed by the PNA extends to the Gaza Strip.[18]

While this article concludes that the ICC Prosecutor should not admit the declaration as a basis for jurisdiction, it should be emphasized that ICC proceedings are only one element in the international community's endeavour to secure accountability for violations international law, in general and with respect to the Gaza Strip specifically. The ICC is not the only mechanism for accountability, even if it is the most structured and visible one. Moreover, its mandate is by definition limited to individual conduct, and does not extend to violations of the laws of armed conflict that do not amount to criminal acts.[19] In the circumstances, accountability could more usefully be pursued through other mechanisms, such as the exercise of universal jurisdiction by individual states, effective incentives for involved parties to enforce the law within their domestic systems, and invocation of state responsibility.

---

[16] E.g. Boyle 1990, and response by Crawford 1990; Quigley 2002. The same arguments are essentially reproduced in Quigley 2009; Prince 1989; Silverberg 1989–1999; McKinney 1994–1995; de Waart 1994–1995; Becker 1998; Blum et al. 1988; Kohen 2006; Goldsmith 2003, p. 94, ft 18, considers the question briefly specifically in the context of Article 12(3) ICCSt. To the issues raised traditionally, one may add certain challenges that have emerged in the last few years, such as the legal and practical consequences of Israel's disengagement from the Gaza Strip, and the implications of the political rift between the West Bank and the Gaza Strip.

[17] Cf. Quigley 2009 who considers the question of statehood in the same context as the present article but only relates to that context in the penultimate paragraph of the conclusion.

[18] On the one hand there is an international commitment to the unity of the two areas as a single political entity. On the other hand, since June 2007, when Hamas took over control of the Gaza Strip, the PNA has lost control over that area. One may argue that a state of Palestine asserted by the PNA must be limited to the West Bank; alternatively, if the Gaza Strip constitutes a sovereign state, its government is not the PNA but the Hamas, which has not lodged any declaration with the ICC. Resolution of this issue requires an analysis of the relationship between the PNA and Hamas, which is outside the scope of this article.

[19] See 'OTP response to communications received concerning Iraq', available online at http://www.icc-cpi.int/NR/rdonlyres/04D143C8-19FB-466C-AB77-4CDB2FDEBEF7/143682/OTP_letter_to_senders_re_Iraq_9_February_2006.pdf.

13.2 Preconditions for ICC Jurisdiction

The ICC may only exercise its jurisdiction over genocide, crimes against humanity and war crimes if the accused is a national of a state which has accepted the jurisdiction of the ICC; if the crime took place on the territory of a state which has accepted ICC jurisdiction; or if the United Nations Security Council refers the situation to the Prosecutor, irrespective of the nationality of the accused or the location of the crime.[20] In the circumstances of the Gaza Strip, none of the preconditions for ICC jurisdiction (a territorial or nationality nexus, or a Security Council referral) are met in a manner which offers a straightforward basis for ICC jurisdiction. Indeed, according to media reports the ICC Prosecutor has initially announced that he was unable to open investigations into alleged Israeli violations of the laws of armed conflict during the Gaza Conflict, because the Court lacked jurisdiction.[21] The nationality nexus is not directly applicable with respect to Israelis, because Israel is not party to the ICC Statute.[22] It may be possible to bring Israeli nationals before the ICC if they are also nationals of other states, that are party to the ICC Statute.[23] Even the fact that a person is a national of one state when the alleged crime was committed in his or her capacity as an organ of another state is no bar to jurisdiction, in view of the distinction underlying international criminal justice between individual and State responsibility.[24] Nonetheless, reliance on multiple nationalities as the basis for initiating an investigation raises various challenges and difficulties. One is whether the fact that an individual in a particular conflict is a national of an ICC state party means that the Court now has jurisdiction to investigate the entire 'situation'.[25] Another is whether the nationality nexus hinges on a formal or on an effective link with a second state of nationality.[26] Particularly with respect to members of military forces, the link with the state party may be only formal: service in the military forces of another state ordinarily accompanies permanent residence in it (or even the possession of its nationality) and allegiance to it, which often runs counter to an effective link with the state of nationality. Accordingly, multiple nationality may afford a nexus only if a formal link is considered sufficient. A third problem is that prosecutions based on individuals' multiple nationality are likely to be available randomly rather than according to the gravity of the individuals' crimes. The 'interests of justice' might therefore suggest that the ICC Prosecutor should

---

[20] Acceptance can be effected by accession to the ICC Statute or by an *ad hoc* declaration, Articles 13, 12(3) ICCSt.
[21] RNW International Justice, *supra* n. 8; Simons 2009.
[22] On Israel's position toward the ICC see Shany 2003; Goldstone 2003; Blumenthal 2002, p. 593.
[23] According to the press, the ICC Prosecutor 'is considering' taking such a step against an Israeli reserve officer who is also a national of South Africa, see Ephron 2009.
[24] See also Akande 2003, pp. 634–635.
[25] Article 13 ICCSt.
[26] Deen-Racsmany 2001, pp. 611–612.

not give priority to investigating cases where jurisdiction is based on multiple nationality.[27] The practice of the ICC Prosecutor to date indicates a reluctance to rely on multiple nationality as a nexus in instances involving large contingencies of military and other persons who act on behalf of non-party states.[28]

Referral of the situation to the Prosecutor by the Security Council acting under Chapter VII of the UN Charter[29] is also an unlikely scenario: the United States, despite its gradual warming toward the ICC,[30] is likely to veto any attempt to pass the necessary resolution.[31] This is probably the background for the Fact Finding Mission's proposal that the General Assembly has recourse to Resolution 377(V), 'Uniting for Peace,'[32] as a means of initiating criminal prosecutions, even though this approach is unprecedented. However, as a matter of UN law, the use of this Resolution to situations where there is no immediate urgency is controversial.[33] Moreover, it is difficult to see how it can be used for international criminal law purposes. The Resolution concerned situations where the Security Council fails to exercise its responsibility to maintain international peace and security due to aggression, breach of the peace or a threat to the peace.[34] Prima facie, this responsibility does not include prevention of impunity.[35] Finally, the Resolution

---

[27] Article 53(2)(c) ICCSt.

[28] In February 2006 the ICC Prosecutor made public his reasons not to initiate investigations on the basis of the nationality nexus with respect to crimes allegedly committed on the territories of Iraq and Venezuela, both non-parties to the ICC Statute. 'OTP response to communications received concerning Iraq', *supra* n. 19, and 'OTP response to communications received concerning Venezuela', available online at http://www.icc-cpi.int/NR/rdonlyres/4E2BC725-6A63-40B8-8CDC-ADBA7BCAA91F/143684/OTP_letter_to_senders_re_Venezuela_9_February_2006.pdf.

[29] Article 13(b) ICCSt.

[30] For a review of US policy toward the ICC see ASIL 2009, at 5–17.

[31] JTA 2009. Previously, the US did not oppose the referral of the situation in Sudan to the ICC (SC Res. 1593(2005), 31 March 2005). At the same time, the statement of the US Permanent Representative to the UN, *supra* n. 7, does not offer much prospect for the US acquiescing in a referral of the Gaza Conflict to the ICC.

[32] Goldstone Report, para 1971. The Arab League Committee also suggested that if the Security Council fails to refer the situation to the ICC, the League of Arab States should request the General Assembly to 'endorse Palestine's declaration', in a meeting constituted in terms of the Uniting for Peace Resolution, GA Res. 377(V)A, 3 November 1950.

[33] Zaum 2008, pp. 160–161

[34] GA Res. 377(V), *supra* n. 32, para 1.

[35] But see the ICTR stating that international peace and security cannot be said to be re-established adequately without justice being made, thus rejecting the claim that establishment of the ad hoc Tribunal was in excess of the Security Council powers under Chapter VII of the UN Charter. Decision on the Defence Motion on Jurisdiction, *Kanyabashi* (ICTR-96-15-T), Trial Chamber, 18 June 1997, § 27. This does not mean that any individual measure in the context of the international criminal tribunals is mandated under Chapter VII.

authorizes the General Assembly to make recommendation to states on collective action.[36] This raises the question whether a referral made collectively should be regarded as multiple referrals or as a referral from an international organization, which the ICC Statute does not permit.

The territorial basis for jurisdiction, which requires acceptance of ICC jurisdiction by the state on the territory of which the alleged crimes were committed, does not provide a simple basis for ICC jurisdiction either.[37] The crimes are alleged to have been committed in the Gaza Strip, which is not under the sovereignty of any state presently party to the ICC Statute. The Palestinian declaration is an attempt to provide the territorial nexus necessary for jurisdiction. It invokes ICC Statute Article 12(3), which provides that where 'the acceptance of a State which is not a Party' to the Statute is required for the ICC to have jurisdiction over a crime, that state may accept the exercise of jurisdiction by the Court by lodging a declaration with the ICC Registrar. The purported acceptance of jurisdiction is not limited to acts committed during the December 2008–January 2009 conflict, but extends retroactively to 1 July 2002, the date of entry into force of the ICC Statute and the earliest date regarding which the Court may exercise jurisdiction. The prevalent view is that a declaration under Article 12(3) only provides jurisdiction but does not constitute a referral,[38] and must therefore be followed either by a referral by a state party or by the Prosecutor's initiation of an investigation *proprio motu*. The ICC Prosecutor responded to the Palestinian declaration by announcing that he 'will carefully examine all relevant issues related to the jurisdiction of the Court, including whether the declaration by the Palestinian National Authority accepting the exercise of jurisdiction by the ICC meets statutory requirements;

---

[36] *Supra* n. 32, para 1.

[37] Neither Jordan nor Egypt, both of which had previous territorial links to the Palestinian territories, can be considered the territorial states. Jordan, an ICC state party, purported to annex the West Bank in 1950. Only two states have ever recognized this annexation. In 1988 Jordan renounced its legal and administrative claims to the West Bank (Jordan: Statement concerning Disengagement from the West Bank and Palestinian Self-Determination, 31 July 1998, 28 International Legal Materials (ILM) (1988) 1637). Reliance on a territorial nexus to Jordan is therefore weak because it is based on a disputed claim that has voluntarily been terminated twenty-one years ago. It may also be contrary to the peremptory obligation to respect the right of the Palestinians to self-determination within (at least) the West Bank and Gaza Strip (*East Timor Case (Portugal v Indonesia)*, International Court of Justice, 30 June 1995, ICJ Reports (1995) 90, at 120, § 29; ILC Draft Articles on State Responsibility for Internationally Wrongful Acts, UN Doc. A/56/19 (2001), 113, commentary to Article 40, § 5). Finally, the Jordan territorial link does not cover the Gaza Strip. The latter had been from 1948 until 1967 under Egyptian military rule. Egypt (not an ICC state party) held the Gaza Strip under occupation from 1948 to 1967, never claiming sovereignty over it. In an era of post-conflict State-building occupation, the notion that an occupying power as representing the interests of the population, including through delegation of jurisdiction to the ICC, is not unthinkable. But a leap of logic would be required to regard Egypt as the relevant occupying power rather than Israel, which is either the current occupant or the most recent occupant.

[38] Williams and Schabas 2008, p. 569 marginal 15; Stahn et al. 2005, p. 423. For a critique of this view see Freeland 2006, p. 224.

whether the alleged crimes fall within the category of crimes defined in the Statute, and whether there are national proceedings in relation to those crimes'.[39]

Against this background, the potential significance of the Palestinian declaration under Article 12(3) becomes apparent. Yet since Article 12(3) speaks of a declaration by a *state* not party to the ICC Statute, prima facie, the declaration is inadmissible. The following analysis considers three aspects of this question.

13.3 Admission of the Palestinian Declaration as that of a Full-Fledged State

Under a straightforward, literal interpretation of Article 12(3), for the Palestinian declaration to be admitted under Article 12(3) it must be regarded as having been issued by a state. In 1988 the PLO issued a proclamation from Algiers declaring the independence of the state of Palestine. According to the Palestinian Ministry of Foreign Affairs, 94 states have subsequently recognized the statehood of Palestine,[40] although as argued below, this was not recognition of an established Palestinian statehood Palestine is a member state of the Organisation of the Islamic Conference[41] and the Non-Aligned Movement.[42] It participates in the Arab League on the same footing as member states, although its admission followed a special procedure to allow it to participate in the League's work 'until that country enjoys actual independence', since '[h]er existence and her independence among the nations can, therefore, no more be questioned *de jure* than the independence of any of the other Arab States'.[43]

The 1988 proclamation of independence had a profound political impact, but its legal significance should not be overstated. First, the proclamation appears to have been largely a symbolic gesture, as implied by the call 'upon the members of the Arab nation for their assistance in achieving its *de facto*

---

[39] ICC Office of the Prosecutor Press Release 2009. The ICC Prosecutor has announced that if he finds that he can investigate the Gaza situation on the basis of a territorial nexus, he will examine the conduct of both sides, interview with Luis Moreno-Ocampo, *supra* n. 8. This statement is in line with Rule 44(2) ICC RPE, which is intended to prevent an interpretation of Article 12(3) ICCSt. which allows a one-sided declaration aimed at the adversary while sheltering the declaring state. Williams and Schabas 2008, at 559. In the circumstances, the problem does not seem to arise as the declaration is drafted in a general manner. For doubt as to the effectiveness of rule 44(2) see J. Goldsmith 2003, pp. 92 ft 11.

[40] http://www.pna.gov.ps/Government/gov/recognition_of_the_State_of_Palestine.asp (broken link).

[41] Palestine has been a member of the OIC since the establishment of the organization in 1969, http://www.oic-oci.org/member_states.asp.

[42] http://www.nam.gov.za/background/members.htm.

[43] Pact of the League of Arab States, Annex on Palestine (emphasis added).

emergence'.[44] More importantly, a proclamation of independence, even with limited recognition subsequently, does not suffice to create a state. While statehood is no longer exclusively a factual matter, it is still dependent primarily on fulfilment of factual requisites, namely effective governmental control over a population in a specified territory. Yet until 1994 at the earliest, the Palestinians did not fulfil the factual requisites of statehood, as they had no control over the territory they claimed.[45] Without even a minimum foundation of control, recognition of Palestinian statehood was or would have been premature and legally incorrect.[46]

Although there are precedents of recognition of statehood being extended on the basis of the right to self-determination before effective control was exercised by the aspirant government over the entire territory it claimed, in the other instances such early recognition either envisaged the attainment of effective control within the foreseeable future (Congo in 1960), or was extended when effective control was already being exercised over at least part of the territory claimed (Guinea-Bissau in 1973,[47] Bosnia and Herzegovina in 1992[48]). An exceptional case is that of Namibia, where the United Nations Council for Namibia (UNCN)[49] was appointed to govern Namibia despite the fact that the territory was wholly controlled by South Africa, and there was no expectation of a change of control in the then-foreseeable future. UNCN acceded to various treaties and joined certain international organizations on behalf of Namibia,[50] and issued Decree No. 1, prohibiting cooperation with South Africa in exploitation of Namibian natural resources.[51] Yet even UNCN, whose controversial status has never been judicially determined, did not assume any functions premised on a fiction of effective control. In fact, Decree No. 1 was passed in order to minimise the consequences of South Africa's acknowledged exclusive effective control over Namibia. In short, the notion of statehood-based exclusively on entitlement without realization of the factual criteria has not been accepted in international practice.[52]

In accordance with this principle, the majority of states responding to the Palestinian proclamation qualified their so-called recognition, referring to Palestinian independence as a legitimate aspiration rather than an existing reality.[53]

---

[44] Letter dated 18 November 1988 from the Permanent Representative of Jordan to the United Nations addressed to the Secretary-General, UN Doc A/43/827-S/20278, 18 November 1988, § 16.
[45] Dajani 1997, pp. 48–49.
[46] Lowe 2007, p. 164.
[47] MacQueen 2006.
[48] Raič 2002, pp. 414–415.
[49] GA Res. 2248(S–V), 19 May 1967, GA Res. 2372(XXII), 12 June 1968.
[50] Namibia was not admitted to the UN until South Africa withdrew from its territory in 1990.
[51] Decree No. 1 (1974), UN Doc. A/9624/Add.1.
[52] Crawford 2006, pp. 447–448.
[53] Dajani 1997, p. 60.

Contrary to popular contentions,[54] the UN has not recognized the state of Palestine as a state. Following the Algiers proclamation the General Assembly Resolution merely 'acknowledges the proclamation of the State of Palestine by the Palestine National Council on 15 November 1988', and substitutes the designation 'Palestine' for the designation 'Palestine Liberation Organisation'. It expressly stipulates that this change was 'without prejudice to the observer status and functions of the Palestine Liberation Organization within the United Nations system'.[55] The UN Secretariat's book of Permanent Missions to the United Nations lists 'Palestine' as an 'entity having received a standing invitation to participate as observer' in the work of the General Assembly.[56] While the PLO, in its designation as Palestine, enjoys a status that is higher than that of other non-state observers to the UN,[57] it remains the representative of a non-state entity.

Since the first transfer of autonomous government power to the Palestinians in 1994 they may have acquired sufficient control to substantiate a claim of effective control.[58] Here the normative aspect of statehood comes into play: statehood is a claim of right and not only of fact.[59] Even if the PNA has in fact acquired extensive control over the population in the territory, effective control and recog-nition cannot consolidate the statehood of an entity which does not claim such status.[60]

---

[54] Quigley 2009 and Boyle 1990, p. 302.

[55] GA Res. 43/177, 15 December 1988, paras 1, 3.

[56] Permanent Missions to the United Nations No. 295, April 2006, last updated with ST/SG/SER.A/295/Add.5, 3 October 2006. For a detailed description of Palestine's status in the UN see Dajani 1997, pp. 53–56.

[57] The PLO's observer status, granted in GA Res. 3237(XXIX), 22 November 1974, was upgraded in GA Res. 43/160A, 9 December 1988, paras 1, 2. The same privilege was only ever granted to SWAPO, in the same resolution. Palestine's rights were expanded in GA Res. 52/250, 7 July 1998. Palestine is invited under Rule 37 of the Security Council provisional Rules of Procedure and permitted to participate in Security Council debates with the same rights of participation as those conferred upon a UN member state which is not a member of the Security Council. Shaw 2008, p. 246. In the proceedings on the *Legal Consequences of the Construction of a Wall in the Occupied Palestinian Territory*, the Court, taking into account Palestinian's special status and that it was co-sponsor of the draft resolution requesting the advisory opinion, permitted Palestine to submit to the Court a written statement on the question within the time limit fixed for member states. It also permitted it to participate in the oral hearings. *Legal Consequences of the Construction of a Wall in the Occupied Palestinian Territory*, Order of 19 December 2003, [2003] ICJ Reports (2003) 428, at 429. The OIC and the Arab League—clearly non-state entities—were later given the same permission, ICJ Press Releases Press Release 2004/1 (14 January 2004) and 2004/2 (22 January 2004) respectively.

[58] But see Dajani 1997, pp. 82–89, who rejects this proposition in so far as concerns the situation prevailing in 1997.

[59] Crawford 2006, p. 211.

[60] O'Connell 1956, p. 415; Restatement (Third) of the Foreign Relations Law of the United State, Section 201. Cf. Crawford 2006, p. 211 and Lowe 2007, p. 165, who see the absence of an unequivocal claim of statehood as the only bar to recognition of Taiwan as an independent state. Roth criticizes this approach both in principle and on factual grounds, indicating certain equivocal statements and practice on the part of the Taiwanese leadership. Roth 2009.

Yet neither the PLO nor the PNA[61] claims that a state of Palestine already exists. Instead, they continue to *demand* the establishment of a sovereign and independent state.[62] The agreements that the PLO has signed with Israel[63] and the rhetoric of the PNA all indicate that independence is regarded as a goal rather than a status already achieved.[64] This is more than a political stance; the Palestinians argued before the ICJ that as a matter of law, a state of Palestine does not yet exist, expressly stating that 'Israel and Palestine are not two States Members of the United Nations', that '[t]he people of Palestine have an unfulfilled right to self-determination',[65] and that the court is 'not asked to determine the boundaries of a *future* Palestinian State'.[66] That the Palestinians demand to exercise the right to self-determination is undeniable—but the demand itself toward an addressee apparently capable of enabling that exercise indicates that the Palestinians themselves are at least ambivalent as to whether they exercise the requisite territorial control, and at any rate do not yet wish to be regarded as independent. Ironically, pronouncing that a Palestinian state exists despite the absence of a Palestinian claim to this effect may even amount to a

---

[61] The term 'PNA' is not mentioned in any of the Israeli–PLO agreements. It is the term used by the Palestinians to indicate the collective of institutions which, as acknowledged by the Palestinians, were established in the framework of the agreements. Website of the Permanent Observer Mission of Palestine to the UN, available online at http://www.un.int/palestine/thepaintro.shtml. The relationship between the PNA and the PLO is a question which exceeds the scope of this article.

[62] E.g. Palestine Liberation Organization, Negotiations Affairs Division, 2009 Negotiations Primer, at 12, available online at http://www.nad-plo.org/news-updates/magazine.pdf ('The PLO's primary goals in engaging in direct negotiations with Israel are... fulfilment of the Palestinian right to self-determination through the establishment of an independent and sovereign Palestinian state in the West Bank and Gaza Strip with East Jerusalem as its capital...'); A/63/PV.57, 24 November 2008, at 9, 11 ('Moreover, the Palestinian people and their leadership remain convinced that... the international community will ultimately fulfil its responsibilities by upholding international law and the Charter of the United Nations so as to achieve a peaceful settlement that will give our people the freedom for which they have waited so long and allow them to take their rightful place among the nations of the world...' and 'We also call for their help in realizing the Palestinian people's inalienable rights, including their right to self-determination and to their independent State of Palestine...').

[63] Declaration of Principles on Interim Self-Government Arrangements, 13 September 1993, 32 ILM 1525 (1993); Agreement on the Gaza Strip and the Jericho Area, 4 May 1994, 33 ILM (1994) 622. Israeli–Palestinian Interim Agreement on the West Bank and the Gaza Strip, signed 28 September 1995, 36 ILM 557 (1997) (hereinafter 'Interim Agreement'); Dajani 1997, p. 90 notes that the Declaration of Principles and Interim Agreement elicited the support of the Palestinian population only insofar as they were transitional.

[64] Quigley 2009 argues that Israel's demand in 1993 that the PLO recognize it implied Israel's recognition of a Palestinian state, since only states may recognize others. Since an existing state does not require recognition from a new state (although Quigley does suggest that post-1988 Palestine is identical to post-Ottoman Palestine, essentially claiming that the mandate territory constituted a state and disregarding events since 1948), Israel's demand had purely political objectives. It therefore makes no sense to attach any implicit legal significance to it. Israel's demand in 1993 was political in the same sense that today it demands that Hamas recognize its right to exist, without in any way implying that it is the government of a state in the Gaza Strip.

[65] Both statements in *Legal Consequences of the Construction of a Wall (Advisory Opinion)*, Oral Proceedings CR 2004/1, 23 February 2004, para 22.

[66] Ibid., para 33 (emphasis added).

violation of that Palestinian right to self-determination, because it would impose a political status on the Palestinian people which they have not yet asserted.

One might argue that the deposit of the declaration is itself an implicit claim of statehood. However, claims to statehood cannot be inferred from statements or actions short of explicit declaration.[67] Moreover, the ambiguity of the Palestinian declaration precludes the conclusion that it implicitly asserts statehood. In particular, the term 'PNA' invokes a governmental apparatus which was established by an Israeli–PLO agreement, premised on the non-sovereignty of the PNA. Since this term acknowledges a non-state status, its use is irreconcilable with a claim to statehood.[68]

The absence of a Palestinian assertion of statehood as an already-established status is not surprising. Such an assertion at the present time might be interpreted internationally as a Palestinian acquiescence in the existing state of things *vis-à-vis* Israel, in particular as regards the breadth of territory claimed by Palestine and the right of Palestinian refugees to return to homes within Israeli territory. It may also weaken the Palestinian demands by making them a matter of post-conflict resolution between formally-equal sovereign states rather than a condition for the resolution of the conflict on the basis of a legal entitlement to the exercise of self-determination. In the immediate term, an assertion of Palestinian statehood would also undermine the claim that Israel remains an occupying power in the Gaza Strip even after its disengagement.[69] Statehood and occupation are of course not mutually exclusive, in the sense that occupation of a state does not extinguish sovereignty despite the loss of effective control by the ousted sovereign.[70] But since the West Bank and Gaza Strip were not under independent sovereignty prior to their occupation by Israel, the claim can be, at best, that independence *emerged*

---

[67] Crawford 2006, p. 211. As demonstrated by the Taiwanese applications for participation in the work of the UN, even a request to perform a function reserved for states can be drafted sufficiently vaguely so as to avoid a claim of statehood or even that the request itself implies a claim of statehood. Mainland Affairs Council, Position Paper Regarding the Referendum on Joining the United Nations Under the Name of Taiwan, 7 September 2007 available online at http://www.mac.gov.tw/english/english/un/02e.pdf.

[68] The mention of the PNA alongside the 'Government of Palestine' may have been intended to enable the ICC Prosecutor to interpret the declaration as claiming statehood without being explicit about it. Alternatively, it may serve to emphasize that the PNA is the only legitimate executive arm of government for all of Palestine, and avoids any charge of illegitimacy that may be claimed if it is attributed in any way to Hamas.

[69] Report of the Special Rapporteur on the Situation of Human Rights in the Palestinian Territories Occupied Since 1967 UN Doc A/62/275, 17 August 2007, paras 9–10; Goldstone Report, para 279; A/HRC/RES/S-12/1 C preambular para 5 (21 October 2009); Bashi and Mann 2007; Report of the Arab League Committee, para 15; Scobbie 2004–2005. The official Palestinian position is unclear. PNA President Mahmoud Abbas referred in his speeches in the UN exclusively to 'siege' and 'blockade' over the Gaza Strip, UN Doc A/63/PV.11, 26 September 2008, at 38, S/PV.6061, 6 January 2009, at 5. But see also statements of Palestine referring to the Gaza Strip as occupied territory and to Israel as the occupying power in it in the context of the 2008–2009 offensive, e.g. S/PV.6201, 14 October 2009, at 6, S/PV.6216 (Resumption 1), 11 November 2009, at 20, 21.

[70] Crawford 2006, p. 73.

from under occupation, namely that non-sovereign territory has become independent *in the face of* occupation.[71] Since both occupation and independence assume effective control by opposing parties, independence implies that the occupant has been repelled, even if only partially.[72] Thus, in order to claim independence the Palestinians must indicate some area over which they already exercise effective control to the exclusion of Israel. The likely candidate territory is the Gaza Strip, where Israel has far less control than in the West Bank. While the question whether the territory is occupied depends on objective facts rather than on the parties' claims, the Palestinians cannot argue that the territory is both independent and occupied at the same time. Indeed, some of the Palestinian arguments on why the declaration should be accepted as that of a state reportedly rely on Israel's denial of its status as an occupying power.[73] As noted earlier, a claim of statehood would also raise the question of the relationship between the West Bank and Gaza Strip, given that each area is controlled by a different authority.[74]

In conclusion, the main obstacle to regarding the Palestinian declaration of 21 January as a valid acceptance of ICC jurisdiction under ICC Statute Article 12(3) is the absence of a Palestinian claim of statehood, which is a prerequisite for the exercise of the power under Article 12(3).

13.4 Admission Under Article 12(3) of a Declaration by a Quasi-State

Absence of a full-fledged state does not mean that the PNA has no international status.[75] For many years it has been referred to as *in statu nascendi*,[76] although the rights that attach to this status remain controversial. Against this background, the question arises whether the term 'state' in Article 12(3) should be interpreted more widely, so as to encompass quasi-state, namely territorial entities in which a governmental authority exercises control but which fall short of full-fledged statehood. For this, it must be demonstrated that the mechanism currently available under the ICC Statute, which reflects a carefully-achieved balance of interests, is inadequate.

From a normative perspective, the question is whether there is indeed justification to single out ICC jurisdiction as a matter which justifies expansion of the term 'state'. The entire framework of international criminal law and of the ICC mechanism within it is premised on the interest in ending impunity being an international, communal

---

[71] For present purposes it does not matter whether this took place in 1988 or through the implementation of the Interim Agreement, *supra* n. 63.
[72] E.g. the case of Guinea-Bissau, MacQueen 2006.
[73] Philp and Hider 2009.
[74] *Supra* n. 18.
[75] Crawford 2006, p. 219. This is by no means a novel notion: R. Roxburgh 1921, pp. 128, 133.
[76] E.g. Giegrich 1999, p. 195.

one, rather than that of individual states.[77] Arguably, this communal interest should not be constrained, in the context of the ICC Statute and more specifically of Article 12(3), by limitations of the traditional meaning of statehood, which makes status subject to political, subjective stances on assertion and recognition of statehood. This is particularly true with respect to the Palestinian territories, which are unique in being neither claimed by any existing state nor recognized as belonging to one. Admission of an Article 12(3) declaration by the PNA would therefore not encroach on any state's sovereignty, and not jeopardise the basic tenets of the ICC mechanism.

It could be suggested by advocates of admitting the Palestinian declaration that expanding the interpretation of the term 'state' in Article 12(3) is the only way to prevent a vacuum in criminal accountability insofar as the territory of the PNA is concerned. But the Palestinian territories are not in a legal jurisdictional vacuum. The ICC provides a mechanism that can cover them, namely a referral by the Security Council. Had the situation been one where jurisdiction could not be granted to the Court under any existing mechanism, one might have argued that new, innovative measures are called for. But there is no such situation, in the Palestinian territories or elsewhere, since the Security Council's power to grant jurisdiction is territorially and personally unlimited. If the Council refuses to exercise its power, it is acting on the political prerogative which the ICC Statute drafters knew it to possess and have agreed to tolerate.[78] Moreover, the inapplicability of a statute of limitations to international crimes is designed to overcome political impediments to accountability in the short term. This leaves open, at least in theory, the possibility of a future referral by the Security Council. The fact that at a specific moment in time, with respect to a specific situation, none of the three bases for jurisdiction (territory, nationality or a Security Council referral) has successfully led to acquisition of jurisdiction does not mean that the rules on jurisdiction are inadequate, but merely demonstrates that the ICC is not omnipotent.

One might argue that given the political constraints on Security Council action, reliance on its powers to reject innovative alternatives is overly formalistic. But the ICC is nothing but a formal mechanism: it is aimed to fill an institutional gap so as to enable implementation of international legal norms that for the most part already exist under substantive international law. Its structure may have no other advantage over alternative ones other than having been agreed upon. Since it is this agreement that gives it legitimacy and enables it to fill the prior institutional gap, there is merit in a strict adherence to it.

To conclude, while it is not unthinkable that the meaning of the term 'state' for the purposes of the Article 12(3) be different than its meaning for the purposes of customary international law,[79] the ICC Statute should be interpreted in good faith in accordance with the ordinary meaning to be given to its terms in their context

---

[77] Preambular para 5 ICCSt.

[78] Bergsmo and Pejic 2008, pp. 595, 598.

[79] Kirgis 1990, p. 220. Kirgis' example, however, is unsatisfactory: he notes divergence of meaning between domestic US law and international law.

and in the light of its object and purpose.[80] The object and purpose of the ICC Statute do not call for any digression from this ordinary meaning. It is worth noting that the status of the Palestinian territories as non-sovereign territory under control of a non-state entity never arose during the drafting of the Statute. Arguably, given the prominence of the territories in other aspects of the negotiations, the absence of territorial nexus can hardly be considered an oversight; rather, it seems that the drafters were content to accept the consequences of the limits of that nexus.

Doctrinally, to apply Article 12(3) to non-state entities it is essential that the entity in question be capable of fulfilling the functions envisaged by the Statute, in this case the delegation of criminal jurisdiction.[81] The requisites for this are possession of jurisdiction over criminal matters (a requisite also underlying the principle of complementarity) and delegation of that jurisdiction to the ICC.[82] The requirement of possessing jurisdiction should be read strictly, as it is not merely a procedural requirement but a substantive one. Without such jurisdiction, an entity might be unable later to cooperate with the ICC under Part 9 of the Statute. For example, one might ask how 'Palestine' would surrender a person arrested in Gaza to the court without the consent and cooperation of Israel which controls the borders of the Palestinian territories. Different opinions have been proffered as to whether the PNA enjoys criminal jurisdiction in the territories under its control, generally and specifically over Israelis. These usually focus on the regulation of the matter under the Israeli–PLO Interim Agreement[83] and on the validity of this Agreement.[84] However, whether the Palestinians have criminal jurisdiction over the Gaza Strip for the purpose of delegating that jurisdiction to the ICC is not a

---

[80] Vienna Convention on the Law of Treaties (adopted May 23, 1969, entered into force 27 January 1980) 1155 UNTS 331 (hereafter 'VCLT') Article 31.

[81] Kirgis 1990, p. 221.

[82] Kaul 2002, pp. 607–610, Akande 2003.

[83] Interim Agreement, *supra* n. 63, Annex IV (Protocol Concerning Legal Affairs) Article 1.

[84] Under the Interim Agreement criminal jurisdiction over Israelis remains with Israel. The Interim Agreement was foreseen to exist for a period of five years, until an agreement were concluded on the permanent status of the West Bank and Gaza Strip. Such agreement was never concluded, leaving the continued validity of the Interim Agreement since 1999 a matter of controversy. Israel maintains that the Interim Agreement continues to govern relations between Israel and the PNA and therefore the PNA does not have jurisdiction over Israelis. Another view is that the Interim Agreement has expired by its own terms in 1999. This may imply either that Israel's occupation has then ended, provided that the PNA continued to exercise at least the powers and responsibilities allocated to it under the Agreement (Benvenisti 1993, p. 551), or that any powers and responsibilities delegated to the PNA reverted in 1999 to Israel: Singer 1994. This leads to a further question, whether at any time since 1999 Israel has ceased to be the occupying power in the Gaza Strip. According to a third view, even if the Interim Agreement continues to exist, Israel's disengagement from the Gaza Strip and its designation of the Gaza Strip as 'hostile entity' imply the lapse of its claim, under the Interim Agreement, to exclusive criminal jurisdiction over Israelis for acts committed within the Gaza Strip. By default, such jurisdiction now lies with the PNA, which may also delegate it to the ICC (Report of the Arab League Committee, *supra* n. 14, paras 601, 604). Since the Report emphasizes that Palestine is a state unconstrained by the Israeli–PLO agreements (para 602), it is not clear why the question of its criminal jurisdiction was treated separately.

matter which is governed by the Interim Agreement, which is a bilateral instrument, and its effect as against third parties is limited. Rather, the criminal jurisdiction of the PNA for the purpose of its delegation to a third party depends on the PNA's status in the territory, which in turn hinges on the objective status of the territory itself that is applicable *erga omnes*. The same holds true with regard to the delegation of jurisdiction. If Israel continues to be held an occupying power, it must be regarded as continuing to have criminal jurisdiction.[85] If, on the other hand, the occupation of the Gaza Strip has ended by virtue of Israel's disengagement from it in 2005, jurisdiction may well have passed into the hands of the Palestinians.[86] Yet since June 2007, it is also not the PNA who is in effective control over the Gaza Strip but Hamas. In short, the governmental authority lodging the declaration is not the one exercising criminal jurisdiction.

Reliance on the absence of sovereignty raises additional difficulties: in the West Bank Israel does not claim sovereignty (except over East Jerusalem) but still claims and exercises criminal jurisdiction over Israelis. If the justification for expanding the term 'state' is the absence of competing claims, does it apply to a situation where there are (apparently, in light of the Palestinian declaration) competing claims of jurisdiction over criminal matters, but not of sovereignty? A similar question arises with respect to situations of competing claims of both sovereignty and jurisdiction which do not parallel each other. With respect to Kosovo, for example, Serbia claims sovereignty but concedes that it lacks territorial jurisdiction, which is in the hands of the UN through UNMIK.[87]

Re-interpreting the term in Article 12(3) may have a destabilizing effect on the interpretation of other provisions of the Statute applicable to states not parties, such as those concerning the principle of complementarity and challenges to jurisdiction.[88] There may also be a spill over effect to other terms used in the Statute. For example, it might be suggested that the term 'national' in Article 12(2)(b) includes permanent residents.[89] In the context of the laws of armed

---

[85] In this respect the view taken by the Arab League Committee is inconsistent, as it claims both that Israel continues to be the occupying power, and that the Palestinians have criminal jurisdiction.

[86] See sources *supra* n. 69; for a contrary view see Shany 2005, p. 369.

[87] Accordance with International Law of the Unilateral Declaration of Independence by the Provisional Institutions of Self-Government of Kosovo (*Request for advisory opinion submitted by the General Assembly of the United Nations*), International Court of Justice, CR 2009/24, statement by Serbia § 44.

[88] Articles 17, 19 ICCSt. It would probably be unrealistic to suggest that a question on the meaning of 'state' would arise with respect to the right to accede to the Statute ICC (Article 125(3) ICCSt.).

[89] Indeed, there is a trend of increasing assimilation of permanent residents to nationals in terms of the State's human rights obligations toward them. At present this trend seems limited to domestic implementation. States still distinguish between nationals and permanent residents for purposes of international protection. One may argue in favor of such an assimilation along lines similar to those put forward with respect to states: permanent residence is a sufficiently-stable relationship with a State so as to justify the imposition on the individual of certain obligations without putting the individual at an unexpected detriment. Moreover, since non-accession of a

conflict the ICTY has already expanded the term, ruling that the term 'national' in Article 4 of the Fourth Geneva Convention should be interpreted as relating to ethnicity rather than to formal bonds and purely legal relations.[90] However, that interpretation was given 'within the context of the changing nature of the armed conflicts since 1945, and in particular of the development of conflicts based on ethnic or religious grounds'.[91] If the immense legal and political changes that the world has undergone during over half a century permit a purposive interpretation of the Fourth Geneva Convention, the same cannot yet be said for the ICC Statute, adopted only a decade ago. Moreover, unlike the Fourth Geneva Convention, the ICC Statute is a criminal code which is subject to principles of interpretation applicable within penal law. These call for a strict reading of terms, less amenable to policy considerations. An exceptionally liberal interpretation of the Statute that departs from this interpretative standard also risks deterring other states still not party to the ICC Statute from joining, making a novel interpretation of the term 'state' untimely as well as legally dubious.[92]

13.5 Institutional Considerations

Given the indeterminate status of the PNA, any pursuit of its declaration by the ICC Prosecutor would constitute at least an implicit recognition of the international status of that entity, whether as a full-fledged state or as a state for the purpose of Article 12(3). In addition to the substantive objections to admission of the Palestinian declaration under Article 12(3), there are also institutional considerations militating against such admission.

Although recognition of statehood is commonly regarded as a declaratory act and not as a constitutive requisite for statehood,[93] in borderline cases such as that of the PNA it may constitute a step toward consolidating an indeterminate general legal status.[94] For this reason, a determination by a legal body such as the ICC (the Prosecutor and, at a later stage, the Court) that a state of Palestine exists (either generally or for the purpose of Article 12(3)) would carry significant weight.

(Footnote 89 continued)
state to the ICC Statute does not confer immunity on its nationals, such residence-based jurisdiction does not encroach on the state of nationality's sovereignty. On the other hand, interpreting the Statute in this way would be clearly contrary not only to the ordinary meaning of the term but also to the intention of the drafters (VCLT, *supra* n. 80, Article 32).

[90] Appeals Judgment, *Tadić* (IT-94-1), Appeals Chamber, 15 July 1999 para 168; Appeals Judgment, *Delalić* et al. (IT-96-21), Appeals Chamber, 20 February 2001, paras 56–73.

[91] Ibid.

[92] A matter which is no longer an issue with respect to the Geneva Conventions, in which membership is universal.

[93] Opinion no 1 § 1 of the Badinter Arbitration Committee, appendix to Pellet 1992; Grant 1999, Chap. 2.

[94] E.g. the cases of Croatia and Bosnia and Herzegovina, which were recognized while not yet in effective control over most of their territories. Rich 1993, p. 49; Türk 1993, p. 69.

Recognition of an entity as a state is a political act, traditionally within the prerogative of states. There is nothing in international law precluding an international actor such as the ICC Prosecutor or Court from extending recognition to a state, but such an act would constitute exceptional practice. An example occurred in July 2008 when the International Monetary Fund (IMF) received an application for admission to membership from the Republic of Kosovo. The IMF's management determined that Kosovo has seceded from Serbia to form a new independent state.[95] Subsequently, the IMF board of governors, where all IMF members (states) are represented, voted to invite Kosovo to join the IMF.[96] This case is unique in that it was the IMF bureaucracy—and not member states, individually or collectively—which took a position on Kosovo's status, leaving to member states only the subsequent decision on admission. Ordinarily, however, international organizations and their organs do not recognize states. Their treatment of entities as states is only a consequence of the prior recognition by member states of those entities' statehood. Even individual states are reluctant to extend recognition of statehood when acting in their capacity as institutional organs. For example, when the PLO attempted to accede to the Geneva Conventions and their Additional Protocols on behalf of the state of Palestine, the depositary Swiss Federal Council informed the states parties that it was not in a position to decide whether the letter constituted an instrument of accession, 'due to the uncertainty within the international community as to the existence or nonexistence of a State of Palestine'.[97] It is noteworthy that the depositary in that event, the Swiss Federal Council, was

---

[95] Statement on Membership of the Republic of Kosovo in the IMF, Press Release no 08/179, 15 July 2008, available online at http://www.imf.org/external/np/sec/pr/2008/pr08179.htm, Reuters, 'IMF recognizes Kosovo, begins to weigh membership', 15 July 2008, available online at http://www.reuters.com/article/newsMaps/idUSN1528175520080715. A request for an advisory opinion on the status of Kosovo is currently before the International Court of Justice, GA Res. 63/3, 8 October 2008.

[96] Transcript of a Press Briefing by David Hawley, Senior Advisor, External Relations Department, International Monetary Fund, Washington, DC, 7 May 2009, available online at http://www.imf.org/external/np/tr/2009/tr050709.htm.

[97] Embassy of Switzerland, Note of Information sent to States parties to the Convention and Protocol, 13 September 1989. On 21 June 1989 the Swiss Federal Department of Foreign Affairs received a letter from the Permanent Observer of Palestine to the UN informing the Swiss Federal Council "that the Executive Committee of the Palestine Liberation Organization, entrusted with the functions of the Government of the State of Palestine by decision of the Palestine National Council, decided, on 4 May 1989, to adhere to the Four Geneva Conventions of 12 August 1949 and the two Protocols additional thereto."

The 1989 attempt at accession is also indicative of the lack of international recognition of a Palestinian state at the time. This is particularly blatant when contrasted with the practice in the case of accession by the Provisional Government of Algeria in the 1960s, see Talmon 1998, pp. 123–125.

undoubtedly capable and authorized to take a decision as to its own recognition of the applicant.[98]

Thus, if the Prosecutor, or later the Pre-Trial Chamber, determines that the Palestinian declaration fulfils the requirements of Article 12(3), they would be assuming an almost unprecedented competence, which incurs onto the political sphere which is the traditional prerogative of states. The converse would not be unprecedented: a determination that the PNA has not established itself universally as a state would not exceed the ordinary powers of a non-state actor.[99]

Importantly, unlike organs of other international institutional organs such as treaty depositaries, the ICC Prosecutor cannot refer the decision elsewhere. He alone is mandated with the power and responsibility to make the preliminary decision whether to initiate an investigation.[100] Although the Court will always make the final determination as to jurisdiction, even the Prosecutor's initial decision to investigate could be deemed an act of recognition, thereby politicizing the functions of his office. The Pre-Trial Chamber's will have automatic power of judicial review over the Prosecutor's decision if the Prosecutor decides that the ICC has and should exercise jurisdiction. If the Prosecutor decides in the negative, the review by the Pre-Trial Chamber is dependent on a request by the state making the referral.[101] The question would then arise directly before the Pre-Trial chamber whether 'Palestine' constitutes a state capable of making a request for a review by the Pre-Trial chamber.

With respect to recognition of statehood, the Assembly of States Parties (ASP) is a possible forum from which the ICC Prosecutor may wish to take guidance. In view of the administrative and managerial character of the specific tasks allocated to the ASP,[102] it is doubtful whether the drafters intended for this power to extend to political questions that have a direct effect on the jurisdiction of the Court, which has been so rigorously negotiated;[103] yet the ASP may engage in any function necessary or essential for the Court and consistent with the Statute.[104] The ASP also has authority to settle disputes between states parties as to interpretation

---

[98] According to a news report, the Palestinians are pursuing membership in the ICC through accession to the Statute. Ma'an News Agency 2009. The report suggests that these efforts are made vis a vis the ICC Prosecutor. However, accession is done by deposition of the relevant instrument with the UN Secretary General, who is the ICC Statute's depositary.

[99] See *Loizidou v Turkey (Merits)*, ECtHR, 18 December 1996, Reports of Judgments & Decisions 1996-VI 2216, para 23.

[100] Articles 15(1), 15(4) and 42 ICCSt.

[101] Article 53(3) ICCSt.

[102] Article 112(2) ICCSt. A notable exception is the transitional power in Article 112(2)(a) ICCSt. to adopt recommendations of the Preparatory Commission, among which are proposals on aggression.

[103] Arsanjani 2001, p. 50.

[104] Bos 2002, p. 308.

or application of the Statute.[105] This may include interpretation of the term 'state' for the purpose of Article 12(3) or even recognition of statehood. How the ASP's decisions on such matters will affect the powers of the Prosecutor's and pre-Trial Chamber remains unclear.

It may be argued that the consequences of admission of the Palestinian declaration as that of a state should not be overstated. The direct effect of such admission would be only to grant jurisdiction to the ICC with respect to a specific situation. It would not determine status for general purposes, nor even for other provisions of the ICC Statute. Interestingly, the concept of Palestinian statehood for a limited purpose was recently embraced by no other than Israeli courts: the Jerusalem District Court has in two cases enquired whether the PNA was recognized (by Israel) as a state for the purpose of state immunity, notwithstanding the clear absence of recognition by Israel of Palestinian statehood in general. Although the cases resulted in different conclusions both on the facts and on the courts' power to decide the issue of statehood (in one case, later confirmed by the Supreme Court, the Court ruled that it must defer to the determination by the executive whether the PA is a state;[106] in the other, later reversed by the Supreme Court, it found that the PNA qualified as a state for the purpose of state immunity[107]), of interest is the willingness of the judges to engage in examination of the notion of 'statehood for the purpose of state immunity'.[108]

However, the notion that a determination by the ICC Prosecutor or Court can be isolated and restricted to the specific context of ICC territorial jurisdiction is largely illusory.[109] Statehood is for the most part a package deal. Where non-states have been granted rights and obligations which ordinarily attach only to states, this was usually not through *ad hoc* recognition or limited statehood but through express extensions of those rights and obligations to non-state entities[110] or through the gradual expansion of international law to non-state entities.[111] There are few and remote precedents of an entity being regarded under international law

---

[105] Article 119(2) ICCSt.

[106] *Norwich* et al. *v. the Palestinian Authority and Yasser Arafat*, Jerusalem District Court Civil Case 2538/00, Judgment, 30 March 2003, para 11, confirmed in *Palestinian Authority v. Dayan* et al., Request of Right to Appeal 4060/03, High Court of Justice, Judgment, 17 July 2007, para 4.

[107] *Elon Moreh College v State of Israel*, Jerusalem District Court, Judgment on Civil Case Request 1008/06, 24 June 2006, para 12, reversed by *Elon Moreh College v State of Israel* et al., Judgment on Civil Appeal 5093/06, 6 August 2008.

[108] The possibility of granting immunity to a 'political entity that is not a state' has since been made available in the 2008 Foreign States Immunity Law, Article 20.

[109] Brubacher 2004, p. 83.

[110] E.g. Article 305(1) of United Nations Convention on the Law of the Sea, Article XII(1) of the Agreement establishing the WTO.

[111] Decision on the Defence Motion for Interlocutory Appeal on Jurisdiction, *Tadić* (IT-94-1), Trial Chamber, 2 October 1995, para 70 ('an armed conflict exists whenever there is a resort to armed force between States or protracted armed violence between governmental authorities and organized armed groups or between such groups within a State').

as a state for some purposes but not for others.[112] Thus, it would be *naïve* to expect that recognition by a legal organ of an international organization which brings together over half of the worlds' states would have no repercussions outside the immediate context in which such recognition was made.

A further argument against the Prosecutor undertaking a decision as to the status of the PNA is that this would create a precedent for use of the ICC as a forum from which non-state actors could publicly assert political independence from their parent states. It would be an invitation to aspirant entities of diverse types, such as Kosovo, Taiwan, South Ossetia, Abkhazia, Transdnistria, Somaliland and the Turkish Republic of Northern Cyprus, which have not managed to garner sufficient international support for a status they claim, to try to advance their goals though the ICC. Regardless of the prospects of success, the existence of a new, international forum which recognizes states by reference to non-classical considerations (i.e. criminal jurisdiction and capacity to delegate it to the ICC) invites its abuse. For example, if crimes were committed in Kosovo by nationals of states not parties to the ICC Statute, could the Prosecutor or Court rely on a Kosovar declaration under Article 12(3)?[113] Similarly, Polisario, the internationally-recognized representative of the Saharawi people[114] and governing body of the aspirant Saharawi Arab Democratic Republic (SADR),[115] might lodge a declaration with respect to crimes perpetrated by nationals of non-party states in the territory it controls. Another case in point may be that of Taiwan. China is not a party to the Statute (nor is Taiwan, of course). Could the ICC Prosecutor assert ICC jurisdiction over these crimes on the basis of a Taiwanese declaration under Article 12(3)? In all these cases the answer would depend on whether the Prosecutor and later Court consider the aspirant entities to be states.

Arguably, the ICC can be prevented from becoming the fighting ground over status claims if Article 12(3) is interpreted as allowing declarations to be lodged only by non-state entities governing territories over which there is no competing territorial claim. This would bar potential declarations by Kosovo or Taiwan, for example. Should the SADR lodge a declaration, the situation would be more complicated: although Morocco claims Western Sahara as sovereign territory, the ICC Prosecutor would be hard put to take account of this claim, because this may be interpreted as contrary to the findings of the ICJ in its advisory opinion, and

---

[112] Examples of exceptions were 'A' Mandated territories which were treated as states for the purpose of nationality but were much less certainly states for other purposes. The Free City of Danzig was a state for the purposes of Article 71(2) of the Rules of the Permanent Court, but whether it was a state for all purposes has been doubted, Crawford 2006, p. 31.

[113] The same scenario would be applicable to South Ossetia and Georgia. Even if jurisdiction is based on the territorial nexus with a member state, Serbia, the problem may arise with respect to the decision on admissibility, when the question might arise whether '[t]he case is being investigated or prosecuted by a State which has jurisdiction over it' (Article 17(1)(a) ICCSt.).

[114] GA Res. 34/37, 21 November 1979, para 7.

[115] The SADR claims to be a state. For present purposes, it is taken as an example of a non-state entity in effective control over territory and population.

consequently to the international commitment to the right to self-determination of the Saharawi people.[116] But more generally, as argued above, there is no situation which cannot be addressed by the Security Council and which requires additional means of granting the ICC jurisdiction. Under these circumstances, any permissive criterion would be suspect of reflecting a political desire to apply special criteria to the PNA rather than an objective policy.[117]

In theory, barring Article 12(3) declarations by quasi-states would not prevent issues relating to jurisdiction over disputed territory from arising in the ICC. For example, if an established state (e.g Serbia, China or Morocco) asserts that its consent to jurisdiction provides a territorial nexus to territory under the aspirant entity's administration, the ICC Prosecutor would still have to take a decision on territorial jurisdiction in light the status of the competing claim by the aspirant state. However, in practice such a scenario is not likely to occur. For example, it seems unlikely that China or Morocco would lodge a declaration under Article 12(3) with respect to acts committed in Taiwan or Western Sahara, respectively. This is because non-party states are unlikely to put their territorial status under international legal scrutiny in order to secure accountability of a handful of individuals. If they do lodge such declarations, this will more likely be in furtherance of their own territorial claims. Such use of the Court should not be encouraged any more than declarations by non-state entities. The likelihood that territorial disputes arise through referral by other states is even less likely, simply because states that are not directly involved have so far demonstrated reluctance to engage in referrals, even in territorially-undisputed situations.[118] Finally, a referral by the Security Council obviates the question of territorial nexus. Thus, the potential admission of an Article 12(3) declaration by quasi-states holds the greatest risk for politicizing the ICC in this context.

In conclusion, a decision by the ICC Prosecutor granting status under the ICC Statute to a non-state entity would be an irregular event in the practice of international organizations, the merit of which would be seriously outweighed by negative costs to both the ICC as an institution and to the discipline of international criminal justice more broadly.

---

[116] The ICJ found that at the time of Spanish colonization, neither Morocco's nor Mauritania's ties to Western Sahara were of territorial sovereignty. *Western Sahara* Advisory Opinion, International Court of Justice, Reports (1975) 12, para 162; GA Res. 63/15, 18 December 2008, preamble.

[117] If the existence or absence of a territorial claim is taken as a criterion for admitting a declaration under Article 12(3) ICCSt., Israel could theoretically block admission of a Palestinian declaration simply by making a claim to the territory of the Gaza Strip and the West Bank. This is nonetheless an improbable scenario, given Israel's policy in the last 42 years and its formal disengagement from the Gaza Strip in 2005.

[118] Jordan is reported to have been contemplating submitting a referral of the Gaza situation to the ICC Prosecutor, Malkawi 2009.

13.6 Conclusion

The present article considers the possibility of ICC jurisdiction over crimes allegedly committed in the Gaza Strip based on a territorial nexus asserted by the PNA. From the analysis it appears that creating such a nexus has no legal ground and is politically precarious. There is no doubt that the PNA is very close to becoming a state; in fact, the only bar may be the absence of declaration of statehood on its part, as the requisites of effectiveness may have already been fulfilled at least to a minimal level that together with the right to self-determination can create a presumption of statehood. However, at present the Palestinian leadership does not assert statehood. Thus, it would be premature for the ICC Prosecutor or Court to recognize the Palestinian declaration as that of a state, even for the limited purpose of Article 12(3). Interpreting Article 12(3) more widely to include entities effectively governing non-sovereign territory also seems unwarranted, as such interpretation flies in the face of the ICC Statute's wording and the intention of its drafters. Any involvement in issues of recognition risks exposing the Prosecutor and the Court to accusations of politicization and subjectivity.

The ICC's goal of ending impunity is channeled through a state-centered mechanism. Despite being an international tribunal, the ICC is more restricted than states since it does not have original, universal jurisdiction. Undoubtedly, the ICC mechanism sometimes leaves justice hostage to political forces. In particular, involvement in unresolved political conflicts may entangle it in questions exceeding its mandate as envisaged by its founders.[119] Extricating the ICC from these entanglements should be done through careful, measured tugs at the limits of the delicate balance achieved between accountability and sovereignty. These limitations of the ICC have been candidly admitted by the former president of the ASP and head of the Jordanian delegation to the ASP, His Royal Highness Prince Zeid Raad Al-Hussein, who noted, with regard to the Palestinian declaration, that '…whenever we believe injustice has intruded upon our lives in the Middle East we scream for the International Criminal Court and yet many of us never seem to read the Statute properly, and in particular Articles 12 and 13. If more of us read those articles, we would be more understanding of how the Court—rightly or wrongly—was designed to operate'.[120]

The ICC is not and should not be regarded as a panacea. Its limits should not be disregarded, as this would jeopardise the Court's legitimacy and effectiveness. Yet accountability should be ensured. It should be sought in other international institutions. Some address themselves directly to individual criminal responsibility, such as the principle of universal jurisdiction. Others address themselves to the

---

[119] The seminal commentary on the ICC Statute does not even mention the issue of non-state entities in the context of Article 12, Williams and Schabas 2008.

[120] ASP Newsletter Special Edition #1 (May 2009), at 8, available online at http://www.icc-cpi.int/NR/rdonlyres/027351FC-E588-4440-AD59-340593F49A3A/0/NewsletterASP1ENGweb_version.pdf.

responsibility of states, such as the principles of state responsibility for wrongful acts under international law. Others still may exist that concern the international responsibility of states, e,g, under international human rights law, to ensure individual accountability under its domestic law. These and other institutions may be preferable to resorting to the ICC, for example where they cast a wider net of accountability, or provide an effective incentive for policy changes that further peace, security and wellbeing.[121] They should not be discarded in favor of the ICC, simply because it is the newest addition to the architecture of international adjudication.

References

ACRI and Organizations (2009) Investigate Israel's Attacks on Civilians, 20 January 2009. http://www.acri.org.il/eng/story.aspx?id=602

Akande D (2003) The Jurisdiction of the International Criminal Court over Nationals of Non-Parties: Legal basis and limits. J Int Crim Justice 1:618

Al Jazeera Television (2009) Interview with Luis Moreno-Ocampo, ICC Prosecutor, on the *Riz Khan* show. http://english.aljazeera.net/programmes/rizkhan/2009/03/200931984142361861.html

Amnesty International (2009a) Evidence of misuse of US-weapons reinforces need for arms embargo, 23 February 2009. http://www.amnesty.org/en/for-media/press-releases/israeloccupied-palestinian-territories-evidence-misuse-us-weapons-reinfo

Amnesty International (2009b) Growing calls for investigations and accountability in Gaza conflict, 14 January 2009. http://www.amnesty.org/en/news-and-updates/news/growing-calls-investigations-and-accountability-gaza-conflict-20090114

Amnesty International (2009c) Sixteen international lawyers in a letter entitled 'Find the truth about the Gaza war', 16 March 2009. http://www.amnesty.org.uk/news_details.asp?NewsID=18109

Arsanjani M (2001) The Rome Statute of the International Criminal Court; Exceptions to the Jurisdiction. In: Politi M, Nesi G (eds) The Rome Statute of the International Criminal Court a challenge to impunity. Ashgate, Aldershot

ASIL Independent Task Force (2009) 'U.S. Policy Toward the International Criminal Court: Furthering Positive Engagement', March 2009.http://www.asil.org/files/ASIL-08-DiscPaper2.pdf

Bashi S, Mann K (2007) Disengaged Occupiers: The Legal Status of Gaza, Gisha: The Legal Center for Freedom of Movement

Becker T (1998) Self-determination in perspective: Palestinian claims to statehood and the relativity of the right to self-determination. Israel Law Rev 32:301

Benvenisti E (1993) The Israeli-Palestinian Declaration of Principles: a framework for future settlement. Eur J Int Law 4:542

Bergsmo M, Pejic J (2008) Article 16: Deferral of Investigation or Prosecution. In: Triffterer O (ed) Commentary on the Rome Statute of the International Criminal Court, 2nd edn. Nomos Verlagsgesellschaft, Baden-Baden

Blum Y, Gerson A, Quigley J, Nakhleh I (1988) Self determination: The Case of Palestine. Proc Am Soc Int Law 82:335

Blumenthal D (2002) The Politics of Justice: Why Israel signed the International Criminal Court Statute and what the signature means. Georgia J Int Comp Law 30:593

---

[121] Preamble, ICCSt.

Bos A (2002) From the International Law Commission to the Rome Conference (1994–1998). In: Cassese A, Gaeta P, Jones J (eds) The Rome Statute of the International Criminal Court; a Commentary, vol I. Oxford University Press, Oxford, p 308

Boyle A (1990) Creation of the State of Palestine. Eur J Int Law 1:301

Brubacher M (2004) Prosecutorial Discretion within the International Criminal Court. J Int Crim Justice 2:71

Crawford J (1990) The Creation of the State of Palestine: Too much too soon? Eur J Int Law 1:307

Crawford J (2006) The Creation of States in International Law, 2nd edn. Oxford University Press, Oxford

Dajani O (1997) Stalled between seasons: The International Legal Status of Palestine During the Interim Period. Denver J Int Law Policy 26:27

de Waart P (1994–1995) Self-rule under Oslo II: The State of Palestine Within a Stone's Throw. Palestinian Yearbook of International Law, vol 8

Declaration recognizing the Jurisdiction of the International Criminal Court. http://www.icc-cpi.int/NR/rdonlyres/4F8D4963-EBE6-489D-9F6F-1B3C1057EA0A/279764/20090122PalestinianDeclaration.pdf

Deen-Racsmany Z (2001) The Nationality of the Offender and the Jurisdiction of the International Criminal Court. Am J Int Law 95:606

Ephron D (2009) ICC Prosecutor may Charge Israeli with War Crimes, Newsweek, 21 September 2009 http://blog.newsweek.com/blogs/wealthofnations/archive/2009/09/21/icc-prosecutor-may-charge-israeli-with-war-crimes.aspx

Freeland S (2006) How open should the door be—Declarations by Non-States Parties under Article 12(3) of the Rome Statute of the International Criminal Court. Nord J Int Law 75:211

Giegrich T (1999) The Palestinian Autonomy and International Human Rights Law: Perspectives on an Ongoing Process of Nation-Building. In: Shapira A, Tabory M (eds) New Political Entities in Public and Private International Law. Kluwer Law International, The Hague, p 183

Goldsmith J (2003) The Self-Defeating International Criminal Court. Univ Chic Law Rev 70:89

Goldstone R (2003) Israel and the International Criminal Court. Hamishpat (in Hebrew), vol 15

Grant T (1999) The Recognition of States: Law and Practice in Debate and Evolution. Praeger, Westport

Human Rights Watch (2009a) Israel/Gaza: International Investigation Essential, 27 January 2009. http://www.hrw.org/en/news/2009/01/27/israelgaza-international-investigation-essential

Human Rights Watch (2009b) Q&A: Accountability for Violations of International Humanitarian Law in Gaza, 6 February 2009. http://www.hrw.org/en/news/2009/02/06/qa-accountability-violations-international-humanitarian-law-gaza

ICC Office of the Prosecutor Press Release (2009) Visit of the Minister of Justice of the Palestinian National Authority, Mr. Ali Khashan, to the ICC (22 January 2009), 6 February 2009. http://www.icc-cpi.int/menus/icc/structure%20of%20the%20court/office%20of%20the%20prosecutor/reports%20and%20statements/statement/visist%20of%20the%20minister%20of%20justice%20of%20palestine?lan=en-GB

Independent Fact Finding Committee on Gaza (2009) No Safe Place. http://www.arableagueonline.org/las/picture_gallery/reportfullFINAL.pdf

Israel Ministry of Foreign Affairs (2009) The operation in Gaza—Factual and Legal Aspects, July 2009. http://www.mfa.gov.il/MFA/Terrorism-+Obstacle+to+Peace/Terrorism+and+Islamic+Fundamentalism-/Operation_in_Gaza-Factual_and_Legal_Aspects.htm

Israeli Ministry of Foreign Affairs (2008) http://www.mfa.gov.il/MFA/Terrorism-+Obstacle+to+Peace/Hamas+war+against+Israel/Israel_strikes_back_against_Hamas_terror_infrastructure_Gaza_27-Dec-2008.htm#statements

JTA (2009) 'White House: Official "misspoke" on Goldstone Report', 23 September 2009. http://jta.org/news/article/2009/09/23/1008097/us-pledges-to-quashgoldstone

Kaul H (2002) Preconditions to the Exercise of Jurisdiction. In: Cassese A, Gaeta P, Jones J (eds) The Rome Statute of the International Criminal Court; A Commentary, vol I. Oxford University Press, Oxford, p 583

Kirgis F Jr (1990) Admission of "Palestine" as a Member of a Specialized Agency and with Holding the Payment of Assessments in Response. Am J Int Law 84:218

Kohen M (2006) Introduction. In: Kohen M (ed) Secession, International Law Perspectives. Cambridge University Press, Cambridge, p 1

Lowe V (2007) International Law. Oxford University Press, Oxford

Ma'an News Agency (2009) Justice minister: PA prepping for ICC membership, 17 October 2009. http://www.maannews.net/eng/ViewDetails.aspx?ID=232793

Macintyre D, Sengupta K (2009) Civilian casualties: Human rights groups accuse Israelis of war crimes The Independent on Sunday. http://www.independent.co.uk/news/world/middle-east/civilian-casualties-human-rights-groups-accuse-israelis-of-war-crimes-1366727.html

MacQueen N (2006) Belated Decolonization and UN Politics against the Backdrop of the Cold War: Portugal, Britain, and Guinea-Bissau's Proclamation of Independence, 1973–1974. J Cold War Stud 8:29

Mainland Affairs Council (2007) Position paper regarding the referendum on joining the United Nations under the name of Taiwan. http://www.mac.gov.tw/english/english/un/02e.pdf

Malkawi K (2009) House approves action to Sue Israel Jordan Times. http://www.jordantimes.com/?news=13888

McKinney K (1994–1995) The Legal Effect of the Israeli-PLO Declaration of Principles Toward Statehood for Palestine. Seattle Univ law Review 18:93

O'Connell D (1956) The Status of Formosa and the Chinese recognition problem. Am J Int Law 50:405

Pellet A (1992) The Opinions of the Badinter Arbitration Committee: a second breath for the self-determination of peoples. Eur J Int Law 3:178

Philp C, Hider J (2009) Prosecutor looks at ways to put Israeli officers on trial for Gaza "war crimes", Times Online. http://www.timesonline.co.uk/tol/news/world/middle_east/article5636069.ece

Prince J (1989) The International Legal Implications of the November 1988 Palestinian Declaration of Statehood. Stanf J Int Law 25:681

Quigley J (2002) Competing Claims to the Territory of Historical Palestine. Guild Pract 59:76

Quigley J (2009) The Palestine Declaration to the International Criminal Court: The Statehood Issue. Rutgers Law Record 35:1–10 [also in this Volume, Chapter 10]

Raič D (2002) Statehood and the Law of self-determination. Kluwer Law International, The Hague

Rich R (1993) Recognition of States: The Collapse of Yugoslavia and the Soviet Union Eur J Int Law 4:36

Roth B (2009) The Entity that dare not speak its name: unrecognized Taiwan as a Right-Bearer in the International Legal Order. East Asia Law Rev 4:91

Roxburgh R, Oppenheim L (1921) International Law: a Treatise, vol I, 3rd edn. Longman Green, London

Schabas W (2007) Introduction to the International Criminal Court, 3rd edn. Cambridge University Press, Cambridge

Scobbie I (2004–2005) An intimate disengagement: Israel's withdrawal from Gaza, the Law of Occupation and of Self-Determination. Yearb Islam Middle East Law 11:3

Shany Y (2003) The Entry into force of the Rome Statute: What are its implications for the State of Israel. Hamishpat [in Hebrew] 15:28

Shany Y (2005) Faraway, so close: the Legal Status of Gaza after Israel's Disengagement. Yearb Int Humanit Law 8:369

Shaw M (2008) International Law, 6th edn. Cambridge University Press, Cambridge

Silverberg S (1989–1999) Diplomatic Recognition of States in Statu Nascendi: The Case of Palestine. Tulsa J Comp Int Law 6:21

Simons M (2009) Palestinians Press for War Crimes Inquiry on Gaza New York Time, 10 February 2009. http://www.nytimes.com/2009/02/11/world/middleeast/11hague.html?_r=1

Singer J (1994) The Declaration of Principles on Interim Self-Government Arrangements: Some Legal Aspects. Justice 1:4

Stahn C, El Zeidy M, Olásolo H (2005) The International Criminal Court's Ad Hoc Jurisdiction Revisited. Am J Int Law 99:421
Talmon S (1998) Recognition of Governments in International Law. Clarendon Press, Oxford
The Sunday Times (2009) Statement by 31 International Lawyers, Israel's Bombardment of Gaza is not Self-defence—It's a War Crime, 19 January 2009. http://www.timesonline.co.uk/tol/comment/letters/article5488380.ece
Türk D (1993) Recognition of States: A Comment. Eur J Int Law 4:66
Williams S, Schabas W (2008) Article 12. In: Triffterer O (ed) Commentary on the Rome Status of the International Criminal Court, 2nd edn. C.H. Beck, Hart, Nomos, München, p 547
Zaum D (2008) The Security Council, the General Assembly and War: The Uniting for Peace Resolution. In: Lowe V, Roberts A, Welsh J (eds) The United Nations Security Council and War. Oxford University Press, Oxford, p 188

Chapter 14
In Defence of Functional Interpretation of Article 12(3): A Response to Yaël Ronen

Yuval Shany

Contents

14.1 The Statute's Delegation-Based Jurisdiction 498
14.2 The Interpretative Question: Can a Non-State Entity be Regarded as a State? 500
14.3 The Rome Statute's Object and Purpose is Well-Served by a Functional
      Approach to Delegation 503
14.4 The Plot Thickens: The Oslo Accords 506
14.5 Conclusions 510
References 511

In a recent article, Dr. Yaël Ronen considers the declaration on 21 January 2009 by the Palestinian National Authority (PNA) that recognized the Court's jurisdiction over the events which took place in Gaza in 2008–2009.[1] Dr. Ronen surveys a host of considerations militating both in favour of and against the assumption of jurisdiction by the ICC Prosecutor. The question was raised by the declaration

---

Hersch Lauterpacht Chair. Public International Law, Law Faculty, Hebrew University. This paper was first published in Journal of International Criminal Justice (2010) 8(2), 329–343. The editors wish to thank OUP for kindly granting permission to republish the article [For author's acknowledgments, please refer to J Int Crim. Justice (2010)].

---

[1] *Supra* Chap. 13; previously published as Ronen 2010. For a copy of the declaration, see Palestinian National Authority—Minister of Justice, Declaration Recognizing the Jurisdiction of the International Criminal Court, 21 January 2009, http://www.icc-cpi.int/NR/rdonlyres/74EEE201-0FED-4481-95D4-C8071087102C/279777/20090122PalestinianDeclaration2.pdf. Although the declaration was issued in response to the events in Gaza 2008–2009, its language is much broader and covers all "acts committed in the territory of Palestine since 1 July 2002".

Y. Shany (✉)
Hebrew University, Jerusalem, Israel

C. Meloni and G. Tognoni (eds.), *Is There a Court for Gaza?*,
DOI: 10.1007/978-90-6704-820-0_14,
© T.M.C. ASSER PRESS, The Hague, The Netherlands, and the authors/editors 2012

Dr. Ronen ultimately concludes that the Prosecutor would be well advised to refrain from assuming jurisdiction:

> There is no doubt that the PNA is very close to becoming a state... However, at present the Palestinian leadership does not assert statehood. Thus, it would be premature for the ICC Prosecutor or Court to recognise the Palestinian declaration as that of a state, even for the limited purpose of Article 12(3). Interpreting Article 12(3) more widely to include entities effectively governing non-sovereign territory also seems unwarranted, as such interpretation flies in the face of the ICC Statute's wording and the intention of its drafters. Any involvement in issues of recognition risks exposing the Prosecutor and the Court to accusations of politicisation and subjectivity. The ICC's goal of ending impunity is channelled through a state-centred mechanism.[2]

This short response to Dr. Ronen's well-argued article will revolve around four points. First, Article 12 of the ICC Statute is premised on a delegation-based theory, according to which states may delegate to the ICC criminal jurisdiction over certain crimes that would have otherwise fallen within the jurisdiction of their national courts (i.e. crimes committed within their territory or by their nationals). Second, the object and purpose of the ICC Statute would not be well-served if state-like entities such as the PNA that exercise criminal jurisdiction over certain areas pursuant to broadly-accepted international agreements would be barred from delegating jurisdiction to the ICC under Article 12(3) of the ICC Statute. Next, although I agree with Dr. Ronen that the ICC should not be utilized to advance controversial sovereignty claims, the PNA declaration—as far as it pertains to the situation in Gaza—does not impinge on the sovereignty of any other state. This is because the alleged crimes which took place in Gaza occurred in an area over which no other state (including Israel) is claiming sovereignty or control. Finally, although the PNA should in principle have been allowed to refer the Gaza situation to the ICC, its actual ability to delegate jurisdiction is limited by the Oslo Accords concluded between Israel and the PLO. These agreements deprive the PNA of jurisdiction over crimes committed by Israeli nationals in the Palestinian territories and seriously limit the PNAs ability to conduct foreign relations. Hence, my conclusions at the end of the day are not radically different than those reached by Dr. Ronen: whereas she rejects ICC jurisdiction over the alleged crimes committed by Israel in Gaza by virtue of the PNAs lack of statehood, I reach a generally similar conclusion by way of reliance on the Oslo Accords.

14.1 The Statute's Delegation-Based Jurisdiction

Two main theories can be invoked to legitimize the operation of international criminal courts—universalism and delegation. According to the universalistic view, international criminal courts embody the collective interest of the international community in effectively ending the impunity of *hostis humani generis*.[3] The same

---

[2] See *supra*, Chap. 13, at Section 13.6 (Ronen 2010, pp. 26–27).

[3] See Kaul 2002, pp. 583, 587.

set of justifications that underlie the exercise of universal jurisdiction by the domestic courts of all states justifies then, *a fortiori*, the exercise of jurisdiction by institutionally superior, and less prone to abuse, international criminal courts.[4] According to this line of thinking, the exercise of international jurisdiction cannot depend on the consent of any specific state implicated or affected by the alleged criminal conduct (including, the "territorial" state or the state of nationality of the alleged perpetrator). In fact, the reluctance of the directly implicated or affected states to hold criminal perpetrators accountable may have been the very source of the problem of impunity, which led to the creation of international criminal courts in the first place.[5]

An alternative understanding of the role of international criminal courts is offered by a delegation-based theory, according to which international criminal courts exercise jurisdiction that was delegated to them by those states that had an internationally recognized right to prosecute the crimes in question before their own domestic courts. Under this approach, a two-stage analysis is required in order to justify the exercise of jurisdiction by an international criminal court. First, one has to substantiate the right of a specific state to exercise jurisdiction. Second, one has to identify a valid act of delegation of jurisdiction from that state to the competent international criminal court.[6] A delegation-based approach would therefore condition the exercise of jurisdiction by international criminal courts upon the consent of specific states.

Note that the two methods of justification are not mutually exclusive and are, at times, almost indistinguishable.[7] Indeed, the Rome Statute itself reflects both approaches: the Security Council referral option corresponds to the universalistic theory[8]; and Article 12 referrals, which are conditioned on membership in the Statute of, or *ad hoc* consent to ICC jurisdiction by, the "territorial" state or the state whose nationality the alleged perpetrator holds, are reflective of the delegation-based approach.[9] It is interesting to note in this regard that the Korean proposal discussed

---

[4] See e.g., Hawkins et al. 2006, p. 14 (international criminal court centralize expertise needed for prosecuting certain crimes).

[5] See e.g., Corell 2005, pp. 11, 16 ("we cannot allow the impunity to continue. The international community has to act in situations where States responsible for bringing perpetrators to justice are either unable or unwilling to do this. It is important to note that it is only in these situations that the ICC would have a role to play").

[6] For a comparable discussion see, Deen-Racsmany 2001, pp. 606, 610–611 (comparing between delegation to the ICC and extradition); Cameron 2004, pp. 65, 77 (comparing ICC delegation with the exercise of representative jurisdiction—instances in which a custodial state is trying individuals who cannot be extradited on behalf of the territorial state).

[7] For example, the International Military Tribunal in Nuremberg can be understood as embodying either the universalistic approach (an international court acting on behalf of the international community) or the delegation-based power approach (an international court acting with the authorization of the four occupying powers in Germany). Scharf 2001, pp. 67, 103–109.

[8] See e.g., Meissner 2005, p. 27 ("In the case of Security Council referrals, however, the Court's jurisdiction becomes truly universal").

[9] Cassese et al. 2002, pp. 1901–1902; Kaul 2002, p. 609; Meissner 2005, p. 46. But see Scheffer 2002, pp. 47, 65 ("The U.S. legal position was that customary international law does not yet entitle a state, whether as a Party or as a non-Party to the ICC Treaty, to delegate to a treaty-based

during the Rome Conference[10] and the German discussion paper circulated before the Conference[11] represented a stronger "hybrid" approach. While they linked state consent and the bestowal of jurisdiction upon the Court—i.e., insisted on some act of delegation—they both envisioned the custodial state (under the Korean proposal) or any member state (under the German paper) as delegating states by virtue of their right to exercise universal jurisdiction under a universalistic theory of jurisdiction.[12]

The question before us—whether the PNA can authorize the ICC to exercise jurisdiction under Article 12(3)—necessarily involves the delegation-based aspects of the Court's jurisdiction. If we have good reasons to regard the PNA, for the purposes of the Statute, as the equivalent of an internationally recognized "natural jurisdiction" state, as understood in the Statue (i.e., a "territorial" state or a state of nationality of the alleged perpetrators), then its letter to the ICC of 21 January 2009 could, in principle, be viewed as a proper act of delegation within the scheme of the Statute. Before addressing that question, some general observations about the meaning of the term "state" under the Statute may be appropriate.

14.2 The Interpretative Question: Can a Non-State Entity be Regarded as a State?

Dr. Ronen is correct in observing that the PNA, the autonomous entity created under the Oslo Accords (a series of agreements concluded between Israel and the PLO in the 1990s),[13] does not meet the definition of a state under international law.

(Footnote 9 continued)
International Criminal Court its own domestic authority to bring to justice individuals who commit crimes on its sovereign territory or otherwise under the principle of universal jurisdiction, without first obtaining the consent of that individual's state of nationality either through ratification of the Rome Treaty or by special consent, or without a referral of the situation by the Security Council").

[10] Proposal Submitted by the Republic of Korea, UN Doc. A/CONF.183/C.1/L.6 (17 June 1998). The idea that the custodial state may be one of the relevant authorizing states (but together with the territorial state) also appears in the ILC Draft Statute. Draft Statute for an International Criminal Court, 1994-II *Yearbook of the International Law Commission* 52, U.N. Doc. A/CN.4/SER.A/1994/Add.1 (Part 2).

[11] The Jurisdiction of the International Criminal Court: An Informal Discussion Paper Submitted By Germany, UN Doc. A/AC.249/1998/DP.2 (13 March 1998).

[12] Crawford 2003, pp. 109, 137 ["If a particular state party to … (one of) the international criminal conventions had both custody of and jurisdiction over the accused, that custodial state could transfer the accused to the ICC—and at the same time in effect transfer its jurisdiction over the accused"]; Kaul 2002, p. 591 ("all states may exercise universal criminal jurisdiction…. Contracting Parties of the Statute can confer through ratification this right on the new institution).

[13] The three main Oslo Accords are the 1993 DOP [The Declaration of Principles on Interim Self-Government Arrangements between Israel and the Palestine Liberation Organization, 13 September 1993, 32 I.L.M. (1993) 1525], the 1994 Cairo Agreement [Israel-PLO Agreement on the Gaza Strip and Jericho Area, 4 May 1994, 33 I.L.M. (1994) 622]; and the 1995 Interim Agreement [Israeli-Palestinian Interim Agreement on the West Bank and the Gaza Strip, 8 September 1995, Article XXXI(7) 37 I.L.M. (1997) 551 (hereinafter 'Interim Agreement')].

The PNA has never proclaimed statehood, or regarded itself as a belated incarnation of the PLOs 1988 Palestinian Declaration of Independence[14]; and statehood cannot be forced on a political entity that chooses (and has legally undertaken) not to claim it.[15] The PNA is thus not a state, but rather a set of quasi-statal institutions governing parts of the Palestinian occupied territories and operating with some degree of autonomy from Israel.[16] Moreover, the PLO—the broader Palestinian national liberation movement (which, unlike the PNA, speaks on behalf of all Palestinians, including the millions of refugees residing outside Palestine)—continues to represent the Palestinian People on the international level, and to conclude international agreements with states and IGOs; whereas the PNA (which is a separate legal entity from the PLO)[17] enjoys more limited legal powers in the field of foreign relations.[18]

Still, international practice has on numerous occasions treated quasi-state entities—political entities with strong state-like features—as if they were they were states *for certain purposes*. Hence, non-state actors such as Taiwan, Puerto Rico and PLO/Palestine, have been allowed to participate in the work of a fair number of international organizations,[19] and/or to sign a number of international treaties.[20] Arguably this practice may be suggestive of the plausibility, under certain circumstances, of a functional approach to statehood. As a general rule, one

---

[14] Palestinian Declaration of Independence, 15 Nov. 1988, http://middleeast.about.com/od/documents/a/me081115f.htm.

[15] The PLO and Israel have undertaken not to take unilateral steps that "will change the status of the West Bank and Gaza Strip pending the outcome of the permanent status negotiations." Interim Agreement, Article XXXI(7). But see Al Haq Position Paper 2009, para 13–15 (discussing Prof. Quigley and Dugard's views on Palestinian statehood).

[16] Davidson 1999, p. 178 (describing the PNA as 'the interim governmental body established to assume partial responsibility for administration in the self-rule areas as provided in the September 1993 Declaration of Principles'); Husseini 2003, p. 505. ('Under the Agreements, the PA functions as an interim, semi-autonomous self-government').

[17] In actuality, given the considerable, though not full overlap between the composition of the leadership of the PLO and PNA, confusion exists as to whether certain functions are performed by one organisational framework or the other. See Nabulsi 2006, pp. 233, 243.

[18] See below text accompanying notes 40–41.

[19] For example, the WHO accorded Puerto Rico associate membership and Palestine and Taiwan observer status; Taiwan, Puerto Rico and the PLO are members of the International Olympic Committee and the International Trade Union Confederation; the PLO is a member of the Arab League; Puerto Rico is an associate member of the World Tourism Organization and the PLO has observer status before that organization. See also, Lin 2004, pp. 133, 149–155 (discussing Taiwan's participation in a number of international organizations); Krasner 1999, pp. 15–16 (discussing the implications of the membership of pre-independence Philippines, India, Belarus and Ukraine in the UN); Desierto 2008, pp. 387, 399 (discussing the participation of British India in the work of the League of Nations); Mushkat 1992, pp. 105, 106–107 (discussing the participation of Hong Kong in the work of the WTO, WHO, IAEA and Interpol).

[20] For example, Taiwan has bilateral investment treaties with six countries (Thailand, Belize, Macedonia, the Marshall Islands and Swaziland) (http://www.unctadxi.org/templates/docsearch.aspx?id=779) and Palestine has established full diplomatic relations with almost 70 countries (http://en.wikipedia.org/wiki/List_of_diplomatic_missions_of_Palestine).

may posit that quasi-states tend to be regarded as functionally equivalent to states if and when the differences between them and "ordinary" states are deemed irrelevant for the purposes of the relevant institution or treaty.[21]

The two recent decisions by the ICJ to allow participation by representatives of Palestine and the Kosovo independent authorities in the advisory proceedings on the Wall and the Kosovo Declaration of Independence, respectively, may be of particular relevance to our discussion. In both cases, the Court did not deem the political entities seeking participation in the proceeding as states; instead, it embraced a functional reading of the Statute provision that regulates the participation of states and international organizations in advisory proceedings,[22] so as to encompass within it the category of quasi-states. In the case of Palestine, the Court justified its decision by reference to the special observer status of Palestine in the UN and its involvement in the diplomatic process that has led to the request for advisory opinion.[23] In the case of Kosovo, the Court justified the participation of "the authors of the unilateral declaration of independence" by the perceived utility of their involvement in the case.[24]

Note, that the aforementioned functional approach is most certainly not universally applicable, nor should it be universally applied. Formal statehood remains an absolute prerequisite for membership in some international organizations, such as the UN, and for participation in many treaties.[25] Furthermore, even for the

---

[21] See generally, Krasner 1999, p. 15, Worster 2009, pp. 115, 129, Cohan 2006, pp. 907, 927–929.

[22] Statute of the International Court of Justice (Annex to UN Charter), Article 66(2)("The Registrar shall also, by means of a special and direct communication, notify any state entitled to appear before the Court or international organization considered by the Court, or, should it not be sitting, by the President, as likely to be able to furnish information on the question, that the Court will be prepared to receive, within a time-limit to be fixed by the President, written statements, or to hear, at a public sitting to be held for the purpose, oral statements relating to the question"). See also ICJ Rules of Court, Rules 105, 108.

[23] *Legal Consequences of the Construction of a Wall in the Occupied Palestinian Territory*, 2003 ICJ 428 ("[The Court decides] further that, in light of General Assembly resolution A/RES/ES-10114 and the report of the Secretary-General transmitted to the Court with the request, and taking into account the fact that the General Assembly has granted Palestine a special status of observer and that the latter is co-sponsor of the draft resolution requesting the advisory opinion, Palestine may also submit to the Court a written statement on the question within the above time-limit").

[24] *Accordance With International Law of the Unilateral Declaration of Independence by the Provisional Institutions of Self-Government Of Kosovo*, decision of 17 Oct. 2008 ("[The Court decides] further that, taking account of the fact that the unilateral declaration of independence by the Provisional Institutions of Self-Government of Kosovo of 17 February 2008 is the subject of the question submitted to the Court for an advisory opinion, the authors of the above declaration are considered likely to be able to furnish information on the question; and *decides* therefore to invite them to make written contributions to the Court within the above time-limits").

[25] Cf. Swiss Federal Council, Note of Information sent to States parties to the Convention and Protocol, 13 September 1989, excerpt at www.icrc.org/IHL.NSF/WebSign?ReadForm&id=375&ps=P (justifying its decision not to register Palestine as a state party to the Geneva Conventions by reference to the uncertainty relating to the status of Palestine).

purposes of the Rome Statute itself, the term "state" may be understood differently in different contexts. It could be argued that quasi-states may confer jurisdiction on the Court under Article 12(3), yet not be allowed to ratify the Charter pursuant to Article 125. This is because the latter provision appears to embody different policy goals and assumes certain functions that quasi-states may not have (e.g., the ability to effectively participate in the diplomatic work of the Assembly of State Parties). In other words, a functional approach may offer quasi-state the opportunity to participate to some extent in the work of the ICC without necessarily conferring upon them the entire gamut of membership privileges associated with full-fledged statehood. The decision whether or not to embrace a functional approach should thus be made on a case-by-case basis, in light of the nature and function of the legal arrangement in question.

14.3 The Rome Statute's Object and Purpose is Well-Served by a Functional Approach to Delegation

The Rome Statute's main *raison d'être* is ending impunity through the exercise of complementary international jurisdiction by an international criminal court.[26] The state delegation mechanism, while representing an important limit on the ICC's jurisdiction (but also an important source for legitimizing the Court's operation), should ultimately be regarded as a means to an end—not an end in itself. Consequently, a tension arises when one interprets in good faith and "in accordance with the ordinary meaning to be given to the terms of the treaty in their context and in the light of its object and purpose",[27] the language of Article 12(3). Whereas the ordinary meaning of the text—*If the acceptance of a State which is not a Party to this Statute is required under paragraph 2, that State may, by declaration lodged with the Registrar, accept the exercise of jurisdiction by the Court with respect to the crime in question*—militates in favor of a traditional understanding of the term "state", the object and purpose of the ICC Statute pull in the opposite direction—i.e., in favor of a broader reading that would contribute to the fulfillment of the Court's mandate to end impunity. The relative strength of these competing "interpretative vectors" may dictate the outcome of the interpretative process.

---

[26] Rome Statute of the International Criminal Court, 17 July 1998, preamble, 2187 U.N.T.S. 90 (hereinafter 'Rome Statute') ("Determined to put an end to impunity for the perpetrators of these crimes and thus to contribute to the prevention of such crimes… Determined to these ends and for the sake of present and future generations, to establish an independent permanent International Criminal Court in relationship with the United Nations system, with jurisdiction over the most serious crimes of concern to the international community as a whole").

[27] Vienna Convention on the Law of Treaties, 23 May 1969, Article 31(1), 1155 U.N.T.S. 331, Article 31(1).

We have already seen that the treatment of quasi-states as states under international practice is quite "ordinary". Hence, the deviation from the "ordinary meaning" of the text, which the inclusion under Article 12(3) of the PNA would entail, appears to be relatively minor.

The PNA is a quasi-state with strong state-like features, and, as Dr. Ronen concedes, all that separates the PNA from statehood may be a formal declaration of statehood on its part.[28] At the same time, preventing the PNA from delegating criminal jurisdiction would compromise the Court's "ending impunity" mission, and prevent it from exercising jurisdiction over a situation where serious crimes may have occurred. Moreover, restricting the contents of Article 12(3) to state-referrals only might create a number of "legal black holes"[29]—land territories over which no state exercises sovereignty. Specifically, no other state would be able to delegate jurisdiction to the ICJ over the situation in Gaza (Israel itself does not claim sovereignty nor effective control over Gaza). Such limits on the Court's delegation-based source of authority would mean that only the Security Council would be in a position to refer to the ICC the Gaza situation (pursuant to the Court's universalistic mandate). While the availability of the Security Council reduces, to some degree, the policy problems created by the formal reading of Article 12(3), it does not fully solve them. First, it could be noted that the Council only has legal authority to refer cases to the Court when acting pursuant to Chap. 7 of the Charter, whereas the ICC's delegated jurisdiction is potentially broader in scope and does not similarly depend on a preliminary finding that international peace and security have been threatened or breached (or that an act of aggression has occurred). Second, and more importantly, the Council's inclination to actually exercise its referral powers has been so far and is expected to continue to be very limited.[30] As a result, the actual reach of the ICC depends on the combined effect of its delegation-based and universalistic jurisdictional powers. Cutting one "branch" of jurisdiction would leave the ICC with truncated capabilities.

---

[28] *Supra* Chap. 13, Section 13.6.

[29] See e.g., *R v Al Jedda*, [2007] QB 621, at para 108 (per Brooke LJ) ("He is not being arbitrarily detained in a legal black hole, unlike the detainees in Guantanamo Bay in the autumn of 2002"). On the need to reduce "legal vacuums" in human rights litigation see *Loizidou v Turkey*, 1996-VI Eur. Ct. H.R. at para 49 ("Since the Republic of Cyprus obviously cannot be held accountable for the part of the island occupied by Turkey, it must be Turkey which is so accountable. Otherwise the northern part of Cyprus would constitute a vacuum as regards responsibility for violations of human rights, the acceptance of which would be contrary to the principle of effectiveness which underlies the Convention"). But see *Bankovic v Belgium*, 2001–XII Eur. Ct. H.R. at para 80 ("the desirability of avoiding a gap or vacuum in human rights' protection has so far been relied on by the Court in favour of establishing jurisdiction only when the territory in question was one that, but for the specific circumstances, would normally be covered by the Convention").

[30] See e.g., Simpson 2004, 47, 59.

At the end of the day, a functional reading of Article 12(3) appears preferable given the weakness of the policy arguments that support the formal approach. Specifically, I am of the view that Dr. Ronen's main policy argument in favor of the formal approach—i.e., the fear of opening the floodgates of the ICC to a hodgepodge of secessionist entities, which will embroil the ICC in high-profile international disputes[31]—can be addressed through means other than a restrictive interpretation of Article 12(3). For example, if Abkhazia, Kosovo or Saharawi were to approach the Court and ask for the exercise of jurisdiction over crimes allegedly committed by Georgians, Serbs or Moroccans, a decision by the Prosecutor on the basis of "interests of justice" to refrain from acting upon such referrals because they involve competing sovereignty claims,[32] which the ICC cannot or should not decide upon, appears to me to be plausible.[33] In any event, I do not see how the Prosecutor can reject such claims on the basis of a narrow reading of the text of Article 12(3) without taking a position on the validity of the relevant statehood claims. In the same vein, the formal approach is unhelpful in addressing other "sensitive" sovereignty-related referrals requiring a determination of the location of international boundaries[34]

In any event, the PNA case is different. The fact that the Palestinian territories (with the exception of East Jerusalem) are not the object of a competing sovereignty claim by Israel or any other state, means that by accepting the PNA declaration and relying on it to investigate the situation in Gaza, the Prosecutor or the Court would not be required to decide a contentious sovereignty claim. Nor would the adoption of the functional approach entail "international recognition" of the PNAs nascent statehood. Quite the opposite would be true. By embracing a functional approach, the Prosecutor would be able to assume jurisdiction over the case without taking a position on the precise statehood status or borders of the authorizing entity. As a result, the functional approach can actually help the Prosecutor separate the criminal law aspects of the referred case from its more contested sovereignty or diplomatic attributes.

In short, problems relating to the uncertain or sensitive status of certain states or quasi-states would be better dealt with through the exercise of case-by-case discretion by the Prosecutor as to whether to initiate proceedings (which the Court would monitor pursuant to Articles 19 and 53 of the ICC Statute), and not through a narrow reading of Article 12(3), which will create as many problems as it seeks to avoid. The PNA has obvious quasi-statal features. For our purpose, the most

---

[31] *Supra* Chap. 13, Section 13.6.

[32] See Rome Statute, Article 53(1)(c).

[33] Note that the three mentioned polities have all claimed formal statehood, and thus represent a stronger *prima facie* case than the PNA that does not regard itself as a state.

[34] For a discussion, see Schabas 2007, pp. 76–77 (noting that more than 50% of international boundaries may be contested and that such disputes may cause difficulties for the ICC).

important are: (1) a legal system invested with territorial jurisdiction over criminal offences pursuant to broadly-accepted international agreements (see *infra*, Sect. 14.4); and, (2) an international legal personality that permits it to interact, to some extent, at the international level with states and IGOs (see also Sect. 14.4). As such, the PNAs declaration could, in theory, be viewed under the proposed functional approach as falling under the scope of Article 12(3).

If this is correct and quasi-states can delegate criminal jurisdiction to the ICC, it would seem as if the loss of effective control by the PNA over the Gaza Strip in 2006 is immaterial to ascertaining its competence to delegate. Since the PNA remains the only internationally recognized government of the Palestinian territories, it is the sole political entity that can exercise jurisdiction over these territories in accordance with international law (leaving aside the question of the ability of Israel—the occupying power—to exercise parallel jurisdiction).[35] The right to delegate jurisdiction is reflective of an internationally recognized legal authority, and not of the material ability of actually exercising jurisdiction over either the territory in question or over certain individuals within or outside that territory. In fact, situations in which states (or quasi-states) lose control over parts of their territory represent a paradigmatic case for self-referral of situations to the ICC in so far as they reflect the "inability of the State genuinely to prosecute".[36]

14.4 The Plot Thickens: The Oslo Accords

The right of the PNA to delegate cases to the ICC is, however, not unlimited, and the limits of the right corresponds to the scope of criminal jurisdiction the PNA has under international law to begin with and possibly also to any undertakings it may have assumed relating to its ability to delegate authority. Obviously, neither a state nor a quasi-state can delegate more rights than it actually possesses.[37] Nor should states or quasi-states be encouraged to breach their international obligations via ICC referrals.

In this regard, the unique status of the PNA as an autonomous entity affects the analysis of its legal competence. Whereas "ordinary" states are endowed by virtue of their full sovereignty with comprehensive criminal jurisdiction over their

---

[35] See e.g., Committee on the Exercise of the Inalienable Rights of the Palestinian People. Programme of Work for 2008, UN Doc. A/AC.183/2008/1, at para 9 ("The Committee reiterates its long-standing position that the Palestine Liberation Organization is the sole legitimate representative of the Palestinian People").

[36] See e.g., Fletcher 2005, pp. 547, 555 ("Today, there are more likely to be instances in which states such as the Congo and the Sudan are 'unable genuinely to carry out the investigation or prosecution'"). The recognition afforded to the PLO reflect on the status of the PNA, the PLO's subsidiary.

[37] *Island of Palmas (Netherlands v US)*, 2 RIAA (1928) 829, 842 ("Spain could not transfer more rights than she herself possessed").

territory and nationals, the PNA, whose legal powers were created and defined by the Oslo Accords, has been endowed from the start with only limited jurisdictional powers over criminal matters. Of most relevance to our topic is the legal protocol to the 1995 Interim Agreement between Israel and the PLO, which delineates the criminal jurisdiction of the PNA (referred to in the text as the Council or Palestinian Council), and provides in Article 1:

1. a. The criminal jurisdiction of the Council covers all offenses committed by Palestinians and/or non-Israelis in the Territory, subject to the provisions of this Article. For the purposes of this Annex, "Territory" means West Bank territory except for Area C which, except for the Settlements and the military locations, will be gradually transferred to the Palestinian side in accordance with this Agreement, and Gaza Strip territory except for the Settlements and the Military Installation Area.
   b. In addition, the Council has criminal jurisdiction over Palestinians and their visitors who have committed offenses against Palestinians or their visitors in the West Bank and the Gaza Strip in areas outside the Territory, provided that the offense is not related to Israel's security interests [...].
2. Israel has sole criminal jurisdiction over the following offenses:
   a. offenses committed outside the Territory, except for the offenses detailed in subparagraph 1.b above; and
   b. offenses committed in the Territory by Israelis.[38]

As a result, both the personal and territorial criminal jurisdiction of the PNA are partial.[39] The PNA cannot exercise jurisdiction over "Area C" in the West Bank, which remains subject to Israeli control. (No such limits appear to exist nowadays with regard to Gaza following the removal of Israeli settlements and military installations in 2005.) More significantly, under the Interim Agreement the PNA cannot exercise criminal jurisdiction over Israeli nationals.[40]

---

[38] Interim Agreement, *supra* n. 13. See also ibid, at Article XVII(1) ("the jurisdiction of the Council will cover West Bank and Gaza Strip territory as a single territorial unit, except for: a. issues that will be negotiated in the permanent status negotiations: Jerusalem, settlements, specified military locations, Palestinian refugees, borders, foreign relations and Israelis; and b. powers and responsibilities not transferred to the Council"

[39] See also *Legal Consequences of the Construction of a Wall in the Occupied Palestinian Territory*, 2004 ICJ 136, at para 77 ("a number of agreements have been signed since 1993 between Israel and the Palestine Liberation Organization imposing various obligations on each party. Those agreements inter alia required Israel to transfer to Palestinian authorities certain powers and responsibilities exercised in the Occupied Palestinian Territory by its military authorities and civil administration. Such transfers have taken place, but, as a result of subsequent events, they remained partial and limited").

[40] But see Al-Haq 2009 at para 36 ("The exclusion of Israelis from PA jurisdiction as provided for in the Interim Agreement cannot legitimately be considered as extending to the international crimes of war crimes and crimes against humanity as to do so would be incompatible with international law"). Note that similar arguments were however rejected by international courts with relation to sovereign immunity and head of state immunity. *Al-Adsani v. UK*, judgment of 21 Nov. 2001 [2001] E.C.H.R. (App 35763/97); *Arrest Warrant of 11 April 2000* (DRC v. Belgium), 2002 ICJ 3. Furthermore, Article 98 of the ICC Statute supports the proposition that states may validly undertake to exclude international crimes from the jurisdiction of the Court.

In addition, the Oslo Accords seriously limit the power of the PNA to engage in foreign relations. For example, Article IX(5) of the Interim Agreement provides that:

(a) In accordance with the DOP, the Council will not have powers and responsibilities in the sphere of foreign relations, which sphere includes the establishment abroad of embassies, consulates or other types of foreign missions and posts or permitting their establishment in the West Bank or the Gaza Strip, the appointment of or admission of diplomatic and consular staff, and the exercise of diplomatic functions.
(b) Notwithstanding the provisions of this paragraph, the PLO may conduct negotiations and sign agreements with states or international organizations for the benefit of the Council in the following cases only:
   (1) economic agreements […],
   (2) agreements with donor countries for the purpose of implementing arrangements for the provision of assistance to the Council,
   (3) agreements for the purpose of implementing the regional development plans […], and
   (4) cultural, scientific and educational agreements.
   Dealings between the Council and representatives of foreign states and international organizations, as well as the establishment in the West Bank and the Gaza Strip of representative offices other than those described in subparagraph 5.a above, for the purpose of implementing the agreements referred to in subparagraph 5.b above, shall not be considered foreign relations.

Since Article IX(5) limits the powers of the PNA to conduct foreign relations (other than in specific fields of international relations),[41] its attempt to authorize the ICC to exercise jurisdiction appears to run contrary to its obligations under the Oslo Accords, and can be viewed as an *ultra vires* act—i.e., an act performed in excess of the legal powers conferred upon the PNA under the Oslo Accords.[42] Note, however, that the Oslo Accords did not limit in any comparable manner the international personality of the PLO, which continues to possess broad powers to represent the Palestinian self-determination unit on the international plane (including, the power to conclude agreements on behalf of the PNA) The legal situation may therefore have been different had the letter of authorization to the ICC been issued by the PLO and not the PNA.[43]

---

[41] For a discussion, see Singer 2004, pp. 268, 280–291.

[42] But see Al-Haq 2009, para 28 ("state practice over the past decade has demonstrated that the limits placed on the PA in this regard by Oslo are no longer recognized or considered legitimate by the international community and as such the question whether the PA presently has the ability to enter into international agreements can only be answered positively").

[43] While it is not fully clear whether the PLO possesses jurisdiction over the Palestinian territories for the purposes of the Statute, the aforementioned aversion against creating "legal black holes" would support considering the PLO as the international representative of the PNA for the purpose of delegation. Still, the PLO, which is a signatory to the Oslo Accords, is equally bound by the jurisdictional limits specified therein.

Although questions have often been raised at times concerning the continued validity of the Oslo Accords,[44] none of the parties to the agreements have renounced them until now. Moreover, if the Accords have been rendered legally obsolete that could mean that any legal powers that the PNA may have obtained under them has already expired. In any event, there are strong indications that, as a practical matter, Israel, the PNA and the international community continue to regard the Oslo Accords as a principal benchmark for assessing the legal rights and powers attendant to the PNA.[45] Specifically, it is hard to find any basis for a broad international acceptance of the right of the PNA to exercise criminal jurisdiction outside the parameters of the Oslo Accords.

The notion that the delegation powers of PNA should be limited by its international obligations is confirmed by powers of the text of Article 98 of the ICC Statute. Although Article 98 does not directly apply with regard to the PNA (the PNA is not a member state; nor are the agreements with Israel immunity agreements), its existence confirms the drafters' desire to prevent legal conflicts between the application of ICC jurisdiction and other international agreements governing the rights and obligations of nationals of third states. This rationale applies *a fortiori* to the PNA case, given that the international agreements in question established its authority, and delineated its initial scope of criminal jurisdiction and power to engage in foreign relations.

Admittedly, at the end of the day, the analysis offered here does generate as a practical matter a "legal black hole" in the Palestinian territories, illustrating the inability of functional analysis to resolve all of the Statute's shortcomings. Although, it could be argued that a functional approach along the lines that were proposed here would have enabled the PLO to authorize the Court to exercise jurisdiction over crimes committed by non-Israelis in the Palestinian territories and Israel to authorize the Court to investigate crimes committed by Israelis, and that the combined effect of both authorizations would amount to a full delegation of the situation in the Palestinian territories to the ICC, it is highly unlikely that Israel would grant such an authorization. Nor is it likely that the Security Council will step into the breach.

---

[44] See e.g., Shany 2007, pp. 369, 381. But see Watson 2000, p. 91 *et seq*; Orkand 2006–2007, pp. 390, 426–429.

[45] See e.g., Security Council Resolution 1515 2003 (endorsing the "Roadmap to a Permanent Two-State Solution"); A Performance-Based Roadmap to a Permanent Two-State Solution to the Israeli-Palestinian Conflict, 20 April 2003, Phase I, http://www.mfa.gov.il/MFA/Peace+Process/Guide+to+the+Peace+Process/A+Performance-Based+Roadmap+to+a+Permanent+Two-Sta.htm ("Israel withdraws from Palestinian areas occupied from September 28, 2000 and the two sides restore the status quo that existed at that time").

14.5 Conclusions

It is possible to read Article 12(3) of the ICC Statute in a functional manner and to construe its reference to a "State which is not a Party to this Statute" as encompassing also certain quasi-states, such as the PNA. This is because the differences between "ordinary" states and certain quasi-states do not appear to be particularly relevant for the purposes of applying criminal jurisdiction under the ICC Statute. Specifically, if the PNA may exercise criminal jurisdiction over a territory to which it or the PLO—the overarching political entity—has an internationally recognized sovereignty claim (and which, in the case of Gaza at least, no other state is contesting), then the PNAs lack of formal statehood appears insignificant for the purposes of invoking the ICC's delegation-based jurisdiction. The adoption of such a functional approach does not mean that the ICC should (or could) regard the PNA as a state for all means and purposes. To the contrary, it would mean that quasi-states may at times confer upon the Court a valid jurisdictional title. As I have argued above, while the adoption of the functional approach is not inevitable, as certainly not all international instruments and institutions have embraced this approach, I am of the view that the object and purpose of the ICC strongly militate in favor of introducing some degree of interpretative flexibility to the term "State" in Article 12(2).

At the same time, the ability of quasi-states such as the PNA to delegate jurisdiction is sometimes limited by international agreements, especially those that facilitated their creation. In our case, the Oslo Accords that established the PNA deprived it from exercising jurisdiction over Israelis, and seriously restricted its ability to conduct foreign relations. Acceptance of ICC jurisdiction by way of delegation must respect these limitations, both as a conceptual matter (an entity cannot delegate more rights than it posses), and also as a practical matter, in order to minimize the disruptive effects of the exercise of ICC jurisdiction on the international legal system.

At the end of the day, my conclusions are not radically different from those reached by Dr. Ronen: whereas she rejected ICC jurisdiction over the alleged crimes committed by Israel in Gaza by virtue of the PNA's lack of statehood, I reached a similar—though not identical–conclusion by way of relying on the Oslo Accords.[46] The existing jurisdictional gap—or accountability gap—over the events that unfolded in Gaza in 2008–2009, which both of our notes confirm, is nonetheless regrettable. This gap ought to be addressed through a robust application of domestic accountability mechanisms by Israel and the PNA (a result independently supported by the complementary nature of ICC jurisdiction). If and when such mechanisms fail to operate, international avenues for imposing state

---

[46] Technically, under the functional approach proposed here, the Prosecutor may still assume jurisdiction over crimes committed by Non-Israeli in the Palestinian Occupied Territories. Such a course of action is, however, highly problematic, as it will lead to Court to literally apply the Statute in a one-sided manner.

and individual legal responsibility, other than ICC proceedings based on the PNA letter of authorization, should be explored.

References

Al Haq Position Paper (2009) On Issues Arising from the Palestinian Authority's Submission of a Declaration to the Prosecutor of the International Criminal Court under Article 12(3) of the Rome Statute, 14 December 2009
Cameron I (2004) Jurisdiction and Admissibility Issues under the ICC Statute. In: McGoldrick D, Towe P, Donnelly E (eds) The Permanent International Criminal Court: Legal and Policy Issue, Hart Publishing, Oxford, p 65
Cassese A, Gaeta P, Jones J (2002) The Rome Statute: A Tentative Assessment. In: Cassese A, Gaeta P, Jones J (eds) The Rome Statute of the International Criminal Court, Oxford, p 1901
Corell H (2005) International Criminal Law—How Long Will Some Miss the Missing Link? Case West Res J Int Law 37:11–16
Cohan J (2006) Sovereignty in a Postsovereign World, Fla J Int Law, 18:907
Crawford J (2003) The Drafting of the Rome Statute. In: Sands P (ed) From Nuremberg to The Hague, Cambridge University Press, p 109
Davidson C (1999) The Challenge to Democratization: Arafat and the New Elite. Fletcher Forum World Aff 23:171
Deen-Racsmany Z (2001) The Nationality of the Offender and the Jurisdiction of the International Criminal Court. Am J Int Law 95:606
Desierto D (2008) Postcolonial International Law Discourses on Regional Developments in South and Southeast Asia. Int J Legal Info 36:387
Fletcher P (2005) Justice and Fairness in the Protection of Crime Victims. Lewis Clark Law Rev 9:547
Hawkins D et al. (2006) Delegation under Anarchy: States, International Organizations and Principal-Agent Theory. In: Hawkins D et al. (eds) Delegation and Agency in International Organizations, Cambridge University Press, p 14
Husseini H (2003) Challenges and Reforms in the Palestinian Authority. Fordham Int Law J 26:500
Kaul H-P (2002) Preconditions to the Exercise of Jurisdiction. In: Cassese A, Gaeta P, Jones J (eds) The Rome Statute of the International Criminal Court, Oxford, pp 583, 587
Krasner S (1999) Sovereignty: Organized Hypocrisy. Princeton University Press, Princeton
Lin C (2004) The International Telecommunication Union and the Republic of China (Taiwan): Prospect of Taiwan's Participation. Ann Surv Int Comp Law 10:133
Meissner P (2005) The International Criminal Court Controversy: An Analysis of the United States' Major Objections Against the Rome Statute, University of Michigan
Mushkat R (1992) Hong Kong as an International Legal Person. Emory Int Law Rev 6:105
Nabulsi K (2006) Justice as the Way Forward. In: Hilal J (ed) Where Now for Palestine? The Demise of the Two-State Solution. Zed Books, London, p 233
Orkand S (2006–2007) Coming Apart at the Seamline—The Oslo Accords and Israel's Security Barrier: A Missed Opportunity at the International Court of Justice and the Israeli Supreme Court. González J Int Law 10:390
Ronen Y (2010) ICC Jurisdiction over Acts Committed in the Gaza Strip: Article 12(3) of the ICC Statute and Non-State Entities. J Int Crim Just 8:3 [Also in this Volume, Chapter 13]
Scharf M (2001) The United States and the International Criminal Court: The ICC's Jurisdiction over the Nationals of Non-Party States: A Critique of the U.S. Position. Law Contemp Prob 64:67

Scheffer D (2002) Staying the Course with the International Criminal Court. Cornell Int Law J 35:47
Schabas W (2007) An Introduction to the International Criminal Court, 3rd edn. Cambridge University Press, Cambridge
Shany Y (2007) Faraway So Close: The Legal Status of Gaza After Israel's Disengagement. Yearbook Int Hum Law 369:2005
Simpson G (2004) Politics, Sovereignty, Remembrance. In: McGoldrick D, Towe P, Donnelly E (eds) The Permanent International Criminal Court: Legal and Policy Issues, Hart Publishing, Oxford
Singer J (2004) Aspects of Foreign Relations Under the Israeli-Palestinian Agreements on Interim Self-Government Arrangements for the West Bank and Gaza. Is Law Rev 28:268
Swiss Federal Council (1989) Note of Information sent to States Parties to the Convention and Protocol. http:www.icrc.org/IHL.NSF/WebSign?ReadForm&id=375&ps=P
Watson G (2000) The Oslo Accords: International Law and the Israeli-Palestinian Peace Agreements, Oxford University Press, Oxford
Worster W (2009) Law, Politics, and the Conception of the State in State Recognition Theory. Boston Univ Int Law J 27:115

Chapter 15
Note on the Legal Effects of Palestine's Declaration Under Article 12(3) of the ICC Statute

Vera Gowlland-Debbas

Contents

15.1 A Functional Approach to Statehood for Purposes of Article 12(3) 514
15.2 Interpretative Approaches to Article 12(3) of the Statute 515
15.3 The International Status of Palestine Under the Relevant Rules
of International Law 517
    15.3.1 Obligations Toward the United Nations 517
    15.3.2 Palestine's International Status and the Legitimacy of Statehood 518
    15.3.3 Obligations Under International Law of the States Parties to the ICC
    Statute 523
References 524

1. The following remarks were submitted at the OTP-NGO Roundtable discussions of 20 October 2010 on whether the declaration lodged by the Palestinian National Authority on 21 January 2009 under Article 12(3) of the Court's Statute meets statutory requirements. My remarks follow from the Opinion which I signed entitled *Les effets de la reconnaissance par la Palestine de la compétence de la C.P.I.* submitted by Professor Alain Pellet at the request of Maître William

---

Emeritus Professor of International Law. This Opinion was presented by the author on the occasion of the ICC, Office of the Prosecutor-NGO Roundtable session on Palestine of 20 October 2010 and has been posted on the Court's website.

V. Gowlland-Debbas (✉)
Public International Law, Graduate Institute of International
and Development Studies (IHEID), Geneva, Switzerland

C. Meloni and G. Tognoni (eds.), *Is There a Court for Gaza?*,
DOI: 10.1007/978-90-6704-820-0_15,
© T.M.C. ASSER PRESS, The Hague, The Netherlands, and the authors/editors 2012

Bourdon and which was endorsed by 40 well-known international lawyers.[1] I also draw on a follow-up note which I addressed to the Prosecutor last May.

15.1 A Functional Approach to Statehood for Purposes of Article 12(3)

2. The gist of Professor Pellet's Opinion is that although there is an on-going debate as to whether Palestine is at present a state or not under international law, it does not fall to the Court to determine this in the abstract since this is a matter for states to decide; ICC acceptance that Palestine may make an effective declaration under Article 12(3) under the Statute does not imply that the ICC takes any position regarding Palestine's statehood under international law. In our view, the validity of the Palestinian declaration should be examined from a functional perspective which focuses on the question of whether Palestine may be considered a state for purposes of the ICC Statute, that is for the purpose of determining the admissibility of Palestine's declaration under Article 12(3) of the Statute and ascertaining whether the necessary conditions for the exercise of the Court's competence have been fulfilled.

3. Recourse to such a functional approach is fairly common in international law; to borrow the term from Judge Rosalyn Higgins, albeit writing with reference to federated entities, the concept of the "state" is one of "variable geometry"; it therefore depends on the particular context or norm which is being applied. Multilateral treaties have encompassed various entities in the term State for purposes of the respective treaty, such as regional integration organizations or state enterprises, and regional courts have on occasion equally done so when it was proved necessary for the promotion of their respective instrument.[2] Entities have been considered as states also for admission to international organizations whenever this has served the purposes of the organization; the best known example is the admission of Ukraine and Byelorussia, as well as India before independence, to membership in the United Nations for purposes of Article 3 of the UN Charter, but it is not the only organization to have done so.

4. Without prejudice to the question of its statehood under international law, it is notable that Palestine has been assimilated to a state for a variety of purposes. The General Assembly has granted Palestine not only observer status, but also additional rights and privileges of participation in its work normally reserved for member states, including the sponsorship of draft resolutions related to the question of Palestine.[3] Since 1975 the PLO has been invited routinely to participate in the discussions on Palestine in the Security Council under rule 37 which applies to "any member of the United Nations" which is not a member of the

---

[1] See *supra*, Chap. 9.

[2] For illustrations, reference should be made to the Opinion of Professor Pellet [See *supra* in this Volume Chap. 9].

[3] See, e.g. GA Res. 3210(XXIX), 3236 (XXIX), 3237 (XXIX), and 52/250.

Security Council,[4] for purposes of the effective exercise of the Security Council's functions under Chaps. 6 and 7. The International Court of Justice has also considered that in view of Palestine's special status in the UN, it could participate in the advisory proceedings relating to the construction of a Wall in the OPT even though the Court's Statute reserves this privilege only to states and IOs, thereby assimilating Palestine to a State in order to allow the Court to effectively address the request for an advisory opinion put to it by the General Assembly.[5]

15.2 Interpretative Approaches to Article 12(3) of the Statute

5. Whether Palestine can be assimilated to a State *for purposes of Article 12(3)* is a matter of interpretation of the Statute's provisions in regard to the Court's jurisdiction for which the Court has, according to the well-known principle of international law, *kompetenz kompetenz* (see also Article 19 of its Statute). It is accepted that the rules of interpretation laid down in Article 31(1) of the 1969 Vienna Convention on the Law of Treaties apply under which the interpretation of a treaty shall be carried out in good faith in accordance with the ordinary meaning of the term, in their context, and in the light of the treaty's object and purpose.

6. It must be underlined, however, that the ICC Statute is not an ordinary multilateral treaty, but a treaty with a collective interest which establishes obligations of an essentially objective character. The International Court of Justice has given voice to the concept of collective interest embedded in multilateral treaties having a humanitarian purpose for in "a convention of this type one cannot speak of individual advantages or disadvantages to States, or of the maintenance of a perfect contractual balance between rights and duties..."[6] In approaching such treaties, judicial bodies have resorted to teleological interpretation of the relevant instrument, including the doctrine of implied powers of international organizations, or have invoked their inherent judicial powers. As the Court stated in the well-known *Reparations* case in considering that United Nations international personality could be extrapolated from a teleological reading of the Charter:

---

[4] "Any Member of the United Nations which is not a member of the Security Council may be invited, as the result of a decision of the Security Council, to participate, without vote, in the discussion of any question brought before the Security Council when the Security Council considers that the interests of that Member are specially affected, or when a Member brings a matter to the attention of the Security Council in accordance with Article 35(1) of the Charter."

[5] *Legal Consequences of the Construction of a Wall in the Occupied Palestinian Territory*, Advisory Opinion, Order of 19 December 2003, paras 2 and 4, and para 4 of the ICJ Advisory Opinion of 9 July 2004 (hereinafter: *Wall Opinion*).

[6] *Reservations to the Convention on Genocide*, Advisory Opinion of 18 May 1951, ICJ Reports 1951, at 23.

> It must be acknowledged that its Members, by entrusting certain functions to [the United Nations]...have clothed it with the competence required to enable those functions to be effectively discharged.[7]

7. The meaning of the term "state" in Article 12(3) should be interpreted by looking at the overall context and object and purpose of the Statute. The latter bestows on the Court the means to fulfill its statutory mission to end impunity for the most serious international crimes over which the Court has jurisdiction, i.e. those that are so grave that they "threaten the peace, security and well-being of the world"; such crimes affect the international community as a whole. In the context of Palestine, a number of fact-finding missions have alleged that crimes of the kind that the Court was established to try have been committed. Declarations under paragraph 3 are one of the necessary conditions for the Court to fulfill this mission and the Court would be doing so by treating Palestine as a state solely for the purposes of Articles 12(3) since only Palestine holds sovereignty over the territory in question as well as a duty under international law to investigate and prosecute offences within the jurisdiction of the Court; at the same time, Palestine has given the consent necessary which underlies the Court's jurisdiction. On the contrary, were it to decline jurisdiction, the Court would be interpreting the Rome Statute in a manner that prevented it from the effective discharge of its mission and establish a zone of impunity in the Occupied Palestinian territory.

8. In addition to a teleological approach, recent judgments by the ICJ, regional courts and quasi-judicial bodies such as the WTO dispute settlement bodies, have drawn on Article 31(3)(c) of the Vienna Convention which states that in interpreting treaty provisions, "there shall be taken into account, together with the context... any relevant rules of international law applicable in the relations between the parties". As the European Court of Human Rights has held:

> (T)he Convention...cannot be interpreted in a vacuum. The Court must be mindful of the Convention's special character as a human rights treaty, and it must also take the relevant rules of international law into account. The Convention should so far as possible be interpreted in harmony with other rules of international law of which it forms a part....[8]

This is echoed in Article 21 of the Statute which calls on the Court to apply in addition to its own instruments, applicable treaties and relevant rules of general international law, including general principles of law, providing they are consistent with internationally recognized human rights.

---

[7] *Reparations for Injuries Suffered in the Services of the United Nations*, ICJ Reports 1949, at 179.

[8] *McElhinney v. Ireland*, Application no. 31253/96, Judgment of 21 November 2001, European Court of Human Rights, Grand Chamber, para 36. See also *Al-Adsani v. the United Kingdom*, Application no. 35763/97, Judgment of 21 November 2001, European Court of Human Rights, Grand Chamber, para. 55.

15.3 The International Status of Palestine Under the Relevant Rules of International Law

9. The relevant rules of international law applicable to the case are: the Court's obligations toward the United Nations which has responsibility for Palestine, the international status of Palestine and the legitimacy of statehood, and the obligations of state parties toward Palestine.

15.3.1 Obligations Toward the United Nations

10. The ICC while an independent organization based on its own treaty, has entered into a "mutually beneficial relationship" with the United Nations as expressed in its relationship agreement, in which the ICC has pledged to coordinate and cooperate with the United Nations in the fulfillment of their mutual responsibilities; this includes for the United Nations, a responsibility toward Palestine. For the reasons I will set out shortly, acceptance of Palestine as a "state" under Article 12(3) for the strictly functional purposes of the Statute would not be counteracting but on the contrary supporting the United Nations responsibilities toward Palestine. It will be recalled that, as the ICJ has pointed out, Palestine remains the special and permanent responsibility of the United Nations "…until the question is resolved in all its aspects in a satisfactory manner in accordance with international legitimacy". As a question of international community concern, the question of Palestine cannot therefore be regarded as only a bilateral matter between Israel and Palestine.[9] In its *dispositif* the Court has called on all UN organs, and this would include organisations within the UN system, to take what further action would be required to bring to an end the illegal situation (while the Court was addressing here the illegal construction of a wall in the Occupied Palestinian Territory, this applies to the general situation in Palestine which the ICJ addressed in the rest of its Opinion).[10] The General Assembly has also urged "the specialized agencies and organizations of the United Nations system to continue to support and assist the Palestinian people in the early realization of their

---

[9] *Wall Opinion*, paras 49–50.

[10] It should be stated from the outset, as this has been contested, that the Court's Advisory Opinion cannot simply be dismissed as nonbinding. States cannot ignore the existence of the fundamental rules that the Court has underlined which bind them in international law nor the automatic legal consequence of their violation. Moreover, the Opinion provides an authorization for them to act in consequence. Most important, the Advisory Opinion which the Court addressed to the General Assembly has been formally accepted and endorsed by the organ which requested it in its resolution ES-10/15 in July 2004. It therefore binds UN organs, including the Secretary-General of the United Nations.

right to self-determination."[11] The exercise of this responsibility may also be linked to the emerging "responsibility to protect" under international law.

15.3.2 Palestine's International Status and the Legitimacy of Statehood

11. Acceptance of Palestine as a state for purposes of the Statute would be in conformity with the international legitimacy bestowed on Palestinian statehood by the international community as a whole acting through the United Nations. Palestine is not a *territoire sans maître* but a territory with an international status confirmed as such by the International Court of Justice. This special status flows from the fact that it was a former Class A Mandate, a self-determination unit and occupied territory.

Palestine as a Former Mandate

12. Palestine was a former "Class A" Mandate, in accordance with Article 22 of the League of Nations Covenant, whose "existence as independent nations can be provisionally recognized subject to the rendering of administrative advice and assistance by a Mandatory until such time as they are able to stand alone." Mandates were guided by two fundamental principles: the principle of non-annexation and the principle of "sacred trust of civilization".[12] The Mandate could not therefore impair or destroy the rights of the original inhabitants and its essence was based on international supervision and accountability. The "ultimate objective" of the sacred trust was the "self-determination and independence of the peoples concerned."[13]

13. The separate status of Palestine and a limited international personality was recognized in the inter-war period. It had certain treaty-making capacity, the treaties it concluded with other states being registered with the League of Nations; a separate Palestinian nationality was also recognized by the League of Nations and in the courts of other states.[14] Referring to South-West Africa, which was even further removed from independence as a "Class C" territory, the ICJ underlined that the mandate system "did not involve any cession of territory or transfer of

---

[11] GA Res. 64/150, 26 March 2010.

[12] *International Status of South-West Africa*, Advisory Opinion, ICJ Reports 1950, at 131.

[13] *Legal Consequences for States of the Continued Presence of South Africa in Namibia (South-West Africa) Notwithstanding Security Council Resolution 276 (1970)*, Advisory Opinion, ICJ Reports 1971, at 31.

[14] For a comprehensive overview of the status of Palestine under mandate, see Qafisheh 2008.

sovereignty"[15]; it was also widely recognized that these mandates enjoyed international personality distinct from the Mandatory Power.[16]

14. With the end of the League, the rights conferred on the people under mandate were safeguarded under Article 80(1) of the UN Charter and the responsibilities and supervisory functions over the administration of the Mandate devolved upon the United Nations.[17] Resolution 181 (II), the Partition Plan, adopted by the General Assembly on 29 November 1947 in exercise of its responsibilities and which terminated the Mandate, laid down the concept of a two-State solution and has since become the express foundation of the legitimacy of the establishment both of the State of Israel in 1948 and of the Palestinian State declared by the Palestine National Council at its 19th Extraordinary Session in Algiers on 15 November 1988.[18]

Palestine as a Self-Determination Unit

15. The General Assembly's responsibility for the Territory beyond the termination of the Mandate did not end, but now flowed from the collective recognition by the international community expressed through the General Assembly of the right to self-determination of the Palestinian people which comprised a right to statehood.[19] This has been endorsed in numerous UN resolutions and confirmed in the Advisory Opinion in the *Wall* case. The right to self-determination is a sovereign right of peoples. The Court considered that the existence of a "Palestinan people" is no longer in issue and that the reference to the "legitimate rights" of the Palestinian people in the Israeli-Palestinian Interim Agreement on the West Bank and Gaza Strip of 28 September 1995 also included the right to self-determination.[20]

16. Since this right can only be exercised over a territory, the affirmation of the right to self-determination of the Palestinian people has meant recognition of a

---

[15] *International Status of South-West Africa*, at 132.

[16] See the 1931 Resolution of the Institute of International Law.

[17] *International Status of South-West Africa*, at 128, 133. The Court derived the competence of the General Assembly to exercise such supervisory functions in part from its broad powers under Article 10 of the Charter as well as Article 80(1) of the Charter.

[18] The Israeli Declaration of Independence states that the establishment of a Jewish State was made "by virtue of our natural and historic right and on the strength of the Resolution (181) of the United Nations General Assembly" (see website of the Israeli Foreign Ministry). The Palestinian declaration states: "By virtue of the natural, historical and legal right of the Palestinian Arab people to its homeland, Palestine... on the basis of the international legitimacy embodied in the resolutions of the United Nations since 1947" (27 ILM, 1998, 1637–1654). See Gowlland-Debbas 1990, pp. 135–153. In its Resolution 273(III) admitting Israel into the United Nations on 11 May 1949, the General Assembly took note of the declarations made by the representative of Israel before the *ad hoc* Committee respecting Israel's implementation of Resolutions 181(II) and 194(II).

[19] GA Res. 2535/B(XXIV), 2628 (XXV), 2672/C(XXV) and since reaffirmed in countless resolutions.

[20] *Wall Opinion*, para 118.

self-determination unit; this corresponds to the territory occupied by Israel since 1967. Thus the borders of the state of Palestine are not in question and have been recognized by the international community.

17. The right to self-determination has been recognized as a norm of *jus cogens*, a peremptory norm of international law, which cannot be derogated from even by the parties concerned. The Court has likewise confirmed its *erga omnes* character, a right in which every State has a legal interest and a duty in its protection.[21] The right to self-determination therefore entails a right to respect for the territorial integrity and unity of the whole Territory under occupation,[22] and the obligation to promote the realization of that right.

Palestine as Occupied Territory

18. The international status of Palestine also flows from the fact that it is an occupied territory and that that regime is regulated by international law from which flows rights and obligations, in particular the application of the Fourth Geneva Convention; the latter is evidence that there are two parties to an international conflict who potentially may be in violation of its grave breaches provisions.

19. In its Advisory Opinion, the ICJ confirmed the series of pronouncements embedded in countless Security Council resolutions since 1948 which underline the legal consequences ensuing from this status. The Security Council has reaffirmed the well-established principle of the inadmissibility of the acquisition of territory by force in its resolutions on Palestine and has called for the withdrawal of Israeli armed forces from the Occupied Palestinian Territory, including Jerusalem.[23] Security Council resolutions have also declared that all legislative and administrative measures taken by Israel which purported to alter the character and status of the Occupied Palestinian Territory, including East Jerusalem, such as its 1980 Basic Law establishing Jerusalem as the "complete and united" capital of Israel, are null and void.[24] The Court has also upheld Security Council resolutions declaring the illegality of the Israeli settlements in the OPT established in breach of Article 49(6) of the Geneva Conventions, a view which was endorsed also by its sole dissenting Judge.[25]

---

[21] *Barcelona Traction, Light and Power Company, Limited*, Second Phase, Judgment, ICJ Reports 1970, at 32; *East Timor (Portugal v. Australia)*, Judgment, ICJ Reports 1995, at 102.

[22] GA Res. 63/165.

[23] E.g., Resolutions 242(1967) and 338(1973). For the drafting history of SC Res. 242 which indicates that the Security Council had no intention of endorsing Israeli annexation of any part of the West Bank or Gaza Strip, see McHugo 2002, pp. 851–882.

[24] See e.g. SC Res. 298 (1971), 446 (1979), 476 and 478 (1980) and 1322 (2000).

[25] *Wall Opinion*, para 120. The Court cites Resolution 237 (1967), 271 (1969), 681 (1990), 799 (1992) and 904 (1994) regarding the applicability to the OPT of the Geneva Conventions in which the Security Council considered that those settlements had "no legal validity". See Declaration by Judge Buergenthal.

20. Unilateral acts by Israel to change the character of the OPT are therefore proscribed and this is confirmed by Article XXXI.7 of the Interim Accord on the West Bank and Gaza Strip which states that neither party will take the initiative nor adopt any measures which would modify the status of the West Bank and the Gaza Strip until a permanent agreement is reached. A declaration of Palestinian statehood would be in line with, rather than affect, the status of the West Bank and Gaza which as stated above, includes the right to self-determination and statehood. The arguments which have so far been presented to the Court urging it not to give effect to the Palestinian declaration under Article 12(3), remain strangely silent on the fact that restrictions on Palestinian independence are solely due to belligerent occupation. It should be stressed that the status of Gaza as occupied territory continues to be recognized by the United Nations. The Security Council in its Resolution 1860 (2009) adopted on 8 January 2009 stresses "that the Gaza Strip constitutes an integral part of the territory occupied in 1967 and will be a part of the Palestinian state".[26]

The Legitimacy of Palestinian Statehood

21. The legitimacy of Palestinian statehood has been confirmed on numerous occasions by the United Nations. In its Resolution 43/1977, adopted by an overwhelming majority with only two votes against, the General Assembly in 1988, "acknowledged" the proclamation of the State of Palestine by the Palestine National Council and declared it to be "in line with General Assembly resolution 181 (II) and in exercise of the inalienable rights of the Palestinian people" and affirmed "the need to enable the Palestinian people to exercise their sovereignty over their territory occupied since 1967". The resolution thus recognized and affirmed the intrinsic legality of a situation considered to be in conformity with the right to self-determination, and the consequent intrinsic illegality, despite its effectiveness, of the Israeli occupation which was preventing the State of Palestine from exercising authority over this territory. By implicitly acknowledging that the conditions for the establishment of a Palestinian State had now been met,[27] the Assembly was asserting its competence to determine the forms and procedures by which the right to self-determination of territories over which it exercised responsibility was to be realized.[28] The right to statehood has been constantly reiterated, including by the Security Council which called for the achievement of the two-state solution.[29] The ICJ has also considered in the *Wall* case that it had a

---

[26] See also the Reports of the Fact-finding Missions established by the Human Rights Council.

[27] The debate surrounding the adoption of this resolution supports this view. Even those States which had not recognized the state of Palestine stated that they nevertheless welcomed the proclamation as the exercise of the right of self-determination, differing only on the timing of recognition (see e.g. A/43/PV.79, Sweden, p. 74; A/43/PV.80, Chile, pp. 18–20, Austria, pp. 21–22, New Zealand, p. 132, Canada, pp. 172–176; A/43/PV.82, Japan, p. 82, and France, pp. 87–88).

[28] See *Western Sahara,* Advisory Opinion, ICJ Reports 1975, at 36.

[29] SC Res. 1397 (2002) and 1515 (2003).

duty to draw the attention of the General Assembly, *inter alia*, to the need to encourage efforts to establish a Palestinian State.[30]

22. In short, far from emerging in violation of international law, Palestine's statehood is a necessary consequence of a fundamental principle of international law, the right to self-determination. The collective recognition of this international status within the United Nations is therefore what distinguishes Palestine from entities such as the former South African Bantustans or the self-proclaimed "Turkish Republic of Northern Cyprus" and other such entities, in regard to which the United Nations has refused to bestow legitimacy.

23. Under international law, illegal effectiveness does not affect the sovereignty of States victims of an illegal occupation. While the Security Council declared null and void the unilateral declaration of independence of Southern Rhodesia in 1965, despite its fulfillment of the criteria of statehood, including that of effectiveness, because contrary to the right to self-determination, conversely in several instances recognition of statehood was bestowed on peoples still under foreign occupation because this was in line with their legitimate rights. Namibia was admitted to membership of the ILO and other specialized agencies (where membership is contingent on statehood) on the basis that its legitimate rights should not be frustrated by the illegal occupation of South Africa.[31] The ILO Resolution reads:

> Noting that Namibia is the only remaining case of a former mandate of the League of Nations where the former mandatory Power is still in occupation,
>
> Considering that an application for membership in terms of article 1 is prevented only by the illegal occupation of Namibia by South Africa, the illegal nature of this occupation having been confirmed by the ICJ in its Advisory Opinion of 21 June 1971,
>
> Affirming that the ILO is not prepared to allow the legitimate rights of the Namibian people to be frustrated by the illegal action of South Africa,
>
> Making it clear that in now granting the application for membership it does not overlook the wording of article 1 and believes that in the near future the illegal occupation of Namibia by South Africa will be terminated,
>
> 1) Decides to admit Namibia to membership in the Organisation it being agreed that, until the present illegal occupation of Namibia is terminated, the United Nations Council for Namibia [...] will be regarded as the Government of Namibia for the purpose of the application of the Constitution of the Organisation.

24. There are other examples of recognition of states emerging from the exercise of the right to self-determination, even under occupation, include the accession to independence of the people of Guinea-Bissau, thereby creating a sovereign State recognized by the General Assembly even while still occupied by Portugal.[32]

---

[30] *Wall Opinion*, para 162.
[31] ILO 64th session (Geneva, June 1978), Provisional Record, No. 24, pp. 19–20.
[32] GA Res. 3061 (XXVIII).

15.3.3 Obligations Under International Law of the States Parties to the ICC Statute

25. The fact that Palestine is a territory with an international status and is therefore of international concern has several implications, including the imposition of obligations on third parties. Therefore to give effect to Palestine's declaration under Article 12(3) would not be contrary to the ICC state parties' obligations under international law.

26. As stated above, the right to self-determination has been recognized as a norm of *jus cogens*, also having an *erga omnes* character. In view of this, the states parties to the Statute have a duty under general international law to promote the realization of the right to statehood of the Palestinian people and not to recognize the illegality of the situation.[33]

27. As parties to the Geneva Conventions, the states parties to the ICC Statute also have a duty to ensure that the grave breaches provisions do not remain a dead letter; common Article 1 of the Geneva Conventions calls on them not only to respect but also to ensure respect for the terms of the conventions; they therefore have a duty to enforce the system of repression of grave breaches under the Fourth Geneva Convention through all the means at their disposal, as the Court has confirmed in its *dispositif* in the *Wall* case.

28. Palestine also has duties under international humanitarian law as the entity which holds exclusive title to the territory of Palestine within its 1967 borders. Much has been made of the limiting effects of the Oslo Accords on Palestinian jurisdiction over its territory. The Oslo Accords however should not be taken to be more than the transfer of belligerent administrative powers and responsibilities from the occupying Israeli military administration to the Palestinian National Authority in preparation for full Israeli withdrawal from the OPT. As stated above, these agreements do not affect the status of Palestine nor the external capacities it has under international law in accordance to which, *inter alia*, it has been admitted to international organizations, concluded a number of treaties in its own right and established official relations with a large number of states. Moreover, not only is the legal status of the Oslo Accords far from clear in that, not having been registered with the UN, they cannot be invoked before any organ of the United Nations [Article 102(2) of the UN Charter], but also Article 103 of the UN Charter ensures that in case of conflict, the obligations of Israel under the Charter would prevail over any other agreement. The General Assembly has also considered that any "partial agreement or separate treaty which purports to determine the future of

---

[33] *Wall Opinion*, para 159. As stated in the *Namibia Opinion* "It would be an untenable interpretation to maintain that, once such a declaration (of illegality) had been made by the Security Council under Article 24 of the Charter, on behalf of all member States, those Members would be free to act in disregard of such illegality or even to recognize violations of law resulting from it". ICJ Reports 1971, at 52.

the Palestinian territories occupied by Israel since 1967 in violation of their right to self-determination", would lack validity.[34]

29. The Oslo Accords cannot, moreover, purport to have the effect of depriving protected persons in the occupied Palestinian territory of their intransgressible rights under international humanitarian law, nor restrict the right and duty of the Palestinian authorities to exercise their jurisdiction fully in respect of the grave breaches of Geneva Convention IV, whatever legal effects the Oslo Accords may have in respect of everyday crimes. Article 47 of the Fourth Geneva Convention (which is effective over the whole duration of the occupation) clearly states:

> Protected persons who are in occupied territory shall not be deprived, in any case or in any manner whatsoever, of the benefits of the present Convention by any change introduced [...] **by any agreement concluded between the authorities of the occupied territories and the Occupying Power** [...] (emphasis added).

On the other hand, if for the sake of argument it can be construed that the Palestinian authorities are *unable* because of the Oslo Accords to proceed in respect of crimes within the ICC's jurisdiction, for which the UN has called specifically on them to investigate, then the admissibility requirements under Article 17(1)(b) of the Statute would be fulfilled. In view of all the above arguments, the Oslo Accords may not be construed in any way as constituting an obstacle to the effectiveness of a Palestine declaration under Article 12(3).

30. In short, were the ICC to give effect to Palestine's declaration under Article 12(3) of the Statute, it would be acting not only in line with the object and purpose of its Statute, but also with the legitimacy bestowed by the international community on Palestinian statehood under international law.

31. In conclusion, as stated in the Opinion by Professor Alain Pellet, all the conditions (*ratione materiae, temporis, loci* and *personae*) exist for the Palestinian declaration to deploy its effects.

References

Gowlland-Debbas V (1990) Collective responses to the unilateral declarations of independence of Southern Rhodesia and Palestine: an application of the legitimizing function of the United Nations, 61 BYIL:135–153

McHugo J (2002) Resolution 242: a legal reappraisal of the right-wing Israeli interpretation of the withdrawal phrase with reference to the conflict between Israel and the Palestinians. ICLQ 51:851–882

Qafisheh M (2008) The International Law Foundations of Palestinian Nationality. Martinus Nijhoff, The Hague, Boston, London

---

[34] See Resolutions 34/70 and 35/169B.

Part IV
Non Judicial Responses: The Russell Tribunal on Palestine

Chapter 16
The Russell Tribunal on Palestine

Frank Barat and Daniel Machover

Contents

16.1	Introduction	527
16.2	Background to the RToP	530
16.3	The First International Session of the Russell Tribunal on Palestine	532
16.4	The Call for the Suspension of the EU-Israel Association Agreement	535
16.5	The Second International Session of the Russell Tribunal on Palestine	537
16.6	Corporate Liability for Complicity in International Law Violations	538
16.7	The Third International Session of the Russell Tribunal on Palestine	540
16.8	Russell Tribunal on Palestine: An Enduring Legacy	541
References		542
Annex to Chapter 16		543

16.1 Introduction

The Russell Tribunal on Palestine (RToP) is a citizen's initiative that is sustained by numerous contributions from individuals, associations, organizations and solidarity movements. Its independence relies on the great variety of volunteers and on the material and financial help it receives from multiple sources. Thanks to a network of National Support Committees (Spain, United Kingdom, Ireland, the Netherlands, Belgium, Luxembourg, Germany, France, Italy and Portugal), two

---

Frank Barat, Co-ordinator of the Russell Tribunal on Palestine (RToP) and Daniel Machover, Partner at London Law Firm Hickman and Rose, and legal adviser to RToP.

F. Barat (✉)
Russell Tribunal on Palestine (RToP), London, UK

D. Machover
Law Firm Hickman and Rose, London, UK

C. Meloni and G. Tognoni (eds.), *Is There a Court for Gaza?*,
DOI: 10.1007/978-90-6704-820-0_16,
© T.M.C. ASSER PRESS, The Hague, The Netherlands, and the authors/editors 2012

successful evidence sessions have taken place in Barcelona (March 2010) and London (November 2010), creating a significant impact on the audiences and receiving considerable media attention.[1] At the time of writing, preparations are in hand for two further sessions, firstly in Cape Town (November 2011), where the focus will be on the crime of apartheid, and a final session in 2012 in the USA, which will focus on UN and US possible complicity in Israel's violations of international law. From the experience of past Russell Tribunals—on US military intervention in Vietnam (1966/1967) and internal repression (with outside interference) in Latin America (1973/1975), as to both of which see further below— and judging from the conclusions of the first two sessions of the RToP, it is clear that findings of the Tribunal provide a legally grounded body of arguments, constituting an important tool to be used by those who seek to ensure respect for the rule of international law, and the rights of the Palestinian people.

The RToP is an international people's tribunal, created in 2009 as a response to the failure of the international community to act appropriately to bring to an end Israel's recognized violations of international law. In particular, the organizers of the RToP were very concerned by the inadequate international response to the Advisory Opinion of 9 July 2004 of the highest judicial body in the world, the International Court of Justice (ICJ), on the legal consequences of the establishment of a wall in the Occupied Palestinian Territories ('the Advisory Opinion'), which called for the wall to be dismantled and which reiterated the need to respect past resolutions of the United Nations (UN).[2]

International law is very clear when it comes to Israel/Palestine and should be at the core of any negotiations. Many UN Resolutions (181, 194, 242, 338, 1322, 1397 and 1435) call for a State of Palestine to be established, while the right to self-determination was at the heart of the Advisory Opinion.[3] The Advisory Opinion also placed a strong emphasis on the duties of third party states to ensure that the Palestinians are able to exercise their right of self-determination:

---

[1] The complete documentation of the RToP can be consulted at http://www.russell tribunalonpalestine.com/en/.

[2] http://www.icj-cij.org/docket/index.php?pr=71&code=mwp&p1=3&p2=4&p3=6&case=131&k=5a; and http://domino.un.org/unispal.nsf/0/b59ecb7f4c73bdbc85256eeb004f6d20?OpenDocument.

[3] See in particular para 118, which states: "As regards the principle of the right of peoples to self-determination, the Court observes that the existence of a "Palestinian people" is no longer in issue ... The Court considers that [the 'legitimate rights' of the Palestinian people] include the right to self-determination, as the General Assembly has moreover recognized on a number of occasions (see, for example, Resolution 58/163 of 22 December 2003) and also para 149, which states: "The Court notes that Israel is first obliged to comply with the international obligations it has breached by the construction of the Wall in the Occupied Palestinian Territory (see paras 114–137 above). Consequently, Israel is bound to comply with its obligation to respect the right of the Palestinian people to self-determination [...]" and para 155.

156. [T]he Court has already observed [...] that in the *East Timor* case, it described as "irreproachable" the assertion that "the right of peoples to self-determination, as it evolved from the Charter and from United Nations practice, has an *erga omnes* character" (*I.C.J. Reports 1995*, p. 102, para 29). The Court would also recall that under the terms of General Assembly Resolution 2625 (XXV), already mentioned above [...]
"Every State has the duty to promote, through joint and separate action, realization of the principle of equal rights and self-determination of peoples, in accordance with the provisions of the Charter, and to render assistance to the United Nations in carrying out the responsibilities entrusted to it by the Charter regarding the implementation of the principle [...]"

Indeed, the International Court of Justice went on to articulate a strong and active duty on states to act to bring to an end the practical and legal consequences of the wall (and by clear implication any other established systematic violations of Palestinian human rights and their rights under international humanitarian law):

159. Given the character and the importance of the rights and obligations involved, the Court is of the view that all States are under an obligation not to recognize the illegal situation resulting from the construction of the wall in the Occupied Palestinian Territory, including in and around East Jerusalem. They are also under an obligation not to render aid or assistance in maintaining the situation created by such construction. It is also for all States, while respecting the United Nations Charter and international law, to see to it that any impediment, resulting from the construction of the wall, to the exercise by the Palestinian people of its right to self-determination is brought to an end. In addition, all the States parties to the Geneva Convention relative to the Protection of Civilian Persons in Time of War of 12 August 1949 are under an obligation, while respecting the United Nations Charter and international law, to ensure compliance by Israel with international humanitarian law as embodied in that Convention.
160. Finally, the Court is of the view that the United Nations, and especially the General Assembly and the Security Council, should consider what further action is required to bring to an end the illegal situation resulting from the construction of the wall and the associated régime, taking due account of the present Advisory Opinion.

Despite the ICJs Advisory Opinion, the Court's above injunction to states and recommendation to the UN have yet to be acted upon: the wall is planned to be 810 km long, but whereas around 300 km had been constructed in 2004, by the summer of 2010 it was already at least 520 km long (i.e. almost two-thirds completed).[4]

---

[4] http://www.stopthewall.org/downloads/pdf/2010wallfactsheet.pdf

16.2 Background to the RToP

The RToP stems from a long history of popular tribunals dating back to 1966 with the establishment, by Lord Bertrand Russell and French philosopher Jean-Paul Sartre, of the Russell Tribunal on Vietnam.[5] The inaugural people's tribunal investigated U.S. foreign policy and its military intervention in Vietnam. The extent of U.S. aggression was little known at the time by the general public and the tribunal, through its detailed analysis and thorough testimonies, helped engender a well-informed enormous peace movement that, from the late 1960s, made the continued U.S. intervention in Vietnam more and more difficult until it finally became untenable. The Russell Tribunal on Vietnam had a very positive impact on American university campuses and highlighted the hypocrisy and lies of the U.S. government at the time. Sessions were held in Sweden and Denmark.

This was followed in the mid-1970s by the Russell Tribunal on Latin America.[6] After examining the US war against Vietnam, a war of aggression, the second people's tribunal this time focused on the internal war waged by military juntas all over Latin America. One crucial historical event led to the creation of the second Russell Tribunal, namely the assassination of Chile's socialist President, Salvador Allende, on 11 September 1973. On this day, fighter jets bombed Chile's capital city, Santiago de Chile, and destroyed Al Moneda Palace. This coup was led by General Pinochet but was financed, planned and executed with CIA support. Pinochet established the first military junta in Latin America. A few years later, most Latin American countries were governed by repressive military regimes. Dissent was not authorized, torture became widespread, the number of political prisoners grew by thousands and thousands of people simply vanished. They became known as *"desaparecidos"*.

The Tribunal was chaired by Hortensia Bussi de Allende, Salvador Allende's wife and took place in Brussels and Rome. It led to the creation of the Permanent Peoples Tribunal in Rome in 1979.

On 4 March 2009, more than 35 years after the Tribunal on Latin America and a few weeks after the end of "Operation Cast Lead" (Israel's assault on Gaza which left more than 1,400 Palestinians dead including hundreds of women and children), a press conference, chaired by Tribunal's general coordinator Pierre Galand, held in Brussels, launched the RToP. Ken Loach, Paul Laverty, Stephane Hessel, Jean Ziegler, Raji Sourani, Leila Shahid, Nurit Peled and the late Ken Coates explained to an audience composed mainly of local and international press, as well as various European political figures, why the Russell Tribunal on Palestine was needed and why such a tribunal could, by its nature, have a very powerful and lasting impact on public opinion.[7]

---

[5] http://www.vietnamese-american.org/contents.html

[6] http://www.internazionaleleliobasso.it/

[7] http://www.dailymotion.com/RussellTribunalPalestine#videoId=xc3xp8

The RToP proceedings, which comprise a number of sessions, deal with different aspects of the complicity and responsibilities of states, international organizations and corporations in the ongoing occupation of Palestinian territories by Israel and the perpetuation of the violations of international law committed by Israel. They also aim to highlight the continuity and comprehensiveness of Israeli policies that appear to have the ultimate aim of preventing the exercise of Palestinian self-determination. The Tribunal is also interested in empowering civil society and reinforcing the work of already existing campaigns by providing additional legal arguments and ideas that will assist in future litigation and legal lobbying. Most people outside the region do not realize the profound domestic legal consequences of the Israel–Palestine conflict. By actively providing Israel with financial, political, military and even moral support, Governments as well as international organizations and corporations, simply make the resolution of this conflict impossible. They are deeply involved in the fact that, over six decades since it was raised, the Palestine question is still waiting for an answer.

As one of its founders explained: "the legality of the Russell Tribunal comes from both its absolute powerlessness and its universality."[8] Thus, although the RToP has no legal status, and draws its strength from the will of citizens who wish to put an end to the impunity that Israel enjoys, while denying the Palestinians their most basic rights, it fulfills a real legal function by promoting and stimulating the implementation of the rule of law. It does not compete with other jurisdictions (domestic or international), but works in complementarity with them to enforce the law in Palestine.

Members of the International Support Committee of the RToP include Nobel Prize laureates, a former United Nations Secretary-General, two former Heads of State, other personalities who have held high political office and representatives of civil society, such as writers, journalists, poets, actors, film directors, scientists, professors, lawyers and judges.[9] The jury of the RToP is composed of international personalities known for their stand against injustice and their moral integrity.[10]

---

[8] Jean-Paul Sartre, Inaugural Statement at the Russell Tribunal on Vietnam, 1967.

[9] http://www.russelltribunalonpalestine.com/en/about-rtop/patrons

[10] Stephane Hessel, Secretary of the Committee that drafted the UN Universal Declaration of Human Rights 1948, is the honorary President of the RToP. Jury members include Mairead Corrigan Maguire, Nobel Peace laureate 1976, Northern Ireland; John Dugard, Professor of International law, UN Special Rapporteur on the Situation of Human Rights in Palestinian Territories occupied since 1967 (2001–2008), South Africa; Lord Anthony Gifford, senior barrister and hereditary peer, United Kingdom; Gisèle Halimi, lawyer, former Ambassador to UNESCO, France; Ronald Kasrils writer and activist, South Africa; Michael Mansfield, barrister, President of the Haldane Society of Socialist Lawyers, United Kingdom; José Antonio Martin Pallin, emeritus Judge, Chamber II, Supreme Court, Spain; Cynthia McKinney, former member of the US Congress and 2008 presidential candidate, Green Party, USA; Alberto San Juan, actor, Spain; Aminata Traoré, author and former Minister of Culture of Mali and Alice Walker, author and activist, USA.

16.3 The First International Session of the Russell Tribunal on Palestine

On 1–3 March 2010, the first international session of the RToP took place in Barcelona.[11] The jury heard evidence about the complicity and responsibility of the European Union and its Member States in the ongoing occupation of Palestinian territories by Israel and the perpetuation of the violations of international law by Israel, with complete impunity.

Barcelona was chosen ahead of other cities for its importance in EU affairs in regard to the Israel–Palestine question. In 1995, the "Barcelona process" and Euro-Arab economic relations was established.[12] This agreement was signed by all Mediterranean countries, including Israel and Palestine. One clause acknowledged that an essential element of the agreement was the respect for human rights by all parties. At the time of the first RToP session, Spain was also the President of the European Union.

Prior to considering the relations of the European Union and its Member States with Israel, the Tribunal made findings in relation to a number of violations of international law by Israel. Israel's absence from the proceedings was not deemed an impediment to the admissibility of the expert reports on those violations. In making these findings regarding violations of international law allegedly committed by a state that was not represented before the Tribunal, the Tribunal was not breaching the rule of mutual agreement among the parties that is applicable before international judicial bodies responsible for the settlement of disputes between states (see the Monetary Gold and East Timor cases, ICJ Reports, 1954 and 1995).[13] The work of the RToP is not comparable to that involved in a dispute referred, for instance, to the International Court of Justice: the facts presented as violations of international law committed by Israel in the Occupied Palestinian Territories have been characterized as such by the United Nations General Assembly and the Security Council, and also by a number of reports such as those of the Special Committee to Investigate Israeli Practices Affecting the Human Rights of the Palestinian People and Other Arabs of the Occupied Territories. Hence, the Tribunal began its work by simply drawing attention to circumstances that were already widely recognized by the international community.

Testimonies presented in Barcelona over two days by 21 experts and witnesses concerned, *inter alia*, the right to self-determination of the Palestinian people; the closure of the Gaza Strip and the operation "Cast Lead"; the illegal settlements and the plundering of natural resources; the annexation of East Jerusalem; the Wall

---

[11] http://www.russelltribunalonpalestine.com/en/sessions/barcelona-session

[12] http://meria.idc.ac.il/journal/2005/issue2/jv9no2a6.html

[13] Case of the Monetary Gold Removed from Rome in 1943 (Preliminary Question), Judgment of June 1954: I.C.J. Reports 1954, p. 19, at http://www.icj-cij.org/docket/files/19/4761.pdf; and East Timor (Portugal v. Australia), Judgment, I.C.J. Reports 1995, p. 90, at http://www.icj-cij.org/docket/files/84/6949.pdf.

built in occupied Palestinian territory and the EU-Israel Association Agreement and military cooperation.

After its deliberations, the jury published its conclusions initially at an international press conference.[14] As indicated above, the preliminary task of the jury was to reach findings about Israel's violations of international law, which it did at para 19 of its findings by reference to the following conduct:

19.1 By maintaining a form of domination and subjugation over the Palestinians that prevents them from freely determining their political status, Israel violates the right of the Palestinian people to self-determination inasmuch as it is unable to exercise its sovereignty on the territory which belongs to it; this violates the Declaration on the granting of independence to colonial countries and peoples (A/Res. 1514(XV), 14 Dec. 1960) and all UN General Assembly resolutions that have reaffirmed the right of the Palestinian people to self-determination since 1969 (A/Res. 2535 B(XXIV), 10 Dec. 1969, and, inter alia, A/Res. 3236 (XXIX), 22 Nov. 1974, 52/114, 12 Dec. 1997, etc.);

19.2 By occupying Palestinian territories since June 1967 and refusing to leave them, Israel violates the Security Council resolutions that demand its withdrawal from the territories concerned (SC/Res. 242, 22 Nov. 1967; 338, 22 Oct. 1973);

19.3 By pursuing a policy of systematic discrimination against Palestinians present in Israeli territory or in the occupied territories, Israel commits acts that may be characterized as apartheid; these acts include the following:

- closure of the borders of the Gaza Strip and restrictions on the freedom of movement of its inhabitants;
- prevention of the return of Palestinian refugees to their home or land of origin;
- prohibition on the free use by Palestinians of certain natural resources such as the watercourses within their land;

19.4 Given the discriminatory nature of these measures, since they are based, *inter alia*, on the nationality of the persons to whom they are applied, the Tribunal finds that they present features comparable to apartheid, even though they do not emanate from an identical political regime to that prevailing in South Africa prior to 1994; these measures are characterized as criminal acts by the Convention on the Suppression and Punishment of the Crime of Apartheid of 18 July 1976 which, though it is not binding on Israel, does not exonerate Israel in that regard;

19.5 By annexing Jerusalem in July 1980 and maintaining the annexation, Israel violates the prohibition of the acquisition of territory by force, as stated by the Security Council (SC/Res. 478, 20 August 1980);

---

[14] http://www.russelltribunalonpalestine.com/en/sessions/barcelona-session/findings

19.6 By constructing a Wall in the West Bank on Palestinian territory that it occupies, Israel denies the Palestinians access to their own land, violates their property rights and seriously restricts the freedom of movement of the Palestinian population, thereby violating Article 12 of the International Covenant on Civil and Political Rights to which Israel has been a party since 3 October 1991; the illegality of the construction of the Wall was confirmed by the International Court of Justice in its Advisory Opinion of 9 July 2004, which was endorsed by the UN General Assembly in its Resolution ES-10/15;

19.7 By systematically building settlements in Jerusalem and the West Bank, Israel breaches the rules of international humanitarian law governing occupation, in particular Article 49 of the Fourth Geneva Convention of 12 August 1949, by which Israel has been bound since 6 July 1951. This point was noted by the International Court of Justice in the above-mentioned Advisory Opinion;

19.8 By pursuing a policy of targeted killings against Palestinians whom it describes as "terrorists" without first attempting to arrest them, Israel violates the right to life of the persons concerned, a right enshrined in Article 6 of the International Covenant on Civil and Political Rights;

19.9 By maintaining a blockade on the Gaza Strip in breach of the provisions of the Fourth Geneva Convention of 12 August 1949 (Article 33), which prohibits collective punishment;

19.10 By inflicting extensive and serious damage, especially on persons and civilian property, and by using prohibited methods of combat during operation "Cast Lead" in Gaza (December 2008–January 2009).

The jury also found that, even though the European Union and its Member States were not the direct perpetrators of these acts, they nevertheless violate international law, either by failing to take the measures that Israel's conduct requires them to take, or by contributing directly or indirectly to such conduct. Moreover, the jury found that the European Union and its Member States do not comply with the relevant provisions of its own constitution, which confirms the attachment of the European Union to fundamental rights and freedoms, states its willingness to uphold and promote the respect of international law and take appropriate initiatives to that end (European Union Lisbon Treaty, Preamble, Articles 2, 3, 17 and 21). Further, at para 34 of its findings, the jury made the following calls:

(i) The European Union and its Member States to fulfill their obligations forthwith by putting an end to the wrongful acts committed by Israel;

(ii) The European Union, in particular, to implement the European Parliament's resolution calling for the suspension of the EU-Israel Association Agreement, thereby putting an end to the context of irresponsibility that Israel continues to enjoy;[15]

---

[15] For an elaboration on this point see the next paragraph.

(iii) European Union Member States to implement the recommendations set out in para 1975 (a) of the UN Fact-Finding Mission Report on the Gaza Conflict (Goldstone Report) regarding the collection of evidence and the exercise of universal jurisdiction in respect of the crimes attributed to Israeli and Palestinian suspects;

(iv) European Union Member States to repeal any restriction under domestic law that would impede compliance with the duty to prosecute or extradite (*judicare vel dedere*) any alleged perpetrator of a war crime or a crime against humanity;

(v) European Union Member States to strengthen mutual legal assistance and cooperation in criminal matters through the EU contact points, EUROPOL, INTERPOL, etc.;

(vi) European Union Member States to refrain from limiting the scope of universal jurisdiction so as to ensure that no EU Member State becomes a safe haven for suspected perpetrators of war crimes or crimes against humanity;

(vii) The Parliaments of Austria, France, Greece and Italy to enact laws which, in conformity with Article 146 of the Fourth Geneva Convention, would facilitate the exercise of universal jurisdiction in those states;

(viii) individuals, groups and organizations to take all necessary measures to secure compliance by the European Union and its Member States with their aforementioned obligations including, in particular, the exercise of universal jurisdiction in civil and criminal matters against any alleged perpetrator—an individual or a state agent—of a war crime or a crime against humanity;

(ix) the existing legal actions in the context of the Boycott, Divestment and Sanctions campaign (BDS) to be stepped up and expanded within the European Union.

The RToP went on to call on the European Union and on each of its Member States to impose the necessary sanctions on its partner—Israel—through diplomatic, trade and cultural measures in order to end the impunity that it has enjoyed for decades. Should the European Union and its Member States lack the necessary courage to do so, the Tribunal called on the citizens of Europe to bring the necessary pressure to bear on the EU by all appropriate means.

16.4 The Call for the Suspension of the EU-Israel Association Agreement

Of particular importance among the findings of the Barcelona Session is the call to suspend the EU-Israel Association Agreement. According to Article 3 of the Treaty on European Union, in its relations with third parties, the EU shall contribute to the protection of human rights and the observance of international law. Since 1995 the European Commission has formalized a policy of including human rights and democracy clauses in all agreements with other countries. These clauses aim both at encouraging third states to respect human rights and at ensuring that the EU does not contribute to any violations of its core principles and values when setting economic policies with other countries.[16]

To this aim, Article 2 of the EU-Israel Association Agreement states that:

"Relations between the Parties, as well as the provision of the Agreement itself, shall be based on respect for human rights and democratic principles, which guides their internal and international policy and constitutes an essential element of this Agreement."

Therefore, respect for human rights and democratic principles constitute an 'essential element' of this agreement, which has definite legal consequences; the violation of an essential element of a treaty is in fact a ground for suspending the operation of the treaty in whole or in part.[17]

This legal consequence is reinforced by the terms of Article 79(2) of the same Agreement, which stipulates that "If either Party considers that the other Party has failed to fulfill an obligation under the Agreement, it may take appropriate measures", including the suspension of the agreement. It is for the High Representative of the Union for Foreign Affairs and Security Policy to propose the suspension of an association agreement pursuant to Article 218(9) of the Treaty on European Union.[18]

It is notable that, even during the ratification process of the EU-Israel Agreement, several national Parliaments raised doubts regarding Israel's commitment to the respect of human rights, which led to a delayed entry into force of the agreement itself.[19]

However, and notwithstanding the increased level of violations of human rights and humanitarian law committed by Israel in the last years, the EU has consistently adopted a position of 'quiet diplomacy' in response to Israel's persistent violations of international law.[20]

As Palestinian human rights organizations have clearly pointed out, 10 years after the EU-Israel Association Agreement entered into force, it is apparent that this approach has failed.[21] A new approach firmly grounded in the rule of

---

[16] Directorate-General for External Policies of the Union, *Human Rights and Democracy Clauses in the EU's International Agreements*, DGExPo/B/PolDep/Study/2005/06, 29.09.2005.

[17] Article 60(3)(a), Vienna Convention on the Law of Treaties, Vienna, 23 May 1969, United Nations *Treaty Series* vol. 1155, p. 331.

[18] See PCHR 2010

[19] The British government, for instance, stated that "assent to the EU-Israel Association Agreement did not imply acceptance by the Government of by Parliament of Israel's current standard of human rights practice, nor indeed of Israel's conduct under certain key provisions of the existing EU-Israel Interim Agreement on trade-related matters." See V. Miller 2004

[20] "The EU and the Middle East Peace Process", 2002.

[21] See PCHR Open Letter 2010.

international law is required, in keeping with the EU's own obligations, specifically Article 21(3) of the Treaty of European Union. As the Tribunal indicated, by its inaction, and specifically by failing to suspend the EU-Israel Association Agreement, the EU also becomes complicit in Israel's policy of disregard for fundamental human rights and its violations of international law.

16.5 The Second International Session of the Russell Tribunal on Palestine

The second international session of the RToP took place in London, on 20–22 November 2010.[22] It examined corporate complicity in Israel's violations of international human rights law and international humanitarian law.

During this session, some 30 experts and witnesses gave detailed presentations on the conduct of different corporations involved in assisting in some way in Israel's occupation and colonization of Palestinian territories. The evidence set out how corporations had been acting illegally, and showed how states and international organizations could and should be held accountable for such conduct, providing the legal space for those actions to take place. In London, the jury focused on the following three questions:

1. Which Israeli violations of international law are corporations complicit in?
2. What are the legal consequences of the activities of corporations that aid and abet Israeli violations?
3. What are the remedies available and what are the obligations of states in relation to corporate complicity?

The corporations that came under the spotlight (i.e. Veolia, Cement Roadstone Holdings, Ahava, Dexia, EDO ITT, Caterpillar, G4S, Elbit Systems, Agrexco, Soda Stream and the pension fund PFZW) were invited to submit their views. Only Veolia, PFZW and G4S replied to their invitation letters, which were presented to the jury for consideration as part of the jury's deliberations.

The jury concluded that the corporations in question were complicit in Israeli violations of international law, including war crimes.[23] Corporations may therefore be liable under civil or criminal law in domestic law courts, and corporate actors may be liable under international criminal law and/or under domestic criminal law if they have taken decisions as a result of which corporations have become involved in assisting Israel's violations of international law. States have an obligation to enforce existing law against corporations where they are acting in violation of international human rights and humanitarian law standards. The Tribunal

---

[22] http://www.russelltribunalonpalestine.com/en/sessions/london-session.

[23] http://www.russelltribunalonpalestine.com/en/sessions/london-session/findings.

also called upon individuals, groups and organizations to take all necessary measures to secure compliance of corporations with international human rights and humanitarian law standards.

The RToP London findings are likely to form not only the basis of legal advocacy for years to come, but also legal briefs to 'national contact points' within the OECD system and litigation against some of the named corporations. This likelihood arises because of the increase in corporate accountability for human rights abuses, exemplified by a number of recent cases and the sharing of legal information about such cases, assisted by resources such as those of the Business and Human Rights Resource Centre.[24]

16.6 Corporate Liability for Complicity in International Law Violations

There are several precedents regarding corporate liability for complicity in serious violations of international law, and particularly of human rights law, which were established in the past few years. Key litigation includes several US cases. For example, in a very recent decision in a case brought by 15 Indonesian citizens against the US corporation ExxonMobil for alleged complicity in abuses by the Indonesian security forces in Aceh, on 8 July 2011 the US Court of Appeals for the District of Columbia Circuit handed down a landmark ruling.[25] The Court held that the claimants had alleged sufficient facts to prove ExxonMobil was guilty of aiding and abetting and that "neither the text, history, nor purpose of the Alien Tort Statute (ATS) supports corporate immunity for torts based on heinous conduct allegedly committed by its agents in violation of the law of nations." Indeed, during 2011 US federal courts have allowed at least two other major civil claims to proceed, involving alleged violations of the ATS and Torture Victims Protection Act (TVPA) for violence overseas by paramilitary troops hired by US corporations.[26] The scene is therefore set for the US Supreme Court to rule on some of the

---

[24] http://www.reports-and-materials.org/Press-release-Legal-Accountability-Portal-29-Oct-2008.pdf

[25] http://www.cadc.uscourts.gov/internet/opinions.nsf/ 567B411C56CD7A6F852578C700513FC8/$file/09-7125-1317431.pdf. The claimants allege that ExxonMobil's wholly owned subsidiary hired Indonesian military as security forces that committed numerous human rights abuses including genocide, extrajudicial killing, torture, crimes against humanity, sexual violence and kidnapping in violation of the Alien Torture Statute (ATS) [28 USC § 1350] and the Torture Victims Protection Act 1991.

[26] In June 2011, a judge for the US District Court for the Southern District of Florida permitted lawsuits under the ATS and TVPA against Chiquita Brand International to move forward. Family members of several thousand victims of paramilitary violence in Colombia brought the claim against Chiquita Brand International, which admitted funding United Self-Defense Forces of Colombia (AUC), a right-wing paramilitary group in Colombia, see http://www.flsd.uscourts.gov/wp-content/uploads/2011/06/008md01916_412.pdf; and (2) in May 2011, the US Court of Appeals for the Ninth Circuit allowed a claim to proceed that was brought by Argentine

issues raised by these raft of ATS and TVPA cases when it considers the appeal of the claimants in *Kiobel* v. *Royal Dutch Petroleum*, where in September 2010 the Second Circuit Appeals Court became the first federal court to rule that ATS does not apply at all to corporations, but only to individuals.[27] Meanwhile, Yahoo has been the subject of several claims brought by Chinese dissidents regarding assistance allegedly provided by it to the Chinese authorities.[28] There are also several claims against corporations being brought across several European countries. For example, a notorious successful claim was brought in the UK arising from events that occurred in August 2006, when the ship Probo Koala unloaded a waste shipment at Abidjan, Côte d'Ivoire, disposing it in open air sites around Abidjan. The ship that dumped this toxic waste, which killed 16 people and caused illness to many thousand local residents (e.g. a range of short-term low-level flu-like symptoms and anxiety), was chartered by the London office of Trafigura, a Dutch international petroleum trader. The claims brought by the victims in a class action in the UK were settled in September 2009.[29] In France, there is pending litigation against Veolia and Alstom for their involvement in the construction of the Jerusalem Light Railway which links communities inside the Green Line with illegal Israeli settlements inside East Jerusalem. In May 2011 the Nanterre High Court ruled against the claimants, the Association France Palestine Solidarity (AFPS), but on preliminary legal issues that did not consider the alleged aiding and abetting of Israeli violations of international humanitarian law.[30] AFPS have therefore lodged an appeal to the Versailles Court of Appeal, which will consider the issues afresh, probably in 2012.[31] Scope also exists for legal action

---

(Footnote 26 continued)
citizens against Daimler AG for the actions of Mercedes-Benz Argentina during the nation's 1976–1983 "Dirty War". The claim, originally dismissed by the US District Court for the Northern District of California in 2005 due to a lack of jurisdiction, alleges that Mercedes-Benz Argentina "collaborated with state security forces to kidnap, detain, torture, and kill the plaintiffs and/or their relatives." See http://www.ca9.uscourts.gov/datastore/opinions/2011/05/18/07-15386.pdf.

[27] http://www.law.smu.edu/getmedia/4c249363-9801-4193-876a-c5600aafa903/Kiobel-v-Royal-Dutch-Petroleum-Co. The claimants in Kiobel, residents of the Ogoni Region of Nigeria, allege that Royal Dutch Petroleum Company and Shell Transport and Trading Company PLC, through a subsidiary named Shell Petroleum Development Company of Nigeria, Ltd, aided and abetted the Nigerian government in committing human rights abuses. The U.S. Supreme Court will begin considering the petition to appeal the ruling in October 2011—http://conflictoflaws.net/2011/new-alien-tort-statute-case-at-the-united-states-supreme-court-kiobel-etal-v-royal-dutch-petroleum-petition-filed/.

[28] http://www.pcworld.com/article/142963/yahoo_sued_again_by_chinese_dissidents.html.

[29] http://www.trafigura.com/pdf/Official%20Transcript%20of%20Judge%20MacDuff%20hearing,%2023%20September%202009.PDF.

[30] http://www.veolia.com/veolia/ressources/documents/1/9907,Translation-TGI-de-Nanterre-Judgeme.pdf; and see http://electronicintifada.net/content/french-court-decision-jerusalem-light-rail-must-be-challenged/10115.

[31] http://www.france-palestine.org

in Israel against Israeli corporations that are complicit in Israeli human rights violations.[32]

The issue of criminal accountability for corporate complicity in human rights violations is more complicated than civil liability. The application of international criminal law to corporate actors and corporations raises particularly difficult legal issues. Attempts to establish corporate criminal complicity in human rights violations date back to the German corporate defendants at the Nuremberg trials after the Second World War. Current test cases include a criminal complaint lodged in France in November 2009 against Dalhoff, Larsen and Horneman (DLH) by four NGOs and a Liberian activist, who allege that during the Liberian civil war, from 2002 to 2003, DLH bought timber from Liberian companies that provided support to Charles Taylor's regime and that were named in UN reports as committing gross human rights violations. The complainants alleged that the French arm of DLH is guilty of 'recel'—the handling of and profiting from goods obtained illegally, punishable under French criminal law.[33]

Finally, legal lobbying and litigation against corporations can combine to achieve accountability. For example, residents of the Indian town of Plachimada have long claimed that the activities of Coca-Cola's Indian subsidiary had resulted in water scarcity and environmental pollution. These residents brought a civil claim in 2003 against Hindustan Coca-Cola Beverage, and their appeal of a dismissal of the case has been pending before the Indian Supreme Court since November 2005. However, in February 2011 the Kerala State Assembly passed a bill establishing a three-member tribunal to hear compensation claims from individuals alleging they were harmed by that company.[34]

16.7 The Third International Session of the Russell Tribunal on Palestine

The third international session of the RToP will take place in November 2011 in South Africa. It will hear evidence about Israeli actions indicating the alleged commission of the crime of apartheid with regard to the treatment of the Palestinians in the OPT and, in a different factual context, in Israel itself.

Experts and witnesses from all over the world are invited to testify in front of the tribunal. The jury will reach findings in particular on whether or not Israel's

---

[32] See: http://harvardhrj.com/2011/07/corporate-accountability-to-human-rights-the-case-of-the-gaza-strip/.

[33] http://www.globalwitness.org/library/international-timber-company-dlh-accused-funding-liberian-war

[34] http://www.business-humanrights.org/Categories/Lawlawsuits/Lawsuitsregulatoryaction/LawsuitsSelectedcases/Coca-ColalawsuitreIndia

practices in Israel and the OPT amount to (i) a breach of the prohibition against apartheid; and/or (ii) persecution (a crime against humanity, as set out in the Rome Statute of the International Criminal Court).

As with previous sessions, any adverse findings are likely to form an authoritative basis for legal advocacy in seeking changes to the conduct of states toward Israel, with the potential for the evidence and/or the findings to stimulate litigation challenging aspects of state complicity with Israeli violations.

16.8 Russell Tribunal on Palestine: An Enduring Legacy

The Russell Tribunal on Palestine is an expression of the strong demand coming from globalized civil society that their governments are more accountable and committed in ensuring that democracy, the rule of law, and the fundamental human rights of people are respected in every part of the world. The 'Arab Spring' of 2011, with the various uprisings that are taking place in the Middle East, have proven that people are resolute, driven and will not remain silent when confronted with terrible repression by 'their' governments. The fairly surprising popular revolutions in Tunisia and Egypt, in particular, mark a new dawn in world politics. Popular actions have seriously challenged authoritarian governments, delegitimizing them in front of the entire world, which has also had a profound impact on western societies and western governments.

Although adopting different means, it can be said that the Russell Tribunal on Palestine, a People's tribunal founded on humanist and internationalist principles, is part of this movement of resistance, directly led by the people, for the people. In the end, the legacy and most significant achievement of the Russell Tribunal is represented by its very detailed findings, which are soundly grounded in international law, will provide everyone with an additional tool to demand that our governments, institutions and other actors, including corporations, stop being complicit in the international law and human rights violations perpetrated by Israel against the Palestinian people.

The Russell Tribunal on Palestine, like its predecessors, is history in the making: peoples' history.

References

European Union (2002) The EU and the Middle East Peace Process. http://europa.eu.int/comm/external_relations/mepp/faq/index.htm#6

Miller V (2004) The Human Rights Clause in the EU's External Agreements, House of Commons Library, 16 April 2004. www.parliament.uk

PCHR (2010) Open Letter to the High Representative of the European Union for Foreign Affairs and Security Policy, Baroness Ashton. www.pchrgaza.org, under Publications/Interventions

Sartre J-P (1967) Inaugural Statement at the Russell Tribunal on Vietnam. http://www.vietnamese-american.org/a1.html

The complete documentation of the Russell Tribunal can be found at: http://www.russelltribunalonpalestine.com/en/

Annex to Chapter 16

RESPONSIBILITY OF THE EUROPEAN UNION,
ITS MEMBER STATES AND CORPORATIONS IN THE ONGOING
OCCUPATION OF PALESTINIAN TERRITORIES

PROVIDING ILLEGAL ASSISTANCE TO ISRAEL ?

Executive summaries of the findings of the international sessions of the Russell Tribunal
on Palestine organised in Barcelona in March 2010 and in London in November 2010

Table of contents

List of abbreviations and acronyms	2
Preface by Stéphane Hessel, Honorary President of the RToP	3
Introduction by Pierre Galand, General Coordinator of the RToP	4

OBJECTIVES AND FUNCTIONING
OF THE RUSSELL TRIBUNAL ON PALESTINE

organisation of the sessions	5
The mandate of the RToP	6
Procedure	6
Admissibility	7
Jury members	7
Findings of the jury	7

FIRST INTERNATIONAL SESSION
OF THE RUSSELL TRIBUNAL ON PALESTINE

programme	9
Executive summary of the findings of the first session of the RToP	11
A. Violations of international law committed by Israel	11
B. Breaches by the EU and its member states of certain specific rules of international law	12
C. Breaches by the EU and its member states of certain general rules of international law	14
D. Failure by the EU and its member states to take measures against the violations of international law committed by Israel and to identify what remedies may be available	16
E. Findings of the jury	18

SECOND INTERNATIONAL SESSION
OF THE RUSSELL TRIBUNAL ON PALESTINE

programme	21
Executive summary of the findings of the first session of the RToP	23
A. Which Israeli violations of international law are corporations complicit in?	23
B. What are the legal consequences of the activities of corporations that aid and abet Israeli violations?	24
C. What are the remedies available and what are the obligations of states in relation to corporate complicity?	29
D. Findings of the jury	33

Russell Tribunal on Palestine
115 Stévin Street
1000 Brussels
Email : trp_int@yahoo.com
Website : **www.russelltribunalonpalestine.com**

Responsible publisher : Pierre Galand - layout : www.loasis-studio.com - cover photo : José Sanchez (imagenenaccion.org)
The Russell Tribunal on Palestine permits free reproduction of extracts from this publication provided that due acknowledgement is given.

List of abbreviations and acronyms

AP	Additional Protocol
AECA	Arms Export Control Act
ATCA	Aliens Tort Claims Act
BDS	Boycott, Divestment and Sanctions
CJEC	Court of Justice of the European Communities
ECHR	European Court of Human Rights
EU	European Union
GC(s)	Geneva Convention(s)
GDP	gross domestic product
Guidelines	OECD Guidelines for Multinational Enterprises
ICC	International Criminal Court
ICCA	International Criminal Court Act
ICJ	International Court of Justice
ICTY	International Criminal Tribunal for the Former Yugoslavia
IDF	Israel Defense Forces
IHL	international humanitarian law
IHRL	international human rights law
ILC	International Law Commission
IOC	International Organising Committee
NCP	OECD National Contact Point specific to each country.
OECD	Organisation for Economic Co-operation and Development
OPT	Occupied Palestinian Territory
PA	Palestinian Authority
Res.	Resolution
RICO	Racketeer Influenced and Corrupt Organizations Act
Rome Statute	Rome Statute of the International Criminal Court, 17 July 1998
RToP	Russell Tribunal on Palestine
The Norms	Norms on the Responsibilities of Transnational Corporations and Other Business Enterprises with Regard to Human Rights, 2002
TVPA	Torture Victims Protection Act
UNSC	United Nations Secretary-General
UNGA	United Nations General Assembly

Preface

Since the creation of the State of Israel, which I witnessed while at the United Nations in New York, the need to find a solution to the Palestinian issue, as a prerequisite for the survival and prosperity of that State, has seemed obvious to me.

Unfortunately, after the Israeli victories in the Six-Day War and the Yom Kippur War, Israeli governments have failed to comprehend that need and have pursued a policy that is in breach of international law, a policy of occupation of territories to which they have no title and of colonisation of the territories concerned.

Israel's European and American partners have failed to compel Israeli leaders to pursue a policy of genuine negotiations with the Palestinians that would have led to a just solution. It has therefore proved necessary to mobilise citizens of good will to highlight the failures of the past forty years and to call for decisive action.

Forty-five years ago, a people's tribunal that assumed the name of the great humanist Bertrand Russell was convened to call on the United States to withdraw from Vietnam. It seemed appropriate to apply the experience thus gained to a similar situation in which the voice of enlightened public opinion could be brought to bear on the real culprits: the Israelis, but also the Europeans, the Americans, and corporations that permit the inalienable rights of the Palestinians to be violated.

I perceive the influence of this new Tribunal, especially vis-à-vis the media, as a modest, sincere and resolute contribution to a process which is equally necessary for the Israeli and the Palestinian people, namely progress towards the harmonious coexistence of two peoples whose future will necessarily be shared.

Stéphane Hessel
Honorary President of the Russell Tribunal on Palestine

ANDREAS VAN AGT • GILBERT ACHCAR • TARIQ ALI • HENRI ALLEG • MARTIN ALMADA • KADER ASMAL (†)

Introduction

On 9 July 2004, the International Court of Justice rendered an opinion on the legal consequences of the Wall in the Palestinian territories occupied by Israel. The opinion was adopted a few days later by the United Nations General Assembly by 150 votes in favour, 6 against and 10 abstentions. The votes in favour included all countries of the European Union.

Campaigners for the Palestinian people's inalienable right to self-determination welcomed this opinion and the subsequent resolution as a turning point: the violations of international law committed by Israel were clearly identified, Israel was asked to comply with its legal obligations, and UN member states undertook to ensure that the resolution would be implemented by Israel. It was a great breakthrough, and things were bound to change.

Three years later, we noted with disappointment that this was not the case. Israel had proceeded with its colonisation, the construction of the Wall, deportations and imprisonment, and had begun to impose a blockade on the Gaza Strip while benefiting from political, financial, military and strategic support from the United States, the European Union, multinational corporations and many others. To make matters worse, the Israeli government launched operation "Cast Lead" on the Gaza Strip in winter 2008, causing more than 1,300 fatalities and wreaking massive destruction that has not yet been repaired owing to the continuing blockade.

It was no longer enough simply to condemn Israeli abuses. The time had come to focus in addition on the responsibilities of other international state and non-state actors that allow Israel to continue violating international law with absolute impunity. Highlighting the role played by different actors in this drama would also pave the way for a broad mobilisation to bring an end to the injustice suffered by an entire people.

An international organising committee was established with broad support from major international figures, and on 4 March 2009 we decided to launch, with the support of the Bertrand Russell Peace Foundation, a new citizen's court called the Russell Tribunal on Palestine (RToP). Since then we have held two international sessions in 2010 in Barcelona and London on the complicity and omissions of the European Union and of multinational corporations. They have been widely reported and their findings, which are summarised in this publication, provide a legally grounded body of arguments that may be invoked by all those militating for the primacy of international law and for respect for the rights of the Palestinian people.

Pierre Galand
General Coordinator of the Russell Tribunal on Palestine

ALAA AL ASWANY • RAYMOND AUBRAC • LUCIE AUBRAC (†) • AGNÈS B • BOUTROS BOUTROS-GHALI

Objectives and functionning of the RToP

The Russell Tribunal on Palestine (RToP) is an international people's tribunal created as a result of inaction by the international community in relation to proven violations of international law committed by Israel.[1]

The RToP proceedings, which comprise a number of sessions, deal with different aspects of the complicity and responsibilities of states, international organisations and corporations in the ongoing occupation of Palestinian territories by Israel and the continuous violations of international law committed by Israel. They also aim to highlight the continuity and comprehensiveness of the Israeli policy that aims ultimately to render impossible the establishment of a Palestinian state.

"The legality of the Russell Tribunal comes from both its absolute powerlessness and its universality."[2] The RToP has no legal status, and draws its strength from the will of citizens who wish to put an end to the impunity that Israel enjoys while denying the Palestinians their most basic rights. It does not compete with other jurisdictions (domestic or international), but works on a complementary basis to enforce the law in the Israeli-Palestinian conflict.

The eminence of the RToP stems from its extensive International Support Committee, which includes Nobel Prize laureates, a former United Nations Secretary-General, two former Heads of State, other personalities who have held high political office, and representatives of civil society, writers, journalists, poets, actors, film directors, scientists, professors, lawyers and judges (see the list on the Tribunal website: www.russelltribunalonpalestine.com).

The RToP is supported by numerous contributions from individuals, associations, organisations and solidarity movements, some of whom are organised as National Support Committees (Belgium, Catalonia, France, Germany, Ireland, Italy, Luxembourg, Netherlands, Portugal, South Africa and the United Kingdom). The independence of the RToP is guaranteed by the diversity and scale of the voluntary material and financial assistance it receives.

Organisation of the sessions

The first international session of the RToP was organised in Barcelona from 1 to 3 march 2010 to consider the **complicity and omissions of the European Union and its Member States** in the ongoing occupation of Palestinian territories by Israel and the continuous violations of international law by Israel.

The second international session of the RToP was held in London from 20 to 22 November 2010. It examined **international corporate complicity** in Israel's violations of international human rights law and international humanitarian law.

The third international session of the RToP will be held from 5 to 7 November 2011 in South Africa. It will deal with the following question: " **is the crime of apartheid applicable to Israel? Consequences** ".

1. An International Organising Committee, chaired by Stéphane Hessel, Ambassadeur of France, and composed of Pierre Galand, Marcel-Francis Kahn, Robert Kissous, François Maspero, Paulette Pierson-Mathy, Bernard Ravenel, Brahim Senouci and the late Ken Koates, is in charge of the overall management of the RToP. An office based in Brussels ensures general coordination. It is run by Pierre Galand with the assistance of Frank Barat and Virginie Vanhaeverbeke.
2. Jean-Paul Sartre, Inaugural Statement at the Russell Tribunal on Vietnam, 1967.

The fourth international session of the RToP to be held in 2012 in New York will consider the **complicity and omissions of the United Nations and the United States of America** in the ongoing occupation of Palestinian territories by Israel and the continuous violations of the rights of the Palestinian people by Israel.

The sessions are always followed by a solemn sitting during which the jury announces the findings of the RToP.

The mandate of the RToP

The RToP takes it as an established fact that some aspects of Israel's behaviour have been characterised as violations of international law by a number of international bodies, including the Security Council, the United Nations General Assembly (UNGA) and the International Court of Justice (ICJ).

The question referred to the jury of the RToP by the International Organising Committee at the Barcelona session was whether the relations of the EU and its member states with Israel could be characterised as wrongful acts within the meaning of international law and, if so, what the practical implications were and what means could be used to remedy them.

The question submitted to the jury of the RToP by the International Organising Committee at the London session was whether the relations of certain corporations with Israel could be deemed to constitute assistance for such violations of international law and, if so, whether it followed that the relations themselves were illegal under international law and under the domestic law of states. If they were, what were the practical consequences of those findings and what action should be taken thereon?

Procedure

The IOC submitted the aforementioned questions to experts who were selected on the basis of their familiarity with the facts of the situation. With a view to respecting the adversarial principle, the questions were also submitted to states, corporations, and natural or legal persons who had been charged by the Tribunal so that they could express their opinion. Experts submitted written reports to the RToP.

At the Barcelona session Mr. Barroso, the President of the European Commission, wrote a letter to the RToP which arrived during the session. President Barroso referred to the conclusions adopted by the Council of Ministers of Foreign Affairs on 8 December 2009. Only one member state of the EU responded to the RToP's request. In a letter dated 15 February 2010, Germany drew attention, as President Barroso had done (see above), to the Council conclusions of December 2009.

At the London session, the following corporations and institutions responded to the RToP: Olivier Orsini, General Secretary of Veolia Environment, letter dated 8 November 2010; Hans Alders, Chairman of the Board of Stichting Pensioenfonds Zorg en Welzijn (PFZW), letter dated 12 November 2010; Ilkka Uusitalo, Head of Unit of the EU Directorate on the Middle East, Southern Mediterranean and Near East, letter dated 12 November 2010 and written on behalf of European Commission President Barroso; Michael Clarke, Public Affairs Director of G4S plc, electronic mail dated 18 November 2010.

The RToP took these letters into consideration as well as any other manifestations of cooperation on the part of the accused. It regrets the fact that the EU, its member states and the corporations that were charged proved reticent in presenting their arguments concerning the issues that were addressed at the first two sessions and that the RToP was unable to benefit from the assistance that their arguments and supporting evidence might have provided.

The written stage of the proceedings is followed by an oral stage during which members of the RToP hear statements by experts.

Annex to Chapter 16

The RToP then hears the witnesses, who are also designated by the IOC. The full list of experts and witnesses[3] heard during the first two sessions of the RToP is available in the full versions of the findings of the RToP, which are available online.

The procedure followed by the RToP is neither that of the ICJ nor that of a domestic or international criminal court, but is based on the methodology applicable by any judicial body in terms of the independence and impartiality of its members.

In this document the RToP uses, depending on the context, the terms Palestine, Palestinian territory, occupied Palestinian territories, Occupied Palestinian Territory and Palestinian people without prejudice to the judgment that will be rendered at the final session.

Admissibility

When considering the relations of the accused with the Israeli state, and the nature of practices undertaken or allowed by the Israeli state in the OPT, the RToP rules on a number of alleged violations of international law by Israel. Israel's absence from the proceedings is not an impediment to the admissibility of the expert reports on the violations. In passing judgment on violations of international law allegedly committed by a state that is not represented before the RToP, the RToP is not breaching the rule of mutual agreement among the parties that is applicable before international judicial bodies responsible for the settlement of wdisputes between states (see the *Monetary Gold* and *East Timor* cases, *ICJ Reports*, 1954 and 1995). The work of this body is not comparable to that involved in a dispute referred, for instance, to the International Court of Justice: the facts presented as violations of international law committed by Israel in the OPT have been characterised as such by the United Nations General Assembly and the Security Council, and also by a number of reports such as those of the Special Committee to Investigate Israeli Practices Affecting the Human Rights of the Palestinian people and Other Arabs of the Occupied Territories. Hence, at this stage, the RToP will simply draw attention to circumstances that are already widely recognised by the international community.

Jury members

The jury of the RToP is made up of international personalities known for their actions and moral integrity:

Stéphane Hessel, Ambassador of France, honorary president of the RToP, France; **Mairead Corrigan Maguire**, Nobel Peace laureate 1976, Northern Ireland; **John Dugard**, Professor of international law, Former United Nations Special Rapporteur on Human Rights in the Palestinian Territories, South Africa; **Lord Anthony Gifford**, senior barrister and hereditary peer, founder of the law firm Gifford Thompson & Bright, United Kingdom; **Gisèle Halimi**, lawyer, former Ambassador to UNESCO, France; **Ronald Kasrils**, writer and activist, former Minister, South Africa; **Michael Mansfield**, barrister, President of the Haldane Society of Socialist Lawyers, United Kingdom; **José Antonio Martin Pallin**, Emeritus Judge, Chamber II, Supreme Court, Spain; **Cynthia McKinney**, former Member of the US Congress and 2008 presidential candidate, Green Party, USA; **Alberto San Juan**, actor, Spain; **Aminata Traoré**, author and former Minister of Culture of Mali; **Alice Walker**, poet and writer, USA.

Members of the jury do not all sit at each session and new members may be designated for future sessions.

Findings of the jury

The documents presented in this edition are executive summaries of the findings of the

---

3. The International Organising Committee wishes to thank the experts, witnesses, members of the jury and of the committee of expert lawyers for their voluntary contributions.

jury of the RToP issued after the Barcelona and London sessions. The original versions of the findings are available on the website of the RToP at **www.russelltribunalonpalestine.com**

These are provisional findings: they are the result of a *prima facie* assessment of the facts brought to the Tribunal's knowledge and are without prejudice to the final verdict that the RToP will deliver at its closing session. The RToP hopes that the EU, its member states and corporations will participate more actively in future sessions of the proceedings by making known their views, thereby preventing the RToP from drawing erroneous conclusions due to their silence and their absence.

Annex to Chapter 16

First international session of the Russell Tribunal on Palestine

Barcelona, 1-3 March 2010

COMPLICITY AND OMISSIONS OF THE EUROPEAN UNION AND ITS MEMBER STATES IN THE ONGOING OCCUPATION OF PALESTINIAN TERRITORIES BY ISRAEL AND THE CONTINUOUS VIOLATIONS OF INTERNATIONAL LAW BY ISRAEL

Programme[1]

MONDAY, 1 MARCH 2010

Opening speech by **Stéphane Hessel**, Ambassador of France, who participated in the drafting of the Universal Declaration on Human Rights.

Presentation of the organisation and aims of the first session of the Russell Tribunal on Palestine by **Pierre Galand** (Belgium) on behalf of the IOC.

Statements on the violations of international law and UN resolutions committed by the State of Israel by: **Felicia Langer** (Germany), human rights attorney, author, recipient of the Right Livelihood award, Bruno Kreisky Award and German Federal Cross of Merit; **Vicky Peña** (Spain), film, theatre and television actress; **Gustave Massiah** (France), economist, town planner and political analyst, founder of ATTAC France; **Pilar Sampietro** (Spain), broadcaster, "Mediterráneo" on Radio Nacional de España (Radio 3); and **Lluís Llach** (Spain) composer and songwriter (one of the main representatives of "Nova Cançó" a movement of musicians and singers who defied Franco).

I. The right to self determination of the Palestinian people

Statements by: **Madjid Benchikh** (Algeria), expert, Professor of Public International Law and former Dean at the Faculty of Law, Algiers; **David Bondia** (Spain), expert, Professor of Public International Law and International Relations at the University of Barcelona; and **Daragh Murray** (Ireland/Palestine), witness, Legal Advisor to the Palestinian Centre for Human Rights.

II. The Annexation of East Jerusalem

Statements by: **Ghada Karmi** (Palestine), expert, author and physician; **Meir Margalit** (Israel), witness, member of the Jerusalem City Council and the Israeli Committee Against House Demolitions; **Charles Shamas** (Palestine), witness, founder of the MATTIN group and former Legal Advisor to the ICRC.

III. Settlements and the plundering of natural resources

Statements by: **James Phillips** (Ireland) expert, barrister; **Michael Sfard** (Israel) witness, barrister; **Charles Shamas** (Palestine) witness, founder of the MATTIN group and former Legal Advisor to the ICRC.

TUESDAY 2 MARCH 2010

IV. The EU-Israel Association Agreement

Statements by: **Agnes Bertrand** (Belgium), expert, researcher and Middle East specialist with APRODEV; **Patrice Bouveret** (France), expert, President of the Armaments Observatory; **Veronique De Keyser**

1. Representatives of the EU and its member states were contacted by mail and invited to attend the session.

NOAM CHOMSKY • VICENZO CONSOLO • JULIE CHRISTIE • JONATHAN COOK • GEORGES CORM ——— 9

(Belgium), witness, Member of the European Parliament; and **Raül Romeva** (Spain), witness, Member of the European Parliament. Statements by: **Phil Shiner** (United Kingdom), expert, barrister; and **Clare Short** (United Kingdom), witness, Member of Parliament and former Secretary of State for International Development.

V. The Gaza Blockade and "Operation Cast Lead"

Statements by: **Derek Summerfield** (United Kingdom), expert, honorary senior lecturer at London's Institute of Psychiatry; **Desmond Travers** (Ireland), witness, retired colonel and member of the UN Fact-Finding Mission that produced the Goldstone Report; **Ewa Jasiewicz** (Poland), witness, journalist and volunteer with emergency medical services during "Operation Cast Lead"; and **Raji Sourani** (Palestine), witness, founder and Director of the Palestinian Centre for Human Rights in Gaza.

VI. The Wall built in the occupied Palestinian territories

Statements by: **Francois Dubuisson** (Belgium), expert, Law Professor at the Université Libre de Bruxelles; and **Francis Wurtz** (France), witness, former Member of the European Parliament.

The jury withdrew for deliberations.

WEDNESDAY, 3 MARCH 2010

PRESS CONFERENCE to present the jury's findings at the first session of the RToP.

Annex to Chapter 16

EXECUTIVE SUMMARY OF THE FINDINGS OF THE FIRST SESSION OF THE RTOP

The full document is available at www.russelltribunalonpalestine.com

After meeting in Barcelona from 1 to 3 March 2010 (first session), the jury of the RToP issued findings dealing with:

A. Violations of international law committed by Israel;

B. Breaches by the EU and its member states of certain specific rules of international law;

C. Breaches by the EU and its member states of certain general rules of international law;

D. Failure by the EU and its member states to take measures against the violations of international law committed by Israel and to identify what remedies may be available.

A. VIOLATIONS OF INTERNATIONAL LAW COMMITTED BY ISRAEL

Having taken note of the experts' reports, and having heard the witnesses summoned by the latter, the RToP finds that Israel has committed, and continues to commit, grave breaches of international law against the Palestinian people. In the RToP's view, Israel violates international law by the conduct described below:

(1) By maintaining a form of domination and subjugation over the Palestinians that prevents them from freely determining their political status, **Israel violates the right of the Palestinian people to self-determination** inasmuch as it is unable to exercise its sovereignty in the territory which belongs to it; this violates the Declaration on the Granting of Independence to Colonial Countries and Peoples (A/Res. 1514(XV), 14 Dec. 1960) and all UN General Assembly resolutions that have reaffirmed the right of the Palestinian people to self-determination since 1969 (A/Res. 2535 B (XXIV), 10 Dec. 1969, and, inter alia, A/Res. 3236 (XXIX), 22 Nov. 1974, 52/114, 12 Dec. 1997, etc.);

(2) By occupying Palestinian territories since June 1967 and refusing to leave them, **Israel violates the Security Council resolutions that call for its withdrawal from the territories concerned** (SC/Res. 242, 22 Nov. 1967; 338, 22 Oct. 1973);

(3) By pursuing a policy of systematic discrimination against Palestinians present in Israeli territory or in the occupied territories, Israel commits acts that may be characterised as **apartheid**; these acts include the following:

- closure of the borders of the Gaza Strip and **restrictions on the freedom of movement of its inhabitants**;

- prevention of the **return of Palestinian refugees** to their home or land of origin;

- prohibition on the free use by Palestinians of **certain natural resources such as the watercourses within their land**;

Given the discriminatory nature of these measures, since they are based, *inter alia*, on the nationality of the persons to whom they are applied, the RToP finds that they present features **comparable to apartheid**, even though they do not emanate from an identical political regime to that prevailing in South Africa prior to 1994; these measures are characterised as criminal acts by the Convention on the Suppression and Punishment of the Crime of Apartheid of 18 July 1976 which, though it is not binding on Israel, does not exonerate Israel in that regard;

(4) **By annexing Jerusalem in July 1980** and maintaining the annexation, Israel violates the prohibition of the acquisition of territory by force, as stated by the Security Council (SC/Res. 478, 20 August 1980);

(5) **By constructing a Wall in the West Bank on Palestinian territory that it occupies,** Israel denies the Palestinians access to their own land, violates their property rights and seriously restricts the freedom of movement of the Palestinian population, thereby violating Article 12 of the International Covenant on Civil and Political Rights to which Israel has been a party since 3 October 1991; the illegality of the construction of the Wall was confirmed by the International Court of Justice in its Advisory Opinion of 9 July 2004, which was endorsed by the UN General Assembly in its resolution ES-10/15;

(6) **By systematically building settlements in Jerusalem and the West Bank,** Israel breaches the rules of international humanitarian law governing occupation, in particular Article 49 of the Fourth Geneva Convention of 12 August 1949, by which Israel has been bound since 6 July 1951. This point was noted by the International Court of Justice in the above-mentioned Advisory Opinion;

(7) By pursuing a policy of **targeted killings against Palestinians** whom it describes as "terrorists" without first attempting to arrest them, Israel violates the right to life of the persons concerned, a right enshrined in Article 6 of the International Covenant on Civil and Political Rights;

(8) By maintaining a **blockade on the Gaza Strip** in breach of the provisions of the Fourth Geneva Convention of 12 August 1949 (Art. 33), which prohibits collective punishment;

(9) By inflicting extensive and serious damage, especially on persons and civilian property, and by **using prohibited methods of combat during operation "Cast Lead"** in Gaza (December 2008 – January 2009).

While the EU and its member states are not the direct perpetrators of these acts, they nevertheless violate international law, either by failing to take the measures that Israel's conduct requires them to take, or by contributing directly or indirectly to such conduct. Moreover, the EU and its member states do not comply with the relevant provisions of its own constitution, which confirms the attachment of the EU to fundamental rights and freedoms, states its willingness to uphold and promote respect for international law and take appropriate initiatives to that end (EU Lisbon Treaty, preamble, Arts. 2, 3, 17 and 21).

B. BREACHES BY THE EUROPEAN UNION AND ITS MEMBER STATES OF SPECIFIC RULES OF INTERNATIONAL LAW THAT REQUIRE THE EUROPEAN UNION AND ITS MEMBER STATES TO RESPOND TO VIOLATIONS OF INTERNATIONAL LAW COMMITTED BY ISRAEL

Certain rules of international law require the EU and its member states to take action to prevent Israel from committing specific violations of international law. Thus,

(1) With regard to the right of peoples to self-determination, the UN General Assembly Declaration on friendly relations (A/Res. 2625 (XXV), 24 Oct. 1970) states, as its fourth principle (2nd para.) that "Every State has the duty to promote, through joint and separate action, realization of the principle of equal rights and self-determination of peoples [...] and to render assistance to the United Nations in carrying out the responsibilities entrusted to it by the Charter regarding the implementation of the principle[...]". In the *Wall* case, the International Court of Justice also referred to this clause (ICJ, *Reports 2004*, § 156).
Similarly, the 1966 International Covenant on Civil and Political Rights, which binds Israel since October 1991, stipulates that "The States Parties [...] shall promote the realization of the right to self-determination";

(2) With regard to human rights, the aforementioned Declaration on friendly relations states

Annex to Chapter 16

in its fourth principle (3rd para.) that "Every State has the duty to promote through joint and separate action universal respect for and observance of human rights and fundamental freedoms in accordance with the Charter" (see also the 5th principle, 2nd para.);

(3) Furthermore, the Euro-Mediterranean Association Agreement of 20 November 1995 (*OJEC* L 147/1 of 21 June 2000), states that "Respect for democratic principles and fundamental human rights […] shall inspire the domestic and international policies of the Parties and shall constitute an essential element of this Agreement" (Art. 2).

This provision requires the EU and its member states to ensure that Israel respects fundamental rights and freedoms, and it follows that, by refraining to do so, the EU and its member states are violating the agreement; as shown by the Court of Justice of the European Communities in the *Brita* case (CJEC, 25 February 2010), EU law is also applicable to the EU's relations with Israel. While the agreement also stipulates that this does not prevent "a Party from taking any measures […] (c) which it considers essential to its own security in the event of serious internal disturbances affecting the maintenance of law and order, in time of war or serious international tension constituting a threat of war or in order to carry out obligations it has accepted for the purpose of maintaining peace and international security" (Art. 76), the RToP does not consider that this possibility accorded to the contracting parties can be invoked to justify the failure of the EU and its member states to fulfil their obligation of due diligence to ensure respect for human rights by the other party; on the contrary, fulfilment of the obligation in question may contribute to the maintenance of "peace and international security";

(4) With regard to international humanitarian law, common Article 1 of the four Geneva Conventions of 1949 stipulates that "The High Contracting Parties undertake to respect and to ensure respect" for the Conventions; as noted by the International Court of Justice in the *Wall* case, "it follows from that provision that every State party to that Convention [the Fourth Geneva Convention], whether or not it is a party to a specific conflict, is under an obligation to ensure that the requirements of the instruments in question are complied with." (ICJ, *Reports, 2004*, § 158).

The official International Committee of the Red Cross commentary emphasised the significance of common Article 1, stating as follows: "It is not an engagement concluded on a basis of reciprocity, binding each party to the contract only in so far as the other party observes its obligations. It is rather a series of unilateral engagements solemnly contracted before the world as represented by the other Contracting Parties. Each State contracts obligations vis-à-vis itself and at the same time vis-à-vis the others. The motive of the Convention is such a lofty one, so universally recognized as an imperative call of civilization, that the need is felt for its assertion, as much out of respect for it on the part of the signatory State itself as in the expectation of such respect from an opponent, indeed perhaps even more for the former reason than for the latter.

The Contracting Parties do not undertake merely to respect the Convention, but also to *ensure respect* for it. The wording may seem redundant. When a State contracts an engagement, the engagement extends *eo ipso* to all those over whom it has authority, as well as to the representatives of its authority; and it is under an obligation to issue the necessary orders. The use in all four Conventions of the words 'and to ensure respect for' was, however, deliberate: they were intended to emphasize the responsibility of the Contracting Parties. [….]

In view of the foregoing considerations and the fact that the provisions for the repression of violations have been considerably strengthened, it is clear that Article 1 is no mere empty form of words, but has been deliberately invested with imperative force. It must be taken in its literal meaning."

The fact that the EU is not a party to the Geneva Conventions does not preclude the applicability of their rules to the EU; thus, in the aforementioned *Wall* case, the International Court of Justice held that an international organisation such as the United Nations, which was not a party to the Conventions either, should take action to ensure that they were respected; according to the Court, the UN and "especially the General Assembly and the Security Council, should consider what further action is required to bring to an end the illegal situation resulting from the construction of the wall and the associated regime, taking due account of the present Advisory Opinion" (ICJ, *Reports. 2004*, § 160).

Moreover, the International Committee of the Red Cross study on customary international humanitarian law notes that states "must exert their influence, to the degree possible, to stop violations of international humanitarian law" (rule 144). As this is a rule of customary law, it is also applicable to international organisations.

Pursuant to international humanitarian law, beyond common Article 1, the member states of the EU are under a specific duty to apply universal jurisdiction to individual criminal suspects, especially in the light of the recommendations of the UN Fact-Finding Mission at paragraphs 1857 and 1975 (a) of its report to the UN Human Rights Council of September 2009 (UN Doc. A/HRC/12/48, 12 September 2009, para. 1857 and 1975).

Further, Article 146 of the Fourth Geneva Convention provides that each state "shall take measures necessary for the suppression of all acts contrary to the provisions of the present Convention other than the grave breaches defined in [Article 147]".

It should be noted that Austria, France, Greece and Italy are four EU countries that have failed to comply with Article 146 (1) in that their internal legal order does not enable universal jurisdiction to be exercised over those suspected of violations of the crimes listed in Article 147.

Article 146 (3) requires not only that parties to the Fourth Geneva Convention apply universal jurisdiction to those suspected of criminal liability for grave breaches defined in Article 147, but also that they take effective measures to repress non-grave breaches. This is explained in the official International Committee of the Red Cross commentary to the Convention as follows: "under the terms of this paragraph, the Contracting Parties must also suppress all other acts contrary to the provisions of this Convention. The wording is not very precise. The expression 'faire cesser' used in the French text may be interpreted in different ways. In the opinion of the International Committee of the Red Cross, it covers everything which can be done by a State to avoid acts contrary to the Convention being committed or repeated. ...[T]here is no doubt that what is primarily meant is the repression of breaches other than the grave breaches listed and only in the second place administrative measures to ensure respect for the provisions of the Convention."

C. BREACHES BY THE EUROPEAN UNION AND ITS MEMBER STATES OF THE GENERAL RULES OF INTERNATIONAL LAW WHICH REQUIRE THE EUROPEAN UNION AND ITS MEMBER STATES TO RESPOND TO VIOLATIONS OF INTERNATIONAL LAW COMMITTED BY ISRAEL

Israel's violations of international law are frequently violations of "peremptory norms" of international law (*jus cogens*): targeted killings that violate the right to life; deprivation of the liberty of Palestinians in conditions that violate the prohibition of torture; violation of the right of peoples to self-determination; living conditions imposed on a people that constitute a type of apartheid.

The peremptory character of these norms is attributable to the fact that they cannot be derogated from (see, for the right to life and the prohibition of torture, the International Covenant on Civil and Political Rights, Art. 4, § 2, and the Convention of 10 December 1984 against torture, Art. 2, §§ 2-3) or that they have been explicitly assimilated to "peremptory norms" by the most authoritative scholarly opinion, namely that of the International Law Commission (ILC) (on the prohibition of apartheid and respect for the right of peoples to self-determination, see the ILC draft articles on state responsibility, commentary on Art. 40, *ILC Report,* 2001, pp. 305-307).[2]

When they witness a violation of such norms, even at a considerable distance, states and international organisations cannot remain passive and indifferent. In Article 41 of the draft articles on state responsibility, the International Law Commission adopted a provision to the effect that: "States shall co-operate to bring to an end through lawful means any serious breach within the meaning of Article 40" [breach of a peremptory norm of international law].

In its commentary, the International Law Commission makes it clear that "the obligation to co-operate applies to States whether or not they are individually affected by the serious breach. What is called for in the face of serious breaches is a joint and co-ordinated effort by all States to counteract the effects of these breaches" (*ILC Report,* 2001, p. 114).

The EU and its member states are therefore under an obligation to react in application of international law to prevent violations of peremptory norms of international law and to counteract their consequences. By failing to take appropriate action to that end, the EU and its member states are breaching an elementary obligation of due diligence pertaining to respect for the most fundamental rules of international law.

The RToP considers that this obligation to react implies, in accordance with the rules of good faith and due diligence, the obligation to ensure that the reaction against violations of peremptory norms of international law complies with the principle of reasonable effectiveness. To that end, the EU and its member states must use all available legal channels to ensure that Israel respects international law. It therefore calls for a response that goes beyond mere declarations condemning the breaches of international law committed by Israel. Of course, the RToP takes note of these declarations, but they are no more than a first step when it comes to meeting the international obligations of the EU and its member states; they are not fully performing the duty of reaction imposed by the rules of international law.

Lastly, the RToP wishes to emphasise that the obligation to react against violations of peremptory norms of international law must be subject to rules of non-discrimination and of the unacceptability of double standards: the RToP is perfectly well aware that states have not codified a rule of equidistance in respect of the obligation to react, but it holds that such a rule is inferable as a matter of course from the principles of good faith and reasonable interpretation of international law. Refusing to accept it will inevitably lead to "a result which is manifestly absurd or unreasonable" and which is ruled out by treaty law (1969 Convention on the Law of Treaties, Art. 32 b). In these circumstances, the RToP considers that it is unacceptable and contrary to the aforementioned juridical logic for the EU to suspend its relations, *de facto,* with Palestine when Hamas was elected in the Gaza Strip and to maintain them with a state that violates international law on a far greater scale than Hamas.

2. As a reminder, the International Law Commission is a subsidiary organ of the UN General Assembly, created in 1947 to codify international law. It comprises 34 members "of recognized competence in international law" A/Res-174(II) on 21 November 1947, 2nd para.

D. FAILURE OF THE EUROPEAN UNION AND ITS MEMBER STATES TO REFRAIN FROM CONTRIBUTING TO THE VIOLATIONS OF INTERNATIONAL LAW COMMITTED BY ISRAEL

The RToP notes that reports by experts have brought to light passive and active forms of assistance by the EU and its member states for violations of international law by Israel. Attention has been drawn, for instance, to the following:

- exports of weapons and components of weapons by EU states to Israel, some of which were used during the conflict in Gaza in December 2008 and January 2009;

- exports of produce from settlements in occupied territories to the EU;

- participation by the settlements in European research programmes;

- failure of the EU to complain about the destruction by Israel of infrastructure in the Gaza Strip during the Cast Lead operation;

- failure of the EU to demand Israeli compliance with clauses concerning respect for human rights contained in the various association agreements concluded by the EU with Israel;

- the decision by the EU to upgrade its relations with Israel under the Euro-Mediterranean Partnership Agreement;

- tolerance by the EU and its member states of certain economic relations between European companies and Israel involving commercial projects in the occupied territories, such as the management of the Tovlan landfill site in the Jordan valley and the construction of a tramline in East Jerusalem.

For these acts to qualify as unlawful assistance or aid to Israel, two conditions must be met: the state providing assistance must do so with the intention of facilitating the wrongful act attributable to Israel and it must do so knowingly; Article 16 of the International Law Commission's draft articles on state responsibility reads: "A State which aids or assists another State in the commission of an internationally wrongful act by the latter is internationally responsible for doing so if:

(a) That State does so with knowledge of the circumstances of the internationally wrongful act; and

(b) The act would be internationally wrongful if committed by that State."

In its commentary the International Law Commission (ILC) makes it clear that the state which assists the perpetrator of the wrongful act must intend to facilitate the wrongful conduct and the assisted state must effectively engage in such conduct; the assisting state incurs responsibility even if such assistance is not essential to the performance of the wrongful act; it is sufficient if it "contributed significantly to that act" (*ILC Report*, 2001, p. 66). The assisting state must therefore be aware of the fact that Israel is violating international law and that the assistance given to Israel was intended to facilitate such violations.

In casu, the EU and its members states could not have been unaware that some forms of assistance to Israel contributed or would perforce have contributed to certain wrongful acts committed by Israel. This is applicable to:

- exports of military equipment to a state that has maintained an illegal occupation for more than forty years;

- imports of produce from settlements located in occupied territories and no real control by the customs authorities of EU member states of the origin of such produce save in exceptional circumstances (Court of Justice of the European Communities, 25 February 2010, *Brita*), whereas the exception should become the rule;

- evidence of a report repressed in 2005 and repeated internal reports by EU officials to EU bodies listing violations accurately, only to be ignored by those bodies.

In both cases, this conduct contributed "significantly" to the wrongful acts committed by Israel even if they did not directly cause such acts, and it is reasonable to assume that the EU could not possibly have been unaware of this. In these cases, the EU may be held to have been complicit in the wrongful act committed by Israel and hence to incur responsibility.

The participation of the settlements in European research programmes, the failure of the EU to complain during the "Cast Lead" operation about the destruction by Israel of infrastructure that the EU had funded in the Gaza strip, and the proposed upgrading of bilateral relations between the EU and Israel are characterised by a number of experts as assistance to Israel in its alleged violations of international law. The ILC considers that one must, in cases of this kind, "carefully" examine whether the state accused of wrongful assistance was aware that it was facilitating the commission of the wrongful act. According to the ILC, "Where the allegation is that the assistance of a State has facilitated human rights abuses by another State, the particular circumstances of each case must be carefully examined to determine whether the aiding State by its aid was aware of and intended to facilitate the commission of the internationally wrongful conduct." (*ILC Report 2001*, p. 68)

Even if the acts of the EU and its member states do not contribute directly to the violations of international law committed by Israel, they provide a form of security for Israel's policy and encourage it to violate international law because they cast the EU and its member states in the role of approving spectators. As the International Criminal Tribunal for the Former Yugoslavia (ICTY) put it: "While any spectator can be said to be encouraging a spectacle - an audience being a necessary element of a spectacle - the spectator in these cases [German cases cited by the Chamber] was only found to be complicit if his status was such that his presence had a significant legitimising or encouraging effect on the principals" (ICTY, *Furundzija* case IT-95-17/1-T, 10 Dec. 1998, § 232).

The European Court of Human Rights (ECHR) has held that lack of effort by a state party to the European Convention on Human Rights to ensure respect for the Convention in a territory under its jurisdiction may engage its responsibility for violations of the Convention committed in the territory concerned, even if the state does not exercise de facto authority there. *In casu*, the Court found that Moldova had failed to exercise due diligence vis-à-vis the secessionist government of Transdniestria and vis-à-vis Russia, which supported it, in order to halt the violations of the Convention that were being committed by the Transdniestrian authorities. Thus, the Court noted that "In their negotiations with the separatists, the Moldovan authorities have restricted themselves to raising the question of the applicants' situation orally, without trying to reach an agreement guaranteeing respect for their Convention rights" (ECHR, *Ilascu and others* v. *Moldova and Russia*, 8 July 2004, § 348).

It added that "the Court notes that the negotiations for a settlement of the situation in Transdniestria, in which the Russian Federation is acting as a guarantor State, have been ongoing since 2001 without any mention of the applicants and without any measure being taken or considered by the Moldovan authorities to secure to the applicants their Convention rights" (*ibid*, § 350).

The Court also noted that the Russian Federation has signed military and economic agreements with Transdniestria, which show that "it survives by virtue of the military, economic, financial and political support given to it by the Russian Federation", that the latter has "made no attempt to put an end" to violations of the Convention and that even if its agents have not participated directly in them, "its responsibility is engaged with regard to the acts complained of" (ibid., §§ 392-394). Although the Russian Federation is clearly much more involved in the events in Transdniestria than the EU in those occurring in Palestine, it is significant that the ECHR bases the responsibility of the Russian Federation and Moldova for violations of the European Convention on Human Rights committed by a third-party authority – Transdniestria – on their inaction or passivity with respect to the violations concerned. This inaction is broadly similar to that of the EU and its member states with respect to the violations of international law committed by Israel in Palestine.

In a partly dissenting opinion in which he was joined by four other judges, Judge Casadevall adopts a similar approach: "I consider that the efforts made by the Moldovan authorities with a view to securing the rights set forth in the Convention after its ratification in 1997 were not pursued with the firmness, determination and conviction required by the serious situation in which the applicants found themselves. [...] It should be noted that, while taking steps to promote co-operation with the secessionist regime with the avowed aim of making life easier for the population of Transdniestria, the Moldovan authorities have not displayed the same diligence with regard to the fate of the applicants. In their negotiations with the separatists, whether before or after May 2001, the Moldovan authorities have restricted themselves to raising the question orally, without trying to reach a written agreement providing for the applicants' release" (ibid., Partly dissenting opinion, Casadevall, Ress, Tulkens, Birsan and Fura-Sandström, §§ 9-10).

Similarly, according to Judge Ress, "if one recognises that the Russian Federation had jurisdiction over Transdniestria at the material time, and continues to exercise control, then one realises that there was an obvious lack of formal protests, declarations or other measures towards the Russian Federation, third countries, the UN and other international organisations, in an attempt to influence them to bring the illegal situation in Transdniestria and the applicants' unacceptable situation to an end" (ibid., Partly dissenting opinion. Ress, § 6).

The situation of the EU and its member states with respect to Israel is, of course, entirely different from that of Russia and Moldova with respect to Transdniestria; nevertheless, the reasoning of the ECHR in this case is perfectly applicable, *mutatis mutandis*, to the responsibilities of the EU and its member states vis-à-vis Israel.

In the light of the foregoing, and as noted by an expert, it is logical to interpret the silence of the EU and its member states as tacit approval or a sign of acceptance of violations of international law by Israel. As it is inconceivable that the EU and its member states are unaware of the violations of international law being committed by Israel, the RToP concludes that the acts in question constitute wrongful assistance to Israel within the meaning of aforementioned Article 16 of the ILC draft articles on state responsibility.

E. FINDINGS OF THE JURY

At this stage of the proceedings, the Russell Tribunal on Palestine calls on:

(i) the EU and its member states to fulfil their obligations forthwith by putting an end to the wrongful acts specified in section C and D of this document;

(ii) the EU, in particular, to implement the European Parliament's resolution calling for the suspension of the EU-Israel Association Agreement, thereby putting an end to the context of irresponsibility that Israel continues to enjoy;

(iii) EU member states to implement the recommendations set out in para 1975 (a) of the UN Fact-Finding Mission Report on the Gaza Conflict (Goldstone Report) regarding the collection of evidence and the exercise of universal jurisdiction in respect of the crimes attributed to Israeli and Palestinian suspects;

(iv) EU member states to repeal any restriction under domestic law that would impede compliance with the duty to prosecute or extradite (*judicare vel dedere*) any alleged perpetrator of a war crime or a crime against humanity;

(v) EU member states to strengthen mutual legal assistance and cooperation in criminal matters through the EU contact points, EUROPOL, INTERPOL, etc;

(vi) EU member states to refrain from limiting the scope of universal jurisdiction so as to ensure that no EU member state becomes a safe haven for suspected perpetrators of war crimes or crimes against humanity;

(vii) the Parliaments of Austria, France, Greece and Italy to enact laws which, in conformity with Article 146 of the Fourth Geneva Convention, would facilitate the exercise of universal jurisdiction in those states;

(viii) individuals, groups and organisations to take all necessary measures to secure compliance by the EU and its member states with their aforementioned obligations including, in particular, the exercise of universal jurisdiction in civil and criminal matters against any alleged perpetrator – an individual or a state agent – of a war crime or a crime against humanity;

(ix) the existing legal actions in the context of the Boycott, Divestment and Sanctions campaign (BDS) to be stepped up and expanded within the EU.

The RToP calls on the EU and on each of its member states to impose the necessary sanctions on its partner - Israel - through diplomatic, trade and cultural measures in order to end the impunity that it has enjoyed for decades. Should the EU and its member states lack the necessary courage to do so, the RToP counts on the citizens of Europe to bring the necessary pressure to bear on the EU by all appropriate means.

Second international session of the Russell Tribunal on Palestine

London 20-22 November 2010

INTERNATIONAL CORPORATE COMPLICITY IN ISRAEL'S VIOLATIONS OF INTERNATIONAL HUMAN RIGHTS LAW AND INTERNATIONAL HUMANITARIAN LAW

Programme[1]

SATURDAY, 20 NOVEMBER 2010

Pierre Galand (Belgium) opened the London session on behalf of the International Organising Committee of the RToP. The second session of the Russell Tribunal on Palestine was introduced by Ambassador of France **Stéphane Hessel** (France) and **Michael Mansfield QC** (United Kingdom).

I. The legal framework relevant to corporate conduct

hocine Ouazraf (Belgium) presented the framework for corporate complicity in international law.

Legal experts **Richard Hermer QC** (United Kingdom), **Yasmine Gado** (United States) and **Dr. William Bourdon** (France) discussed the details of British, United States and French law respectively, their relevance to the application of international law and their relevance to the second session's focus on corporate complicity.

II. Implication of corporate activities in and around settlements

Dr. Dalit Baum (Israel) and **Hugh Lanning** (United Kingdom) provided an overview of issues relating to business practices in relation to settlements and the settlement industry.

Fayez Al Taneeb* (Palestine) and **Wael Natheef** (Palestine) spoke about the direct impact this was having on Palestinians as workers and residents in and around settlements.

Adri Nieuwhof (Netherlands) spoke as the lead expert on public contract regulations and the French multinational Veolia, and its business practices in the occupied Palestinian territories.

Ghaleb Mashni (Palestine) presented an account of the impact this has had on Palestinians.

John Dorman (Ireland) rounded off the session with an account of the relations between Cement Roadstone Holdings and the construction of the Wall.

III. Trade and labelling of settlement goods

Salma Karmi from Al Haq (Palestine) provided an overview of the legal issues relating to the trade in and labelling of settlement goods.

Christophe Perrin (France) followed with an account of the business practices of the agro-food company Carmel Agrexco.

Nancy Kricorian and **Rae Abileah** (United States) discussed the cosmetics company Ahava and its production of spa products.

Phon Van Den Biesen (Netherlands) discussed issues relating to the labelling of products from Israeli

---

1. All corporations whose business practices were queried during the session had been contacted by registered mail and invited to attend the session.

Annex to Chapter 16

settlements, and **Genevieve Coudrais** (France) spoke about the case of Soda Stream.

SUNDAY, 21 NOVEMBER 2010

IV. Financial services sector

Merav Amir (Israel) presented an overview of both Israeli and international finance companies and their connection to the Israeli occupation of Palestine.

Mario Franssen (Belgium) spoke about the Dexia group.

Saskia Muller (Netherlands) spoke about the PFZW Pension Fund.

V. The security industry and the war industry

John Hilary (United Kingdom) presented an overview of the security industry and the nature of corporate involvement.

Maria LaHood (United States) provided information about Caterpillar and the use of its equipment in Israeli military practices, and Josh Ruebner (United States) presented additional information and evidence relating to Caterpillar's business practices.

Merav Amir (Israel) and **Dr. Dalit Baum** (Israel) followed with an account of the British private security firm G4S.

Shir Hever (Israel) and **Jamal Juma'a*** (Palestine) spoke about Elbit Systems and their role in security practices by the Israeli state.

Paul Troop (United Kingdom.) discussed recent court cases against UK-based arms manufacturing companies EDO ITT and Raytheon.

Terry Crawford (South Africa) spoke about the SWIFT international financial system.

The final speaker **Ben Hayes** (United Kingdom) provided details of EU subsidies to the security industry.

Speaking time for corporations

 Wrap-up questions

Round up: Overview of the two days and the way forward

The jury withdrew for deliberations.

MONDAY, 22 NOVEMBER 2010

PRESS CONFERENCE setting out the jury's findings at the second session of the RToP.

---

* These witnesses did not obtain a visa to appear before the RToP in London. Their written statements were heard by the RToP.

EXECUTIVE SUMMARY OF
THE FINDINGS OF THE
SECOND SESSION OF THE RTOP

The full document is available at
www.russelltribunalonpalestine.com

The London session focused on the following three questions:

A. Which Israeli violations of international law are corporations complicit in?

B. What are the legal consequences of the activities of corporations that aid and abet Israeli violations?

C. What are the remedies available and what are the obligations of states in relation to corporate complicity?

A. VIOLATIONS OF INTERNATIONAL LAW BY ISRAEL ATTRIBUTABLE TO CORPORATIONS

Violations of international law by Israel in which corporations are particularly closely involved are:

- **The systematic establishment of settlements**[2] in East Jerusalem and the West Bank breach the rules of IHL governing the occupation, in particular Article 49 of GC4 of 12 August 1949 by which Israel has been bound since 6 July 1951 (this breach has been recognised by the ICJ in its Advisory Opinion of 09 July 2004 on *The Legal Consequences of the Construction of a Wall in the Occupied Palestinian Territory* (§ 120), an Opinion endorsed by the UNGA in its resolution ES-10/15. The establishment of settlements also constitutes a war crime pursuant to Additional Protocol I (Art. 85, § 4 (a)) to the 1949 GCs and the Statute of the International Criminal Court (Art. 8, § 2 (b) (viii)). Although these instruments do not bind Israel, the provisions cited reflect the current state of customary international law; moreover, the ILC included this crime in its draft Code of Crimes against the Peace and Security of Mankind adopted in 1996 (Art. 20 (c) (i));

- **The systematic policy of discrimination** pursued by Israel in the occupied territory amounts to acts of apartheid vis-à-vis the Palestinian population (apartheid is defined as a crime by the UN Convention of 30 November 1973, API (Art. 85, § 4 (c)) and the ICC Statute (Art. 7, § 1 (j)); although these instruments do not bind Israel, they arguably reflect the current state of customary international law;

- **The violations of IHL committed by Israel in Gaza during "Operation Cast Lead"** (December 2008 – January 2009). The RToP particularly notes the destruction of civilian goods "without military necessity", which also constitutes a war crime (Goldstone Report, 15 September 2009, UN doc. A/HRC/12/48: see. i.a., §§ 388, 703 et seq., 928, 957, etc.); the report also mentioned that possible crimes against humanity were committed during "Operation Cast Lead";

- **The construction of a Wall in the occupied Palestinian territory** is a violation of, in particular, Articles 46 and 52 of the 1907 Hague Regulations, Article 53 of GC4 of 1949, and Article 12 of the International Covenant on Civil and Political Rights, which bind Israel.

The ICJ found that the construction of the Wall was illegal (*Wall, loc. cit.*, §§ 114-137.) and called upon Israel to:

(a) Respect the Palestinian right to self-determination;

(b) Put an end to its violations of international law, in particular violations of international humanitarian and human rights law, arising from the construction of the Wall;

(c) Dismantle sections of the Wall built on occupied Palestinian territory;

2. According to the Security Council (S/RES/446, 452, 465) and the ICJ.

Annex to Chapter 16

(d) Repeal or render ineffective all legislative and regulatory acts adopted with a view to constructing the Wall;

(e) Make reparation for all damage suffered by all natural or legal persons affected by the Wall's construction.

The Court added that *all* States must, according with their *erga omnes* obligations, adhere to the following negative and positive duties:

(a) Not to recognise the illegal situation created by the construction of the Wall;

(b) Not to render aid or assistance in maintaining the situation created by the construction of the Wall, and to remove every impediment to the exercise by the Palestinian people of its right to self-determination;

(c) To bring to an end, by lawful means, the illegal situation brought about by the construction of the Wall;

(d) To ensure respect of IHL by Israel.

B. LEGAL IMPLICATIONS OF CORPORATE ACTIVITIES

The acts of the various corporations that support and contribute to the violations of international law committed by Israel can be divided into three categories:

(I) supply of military equipment, materials and vehicles to Israel that were used in the Gaza Strip during "Operation Cast Lead", supply of security equipment used at checkpoints on routes leading to the construction of the Wall and supply of security equipment to the Israeli settlements in the OPT;

(II) various types of assistance provided to the Israeli settlements in the OPT;

(III) forms of assistance for the construction of the Wall in the OPT.

The RToP considered the above with reference to the UK, French and US legal frameworks and also considered the way in which international law has been interpreted by these states.

(I) Supply of military equipment

The RToP heard evidence that the Israeli security and war industry has a symbiotic relationship with those of other states, including many EU and Western states which mutually benefit and profit from procuring arms from and selling arms to Israel and Israeli corporations. The Government of Israel consistently devotes large-scale resources to military expenditure (7-9% of its GDP), but it also benefits from very significant military and economic aid from the United States (since 1949) and from the EU (evidence of J. Hilary).

(1) **Brimar:** This British firm manufactures the display components used in the Israeli Air Force's AH-64 Apache helicopters. The British Government has conceded that components licensed for export from Britain were "almost certainly" used by the Israeli armed forces in the Gaza Strip during "Operation Cast Lead" (evidence of J. Hilary).

(2) **G4S:** This British/Danish multinational corporation owns 90% of G4S Israel, which has assisted Israel in the illegal activities (evidence of M. Amir and D. Baum) by:

- supplying luggage, scanning equipment and full body scanners to several military checkpoints in the West Bank, including the Qalandia, Bethlehem and Irtah checkpoints, all of which have been built as part of the separation Wall whose route was declared illegal by the ICJ in its Advisory Opinion of 9 July 2004;

- supplying equipment to the Erez checkpoint which serves as part of the Israeli blockade policy over the Gaza Strip;

- supplying security services to businesses, such as supermarkets, in the illegal settlements in the West Bank and in the settlement areas of East Jerusalem;

- providing a defence system for the walls of Ofer Prison (which specifically hosts Palestinian political prisoners) and installation of a central command room in the facility, from which the entire facility can be monitored. Ofer Prison is located in the "Seam Zone" of the West Bank. Access to this area is severely restricted for Palestinians (especially from the West Bank), who depend on obtaining a special access permit from G4S. The practical impact of these restrictions on movement is that Palestinians from the West Bank have very limited access for the purpose of visiting detainees or attending military court hearings;

- providing the entire security system for Ketziot Prison and a central command room in Megido Prison. These are facilities to hold "high security prisoners", i.e. Palestinian political prisoners from the OPT, who are illegally held in Israel.

According to Article 76 of the Fourth Geneva Convention, "[p]rotected persons accused of offences shall be detained in the occupied country, and if convicted they shall serve their sentences therein." As Megido and Ketziot prisons are both well inside Israel, Israel violates international humanitarian law by holding Palestinians and G4S is complicit in this violation.

(3) **Caterpillar** has supplied the Israeli army with militarised D9 bulldozers, which have been used extensively to demolish Palestinian houses, have resulted in injuries and deaths, and have provoked the forced displacement of more than 50,000 Palestinians (evidence of M. LaHood). They have further been used in the construction of the Wall and for urban warfare during "Operation Cast Lead".

- In the United States all arms transfers and military aid, which include Caterpillar's D9 bulldozers, are subject to laws that are intended to prevent weapons from being misused to commit human rights abuses.

- The *Arms Export Control Act* (AECA) stipulates (P.L.8-829) that foreign countries either purchasing US weapons or receiving them as military aid must use them for "internal security" and "legitimate self-defence" (P.L.97-195).

- The Foreign Assistance Act (P.L. 97-195), which regulates all US military and economic aid programmes, stipulates that "No assistance may be provided ... to the government of any country which engages in a consistent pattern of gross violations of internationally recognized human rights". It also prohibits military aid to "any unit of the security forces of a foreign country if the Secretary of State has credible evidence that such unit has committed gross violations of human rights".

Yet, in apparent violation of the United States' own laws, the US Defence Security Cooperation Agency (an agency within the US Department of Defence) certified that the military procurement of Caterpillar bulldozers was consistent with the AECA and the applicable Foreign Military Financing Program (FMF) (evidence of J. Ruebner).

(4) **Elbit** is a leading Israeli multinational in the defence and war industry, founded in 1967. Once Elbit develops a weapon or military system, it is first used by the Israeli army as part of its military operations. The company is then able to market its products to other armies around the world as having been "tried and tested" in real combat conditions rather than simulated trials, giving it a clear edge over its rivals. Ongoing armed conflict is therefore in Elbit's commercial interest to ensure that its new products are tested in combat.

Despite Elbit's relationship with the Israeli military, Western states continue to do business

Annex to Chapter 16

with it, purchasing its products and awarding military and defence contracts to Elbit and/or its numerous subsidiaries around the world. Some examples of this are set out below:

- Elbit's Hermes 450 UAVs were widely employed in Gaza during "Operation Cast Lead" (evidence of J. Hilary). Countries all over the world, including Australia, Canada, Croatia, France, Sweden, the United Kingdom and the United States, have procured UAVs developed by Elbit;

- Despite the above, the British Army has awarded Elbit Systems and its partner company Thales UK a contract worth over US $1 billion for the development of the Watchkeeper Programme, the next generation of UAVs;

- The British company UAV Engines Limited, a wholly owned Elbit subsidiary, will produce the plane's engines. U-Tacs, another British subsidiary of Elbit, operates the Watchkeeper Programme (evidence of J. Hilary).

(II) Assistance provided to the Israeli settlements in the Occupied Palestinian Territory

Numerous corporations provide a range of services that assist in the construction and maintenance of illegal Israeli settlements in the OPT. One thousand four hundred Israeli corporations are highly active in settlements. The database of "Who Profits from the Occupation" documents that a further 400 corporations, Israeli and non-Israeli, are supporting illegal settlements (http://www.whoprofits.org/). Among these, the following corporations' activities were detailed and documented during the RToP session:

(1) Israeli corporations: including **AFIGROUP, AVGOL, AHAVA** – Dead Sea Laboratories Ltd, **Tishbi Estate Winery, Soda-Club, Alon Group,** Leumi and **Hapoalim** banks, and **Carmel Agrexco**;

(2) Foreign corporations: **Shamrock Holdings of California** (Burbank, California, USA); **Alstom** (S.A., Levallois-Perret, France), **Veolia Transport** (S.A., Nanterre, France), **Dexia** (Brussels, Belgium), **Caterpillar, AIG** (American International Group, New York, USA), **Cement Roadstone Holdings** (Irish company), **Pensioenfonds Zorg en Welzijn** (PFZW, the Netherlands), **G4S** (British/Danish corporation), **Society for Worldwide Interbank Financial Telecommunication** (SWIFT).

The establishment of Israeli settlements in the OPT constitutes a war crime. As settlements almost always involve extensive appropriation of property that is not justified by military necessity, this appropriation is also a war crime according to Article 147 of GC4, which Israel has ratified. The primary acts of Israelis in building and living in illegal settlements can therefore entail their individual criminal liability, which can be extended to all those who aid and abet Israelis in building and living in those settlements.

In view of the criminal nature of the Israeli settlements and the actions aimed at maintaining them, economic relationships between corporations and the settlements may be viewed as participation in these crimes. Depending on the form that the relationship assumes, and depending on the criminal law of the state whose jurisdiction has been seized, **participation in a crime may be characterised**, depending on the case, **as complicity, handling and/or receiving stolen goods, or laundering.**

Complicity: a corporation's business relationship with a settlement is a type of conduct that "abets [...] or [...] assists" (ICC Statute, Art. 25, § 3 (b) & (c)) the settlements' continued existence. The fact that such participation occurs after the crime was committed does not preclude its designation as "complicity" since the settlements constitute a *continuing* offence.

The offence is continuous given the permanent nature of the settlements and Israel's consistent refusal to comply with Security Council resolutions. In addition, as the Israeli settlements are a known phenomenon, corporations cannot be unaware that their activities are assisting in Israel's activities.

This applies to:

- **AFIGROUP**: construction of buildings in the settlements, either directly or through its subsidiaries;

- **AHAVA** – **Dead Sea Laboratories Ltd.** and **Shamrock Holdings of California**: manufacture, sale and export of cosmetic products produced with Dead Sea mud obtained from Mitzpe Shalem, a settlement established in the West Bank in 1977 (evidence of S. Karmi, N. Kricorian and R. Abileah);

- **Alon Group**: running of service stations and businesses in multiple settlements throughout the West Bank;

- **Dexia**: bank funding of Israeli settlements in the West Bank via its subsidiary Dexia Israel Public Finance Ltd (evidence of M. Franssen);

- **Leumi** and **Hapoalim** banks: granting of mortgages to settlers to purchase property in the settlements. In October 2010, *Who Profits*? published a comprehensive report about the involvement of Israeli banks in the financing of the occupation;

- **Alstom** and **Veolia Transport**: construction and running of a tramline in East Jerusalem that passes through East Jerusalem, which has been annexed by Israel, and links West Jerusalem to the Israeli settlements (evidence of A. Nieuwhof). Veolia also operates bus services to Israeli settlements.

In conclusion, the economic activities undertaken by corporations in the Israeli settlements contribute to the perpetuation of the settlements and thereby constitute complicity in a war crime.

Handling and/or receiving stolen goods: Under English law it is a criminal offence to knowingly receive or handle stolen goods, although this does not apply to land.[3] Similar offences, which are defined in the domestic criminal codes of most civil law states[4] as the possession or holding of something that one knows was obtained by means of a felony or misdemeanour committed by a third party, may be applied to the holding of settlement property acquired from Israelis who purport to hold legitimate title. The incrimination bases itself on the illegality of the settlements.

Individuals who handle or receive agricultural produce from the settlements (for example oranges, olives, avocadoes, etc. harvested by **Agrexco**) or who acquire goods manufactured in the settlements are liable under these offences. In this context, the basis of the incrimination is not only the illegality of the settlements, but also the unjustified appropriation, by military means, of the natural resources of the occupied territory (violation of Art. 55 of the Hague Regulations; a war crime according the 4th GC, Art. 147, the ICC Statute, Art. 8, § 2(b) (xiii) and the ILC draft Code of Crimes against the Peace and Security of Mankind, Art. 20 (a) (iv)).

Laundering: Money laundering is the practice of converting products of illegal origin into assets that appear to have a legitimate origin.[5] The mere possession or the depositing in a bank account of funds that are the product of a criminal offence constitutes laundering[6] unless the law of the state concerned does not criminalise the possession of assets obtained by the perpetrator of the main offence;[7] under some legislation, two offences are not committed if property is both stolen and laundered.

3. Sections 22(1) and 34(2)(b) of the Theft Act 1968.
4. E.g. Belgian Criminal Code, Article 505, section 1, § 1; new French Criminal Code., Article 321-1.
5. See, *inter alia*, the Council of Europe Conventions signed in Strasbourg on 8 November 1990 and in Warsaw on 16 May 2005.
6. Conventions signed in Strasbourg, Article 6, § 1(c), and Warsaw, Article 9, § 1(c).
7. "Property" includes property of any description, whether corporeal or incorporeal, movable or immovable, and legal documents or instruments evidencing title to, or interest in such property.

Annex to Chapter 16

Banking institutions (**Leumi, Hapoalim, Dexia** banks) that knowingly receive funds originating from economic activity within Israeli settlements are liable under these offences.

Supplying the settlements with goods intended for the violation of Palestinian rights: Deliveries of certain types of equipment such as the **Caterpillar D9** bulldozers, which are used to demolish houses or to damage land belonging to Palestinians and to construct Israeli buildings, constitute complicity in war crimes, such as not only the creation and maintenance of settlements but also the destruction or arbitrary and large-scale appropriation of goods without military justification (see Nuremberg IMT Statute, Art. 6, b; Fourth Geneva Convention, Art. 147).

As to the criminal and civil liability of these corporations and corporate actors, see the conclusion set out below.

(III) Assistance for the construction of the Wall in the OPT

Construction of the Wall and its associated regime is illegal (see above, § 4). The RToP heard evidence that Israeli and foreign corporations provide or have provided assistance for the construction and maintenance of the Wall. The following examples were presented in written and oral evidence before the RToP:

- **Caterpillar** supplies D9 bulldozers to Israel, which are used *inter alia* to prepare the ground for the building of the Wall in occupied territory (evidence of M. LaHood and J. Ruebner).

- **G4S Israel** supplies luggage scanning equipment and full body scanners to several military checkpoints in the West Bank, many of which were built as part of the Wall (evidence of M. Amir and D. Baum).

- **Elbit** is one of Israel's largest private military technology firms and is responsible for sections of the Wall.[8] The Norwegian Government's pension fund announced its divestment from Elbit Systems in September 2009 as a result of the company's involvement in the construction of the Wall.[9] This decision was followed by divestment by other Swedish and Dutch pension funds (evidence of Hever). In May 2010, Denmark's Danske Bank divested from the firm[10] (note that the basis of this decision was the view that Elbit was on the brink of losing market value as a result of such divestment; Danske Bank did not explicitly object to the company's immoral and/or potentially illegal conduct but rather made a profit-oriented decision (evidence of S. Hever)).

- **Riwal Holding Group** (based in Dordrecht in the Netherlands) leased cranes used to construct parts of the Wall (evidence of J. Dorman).

- **Shamrock Holdings of California** (Burbank, California, USA) has invested in the ORAD Group, an Israeli company specialising in defence and security services, which has provided Israel with electronic surveillance equipment for the Wall.

- **Ashlad Ltd.** (Tel Aviv, Israel), a subsidiary of the **Ashtrom Group**, is an Israeli construction company that manufactures, among other things, concrete slabs for the construction of the Wall.

- **IDB Holding Corporation Ltd.** is an Israeli holding company that holds 61% of the shares in the CLAL Company.

- **Magal Security Systems** (Yehud, Israel) is an Israeli company that specialises in electronic surveillance and detection systems that have been supplied to Israel for the construction of the Wall.

---

8. B. Hayes, *European Union R&D Subsidies for Israeli Security Actors*.
9. J. Hillary, *Corporate Complicity in Violations of IHL and Human Rights Law - The Israeli Arms Trade and the Apparatus of Repression*, and the evidence of S. Hever.
10. *Ibidem*.

These corporations materially assist Israel in its construction and maintenance of the Wall. As explained above (§ 4), (i) the Israeli construction and maintenance of the Wall violates international law; and (ii) *all* States have obligations under international law to bring Israel's violations to an end. The RToP finds that corporations have an obligation not to assist in any way in maintaining the situation created by the Wall, and to refrain from profiting from Israel's violations of international law.

C. LEGAL INSTRUMENTS OF COERCION AND OBLIGATIONS OF STATES

The Netherlands provides an example of domestic enforcement of international law against corporations. Pursuant to the Dutch *Wet Internationale Misdrijven* (law on international crimes), Dutch corporations are required to adhere to specific provisions of international criminal and humanitarian law (evidence of S. Muller). To this end, Dutch police raided the offices of Riwal Holding Group in October 2010. The police confiscated computers relating to the leasing of cranes used in the construction of the Wall and the settlements (evidence of J. Dorman and S. Muller). As of November 2010, the police investigation had passed to the Dutch State Prosecutor, who was to decide whether to prosecute the corporate executives on charges of violating international law.

As a result of assisting Israel in its violations of international law, the above corporations infringe the rights enshrined in international humanitarian and human rights law. These corporations and their corporate actors may be subject to legal actions in the countries where they are domiciled or have a significant presence: civil claims under domestic law for violations of domestic civil law and/or international law; and criminal prosecution for breach of domestic law and/or the commission of international crimes (see below).

(I) The basis of corporate criminal liability under international law

Under international criminal law those involved in a criminal offence under international law can be held responsible as principal perpetrators or as accomplices.[11] For instance, Article 25 of the Rome Statute stipulates that a person is criminally responsible for a crime within the jurisdiction of the ICC, if that person "for the purpose of facilitating the commission of such a crime, aids, abets or otherwise assists in its commission or its attempted commission, including providing the means for its commission".

Providing the means to facilitate the crime (the *actus reus*) is a material element of complicity, which "requires practical assistance, encouragement, or moral support which has a substantial effect on the perpetration of the crime".[12]

This material element of complicity includes various forms of support provided by individuals (including corporate actors), such as the provision of arms and associated material, communication equipment, and other means intended to facilitate the commission of international crimes.[13]

The RToP concluded that the corporations designated here knowingly acted in a manner to aid or even encourage Israel's violations of international law.

Criminal liability implies the *actus reus* and the *mens rea*: it must be established that corporations knew or intended that Israel would use their equipment and/or services to perpetrate violations of

---

11. This principle is codified in Article 7(1) of the Statute of the International Criminal Tribunal for the former Yugoslavia (ICTY), Article 6(1) of the Statute of the International Criminal Tribunal for Rwanda (ICTR) and Article 25 of the ICC Statute.
12. ICTY, *Prosecutor v. Anto Furundzija*, trial judgment, 10 December 1998, IT-95-17/1-T.
13. See, for example, the Nuremberg "industrialist trials" of Walther Funk, the Zyclon B case and the Krupp Trials. The Zyclon B case is discussed in Annex C.

international law.[14] From the evidence presented to the RToP, this should be a relatively straightforward conclusion in respect of the assistance provided by corporations for the building and maintenance of the Israeli settlements.

With regard to direct knowledge of corporations in relation to the wrongful use of military equipment, evidence provided by S. Hever and J. Hilary revealed that some corporations have declared in their own promotional materials that their equipment was used during "Operation Cast Lead".

And yet it was common knowledge throughout "Operation Cast Lead" that the Israeli military operation was inflicting extensive damage on Palestinian civilians and their goods. These facts were widely reported in the media. It therefore follows that corporations that delivered military equipment to Israel during "Operation Cast Lead" were aware that their equipment would or could assist Israel in committing war crimes and/or crimes against humanity. There is therefore evidence that would easily establish the relevant "*mens rea*" in the complicity of corporate actors in such crimes.

Examples from Israel's military history permit the prediction of violations of international law by Israel. Corporations should therefore have foreseen well before 27 December 2008 the likelihood of their equipment being used in violations of international law. On the basis of this knowledge, they should have refused to sell such equipment to Israel. There can be no basis for maintaining these sales to Israel.

For the reasons set out above, the RToP concludes that the corporations that delivered weapons to Israel during or before "Operation Cast Lead" can be seen to be accomplices to the war crimes committed by Israel during that Operation. As such, they may be held accountable in civil and criminal law courts.

(II) The basis of corporate civil and criminal liability under French law

(1) French criminal law

In a case concerning the Dutch charity Al-Aqsa, which had sent money to Hamas for what it presented as humanitarian purposes, the court of first instance of the CJEC placed the foundation on the list of terrorist organisations and froze its bank assets.[15] As Hamas had been placed by the Council of the EU on the list of terrorist organisations, the Netherlands considered that funds sent by Al-Aqsa could be used by Hamas for terrorist purposes.

If a group's history of terrorist acts may be invoked in support of the existence of a serious risk of terrorism, the violations of IHL committed by Israel in the past should also induce corporations to refrain from supplying it with military equipment that could be used by Israel to violate IHL – a hypothesis that was confirmed by "Operation Cast Lead". The same reasoning applies to corporations that repeatedly assist Israel in building and maintaining Israeli settlements and the Wall.

Under French criminal law, Israel's ongoing war crimes may be viewed as a habitual offence, which traditionally constitutes an aggravating circumstance in criminal offences. A habitual offence exists as soon as a first act constituting an offence is repeated.[16]

The systematic/ongoing nature of the war crimes committed by Israel requires increased caution and vigilance by suppliers of weaponry and of materials and services to Israeli settlements and to the builders of the Wall. The obligation is particularly stringent in the context of armed conflict. In this situation, as the

---

14. Article 30 of the ICC Statute, which reflects customary international law. Under national criminal law the subjective elements of intent and knowledge constitute elements of accomplice liability.
15. CJEC, GC, case T-348/07, *Al-Aqsa*, 9 Sept. 2010, s. 1 *et seq.*
16. Court of Cassation, Criminal Chamber, 24 March 1944, *Gaz.Pal.* 1944, I, 254; *id.*, 24 July 1967, *Bull.crim.* No. 23 p.548; *id.*, 3 March 1971, *Gaz.Pal.* 1971, I, 362.

most fundamental human rights (right to life, right to respect for physical integrity) are more at risk of violation, IHL imposes on the parties to the conflict a specific obligation of precaution in the conduct of hostilities (AP 1, Art. 57; customary IHL, rules 15 et seq.; UNSG Circular on respect for IHL by UN forces, Art. 5, § 3; etc.). While this special obligation of precaution is primarily binding on the belligerents as direct parties to the conflict, its scope extends as a core principle of IHL to indirect parties to an armed conflict. In particular, this obligation would apply to suppliers of military materials and equipment on account of the absolute need to respect the principle of distinction between combatants and non-combatants, which is an overriding IHL obligation (St. Petersburg Declaration of 1868, preamble, para. 2; AP 1, Art. 48; customary IHL rule 1).

French criminal law permits the prosecution of corporations for all criminal offences.

(2) French civil law

Articles 6, 1131 and 1133 of the French Civil Code provide that a contract may be terminated if its aim contradicts public morals or public policy. In 2007 the PLO and the Association France Palestine Solidarité (AFPS) took Veolia and Alstom to court in France, seeking the termination of the contracts between Alstom, Veolia and the City Pass Consortium concerning the construction and running of the Jerusalem Light Railway, which will link West Jerusalem with Israeli settlements. **Depending on the outcome of this case, similar actions may be possible in France in the future.**

(III) Remedies under UK law

There may be a possibility of criminal and civil redress before the British courts in respect of the following corporations:

- **G4S**: Possibility of bringing a civil claim under tort law in respect of G4S UK and G4S Israel for their roles in the provision and supply to the Israeli state of equipment used in the checkpoints, which are part of the separation Wall. The other option is to judicially review the British Government's decision to grant contracts to G4S to provide security for UK prisons and immigration deportation services, in light of G4S's complicity in Israel's violations of international law with respect to the settlements and the construction of the Wall.

- **Brimar**: Possibility of bringing a civil claim under tort law relating to display components manufactured by Brimar used in the Israeli Air Force's AH-64 apache helicopters which, as the British Government has acknowledged, were probably used in "Operation Cast Lead". Again this is subject to a number of issues to be determined (see Annex C of the main document).

A possible criminal action for breach of the ICCA (International Criminal Court Act 2001).[17] However, see Annex C of the main document, which sets out the difficulties involved in establishing jurisdiction, identifying the person who was the "controlling mind" of the company at the material time, and the difficulties in extraterritorial application of UK laws.

- **Elbit**: Following the involvement of Elbit in a series of war crimes committed during "Operation Cast Lead" and while monitoring sections of the Wall for which it is responsible, it is permissible to bring a public law challenge (judicial review) of the Government's decision to award Elbit Systems a contract worth over US $1 billion for the development of the Watchkeeper programme.

With regard to the **OECD**, the various corporations mentioned above may be referred to the relevant National Contact Points (NCPs) (see Annex C of the main document, which sets out the procedure for the British NCP).

---

17. The ICCA is implementing the Rome Statute of the International Criminal Court in English, Irish and Welsh law.

(IV) The legal basis of possible remedies under United States law

(1) Alien Tort Claims Act (ATCA)

In 2005, the Centre for Constitutional Rights brought a claim against Caterpillar Inc. on behalf of the family of Rachel Corrie,[18] a 23-year-old American citizen who was intentionally killed by the Israel Defense Forces (IDF) during the demolition of Palestinian homes with Caterpillar bulldozers to make way for a buffer zone near the Egypt-Gaza border. The Caterpillar company was alleged to have been complicit in her death in a claim under the ATCA. In supplying modified D9 Bulldozers, Caterpillar had aided and abetted Israel's war crimes, which included: collective punishment, the destruction of property not justified by military necessity, and attacks targeting civilians (violating Arts. 27, 32, 33, 53 and 147 of the Fourth Geneva Convention). In addition, the demolition of Palestinian homes – as civilian property – constitutes a war crime.

Both the US District Court and the Ninth Circuit Appeals Court dismissed the case. The Appellate Court dismissed the case, but ruled that it did not have jurisdiction to decide the case because it would intrude on the US Administration's foreign policy decisions. Rachel Corrie's family sought a rehearing, which was denied by the Appellate Court in 2009.

The recent decision in *Kiobel*[19] suggests that a suit may not be brought against corporations. However: (i) this is not the final word on the issue – cases may be brought outside the Second Circuit and the issue has yet to be determined by the US Supreme Court; and (ii) suits may be brought against corporate executives (see below): the possibility of bringing suits against individuals was explicitly confirmed by both the majority and the concurrence in the *Kiobel* case.

Notwithstanding the decisions in *Caterpillar* and *Kiobel*, the law and practice in cases based on the ACTA continue to evolve, and each claim against a corporation or its agents will need to be considered on its merits. **On this basis, the RToP encourages parties to continue bringing such claims in the future.**

(2) Shareholder breach of fiduciary duty claim

Under US corporate law, **shareholders of any nationality can bring an action against the directors of Caterpillar or any corporations complicit in Israel's violations of international law** on the grounds that: by approving or condoning the aiding and abetting of war crimes or gross human rights abuses, the directors breached their duties of care, loyalty and good faith to the company and its shareholders and caused them to suffer a loss.

(3) Public law: lawsuit to force a state to revoke a corporate charter or licence

In the US, states have the legal right to **revoke licences** granted to corporations to do business with a particular state authority where, for example, the company is deemed to have abused or misused its power or is deemed to have engaged in crimes considered to be a serious breach of the public trust. Consistently approving or condoning illegal action that results in widespread human rights abuses, including war crimes, lies outside the power granted to corporations and should justify revoking their licences (see the potential difficulties set out in Annex C of the main document).

(4) Criminal law

Caterpillar Inc. and Shamrock Holdings may be liable under US criminal law for aiding and abetting war crimes committed overseas. US war crimes statutes approve the exercise of extraterritorial jurisdiction to prosecute grave breaches of international criminal law by and against US nationals (see Annex C, which also considers some of the difficulties involved in prosecuting US corporations for complicity in acts which constitute war crimes or gross human

---

18. *Corrie et al. v. Caterpillar*, 403 F.Supp.2d 1019 (2005).
19. *Kiobel v Royal Dutch Petroleum*, No. 06-4876-cv, 2010 WL 3611392 (2d Cir. Sept. 17, 2010).

rights violations when they involve victims of foreign nationality).

D. FINDINGS OF THE JURY

On the basis of the evidence presented during the London session of the Russell Tribunal on Palestine, the jury draws the following conclusions:

- **"Operation Cast Lead"**: Israel committed serious breaches of IHL in the Gaza Strip (December 2008 – January 2009), with the level of damage inflicted on the civilian population and civilian infrastructure demonstrating the disproportionate and indiscriminate nature of the operation. These breaches constitute war crimes, engaging the criminal responsibility of the perpetrators. Corporations provided Israel with weaponry and military equipment that assisted in these crimes. These supplies are material elements of assistance that constitute complicity in the violation of international law by Israel.

- **Settlements**: The establishment and maintenance of settlements in the OPT are war crimes. Corporations assist in the establishment and maintenance of these settlements via their economic relations, provision of services, investments, financing operations or provision of material. These corporations are complicit in Israel's war crimes.

- **The separation Wall**: The construction by Israel, inside the OPT, of this Wall violates international law by seriously restricting, without legal justification, the exercise of civil, economic, social and cultural rights by the affected Palestinian population. Corporations are complicit in these violations of international law by providing Israel with cement, equipment and vehicles that are used in the construction and maintenance of the Wall.

Corporations may be liable under civil or criminal law in domestic courts on the ground of assistance in violations of the international law (e.g. for misdemeanours, money laundering and/or handling or receiving stolen goods), given that many countries' domestic legislation incorporates international law, including international humanitarian and human rights law. Thus:

(a) Under domestic tort law (e.g. in the United Kingdom or the United States), a claim for damages against a corporation that provided goods and services where it was foreseeable that they would cause the claimant (or a class of persons to which the claimant belonged) damage/loss, particularly personal injury, may succeed where it can be shown that damage was caused. The fact that the acts were those of the defendant's subsidiary need not be a bar to claims for recovery against the head office.

(b) In the United States, Palestinians may bring a suit under the ATCA for aiding and abetting war crimes and/or crimes against humanity.

(c) The Special Representative's Guidelines, the Global Compact, the Norms[20] and the OECD Guidelines all specify that corporations should refrain from violating and should actively promote respect for human rights.

(d) Pursuant to Articles 121-7 of the French Criminal Code, it is possible to bring a claim before French courts against corporations present in French territory and providing material support for the construction of the Wall.

(e) As war crimes are also criminal offences under US domestic law, which criminalises aiding and abetting such offences, a corporation could be prosecuted in the United States for aiding and abetting war crimes, even if they were committed overseas. US war crimes statutes approve the exercise of extraterritorial jurisdiction to prosecute grave breaches of international criminal law by and against US nationals.

On a ground that is not criminal or civil, the jury concludes that claims may be submitted to OECD

---

20. The Norms on the Responsibilities of Transnational Corporations and Other Business Enterprises with Regard to Human Rights, 2002.

National Contact Points for mediation and/or investigation and a final statement. The jury recommends that a claim be brought before a domestic NCP where one is available for the state in which the corporation is domiciled. If no such NCP exists, claims should be addressed to an NCP in another state in which the corporation has a permanent representation.

Representations to public bodies should make it clear that continued economic relations with corporations that assist Israel in violating international law would be contrary to their voluntary codes of conduct/guidance and to their government's obligations to promote and protect human rights. Maintaining these relations may give rise to state responsibility.

States are advised to follow the example set by the Dutch public bodies, which have investigated a Dutch corporation alleged to be complicit in violations of international human rights and humanitarian law by supplying materials to Israel for the construction and maintenance of the Wall.

The jury concludes that states have an obligation to enforce existing laws against corporations where they are acting in violation of international human rights and humanitarian law.

States should ensure that there are remedies available, and that these remedies are accessible to victims of corporate violations of international and domestic law.

Finally, the jury calls upon individuals, groups and organisations to take all necessary measures to secure compliance of corporations with international human rights and humanitarian law standards, in particular by means of: boycotts of corporations that assist in violations of international law; shareholder action to hold corporations to account; divestment by pension funds from investments tainted by illegality; and ongoing action to place corporations in the spotlight with the purpose of bringing about a change in corporate culture. The jury relies, for these initiatives, on the Advisory Opinion of the International Court of Justice on the Wall. In this Advisory Opinion, the Court stated that there exists an *erga omnes* obligation to refrain from recognising or in any way supporting the illegality that arises from the conduct of Israel by building the Wall and violating international humanitarian law.

Part V
Concluding Remarks

Chapter 17
International (In)Justice and Palestine

John Dugard

Contents

Annex to Chapter 17 586

In the bleakest days of apartheid in South Africa one could always turn to the international community and its institutions for support. There were international standards and norms that apartheid violated and the international community was not afraid to assert such standards and to condemn South Africa for violating them. The West led the way in this condemnation of apartheid. But it is not so with Palestine. Despite the fact that the violation of international *legal* norms is much clearer in the case of Israel's relations with Palestine, the response of the international community's institutions (as contrasted with that of civil society) has been very different. This is particularly apparent in the response to the wall Israel is presently constructing in Palestinian territory, the invasion of Gaza in 2008/2009 and the attack on the high seas on the humanitarian aid flotilla bound for Gaza in May 2010.

The International Court of Justice in its 2004 Advisory Opinion on *Legal Consequences of the Construction of a Wall in the Occupied Palestinian Territory*[1] found that the wall Israel was constructing in Palestinian territory violated both

---

Professor of International Law, University of Pretoria and Leiden University. Former Special Rapporteur to the UN Human Rights Council on the Human Rights Situation in the Occupied Palestinian Territory.

---

[1] At http://www.icj-cij.org/docket/index.php?p1=3&p2=4&k=5a&case=131&code=mwp&p3=4.

J. Dugard (✉)
Leiden University, Leiden, The Netherlands

international humanitarian law and international human rights law; and that settlements were unlawful. But the political organs of the United Nations, European Union and League of Arab States have done little to enforce this Advisory Opinion. The Security Council, acting through the Quartet and led by the United States, has ignored the Opinion; the Secretary-General of the United Nations has done likewise; the General Assembly has failed to take steps within its limited powers to remind the international community of its obligations under this Opinion; and the Human Rights Council has done nothing. Neither the European Union nor the Arab League has done anything to ensure compliance with the Opinion.

The response of the United Nations to Operation Cast Lead and the attack on the Gaza Flotilla has been little different. The United States by means of its predictable veto has prevented the Security Council from condemning Israel's actions; the General Assembly has done little; and the Human Rights Council has been thwarted from taking action to enforce the recommendations of the Goldstone Commission Report (which it commissioned) by concerted action on the part of the European Union and the Palestinian Authority.

But what about the International Criminal Court? After all, it is the body set up by the international community to fight impunity and promote international justice. What has it done, and what could it do, to secure justice for the Palestinians?

The International Criminal Court (ICC) has strict jurisdictional rules. It has competence to investigate and prosecute international crimes in three situations only: (i) where the crime is committed in the territory of a state party to the ICC Statute [Article 12(2)(a) of the ICC Statute]; (ii) where the crime is committed by a national of a state party [Article 12(2)(b)]; and (iii) where the Security Council refers a situation to the ICC under Article 13(b). Israel is not a party to the ICC Statute—mainly because the ICC Statute criminalizes the transfer of settlers into an occupied territory.

The Security Council will clearly not refer any matter affecting Israel to the ICC—as it has done in the case of Darfur. The American veto guarantees this. There are, however, ways in which the ICC may exercise jurisdiction over Israel's actions. Indeed there are at present two requests before the Prosecutor of the ICC for the investigation and prosecution of Israeli army officers and politicians.

In January 2009 the Palestinian Authority made a declaration under Article 12(3) of the ICC Statute in which it accepted the Court's jurisdiction for any international crimes committed on Palestinian territory—that is crimes committed by both Israelis and Palestinians. This procedure is open to 'a State which is not a party to this Statute'. In order to accept this submission to jurisdiction the Prosecutor of the ICC will not have to decide that Palestine is a 'state' for all purposes but only for the purpose of the ICC. This is a difficult decision for the Prosecutor. Palestine is not a member of the United Nations and the United States and the European Union believe that Palestinian statehood should not be recognized before Palestine and Israel have reached a settlement on boundaries, refugees and East Jerusalem. On the other hand, Palestine is already recognized as a state by over one hundred states and is a member of the Arab League. Moreover it has recently been recognized by a number of prominent South American states—Brazil. Argentina, Uruguay and Bolivia. (The Prosecutor of the ICC, Mr. Luis Moreno Ocampo is himself a national of Argentina.) Palestine is recognized by many more states than Kosovo (recognized by about 70 states), which is seen as a state by the US and EU. In the light of these recognitions and the fact that the declared purpose of the ICC is 'to put an end to impunity', which means that a purposive interpretation of the ICC Statute would support acceptance of the Palestinian declaration, it would not be unreasonable for the ICC Prosecutor to accept the Palestinian declaration and commence investigations into Israel's actions, particularly arising out of Operation Cast Lead. Moreover the Goldstone Commission Report has already laid the foundations for prosecutions of Israeli officers and politicians.

The Goldstone Report was not the only fact-finding report on Operation Cast Lead. Amnesty International, Human Rights Watch and the League of Arab States (whose mission I chaired) [the Executive Summary of the latter Report, titled 'No Safe Place', is included in this Volume, see *infra* Annex to this Chapter - ChM] all produced thorough reports on the conflict. In all reports, including the Goldstone Report, there were accounts of the killings of civilians by Israel Defense Forces (IDF) in a cold, calculated and deliberate manner. But the principal accusation leveled at Israel was that in its assault on Gaza it used force indiscriminately in densely populated areas and was reckless as to the foreseeable consequences of its actions which resulted in at least 900 civilian deaths and 5,000 wounded.

In terms of the Rome Statute of the International Criminal Court it is a war crime to intentionally direct attacks against a civilian population [Article 8(2)(b)(i)]. Such an intention need not be premeditated: it suffices if the person engaging in such action meant to cause the consequence of his action or "is aware that it will occur in the ordinary course of events" (Article 30). Goldstone's op-ed, which appeared in the Washington Post in April 2011[2], may be interpreted to mean that he is now satisfied (although there is no evidence to support this) that Israel did not as a matter of policy deliberately and in a premeditated manner target civilians and that where the calculated killing of civilians occurred this was without the blessing of the Israeli military and political leadership. But he could not possibly have meant that Israel did not "intentionally target civilians as a matter of policy" in the legal sense of intention. This Israel's assault was conducted in an indiscriminate manner with full knowledge that its consequences would be the killing and wounding of civilians is a matter of public record fully substantiated by the Goldstone Report and other equally credible reports.

The Prosecutor of the ICC has now been sitting on this decision for nearly two years. During this time he has given the impression that he is seriously considering the Palestinian application. He has held talks with the Palestinian Authority and

---

[2] The op-ed claimed that the investigations published by the Israeli military and recognized by a follow-up UN Committee Report chaired by Judge Mary McGowan Davis, which appeared in March 2011, "indicate that civilians were not intentionally targeted as a matter of policy", see also the contribution of Richard Falk, *supra* in this Volume, Chap. 3.

the Arab League; sent his staff into the region and encouraged extensive academic debate over the question whether Palestine qualifies as a state. But the sad truth is that the Prosecutor is determined not to make a decision on this matter. It would offend the members of the EU, all states parties to the ICC, Canada and Australia, and, above all, it would ensure that the United States never becomes a party to the ICC Statute. So for political reasons—fear of offending the West—the Prosecutor has decided not to do anything.

The second opportunity for the ICC to exercise jurisdiction arises from the attack on the Gaza Flotilla. Nine persons were killed and some 50 seriously injured when Israeli forces attacked the *MV Mavi Mamara.* This ship was not registered in Turkey but the Union of the Comoros. The Union of the Comoros is a party to the ICC Statute. Article 12(2) (a) of the ICC Statute expressly provides that the Court has jurisdiction if the crime was committed on the territory of a state party or 'if the crime was committed on board a vessel or aircraft, the state of registration of that vessel or aircraft'. In short the conduct in question occurred on the territory of the Union of the Comoros—a party to the ICC Statute. Moreover the Report of an Independent Fact-Finding Mission to the Human Rights Council[3] has found that serious international crimes were committed on board by the *MV M avi Marmara.* The Turkish Foundation for Human Rights and Freedoms and Humanitarian Relief (IHH), under whose auspices the *MV Mavi Marmara* sailed, has filed a complaint with the Prosecutor of the ICC in this matter. It is hoped that the Union of the Comoros will file a complaint too in respect of a crime that was committed on its territory. However, one can imagine the pressure to which it is currently being subjected from the United States to refrain from so doing. As yet the Prosecutor of the ICC has failed to respond to the complaint of the IHH and there are no signs that he is about to do so. This, despite the fact that both the requirements of jurisdiction and gravity are met.

The ICC has therefore followed in the footsteps of the political organs of the United Nations by refusing to investigate, let alone prosecute, crimes committed by Israeli officers and politicians. It would take a brave, independent and courageous Prosecutor to take action against Israel in the face of US and EU protection of Israel.

It is much easier for the Prosecutor of the ICC to concern himself—and the ICC—with Africa. Consequently all the cases at present before the ICC are against Africans—from the DRC, Central African Republic, Uganda, Sudan and now Kenya and Libya. True, the first three countries have themselves referred persons to the ICC for prosecution and the Security Council is responsible for the investigation of President Al Bashir of Sudan and of Muammar Gaddafi in Libya.

But the Prosecutor has himself initiated action against Kenyan politicians. Small wonder that the African Union has accused the Prosecutor of an anti-African bias. The Prosecutor could remove suggestions of anti-African bias by investigating Israeli officers and politicians. But that would offend the West. It is

---

[3] UN Doc A/HRC/15/21 (27 September 2010).

comfortable with the notion that international crimes are committed by Africans. It would be terrible for the West if one of its own kind—an Israeli army officer or politician—was to be brought before the ICC.

The International Court of Justice is the only international institution to emerge with honor from Israeli/Palestinian saga. The political organs of the United Nations have not done so. Nor, sadly, has the International Criminal Court. An end must be put to impunity for the perpetration of international crimes, proclaims the Preamble of the Rome Statute of the ICC—as long as this does not apply to Israel, it should add.

In March 2011 the Goldstone Report was referred to the General Assembly of the United Nations by the Human Rights Council with the request that it be referred by the Assembly to the Security Council and that the Security Council submit the matter to the Prosecutor of the International Criminal Court, as it has done in the cases of Darfur and Libya. Doubtless the General Assembly will refer the Goldstone Report to the Security Council, despite Goldstone's op-ed, but it will end there as the customary United States veto will ensure that Israel remains unaccountable.

The Goldstone Report is a historical milestone. It is a credible, reasoned, comprehensive and thoroughly researched account of atrocities—war crimes and crimes against humanity—committed by Israel in the course of Operation Cast Lead and of war crimes committed by Hamas in the indiscriminate firing of rockets into Israel. It is a serious attempt to secure the accountability of a state that has for too long been allowed by the West to behave in a lawless manner.

Annex to Chapter 17

Report of the Independent Fact Finding Committee On Gaza:

No Safe Place.

Presented to the League of Arab States.
30 April 2009.

17 Annex to Chapter 17

Executive Summary.

1. The Independent Fact Finding Committee on Gaza to the League of Arab States (**the Committee**) was established in February 2009 with the tasks of investigating and reporting on violations of human rights law and international humanitarian law during the Israeli military offensive (hereinafter operation *Cast Lead*) against Gaza from 27 December 2008 to 18 January 2009 and collecting information on the responsibility for the commission of international crimes during the operation. The Committee comprised Professor John Dugard (South Africa: Chairman), Professor Paul de Waart (Netherlands), Judge Finn Lynghjem (Norway), Advocate Gonzalo Boye (Chile/Germany), Professor Francisco Corte-Real (Portugal: forensic body damage evaluator) and Ms Raelene Sharp, solicitor (Australia: Rapporteur).

2. The Committee held an initial meeting with the Secretary-General of the Arab League and his staff in Cairo on 21 February. It then travelled to Gaza on 22 February, which it entered at the Rafah crossing. The Committee was accompanied by three representatives of the League: Mr Radwan bin Khadra, Legal Advisor to the Secretary General and Head of the Legal Department, Mrs Aliya Ghussien, Head of Palestine Department, and Ms Elham Alshejni, from the Population Studies and Migration Department. The Committee was also accompanied by Mr Omar Abdallah from the Egyptian Foreign Ministry.

3. The Committee remained in Gaza from 22 to 27 February. The programme for its visit was organized by the Palestinian Centre for Human Rights, which provided logistical support to the Committee. The Committee met with a wide range of persons including victims of operation *Cast Lead*, witnesses, members of the Hamas Authority doctors, lawyers, businessmen, journalists and members of NGOs and United Nations agencies. It visited the sites of much of the destruction, including hospitals, schools, universities, mosques, factories, businesses, police stations, government buildings, United Nations premises, private homes and agricultural land.

4. The Committee collected a wealth of information from many sources, including the websites of the Israeli Foreign Ministry and Israel Defense Forces (**IDF**), Israeli newspapers and NGO reports, the reports of Palestinian and international NGOs, United Nations publications, Palestinian official documents and the testimony of witnesses to the conflict. On three occasions, the Committee wrote to the Government of Israel requesting its co-operation. Such letters were faxed to the Government in Israel and later delivered to the Israeli embassies in the Netherlands and Norway. The Committee received no response to its requests for co-operation, which compelled it to rely on official websites, publications and the media for information about the Israeli perspective. The Committee regrets the decision of the Government of Israel to withhold co-operation.

5. The Committee's visit to and experiences in Gaza inevitably influenced and shaped its opinions and assisted it in making its findings. The Committee's impressions and the inferences that it drew from what it saw and heard were corroborated by information from other sources. However, it could not have carried out its mandate without the visit to Gaza which allowed it to see for itself the destruction and devastation caused by operation *Cast Lead* and to speak to those who had experienced and suffered through the offensive.

6. The Committee's report is divided into three main parts: a factual description and analysis; a legal assessment and possible remedies; and recommendations. The factual

description includes a report by the body damage evaluator, who examined 10 individuals who sustained injuries during operation *Cast Lead*. Operating under internationally recognised standards, the report documents the injuries suffered and their alleged causes.

The Facts

7. The Committee saw, heard and read evidence of great loss of life and injury in Gaza. Statistics accepted by the Committee show that over 1,400 Palestinians were killed, including at the very least 850 civilians, 300 children and 110 women. Over 5,000 Palestinians were wounded. The Committee was unable to accept the figures given by Israel, which claim that only 295 of those killed were civilians, as they do not provide the names of the dead (unlike Palestinian sources). Moreover, Israel includes policemen as combatants, whereas they should be considered as civilians, and it asserts that only children below the age of sixteen qualify as such, whereas the accepted international age for children is eighteen. The Committee heard disturbing accounts of cold-blooded killing of civilians by members of the IDF, accounts which were later confirmed by Israeli soldiers at the Oranim military college.

8. Four Israeli civilians were killed by Palestinian rockets during operation *Cast Lead* and 182 wounded. Ten Israeli soldiers were killed (three by friendly fire) and 148 wounded.

9. Palestinian fighters had only unsophisticated weapons - Qassam rockets and Grads- whereas Israel was able to employ the most sophisticated and modern weaponry to bombard the population of Gaza from the air, land and sea. Although Israel initially denied it had used white phosphorous in the offensive it later admitted its use but denied it had been used unlawfully. The Committee is, however, satisfied on the available evidence that white phosphorous was used as an incendiary weapon in densely populated areas.

10. There was substantial destruction of, and damage to property during the offensive. Over 3,000 homes were destroyed and over 11,000 damaged; 215 factories and 700 private businesses were seriously damaged or destroyed; 15 hospitals and 43 primary health care centres were destroyed or damaged; 28 government buildings and 60 police stations were destroyed or damaged; 30 mosques were destroyed and 28 damaged; 10 schools were destroyed and 168 damaged; three universities / colleges were destroyed and 14 damaged; and 53 United Nations properties were damaged.

11. It was clear to the Committee the IDF had not distinguished between civilians and civilian objects and military targets. Both the loss of life and the damage to property were disproportionate to the harm suffered by Israel or any threatened harm. There was no evidence that any military advantage was served by the killing and wounding of civilians or the destruction of property.

12. The Committee received evidence of the bombing and shelling of hospitals and ambulances and of obstructions placed in the way of the evacuation of the wounded.

13. The 22-day offensive with bombing and shelling from the air, sea and land traumatized and terrorised the population. Israel dropped leaflets warning the population to evacuate, but in most cases failed to give details of the areas to be targeted and conversely which areas were safe. Phone calls were equally confusing. Generally, the leaflets and phone calls simply served to confuse the population and to cause panic.

14. Israel has defended its actions by arguing that buildings were used to store munitions and hide militants and that the Palestinians made use of women and children as human shields. The Committee received evidence of human shields being used by both Hamas and Israel and has not been able to verify the truth of these allegations. Nevertheless it does not believe that such large scale killing and wounding can be attributed to the use of human shields. Similarly, Israel has produced no credible evidence of buildings being used to harbour munitions and militants. Again, it is likely that this did occur in some cases but it could not possible justify the type and amount of killing and wounding and damage to property that occurred.

15. The IDF conducted an internal investigation into allegations that its forces committed international crimes. It found that although there were a few irregularities international crimes were not committed by its forces. The Committee is unable to accept those findings. The Committee finds the IDF investigation to be unconvincing as it was not independent. There is also no suggestion that it considered Palestinian sources.

Legal Assessment

16. Before making its legal assessment, the Committee considered a number of issues that might affect criminal responsibility for any crimes that were committed. The Committee found that:

    (1) Gaza remains occupied territory and that Israel is obliged to comply with the Fourth Geneva Convention in its actions in Gaza.

    (2) Due to the uncertain meaning of 'aggression' it could make no finding on the question whether Israel's offensive constituted aggression.

    (3) Israel's actions could not be justified as self-defence.

    (4) It could not examine the criminal responsibility of either Israel or Hamas in the context of international terrorism as the meaning of both state terrorism and terrorism by non-state actors is too uncertain; consequently, criminal responsibility was best measured in accordance with the rules of international humanitarian law.

    (5) Principles of proportionality should be applied in assessing criminal responsibility.

17. The focus of the report is on international crimes and the available remedies for prosecuting such crimes. Consequently little attention is paid to violations of human rights law and international humanitarian law that do not constitute international crimes. Nevertheless, the Committee found that there had been serious violations of the International Covenant on Civil and Political Rights, the International Covenant on Economic, Social and Cultural Rights and the Convention on the Rights of the Child. There were also violations of the Fourth Geneva Convention and its Additional Protocols, particularly in respect of the prohibition on collective punishment.

18. The Committee then turned to the question of international criminal responsibility arising from the conflict. Here it considered war crimes, crimes against humanity and genocide.

War Crimes

19. The Committee examined the responsibility of parties to the conflict for the commission of only of those war crimes which are generally accepted and whose meaning and content is clear.

20. The Committee found that the IDF was responsible for the crime of indiscriminate and disproportionate attacks on civilians. In reaching this conclusion the Committee had regard to the number of civilians killed and wounded and to the extent of the destruction to civilian property. It rejected Israel's determination of who is a civilian. Members of the Hamas civil government responsible for administering the affairs of Gaza are not combatants as claimed by Israel. Nor are members of the police force responsible for maintaining law and order and controlling traffic.

21. The Committee also found that Palestinian militants who fired rockets into Israel indiscriminately, committed the war crime of indiscriminate and disproportionate attacks on civilians.

22. The Committee found that the IDF was responsible for the crime of killing, wounding and terrorizing civilians. The Committee based this finding on the number of civilians killed by 22 days of intense bombardment by air, sea and land. The Committee also found the weapons used by the IDF, particularly white phosphorous and flechettes, caused superfluous and unnecessary suffering.

23. The Committee rejected Israel's claim that it had warned civilians to evacuate their homes by leaflets and phone calls. The leaflets and phone calls generally failed to tell civilians which targets were to be bombed and where they might find safety. As a result they only served to cause confusion and panic. Incessant bombing and misleading warnings of this kind served to terrorize the population.

24. The Committee found that Palestinian militants who fired rockets indiscriminately into Israel which killed four civilians and wounded 182 committed the war crime of killing, wounding and terrorizing civilians.

25. The Committee found that the IDF was responsible for the wanton destruction of property and that such destruction could not be justified on grounds of military necessity. The number of civilian properties destroyed was completely disproportionate to any harm threatened and there was no credible evidence that the destruction served any military advantage.

26. There was considerable evidence that the IDF and its members had bombed and shelled hospitals and ambulances and obstructed the evacuation of the wounded. In the opinion of the Committee this conduct also constituted a war crime. The Committee was not able to accept the findings of the IDF internal investigation on this subject as it took no account of Palestinian allegations.

Crimes Against Humanity

27. A crime against humanity comprises acts of murder, extermination, persecution and similar other inhumane acts committed as part of a widespread or systematic attack directed against any civilian population with knowledge of the attack. The Committee found that Israel's offensive met the legal requirements for this crime and that the IDF was responsible for committing this crime.

Genocide

28. Genocide is considered the "crime of crimes". It has been singled out for special condemnation and opprobrium. The very suggestion that a state has committed genocide should therefore be approached with great care. Nevertheless the Committee believes that operation *Cast Lead* was of such gravity it was compelled to consider whether this crime had been committed.

29. The Committee found Israel's actions met the requirements for the *actus reus* of the crime of genocide contained in the Genocide Convention, in that the IDF was responsible for killing, exterminating and causing serious bodily harm to members of a group - the Palestinians of Gaza. However, the Committee had difficulty in determining whether the acts in question had been committed with a special intent to destroy in whole or in part a national, ethnical or religious group, as required by the Genocide Convention. It rejected the argument that Israel had carried out operation *Cast Lead* in self-defence. However, it found the main reason for the operation was not to destroy a group, as required for the crime of genocide, but to engage in a vicious exercise of collective punishment designed either to compel the population to reject Hamas as the governing authority of Gaza or to subdue the population into a state of submission.

30. The Committee found although operation *Cast Lead* had not been carried out by the IDF to destroy the Palestinians of Gaza as a group, individual soldiers may well have had such an intent and might therefore be prosecuted for this crime. This finding was based on the brutality of some of the killing and reports that some soldiers had acted under the influence of rabbis who had encouraged them to believe that the Holy Land should be cleansed of non-Jews.

State Responsibility For Genocide

31. Under international law a state may be held responsible for the commission of internationally wrongful acts that are attributable to it. Such responsibility may arise from customary international law or in terms of treaty obligations. It is clear internationally wrongful acts were committed by Israel in operation *Cast Lead*.

32. Most human rights and international humanitarian law treaties do not confer jurisdiction on the International Court of Justice for the commission of internationally wrongful acts under such conventions. However, the Genocide Convention, in Article 9, confers such jurisdiction on the International Court of Justice in respect of the responsibility of a state for violation of the Convention, at the request of any other state party. It is not be necessary for the other state party to show that it has a national interest in the dispute as the prohibition on genocide is an obligation *erga omnes*.

33. Proof of the commission of genocide is a prerequisite for bringing a claim under the Genocide Convention. It has already been shown that the Committee was not able to find that the state of Israel acting though the IDF had the necessary specific intent to destroy a group as required for the crime of genocide. On the other hand, there is a prospect that such a claim might succeed if it can be proved that individual members of the armed forces committed acts of genocide while they were acting under the direct control of the Government of Israel. Such a scenario would allow Israel to be held responsible under the Genocide Convention for failure to prevent or to punish genocide.

Responsibility Of Israel

34. The Committee has found that members of the IDF committed war crimes, crimes against humanity and, *possibly*, genocide in the course of operation *Cast Lead*. Those responsible for the commission of such crimes are individually responsible for their actions, as are those who ordered or incited the commission of such crimes or participated in a common purpose to commit such crimes. Military commanders and political leaders are likewise responsible for crimes committed under their effective command, authority or control where they knew or should have known the forces were committing such crimes and they failed to prevent or repress the commission of such crimes or to investigate and prosecute those responsible.

Responsibility Of Hamas

35. As the governing de facto authority of Gaza, Hamas may be held responsible for violations of international humanitarian law attributed to it. Individuals who have fired rockets indiscriminately into Israel are criminally responsible for their actions and must be held accountable for them under the law governing the commission of war crimes. In assessing the responsibility of Hamas and individual Palestinian militants there are a number of factors that reduce their moral blameworthiness but not their criminal responsibility. Such factors include the fact Palestinians have been denied their right to self-determination by Israel and have long been subjected to a cruel siege by Israel.

Remedies

36. There are a number of remedies in the criminal law field that may be invoked by states, NGOs and individuals to secure redress for crimes committed in Gaza. These include prosecutions for violation of the Fourth Geneva Convention in national courts in accordance with Articles 146 and 147 of the Convention, prosecutions pursuant to universal jurisdiction statutes which allow a person to be prosecuted in a third country for an international crime committed extraterritorially, and referral to the International Criminal Court. On 22 January 2009 the Palestinian Minister of Justice, Mr Ali Kashan, lodged a declaration with the Registrar of the International Criminal Court on behalf of the Government of Palestine recognizing the jurisdiction of the Court for international crimes committed in Palestine since 1 July 2002 under Article 12(3) of the Rome Statute. At this time the Registrar is still considering her decision. The Committee believes that the International Criminal Court should accept the declaration lodged by the Government of Palestine and investigate the commission of international crimes in the course of operation *Cast Lead*.

37. There are also a number of civil law remedies available to states, NGOs and individuals. As shown above, states may be able to initiate proceedings against Israel for failure to prevent or to punish the commission of the crime of genocide if it can be established that members of it armed forces were responsible for the commission of that crime.

38. The American Alien Tort Act, which allows American Federal Courts to exercise jurisdiction in any civil action brought by an alien for violation of a peremptory norm of international law outside the United States, is another remedy that may be considered.

39. Procedures within the United Nations may also be invoked. States may request the Security Council to refer the situation in Gaza to the International Criminal Court in

the same way that such a referral was made in the case of Darfur in Resolution 1593 of 31 March 2005. States may also request the General Assembly to request the International Court of Justice for an Advisory Opinion on the legal consequences of operation *Cast Lead* for Israel and other states. In 2005 the General Assembly adopted the Summit Outcome Document in which the United Nations undertakes the responsibility to protect states against genocide, war crimes and crimes against humanity. The General Assembly, and possibly the Security Council, might be approached to take action under this commitment.

Recommendations

40. The Committee makes the following recommendations:

Recommendations to Organs of the United Nations.

(1) The League of Arab States should request the General Assembly of the United Nations to request the International Court of Justice to give an advisory opinion on the legal consequences for states, including Israel, of the conflict in Gaza between 27 December 2008 and 18 January 2009 (**the Conflict in Gaza**).

(2) The League of Arab States should request the Security Council to refer the situation in Gaza, arising from Operation Cast Lead, to the Prosecutor of the International Criminal Court under Article 13(b) of the Rome Statute.

(3) The League of Arab States should request the Security Council, failing which the General Assembly, to exercise its Responsibility to Protect, affirmed in the Summit Outcome Document of 2005 in respect of Gaza.

Recommendations involving the International Criminal Court.

(4) The League of Arab States should endorse Palestine's declaration accepting jurisdiction of the International Criminal Court under Article 12(3) of the Rome Statute. If the Security Council fails to refer the situation in Gaza to the International Criminal Court under Article 13(b) of the Rome Statute (Recommendation 2), the League of Arab States should request the General Assembly to endorse Palestine's declaration under Article 12(3) of the Rome Statute in a meeting convened under the Tenth Emergency Special Session, constituted in terms of the Uniting for Peace Resolution 377 A (V).

Recommendations relying on the Geneva Conventions.

(5) The League of Arab States should request the Swiss Government to convene a meeting of the State Parties to the Fourth Geneva Convention to consider the findings of the present Report.

(6) The League of Arab States should request states to consider taking action under Article 146 of the Fourth Geneva Convention to ensure that those suspected of having committed grave breaches of the Convention under Article 147 be investigated and prosecuted.

(7) The League of Arab States should remind State Parties to the Geneva Conventions that they are obliged by Article 1 of the Fourth Geneva Convention "to ensure respect" for the Convention. This obligation was confirmed by the International Court of Justice in its 2004 Advisory Opinion

on "*Legal Consequences of the Construction of a Wall in the Occupied Palestinian Territory*". It may be argued that the obligation contained in Article 1 "to respect and to ensure respect for the present convention in all circumstances" includes an obligation on all states to render whatever assistance they can to a state subjected to violations of the Convention.

Recommendations to other States.

(8) The League of Arab States should recommend to its members that they consider instituting legal proceedings against Israel in accordance with Article 9 of the Convention on the Prevention and Punishment of the Crime of Genocide, with due regard to the caution expressed in the present Report.

(9) The League of Arab States should encourage states to prosecute persons responsible for the international crimes identified in the present Report before their national courts (where universal jurisdiction statutes so permit).

(10) The League of Arab States should recommend to states that incurred damage to their property in the conflict in Gaza that they claim compensation from Israel for such losses.

Recommendations for action by the League of Arab States directly.

(11) The League of Arab States should facilitate negotiations between Fatah and Hamas in order to ensure that the welfare of the people of Gaza is not affected by the conflict between these two parties, particularly in the medical field.

(12) The League of Arab States should establish a documentation centre to keep a record of breaches of international humanitarian law in Palestine. Such an historical archive would ensure that a record is kept of crimes against the Palestinian people, and may assist any future action(s) taken by the League or other bodies.

(13) This report should be referred to the United Nations, the European Union, the African Union, the Organization of American States, the Organization of Islamic Conference, the Association of South East Asian Nations and the International Criminal Court; and distributed to relevant NGO's and the general public.